D1616854

The Urban Experience

OTHER TITLES FROM E & FN SPON

**Crime Prevention Through
Housing Design**
P. Stollard

**The Garden City
Past, present and future**
S. Ward

**The Idea of Building
Thought and action in the design
and production of buildings**
S. Groák

**Housing for Life
A guide to housing management
practices**
C. Davies

**Marketing the City
The role of flagship developments
in urban regeneration**
H. Smyth

**Rebuilding the City
Property-led urban regeneration**
Edited by P. Healey, D. Usher,
S. Davoudi, S. Tavsanoglu and
M. O'Toole

Competitive Cities
H. Duffy

Transport Planning
D. Bannister

Urban Public Transport Today
B. Simpson

**Property Investment Decisions
A quantitative approach**
S. Hargitay and M. Yu

**Urban Regeneration
Property investment and development**
Edited by J.N. Berry,
W.S. McGreal and W.G. Deddis

Property Management
Second edition
D. Scarrett

**Property Valuation
The five methods**
D. Scarrett

**Effective Writing
Improving scientific, technical
and business communication**
Second edition
C. Turk and J. Kirkman

**Good Style
Writing for science and technology**
J. Kirk

Journals

Children's Environments
(Formerly Children's Environment
Quaterly) Editors: R. Hart, S. Bartlett
and L. Chawla

International Play Journal
Editor: B. Hughes

Planning Perspectives
Editors: G. Cherry and
A. Sutcliffe
An international journal of planning,
history and the environment

For more information on these and other titles, please contact
The Promotion Department, E & FN Spon, 2−6 Boundary Row, London SE1 8HN.
Telephone: 071 865 0066.

THE URBAN EXPERIENCE

A people – environment perspective

Edited by S. J. Neary, M. S. Symes and F. E. Brown
Urban Renewal Research Unit
University of Manchester
Manchester, UK

Proceedings of the 13th Conference of the International Association
for People – Environment Studies held on 13 – 15 July 1994

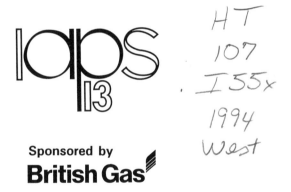

HT
107
. I 55x
1994
West

Sponsored by
British Gas

E & FN SPON
An Imprint of Chapman & Hall

London · Glasgow · Weinheim · New York · Tokyo · Melbourne · Madras

Published by E & FN Spon, an imprint of Chapman & Hall,
2-6 Boundary Row, London SE1 8HN

Chapman & Hall, 2-6 Boundary Row, London SE1 8HN, UK

Blackie Academic & Professional, Wester Cleddens Road,
Bishopbriggs, Glasgow G64 2NZ, UK

Chapman & Hall GmbH, Pappelallee 3, 69469 Weinheim, Germany

Chapman & Hall Inc., One Penn Plaza, 41st Floor, New York NY10119, USA

Chapman & Hall Japan, Thomson Publishing Japan, Hirakawacho
Nemoto Building, 6F, 1-7-11 Hirakawa cho, Chiyoda-ku, Tokyo 102, Japan

Chapman & Hall Australia, Thomas Nelson Australia, 102 Dodds Street,
South Melbourne, Victoria 3205, Australia

Chapman & Hall India, R. Seshadri, 32 Second Main Road, CIT East,
Madras 600 035, India

First edition 1994

© 1994 E & FN Spon

Printed by St Edmondsbury Press, Bury St Edmunds, Suffolk

ISBN 0 419 20160 2

A catalogue record for this book is available from the British Library

Printed on permanent acid-free text paper, manufactured in accordance
with ANSI/NISO Z39.48-1992 and ANSI/NISO Z39.48-1984 (Permanence of Paper).

Publisher's Note
This book was produced from camera-ready-copy provided by the editors.

Contents

ix

Contributors

Antonio Aiello
Università degli Studi di Roma "La Sapienza", Italy.

Joost van Andel
Department of Social Sciences, Eindhoven University of Technology, Netherlands.

Rita Grazia Ardone
Università degli Studi di Roma "La Sapienza", Italy.

Helen B. Armstrong
Cultural Landscape Research Unit, School of Landscape Architecture, University of New South Wales, Australia.

Nazan Aydin-Wheater
Department of Landscape Architecture and Urban Design, Bilkent University, Ankara, Turkey.

Gilles Barbey
Département d'Architecture, Ecole Polytechnique Fédérale, Lausanne, Switzerland.

Bernadette Blanc
INRS-Urbanisation, Montreal, Canada.

Marino Bonaiuto
Dipartimento di Psicologia dei Processi di Sviluppo e Socializzazione, Università degli Studi di Roma "La Sapienza", Italy.

Mirilia Bonnes
Dipartimento di Psicologia dei Processi di Sviluppo e Socializzazione, Università degli Studi di Roma "La Sapienza", Italy.

Edwin S. Brierley
Department of Architecture, De Montfort University, Leicester, UK.

Frank Brown
School of Architecture, Manchester University, UK.

Mervyn Busteed
Department of Geography, Manchester University, UK.

Andreas Cebulla
Northern Ireland Economic Research Centre, Belfast, UK.

Johanne Charbonneau
INRS-Urbanisation, Montreal, Canada.

Swati Chattopadhyay
Department of Architecture, University of California at Berkeley, USA.

J. F. Coeterier
Winand Staring Centre, Wageingen, Netherlands.

Gaye Culcuoglu
Department of Landscape Architecture and Urban Design, Bilkent University, Ankara, Turkey.

Francine Dansereau
INRS-Urbanisation, Montreal, Canada.

Aytanga Dener
Department of Architecture, Istanbul Technical University, Turkey.

Peter Dickens
School of Social Sciences, University of Sussex, Brighton, UK.

David Doughty
Faculty of Design, Kingston University, Surrey, UK.

Cristiane Rose de Siqueira Duarte
Programa de pós-graduaçao en Urbanismo Prédio da FAU/Reitoria - Cidade Universitária, Universidade Federal do Rio de Janeiro, Brazil.

Gary W. Evans
Design and Environmental Analysis, Cornell University, New York, USA.

S. Falchero
Dipartimento di Psicologia, Università degli Studi di Padova, Italy.

Svetlana E. Gabidulina
Moscow Linguistic University, Russia.

Annick Germain
INRS-Urbanisation, Montreal, Canada.

Gert Groening
Fachgebiet Gartenkultur, Fachbereich Architektur, Hochschule der Künste Berlin, Germany.

Rob Hodgson
Department of Geography, Manchester University, UK.

Philip James Hubbard
Department of Geography and Geology, Cheltenham and Gloucester College of Higher Education, UK.

Vacit Imamoglu
Department of Architecture, Middle East Technical University, Ankara, Turkey.

Masao Inui
Tokyo Institute of Technology, Yokohama, Japan.

Barry Jackson
School of Architecture, New Jersey Institute of Technology, USA.

Miki Kondo
Kobe University, Japan.

R. J. Lamb
Department of Architecture, Sydney University, Australia.

Roderick Lawrence
Centre for Human Ecology and Environmental Sciences, University of Geneva,
        Switzerland.

Maria Cristina Dias Lay
Faculdade de Arquitetura e Urbanismo, Universidade Federal do Rio Grande do Sul,
        Brazil.

Stephen J. Lepore
Carnegie Mellon University, USA.

Mats Lieberg
Department of Building Functions Analysis, School of Architecture, University of Lund,
Sweden.

Kiwamu Maki
Tokyo Insitute of Technology, Yokohama, Japan.

Anna Rita Mazzotta
Istituto di Psicologia e Sociologia, Università degli Studi di Lecce, Italy.

Maria Montero y Lopez Lena
School of Psychology, National Autonomous University of Mexico.

Anne Vernez Moudon
College of Architecture and Urban Planning, Washington University, Seattle, USA.

Alejandro Muniz Campos
School of Psychology, National Autonomous University of Mexico.
Yoshiki Nakamura
Tokyo Institute of Technology, Yokohama, Japan.

Susan Neary
School of Architecture, Manchester University, UK.

Ryuzo Ohno
Kobe University, Japan.

O. A. Oyediran
Department of Architecture, Lagos University, Nigeria.

E. Mainardi Peron
Dipartimento di Psicologia, Università degli Studi di Padova, Italy.

A. T. Purcell
Department of Architectural and Design Science, Sydney University, Australia.

Ruth A. Rae
Environmental Psychology Program, City University of New York, USA.

Claude Raffestin
Centre for Human Ecology and Environmental Sciences, University of Geneva, Switzerland.

Antonio Tarcísio da Luz Reis
Faculdade de Arquitetura e Urbanismo, Universidade Federal do Rio Grande do Sul, Brazil.

Leanne G. Rivlin
City University of New York Graduate School, USA.

Marion Ryan
College of Architecture and Urban Planning, Washington University, Seattle, USA.

Henry Sanoff
School of Design, North Carolina State University, USA.

Uwe Schneider
Fachgebiet Gartenkultur, Fachbereich Architektur, Hochschule der Künste Berlin, Germany.

Alex Schroeder
Georgetown University, Washington DC, USA.

Arthur E. Stamps III
Institute of Environmental Quality, San Francisco, USA.

Martin S. Symes
School of Architecture, Manchester University, UK.

Ilhan Tekeli
Department of Regional and City Planning, Middle East Technical University, Ankara, Turkey.

Vesselina Troeva
Department of Civil Engineering and Geodesy, University of Architecture, Sofia, Bulgaria.

Zuhal Ulusoy
Department of Landscape Architecture and Urban Design, Bilkent University, Ankara, Turkey.

Joachim Wolschke-Buhlman
Centre for Studies in Landscape Architecture, Washington DC, USA.

Cecilia Wong
Department of Planning and Landscape, Manchester University, UK.

John Zacharias
Concordia University, Montreal, Canada.

W. G. Zwirner
Faculty of Design, Kingston University, Surrey, UK.

Preface

Cet ouvrage contient les communications présentées lors de la 13ème Conférence Biennale de l'Association pour l'Etude des Relations Homme-Environnement (IAPS) qui s'est déroulée à Manchester en juillet 1994. Dans le passé, l'étendue des thèmes, l'organisation linguistique et la publication du compte-rendu des conférences de l'IAPS ont varié. Pour cette conférence, un thème précis, l'Expérience Urbaine, a été défini, et il a été décidé de n'accepter que les communications qui s'y rapportaient directement. Les communications devaient être faites en anglais ou en français, les résumés seuls étant traduits dans l'autre langue. Enfin, on a choisi, et ce fut une décision importante, de ne publier dans cet ouvrage, disponible dès le début de la conférence, que les communications ayant été approuvées après une procédure d'arbitrage, semblable à celle en vigueur dans les journaux scientifiques. Les participants à la conférence et le public ont pu prendre connaissance des résumés de toutes les communications dans un recueil publié séparément.

This book contains a selection of papers prepared for and presented at the 13th biennial Conference of the International Association for People-Environment Studies (IAPS) held in Manchester in July 1994. IAPS conferences have varied in their scope and in their linguistic framework as well as in the form in which their proceedings have been published. In this case it was agreed that the conference should have a clear theme, the Urban Experience and that papers should be accepted only on topics close to that theme. It was also decided that presentation could be in English or French, with a translation of summaries only into the other language. A final, important, choice was to publish those full papers which passed a review process similar to that used for scientific journals in this book of proceedings which would be available when the conference opened. Summaries of all papers to be presented at the conference were made available to delegates at the same time and also to the general public in a book of abstracts.

The conference programme was organised into three main parts, with a concentration on one part on each of the three days. This subdivision has been followed as far as possible in the organisation of the book, so readers will find the first part deals with Participation and Urban Design, the second with User Needs and Evaluation, the third with Environmental Education and Urban Theory. Within this framework, paper presentation sessions, symposia and workshops were given section titles indicating their general academic content and these have been repeated here. The chapters of the book were then allocated to the sections under which they were presented as papers in the conference. Thus if three papers in one section were selected for inclusion they will all be found as chapters in that section of the book, or if one paper only was selected then that section will only have one chapter, and so on.

The criteria according to which papers were selected to be chapters in this book of proceedings was as follows. Firstly, authors had to submit a full paper set out in the light of the conference call for papers by a date well in advance of publication. For each paper copies were sent, with the name(s) of the author(s) removed, to two referees considered to have knowledge of the topic concerned and to be fluent in the language of submission. Wherever possible these referees were IAPS members or former conference attendees. The referees then reported to the editors on the quality of each paper they had read and suggested, where appropriate, revisions which should be made. Each paper which both of its referees considered publishable as it stood or with minor alterations has been included in this book. The constraint of publishing the book in time for distribution at the conference precluded inclusion of papers for which major rewriting was recommended or which referees felt could not be published in the form in which they were submitted.

As is conventional, the conference organising committee invited a number of established specialists (three in this instance) to present keynote speeches. Their texts have also been included in this book, one in each part. An innovation in the conference was the inclusion, at the request of the IAPS Board's Executive Committee, of an IAPS lecture. The text of this lecture has also been included. Clearly it has not been possible to include reports on the discussions which are expected to take place after all presentations: for this interested readers must await the reviews of the conference which will no doubt appear in due course in various academic and professional journals.

The editors are grateful for the support and encouragement given by the conference organising committee, other members of which were Patrick Malone, Michael Robinson, Gwyn Williams and Necdet Teymur, the latter performing the invaluable role of liaison with the IAPS Board Executive Committee, of which the other members were Arza Churchman, Vittoria Giuliani, Sue-Ann Lee and Jonathon Sime. Further members of the IAPS Board during the conference planning period have been Michel Conan, Gert Groening, Graeme Hardie, Vacid Imamoglu, Lelenis Kruse, Roderick Lawrence, Aristidis Mazis, Toomas Niit, Julia Robinson, David Uzzell and Gilles Barbey.

The panel of referees for paper review included J. Archer, A. Awotona, D. Baldwin, G. Barbey, T. Berry, G. Bizios, M. Bonnes, R. Bristow, S. Brower, M. Bulos, J. Burgess, E. Canniffe, A. Churchman, J. Coeteriere, I. Cooper, I. Donald, T. Duin, G. Evans, R. Feldman, K. Funahashi, B. Goodey, G. Groening, J. Hanson, D. Herman, V. Imamoglu, D. Joiner, A. King, S. Kose, B. Krantz, R. Lawrence, A. Leaman, S.A. Lee, R. Males, W. Marshall, A. Mazis, J. Mellor, B. Mikellides, A. Vernez Moudon, D. Piche, E. Pol, L. Rivlin, J. Robinson, M. Robinson, D. Rudlin, A. Ruff, F. Salmon, H. Sanoff, R. Sebba, M. Segaud, A. Seidel, L. Sheridan, J. Sime, V. Symes, N. Teymur,

K. Tsoukala, C. Twigger, D. Uzzell, A. van Wagenberg, J. van der Wardt, J. Wolschke-Bulman, P. Woods, J. Worthington, D. Yeomans...and these must be thanked for the contributions they have made to the quality of the conference and of this book.

Conference logistics and marketing have been handled with consumate skill by Susan Spibey. In addition we should recognise the valuable preparatory work undertaken by Joyce McLelland and Petra Savage. Our commissioning editor, Madeleine Metcalfe has maintained her confidence in this publication despite what seemed an impossibly tight timetable. Anne Hegerty carried out the sub-editing with eagle eyes. Jonathan Neary co-ordinated the tables and figures. Translations were in some cases made and in others corrected by Valerie Olek, who, with Catherine Foulkes and a number of other helpers in the School of Architecture, provided invaluable secretarial back-up. Bridget Franklin prepared the original conference prospectus and made the presentations to the IAPS Board and members which convinced them that a conference should be held in Manchester and that it should deal with Urban Issues. The Cultural Delegation of the French Embassy supported a "mission" of French specialists attending the conference, the University of Manchester provided technical and accounting assistance and some financial support. The main sponsor, without whom none of this would have been possible, was British Gas, whose Robert Cornish, lately Customer Services Director, North West, also arranged a musical celebration on "le quatorze juillet." The efforts and enthusiasm of all these people have been of enormous assistance in the organisation of the conference and in the preparation of this record of its proceedings.

Susan Neary, Martin Symes, Frank Brown

Part One

PARTICIPATION AND URBAN DESIGN

1

Introduction

Martin S. Symes

Certaines villes, comme Manchester et Athènes, ont représenté des civilisations aujourd'hui disparues. Un nouveau type de civilisation est en train de naître. Les villes, appréciées par les sociologues pour leur anonymat, ont également été perçues comme des lieux de conflits. On considère aujourd'hui qu'elles sont construites par des mythes et des histoires, des systèmes sociaux et des perceptions individuelles. Douze chapitres de cette partie de l'ouvrage sont consacrés à l'étude de l'influence du public sur ces processus. Ils font état de recherches en provenance de tous les continents, traitant aussi bien de l'urbanisation et de la modernisation des pays en voie de développement que des interactions entre les forces du marché et la bureaucratie dans les pays industrialisés. Des contributions à la littérature scientifique, utilisant des paradigmes positivistes et phénoménologues, sont faites. Les voies probables du développement de la littérature de cette sous-discipline sont suggérées dans la revue bibliométrique du chapitre final.

Cities such as Manchester and Athens represented types of civilisation which have now disappeared. A new one is emerging. Sociologists have valued cities for the anonymity they provided but they have also been seen as arenas for conflict. They are now seen as being constructed by myths and histories, social systems and individual perceptions. Twelve chapters in this part of the book consider how the public participates in these processes. They report on research from all continents, covering the urbanisation and modernisation of developing countries as well as the interactions between bureaucratic and market forces in the developed world. Contributions are made to the scientific literature using both positivist and phenomenological paradigms. The final chapter of this part of the book reports on a bibliometric review which suggests how the literature of this sub-discipline may develop.

The historian Asa Briggs (1963) is responsible for the unforgettable comment that Manchester shared with Athens the distinction of being representative of a civilisation which has forever disappeared. Manchester, the location of this conference, and many other cities, developed and grew with explosive force in the wake of the Industrial Revolution and that revolution is now surely over. It engendered a kind of civilisation, an urban civilisation, with fine buildings, grand institutions, new technologies and new structures of social organisation, as well as much poverty, misery and ill-health. A good deal of this, some good, some bad, remains with us, but the driving force has gone. Water transport, coal mining, steam power: these generators of nineteenth-century industry no longer shape our new landscapes, here in Britain or elsewhere. Nor are Greek Revival clubs and galleries, neo-Gothic town halls, schools and universities, cast-iron warehouses and red-brick terraced housing symbols of the growing wealth of cities, nor do public meetings hear impassioned pleas for social and political reform to spread this wealth to those whose manual skills created it. We live in interesting times, as the Chinese are reputed to say, and we see a new civilisation being constructed around us, based in part on the achievements, and problems of what we may perhaps dub "the Manchester civilisation", but not integral with it and not leading in the same direction. This is a period of great change, political, economic and social, and the consequences of this process will be felt in our cities, in all parts of the world, for a long time to come. There will, hopefully, be a new civilisation, but its shape is as yet far from clear.

The conference of which this book provides a partial record, presents an opportunity for reflecting on the nature of this anticipated new urban civilisation from a particular point of view. This is the one offered by people-environment studies. The field, which has been variously known as architectural or environmental psychology or sociology, man-environment or human-factor studies, or just plain environmental studies, investigates the ways in which people create, adapt, use and respond to their physical surroundings. That part of this subject which deals with city-dwellers and city-life, most often owes its fundamental conceptualisation to urban sociology, but this itself is a new and only partly-formed area of application and many of the questions raised in the conference papers, or chapters of this book, defy simple disciplinary classification.

For many specialists, the essential characteristics of city-life, in whatever period of history, have yet to be defined. A start was certainly made by sociologists such as Simmel (1936) and Wirth (1938). Modern cities, it was argued, have the overwhelming benefit of offering great opportunities for personal realisation and social improvement. The very anonymity that is found in high-density concentrations of human beings allows each to find her or his own identity and way of life. Markets can be created to respond to new desires and these do not have to be defined or controlled by tradition. Forms of community can develop which respond to the needs of the previously disenfranchised and unskilled as well as to those of privilege and inheritance.

This tradition of thought is especially associated with the work of the colleagues and students of Park and Burgess (1925) in Chicago and has in recent years been much criticised for its acceptance of the forces of industrialisation, urbanism and migration as well as for an often mechanistic view of the consequences for individual people of these social trends. A major transformation in ways of thinking about urbanism was wrought by Jacobs (1961) who saw more value in the vitality and the diversity of the social groups and small businesses which clustered in the inner areas than the Chicago School theorists, who considered this no more than a zone of transition which those able to do so would soon escape. More radical again were the perceptions of Harvey (1973) and Castells (1972) who presented cities as places of conflict and struggle, where power was created, brokered and exercised and where economies were generated, developed and brought to crisis. Above all, the city was seen as a political arena. Present theorisations tend to stress the conflicts in state and local government policies for urban place-making and to relate these to (Healey et al 1992) to struggles over the use of institutional resources to create desirable forms of employment.

The papers in the first part of the conference, and thus of this book, are concerned with the human aspects of this place-making process on a broader front. They approach it less from the point of view of the professional urban designer, who is concerned with manipulating funding sources, development permissions and aesthetic codifications, than from the point of view of the various types of city dwellers who must find their homes there and make their way of life. As well as being "democratic" in their orientation, these chapters are also "internationalist" on a broad scale, implicitly arguing that lessons can be learnt for other urban situations from the experience of many "exotic" experiences. Thus the substantive chapters in this part of the book deal with urban histories and associated myths, with social structures and movements, with the problems of bureaucracies and with the role of individual, personal experience. So if the picture which emerges is of a society participating, or attempting, to participate in the creation of its own environment, this society also seems to be a global one, or to have global features. The case-study material, which comes from Britain, Switzerland, Hungary, the Czech Republic, the United States, Brazil, Turkey, Nigeria and Australia, makes Simmel's view of the anonymous city-dweller appear rather limited. Urban life in the "post-Manchester" society seems replete with human histories and human emotions. It is surely on the basis of these social dimensions that the city of the twenty-first century is being constructed. An active, rather than a passive, view of the way people bring their own intentions to the appropriation of space is now required in urban theories.

Tikeli's opening chapter introduces the international perspective of the book. It gives a useful corrective to the presumption too easily made in collections of this kind that urban problems are found in the West (or North) and development problems in the East (or South). His argument here is based on the twin assumptions that all of today's cities are affected by rather general social and economic forces, but that each one is different in the particular way in which its history determines their expression. He ties the patronage system brought by Turkish migrants into their urban settings to the form of citizenship which is most often found there, giving a most appropriate lead into the theme of the first part of the book, citizen participation. Indeed the next contributor, Kroll, has a well-established reputation as a facilitator of participatory architectural and urban design. His purpose here is to challenge professional preconceptions. How can geometry respond to life? Why should order be imposed on our homes? What knid of a machine is supposed to be controlling the environment? Can we extract ourselves from the twentieth century? Will artchitects ever find themselves useful? Kroll's examples are intended to show that these questions can have unexpected answers and that organic, not a mechanistic urbanism is possible. These two opening chapters, stressing the global context and the humanist perspective set an agenda to which later chapters respond.

Moving to the broader backdrop, Lawrence reviews the anthropological literature on urban form, showing that myths have had an important role in determining the site layout of ancient cities. Rituals have often been associated with their establishment but in the modern world bureaucratic procedures have tended to suppress these. The chapter argues for a reintegration of the "irrational" with the rational in contemporary urban design. A start in this direction is made with Oyediran's chapter on factors determining the design and construction of home compounds amongst the Hausas and Tivs of Northern Nigeria. Religion is an important influence and attitudes towards the separation of the sexes and the generations are emphasised. These issues are associated in many parts of the world with the spread of the Christian and Islamic religions and reappear in the history of an Anatolian town, Kayseri, discussed by Imamoglu. The city had noticeably different structures of social life contained in equally different physical forms. The author argues that for more than 800 years this led to "a lively but stable social life, cultural and economic life in the town" and regrets that these deep roots have not been exploited in the transformations which have occurred in the last 40 years. Just what this recent "modernisation" may have consisted of is well-illustrated by reference to Dener's chapter, a case study of the development of apartment buildings in Istanbul. The evidence shows the introduction of new typologies by the upper middle classes, who continued to wish to live "modestly" but with higher standards of equipment. This first stage was followed by a rash of higher density construction for the "nouveaux riches" and later, the development of imaginative "build-and-sell" systems for the poorer social groups, as well as increasing regulation over squatter settlements. In the author's words "the elevations had to be spectacular".

The next two chapters both deal with contemporary processes of urbanisation in Brazil. Lay and Reis undertook a complex study of residents' images of mass housing schemes in Porto Alegre. Functional and symbolic features of the schemes were identified in the study: neighbours' and outsiders' opinions about the schemes, standards of maintenance and ease or of orientation were factors determining residents' views, although their own positive or negative attitudes were also shown to be influential. The study contrasts interestingly with that reported by Duarte, a longitudinal study of the first eight years of a scheme for the forced urbanisation of squatters in Rio de Janeiro. A sudden change in the degree of personalisation of the new dwellings was observed and the author shows that this coincided with the development of a stronger sense of community among their residents. Social and spatial communities, it is argued, are constructed together in such situations.

If these chapters suggest their authors are optimistic about the possibilities for realising an expression of social and community values in the urbanisation (and modernisation) of developing countries, those that follow seem less certain that design participation procedures will lead to desired outcomes in the developed countries. Sanoff's case study of workshops in Bangalon in Australia concludes that although community involvement is valued and affects outcomes substantially, "the end product is not the end of the process": an ongoing process of monitoring and adaptation of the environment to changing needs will continue to be needed. Even if this may be difficult, for as Hubbard argues in the next chapter, the values of the professionals who must work with lay people on planning decisions are so different that the former cannot adequately conceptualise the preferences expressed by the latter. The chapter supports this view with evidence from the analysis of a multiple sorting test undertaken in Britain. The question of how the ambitions of popular culture can be applied to the development of a bureaucratically regulated environment comes up again in Doughty's chapter on the spa-towns of three European countries. The conclusions, however, seem to point in a different direction, for the Welsh example seems to need the kind of bureaucratic support which still existed when the chapter's author visited Hungary and the Czech Republic.

Official procedures, market processes and the interests of different social groups interact in a complex way and further research on the range of outcomes to be found in developed countries is still required. A clear and simple example is reported by Stamp. In it various hypotheses concerning preferences for house and block design were tested with San Francisco residents. This chapter is a valuable addition to the scientific literature and could usefully be replicated elsewhere but a fascinating example of an alternative paradigm is given by Barbey in the chapter on personal urban experience. The discussion centres on two aspects of his life world: the experience of having lived in and around a single city for over sixty years and the experiences of having visited a number of other, very different, cities at key moments in a particular twenty-year period of his personal history. The foreign cities are presented as a "kaleidoscope" while the familiar city presents a "panorama"; the former flicker as in the light of a candle while the latter is spread out like tablecloth but both are necessary for a composite image of the city. It is on such personal syntheses, it is argued, that projects for urban design must be founded.

A final chapter in this part of the book, by Montera, gives a bibliometric review of publications on environmental psychology. This will serve as a useful reference point for those seeking to understand the way this field has developed and may develop in the future. Although the definitions of the emerging topics have been somewhat diffuse and the spread of their publication rather wide, it is clear that the field is beginning to cohere. It is to be hoped that the twelve other chapters published in this part of the book will encourage that coherence and that the knowledge this new sub-discipline produces will encourage people the world over to work to make urban places they can feel are their own.

References:

Briggs, A "Victorian Cities", London, Odhams, 1963

Castells, M. "La Question Urbaine", Paris, Maspero, 1972

Jacobs, J. "The Death and Life of Great American Cities", New York, Randon House, 1961

Harvey, D. "Social Justice and the City", London, Edward Arnold, 1973

Healey, P., Davoudi, S., O'Toole, M., Tarsanoglu, S. and Usher, D. (eds) "Rebuilding the City", London, Chapman and Hall, 1992

Park, R.E., Burgess E.W. "The City", Chicago, University of Chicago Press, 1936

Simmel, G. "The Metropolis and Mental Life", Chicago, University of Chicago Press, 1936

Wirth, L. "Urbanism as a Way of Life" in American Journal of Sociology XLIV(1), July 1938, 1-24

2

The patron-client relationship, land-rent economy and the experience of "urbanization without citizens"

Les relations de clientèle, la location de terrains, et l'expérience de "l'urbanisation sans citoyens"

Ilhan Tekeli

Nous avons tenté de comprendre l'urbanisation rapide des pays situés en périphérie du centre capitaliste, du point de vue des formes urbaines spécifiques qui sont apparues, et au regard des transformations culturelles subies - ou non - par les populations urbaines. Nos efforts ont échoué en face de la complexité du phénomène.

Cet exposé présente ces efforts de compréhension et d'éclaircissement à travers les relations internes de trois variables souvent ignorées dans le paradigme dominant. Dans ces pays, les trois variables cruciales dans l'élaboration d'un projet sont: a) les relations de clientèle qui dominent la vie politique; b) l'économie de location de terrains en zone urbaine, encouragée par l'urbanisation rapide et les mécanismes politiques dominants; et c) l'absence de "citoyenneté" dans ces villes, malgré le développement d'un individualisme opportuniste.

Se fonder seulement sur ces trois variables reviendrait à trop simplifier un phénomène urbain complexe. Cependant l'étude détaillée des relations internes et des interactions entre ces trois variables aide à mieux comprendre la reproduction de l'expérience urbaine de ces pays, en termes physiques et culturels, et révèle les obstacles qui s'opposent au développement et à l'enrichissement de leur qualité de vie urbaine.

Mots clé: relations de clientèle; économie de location; citoyenneté; qualité de vie urbaine.

Keywords: Patron-client relations, rent economy, citizenship, quality of city life

I come from Turkey, a country which has been experiencing a rapid urbanization process for fifty years similar to many developing countries. I have been faced with this experience as a citizen, struggling with its daily problems; as a city planner, trying to find solutions to these problems; and as a university professor, trying to make some conceptualizations and theoretical explanations. Throughout these fifty years, both the phenomenon we have been experiencing and our ways of perceiving it have changed continuously partly due to our failures as city planners. These will continue to change in the future as well. With the aim of comprehending this experience, I will try to explore this issue by concentrating on the mutual interaction of three variables which I find worth considering nowadays.

These three variables are; 1) a dominant populist attitude in the political field in those countries or the patron-client relationships, 2) an urban land-rent economy, 3) a lack of the formation of citizenship in those cities, or 'urbanization without citizens'. Presenting the mutual interaction between these variables will expose more clearly the barriers which stand in the way of development of healthy and safe urban forms and the enrichment of the quality of urban life in developing countries. On the other hand, it should be noted that these three variables, though very important, will only partially represent such a phenomenon as complex and overdetermined as urbanization. What I seek to do in this paper is to attract attention to various relationships which have barely been considered.

POPULIST POLICIES AND URBAN PATRON-CLIENT RELATIONSHIPS

After the second world war, the developing countries generally pursued populist policies. Whether they were authoritarian or democratic regimes, this tendency was very strong. It can be claimed that the ways of articulation with the world economy and the modernity project carried out in those countries brought about this tendency. The traditional structures in those countries started to dissolve and a rapid urbanization emerged as a result. However, this dissolution in the traditional relations was not strong enough to give rise to new social relations in the urban areas to be able to integrate migrants. New forms of relationship could not develop; institutions of civil society could not evolve; and social structure and political ideologies could not be crystallized (K²ray, 1982a).

Within such a transitional society, populism had the chance to become an ideology which could bring together different uncrystallized groups. As this ideology could set up coalitions between economic elites, intellectuals, middle-classes, workers and peasants, it could also articulate with different political ideologies. Whether these populist policies were put into practice by multi-party democratic regimes or authoritarian single-party regimes, a wide-spread patronage pattern, comprising partly traditional, partly modern relationships, has been encountered within these (Sunar, 1983).

Within a patron-client relationship, the people holding the political power can allocate the resources they control by favouring the people who show political loyalty and devotion to them and by distorting the legal order in certain degrees. This relationship may take different forms with respect to the resources which are controlled, the size of the groups benefiting from these allocations and different ways of expressing this devotion. When such a relationship is taken into consideration, two results can be drawn. The first one is that these resources can be distributed to a small group of followers because the resources controlled by the people with political power are limited. Therefore, this will create double-standards in terms of the norms of the nation state which assumes all citizens as equal. On the other hand, if the resources are directed to large masses with egalitarian considerations, then the system is likely to experience certain bottlenecks and crises.

Although there are various theoretical inconsistencies in this respect, the patron-client relationship and populist policies have been utilized successfully by politicians in transitional societies for certain periods of time in stabilizing the social structure (Denoeux, 1993). The stabilizing effect of this attitude is generally encountered in the following cases; 1) The existence of a strong central authority and the implementation of these populist policies by a charismatic leader in power. The responsibility of establishing the political order is not expected from the cliente list relationship networks themselves but they can function under the existing central authority. 2) These policies do not lead to crises in the periods when development can be achieved and the political authority can hold together wide coalitions by means of these allocation channels. 3) The maintenance of these populist policies cannot be realized only by means of the allocation channels of patron-client relationships but a political discourse should be developed so as to get the support of the masses. 4) These policies do not lead to destabilization in societies which are not fragmented in terms of ethnic and religious relations or if the patron-client relationships can cut across these groups.

THE IMPORTANCE OF URBANIZATION AND RENT-ECONOMY WITH RESPECT TO POPULIST POLICIES AND PATRON-CLIENT RELATIONSHIPS

In contrast to the expectations, rapid urbanization did not lead to radical political action in the initial years of urbanization in developing countries and it did not become a threat for the existing political authorities. This phenomenon has been explored within various theoretical frameworks. One of these is the

12

theory of relative deprivation. According to this, the new-comers to the urban areas perceive their deprivation in comparison to the conditions in the areas they come from. This, in turn, keeps them away from a radical attitude. Another theoretical explanation is Huntington's hypothesis. According to this, the urban poor is faced with urgent needs that must be fulfilled in a short time. Therefore, they can fulfil these not by reacting against the existing authority groups but by taking side with them. Both of these explanations are relevant for the first-generation migrants but they become inadequate for a longer-term analysis.

The populist policies in allocating the rents created in the urban economy and the patron-client relationships can provide some explanations in this respect. The rents created in the urban economy and their rising surface are influential in making the populist policies gain a stabilizing effect. The magnitude of the urban rents in countries which experience a rapid urbanization and its importance in the allocation of income created in the country should not be underestimated.

The rents which are created in different areas of urban economy can be summed up in two groups. The first type is related to the rents which are created by converting the urban land into building lots and by granting development rights. The second type of rents are created by means of entry barriers established institutionally in various service sectors. In both of these, as the size of the cities increases, the magnitude of the rents that are created also increases. This becomes the major field of activity for local authorities and local political relations. It can be claimed that every local authority programme associated with new service production and activities has always comprised a second meaning, though not expressed explicitly. This is linked to the allocation of urban rents on space and among social groups.

With regard to the establishment and maintenance of patron-client relationships, the allocation of urban rents possesses various advantages compared to the direct allocation of the state resources by politicians. These advantages can be set out in the following way; 1) During the allocation of urban rents, there is not a direct transfer of money from the administration and the people living in the city realize these themselves. Therefore, its legitimization becomes easy within the discourse of market economy and ownership rights. 2) For this reason, the limits of the allocated resources, whether they are exhausted or not is not definitely known. Though easier in growing systems, it is also possible to provide various benefits in this way in systems which are not growing. 3) A wide coalition may be set up in the society by giving different groups the opportunity to create rents against each other. However, it is not possible to make a net account of the gains and losses of different groups so various groups give a support to these populist policies easily within an illusion. 4) As encountered especially in the allocation of urban land rents, due to the social stratification, the real-estate owners in the society are able to maximize their rents while the people without any real-estate can avoid paying rents by seizing public land and get a share of the rents after these plots are given a legal status. The variety and the flexibility in the formation of urban rents and its seizure and allocation provide an ideal medium for maintaining the populist policies and patron-client relationships.

THE LACK OF THE FORMATION OF CITIZENSHIP

When a rapid urbanization process started be experienced in the peripheral countries, it was expected within a positivistic scientific approach that these migrant masses would realize a cultural transformation. This transformation was expected to occur in accordance with the motto of the Chicago School, which was 'urbanism as a way of life' or in accordance with the modernization paradigm. In both cases, the expectation was the same.

It was expected that the new urban dwellers, as atomistic individuals, would live in the city within instrumental and anonymous relationships, without being exposed to direct social control, by switching from primary to secondary relations, by forming diversified and transitional relations and by adopting the urban cultural norms within an individualistic competitive atmosphere.

The urban migrants experienced an important cultural transformation within two or three generations. However, this transformation did not occur parallel to the expectations set out in urban sociology literature (Pickvance, 1976). These people learned how to benefit from all the opportunities provided in urban areas. They obtained a share from urban rents within patron-client relationships. They could also be influential in the political arena. They formed their relationships in an instrumental manner so as to realize their consumption norms. The cultural transformation they experienced had both defensive and offensive elements. The defensive element was associated with the fear of getting lost in the city by becoming atomistic individuals. They reinvented their identities, which they did not acknowledge in their home-lands, with the name of 'hemserilik' in the cities they settled to form a defense mechanism and these relationships enabled the patron-client network to be established more easily. They created a social control to some extent and delayed the weakening of primary relationships. On the other hand, they gained the opportunity of continuously reproducing and spreading their own music and cultural norms by means of various channels of market mechanism. This, in turn, has been perceived to be an offensive attitude by the old urban dwellers.

How can we evaluate the cultural transformation which has been different from what has been expected in the urban sociology literature? Or is it our historical understanding which should be judged? The inadequacy of the modern historical approach which has a strong belief in the determination of historical processes, leaving us devoid of other alternatives has become quite apparent. Consequently, the significance of a critical historical approach has been acknowledged. If it is accepted that history is a critical category as Arendt has claimed, then we cannot be satisfied with explaining only what has happened. We should concentrate on the lack of the formation of the public realm and with reference to this, the opportunities that could not be utilized in the formation of the urban citizen (Hansen, 1993).

In both the expected and the experienced transformation model, we are encountered with a society composed of individuals imprisoned into their individual lives. In fact, the formation of citizens has not constituted an important place in the urban sociology literature. The formation of the nation state and the participation of the individual in the voting process to establish the political authority has been accepted to be adequate in assuming the existence of citizens. In fact, there is no reason in complaining about the patron-client relationship if the formation of the citizen is approached with such a superficial point of view.

However, in a comprehensive definition of citizen, an individual as a member of society is considered instead of atomistic individuals. On the other hand, admitting the existence of a societal level does not lead to the reification of the individual. The individuals are expected to take into consideration in their actions the society and its laws, i.e they will use their rights but at the same time be conscious about their power in changing the society and its rules with their active contribution, as they are performing their responsibilities (Arendt, 1958). Such citizens can emerge only with the formation of the public life and public realm. The people sharing a common world within a sphere of appearance where public problems can be put forward and discussed from different points of view can deal with politics as citizens (Passerin D'Entreves, 1993). They can make sacrifices for the interest of this common world or the city. They feel contented with the formation of such a common public realm and construct a collective identity. With respect to the above framework, citizenship can be perceived as an active debate on the competing projects of collective identity. Only within such a medium, can individual freedom as well as a multidimensional cooperative individualism be realized in society.

If the mode of politics is imprisoned by populism and patron-client relationships in a country, then the possibility of the emergence of citizens tends to disappear. Their point of view is doomed to be blinded by their interests in the private sphere, which can be fulfilled through patron-client relationships. Therefore, they will consider the attempt to make a contribution in forming a public realm within a sphere of appearance as a waste of time. Within the opaque political field constituted by a network of patron-client relationships, they will try to maximize their private interests ignoring the existence of a public realm. The emergence of such a mechanism will create the major obstacle in the formation of citizens.

WHAT KIND OF AN URBAN FORM AND LIFE QUALITY IS EMERGING IN CITIES

In my opinion, we have to do more than mentioning about the important aspects of the urbanization experience. Their consequences should also be considered. In this section, I will attempt to investigate three of these, 1) urban planning, 2) urban form, and 3) the repercussions on the quality of urban life.

Urban planning was introduced in developing countries as a part of the modernity project. Behind this project, there is a definite understanding of politics and citizenship and it gets its legitimization within this framework. The populist attitude in politics encountered in those countries continuously produce very creative ways of ignoring the plans. These unauthorized developments are always legalized, confined to a certain period and area. On the other hand, the modernist urban planning approach maintains its characteristic of constituting the major legitimization framework for constructions in the city. Such a contradiction is continuously being experienced in the system. Since the system cannot establish the public realm and citizens, it can neither construct a planning discipline nor organize the control mechanisms. Therefore, a chronic legitimization crisis is being experienced in developing an alternative legitimization framework to improve the existing practice.

This populist political system is liable to both creating and avoiding rents. Therefore, as it tries to present a planned image, it is also likely to show tolerance to spontaneous unauthorized developments. The possibility of avoiding the urban rents leads to urban sprawls at the fringe, along the main highways (K^{2}ray, 1982b). On the other hand, the tendency to maximize the urban rents results in a continuous increase in the development rights in central areas, development of the process of pulling down and reconstruction and a rapid intensification in vacant areas. In the course of time, the area between the fringe and the city become exposed to construction activities gradually. The rapidly expanding urban population enables these processes to perform their expected functions. Although the housing supply processes and the organization pattern of transportation in the city may allow a decentralized macroform, the cities spread in the form of oil drops dispersed at the fringe. In evaluating this urban macroform, it must be noted that it has some positive features as well as negative ones with respect to the quality of urban life.

The high rents created by the rapid urbanization, the development pattern of urban forms and the urban services affect the urban life in many respects. The rise and enlargement of the rent surface in the city increases the cost of living, i.e. the reproduction of laborforce. The attempts to show the high cost of living in the city as an inevitable result of urbanization remain a matter for debate. Some part of the rents created by the growing cities is unavoidable. However, a considerable part of the rents created in the cities of those countries are absolute rents and It is not possible to justify this avoidable part of rents. If the political practices in a country achieve a decrease in these rents, then it may be possible to lower the cost of laborforce and increase the competitive advantages at the international level. This, in turn, will create a positive chain reaction in the development of the country.

In addition to the above considerations, the rents are, in fact, created by the society so it is not possible for real estate owners to justify their claims of rent ethically (Tekeli, 1991). The populist policies in developing countries allow the real estate owners to obtain these rents and they cannot direct these rents to the central or local administrations through a strict taxation policy. As a result, the cities grow without sufficient infrastructure and urban services. Insufficient infrastructure cannot be explained solely on the basis of low national income. The accumulation of urban rents in the hands of real estate owners instead of the public institutions distorts the balance between the private and public expenditures. People in those countries spend a lot of money to furnish their houses but they still come to their houses passing through muddy streets. In fact, this is a good indicator of how populist policies prevent the development of a public realm and imprison the urban dwellers into their private field of consumption.

Naturally, the repercussions of the urbanization experience, developing within patron-client relationships can be explored more in detail with respect to its implications on the quality of urban life. However, I want to conclude this evaluation by emphasizing one more issue. Within this urbanization experience, the individuals are continuously faced with a kind of hypocrisy in society. The individuals obeying the urban plans and the legal laws of society, i.e the ones who try to be proper citizens are doomed to lose compared to the ones who succeed in breaking these laws. This hypocrisy may continue to exist without leading to serious political tensions due to the lack of the formation of citizens. In fact, the maintenance of the patron-client relationship within a nation state is nothing else, but mere hypocrisy.

SOME FINAL COMMENTS

This analysis concerning the urbanization experience in developing countries seems to pose a pessimistic picture. Despite all these problems, urbanization provides important opportunities for these countries in activating the dynamics of development. The criticism put forward in the present evaluation aims at a better utilization of these opportunities. Therefore, it possesses a hope as well as a kind of optimism. For this reason, it has been attempted to introduce the problematic of the formation of the citizen into the agenda of developing countries. I sincerely believe that even if the individuals are tried to be alienated in society, the motivation for social solidarity cannot be regressed to the point at which it cannot be activated again.

References

Hannah Arendt: The Human Condition, The University of Chicago Press, Chicago, 1958
    Guilain Denoeux: Urban Unrest in Middle East, State University of New York Press, New York, 1993.
Phillp Hansen: Hannah Arendt Politics, History and Citizenship, Polity Press, Cambridge, 1993.
Mubeccel Kiray: "Changing Pattern of Patronage: A Study in Structural Change", Mubeccel Kiray: Toplumbilim Yazilari, Gazi Universitesi, Ankara, 1982, pp. 177-202.
Mubeccel Kiray: "Metropoliten Kent Olgus", Mubeccel Kiray: Toplumbilim Yazilari, Gazi Universitesi, Ankara, 1982, pp. 353-365.
Maurizio Passerin D'Entreves: "Hannah Ardent ve Yurttaslik Kavrami", Birikim, No. 55, November 1993, pp. 67-81.
C. G. Pickvance: "Introduction: Historical Materialist approaches to Urban Sociology", in C.G.Pickvance (ed.), Urban Sociology, Tavistock Publications, London, 1976, pp. 1-32.
Ilkay Sunar: "Demokrat Parti ve Populism", Cumhuriyet Dönemi Türkiye Ansiklopedisi, Vol. 8, Iletisim Yayinlari, 1983, pp. 2076-2088.
Ilhan Tekeli: Kent Planlamasi Konusmalari, TMMOB Mimarlat Odasi Yayinlari, Ankara, 1991.

3

Vers une écologie urbaine

Towards an urban ecology

Lucien Kroll

Some contemporaries - non-moderns, who are thus post-moderns - tell us about their own obvious logic, and not about Reason (which too often gives way when one stops watching it). Matter does not conform with the physicists' great schemes and disobeys their orders. What about planning then?

The town of Curitiba is managed like a compost heap.

We know that the great manoeuvres of our economic (and cultural) mercenaries towards the poor and the distant, towards the Third and Fourth Worlds, require a complicity with offensive mechanization, which, if left unbridled, appears more and more unbearable, unfair and self-destructive. We must give priority to eco-sociology.

Let's not talk about architecture, which leads us to manufacture, artifice and separation. Let's talk about process, and therefore about landscape. A landscape builds itself up, using its personal and communal energy (phytosociology), and without any creator's direction.

A landscape is a living entity (therefore representing more than the sum of its components). It slowly establishes its balance (which is always temporary) through disturbances, in which it answers rationally all the motives of its own creation, even those of the lowest energy. Sometimes a piece of architecture can become a landscape.

Who is rational?

Keywords: non-moderns; Curitiba; eco-sociology; process; landscape.

Mots clé: non-modernes; post-modernes; Curitiba; éco-sociologie; processus; paysage.

l'Anti-moderne ou la Standardisation?
Crise du paysage urbain ou Survivre dans les Ordure?
Paysage et Société, ou comment retrouver l'équité?

ALENÇON

Figure 3.1 Alençon.

ENTRE MODERNE ET CONTEMPORAIN

Des "contemporains" donc des non-modernes, donc des postmodernes, disent leurs logiques vécues, évidente et non la Raison. Celle-ci mollit trop souvent : chaque fois qu'on la quitte du regard. La Raison a dérivé lentement à un tel point que même les innocences de la modernité se brouillent à la vue, deviennent incompréhensibles, barbares même! La nouvelle générosité, l'équité sociale reprise à zéro, la rationalité heureuse, la table rase des complications culturelles, l'interdiction des désordres anciens, la technique rédemptrice, les promesses d'avenir neuf et toute la quincaillerie du progrès mécanique, tout ceci semble subitement poussiéreux et même méchant. Lorsqu'on mesure l'arrivisme des arrivés et les conséquences de leurs productions d'architectes, on se demande bien ce qu'on peut conserver de ces grands tracés urbains froids, de ces utopies parfaites, de ces villes linéaires, circulaires ou quadrillées, de leurs exercices scolaires? Et puis de leurs réalisations si bien mécanisées qu'un grand nombre d'ensembles rationnels, inhabitables, devront être démolis et le reste devra être refourbi pour plus d'argent qu'ils n'avaient coûté! Les innocences du Mouvement Moderne adolescent se sont réalisées en son âge mûr sous forme d'abstractions qui voulaient échapper totalement aux complexités de la vie, à celles de la société et bientôt même aux désordres des sciences exactes (une trahison!). Leur perfection était encore viciée par l'esprit du temps de leur temps qu'aucune raison n'avait réussi à éclairer: le colonialisme, le taylorisme militaire, l'eurocentrisme ou le racisme encore aimable, l'illusion de l'astrophysique comme modèle de mécanique éternelle, l'angélisme, etc. A qui croire encore: l'immaculée conception des schémas, trop transparents, saisis d'un coup d'oeil et répétés à l'infini, démocratiquement, devenait une méchante sociobiologie.

NEWTON OU PRIGOGINE

Car, voici que la matière désobéit aux grands schémas des physiciens qui lui avaient assigné un ordre définitif. Et que seul le désordre, le déséquilibre, lui donnent l'opportunité de se confectionner un ordre bien à elle. Et l'urbanisme alors? Les géométries se déforment, bourgeonnent, l'équilibre fait le tourbillon, du chaos émerge un ordre complexe, les attracteurs sont étranges, d'honnêtes dimensions stables et fiables subitement se jettent vers l'infini, les sols empoisonnés se refont en jardins, le quotidien redevient sacré et le héros risible et parfois des architectes ont l'étrange sentiment d'être utiles. La ville de Curitiba est gérée comme un compost. Puis les urbains s'affairent en comités et poliment transforment enfin des asphaltes en micro-parcs. On renonce aux certitudes chimiques et on demande aux plantes d'assainir nos eaux-vannes turpides dans une grande fête. La systémique moralement confortable devient floue : on s'efforce alors de penser relationnel. Tout s'enchaene et prend un autre sens. Comprendra-t-on ? Qu'importe puisque c'est la vie contemporaine. C'est l'écologie. Mais rien n'est jamais gagné.

L'écologie est d'abord sociale avant d'être "de luxe". On sait comment les grandes manoeuvres de nos mercenaires économiques (aussi bien culturels) face aux pauvres et aux lointains, aux 1/3 & 1/4 mondes, exigent une complicité avec de méchantes mécanisations qui, lorsqu'elles sont effrénées, s'affichent de plus en plus insupportables, inéquitables, auto-destructives.

LE JARDIN OU LE QUARTIER

Même le jardin n'échappe pas: il est, et sans violence, un emblème, un leurre, une maquette de cette angoisse moderne (ou anti-), un exercice, un révélateur, une éprouvette. Il aide à comprendre, à souffrir, à vivre la chose. Encore faudrait-il que le jardinier avoue son rôle, aimablement. Que le jardin ne se contente pas, narcissiquement, d'être un objet, comme la plupart des architectures actuelles! Car s'il se réduit à être rationnel, il est administrativement confortable: on peut le faxer sans rien perdre de sa substance, il est lyophilisé. Il ne peut jamais être plus que ce qu'un créateur a dit qu'il serait: stérile donc.

PAYSAGE

Ne parlons pas d'architecture car nous tombons dans l'ordre du fabricat, de l'artifice, de la séparation. Parlons de processus donc de paysage. Un paysage se construit lui-même, dans son élan personnel et communautaire (phytosociologie) sans directive d'auteur (l'an-archie): ce sont les paysagistes sans doute les seuls à ne pas faire de paysage! Un paysage est un ensemble vivant (donc plus que la somme de ses éléments!) qui à travers ses tumultes, forme lentement son équilibre (toujours provisoire) en répondant de faτon rationnelle à tous les motifs de sa formation, même ceux de la plus faible énergie. Bien l'inverse des attitudes modernes!

ARCHITECTURE

Une architecture peut devenir paysage, parfois: cela dépend de l'ouverture ou de la crispation de son responsable. Nous visons ceci: le chaos et l'écologie travaillent ensemble mais il en est rarement question chez les paysagistes. Pas plus chez les architectes ou les urbanistes: ils imposent leur ordre et s'angoissent à l'idée d'un futur qui leur échapperait! Expliquons : il est proprement académique de mécaniser un métier et de considérer cette activité comme un droit personnel (en soi, solitaire et de plus en plus exclusif) et non comme l'interprétation des mouvements browniens de la vie d'une société. Mais lesquels?

FISSURES

Que s'est-il passé: une nouvelle sauvagerie, la fin d'un fanatisme religieux, un effondrement des certitudes (idéologiques ou morales), une dérive vers le désordre amical, (les défauts, même des méthodologies nouvelles destinées à quitter les habitudes sont plus constructifs que les perfections.

ARCHITECTES

On comprend les malaises et les fuites vers l'absurde. Aucun architecte ne deviendra célèbre simplement parce qu'il est le plus banal de sa génération. Sauf enraciné dans son milieu, il ne peut survivre sans étonner. Les plus fort étonnent fortement. On ne l'appelle que parce qu'on l'a remarqué. Par après, ils rédigent des discours-modes-d'emploi qui disent combien seul l'absurde est légitime et combien donc ils sont uniques. Tous. Leur importance se mesure au nombre d'hectares de quadrichromies qu'ils ont publiées. Et à chaque nouvelle affaire, il doivent étonner plus qu'à la précédente. Et ils le font. Pourtant ça fatigue. Ou bien ils choisissent d'être plus vides encore qu'avant, sans pour autant proposer de nouvelle attitude (Dada déjà...). Puisqu'ils ne peuvent plus montrer leur générosité (elle méprise celui qui reçoit), leur courage (il écrase le laïc), leur rationalité (elle trompe l'émotion populaire), leur culture (elle n'est pas compatible)...   Ou encore le cosmétique : une boεte ornée, c'est parfois plus que non ornée mais la substance n'est pas changée ni sa relation habitant/habité.

   Et le travesti en antique, parfois d'opérette mais souvent savamment sincère mais décalé dans le temps ou l'espace! Au moins, ceci chatouille l'angoisse moderne devant les formes du passé: pendant quelques générations de modernistes ces formes ont été le tabou, l'inceste. Rien de ce que la maman de l'architecte avait pu vivre ne pouvait être rappelé, même par allusion. Aucune forme passée ne pouvait se deviner, sous peine d'excommunication : rien que du neuf, du mécanique, du non-impliqué. La table rase est une malédiction moderne, pour se débarrasser de laquelle, il faut une grande clairvoyance (auto observation) et beaucoup d'énergie. Et encore, on parvient à racler quelques adhérences mais les plus honteuses ce sera seulement dans quelques années qu'elles apparaetront dans la lumière crue!

COMMENT SORTIR ÉLÉGAMMENT DU XX E SIÈCLE?

Les prophètes informatiques prolongent ces schizophrénies de nettoyages éthiques. On calcule durement, on rend logique ce qui était sentimental, géométrique ce qui était intuitif, numérique ce qui était analogique, et à nouveau mécanique ce qui était organique tout en disant rationnel ce qui n'est qu'abstrait. Aux USA, Herbert Simon et Marvin Minski avec des moyens métalliques et brillants retournent aux logiques des années trente et font commerce du general problem solving. Le titre sincère d'une des conférences de Simon est: "les sociétés seront-elles dirigées par des machines?" Tout son livre répond oui. La structure hiérarchique est bien l'inverse du réseau informel, lequel ne peut sans doute être géré ni par une machine mécanique ni par une machine déguisée en homme. La complexité est infinie et sans être massacrée, ne peut se traiter que par l'intuition, par l'instinct, par l'art. On se croirait revenu aux années vingt, comme avec certains architectes nostalgiques de ces certitudes. Le paysage à habiter, c'est pareil.

MACHINES

L'artificialisation gagne, les machines se déguisent en humanoïdes et par une contagion inverse décident que la seule vertu de l'homme, c'est sa logique; son seul art, une mécanique appliquée; son seul motif, une production. On parle alors d'ingénierie de la connaissance et même d'ingénierie de la culture. Nous voici à nouveau conduits par des garagistes. Car l'évolution de ces nouvelles bécanes va refluer en deuxième vague sur les modes de conception, d'expression et de réalisation du milieu habité. On croyait enfin sortir du préfabriqué lourd et étranger et on se précipite dans le cosmétique de peur de laisser créer les usagers eux-mêmes (même en accord avec les spécialistes) de peur de perdre son droit à l'autorité sur les formes et de laisser apparaetre une complexité, un tissu. L'angoisse de devoir opérer dans un champ qui n'ait pas été stérilisé, c'est à dire, où des initiatives d'habitants ou bien les évènements imprévus, devraient pouvoir être pris en compte! Louis Guillaume Le Roy y répond par son action, ordinaire, démesurée et tragique. Un seul outil, le temps. Les écologistes se coincent entre la politique et la "nature" et on les soupçonne de fàchisme! Mais qu'ont-ils proposé au paysage urbain? Conserver, est-ce conservateur? Qui est rationnel?

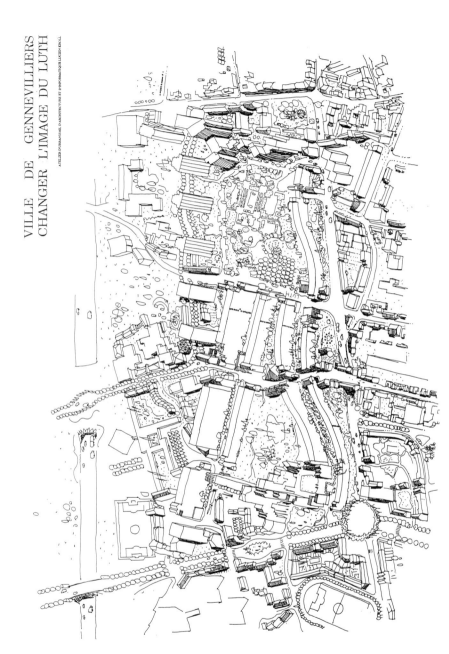

VILLE DE GENNEVILLIERS
CHANGER L'IMAGE DU LUTH

ATELIER D'URBANISME, D'ARCHITECTURE ET D'INFORMATIQUE LUCIEN KROLL

Figure 3.2   Ville de Gennevilliers changer l'image du Luth.

LES MODELES

Il n'y a pas de modèles géométriques des milieux habités: les formes simples ne peuvent rendre compte des complexités naturelles des paysages et des sociétés! L'écologie s'appuie seulement sur des actions humaines, animales, végétales, minérales jamais sur des formes abstraites! Un urbanisme de subsidiarité reᴛoit dans le paysage le résultat de toutes les actions de détails : il les fédère au moyen de connivences, d'instincts, d'empathie. Il procède par convictions et non par règles ni par plans d'ensemble centralisés auxquels doivent obéir les détails.   Encore faut-il percevoir les actions de détails et les unanimités dans leur variétés. Et puis essayer de les interpréter sans les réduire ni les massacrer.

EXEMPLES

Nous ne proposons pas les travaux qui suivent comme des oeuvres, mais comme des étapes, des résultats d'attitudes, de processus (laisser se faire et nager avec le courant). Et puis dans le kaléidoscope des tendances contemporaines, nous reconnaissons de loin quelques fraternités avec des attitudes semblables ou parallèles. C'est obstinément le même projet que notre atelier refait à travers les diverses missions qu'il a pu réaliser : déstabiliser les certitudes qui font les architectures héroïques, démontrer qu'un milieu aimable ne se constitue qu'en dehors des schémas d'autorités et que les outils modernes (organisation méthodique, industrie du bâtiment, informatique, etc.) peuvent aussi bien être utilisés à produire des milieux diversifiés. Nous espérons montrer comment atteindre l'organique, à travers des images apparemment disparates : celles-ci n'obéissent pas à des théories de la forme, mais proposent une enveloppe, un outil, un signe à ces écheveaux d'actions qu'on devine, d'attirances, de mouvements browniens et d'unanimités nécessaires à tisser les textures urbaines. L'ignorance de ces motifs touffus, leur simplification bête ou leur rationalisation anémie l'architecture.

Laroche-Clermault

Dans l'Indre-et-Loire, nous avions discuté avec "tout un village" pour lui greffer dix maisons : elles ne se voient pas. Aussi deux écoles, un petit peu obliques ou molles, en voûtes de bois, éclairées par les diagonales.

La ZUP de Perseigne et le collège Louise Michel à Alençon

C'est en suivant les piétons à la trace, que nous avons découvert une "rue virtuelle" autour de laquelle toutes les interventions se sont organisées. Un collège d'Education Secondaire a été un instrument de réhabilitation de l'ensemble.

Le Lycée Professionnel Diderot à Belfort

Pour qu'il y ait échange avec le quartier le plus proche, le Lycée ne pouvait s'enfermer dans ses murs et sa fonction: nous l'avons éclaté en elots variés, réunis par une place et des rues publiques et différenciées par tous les moyens. Nous avons placé l'extérieur au milieu.

Béthoncourt-Montbéliard

Une barre solitaire de 40 logements, vide depuis sept ans: essayons de lui donner un nouveau rôle de géométrie organique dans le quartier. Elle devient le quatrième côté d'une petite place habitée et se fait envahir par des maisons ordinaires en bout, de côté, par dessus: la voilà devenue .relais d'une continuité, l'inverse de la vocation de sa naissance. Une tour de 14 étages aussi.

Le Luth à Gennevilliers

"Désenclaver", demandait le concours d'architecture: nous avons imaginé une nouvelle voie Sud-Nord qui démolisse et qui remolissse aussitôt mais à l'image des piétons et non de la machine. Et au cours d'ateliers d'habitants, le projet s'est précisé, à leur image.

Vaulx-en-Velin

Après les désordres et l'insécurité, la Ville a à la hâte, organisé un concours entre plusieurs architectes pour élaborer une image dynamique qui motive les acteurs sociaux, économique, etc. Hélas, à nouveau le quartier a pris feu et, curieusement cela a gelé toute initiative : le concours n'a même pas été jugé (c'était la panique!).

Haarlem Zuiderpolder

Cent vingt-neuf logements sociaux dans les règles et dans les budgets coutumiers, mais avec toutes les variations accessibles. Et un pari : les habitants allaient se trouver tellement chez eux qu'ils continueraient spontanément notre projet et à leur façon c'est gagné: ils sont géniaux!

Ecolonia

Les Pays-Bas se sont subitement sentis si pollués qu'ils ont décidé de construire une opération démonstrative : une centaine de maisons amicales envers le milieu. On nous a demandé de (dés)organiser neuf architectes autour d'espaces publics que nous voulions peu autoritaires : aucune forme ne les commande, seulement des connivences urbaines.

Figure 3.3 Vaulx-en-Velin.

Pessac Les Ailes Françaises

Comment concevoir du logement qui convienne au Sud-Ouest? Surtout ne rien inventer: faire comme toujours est bien plus rationnel! Des rues et des places. Puis, nous avons découvert deux mensonges modernes. D'abord, des petits blocs bien rangés sur des pelouses, cela mange plus de terrain que les formes traditionnelles de rue. Ensuite le pavillon est moins cher que le collectif superposé. Pourquoi alors imposer du collectif éparpillé à des locataires qui demandent des pavillons depuis vingt-cinq ans en particulier et depuis plusieurs millénaires en général? Les cent soixante logements sont tous différents, bien sûr.

Cabrini-Green

Un concours sur la réhabilitation d'un quartier sordide à Chicago: nous avons proposé ce que nous savions en Europe. Deuxième place, mais nous n'avons pas compris pourquoi ils nous ont choisis?

et d'autres ...

4

Mythical and ritual constituents of the city

Eléments mythiques et rituels constitutifs de la ville

Roderick Lawrence and Claude Raffestin

"Un mythe exprime, relève et codifie une croyance; il préserve et renforce la moralité il garantit l'efficacité du rite et contient des règles pratiques de conduite. Le mythe est donc un ingrédient vital de la civilisation humaine; ce n'est pas un conte futile mais un récit empreint d'une force active, façonné par des principes actifs." Bronislaw Malinowski*
    On pense souvent que toute activité humaine dérive soit du non-rationnel, non-utilitaire mystique et sacré, soit du rationnel, utilitaire, bon sens et profane. Il en résulte que les comportements dictés par un mythe ou un rite ont souvent été considérés comme appartenant à des pratiques imaginaires, magiques ou religieuses. Toutefois, une telle vision dualiste induit en erreur. Cela s'est produit lors des travaux de recherche en sociologie, en anthropolgie ainsi que dans l'élaboration des théories d'architecture d'urbanisme. La présente étude affirme que la ville est une construction humaine à plusieurs dimensions. Elle ne devrait pas uniquement être considérée comme une solution rationnelle aux problèmes de l'habitat, du marketing; de la communication et des transports. La ville est plutôt comme un palimseste, constitué de couches successives chacune chargée d'histoire de culture, de politique et de symboles. Cette étude prétend que les quartiers urbains contemporains se sont appauvris en partie à cause d'une mauvaise interprétation de la nature composite (tant rationnelle que non rationnelle) de la ville. Chaque ville se compose de nombreux éléments culturels y compris mythes et rituels. Des rites et des mythes sont à l'origine de la fondation et de l'aménagement des villes ainsi que le cours de la vie quotidienne à travers les civilisation humaines. La présente étude propose des définitions et des interprétations de mythes et de rituels dans différents contextes urbains. Dans un deuxième temps, elle affirme que, bien qu'ils aient été ignorés par l'occident en général et par les scientifiques en particulier, le mythe et le rituel ne devraient pas l'être aujourd'hui.*

Mots clés: culture urbaine; mythes; rituels; planification urbaine
Keywords : urban culture; myths, rituals; urban planning

Keywords : urban culture; myths, rituals; urban planning

The city is a human construct par excellence. It is founded by sedentary people who choose to cultivate a particular portion of the landscape. The location of a site for the construction of a city is meant to respond to sets of criteria which a town planner, a surveyor or a geographer would usually classify in terms of its accessibility, climate, available resources, geological conditions and perhaps other rational parameters. Nonetheless, there is abundant evidence today that the siting and the layout of a city are also considered in terms of cosmological beliefs and ideals. These beliefs and ideals have been communicated throughout history, either by written prescriptions, or orally by myths. These myths deal simultaneously with a local environment (e.g. the city) and the universe (e.g. the cosmos). In principle the former is meant to reflect the latter, and explicit relationships are identified between humanity, other forms of life and the cosmos.

One value of myths is that they are visionary. Images are construed and used to interpret and cultivate the landscape, including the siting and layout of cities. Once the territory of a new city has been chosen it is commonly demarcated from its surroundings by a set of conceptual, behavioural, judicial, symbolic, political and physical boundaries. In essence, human-made boundaries are construed in otherwise nonbounded space and time. These boundaries distinguish between "here and there" or "this and that", which include the anthropos and the cosmos, as well as the city and the country.

Since the earliest human civilizations people have used diverse kinds of boundaries to order and control their relationships with other constituents of their local environment and the cosmos. Several anthropologists, including Leach (1976), have discussed how "this" and "that" are distinguished from each other by the use of conceptual boundaries. Given that such boundaries are fundamental constituents of human culture, they should not be overlooked in studies of the foundation, the meaning and the use of cities. Nonetheless, whereas many published studies have examined the siting, the layout and the morphology of cities, too few have simultaneously examined their underlying conceptual foundations using an integrative perspective. Therefore, this paper argues and illustrates that it is important to identify and comprehend the multidimensional nature of the city, both at one point in time and over an extended period.

It is generally recognized that often boundaries have explicit material dimensions, like those of the ancient city with massive fortifications. Nonetheless, the frontier between Italy and Switzerland, or the boundary between my house and that of my neighbour, may only be defined by a line on a map or an ordonnance. However, these representations of boundaries (recurrent in geography and town planning) do not indicate their political and legal, nor their socio-pyschological dimensions. Nonetheless, as Rykwert (1976) has shown, for example, a Romano Etruscan belief in the sacredness of land titles and the inviolability of property boundaries was transmitted and applied throughout the Roman Empire. The legal existence of a new Roman settlement was accompanied by an elaborate foundation act that preceded any construction work on the chosen site. The rectangular boundaries of the new settlement were attributed a religious connotation, because they not only delimited but also symbolically protected the sacred territory of the future city from other constituents of the cosmos. These boundaries were ritually defined by the initial furrow on the surface of the land. The furrowing of the soil was performed by the founder of the new settlement using a bronze plough. The line cut by the plough and the soil it displaced inside the boundary of the future city were considered sacred, whereas the span of the future gateways into the city (that were not furrowed) were subject to civil jurisdiction. Subsequently, the Romans employed diviners to perform purification rites using sacrificial animals that consecrated the boundaries. The city was formally founded only once these rites had been completed, and only then could the construction of the city begin.

This example could be illustrated by numerous others from different societies in each continent of the world. Collectively they show that in order to comprehend the multi-dimensional nature of cities it is instructive to analyse their conceptual and symbolic dimensions by identifying and studying the mythical and ritual constituents of the siting, layout and use of cities. In order to achieve this goal the next section of this paper presents and illustrates interpretations of myth and ritual. Then the paper considers their pertinence in the contemporary western world, in general, and with respect to urban life, in particular. The paper concludes by requesting and suggesting a reorientation and diversification of discourse and praxis about the city and daily urban affairs.

WHAT ARE MYTHS ?

In societies dominated by a quantitative, scientific world view, it may seem unjustified to evoke the notion of myth. On the one hand, this scepticism would be justified if myths were only fictitious fables that have no verification. On the other hand, this scepticism is unjustified given that mythos and logos are not mutually exclusive, but they have the same etymology and meaning. Both refer to those reasons, words and discourse that are personified as the source of order embodying patterns of relationships betwen humanity, other forms of life and the universe.

Myths are a fundamental constituent of human cultures found in all societies since the earliest civilisations. Myths help people to make sense of the universe, and their lives in it, in a comprehensive way. They are not to be misinterpreted as historical statements that can be validated: "Myths do not seek to answer questions in the manner required by modern science" Stewart (1989, p. 18). Rather, they restate, recreate and communicate the existence of the universe and of human life. People use myths as charters for their lives. Myths provide a source of meaning for the origin of humanity, and they enable people to acquire a sense of control of that which cannot be verified.

Several contributions by anthropologists show that myths are culture specific semantic communication systems that enable people to explain unobservable or unknown entities and events in terms of observable phenomena (Leach, 1968). In this sense, all human societies have spoken and/or written fables that function as myths of origin (Turner, 1968). Creation myths form a specific set of myths that transgress the realm of institutional or formal religion. This type of myth is not meant to seek unqualitifed answers to questions beyond the comprehension of ancient human civilisations. Rather, being an integral part of culture they provide "an organic timeless flow of images and narratives within which such questions were bypassed altogether, because the "answers" of mythology come from deep levels of unconsciousness, in which universal patterns or intimations are apprehended" (Stewart, 1989, p.6).

Myths commonly include discourse on the local (known) environment or habitat of people and the universal (unknown) environment. Myths are narratives that describe how one state (e.g. chaos) became another (e.g. the cosmos). In creation mythology there are two predominant models. The first is an image model that commonly adopts an anthropomorphic form (e.g. a human being) or a specific element of the environment such as a tree (e.g. the tree of life). In some applications of this model the origin of humanity precedes the appearance of animals and plants. This conceptual ordering of creation is the antithesis of the scientific concept of evolution commonly accepted today.

The second model in creation mythology is the directional model which attributes directions to the cosmos that are value-laden. There usually are six directions, namely east, south, west, north, above and below. As Stewart (1989, p. 19) noted, although there are distinct geographical and cultural differences between India and Ireland, the societies in these countries shared "the common heritage of the Six Directions as actual zones in the land". This conceptual ordering of the universe was not restricted to Indo-European civilisations, because oriental societies, including the Chinese throughout several dynasties, adopted it too.

The layout of Chinese cities, their urban quarters and their buildings express and communicate these conceptual orders which include cosmology, ideals and beliefs (Needham, 1956; Wheatley, 1971). For more than a millenium, the Chinese have used customs and rituals called feng-shui with the aim of integrating people, their activities and the landscape. Generally, it is believed that the good will of divine powers can be transmitted only in favourable geographical circumstances to establish harmony between the human settlement and the universe. Following consideration of the local features of the landscape, prescriptions and symbols aided the selection of sites for cities, palaces, dwellings and burial grounds. Then rites were performed to consecrate the chosen site. These rites are only performed on the propitious days prescribed in the annual almanacs. These almanacs contained astronomical information about the definition of agricultural cycles, and the dates that should be avoided or used for building construction (Knapp, 1986). These days were attributed with good and bad fortune for preparing building sites, for erecting the structural timber framework of buildings, and for installing the doors and the cooking stove within. By adhering to these customs and prescriptions, it was believed that favourable circumstances for the future inhabitants would be ensured.

It is noteworthy that many of the customs just mentioned are no longer practised in the People's Republic of China, where political ideology has overriden folklore. Consequently, authentic myth and ritual that were transmitted from generation to generation over more than a millenium have been surpressed. However, these customs are still common in Hong- Kong and Taiwan, where they are performed by carpenters and masons. Although these specialists are skilled craftsmen they are not just technically competent, because they are considered to be skilled magiciens who are employed to insure the prospect of good fortune by integrating the habitat and the cosmos of the present, to the past and to the future.

INTERPRETING RITUAL

There is little consensus about the meaning and use of the term ritual and how rites should be understood. The word ritual derives from the latin word ritus, which has been used since the 14th century to mean a social convention or habit. Since then there have been two predominant interpretations of ritual. The first commonly refers to an activity, or sets of activities, that cannot be justified solely by a means-to-end type of explanation of human behaviour. The second interpretation refers to sets of customs specifically associated with religion. Consequently, ritual can be contrasted with ceremony, customs, and routines, that form a part of daily activities. Despite the differences between these interpetations, both imply that ritual refers to "a category of behaviour that follows customs in which their relationship between the means and the end is not intrinsic" as Goody (1961, p. 59) has discussed.

One fundamental purpose of ritual in traditional societies is to articulate the movements of individuals and groups with respect to their physical environment (e.g. their habitat and its surroundings) and their social environment (e.g. between social groups and across the life-cycle). In principle, rites are a means of boundary regulation and control. They involve a physical, social and temporal separation from an initial state of being, then a marginal or liminal phase, followed by the assimilation to a new condition or the reassimilation to a previous condition (Gluckman, 1962). This approach implies that it is necessary to distinguish between rites of religious practice and the ritualization of social relationships in traditional societies. According to Gluckman, in the ritualism of formalized religion, the behaviour of the participants does not reflect the diverse social roles and relationships of the members of the congregation. In contrast, the ritualization of social relationships in the daily affairs of traditional societies is

"a stylized ceremonial in which persons related in various ways to the central actors, as well as these themselves, perform prescribed actions according to their secular roles; and that it is believed by the participants that these prescribed actions express and amend social relationships so as to secure general blessing, purification, protection, and prosperity for the persons involved in some mystical manner which is out of sensory control."

Rituals articulate ideals, beliefs and values about the way human individuals and groups, their immediate environment and the cosmos are interrelated. Myths and rituals do not make clear-cut boundaries between these constituents of the universe; nor do they dissect time into specific units, because past, present and future form a continuum. The enactment of rites occurs between people who share and communicate meaning and values about their lives. In principle, rituals are binding. They illustrate the dependence people feel toward other individuals and their society. Therefore they require communal participation. Indeed, as Pottebaum (1992, p. 88) notes, the quality of a specific rite is largely proportional to the level, frequency and quality of the behaviour of the participants.

If rites are intended to communicate between people, it is important to decipher what they mean. According to several social anthropologists, it is possible to identify the symbolic meaning of a rite by analysing the diverse uses of ritual symbols and practices in every day life. Lévi-Strauss (1955) interprets ritual as integral with human thought at an abstract and metaphysical level. His interpretation implies that ritual is a language and that rites are specific acts, akin to speech. Hence it is instructive to decipher sets of rules that underlie rites. In this sense, the meaning of ritual can be studied by analysing its content in context. This context is dynamic and culturally dependent: many rites are performed at significant times in the seasonal cycle (e.g. at the summer or winter solstice, or at the vernal or autumnal equinox); at liminal stages in the

life-cycle of individuals and groups (e.g. rites de passage associated with birth, puberty, marriage and death), at times of natural catastrophes (e.g. famine, drought, flood and epidemic) and for the consecration of property (e.g. the foundation of a new city and the construction of a new building). According to Gluckman (1962, p. 23) there are four types of ritual, and it is useful to distinguish between them. These are:
1.   Magical action including the acts of mystical powers and substances.
2.   Religious action including the cults of ancestors.
3.   Substantive or constitutive rituals that reflect or alter social relationships by reference to mystical notions.
4.   Factitive rituals that increase the productivity or strength, or purify and protect the material well-being of a group.
Substantive and constitutive rituals includes rites de passage, whereas factitive rituals includes the foundation rites of cities that were practised in many traditional societies.

In each of the above-mentioned situtations, the participants in ritual believe that a rite can invoke power that will alter the state of the world. Consequently, the ideals and beliefs accompanying ritual behaviour distinguish the latter from all other kinds of behaviour. Accordingly, Harrison (1913) stated that ritual can be intrepreted as a dramatisation of myth.

Given the evidence that myth and ritual have been constituents of the conceptual foundations of cities in many civilisations, it is necessary to consider their relevance for the siting and layout of contemporary cities. In the Preface to his historical analysis of Romano-Etruscan urban culture, Rykwert (1976) criticizes the layout and design of modern cities. He also deplores recent approaches applied in town and country planning based largely or solely on functional, economic and other rational parameters. However, although he argues that expressive and symbolic systems should be included in city planning he does not indicate how his historical study can help overcome the shortcomings he has identified. This complex subject will be considered in the next section of this paper.

THE PERTINENCE OF MYTH AND RITUAL IN CONTEMPORARY URBAN SOCIETIES

"One need only ponder what people mean in our time when they counsel us to "be realistic". They mean, at every point, to forego the claims of transcendence, to spurn the magic of imaginative wonder, to regard the world as nothing but what the hard facts and quantitiave abstractions of scientific objectivity make it out to be ....Science is our religion because we cannot, most of us, with any living conviction see around it ....We live in a world whose consciousness of reality ends at the scientific perimeter, hence a world growing more idolatrous by the hour...." Theodore Roszak

The preceding interpretations of myth and ritual show that they are closely interrelated. Collectively, they enable individuals and groups to establish an intimate relationship between themselves, and also with the primordial and generative logic of the cosmos that transcends human society. Both myth and ritual can be interpreted as systems of signs that organize abstract conceptual relationships in terms of concrete images (Geertz, 1968). Hence they serve as catalysts for speculative thought rather than as models for secular behaviour. Whereas empirical language refers to objective facts, myth and ritual refer to "the quintessence of human experience, the meaning and significance of human life" (May, 1991, p 26). Collectively they enable the formulation of "a science of the concrete" which is no less rationale, nor illogical than "the abstract science of the modern world" (Geertz, 1968, p. 405). According to May (991, p. 25) the denial of myth is part of "our refusal to confront our own reality and that of society."

Although there are numerous differences between traditional societies and those of the contemporary western world, the latter do have recourse to myth and ritual. Yet they do not necessarily have the same idioms as those of our ancestors. In Switzerland, for example, William Tell is still a national hero, while in North America the ancient frontier myth has been reinterpreted by novelists, playwriters and those film-makers who characterised the Lone Ranger. Despite these and other examples it has been increasingly common in the western world to label myths as fictitious tales. Nonetheless, the summer solstice is celebrated in many countries including Sweden where it is a national holiday. Elsewhere, the beginning of Spring is widely celebrated around a Maypole on May Day in some rural communities, whereas it has been transformed into a holiday for urban workers in many countries. In the domestic realm, house warming parties (pendre la crémaillère) are given when moving into a dwelling unit. Last but not least, rites de passage associated with birthdays, christenings, confirmations, marriages and deaths are celebrated (van Gennep, 1909). These rites enable individuals and groups to define and communicate their self-, social- and place identities.

Despite the omnipresence of ritual in daily life, there can be little doubt that rites are not as common today in relation to urban planning and architecture as they have been. For example, when a new city, such as Canberra was planned as the capital of Australia earlier this century, the chosen site was primarily selected for political and functional reasons largely to counteract the rivalry between authorities in Sydney and Melbourne, whereas the characteristics of the extant landscape were considered of secondary importance. Such parameters overlooked an adequate supply of potable water for the new city. This kind of reasoning led the official town planner to radically modify the landscape by constructing a large artificial lake. When Canberra was founded the national government did organize a ceremonial occasion. However, this occasion was meant for a selected group of invited officials, when pomp and ceremony negated any participation by members of the community.

The example of Canberra can be complemented by the foundation of other new cities (such as the British New Towns, Brasilia, New Delhi, Washington) as well as other contemporary approaches in urban planning (such as the forced displacement of communities for urban renewal projects or other developments in many countries). These approaches to urban planning underline the fact that it is the processes underlying the foundation and development of contemporary cities that should be examined in tandem with the material characteristics of urban quarters. In principle, apart from small numbers of self-build communities, the processes and practices in contemporary cities are imposed by a limited number of property owners and professionals on the whole community. In fact the community remains voiceless. In such circumstances there are obvious reasons why historical precedent for ritual in urban environments cannot be reapplied in a meaningful way, unless certain principles are borne in mind. These principles can be considered after answering the following questions:

Q1 - What are the mythical and ritual constituents of urban technological culture in the western world?

Q2 - Have ancient myths and ritual become obsolete and replaced wholly or partly by other beliefs and practices owing to the valorization of technology, materialism and progress?

Q3 - What myths and rites reflect the current beliefs and ideals of individuals, groups and communities in western urban societies that are rapidly changing?

Q4 - What prerequisite conditions are necessary if ancient and modern myths and ritual are to assume a significant role in the foundation of new cities and the conduct of urban affairs?

Social anthropologists broadly agree that there is more ritualisation of social relationships in traditional societies compared with modern, industrialised societies. Many reasons have been given for this difference. Gluckman (1962), for example, examines the transformation fo social roles and functions stemming from feudalism. He synthesizes many contributions on this subject to argue that the gradual yet steady shift from "multiplex" and "diffuse" social relations (defined by the multiplicity of social roles of an individual in a traditional society) to monodimensional social relations in modern contemporary societies, has been coupled with the spatial and temporal segmentation and specialization of social roles and functions. This change illustrates that an integrative, holistic world-view common in traditional societies has been replaced by a segregated and segmented one in contemporary societies. Consequently the "rational" has been distinguished from the "irrational" and ethical values, moral beliefs and judgments have become demarcated from the social organisation of daily affairs.

The explicit segmentation and segregation of many constituents of daily life in modern urban societies is for instrumental not moral purposes. Given the fact that social, spatial and temporal distinctions are more formalised in these societies compared with traditional ones, there is less need to use ritual for symbolic differentiation in contemporary urban affairs.

The above-mentioned differences between traditional and contemporary societies are the result of the conceptual, material, legal, and political reordering of our world which began many centuries ago (Eliade, 1959). It can be traced back to the early history of Christianity and the role of institutionalized religion. From the third century A.D. the clergy of the Church deprecated ancient myths and rites handed down by the Greeks and Romans. The clergy argued that only the Christian doctrine was True, whereas any other interpretations were pagan and false; consequently they were prohibited. Nonetheless, the Church ignored the wealth of myth and ritual transmitted through the ages that Christianity had already adopted, including the Garden of Eden in the Book of Genesis, the legends of Christmas and Epiphany, and Satan who personified evil and hell. This example serves to show that authentic myth and ritual which had evolved since the dawn of human civilisation where explicitly challenged by an elite who intended to impose their beliefs and ideals based on intellectual and professional interpretations. This kind of intervention has recurred thoughout human civilisations, and it has not been restricted to institutionalized religion. It has also had a significant impact on many constituents of human life including the siting, foundation, layout and use of cities, their urban quarters and the dwellings of the inhabitants.

Traditionally the siting, layout and construction of cities and buildings resulted from the unselfconscious ordering of (what is commonly termed today) rational and irrational parameters. The case of China summarized above illustrates this approach. In contrast, contemporary cities and their buildings result from explicit intentions formulated by administrators, politicians and corporate clients, as the example of Canberra shows. Hence the ancient city was governed by complex rules and conventions - including rites and prescriptions - that were widely shared and understood by the indigenous population. Both the implicit conceptual parameters and the human-made environment evolve incrementally over time. However, when there are more abrupt societal changes stemming from the unintended consequences of rapid technological innovation, the diversification of construction materials and the specialization of social functions and roles, these incremental adaptive changes were replaced by rapid and decisive developments. Consequently, today the time taken to accomplish the task of erecting a building has been attributed an intrinsic cultural value, whereas traditionally this task was temporally defined by prescriptions in almanacs. Today, in western societies, these and other tasks are measured econometrically by the number of people hours, whereas in countries like Hong-Kong and Taiwan they are still prescribed by eternal time. This distinction illustrates the supremacy of an instrumental and rational approach in the western world, which has become the rationale for recent developments in many academic, scientific and political circles.

Some contemporary economists, statisticians and systems analysts claim that quantitative instruments can be applied to evaluate qualitative values as if the latter are analogous to quantifiable material objects. When this approach cannot be applied, as in the case of myth and ritual, the latter are classified as irrational and then they are discredited. For many they then become obsolete. Consequently, beliefs and ideals that reflected longstanding preoccupations about the origins of the universe, the development of the cosmos, and the status of homo sapiens in relation to all other biological organisms have been relegated to backstage and/or overriden by more recent preoccupations. These concern the nature of progress defined precisely in terms of material wealth, economic growth and technological innovations. Such preoccupations have been coupled with scientific discourse about the genetic and biological determinants of human life and society. This discourse does not include human beliefs, ideals and values. Rather, the innate struggle with other humans and groups to use resources at the expense of all other species has been used frequently by politicians and economists to advocate principles of laissez-faire and market economies. In essence, individuals no longer have ideals and beliefs about the universe and the cosmos, because they have become fully preoccupied in themselves.

The preceding overview suggests that without communal bonds, and devoid of the opportunity to participate in the foundation and construction of cities, too many citizens today are excluded from urban life. Yet isn't this the antithesis of the role of citizens and the purpose of the polis ?

CONCLUSION

This paper has presented and illustrated some generalized interpretations of myth and ritual and some particular examples in relation to the siting, layout and use of cities in several civilisations throughout history. It has been argued that myth and ritual should be studied in order to understand the multidimensional nature of the city. The paper then showed that although myth and ritual are omnipresent, they have acquired different idioms in contemporary urban societies compared with ancient ones. The reasons for these differences are numerous. In this paper attention has only been given to the suppression of authentic myth and ritual by institutionalized religious doctrine, by the political use of ceremony at the expense of citizen participation in the foundation and use of cities, and by the replacement of an integrative, holistic world-view (common in traditional societies) by the increasing segmentation and specialization of many characteristics of contemporary urban life.

In ancient Chinese, Greek and Roman civilisations the city was considered as the privileged locus for public debate on the relationships between the cosmos and human society. Collectively, beliefs, ideals and ritual behaviour ensured a harmony between the good will of the universal orders and the well-being of the citizens of the city. In essence, myth and ritual were not just the means of expressing and communicating self-, social- and place-identities but also the guarantee for ontological security.

Certain types of ritual that are performed in traditional societies (e.g. magical performance and formal religious cults) may not seem compatible with the beliefs and ideals of many individuals and groups that are atheist in contemporary urban societies. Yet, although the threats of drought, flood or warfare have not been fully controlled by scientific or technological means, today rituals are not commonly practised to deal with anxieties about these threats. Nonetheless, the orgins of humanity, the development of human civilisations from primal parentage, and the conceptual foundations of human societies and their settlements have been and still are metaphysical questions. For many, these questions have not been answered satisfactorily by the contributions of scientific enquiry, which often refute or deny the pertinence of ethical and moral orders. The dilemma of much current debate about urban societies is that it does not account for the ambiguity between the "rational" and the "nonrational" interpretations of human civilisation. Such dualistic modes of thinking are outmoded. Until they are replaced by an integrative historical perspective, the layers of contextual meaning attributed to the city will only be partially understood.

References

ELIADE, M. (1959) Cosmos and History : The Myth of the Eternal Return. New York: Harper Row (Translated by William R. Trask from the French Edition).

GEERTZ, C. (1968) Religion : Anthropological Study. In D.L. Sills (Ed.) International Encyclopaedia of the Social Sciences, Vol. 13, pp. 398-406.

GENNEP, A. van (1960) The Rites of Passage. London: Routledge. (Original edition published in French in 1909).

GOODY, J. (1961) Religion and Ritual: The Definitional Problem. British Journal of Sociology, Vol. 12: pp. 142-164.

GLUCKMAN, M. (Ed.) (1962) Essays on the Ritual of Social Relations. Manchester: University of Manchester Press.

HARRISON, J. (1913) Ancient Art and Ritual. New York: Oxford University Press (Second edition, 1951).

KNAPP, R. (1986) China's Traditional Rural Architecture: A Cultural Geography of the Common House. Honolulu: University of Hawaii Press.

LEACH, E. (1968) Ritual. In D. L. Sills (Ed.) International Encyclopaedia of the Social Sciences, Vol. 13, pp. 520-526.

LEACH, E. (1976) Culture and Communication: The logic by which symbols are connected. Cambridge: Cambridge University Press.

LEVI-STRAUSS, C. (1955) The structural study of myth. Journal of American Folklore, No. 68.

MAY, R. (1991) The Cry for Myth. New York: W.W. Norton & Company.

NEEDHAM, J. (1956) Science and Civilisation in China (four Volumes) Cambridge: Cambridge University Press.

POTTEBAUM, G. (1992) The Rites of People: Exploring the Ritual Character of Human Experience. Washington, DC: The Pastoral Press.

RYKWERT, J. (1976) The Idea of the Town. Cambridge, MA: The MIT Press (Second edition, 1988).

STEWART, R. (1989) The Elements of Creation Myth. Shaftesbury, UK: Elements Books.

TURNER, V. (1968) Myth and Symbol. In D.L. Sills (Ed.) International Encyclopaedia of the Social Sciences. Vol. 10, pp. 576-582.

WHEATLEY, P. (1971) The Pivot of the Four Quarters: A Preliminary Enquiry into the Origins and Character of the Ancient Chinese City. Edinburgh: University of Edinburgh Press.

5

Socio-cultural influence of the Hausas and Tivs of northern Nigeria on their traditional architecure and building design

L'influence socio-culturelle des Haousas et des Tivs du Nigeria du nord sur leur architecture et plans de construction

Osuade Oyediran

Cette étude analyse l'influence socio-culturelle des Haousas et des Tivs sur leur milieu physique, et le fait reconnu qu'ils ont des croyances religieuses communes mais un fond culturel différent. Elle traite également des rapports entre leur culture et leur environnement physique, en portant une attention particulière aux modèles de construction, aux matériaux locaux employés et au tracé physique. On a mené une étude sur le terrain dans plusieurs communautés et des entrevues avec certains de leurs membres; on a étudié attentivement les documents disponibles et présenté une analyse exhaustive des conclusions. On s'est efforcé d'identifier les différentes caractéristiques familiales qui déterminent l'environnement habitable de la région.

Mots clé: influence socio-culturelle; architecture et plan de construction; milieu physique.

Keywords: sosio-cultural influence; architecture and building design; physical environement

According to Rapoport (1989)

> "Give a certain climate, the availability of certain materials and the constraints and capabilities of a given level of technology, what finally decides the form of a dwelling and moulds the spaces and their relationship, is the vision that people have of the ideal life. The environment sought reflects beliefs, family and clan structure, socio-organisation ways of gaining a livelihood, and social relation between individuals".

This statement of the philosopher clearly shows his opinion as regard the importance of "culture", which may be described as a set of behaviours and ideas that are generally accepted by members of a particular society. These ideas are usually expressed in different actions and institutions of the society in form of marriages, religions, politics and social settings. A close look at the different culture and social settings of both the Hausas and Tivs of Northern Nigeria confirms the findings.

For example, the varied customs of the Hausas and Tivs of Northern Nigeria greatly influence their modes of building patterns and architectural characteristics within each locality. In particular these patterns are based mainly on the family relationships and occupation. In addition, the Hausas are influenced by the islamic religious culture while the Tivs are more inclined to the kinship culture.

This difference in tradition between the Hausas and Tivs is symptomatic of what is common among other major Nigerian ethnic groups. It is on this basis that a thorough analysis of the influences of socio-cultural values on their living patterns is being undertaken. Their economic growth is influenced by an adherence to their indigenous culture since each ethnic group seems to be closely knit together. Thus the process of urbanisation is slow. The study therefore aims at an in-depth understanding of their different cultures and how that influence their living pattern. It is worth-while to note that although the assumed similarities in the religious belief of both ethnic group is general, their (overall) outlook to urbanisation problems differ greatly. Whereas the study shows flexibility in the urbanization processes in the heart Tiv-land, the Hausas area has a rather rigid formation of kinship based on religion with the exception of some larger urban centres. The study looks at the economic factors arising from their various customs and how these have affected their urbanisation process. It is assumed that with the present global economic recession and women liberation movements, the practised "Purdah" system for women in Hausa-land may be relaxed giving way to a different socio-political structure. It is on the basis of the importance of the effect of culture on the social well-being and urbanisation processes in these two wide regions that this study was conceived. There is some remarkable significance in the influence of culture and social settings on urbanisation process on which a lot of research studies have been carried out (see for Example Rapoport, 1969). Not many of such studies are available for Nigeria in general, and the Hausas and Tivs of Northern Nigeria in particular. Among the few studies available are those of Bohannan (1954); Schwerdtfeger (1982); Gbem (1986) and Ayodele (1987). All these studies are however limited in scope.

The present study is therefore a pioneering one on the relationship between socio-cultural characteristic and urbanisation and architecture in Hausa- and Tiv-land respectively.

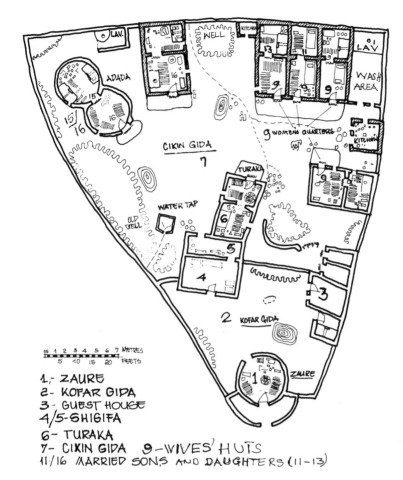

LAV.
WELL
KITCHEN
LAV
WASH AREA
ADADA
9 WOMENS QUARTERS
KITCHEN
CIKIN GIDA
7
TURAKA
WATER TAP
OLD WELL
6
5
4
2 KOFAR GIDA
1 ZAURE
ZAURE

05 1 2 3 4 5 6 7 METRES
5 10 15 20 FEETS

1.- ZAURE
2- KOFAR GIDA
3- GUEST HOUSE
4/5-SHIGIFA
6- TURAKA
7- CIKIN GIDA   9-WIVES' HUTS
11/16 MARRIED SONS AND DAUGHTERS (11-13)

Figure 5.1   Typical plan of a Hausa compound (single storey).

THE STUDY AREAS

The Hausa speaking areas of Northern Nigeria cover Sokoto, Kastina, Kaduna, Kano and Bauchi states. There are also many Hausas in Niger, Plateau, Borno and parts of Adamawa and Taraba states. However the Hausas as a 'people' and the Hausa-speaking people are not synonymous; consequently this study limits itself to the Hausas as a 'people' and the area they occupy in Nigeria. In general, these areas which the Hausas occupy may be regarded as heart of Hausa-land. They include Sokoto, Kano and parts of Kaduna and Katsina States

The study areas cover the Northern Guinea, Sudan and the Sahel Savannas. The mean annual rainfall varies between approximately 1,140 mm in the Guinea savanna areas and less than 600 mm in the Sahel savanna. The rainfall is most concentrated in the rainy season and is characterized by a single maximum. The significance of this pattern of precipitation arises partly because of its impact on the soils and vegetation and the consequent impact of this on building construction.

The mean temperatures are usually between 28° - 32°C. Daily temperatures are however usually as high as 34°C in the afternoons and may be less than 20°C at night. In the Sahel savanna, minimum temperatures may be less than 10°C. Thus normal temperature ranges are usually more than 20°C and may be as high as 25°C. The effect of these temperature ranges on building construction is the need for efficient thermal control to achieve a maximum comfort level inside the building.

The Tivs are located to the south of Hausa-land approximately between 6°30'N and 8°N and 8°E to 10°E. According to Bohanna (1954) the Tivs live on both banks of the Benue river and in parts of Cross River and Plateau states.

Compared with the Hausa-land, the Tiv area is characterized by relatively wetter conditions with more rain, which varies from about 1,250 mm in the south and about 1000 mm in the north. Mean temperatures are generally lower while temperature ranges are less than in the Hausa-land. The vegetation of Hausa-land consists mainly of thorny shrubs locally called "Bagaruwa" and "Anona Senegalensis" (Gwandar-Daji).

Their significance lies in that fact that they are used by masons as reinforcement members for mud armatures and for filling in panels of mud roofs. There are also the Deleb Palms (Giginya) from where the main structural beams (local Azara) for mud walls and roofs of indigenous houses are obtained. Also, the Bamboo (Gora) and Raphia Venifera (Tukurwa) used for roofing construction are found in abundance. The soils are generally sandy, loam or clay with interspersed area of hard stone deposit.

Vegetation in the Tiv-land consists mainly of the Guinea Savanna with tall grasses (Imperata Cylindrica). There is also the Benue river plain where bamboo stalks are found in abundance. These materials and the common bamboo stalks are found in abundance. These materials and the common climber plants are used mostly for roofing purposes. The soil is mainly laterite with clay, which is widely used for wall construction.

FAMILY STRUCTURE AND CULTURE

The family set-up in an Hausa community is based on religious culture and respect for authority. The Emirs occupy the apex of the socio-political scene in the towns and villages. Next to him are his advisers "Saraki" (Masu Sarauta) who are feudal office holders and at the lowest stratum are the ordinary citizens (Talakawas). These "Talakawas" are the artisans of all sorts that form the economic base of the society.

In contrast the Tivs have Tor-tiv at the helm of the socio-political set-up, closely assisted by lesser chiefs among the elders. For both the Hausas and the Tivs, the ordinary citizens are ranked lowest in the family structural set-up.

The culture of both the Hausas and the Tivs is probably noticeable at the family level. In particular, the Hausa culture is mostly rested on the Islamic teaching. At the background are women who are mainly confined to purdah, while their men stay at the centre of activities. The man is the sole head of his family which include his wife or wives, his children and their wives (if any) and his widowed old mother. His household consists of all persons who eat together from the same pot, live together within his compound (sassa) and contribute in kind, cash or labour to the maintenance of the household.

The household head of Hausa community (Maigida) is the sole authority within the family structural set-up. He can take and execute independent actions and his decisions are well respected. For example, he can take decisions to extend the compound and build new huts. In contrast, the other people in the household cannot take or execute any such decisions that affect the compound without reference to the "Maigida", otherwise such decisions would not hold.

Since the main occupation of the people in Hausa-land is mostly agriculture, it is usual for each household to form a single work force (Gandu) with the "Maigida" as the leader of the group. They farm a common field during the farming (rainy) season. They also cook and eat together, with the meals prepared in turn by each of the member's wives. This culture helps to hold everyone together.

For the first marriage of a young male compound member, all resident household heads of the compound meet to contribute towards the bride price (dowry). They also contribute towards building a new hut for the young couple within the greater fence.

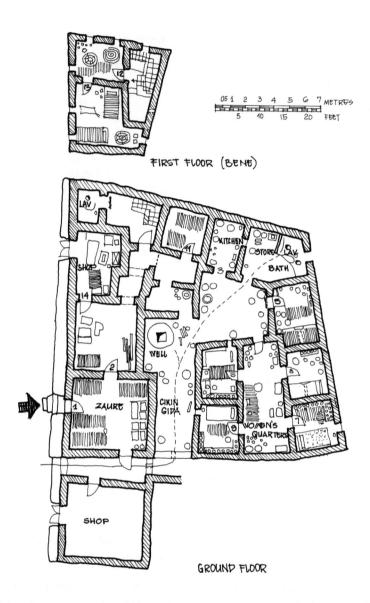

Figure 5.2   Plan of Hausa compound with upper floor. Key as figure 5.1

Like the Hausa, the Tiv communities have their own cultural characteristics which significantly influence traditional architecture and building designs. The head of the family is the father while other members are wives or children. However a compound household is very much larger than in the Hausa set-up. The household is parti-linear whereby all male adults from the same parent (father) settle together with their own individual family to form the household. The effect if that a Tiv's compound contains many single huts connected only by a central place. The culture recognises the patri-linear kinship but independent family units.

SOCIO-CULTURAL INFLUENCE ON INDIGENOUS ARCHITECTURE

The cultural characteristics discussed above considerably affect the architectural differences between the Hausas and the Tivs. The Islamic culture observed in Hausa compounds makes the architecture a homogenous set-up (Figure 5.1). The women who are in purdah live in the innermost part of the compound (Cikin-gida)(Figure 5.2). At the main entrance (Zaure) is the family head who uses this area to receive visitors and sometimes uses the spaces to further his economic livelihood if he is Koranic school teacher. The space is also the visitors sleeping area (Figure 5.2).

From here, a door leads to the fore-court (Kofar-gida) behind which the man has his main reception hut (Shigifa). Here the wives also receive their adult male visitors, mainly their relations and well-known people to their husband. The husband's sleeping hut (Turaka) is also directly behind the shigifa, through which a door leads to the innermost courtyard (Cikin-gida). The guest house, also located within the Kofar-gida area is for the visitors staying overnight or for several days (Figure 5.1).

In the inner courtyard (Cikin-gida) the huts of the wives are arranged facing the husband's sleeping hut (Turaka) directly. Notice in Figure 5.1 for example, the four huts belonging to four wives are facing the Turaka. Nearby are the toilet, washing-area, wet season kitchen or other kitchen and a well for domestic use. Stores are usually provided with granaries and poultry-pens where they are needed.

Within this inner courtyard, the huts for the married male children and their wives are built adjacent to the women's huts. They may be provided with separate toilet, washing area and kitchen. An optical demarcation is erected with woven grass-reeds (Zana) which is for multi-purpose use. However, access to the inner courtyard is mainly through the husband's living area (Turaka) as already noted. The entire compound is fenced round with a high wall fence, which also acts as security and as privacy and screening device.

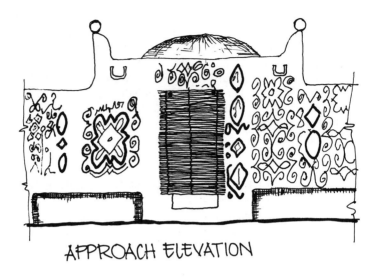

APPROACH ELEVATION

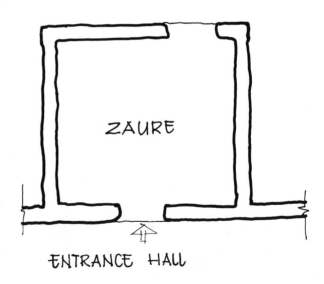

ZAURE

ENTRANCE HALL

Figure 5.3   Approach elevation and entrance hall Hause Zaure.

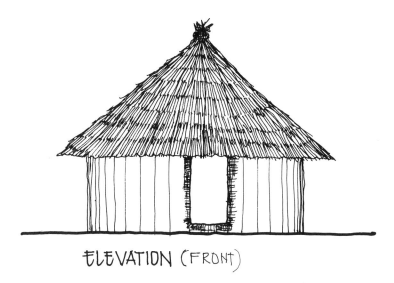

ELEVATION (FRONT)

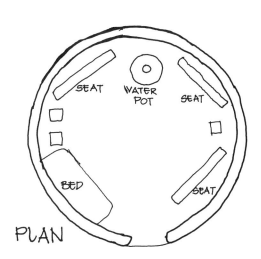

PLAN

Figure 5.4   Elevation and plan of Tiv hut source: field work.

In addition to the structural patterns of the Hausa traditional architectural designs, building decorations are other aspects which portray traits of the Hausa culture. These decorations are beautifully carved or sometimes created to portray some historical or religious effect or background (Figure 5.3).

The decorative impressions on the Hausa buildings is missing in Tiv compounds since the huts are individually created, with possible hand impression on the wall of an individual huts (Figure 5.4). Also in contrast to the Hausa, each Tiv family has a distinct family area (Hunda) within the compound where their huts are placed with their reception hut (Ate), in the centre (Figure 5.4). The totality of all families' huts form a circular area with a common central space (Tembes) where adult men meet to discuss or hold family meetings. The individual family's reception hut is also the playing area for the children.

CONSTRUCTION MATERIALS AND METHOD

While the individual building plans and architectural designs considerably depend on the cultural set-up and historical background of the people, the construction materials depend mainly on socio-economic factors of the people. For both the Hausas and the Tivs, particularly those who are less exposed to the western culture and civilization, the mode of living is mainly subsistence, with very low capital income. Consequently resources for the introduction of building facilities from outside the local environment are considerably limited. For example, because of the limited resources, building materials are mainly those adapted from the local environment. Such materials include those used in constructing the walls and the roofs.

The construction materials and methods of the various huts however vary in both the Hausa-land the Tiv area. In particular, there are variations in the composition and use of locally available building materials. In general however, mud huts and thatched roofs are common to the two study areas.

The Hausa mud bricks (Tubali) used for foundation are conical in shape. The mud bricks are made up of wet earth with pieces of grass obtained from the environment. They are then left to dry for about two weeks in the sun. These bricks are used as foundation on good building grounds where a trench of about twenty centimetre (20cm) is dug and the bricks arranged closely to each other. They are then bound together with the mud mortar. Where the building is more than one storey, the foundation is usually made up of a special ferrous stone (Marmara) which are equally set together and bound with mud mortar. These stones are also obtained from the local environment.

The foundation of the Hausa building is usually between seventy centimetre to one meter (70cm - 100cm) wide. The walls of the hut are also made out of specially earth mud. This earth mud is a mixture of wet earth, dried animal faeces (from their cattle, donkeys and horses) and sometimes strengthened with grass pieces. The essence of the animal faeces is to ensure good bounding while the grass allegedly gives added strength.

In some cases certain residual materials from dyeing pit are mixed with the mud and faeces to give a smooth and relatively water resistant surface. The walls are usually about fifty centimetre (50cm) thick. The roofing system in the Hausa architecture is usually flat, dome shaped or thatched with grass. When flat, it is usually constructed of mud, but if dome-shaped or thatched, it is constructed with grass. The vaulted (Dome) roof is supported by arches made of Azara beams (Figure 5.6) laid closely with woven light wood purlins made out of Anona Senegalensis (Gwandar-daji) and covered with mud mixed with grass and animal faeces. Drainage of rain-water is done through spouts made of metal sheets.

The flat roof is usually preferred for rectangular shaped huts. Beams are laid from the corners of the hut diagonally until the whole roof area is covered. A mud mixture of about five centimetre (5cm) thick is then laid on the roof. After drying a further earth layer of about fifteen centimetres (15cm) is again spread on the roof with a final thin layer of mud mixture of bounding materials from the locust-bean fruit pods (Makuba) or the remnants of dyeing pit.

The walls are normally constructed with minimal openings towards the inner courtyard to prevent any optical intrusion from outside since the women are usually in purdah. Due to the thickness of the wall (about 50cm), it is possible to have a cool internal temperature during the day with the already stored heat from the wall released inwards during the cold night.

As already noted, the whole compound is massively fenced with a high wall. This is in line with the culture of keeping away strangers from intrusion and maintaining their privacy and security. The main entrance door and wall are usually decorated with beautiful motifs to reflect the historical and religious culture of the people (Figure 5.3).

Unlike the Hausas, the Tiv compounds are casually and ordinarily constructed. The materials usually employed in the construction of the hut in the Tiv-land is wet earth mud for walls, the hard wood or bamboo for roofing and thatched with grass. Unlike in the Hausa-land, the culture of flat or domed mud roofs is not common among the Tivs. All the huts are built on circular bases. The size of the rooms depend on the use they are built for. There are no internal partitions made. The big hut (Iyou - Kyunda) is usually about five meters in diameter and is big enough to contain the whole family. Beds are arranged at the side of the walls with space for movement in the middle. A big pot for drinking water is kept in the same hut. Some chairs for important visitors are arranged near the door while a wardrobe or table for keeping valuables are kept at one extreme end (see Figure 5.4).

56

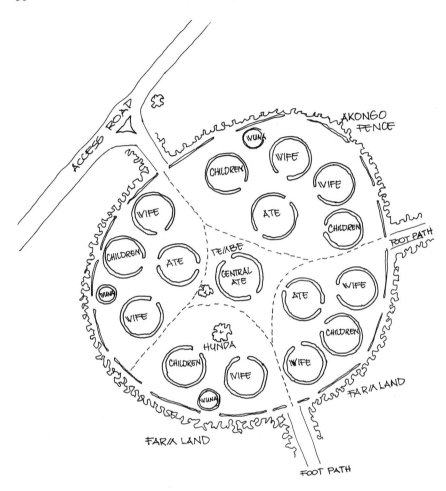

Figure 5.5   Tiv compound showing Ihinda. There are four Hundas with a central Ate.
Source: field work of Gbem T. Felix (1989).

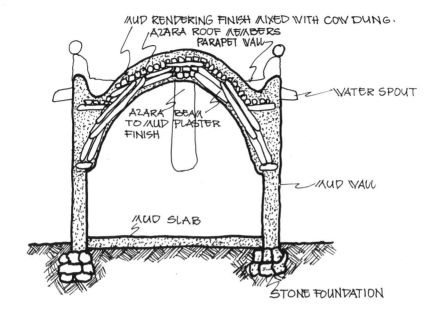

MUD RENDERING FINISH MIXED WITH COW DUNG.

AZARA ROOF MEMBERS

PARAPET WALL

WATER SPOUT

AZARA BEAM
TO MUD PLASTER
FINISH

MUD WALL

MUD SLAB

STONE FOUNDATION

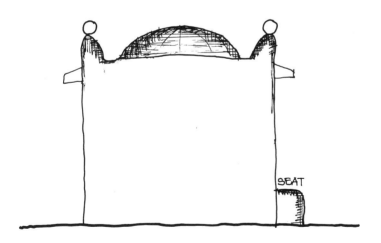

SEAT

LEFT SIDE ELEVATION.

Figure 5.6   Section and elevation of Zaure showing dome roof structure.

Another type of living in Tiv culture is known as the "Iyou - Iyorun", which although it is basically built for cooking and dinning, is sometimes used as sleeping room for children. In the middle of this hut, a storage unit (Dsaar) is constructed with strong timber posts above the fireplace. Under this storage unit is another space (Shaase) constructed to perform the function of an oven. Here, fresh meat and other food items are kept to dry.

As already noted, the "out of way" hut constructed in a Tiv compound is the "Ate" where visitors are received and the men sit to eat and drink just like in a lounge. The mud wall of this hut is usually about ninety centimetre (90cm) high.

The construction work in the Tiv community is done communally with every member involved. The women and children provide help in arranging the building materials for use while the men do the building work. The walls are from purely clay sand mud and are about fifty centimetres thick. This is erected in layers on simple foundation also made of mud. Each layer is allowed to dry before the next one is built on it. The in-situ building system (Imbyar-Imbyar) allows local builders (Masons) to use their fingers and palms impression to create motifs and decorations on the wall when they are still wet. The ant-hill earth dust is usually collected and mixed with the mud to give the walls a smooth and shining surface. To finish the construction, the floor is filled with laterite and wet with water. This allows the floor to become hardened and properly consolidated for effective occupation. A final layer of dust from ant-hill is prepared to give the floor a hard and smooth finish. Unlike in Hausa-land, huts in Tiv-land are not connected together with a solid wall fence. Only a porous planted edge is used for this purpose.

CONCLUSION

The significance of the socio-cultural factors as emphasized in this paper could be made effective if such factors were integrated in their mode of living and behaviours. Achieving this aim may necessitate government encouragement of mixed settlements whereby the various house types would be modernized and built in settlement forms. Such settlements should be encouraged to generate economic activities like farming and petty trading at the local level. The various local artisans who are responsible for the various cultural building arts should be re-trained and encouraged to move out of their own location to train others elsewhere. The cultural farming system of the Hausas could be modernised by transforming them into co-operative societies. These cooperative societies could in turn be organised as the nucleus of an urban based economic stimulant. Goods produced collectively in the farms would then change hands within the urban areas. Another significant part of the development will be an attempt to encourage the use of other modern building materials to replicate the interesting Doms, flat-roofs and ornament as constructed by the Hausa and Tiv builders. This singular attempt will help the urbanisation process. The clustering of the Tivs within the compound "Ihinda" would thereby be made less interesting since people would be able to erect the same type of building elsewhere and at the same time pursue other economic activities.

The findings also show that much research work still needs to be done in the field of socio-cultural influences on the urban living pattern. The cultural influence of each ethnic group cuts across one another and this could be furthered and sustained through marriages, settlements and economic integration.

References:

1. Rapoport, A. (1969) House Form and Culture, New Jersey, Prentice Hall, Inc. England
2. Bohannan, P. (1954) The Tiv farm and Settlement HMSO, London 1954
3. Schwerdtfeger, F.W. (1982) Traditional Housing in African Cities. John Wiley & Sons, New York
4. Gbem, T.F. (1986) Tiv Domestic Architecture and Building Materials, Unpublished B.Sc (Thesis) Dept of Architecture, Ahmadu Bello University, Zaria.
5. Ayodele R.A. (1987) Hausa and Yoruba Traditional Architecture, Unpublished B.Sc. (Thesis) Dept of Architecture, Ahmadu Bello University, Zaria

6

Urban experience in an Ottoman town in central Anatolia

Expérience urbaine dans une ville ottomane en Anatolie centrale

Vacit Imamoglu

Kayseri est une ville marchande qui date du premier millénaire A.J. Stratégiquement, elle se situe sur les routes commerciales et bénéficie d'un riche héritage architectural. Dans les dernières quarantes années, cependant, d'importantes transformations ont eu lieu, causant la disparition d'une grande partie des quartiers traditionnels urbains.

Cet article traite des caractéristiques générales de la ville en fonction de son emplacement physique et social, de sa vie économique et de la place que tiennent dans l'habitat des différences climatiques (ete-hiver) et des soucis de sécurité, de gendre et d'intimité.

Mots clé: ville de Kayseri, habitations urbaines Ottomanes, voisinages Ottomans, différence de genre dans l'occupation de l'espace.

Keywords: town of Kayseri, Ottoman urban houses, Ottoman neighbourhoods, gender difference in space usage.

This paper aims at exploring some dimensions of urban experience and general characteristics of the architectural environment in Kayseri at the first half of the 20th century. In addition, it attempts to explain how people lived, what hardships they faced in their daily lives, what attitudes they had and which values they wanted to keep in relation to their town and neighbourhoods. A final aim might be to draw some inferences concerning people-environment relationships that might be of relevance today.

One of the difficulties of researching past urban life in Turkey is the shortage of written sources in the field. Although general impressions of travellers about town layouts and urban living can be found occasionally, these are far from being useful. Since official records and judicial files were only recently opened to the public in Turkey, at the present time one cannot depend on this kind of material, which is usually piecemeal. Novels or written stories are almost non-existent, and oral testimony is quickly disappearing.

Another difficulty is related to the old city fabric; in the last 40 years a silent demolition went on and most of the neint.

METHOD

Three ad hoc approaches were employed in understanding urban experience in Kayseri:

1) Streets, public open spaces and houses within the historical core of the city were surveyed and photographed. In addition, 12 houses were examined thoroughly;they were photographed; their 1/50 scale architectural drawings were prepared. Additionally approximately 60 houses and their immediate surroundings were examined and photographed.

2) Present and previous householders and descendents of families who have built the houses were interviewed. Their statements and evaluations of urban and domestic experiences were recorded.

3) Oral reports of old citizens of Kayseri, as well as my own memories about the demolished quarters of the city and the houses were also utilized to complete the picture.

THE TOWN

Kayseri is a historical town in central Anatolia on the famous Silk Road. Although its history may be traced back to earlier periods, during the first millennium B.C., Kayseri was a merchant town named as Mazaca. Later, after the establishment of the Roman province in 17 A.D., it became the capital of Capadoccia and was called Caesarea. Byzantines constructed the present citadel and outer city walls. Later on, during the Seljuk period (12th to 15th centuries), Kayseri became one of the most important centers of Anatolia with a lively economic and social life. The flourishing city spread beyond the citadel and a number of town quarters, as well as many religious and secular buildings were established outside the city walls. In the late sixteenth century, under the Ottoman rule Kayseri had a population of 40000. It was the largest town of Anatolia after Bursa, four-fifths of its population being muslim and the remaining christian. For various economic, political and military reasons its population fluctuated until the establishment of the Turkish Republic in 1923. At the beginning of this century, the town had a population of 56000. It increased to 65000 in 1950 and is over 450000 today.

Figure 6.1   Plan of Kayseri in the early twentieth century (source: A. Gabriel, 1931).

The economic boom after the Second World War gradually forced Kayseri to turn into a so-called "modern" town with medium-height, densely built apartments, offices and government buildings, at the expense of destroying most of its historical quarters. Although public and religious buildings - mostly from Seljuk period - were kept in good condition, residential buildings were widely ignored or deliberately destroyed, mostly for their prospective land value.

Physical Setting: The town of Kayseri lies on the plain of Karasu river on the northern side of Mount Erciyes (Argaeus), which is an extinct volcano of 3916 m in height. Until 1950's the town had a medieval character: inner and outer city walls were the most dominant structures in the town (Figure 6.1). To the west of the citadel, the covered bazaar and most of the hans were located. In general the town was made of maze-like narrow streets and organic open spaces at the intersection of roads or in front of public buildings. The width of the winding streets could hardly let two carriages pass. The continuity of these streets was interrupted either by projections of upper rooms of houses or by surprise landmarks like pyramidal caps of tombs (kümbet), hemispherical domes of mosques or Turkish aths, minarets or public fountains (Figures 6.2).

Figure 6.2   Bayram Street in the Tavukcu neighbourhood, 1986.

At the beginning of this century, Kayseri had 3722 shops, 120 bakeries, 30 hans, 11 Turkish bath houses, 150 mosques or mesjids, 4 churches, 39 primary schools, a high school, two libraries, 39 medreses, eight külliyes, 123 public fountains (Ahmed Nazif, 1987; Imamoglu, 1992). Although central business district of the town was on the west side of the citadel and there were concentration of shops near the five gates of the town, neighbourhoods had their commercial and cultural facilities too. Each neighbourhood had a mosque together with a neighbourhood school, or sometimes a church when the population of the neighbourhood was christian. The use of cutstone as the main building material in nearly identical dimensions helped to create a mathching scale along streets and somewhat unified the environment. Few trees were found near fountains or mosques; greenery was concentrated mainly in private gardens or courtyards. This in turn provided a contrast between public and private domains. Compared to the monotonous, stone-paved, stone-surrounded streets - dazzling under sunshine - courtyards of houses provided a different atmosphere. Here, carefully arranged volumes of rooms and sheds dynamically interacted with the open space and greenery, enhancing a rich play of light and shadow, colour and texture. Thus, upon entering a private courtyard, the harshness of public domain suddenly disappeared and a humane, domestic atmosphere suitable for a simple, yet colourful everyday life came into being (Figure 6.3).

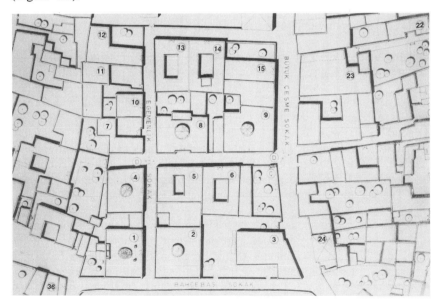

Figure 6.3   A portion of the Bahcebasi neighbourhood in Kayseri towards the end of 1940. The grid-iron pattern in the middle part was developed at the end of the nineteenth century.

Economic Life: The main income of the city was dependent on trade. The number of shops, hans and bazaars are some indications of the domination of this sector. Kayseri also had a long tradition of producing dyes, leather, textiles, carpets, pastrami and sausages. Its moderately rich agricultural hinterland provided grain, fruits and vegatables. Natives of Kayseri had a sort of subsistence economy. Grains, peas and beans were brought from nearby villages, while live-stock and poultry were raised within the family units. Horticulture was carried out around the town. Very few items were bought and sold for household usage: salt, sugar, fabrics or products that were difficult to produce within a family circle. Nothing was wasted or misused, nothing was thrown away; edible things were fed to animals; flammable things, such as, weeds, nut-shells were utilized as fuel for cooking or heating. Careful use of material and prevailing scarcity determined the character of traditional life.

Social and Cultural Setting: The town of Kayseri housed different religious groups for centuries. Muslims and christians lived in a friendly atmosphere, sharing most of the cultural values. Towards the end of the sixteenth century there were 50 muslim, 13 christian and nine mixed neighbourhoods (Jennings, 1976, p.32). In the seventeenth century all-muslim neighbourhoods declined to 35, the number of christian quarters was 14, while 12 town-quarters contained a mixed population (Faroqhi, 1987, p.59). Although thorough research is not available for the later periods, one can infer from the available sources that this proportion was more or less steady until the 1920's.

Until the deterioration of traditional life, the concept of neighbourhood was very important in Kayseri. Neighbourhood was not only a physical entity within the city, but also a social unit, providing social and economic cooperation among neighbours. Neighbourhood cohesion was strong and widespread. Families were concerned with their neighbours and neighbourhoods. They were on good terms with nearby households and respectful to all. (Although compared to the first half of this century neighbourlines has lost its strength to a great extent, in comparison with the western societies, still it is a continuing characteristic of the interdependent Turkish culture prevalent in Kayseri and other Turkish towns - Imamoglu and Imamoglu, 1993; Imamoglu, E.O. et al. 1993.)

Marriages, religious holidays, circumcision ceremonies of muslim children, and funeral ceremonies were important occasions that brought the neighbours together. Neighbours shared common facilities like a bakery, a Turkish bath, a school, one or two fountains, and sometimes a grocery shop. Drinking water was fetched from the street fountains; traditional pastries and sweets were prepared at home and taken to the bakery, which was at the same time a kind of winter public room for the elderly and local officials like the neighbourhood guard. Children of similar ages played together and formed sub-groups according to the streets or areas they lived in and identified themselves as such. Proximity rather than religion was the important tie in interaction. Although houses included at least a small bathing cubicle, public baths were important facilities. People used to go to Turkish baths at periodic intervals (once a week, once in two or three weeks). These were social events especially for women; family members with their neighbours and relatives used to spend the greater portion of a day eating and entertaining themselves in addition to cleansing.

Summer-Winter Differentiation in Town Life: There used to be a seasonal differentiation of living in many parts of Anatolia in the past. Depending on the severity of summers and the economic level of families, this differentiation could be quite modest, even unnoticable, like using north-oriented portions of the house or the upper levels more often in summer, or quite elaborate such as having a simple house at a higher altitude nearby the town, and moving there during summer. Kayseri was a town where the latter trend prevailed at least for the last four centuries. Evliya Çelebi, well-known Ottoman traveller visited Kayseri in 1650 and reported that there was a total of 103 such resorts "for enjoyment and entertainment" in and around the city (p.75). With the exception of very few families too poor or who did not have adult males capable of arranging the families' interaction with the external world, Kayseri natives moved to summer resorts on the outskirts of Mount Erciyes. These resorts (called "bag", meaning vineyards) were on higher elevations than the town and received cooling summer breezes. Scattered houses formed a kind of low-density community and provided informal living for every family. Fruit and vine trees, vegetables and flowers created a rich country atmosphere different from the one in the town where a concentrated urban life was prevalent.

During summer, men rode on horseback or drove carts to the town for their business every morning and returned home at sunset. Most of the houses in the town were empty and residential areas looked deserted.

Concern for Security: With her strong citadel and outer city walls and ditches Kayseri was well equipped against military threats during Byzantine era. However, with its fast growth and prosperity under Seljuk rule, the town expanded outside the walls and became more vulnerable. At the end of the nineteenth century the citadel was in a good condition but the outer walls have been extensively destroyed.

In general, house layouts and their relations with streets indicate that there was a deep concern for security and even for defence in the design of Kayseri houses. A close look at the history of the town indicates that it suffered extensively from skirmishes and wars for long periods. This must have influenced the security concepts of the inhabitants and shaped their attitudes towards their physical environment.

If one of the reasons for creating safe houses was protection in wars and street fights, the other was the custom of moving up to summer resorts in summer time. At that time empty streets and neighbourhoods attracted thieves. In the nineteenth century the town was peaceful. However, houses in Kayseri had small windows regardless of the position or orientation - whether towards the courtyards or streets -and were equipped with iron bars, sometimes with additional rabbit or chicken-mesh. Furthermore, almost all windows facing the street had shutters helping to create better environmental control but at the same time acting as efficient devices to shut off the interior spaces for security and defence. Walls around gardens or courtyards were four to five-meters high. Although half of that height would be sufficient for separation from the street or maintenance of visual privacy, it was a common practice to build them so high. This is, most probably a precaution against somebody peeping in or jumping inside from a horse or carriage in a street clash or pillage.

Dwellings: Unlike the Western World, house in Anatolia was seldom used to express the wealth and nobility of its owner. Spontaneous and informal development of plans and the repetition of houses on narrow, winding streets created a humble and friendly atmosphere. Only towards the end of the nineteenth century did christian families look to a European type of living and build pretentious houses in Kayseri.

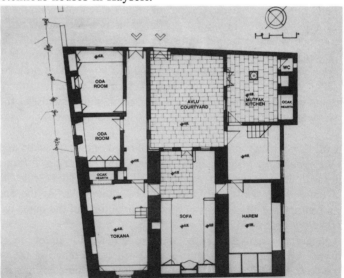

Figure 6.4   Groundfloor plan of a typical traditional town house (Baldöktü House). Date of construction 1860−70.

As is seen in Figure 6.4, a typical traditional town house in Kayseri is a product of rooms planned around an open space in a free yet dynamic equilibrium. Some of the important design features are the use of courtyard as an extension of the house, a sensitive site treatment solving problems related to odd-shaped building lots, and an ultimate respect for privacy of neighbours.

Gender and Privacy: Anatolia, mainly a muslim region for the last 800 years, carries in varying degrees an "Islamic" character in its buildings. According to Islamic interpretation, men and women are to be segregated for most social and public events. Thus, plans of large houses provided two separate (or separable) sections: one for women called haremlik (dahiliye) and one for men called selamlik (or hariciye). In general haremlik area constituted the major spaces and services where the family lived. In the selamlik, men received and entertained their guests. Sometimes in some of the upper and middle socio-economic-status dwellings these two sections became completely independent adjacent buildings with separate entrances, courtyards and service spaces.

Women cooked, cleaned and maintained the house. In well-to-do families female servants and cooks recruited from the nearby villages were employed. Men earned the money or secured the living and did the shopping. They lived in an almost female-free world during the day and even on some nights when they came together for "men-only" social gatherings and celebrations both in the town and summer resorts. Circumcision, engagement and wedding ceromonies were carried out for men and women separately in muslim community until the 1950's. This segregation created two different worlds of gender and alienated each one from the problems and privileges of the other.

Visual privacy for women was one of the primary requirements in a muslim house. Constructing high peripheral walls around the courtyards, opening no windows to the streets on the ground level, sometimes employing wooden grills in front of the upper floor windows, in addition to situating the living quarters away from the streets, were important features to secure privacy in traditional design. Women should be able to work or entertain their guests at home without the interference of men. This is one of the reasons why a selamlik room or section was oriented to the street, away from the courtyards and living quarters. When a muslim house was put up for sale, one of its important assets was its privacy, well expressed by the saying: "as private as a well".

Living Styles of Different Religious Groups: Kayseri was one of the few Anatolian towns in which a substantial christian minority lived. In the sixteenth century there were four churches and 12 mosques in Kayseri. The proportion of christian population varied between one fifth to one third until the establishment of the Republic. Two subgroups, Gregorian Armenians and

Orthodox Greeks, lived together with the Muslims in a friendly and cooperative way. The Greeks were mainly involved in trade and were better off than Armenians who dealt with handicrafts like dress-making, shoe-making, carpet weaving, carpentry, sculpting, constructing, playing music, running a pub, producing pastrami, etc. Muslims were landowners or traders, and they served in the army sometimes for years.

Christians, especially Greeks, lived a prosperous life. They had close contacts with ijstanbul and Europe and were influenced by the prevailing value systems and life styles: they had built spectacular houses in and around the town. Instead of using traditional, introverted house plans, they used European-type, extraverted layouts, and took all precautions available to make the house comfortable. Since they did not need to segragate the women, their designers had more chance to conceptualize their ideas and create more contemporary type town houses.

DISCUSSION

In congruence with formulations of social theorists like Giddens (1986), this study indicated that in a given period of time, different components of the socio-architectural environment produce an rds the end of Ottoman rule are few of the evidences of a lively but stable social, cultural and economic life in the town.

The attitude of Kayseri natives towards life was humble and informal. They were religious and moderately conservative, yet open-minded and tolerant. The "merchant city" character, and the rich cultural background of the town were few of the reasons for such qualities. The population did not vary for a long time and some values were maintained jealously, one being respect for other religions and value systems. Due to this character, Kayseri was a good Ottoman town: people of different origins and religions lived side by side, different religious groups complementing each other by specializing in different professions and living in a harmonious manner. Reflection of this attitude in social and cultural climate onto the physical environment was clear: although the public buildings exhibited an image of stability in community by their large sizes and monumental character, dwellings were humble, additive and unpretentious.

Houses reflected accumulation of a long history of built culture by their skillful, innovative and evocative characters. Religious groups easily reflected their value systems, beliefs and attitudes towards their houses and neighbourhoods. They shared many things in urban and cultural life with other citizens but at the same time kept their identities.

Figure 6.5 Elevation of a Muslim house (Güpgüpogullari Konak). Date of construction 1419

Arrangement of houses and public domains were such that privacy requirement of each religious group was easily met. Houses were interrelated but each had its own privacy. This was achieved mainly by the use of private courtyards and gardens in houses. Today the use of such spaces disappeared. In a relatively short period people gave up living in the courtyards, gardens and verandas, and became adapted to a concentrated urban life, generally squeezed into apartment flats. However, there is a continuing use of summer resorts which may be interpreted as a compensation for such a change.

The builders were professionals who acted as agents for integrating forms of the past with the current needs and desires of people, usually reflecting the ideas of "the other" religion or a higher social class in his new task. Hence an eclectic and rich combination of architectural forms, elements, decorations came into being in the built environment (Figure 5). Standards of comfort and lack of technical amenities were major problems in urban life. On the other hand, there was a strong social support system within the different generations of the family, relatives and neighbours. Furthermore, the possibility of employing servants made life relatively easier for the middle and upper socio-economic status groups. Today, traditional way of living, with a religious interpretation of the cosmos, changed into a modern, time-conscious and relatively materialistic one. With the acceptance of secularism, religion has somewhat lost its power as an organizer of social life. Consequently, segregation of spaces for men and women for social and public events disappeared and strict privacy requirements for women loosened because in Giddens' (1986) terms it was no longer functional.

The most noticable change in Kayseri however, is the clear contrast between the traditional and contemporary use of space and environmental quality. Although the town has grown in size and complexity enormously, it is unfortunate that deep roots of an exciting past were not utilized in designing buildings or open spaces. What exists with a real architectural or urban design quality in the town today, generally belongs to the past.

References

Ahmed Nazif (1987). Kayseri Tarihi (History of Kayseri). Mehmet Palamuto°lu prepared the manuscript from the original Ottoman text. Kayseri: Özel ijdare Md. ve Belediye Yayìnlarì.

Evliya Çelebi Seyahatnamesi (1970). Besinci kitap. Türkçelestiren: Zuhuri Danìsman, Istanbul: Zuhuri Danìsman Yayìnevi, 60-79.

Faroqhi, S. (1987). Men of modest substance - House owners and house property in seventeenth-century Ankara and Kayseri. Cambridge: Cambridge University Press.

Giddens, A. (1986). Central problems in social theory. Berkeley, CA: University of California Press.

Gabriel, A. (1931). Monuments Turcs d'Anatolie. 2 Vols Paris: 1931-1934, Vol.1, Kayseri-Nigde.

Imamoglu, V. (1992). Traditional dwellings in Kayseri. Ankara: Türkiye Halk Bankasì, Laga.

Imamoglu, E.O. and ijmamo°lu, V. (1992). Life situations and attitudes of the Turkish elderly toward institutional living within a cross-cultural perspective. Journal of Gerontology: Psychological Sciences, 47, 2, 102-108.

Imamoglu, E.O., Küller, R., ijmamo°lu, V. and Küller, M. (1993). The social psychological worlds of Swedes and Turks in and around retirement. Journal of Cross Cultural Psychology, 24, 1, 26-41.

Jennings, R.C. (1976). Urban population in Anatolia in the sixteenth century: a study of Kayseri, Karaman, Amasya, Trabzon and Erzurum. Int. Jr. Middle East Stud., 7, 21-57.

7

The effect of popular culture on urban form in Istanbul

L'effet de la culture populaire sur la forme urbaine à Istambul

Aytanga Dener

La Turquie étant un pays en voie de développement, le gouvernement n'a pas pu mettre en place un programme d'aménagement de logements. Les gens ont donc eu recours à un système unique pour résoudre leurs problèmes, utilisant à la fois des moyens officiels et non-officiels. Dans les grandes villes turques après les années soixante, de petits entrepreneurs ont eu l'occasion de construire des pâtés de maisons à très faible coût pour les familles de la classe moyenne, qui n'avaient aucun autre moyen de posséder une maison. Petit à petit, ces relations entre l'offre et la demande ont déterminé le paysage urbain. Une comparaison est faite des rapports avec l'espace et les matériaux utilisés pour ce type de maisons et pour les appartements des membres de l'élite riche de la Nouvelle République, qui avaient été construits auparavant. Plusieurs exemples de maisons ont été recueillis dans des magazines et une étude d'archives a été réalisée dans quatre arrondissements de la ville d'Istambul. Ces arrondissements sont choisis en fonction de l'aménagement de la ville et des nouvelles zones d'habitation. Les plans et les élévations des maisons sont étudiés, en fonction des autres effets de la culture populaire et des attitudes de consommation dans la société. La forme urbaine contemporaine à Istambul est étudiée en fonction des nouvelles tendances apparues après les années 80.

Mots clé: culture populaire; relations avec l'espace; logements pour familles de la classe moyenne; forme urbaine.

Key words: popluar culture, space relations, middle class family housing, urban form

In 50s, with the new Government, the first liberalization attempts have begun and different local business groups and artisans have become effective in both

Housing blocks for middle and lower class families have covered a considerable percentage of land in great cities within three decades. In these years, not the professional designers but the constructors determined the form of the buildings according to current values and preferences. The role of planned development has stayed at a minimum while popular approval has come forward. Formal endeavors have always been inadequate and people tried to find their own solutions. They usually have achieved alternative systems and prevented a social breakdown. The mutual inclinations have led to these spontaneous solutions. The houses have met the needs of middle class families at minimum costs and they embodied the minimum standards.

At this point, "popular culture", can be accepted as the common behavior of middle and lower class people which is developed spontaneously in their daily lives. It is the reproduction of a certain life style and sometimes an escape from negative aspects of real life. Generally, governors approve this behavior because in this way protest or uprisings are prevented. However people without question accumulate some concepts or forms in their brains and build "banks of icons" for using as a template. They usually use similar elements in a simple and schematic way in order to realize popular products. In this way, people get used to stereotypes while it becomes easy and less painful to accept the present negative situation. (Oktay, A., 1993)

The same approach is valid for house building. Neither the formation of space nor the selection of building materials need much effort for a large number of people. There are neither much varying options nor new creations. Having necessary cliches in their minds people try to adapt some parts of the elite life style into their own houses in a simplistic way. They miss living like wealthy people but owning a house in the cheapest way directs the whole procedure. The more the share of professional work diminishes the weaker space solutions and the more identical facades dominate the buildings. However, it is obvious that people have found the way to solve the housing problem and lessen the social tension within certain limits. On the other side, low quality housing itself comes to be the following problem. Sometimes people even can not use the houses before reconstructing some sections. Besides physical difficulties there is also visual discomfort to be relieved. The inner spaces and urban environment should be rehabilitated taking into consideration the various social and economic aspects. At least this very important issue must be discussed to supply a certain consciousness on a large scale.

This paper also aims to discuss how and why urban housing in Turkey has been this much affected by popular culture and some developments that can not be prevented have occured. For evaluating the state of housing in Turkey after 1923 (the establishment of Republic) the research has beeen realised in two phases. At first, the projects of houses that are built between 1923-50 are gathered from periodicals and a typological analysis is constituted. Then, an examination is made of the houses that are built after 1950 using certain district municipality archives. In order to select the municipalities the new housing regions and general development of Istanbul is scrutinized. Parallel to the social transition, the city has grown from the shores of the Marmara Sea to the inner parts layer by layer. (Dener, A., 1994) Drawing sections perpendicular to shores gives an idea about a social and economic panorama which makes it clear that the position and the history of Turkey have articulated the process of urban formation for years. From this point of view, the conditions of a developing country can be better understood within a historical perspective.

With an Eastern background, the Ottomans adapted some of the social and economic structures of local communities to their new system when they come to Anatolia. They established a different type of agricultural relations that depended on the absolute authority of the Sultan and the central leading group. For a long time, till the 19th century, military forces who also gathered taxes from the peasants were not allowed to own land. Thus the central authority prevented owning private possessions and deccelerated the development of the capitalist economy. In addition to differences in the economy economy the social institutions also came to work in a special way. Unlike in Western countries, close relations between family members or informal liaisons were more important in the solution of social problems.

Before the Republican Period, during the last years of the Ottoman Empire, the ottoman elites who were living in Istanbul accepted the Western way of living as civilized and tried to live and behave in the same way. They hired foreign teachers in order to educate their children. Young girls and boys spoke in a foreign language, they played the piano, singing and dancing just like the youth in West European countries. They even could not accept traditional clothes and did not mind changing their appearance. At the same time, the effect of this ideology, was able to be traced at their houses. The rich elites were eager to live in the regions where minorities and other foreign people were living in Istanbul because they admired the Western way of life in concrete buildings that were installed with electric, heating and water systems. They were not able to live in the way they used to in big, wooden houses of the 19th century. Yakup Kadri Karaosmanoglu, novelist of the new Republic, recounted this period in a realistic way. In one of his novels he quotes the thought of an Ottoman bureaucrat about the traditional way of living in old style wooden houses: "In reality, there has been no way to be comfortable. For years, six months in winter, I have never able to get warm and six months in summer, I have not even able to breathe. What a small window and what a small door... It is in vain to redecorate the house. You always feel like a refugee. I always tell you. I can never understand the meaning of living here like nomads while it is possible to live in wonderful, new apartments at Sisli.

There is not even a bath room in this huge house. You have to make preparations three days before to warm up that clumsy hamam... In these conditions, you can not take a shower once a month." However, after the death of his mother in law he threw all the furniture away and redecorated every room in a different European style looking at furniture booklets. (Karaosmanoglu, Y.K., 1947) This attitude, increased the difference between the elites and the majority of the people. On the other hand, researches verified that families were nearer Eastern or local families regarding marriage age, number of children and family type. At the end of 19th century, the marriage age was 30 for men and 21 for women while the birth rate was 3.9 in Istanbul. As men and women did not prefer to marry in their youth the birth rate also reduced in a natural way and the nuclear families remained dominant. (Duben, A., Behar, C., 1991) All the groups who came together to establish the Republic have been against Western imperialism and they have always encouraged research about Turkish culture. At this point they were in a dichotamous position. Though they were behind nationalism they tried to give form to the new Republic taking Western civilization as an example.

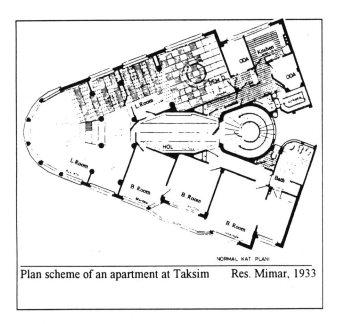

Plan scheme of an apartment at Taksim   Res. Mimar, 1933

Figure 7.1   Plan scheme of an apartment at Taksim (Res. Mimar, 1933).

Sometimes, they even used force to realize the reforms and to show that they could behave like Western people. A vast group of people who were on the side of traditional values could not raise their voice for a long time. The new authorities and the elite families had a dominant role and restricted all kinds of cultural development to their Westernization program. This policy continued in art. Thus this field also remained unproductive and the potential of people faded. The conditions were convenient for the upper class to show their new way of life and that they were different from the Ottomans. They were trying to meet the novels and give information about the life of a minister who has become a contractor later. A Swedish instructor was teaching his children and all the women living in the house dance and good manners. (Karaosmanoglu, Y. K., 1983)

The Space organization at apartments of the new bourgeoisie was not different from the ones in Western countries. Some of these apartments were over 300 m2. Wide living and dining rooms located on the side with the best view were separated from bedrooms. In general, servants were living with these families and they were not only helping house keeping but also serving at big parties given by the family that were also one of the most significant necessities of the new life. The dwellers could also take the advantage of a heating system and an elevator besides gas, water and electric installations. The rooms were totally decorated with European style furniture. Mr. Turk, a newly rich businessman who was introduced in novel of Halide Edip Adivar was living in one of these luxurious apartments with a wonderful sea view. In fact, he had combined four apartments. The entrance had a very rich appearance. Big crystal lamps illuminated carpets, glazed frames and marble tables. (Adivar, H. E., 1981)

On the other side, while a group of people was continuing to live modestly, another group of people was trying to jump up to the rich ostentatious life of elites. The people living in poor quarters were dreaming of living in apartments in favored regions that would that would signify transformation to an upper class. Even the basements of new buildings were favorable. Ms Balkar, was an instructor in Adivar's novel. She was giving lessons to Mr. Turk's daughters and had moved to the basement of the same building. She felt very happy at living in a warm and dry apartment. (Adivar, H. E., 1981) The segregated social life and duality in society had continued for approximately three decades.

In 1950, the liberal wing who was on the side of traditional values gained the elections against governmentalists. The same year, they established the multi-party system. In this way, different groups in society raised their voice and publicized their needs through a rightist party.

NORMAL KAT PLANI

Figure 7.2   Plan scheme of an apartment at Ayazpasa. It is quite large (350 square metres) with a beautiful sea view and meticulous decoration (Res. Arkitekt, 1936).

After the establishment of the Republic, the Government tried to separate religious affairs from formal institutions urging people sometimes by force. Strict Westernization affected democratic life negatively. With the multi-party system, people gained a certain kind of liberty and captured the chance of expressing themselves. There was no reason for them to be afraid of declaring their thoughts and beliefs if they did not pass beyond certain limits. So, 1950 can be evaluated as a fracture point in social transition. The population increased considerably. The migration from rural areas to urban places accelerated and because of these factors it was right to speak about a housing gap especially in great cities. Though the Government decided to subsidize mass housing and the first examples were designed these factors caused serious accommodation problems. The housing gap continued to be the most important issue waiting to be solved. The signs of liberty that appeared in the 50s were substantiated by some new democratic rights in 1960, after the military movements. In the 70s, the Government still continued to protect the economy but servingg industry showed an improvement at a significant rate. However, the share of industry in national income was more than agriculture.

In these years, the new Governments followed a popular program. Personal incomes remained high compared to other developing countries. Mean growth rate was 6.6 %. In 1965, the acceptance of the "Flat Owning Law" brought housing to a new state. Some of the governmental plans about housing could not be applied while others remained inadequate because of the accelerated social transition. The Government could not be effective in housing. From the very beginning of the new Republic, the Government seemed quite decided on developing industry and supporting the bourgeoisie, a group of businessmen. Not only the underdeveloped economy, but the newly built social institutions could not act in the way they were expected to. There were many unemployed people in great cities. They tried to find their own solutions sometimes using their family relations or citizenship, liaisons that have been effective since the Ottoman Period. They established mechanisms that decrease tension in the society.

METHODOLOGY

One of the options for tracing the interaction between spatial and social change is sucritinizing housing projects. It will not be wrong to evaluate the social change of Turkey in two main periods. First, the period between the establishment of the Republic and 1950. Second, the duration beginning with the multi-party system in 1950 and ending in late 1980s. The two periods are also appropriate for the examination of spatial change. The former period, can be identified by governmentalism, the pressure over people, the effort to develop industry and the bourgeoisie and their luxurious apartments while the later comes forward by limited liberalism, small scale business and the cheap house building systems. To see the spatial differentiation the research has been realized in two phases. As it has been impossible to find samples for earlier years of the Republic in the archives of the municipality the periodicals have been examined. For the second period, four districts, Uskudar, Kadikoy, Besiktas and Bakirkoy that still have the capacities to build housing blocks have been selected. The selection has been realized by examining the new development areas and housing regions of Istanbul. It is possible to draw four axes of housing areas-two of them parallel to Bosphorus sides. At the archives of four district municipalities, a research has been completed by random selection in order to gather the projects (plan schemes and the elevations of houses have been evaluated) of house samples belonging to different years (1950-).

RESULTS

The informal way of owning a house in the cheapest way was squatter building. Without paying for the field and using the family's own labor force houses were built in a very short time. Usually people working at marginal jobs lived in squatter settlements and they constituted both economic and social solutions for Turkey applying a method originating in the 18th century. Parallel to the social developments in Turkey and after the Flat Owning Law (1965), an alternative solution came from middle class families and small scale business owners. In a very creative way land owners who could never get the chance to renew their houses, contractors with a very little amount of capital and families who could not save enough to own a house by themselves came together and established the unique build and sell (yap-sat) system. The contractors began to work making an agreement with the land owners and buying their lands promising them a couple of apartments. After they sold the rest of the apartments even before beginning to construct. Money they gathered was helping them to finish construction. Without any suspicion, this was another cheap way to own a house. For this reason, the contractors did not want to pay much for the architects. Some of the architects worked as if practitioners and earned a minimum amount. So they were able to spent very little time on a project and usually used the same schema for different buildings. It was impossible to think over elevations and the harmony between them. On the contrary, it would be a time wasting issue.

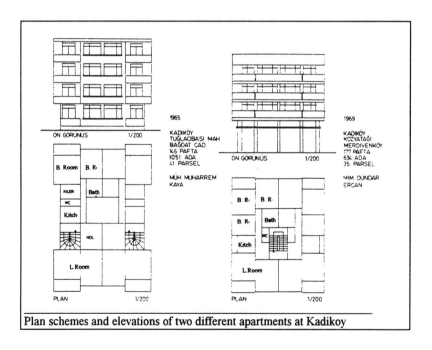

Plan schemes and elevations of two different apartments at Kadikoy

Figure 7.3   Plan schemes and elevations of two different apartments at Kadikoy.

Often contractors who were not well educated were realed the last touches to buildings. Selling the apartments as quickly as possible and attracting the clients was the most important problem for them. Ostentatious forms but the cheapest materials were favoured. Deformed historical forms, the elements of Western architecture or some other local ornaments have been used together.

Thus, unavoidably the popular culture became effective on urban form. Synthesizing both the Western and the Eastern popular culture can easily be marketed and be interesting to a variety of people. The building and selling system process accelerated in the 70s and continued in the 80s. Housing demand has changed gradually. Because of the economic transition, middle class families have lost the chance of buying houses; only the members of the upper middle class and upper class could afford apartments. However, the contractors have become more cautious about materials and design quality. The elevations of buildings have begun to be more important and have had to appeal to different kinds of clients. Though the plan schemes have not changed much the elevations have had to be spectacular. (Dener, A., 1994)

It is possible to get a global idea about the social and economic development of Turkish society by looking to housing groups in great cities that belong to different periods. At first, a historical review of housing regions easily shows the transition of regularities related to some changing administrative decisions of different ideologies. The heights of buildings and dimensions of windows and doors or some other details change through time obviously. Especially politicians wanting to win the elections have periodically let some rights be abused.

For this reason, illegal attempts have increasing caused serious deformations in the urban environment. After a while, abuses have to be tolerated because better solutions needed better economic conditions. In other words, premature economising has determined the formation of cities. A gradual increase in national income after the 60s has only let people build houses for themselves but have never given them the opportunity to hire qualified professional labor because costs had to stay at a minimum. Contemporary architectural styles in Western countries affected the forms of upper class houses and architects take projects published in periodicals as an example but usually deformed their main character with quick and careless labor.

Coming to recent years the gradual improvement of construction systems and building materials can be observed parallel to economic development. At least, the standard of houses has increased by the number of electric tools. The evolution of small industry has made it easier to own a TV, washing machine, refrigerator and a car. This affect the distance between houses and centers.

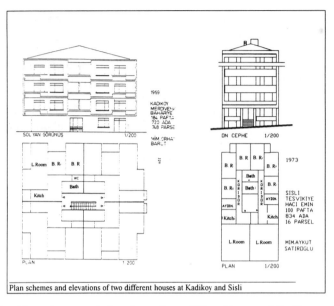

1959
KADIKOY
MERDIVEN
BAHARIYE
184 PAFTA
720 ADA
748 PARSE

MIM.ORHA
BARUT

SISLI
TESVIKIYE
HACI EMIN
100 PAFTA
834 ADA
16 PARSEL

MIM.AYKUT
SATIROGLU

SOL YAN GÖRÜNÜŞ   1/200   ÖN CEPHE   1/200

L.Room   B.R.   B.R.

Kitch

wc

Bath

PLAN   1/200

B.R   B.R.

B.R   B.R.

Bath

B.R.   Bath   B.R.

AYDIN   AYDIN

Kitch   Kitch

L.Room   L.Room

PLAN   1/200

Plan schemes and elevations of two different houses at Kadikoy and Sisli

Figure 7.4   Plan schemes and elevations of two different houses at Kadikoy and Sisli.

With the evolution of social rights the Governments have become obliged to think more about the housing problem and work harder to organize new house building systems and subsidization policies. In recent years, new liberal consumption policies have influenced the whole society. Furthermore, people want to live at higher standards and to try to supply more comfort in their accommodation. It is quite clear that better economic conditions promote the standards of social life and both these developments require administrative renovation. Thus, an entire comprehension about the transition of housing styles and changing administrative, social and economic effects can only be achieved within a historical perspective as they influence each other directly.

Consequently, looking to historical developments neither the social nor the economic conditions give chance for professionals to organize house building as it should be. Parallel to this issue also the other social institutions work ineffectively. Some of the social problems are solved spontaneously which prevents more serious conflicts. Popular approval plays a deterministic role on the quality of solutions. The results are usually simple and beyond satisfying sophisticated necessities but make most of the people feel better. Either the squatters or the houses that are built by the yap-sat (built and sell) system satisfy basic shelter needs. Besides, though with some deformed styles and low quality materials they provide a milieu in which people forget the negative aspects of their daily lives.

References

Adivar, H.E., (1981), Sonsuz Panayir, Atlas Kitabevi

Dener, A., (1994), Sosyal ve Mekansal Degismenin Etkilesimi Cumhuriyet Sonrasi Konutlari (Unpublished Ph D thesis), ITU

Duben, A., Behar, C., (1991), Istanbul Households, Mariage Family and Fertility 1880-1940, NY: Cambridge University Press

Karaosmanoglu, Y.K., (1947), Kiralik Konak, Istanbul: Remzi Kitabevi, pp. 113,114

Karaosmanoglu, Y.K., (1983), Ankara, Istanbul: Iletisim Yay.

Oktay, A., (1993), Turkiye'de Populer Kultur, Istanbul: Yapi Kredi Yay.

8

The impact of housing quality on the urban image

L'impact de la qualité de l'habitation sur l'image urbaine

Maria Cristina Dias Lay and Antonio Tarcísio da Luz Reis

Cet article attire l'attention sur des facteurs liés à l'apparence visuelle et au fonctionnement des grands ensembles collectifs et discute de l'impact de la qualité des logements de masse sur la morphologie urbaine au Brésil. L'examen des relations entre les éléments physiques et symboliques de l'apparence visuelle developée dans l'étude comparative des ensembles collectifs dans la cité du Porto Alegre, a permis lde comprendre comment les attributs espaciaux affectent les attitudes de l'individu par rapport aux résidents et à l'environnement, et comment ces attributs affectent les types de comportement. On a trouvé que les comportements des résidents (positif, neutre ou negatif) ont réfléchi leurs perceptions et évaluations du fonctionnement de l'environnement, affectant directement, positivement ou negativement, l'image de leur environnement residentiel et son contexte urbain.

Mots clé: fonctionnement de l'habitation; apparence visuelle; image de l'environnement; attitude; comportement

Keywords: housing performance; visual appearance; attitudes; environmental image; behaviour

As good or bad environmental performance is specially reflected by the appearance of outdoor spaces, it has a major impact on the perceived image and morphological characteristics both of the residential environments produced and of their urban consequences. In housing developments in Brazil, standardisation of project design and building specifications were established as almost scale of the country, and the marked different regional characteristics of each of the 23 States, the nature of the system of provision based on economy of scale adversely affected the quality of construction by its overemphasized priorities for quantitative targets. Consequently, the design of most housing schemes was not appropriate for the satisfaction of user needs and aspirations.

The housing schemes have been characterised by two main typologies: repetitive block of flats, without lifts and four storey high; and detached houses on small individual plots. While the blocks of flats followed the modernist approach with buildings placed in continuous open space, generally located so as to leave empty areas with sometimes undefined functions between them, without differentiation in the facades and non-related to the street, the detached houses on small plots followed the conventional division of plots with a narrow and long block arrangement. Two storey blocks of flats and row houses were also provided, however the typology most often studied comprised the four storey blocks of flats (probably because problems were more frequently detected). The latter is also the focus in this work.

Despite their common poor building and design quality, dissimilar environmental performance was identified (e.g. Lay, 1992; Reis, 1992), which seemed to be related, inter-alia, to occasional differences in the site layout. It was observed that while some housing schemes were neglected and abused, others were positively used and maintained. This raised the question of what design factors might be positively or negatively affecting user attitudes and environmental evaluation, causing some housing schemes to be perceived as more or less successful than others.

In order to account for the attested influence of the built environment on spatial behaviour and the subsequent impact of spatial behaviour on the built environment (e.g. Proshansky et al., 1970; Holahan, 1978), this investigation focuses on the specification of objectively defined physical and symbolic environmental characteristics affecting user attitudes and the perception of environmental images, and the study of their relationship to behaviourial variables. It attempts to identify some patterns and symbols that might be collectively perceived as fulfilling or not residents' preferences, affecting their satisfaction with the housing scheme and their responses to it through positive or negative behaviour, and higher or lower frequency of use.

Environmental image and visual appearance

The many studies of housing schemes show appearance to be a major factor influencing overall satisfaction (e.g.Cooper 1970; Doe 1971, 1972; Francescato, 1979; Lansing et al. 1970; Coulson, 1980). The process of image-making described by Lynch (1960) provides grounds for assuming that user perception of visual appearance is intrinsic to the process of image-making, and that its components play a major role in facilitating or resisting the creation of a positive collective image of the site, affecting user evaluation of the residential environment, and making the environment more or less desirable and easy to understand and use.

The attribute of visual appearance, as adopted in this paper, is also concerned with the understanding of the aesthetic experience of the built environment as part of the residents' everyday life, and subsequently understanding their judgements of preferences. As Lang (1987) points out, it is closely associated with the subject of empirical aesthetics, which has been debated for centuries (e.g. Santayana, 1896; and Rasmussen, 1959), with the purpose of (1) identifying what gives people pleasurable experience and why, and (2) understanding the nature of the human ability to create and to enjoy creating displays that are pleasing.

The elements put forward in this discussion further suggest that visual appearance might affect user attitudes, motivations and behaviour, encouraging or discouraging activities and experiences. Both extent to which outdoor residential environments might be designed in order to afford specific physical qualities and symbolic values, and also the identification of the 'codes' that their specific population understand and enjoy, might be obtained if the assessment of patterns and symbols that affect the fulfilment of residents' preferences, user attitudes towards the housing scheme, and their behaviour can be accomplished.

In order to account for the source of the impact of those features on user perception of visual appearance, user satisfaction, and the use of spaces, the qualities in the environment which are explored, are grouped according to physical and symbolic environmental characteristics.

Physical characteristics of visual appearance

The site features identified in the literature suggest that the physical appearance of the site originates from two physical qualities: imageability and attractiveness. In order to comprehend the way certain visual attributes in the built environment might affect user perception of imageability and attractiveness and how those attributes interrelate, specific concepts and elements related to both of these two physical qualities were investigated. These include openness, spaciousness, enclosure, level of orientation, territorial definition, the kind and quality of materials used, features on the facades of buildings, the level of maintenance, the arrangement of buildings.

Symbolic qualities of visual appearance

Given the assumption that users produce symbols that represent values and aspirations which are manifested in the environment, the use of certain cues in the appearance of residential areas (e.g. personalisation, destructive behaviour, maintenance) that might have a strong influence in consciously creating and conveying the *social image* of the perceived environment, expressing user attitudes, tastes and identity, and their impact on user motivations and behaviour, were investigated. Moreover, the importance of homelike features and vital considerations in the development of satisfactory residential environments (e.g. designs that maximize the expression of individual place, residence and territory; physical characteristics that reflect residents' self-image or desired status and self-esteem); and the influence of appearance in affecting and reflecting residents' reputation were further explored in the field work.

These specific physical and symbolic components of the housing environment were examined in terms of the environmental messages they transmit, and the dynamic of these environmental messages was investigated: that is to say how environmental images were created, how these images generated or dissipated conflict and misunderstanding between individuals and groups living in the housing schemes arises. Selected physical elements perceived by the residents were analyzed in order to measure the extent to which visual appearance was affected by them. In addition some of the images and associations of their environment which residents hold, how these were influenced by their perception of symbolic characteristics provided or missing in the site, and how the interpretation of the symbolic messages transmitted by these attributes in the environment affected residents perception of visual appearance, were further analyzed.

METHODS

The survey was designed with the purpose of

(i) identifying and analyzing the most frequently perceived attributes, categorized into *physical* and *symbolic* components of the sites, affecting user perception of visual appearance and the resultant image of the scheme;

(ii) identifying and analyzing the effects of user perception of visual appearance of the scheme on user attitudes towards the site;

(iii) identifying and analyzing the effects of user attitudes towards the site on spatial behaviour.

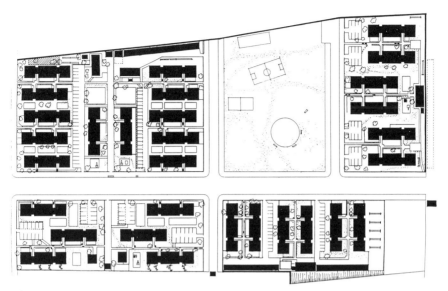

Figure 8.1 Jardim Salomoni housing scheme − positive resident evaluation and high degree of usage of outdoor spaces.

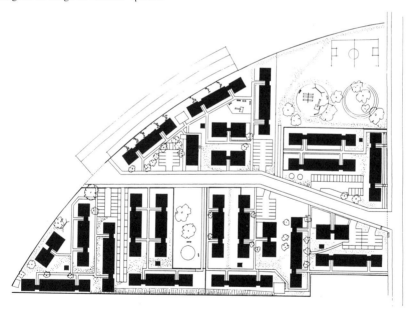

Figure 8.2 Parque Cristal housing scheme − negative resident evaluation and low degree of usage of outdoor spaces.

In addition, it should be possible to measure and compare the level of usage and modifications of outdoor spaces across residential environments having different layouts and to develop a behaviourial portrait of each of these residential environments, including both the range of activities that occur in the outdoor spaces and an identification of the environmental features that support these activities.

The means and methods of measuring the variables and attributes were investigated and tested through a detailed comparative study of outdoor spaces in a sample of two mass housing schemes in the city of Porto Alegre, Brazil. A form of stratified sampling was utilized for the selection of the sample of schemes, which was based on diagnostic explorations conducted in 19 housing schemes provided by governmental housing policy (based on home ownership exclusively) for the low and low/middle-income groups, located within different inner-city neighbourhoods. This preliminary sample selection did permit a coarse selectivity to be applied, in this case to select the most obvious disliked and liked housing schemes. That is, of the two sites selected, Jardim Salomoni housing scheme (figure 8.1) represented projects of positive resident evaluation and high degree of usage of outdoor spaces, and the Parque Cristal housing scheme (figure 8.2) represented projects indicating negative resident evaluation and a low degree of usage of outdoor spaces.

Both sites presented a standardised shape and yet had peculiar characteristics in the site layout. The projects were comparable in age (10 years old), in the quality of design of buildings, and in their form. All accommodation consisted of flats in blocks up to four floors in height. Residents of both sites were comparable along three dimensions: ethnic (multi-racial), socio-economic level and length of residence. Moreover, the two housing schemes, as part of the subsidized housing provided by governmental housing policy, were in private ownership. It was noted that most of the flats were occupied by their owners and only a few were rented from private owners.

The multi-method techniques used for data collection consisted of a combination of observation of physical traces, observations of behaviour, interviews, questionnaires and record analysis. For the appraisal process, three evaluative factors were considered:

(1) **the setting** - the social and physical attributes of each housing scheme evaluated, including quality of maintenance, changes and decorations provided by the users;

(2) **the users** - the background, individual characteristics, needs, preferences, aspirations, attitudes and behaviour of people who are involved with the setting;

(3) **the proximate environmental context** - the ambient qualities, land-use characteristics and neighbourhood qualities that surround the setting.

In order to suit the requirement of maintaining the integrity of the data, non-parametric statistics were adopted. The data analysis provided measures to assess how strongly reactions among residents to living in such housing schemes were related to certain physical and symbolic features in the built environment.

RESULTS AND DISCUSSION

The measures employed enabled objective comparisons between the alternative design proposals provided in the two schemes in terms of the effects variations in the perceived visual appearance had on user evaluation of environmental performance, user attitudes, motivations and behaviour. The study confirmed that:

(i) resident perception of visual appearance is based on user interpretation of the functional and symbolic performance of certain physical attributes and components which form user perception of the overall image of the scheme;

(ii) the perceived image of the scheme affects user attitudes towards the site;

(iii) user attitudes towards the site regulate the type of spatial behaviour occurring in outdoor spaces on the site.

Residents evaluated visual appearance on the basis of their perception of the attributes that expressed or not their values, tastes and social attitudes, in addition to their perception of spatial qualities and structure.

Physical characteristics

The two major physical attributes found to contribute to resident evaluation of the appearance of their housing schemes - *imageability* of the site and *attractiveness* of buildings and landscape - were analyzed through collecting and studying user evaluation of certain physical elements identified in the study as facilitating, or not, imageability, and as determining the attractiveness of the site.

Imageability

The attribute imageability relates to how the environment was perceived and experienced by its users and it was established by both questionnaire answers and by observation. This particular attribute arose from an assessment of the apparent clarity or legibility of the overall image of the scheme to the users, and the ease with which the environment could be mentally organized and recognized by them as a coherent pattern. The magnitude and the nature of this attribute was affected by user ability to structure and identify their residential environment. The criteria used to determine the degree of imageability of each site were defined and analyzed according to the physical characteristics which were likely to be consistently significant to residents in their definition of the character of the spaces and structure of the site.

The absence of order in the placing of buildings (e.g. in Parque Cristal, figure 2 above) adversely affected legibility and resident perception of the appearance of the scheme. When spaces were analyzed, there was a mismatch between spaces that were more physically enclosed and user perception of spatial definition. While in the literature, spatial enclosure refers to physical limitation of spaces, user perception of enclosure was differently perceived. Enclosure was perceived in functional terms rather than in physical terms, that is, user perception of more or less enclosed spaces depended upon how the buildings were functionally related to each other (e.g., front to front, front to back, front to side, back to back, etc.). Enough evidence was found to suggest that the lack of concern with the way buildings and spaces were related, resulted in spaces that did not instill a sense of belonging and identification of territory in residents. The evidence for this was obtained through comparing observations of physical indicators for territorial definition and levels of maintenance, and on-site observations of the way spaces were used on each site. These were the criteria used to indicate user sense of belonging and territorial definition.

The perceived degree of spaciousness and adequacy of spaces tended to be particularly associated with visual appearance, affecting users' perception and evaluation of their residential environment and user perception of outsider evaluation of the site. The inadequacy of spaces identified in Parque Cristal was indicated by the manifestation of conflict of use within specific zones, as the apparent shortage of space did not permit activities to be performed in a functional and beneficial way. When perceived spaciousness was evident (as in Jardim Salomoni), conflicting use of specific spaces among age groups was not found.

The character of the site differed according to the level of orientation perceived by users, was influenced by the structure of the site and residents' memory of past experiences (respondents who came from a small town and previously lived in a house, and respondents who felt that their previous living environment was better than the current one, perceived poor orientation as arising from the design of the schemes). The effects of the structure of the site were analyzed on the basis of findings suggesting that when site design provided a distinct hierarchy of spaces from private through public, conflict among neighbours was reduced, and resident involvement in maintenance activities was beneficially affected. Moreover, resident opinion that visitors to the site readily oriented themselves in it was taken to be an indication that the residents themselves have a clear perception of identity of the site, promoting a 'sense of place' among them.

Poor orientation was mostly affected by factors which were contrary to residents favourable aesthetic criteria (e.g. ugly, dirty, badly kept spaces), and the ways spaces were used, denoting inadequacy of play and meeting spaces. The consistent use and organization of definite cues from the outdoor environment (clearly identified in Jardim Salomoni) appeared to be a necessary condition of the ease of orientation.

Maintenance further influenced user perception of the level of orientation in the two sites. The evidence gathered suggests that if maintenance improves, the level of orientation tends to increase. It was observed that the definition of spatial hierarchy and territories tended to be more strongly correlated with good maintenance over time, like a spiral process -the clearer the structural definition is, the better maintenance will be, and the better maintenance is, the clearer structural definition will be.

Attractiveness

Attractiveness was not judged by the aesthetic standards held by designers, but by resident perceptions of attractiveness; it was associated with the specific appeal of buildings, units and grounds. The common elements identified on the two sites perceived by residents as inducing or obstructing attractiveness, that is, making buildings and spaces more or less pleasant and appealing to be used or contemplated, were classified into two categories: overall *maintenance* of the site and *construction details*.

The evidence showed that well-maintained grounds and the absence of litter was a prerequisite of satisfaction with the visual appearance of the two sites. Attractiveness was closely related to good upkeep, obtained through cleanliness and maintenance of buildings and site landscape. In turn, user perception of living in an attractive building and an appealing landscape was strongly affected by the cleanliness and maintenance of the site, that is by the perception of more or less upkeep of green areas and landscape in general, paths, furniture or the façades of buildings, this varied with residents' initiatives and motivation to improve/repair or modify the environment: the quality of maintenance on each scheme created a particular ambience that affected resident perception of the entire setting: an ambience of dereliction and neglect tended to evoke misuse and carelessness, while good maintenance and surfaces of good quality tended to be valued and appreciated.

Moreover, good maintenance and extensive landscaping were used to distinguish blocks of units and reinforce territorial definition (e.g. in Jardim

Salomoni). Nonetheless, variety among blocks, which is constantly mentioned in the literature as a desirable element to prevent monotony, turned out to be of no importance, and even undesirable, to most residents. The explanation found was that residents were conscious about the effects variety might have on their perception of 'community', which their opinions supposed to mean equitable. The construction elements which were more sensitive to resident perception of attractiveness were entrances to buildings, and the use of colours to differentiate the condominiums.

Symbolic characteristics and components

The fact that residents showed that the outside appearance of the scheme was very important was not related only to the form itself or to the aesthetic character of buildings, but to form as it affected residents' social standing in the community, as well as their own satisfaction. Residents were aware of certain aspects of the visual appearance of the scheme and the 'public image' it presented.

To understand the ways in which the interpretation of components in the physical environment affected user perception of visual appearance, and what the symbolic meaning of components was within each particular context, the social and symbolic significance of certain physical components were examined in terms of (1) the environmental messages they transmitted to residents (based on common image associations and values which residents held); and (2) how physical components satisfied or not resident desire for a home.

Outside appearance was important to users because it reflected residents' good or bad 'reputation' - i.e. well maintained semi-private spaces were important clues for conveying respectability, while poorly maintained and neglected semi-private spaces did not live up to residents' image of respectability or their desire to have their physical environment reflect their good citizenship. Resident pride in their living environment tended to be transmitted to others and interpreted by the residents through their perception of the level of maintenance of the spaces surrounding the buildings. Consequently, resident evaluation of *unappealing attractiveness of the site*, *unpleasant open areas* , and their perception of *adverse outsiders' opinions about the appearance of the scheme* were affected by their interpretation of poor maintenance and the neglect of semi-private and semi-public areas as conveying other residents' lack of desire to have their physical environment reflect a good 'reputation'.

Figure 8.3   The use of ornaments in gardens in Parque Cristal proclaiming tastes.

Objects, when employed, helped to create images, which proclaimed to themselves, friends or passers-by their status, values and tastes . They were viewed as 'social tools' or symbols that functioned both as a means of communication among individuals and as a significant reference (examples are shown in figures 8.3 and 8.4).   The exterior personalization, for example, provided evidence that those who made them were concerned about their living environment, and also indicated the tendency to show aspirational class values.

Nonetheless, rather as Becker (1977) observed, the positive consequences attributed to personalization in the literature by participants' satisfaction with what they produced proved to be easily transformed into dissatisfaction when other residents criticised or damaged those initiatives, generating potential conflict.   Others' reactions to their spatial behaviour and values as expressed, often to a large extent by the physical elements and objects introduced (personalization), adversely affected resident self-esteem and identity with the scheme, which tended to develop through individuals' interactions with other residents.   This had an important influence on people's perceptions and attitudes.

The effects of user attitudes (psychological manifestations) on spatial behaviour (physical manifestations) were investigated through observations made on the two sites. Spatial behaviour appeared to derive from the nature of attitudes residents held towards their residential environment (i.e. residents living in the neglected and abused housing scheme - Parque Cristal - perceived and evaluated their residential environments as unsatisfactory, and vice-versa). Attitudes appeared to motivate differentiated spatial behaviour (positive and negative), affecting user emotional reactions and user motivations for socializing, improving and maintaining the site or not (i.e., poor maintenance provided evidence that residents were not satisfied or proud of their residential environment and, therefore, did not feel motivated to improve its appearance).

Positive attitudes motivating positive behaviour

The findings indicated that physical attributes such as spatial definition, territorial control, adequacy of spaces for child's play and for large-scale socializing, etc., when satisfactory, positively affected residents' attitudes, including sense of belonging, sense of identity with the place and positive evaluation of the image of the scheme. These positive attitudes could have had an effect on resident motivation to improve the scheme through physical changes and maintenance, and consequently affected social interaction among residents, which were than more motivated to increase social and user-environment interaction.

Figure 8.4   Electronic gates introduced by the residents in Jardim Salomoni, perceived as promoting social status.

Negative attitudes motivating detrimental behaviour

Discontent with the spatial arrangements on the site and with conflicting uses caused by the nature of the semi-private and semi-public spaces, with residents reactions to specific activities and attributes, with annoyance caused by neighbours, and with disruption by children, were some of the factors identified as adversely affecting residents' emotional attitudes toward the scheme and other residents. They were assumed to encourage residents' motivations for destructive behaviour, social conflict, dysfunctional behaviour and further neglect. These were mainly manifested through intentional or casual property damage (vandalism), graffiti, poor maintenance and neglect of spaces.

CONCLUSIONS

It has been shown in this paper that resident perception of visual appearance was affected by the type of use and maintenance of buildings and spaces, and that this seemed to have resulted from the way spaces, determined by site layout, were more or less clearly understood. The quality of maintenance created a particular ambience in each scheme and this appears to have affected social activities and resident perceptions of the entire setting. This might have further affected user motivation to improve the scheme or not, and consequently affect the image of the scheme. Besides, as maintenance is under residents responsibility and depends on and further develops a sense of community among them, it appears to be simultaneously one of the propagators of positive or negative interaction among residents and also an indication of how positive or how negative interaction among residents has developed.

Finally, the results suggest that positive attitudes tend to motivate positive behaviour, while negative attitudes tend to motivate detrimental behaviour. The observations carried out indicated that neglected environments tended to remain neglected (atmosphere of dereliction and neglect evoked misuse and carelessness), while well maintained environments tended to remain well kept (good maintenance was respected and valued). This continuous process appears to be self-perpetuating, unless attitudes and motivations, for any reason, are modified (changing external stimuli).

By analogy, it can be assumed that the same applies to larger urban areas. When bad performance exists, the massive scale and number of those projects in Brazil, which replicate poor quality housing schemes has been creating a major negative impact on the cityscape, propagating 'ulcers' in extensive parts of cities. The consequences of this are predictable, in that the attitudes, motivations and behaviour affected by the adversely perceived visual appearance of housing schemes and entire lower-income neighbourhoods might encourage further deterioration of the cityscape, adversely influencing citizens' feelings of self-esteem, their social standing in the community, their relationships to their neighbours, sense of belonging, and sense of identity with the place, and further affecting maintenance of social order, encouragement of self development, and promotion of quality for the population.

However, criticisms cannot be made only against the economy of scale production itself, as the urgent need for housing clearly justifies its use, but concern can be expressed about the effects that this large production of poor quality housing schemes had on the landscape of cities. It is therefore clear that the spatial structure of the mass housing schemes provided in Brazil and its performance need to be further analyzed in terms of quality, as attempted in this study, in order to identify the relevant factors requiring change and the nature of change that will promote significant improvement in mass housing provision. By this means, the 'external stimuli' above mentioned might change.

References

BATLEY, R. (1983). Power through bureaucracy: urban political analysis in Brazil. England, Gower Publishing Company.

BECKER, F.D. (1977). Housing Messages. Stroudsburg, Dowden, Hutchinson and Ross, Inc.

COOPER, C. (1970). Resident attitudes towards the environment at St. Francis Square, San Francisco: A summary of the initial findings. Berkeley, Institute of Urban and Regional Development, University of California. Working paper N°126.

COULSON, N.J.(1980). Space around the home: Do residents like what the planners provide? The Architects' Journal, December, Vol.24, pp.1245-1260.

Department of the Environment (1972). The estate outside the dwelling: reactions of residents to aspects of housing layout. Design Bulletin 25, London, HMSO.

FRANCESCATO, G. et al. (1979). Residents' satisfaction in HUD-Assisted Housing: design and management factors. Washington D.C., US Department of Housing and Urban Development.

HOLAHAN, C.J. (1978). Environment and Behaviour: A Dynamic Perspective. New York, Plenum.

LANG, J. (1987). Creating Architectural Theory: The role of the behaviourial sciences in environmental design. New York, Van Nostrand Reinhold Company Inc.

LANSING, J.B. et al. (1970). Planned residential environments. Ann Arbor, Institute for Social Research, University of Michigan.

LAY, M.C.D. (1992). Responsive site design, user environmental perception and behaviour. Department of Architecture, Oxford Polytechnic, England, Ph.D. Thesis.

LYNCH, K. (1960). The Image of the City. Cambridge, Mass., MIT Press.

PROSHANSKY, H.M. et al. (eds.) (1970). Environmental Psychology: Man and his Physical Setting. New York, Holt, Rinehart and Winston.

RASMUSSEN, S.E. (1959). Experiencing Architecture. Cambridge, Mass., MIT Press.

REIS, A.T.L. (1992). Mass housing design, user participation and satisfaction. Department of Architecture, Oxford Polytechnic, England, Ph.D. Thesis.

SANTAYANA, G. (1896). The sense of Beauty. Reprinted (1955), New York, Dover.

9

Une communauté s'éveille: expérience urbaine dans un ensemble de logements sociaux à Rio de Janeiro

The Raising of a Community: Urban Experience in a low income settlement in Rio de Janeiro.

Cristiane Rose de Siqueira Duarte

The object of this study is "Vila Pinheiros", one of the low income settlements built ten years ago to host a population of 65000 people who lived in a shanty town named Favelas Maré, located in Rio de Janeiro. After being established at the low income settlement, this population, made up essentially of extremely poor rural immigrants, suffered a hard adjusting process to the urban environment. This process, however, ended up in transforming these isolated immigrants in a real community in the social meaning of the term. Currently, this popular neighbourhood is completely transformed by its inhabitants, both in its physical aspect and in the use value of its spaces. This study is supported by a field work which followed the development of Vila Pinheiro's social practices along 4 years. It presents an analysis of a social and cultural process of spatial modifications related to the adjusting period to the urban environment experienced by this population of rural immigrants. In order to contribute to the understanding of the realities of this group of inhabitants through the observation of the social- spatial dialectics, this study tries to bring evidence that while the community builds its spaces, its is at the same time building it self.

Keywords: urban cultures; social housing, social practices, urban neighbourhoods, Rio de Janeiro.

Mots Clés: cultures urbaines, logements sociaux, pratiques sociales, quartiers urbains, Rio de Janeiro.

Vila Pinheiros est un ensemble de logements sociaux uni familiaux construit par l'État pour reloger les habitants des favelas Maré, à Rio de Janeiro. La construction de cet ensemble de logements a été construit dans le cadre d'un programme de planification urbaine très ambitieux nommé "Projeto Rio", qui a été édifié entre 1979 et 1983.

Les anciens habitants des favelas Maré, migrants ruraux pour la plupart, ont dû accepter sans résistance les conditions imposées par les organismes publics de l'époque, poussés beaucoup plus par des intérêts politiques que par des fins sociales. Après son installation dans le quartier, cette population a été "abandonnée" à elle-même, sans avoir pu compter ni avec les plans d'assistance ni avec les titres de propriété des logements, qui leur avait été promis par le gouvernement.

Au long des trois premières années après l'occupation de Vila Pinheiros, très peu de changements physiques ont été registrés. Etant très peu instruits et ne connaissant pas leurs droits en tant que citoyens, cette population avait peur d'être expulsée de leurs maisons. Pendant cette période d'incertitude, beaucoup d'habitants ont considéré leurs maisons comme une rare opportunité d'accéder à des revenus supplémentaires et, quoique interdits par les organismes officiels, ils ont vendu leurs maisons et sont retournés habiter d'autres favelas.

Cependant, l'incertitude, l'angoisse et les difficultés d'assimilation du "genre de vie urbain" renforçaient chez cette population la nécessité de posséder un endroit avec lequel elle pouvait s'identifier.

Un peu plus tard, d'autres événements ont aidé à accélérer le développement de systèmes sociaux capables de se traduire par le sentiment d'appartenance de cette population aux espaces de Vila Pinheiros, tels que le nouveau gouvernement de Rio, élu par le peuple avec des promesses de réglementer la loi de la possession urbaine ou encore l'augmentation de l'influence politique de l'association des habitants des favelas Maré.

A partir de 1986/ 1987, la vitesse de transformation de l'aspect du quartier s'est accélérée (figure 9.1).

Il était étonnant de voir que, sur un court laps de temps, de nouveaux étages étaient bâtis sur les maisonnettes construites par l'État; de nouvelles façades surgissaient, d'autres se recouvraient de faïences et d'ornements; les maisons se multipliaient; les trottoirs étaient envahis par de nouvelles constructions et de petites tentes; des commerces s'installaient; des boutiques d'artisans s'ouvraient un peu partout; des espaces vides gagnaient de nouvelles fonctions; des éléments d'infrastructure qui avaient été le produit de l'intervention publique étaient constamment confrontés aux nouveaux usages inventés par les habitants.

Chaque jour, sous nos yeux, Vila Pinheiros perdait cette ligne monotone et inhumaine caractéristique des logements sociaux construits par le pouvoir public, et son paysage était constamment modifié et réinventé par ses habitants dans un processus extrêmement dynamique.

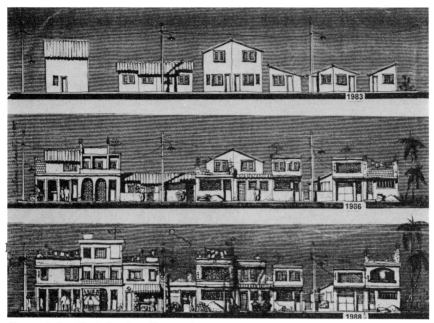

Figure 9.1   Evolution dans l'aspect du quartier Vila Pinheiros.

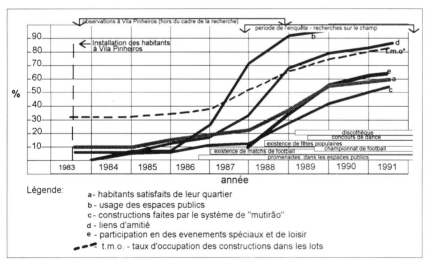

Figure 9.2   Tableau montrant l'évolution des pratiques sociales par rapport à la dynamique des espaces du quartier.

Une recherche sur le terrain qui a eu pour but de comprendre la logique des transformations spatiales de Vila Pinheiros nous a montré que les habitants qui pourraient paraetre tellement démunis et situés en bas de l'échelle humaine, étaient en fait des victimes de leur migration par rapport à l'accueil que pouvait leur réserver la grande ville. Ces migrants sont en réalité des porteurs d'un héritage culturel très enraciné, qui s'est manifesté d'une faron décisive au moment où les espaces de Vila Pinheiros ont commencé à être transformés.

METHODOLOGIE

La première étape du travail de recherche s'est fondée sur la découverte de l'origine de ces habitants, de leur culture, leurs traditions, leur manière de vivre et d'organiser leurs espaces avant leur migration pour Rio de Janeiro. Il nous a fallu comprendre ce qu'ils étaient allés chercher dans une grande ville, ce qu'ils s'attendaient à y trouver et les raisons qui les ont fait quitter leur condition de paysans abandonnant derrière eux toute une existence...

D'autre part, pour mieux saisir l'appropriation des espaces de Vila Pinheiros, il nous a fallu effectuer une ethnographie des espaces publics du quartier.

Au long des quatre années de recherche, nous avons pu suivre les cas d'une centaine de familles; interviewer plusieurs centaines d'habitants et rassembler une nombreuse documentation iconographique. De plus, les résultats de l'observation participative des pratiques sociales, des techniques de construction, des données anthropologiques, sociales et économiques ainsi que des données statistiques ont été rassemblées et analysées au long de cette période de recherche.

Bien qu'il s'agisse d'un processus qui dépend du facteur "temps" et bien que ce processus soit encore en cours, il nous a été possible d'observer, pendant nos quatre années de recherche, une évolution significative des phénomènes sociaux.

Cependant, certaines recherches en sciences sociales confirment mal leurs hypothèses en s'appuyant sur des propos parfois trop subjectifs. Si les modifications spatiales du quartier pourraient être mesurées et photographiées, si le flux des passants dans les rues et la fréquence des fêtes populaires pouvaient être estimés, il n'était pas de même en ce qui concerne, par exemple, le "lien d'amitié".

L'évaluation de ces phénomènes sociaux a donc dû être établie par le biais des remarques des habitants eux mêmes. Les questions qui leur ont été posées sur ce sujet ont été pensées de faron à éviter toute sorte d'induction de notre part.

Quelques-uns des résultats ont pu être transformés sous forme graphique, comme le montre l'exemple de la figure 2.

Ainsi, l'habitant qui a répondu être satisfait de son quartier, a été invité à estimer depuis quelle date (ou depuis combien de temps) il avait ce sentiment. La même méthode a été utilisée pour les questions concernant les liens d'amitié, la participation en des événements spéciaux ou des loisirs (fêtes populaires, matchs de foot,, jeux aux cartes, discothèque, etc.) ou encore l'usage des rues pour des simples promenades.

D'un autre coté, les données concernant l'augmentation des taux d'occupation des constructions dans les lots, ont été calculées d'après les plans relevés pendant notre recherche.

Au long de la recherche nous avons pu connaetre les moyens par lesquels se forme et en quoi consiste l'ensemble d'images qui composent les aspirations du paysan qui décide migrer pour Rio de Janeiro. Il nous a été également possible de vérifier que, après l'installation en milieu urbain, le contact avec la grande ville augmente le répertoire des références symboliques utilisées par le migrant pour donner des significations à l'espace. D'autre part, ces références souffrent, elles aussi, des changements importants au long des différentes phases des mécanismes d'adaptation au milieu urbain vécues par ce migrant. Ces mécanismes d'adaptation sont étroitement liés à deux facteurs antagoniques soumis à une permanente interaction entre les contraintes urbaines et la culture d'origine rurale.

Ainsi, si d'un coté l'urbain est pour le migrant un symbole d'une "vie meilleure", d'un autre coté les transformations sociales et spatiales ne pourront exister que si elles se fondent sur la reproduction de modèles ruraux. La ré interprétation permanente de ces modèles est un processus dynamique qui se traduit par les dynamiques de moulage de l'espace.

Nous avons constaté que les transformations sociales et spatiales se sont déclenchées par un processus d'appropriation symbolique et matérielle des espaces du quartier et que les logiques de l'usage des espaces se sont construites au long d'un processus de développement d'un système de relations sociales. Les logiques de ce système ont comme résultat le surgissement de mœurs qui délimitent le comportement social le transformant en des "codes d'usage" des espaces. Ainsi, l'habitant qui commence à s'approprier de ses espaces réussit simultanément à conquérir un "espace" dans sa société.

A Vila Pinheiros, l'appropriation matérielle s'est produite, au départ, par le moyen des transformations que l'usager a effectué dans son habitation. Elles ont prouvé, d'une certaine manière, que l'habitant a adopté sa maison comme étant son patrimoine définitif. A partir du moment o· les modifications spatiales se sont déclenchées, le nombre de maisons mises en vente a chuté très fortement et les taux d'émigration du quartier s'est approché de zéro.

RESULTATS

Le graphique traduisant la vitesse des modifications des maisons montre que les constructions de Vila Pinheiros ne se modifient plus avec une aussi grande rapidité qu'il y a quelques années (figure 9.2). Il est également clair qu'il y a maintenant une harmonie formelle dans le quartier.

D'après Sorre (1952), le "genre de vie" a une influence décisive dans la "forme de l'habitation". L'auteur utilise cette expression pour se référer au contexte des forces socioculturelles où sont inclues les croyances, la structure familiale, l'organisation sociale, l'économie et les relations sociales.

Si ces notions empiriques sont incontestables, le quartier doit traduire, aussi dans son aspect formel, le fait que ses habitants possèdent des valeurs en commun. C'est bien le cas de Vila Pinheiros car, à présent, malgré la diversité des couleurs et de quelques autres éléments, les constructions commencent peu à peu à acquérir un même langage architectural.

La majorité des maisons du quartier présentent maintenant une tendance à avoir deux étages et une terrasse très souvent couverte. La volumétrie des constructions devient la même partout et les façades se "collent" à l'alignement des trottoirs.

Construites en alignement continu, ces maisons établissent un système de symboles qui reflètent le "genre de vie" des habitants. Les portes, toujours ouvertes, permettent la vision des équipements et des meubles du salon, exposés au regard du passant pour être perçus plutôt comme des symboles d'ascension sociale et d'assimilation aux cultures urbaines.

Les cuisines sont cachées de la vue du "passant" et les "cours" aux aspects ruraux sont aussi éloignées qu'un passé rural, que l'habitant ne réussira pourtant pas à cacher.

Les façades, colorées et recouvertes d'un matériau céramique (si la situation de l'habitant le lui permet), exhibent des images de "saints", des crucifix et des statues d'anges, qui "parlent" de l'origine des habitants, de leurs croyances, leur religiosité et leur relation avec le monde de "l'Au-delà".

Les petits commerces et industries informelles, qui surgissent un peu partout, "parlent" d'une vie où il faut essayer à tout prix de survivre; alors que les modèles économiques jettent la majeure partie de la population dans l'illégalité, obligeant les habitants à inventer, à chaque jour, une façon de réussir à subsister.

Les couleurs vives et les dessins géométriques des barreaux aux fenêtres adoucissent l'image d'une réalité frappante: celle des relations d'assujettissement aux systèmes de "pouvoir informel", de la peur et des lois des "gangs" liées au trafic de drogues. En fait, dans le cas de Vila Pinheiros, la capacité des gangs à imposer leur ordre est très renforcée par l'héritage culturel des migrants ruraux. Issus d'un passé d'esclavage ou de travailleurs colonisés, ces anciens paysans auront des modèles de réaction d'assujettissement à l'égard des "détenteurs du pouvoir". Ces références symboliques seront constamment utilisées par le migrant pendant qu'il construit son identité en tant qu'habitant d'une ville.

Cependant, il est intéressant de noter que, bien que ce passé rural des habitants de Vila Pinheiros leur impose certains comportements de passivité, il sera aussi le point de départ de la construction de liens sociaux et de pratiques sociales qui vont commencer à se manifester dans le quartier. Nous avons relevé que les pratiques sociales développées par les habitants de Vila Pinheiros partent toutes dans le même sensá: celui de l'établissement de liens sociaux et de systèmes d'échange entre voisins.

Beaucoup de formes de réseaux sociaux ont commencé à exister. La naissance d'un phénomène d'identification mutuel entraene des pratiques d'entraide de plus en plus fréquentes.

Nous avons relevé, par exemple, un grand nombre de "mutiroes", des petits "chantiers domestiques" sur lesquels les habitants se réunissent pour aider à la construction ou à l'agrandissement de la maison d'un voisin. Cela se passe normalement le dimanche, le seul jour o· la population ne travaille pas "en ville", mais travaille pour son voisin, sans se donner droit au repos.

Le rassemblement en vue d'installer les poteaux d'illumination dans le terrain de foot et bien d'autres exemples, nous ont surpris par le fait que, dans plusieurs cas, l'habitant n'a pas hésité à donner un argent qui lui manquera pour assurer les conditions de survie de sa famille, au profit d'un équipement perʒu comme "appartenant à tous".

Finalement, l'exemple le plus frappant d'appropriation d'un espace public par la collectivité a été relevé dans la dernière rue d'un pâté de maisons o· les habitants se sont réunis et ont construit une piscine en plein milieu de la rue!

Autre trait significatif relevé dans nos enquêtes est l'étude de l'imaginaire commun, le "home idéal" recherché par la population. L'ensemble d'aspirations, des souffrances et la vie en commun font les habitants construire un idéal imaginaire du lieu où ils vivent.

A Vila Pinheiros, la description de ce "home idéal" a très souvent été lié à des aspects sociaux. Dans leurs récits, les habitants ne séparent pas "le lieu" de ses "voisins". Des liens indissolubles se sont formés désormais entre ces deux catégories d'éléments. Ainsi, cette population n'est plus constituée par des simples "habitants", ceux-ci peuvent désormais être classés dans la catégorie "voisins", ayant un même univers culturel et un genre de vie semblable.

Les résultats de notre recherche sont trop nombreux pour être discutés en quelques pages, cependant, ce qu'il est intéressant de commenter est la différence des perceptions présentées par les habitants au début de l'occupation de Vila Pinheiros et maintenant, dix ans après leur installation. Au début, nous pourrions nous référer à Vila Pinheiros comme étant un "quartier" dans le sens du mot employé par les urbanistes. Dans ces cas, le "quartier" est une unité de voisinage dans sa définition théorique. Le "quartier" Vila Pinheiros faisait alors référence à un ensemble de maisons et de rues conᴛues et construites par le gouvernement, en vue de reloger un certain nombre de familles habitant les favelas Maré.

Actuellement, le mot "quartier" peut être utilisé dans le sens employé par les géographes sociaux, les sociologues et anthropologues urbains: d'après Frémont (1984), le "quartier" est une association entre un paysage construit, un ensemble de pratiques sociales et un groupe humain présentant, entre autres choses, le sentiment collectif d'appartenance à la communauté.

DISCUSSION

Ce que nous avons trouvé à Vila Pinheiros nous a fait comprendre que l'espace public d'un ensemble d'habitations peut se transformer en un scénario de rencontres des acteurs concernés. Ce changement de la perception et de l'usage des rues survient si la population réussit à engendrer un processus d'identification et d'ancrage en attribuant des significations et de nouvelles valeurs à ses espaces.

Le processus dynamique des espaces et des relations sociales a rempli les espaces de Vila Pinheiros de repères sociaux et physiques utiles à ses usagers. Les rues s'y sont transformées d'un simple lieu de passage à un scénario où se déroulent des échanges sociaux.

Ainsi, comme le souligne Jacobs (1961), les personnes ne participent pas à la vie du quartier simplement parce qu'il faut vivre, travailler, acheter, prier ou se divertir dans ces endroits. On en participe surtout parce qu'on est inséré dans un système de relations.

Dans ces cas, il sera possible de voir à quel point les valeurs organisationnelles des espaces créés et planifiés par des technocrates sont différents des valeurs symboliques et des valeurs d'usage des espaces transformés par l'imaginaire de la communauté.

Nous savons à présent que certains programmes d'ensembles d'habitations qui avaient prévu l'auto-construction ont échoué car on n'y trouvait pas un vrai sentiment d'identification entre les habitants. Bon nombre de ces programmes étaient crées et mis en place par des technocrates, avec l'aide "d'associations d'habitants" qui, outre le fait qu'elles étaient infiltrées par des intérêts politiques, ne représentaient pas les aspirations culturelles de la communauté concernée. Or, il est prouvé que ces programmes ne peuvent se structurer sans une mobilisation sociale et une identification de la population.

Cependant cette affirmation ne signifie pas que la communauté ait résolu toute seule ses problèmes d'adaptation et d'habitation... La réalité est autre.

Il est vrai qu'il s'est développé tout un processus chez les habitants qui a résulté dans une tendance à la conscience d'une identité commune. Néanmoins, le danger de ce genre d'affirmation est qu'elle peut devenir encore un prétexte pour se croiser les bras.

Le fait que ces populations puissent, dans certains cas, réussir à établir des liens d'entraide et de solidarité, n'efface pas leur vie de pénurie, l'exploitation et la pauvreté à laquelle elles essayent de se conformer, mais contre laquelle elles auraient le droit légitime de se battre... et contre laquelle nous avons le devoir de lutter.

Remerciements

Ce travail n'aurait pas pu être fait sans le relevé sur place effectué par le Groupe de Recherches "Habitaçao" de la Faculté d'Architecture de l'UFRJ qui a travaillé sous notre direction entre les années 1988 et 1991. Nous remercions également notre collègue Osvaldo Silva qui a accepté de partager avec nous la responsabilité de la coordination du Groupe "Habitaçao".

Références

Duarte, Cristiane R. de Siqueira: "Intervention Publique et Dynamique Sociale dans la Production d'un Nouvel Espace de Pauvreté Urbaine: Vila Pinheiros, à Rio de Janeiro"- Thèse de Doctorat de l'Université de Paris -I , 1993

Frémont,A. et al :"Géographie Sociale" - Masson, Paris, 1984
Geertz, Clifford: "Interpretation of Cultures" - Basic Books, New York, 1973
Jacobs, Jane: "The Death and Life of Great American Cities" - Random, New York, 1961
Rapoport,Amos:"House Form and Culture" - Prentice Hall Inc., Englewood Cliffs, 1969
Sorre, Max: "Les fondements de la Géographie Humaine" - VolumeáIII, Armand Collin, Paris, 1952

10

The experience of community action in an australian town

L'impact d'une action communitaire dans une ville austrailienne

Henry Sanoff

On presente une strategie d'action de recherches concernant l'image culturelle d'une petite ville. Le processus d'urbanisation ne presente pas des problemes seulement pour les grandes villes. Beaucoup de petites communautes doivent faire face aux memes problemes, pourtant beaucoup de caracteristiques, comme les dimensions des normes culturelles, la structure sociale, l'economie locale, et le processus par lequel on arrive aux decisions, sont plus intimement liees que dans les grandes villes. Avec l'aide d'un modele participatoire de dessin comme base pour clarifier l'image propre de la ville on a suivi un processus de charrette intensif pendant quatre jours pour developper un plan d'action pour le ville. Une equipe de dessinateurs a mene des interviews, elle a developpe aussi un forum pour preciser des objectifs, et a propose de nombreuses solutions aux problems identifies par les participants. Une partie integrale du processus a ete de developper des strategies pour atteindre certains buts specifiques. Une investigation un an apres a revele des changements physiques de grande portee dans l'apparence de la ville, ce que les habitants de la ville ont cite comme resultat directe du processus de dessin participatoire.

Mot-cles: action de recherches; dessin participatoire; petite ville

Keywords: action research; participatory design; small town;

An emerging methodology of community development is based on the conviction that social improvement does not occur until the people involved believe that improvement is possible (Biddle and Biddle, 1966). As citizens are brought to feel a sense of community, and adopt goals that serve their concept of communty, they develop a stronger sense of social improvement.

During the last two decades, there has been a considerable movement towards the direct involvement of the public in the definition of their physical environment. The increased sense of social responsibility took root in the mid-1960's, when a feeling of community consciousness prevailed in many low income u0rban neighborhoods. The concept of advocacy planning introduced the participation of non-professionals and non-designers in the process of decision making. This means that the citizens ought to be heard, to be well informed about the reasons behind the planning proposals and be able to respond to them in the technical language of professional planners/designers (Davidoff, 1965).

The advocate represents an individual, group or organization who assists the client(s) in clarifying and expressing their ideas. The advocate is responsible to the client, so he/she would seek to express the clients views and interests. ".....citizen participation is a categorical term for city power. It is the redistribution of power that enables the have-not citizens, presently excluded from the political and economic process, to be deliberately included in the future "...participation without redistribution of power is an empty and frustrating process for the powerless. It allows the power holders to claim that all sides were considered but makes it possible for only some of these to benefit. It mainatins the status quo" (Arnstein, 1969).

CURRENT VIEWS OF PARTICIPATION

There has also emerged a new pragmatic approach to participation, one that no longer views participation as Arnstein's (1969) categorical term for "citizen power." The purposes of participation have been more modestly defined to include information exchange, resolving conflicts, and to supplement design and planning. (Participation) reduces the feeling of anonymity and communicates to the user a greater degree of concern on the part of the management of administration. (With) it, residents are actively involved in the development process, there will be a better maintained physical environment, greater public spirit, more user satisfaction and significant financial changes (Becker, 1977). Citizen participation has a different meaning to different people and even a different meaning to the same people according to the situation; different users prefer to participate in different ways according to the situation too. The two main purposes of participation are:

1) To involve citizens in design, planning, and other governmental processes and, as a result increase their trust and confidence in government, making it more likely that they will accept decisions and plans and work within the systems when seeking solutions to problems.

2) To provide citizens with a voice in design and planning decision making in order to improve plans, decisions and service delivery (Sanoff, 1990a).

An important point in the participatory process is individual learning through increased awareness of a problem. In order to maximize learning the process should be clear, communicable and open. It should encourage dialogue, debate and collaboration.

Thus, participation may be seen as direct public involvement in decision making processes: citizens share in social decisions that determine the quality and direction of their lives. This requires the provision of effective communication media in order to provide suitable grounds for citizen participation in designing. There are many benefits accruing from such an approach for the community, the users, and the designers and planners.

Firstly, from the social point of view, participation results in a greater meeting of social needs and increasingly effective utilization of resources at the disposal of a particular community.

Secondly, to the user group, it represents an increased sense of having influenced the design decision making process and an increased awareness of the consequences of decisions made Hester, 1990).

Thirdly, to the designer, it represents more relevant and up-to-date information than was possible before. Creating a methodological framework can enable the use of rational design methods without affecting the creative process.

Since participation has a diversity of expression, a design and planning solution from this approach will need to be made transparent so that the decisions are understood by the people who made them. By convening public forums that encourage community participation, people can openly express their opinions, make necessary compromises, and arrive at decisions that are acceptable. By involving as many interests as possible, not only is the product strengthened by the wealth of input, but the user group is strengthened as well by learning more about itself.

The types and degrees of participation depend on several factors and vary in accord with the circumstances. Burns (1979) classifies participation in four categories or 'experiences' that can lead to agreement about what the future should bring:

Awareness: This experience involves discovering or rediscovering the realities of a given environment or situation, so that everyone that takes part in the process is speaking the same language based on their experiences in the field where change is proposed.

Perception: This entails going from awareness of the situation to understanding it, and its physical, social, cultural, and economic ramifications. It means sharing with each other so that the understanding, objectives, and expectations of all participants become resources for planning, and not hidden agendas that could disrupt the project later on.

Decision-Making: This phase concentrates on working from awareness and perception to a program for the situation under consideration. In it, participants make actual physical designs based on their priorities for professionals to use as a resource to synthesize alternative and final plans.

Implementation: Many community-based planning processes stop with awareness, perception, and descision-making, often with fatal results to a project because it ends people's responsibilities just when they could be of most value: when the how-to, where-to, when-to, and who-will-do-it must be added to what people want and how it will look. People must stay involved, throughout the process, and take responsibility with their professionals to see that there are results (Hurwitz, 1975).

Participation means different things to different people and different things to the same people, depending on the issue, its timing, and the political setting in which it takes place. Participation can be addressed effectively if the task is conceptualized in terms of what is to be accomplished when the need is acknowledged to involve citizens. Conceptualizing the issue means asking simple questions of who, what, where, how, and when?

- Who are the parties to be involved in community participation?
- What are the specifications we wish to have performed by the participation program?
- Where do we wish the participation road to lead?
- How should people be involved?
- When in the planning process is participation needed or desired?

These are simple questions, yet rarely are they asked prior to the development of a community participation program. The planning that accompanies the development of any participation program should first include a determination of goals and objectives. For example:

Is the participation intended to generate ideas?

Is it to identify attitudes?

Is it to disseminate information?

Is it to resolve some identified conflict?

Is it to measure opinion?

Is it to review a proposal?

Or is it merely to serve as a safety valve for pent-up emotions?

The list of possible participation objectives will differ from time to time, and from issue to issue. Once the goals and objectives of community participation are stated, it becomes clear that participation is perceived differently depending on the type of issue and people involved. If differences in perception and expectations are not identified at the outset, and realistic objectives are not made clear, the expectations of those involved in the participation program will not have been met, and they will become disenchanted.

The steps to successful participation planning are (Rosner, 1978):
1. Identify the individuals or groups who should be involved in the participation activity being planned.
2. Decide where in the planning process the participants should be involved; that is in the development, implementation, or evaluation.
3. Articulate the participation goals and objectives in relation to all participants who will be involved.
4. Identify and match alternative participation methods to objectives in terms of the resources available.
5. Select an appropriate method to be used to the achieve specific objectives.
6. Implement chosen participation activities.
7. Evaluate the implemented methods to see to what extent they achieved the desired goals and objectives.

It is not suggested that taking the proposed steps will automatically ensure success, but it can be claimed that the process will minimize failure.

PARTICIPATORY PLANNING IN BANGALOW

Traditional approaches to urban and neighborhood development were based on the master planning model, where policies and action strategies were linked to physical information, such as land use and building condition. More recently, this approach has been replaced by a goal based planning model, where policies and actions are based on social as well as physical information (e.g. client-user goals, census data, and demographic factors). The complexity of big cities with large numbers of people and institutions usually results in a fragmentation of functions, a divison of power, roles and responsibilities so there is a liklihood of many disconnections between dimensions of a community. In a small town the dimensions of cultural norms, social structure, local economy, and decision making are much more interconnected than in a big city. Thus, use of a goal based development plan was the approach used in the small town of Bangalow, Australia, where connections were made between awareness, perception, decision making, and implementation.

Current interest in small towns is associated with the concern for what are believed to be the more manageable scales of human activity. The philosophies of smallness-seekers run the gamut from the anarchists who believe in minimal external control, to the critics of urbanization who find large cities unliveable in, and even unmanageable.

As a result, the apparent changes to the small town have been from an autonomous and distinctive place to live, to one that is no longer independent, or even separable. Once characterized by limited growth and minimum resident control, small communities are experiencing a renewed interest with people returning to the small town being significantly different from those who never left it. There are also indications that small town residents voice higher satisfaction with work, housing, and leisure time activity, and the rate of participation tends to be higher in small communities.

Despite the higher subjective senses of quality of life, small towns are in need of help particularly from the planners who stamp out master plans which look alike. The idiosyncracies and characteristics of each small town are ignored. Every town has a personality, a unique combi- nation of elements that creates its identity. A town's character, or sense of place, is shaped by its architectural style, the natural setting, cultural diversity, use of materials, and countless other local conditions that distinguish one place from another. The relationship of all these elements to each other are important aspects of a town's identity (Sanoff, 1981).

There are four action-modes that are generally used in small town revitalization (Swanson, Cohen, & Swanson, 1979). In some of them, proposed action is a one shot effort, while in others, activities are undertaken sequentially or simultaneously. In some of them, values are made explicit at the outset, while others project values that are implicit, not clarified, or justified. In some outside experts play a prominent role, while in others local residents dominate the process.

The categorical approach tends to carry out one substantive project at a time. The presumption is that each problem may be solved in relative isolation, without regard to its interconnections to other problems. Recreation problems, housing problems, infrastructure problems all receive separate treatments, while the cumulative direction for the community structure go unattended. This piecemeal approach is nurtured by state and federal grants and programs where supoport is available by specific problem areas. This approach encourages local people to think in categorical terms.

The comprehensive planning approach is intended to overcome the piecemeal one through an overall assessment of community facilities and services. The major problems in a community are identified and recommendations are made, often without an analysis of the impact on the residents. This approach examines the problems, but never sets them in a perspective of how they relate to social structures, decision making systems, and community values.

The integrative approach attempts to involve people in a process where they identify their own needs and preferred courses of action. These considerations are part of process of organizing, deciding on priorities, mobilizing support for the proposal, and engaging in the implementation of the project. Thus a specific problem such as housing, sewage, or social services, may be the beginning of a deeper exploration of the community's problem. The integrative approach tries to connect problems to the social, political, and value context of the community. In doing so, the solutions to housing problems may be found in the social structure or political system, instead of in narrowly defined rehabilitation or construction actions which commonly emerge from the categorical approach.

The dialogical approach emphasizes values clarification. It is concerned with having local residents articulate their values up front, to understand how they help or constrain achieving desired goals, and to decide the necessary changes they must make. In many community improvement projects, the values being reinforced have tended to be those of the dominant persons or groups in town. To avoid this, those who advocate the dialogical format of community problem solving encourage community discussions of internal dynamics and values before engaging in specific projects. Basically, this is a process of community education where residents become aware of the forces acting upon a community from within and from outside.

This balance of elements which creates a town's identity is under constant pressure for change. For this reason it is important that new development and change in general be guided by a conservation philosophy, a conscious policy of respect for the exisiting environment, and for the unique identity of towns. Thus a renewed awareness is necessary to guide change within certain desired limits. Awareness is the beginning of a process leading to the understanding of problems, clarification of objectives, and the consequences of the strategies for change.

Bangalow is a small Australian town in New South Wales, with a population of 780 people. The township and its immediate surrounding rural area consists of a population of 3000 people. Bangalow lies in the valley of Byron Creek, 12kms. west of Byron Bay. With the coming of the railway in 1894 and the clearing of the "Big Scrub" rainforest, Bangalow thrived as a dairying district. The comparative wealth of the early 1900's is evidenced by the fine commercial buildings in the town center. The town's historic character was noted in an assessment of environmental heritage (Shellshear, 1983) and efforts have been extended to reinforce the town's continuity with the past. The town of Bangalow was where a design resource team spent four days helping to preserve the town's past and to shape a new future. The team consisted of this author, and four architecture students from the University of Sydney, as well as several local architects and planners who served as consultants and information resources (Sanoff, 1990b). This "charrette" process, a period of intensive planning, was decided as the most expedient and time effective strategy to enable the town to reassess its future, since a proposed by-pass off the Pacific Highway would dramatically effect the potential of Bangalow as a rural tourist center and gateway to the hinterlands.

METHODS

The visit of the design team began with a meeting of community leaders followed by a bus and walking tour with interested citizens. The tour provided the design team with additional insights about the community from local professionals who had conducted feasibility studies of the implications of the by-pass. The second day consisted of interviews with interested townspeople who presented conflicting opinions and attitudes about the town's future. The purpose of the interviews was to identify the range of issues, from the residents perspective, that seemed to be crucial to the economic and social development of Bangalow.

Resident interest was displayed for converting Bangalow into a "heritage village with true charm," while opposing views expressed belief in "not looking back." Many seemed to agree, however, that recognition of the town's history was important. Gateways to Bangalow emerged as a popular issue as well as signage and streetscape enhancement. Keen interest was shown for replacing the traditional verandahs (covered porches) and encouraging reluctant shopkeepers to invest in Main Street improvements.

New and improved facilities for the visual and performing arts were also cited as a need by many residents, with an emphasis on places for the town's youth. Some people lamented the problem of resident apathy, while others remarked about the "good community feeling." It was generally recognized that the community was heterogeneous, with many new families with young children moving to town. Consequently, the services in Bangalow were inadequate, forcing residents to shop in nearby towns.

The results of the interviews provided the necessary background to prepare for a community-wide workshop which was held at the local bowling club on the third evening. This event was planned to provide an opportunity for the residents of Bangalow to meet face to face to consider the goals and strategies that would enable their ideas to be implemented. Public participation in Bangalow's future through a community workshop, was a strategy for bringing together different generations of residents, an event that had not previously occurred in the town. The design team relied upon the expertise of the community participants to shape their future by developing a list of goal statements prepared from previous interviews. The objective for design intervention was to develop a process whereby citizens could identify important issues, outline specific alternatives and implementation procedures, so they could change the plan as they felt it should change. Since conflicting values are inherent in any goal oriented process, an approach was developed which encouraged community members to clarify their differences through a game simulation, where goals and implementation strategies were the key factors that participants could manipulate.

Figure 10.1 Children's workshop.

Since Bangalow's young people represent the future of the town, a special children's workshop was conducted with 5th and 6th grade students from the public school. The young people were involved in developing models of their future town as well as wall murals depicting their likes and dislikes (Figure 1). The message from the ten and eleven year old children was clear; more stuff for the kids. Activities such as a pinball parlor, skating rink and park were specific features identified, though there was a general feeling that Bangalow lacked the necessary services and amenities associated with a self-sufficient community. The results of this two hour activity were exhibited at the community workshop, where many of the young people had attended.

To begin the community workshop, small groups of five persons each were formed where players selected from a goal list provided, four statements that seemed important in developing the town. The individual lists were then pooled, and through a process of collaboration, four mutually agreed upon statements were selected by consensus. Through a similar process, complimentary strategies were selected that could effectively accomplish each of the goal choices. During both phases of the process, group members were urged to support their individual choices, and persuade the total group to include their own particular selection (Table 10.1)

GOALS	STRATEGIES
• Recognize the area's natural and scenic resources as major assets • Heighten public awareness to the town's unique historical character • Provide youth oriented activities • Improve gateways to the town • Enhance the community's natural resources • Promote downtown revitalization • Package and promote an image of innovation and tradition • Encourage the arts to contribute to the development of the community • Promote the town's historic resources • Create avenues for public/private partnerships for community development	• Utilize all forms of media to educate the community on the importance and impact of the town's cultural heritage and environmental issues • Develop a plan for the visual enhancement and preservation of the areas of the town • Develop a link between business and local organizations to solicit support for identified projects • Rehabilitate and reuse significant buildings • Develop an organization to encompass cultural, environmental, and historical interests • Develop community awareness programs for historical preservation • Retain, maintain, and add trees

Table 10.1: Goals and Strategies Organized by Priority and in Categories of Importance

DISCUSSION

The process provided the impetus for discussions with town members, and the subsequent development of goals reflecting the wide range of possibilities for the town of Bangalow. Many ideas were explored by the citizens of Bangalow. These were summarized by a concern for the town's unique heritage, and the provision for services and facilities for special populations and interest groups.

In addition to the goal setting exercise, the design team prepared sketches of proposed changes to features of the town that were identified by the residents during the interviews. This part of the workshop focused on six different aspects of the town, including the town entrance, building signage, infill and open space, adaptive reuse of vacant buildings. The intent was to allow participants to compare the existing situation with proposed changes in order to fully realize the potential impact of the changes (Figure 3).

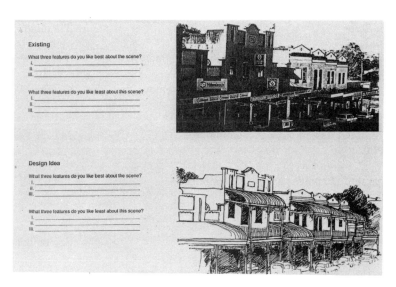

Figure 10.2 Comparison between existing conditions and proposed changes (verandahs).

The results of the workshop were analyzed by clustering similar goals and compatible strategies, and comments made about changes in the town's appearance. On the fourth day, a strategic plan was proposed. A strategic plan is a tool for enabling communities to move towards particular goals. The components of a strategic plan would include a statement of purpose, drawing upon the goals at the community workshop, such as: "To recognize the area's natural and scenic resources as major assets."

This statement defines what should be accomplished through the strategic plan, and it will be the responsibility of the participants in the process to shape this statement into a series of tangible outcomes. Since the goals are broad statements of intent, strategies are measurable tasks that
support the accomplishment of goals. Action steps further advance the strategies by specifying activities which contribute to their achievement (Figure 4).

GOAL:
To create a permanent home for performing and visual arts organizations in Bangalow

STRATEGY:
Renovate the Art gallery into the bangalow Center for the Arts.
Establish steering committee to oversee facility planning and fund raising.

Action Steps	Responsibility	Timeline
Appoint committee	Spirit of Bangalow,Inc.	September 1990
Have support committee work with office staff	Spirit of Bangalow, Inc.	October 1990
Hold national design competition	Committee	March 1991
Hire capital campaign consultant and begin fundraising	Committee	June 1991
Select architect	Committee	September 1991

Table 10.2: An Example of Strategies and Action Plans

Implementation of the strategic plan required the formation of a new organization to provide the needed communication and coordination between civic, historic, government, and arts related organizations. Although this would be an independent organization, it would bring together representatives from exisiting groups with the intention of integrating economic development and the cultural life of the town. Twenty five people agreed to become part of a steering
committee, with task forces created in Natural Resource Development, Urban Design, Cultural Facilities, Cultural Tourism, and Media Communication Education. The identification of the task forces resulted from an analysis of the patterns of goal statements generated at the workshop.

Two months after the formation of a new organization called, the Spirit of Bangalow, task forces reported significant progress towards fund raising and implementation of numerous projects including a community park, restoration of an old movie theater into an arts center, and the restoration of verandahs. One year after the initial community workshop, substantial changes were made including the addition of several verandahs and a children's park.

CONCLUSION

Participation in neighborhoods and with community organizations is widely recognized as a solution to many social problems. Over the last two decades, people in many neighborhoods and small towns have come together to create their own community based organizations to tackle problems which government and the private sector have long neglected. They have formed countless block clubs, self-help groups, neighborhood associations, community organizing fund drives, and community development corporations. The public demand for participation, especially in planning, has grown to where governments have begun to incorporate into their legislation, compulsory provisions for public participation and public authorities have come to regard public involvement as a normal part of their practice (Shearer, 1984). In many situations it can be observed that the participation process is not considered a separate exercise from the design process.

Based on the Bangalow experience, and numerous projects conducted by this author and others, it is possible to synthesize the theories and practices of participation into the following five statements (Sanoff, 1990):

There is no best solution to design problems (Peattie, 1968). Each problem has a number of solutions that are traditionally based on two sets of criteria: (a) facts - the empirical data concerning material strengths, economics, building codes, and so forth; and (b) attitudes - interpretation of the facts, the state of the art in any particular area, traditional and customary approaches, and value judgements. Thus design and planning decisions are by nature biased and depend on the values of the decision-maker(s).

Expert decisions are not necessarily better than lay decisions (Rittel, 1972). Given the facts with which to make decisions, the users can examine the available alternatives and choose among them. The designer involved in such an approach should be considered a participant who is expected to state an opinion, provide technical information, and discuss consequences of various alternatives, just as the users state their opinions and contribute their expertise.

The design process can be made transparent (Rittel, 1972). Steps taken and alternatives considered by the designer, traditionally in their own minds in the privacy of an office, can be brought to the surface for the users to discuss. By understanding the basis of planning and design decisions and comparing alternatives, the users in effect generate their own plan. The final product is more likely to succeed because it is better understood by the people who will use it.

All individuals and interest groups should come together in an open forum. In this way people can openly express their opinions, make necessary compromises, and arrive at decisions that are acceptable to all concerned. By involving as many interests as possible, not only is the product strengthened by the wealth of input, but the user group is strengthened as well by learning more about itself.

The process is continuous and ever changing. The product is not the end of the process. It must be managed, re-evaluated, and adapted to changing needs. Those most directly involved with the product, the users, are best able to assume the tasks.

Community participation is a complex concept. Planning for effective participation requires an analysis of the issues to be discussed, the individuals or groups that are to be affected, the resources that will be needed, and the goals for which the participation is being initiated. While it is necessary to identify goals and objectives in planning for participation, it is also necessary to analyze the techniques that are avaliable and the resources they require. Techniques such as surveys, review boards, neighborhood meetings, conferences, task forces, workshops, and interviews, represent a few of the options available to participatory designers. When people participate in the creation of their environment, they need the feeling of control; it is the only way their needs and values can be taken into consideration.

Acknowledgements

This project was sponsored by the Arts Council of New South Wales, Bangalow By-Pass Ring Road Committee, and the Community Cultural Development Unit, Australia Council. The design team included Matt Devine, Ann McCallum, Roger Ackland, David Young, and David Huxtable. The project Co-ordinator was Rory O'Moore and included Helen O'Moore, Stacey Pollard, and Vicki Reynolds, all from the town of Bangalow.

References

Arnstein, S. (1969). A ladder of citizen participation, AIP Journal 35:216-224.

Becker, F. (1977). Housing Messages. Stroudsburg, PA: Dowden Hutchinson & Ross.

Biddle,W.W. & Biddle, L.J. (1966). The Community Development Process. NY: Holt, Rinehart and Winston.

Burns, J. (1979). Citizens take part in the procss of urban design, National Citizen's Weekly 2:43.

Davidoff, P. (1965). Advocacy and pluralism in planning, AIP Journal 31:331-338.

Delbecq, A.L., Van de Ven, A.H., & Gustafson, D.H. (1975). Group Techniques for Program Planning: A Guide to Nominal Group and Delphi Processes. Glenview, IL: Scott Foresman.

Hester, Jr., R.T. (1990). Community Design Primer. CA: Ridge Times Press.

Hurwitz, J.C. (1975). Participatory planning in a urban neighborhood, DMG-DRS Journal 9:348-357.

Peattie, L. (1968). Reflections on advocacy planning, AIP Journal 34:80-88.

Rittel, H. (1972). Son of Rittelthink, DMG Newsletter 3-10 Berkeley: University of California.

Rosner, J. (1978). Matching method to purpose: The challenges of planning citizen participation activities. In S. Langton (Ed.) Citizen Participation in America. NY: Lexington.

Sanoff, H. (1978). Designing with Community Participation. NY: Van Nostrand Reinhold.

Sanoff, H. (1981). Involving small town citizens: A North Carolina approach. Small Town 12.3:30-33.

Sanoff, H. (1990a). Participatory Design: Theory and Techniques. Raleigh, NC: Sanoff.

Sanoff, H. (1990b). Bangalow: Small Town Image Building. Sydney, Australia: Arts Council of NSW, Ltd.

Shearer, D. (1984). Citizen participation in local government: The case of Santa Monica, California, International Journal of Urban and Regional Research 8:573-586.

Shellshear, T. (1983). Byron Shire Environmental Study: Working Paper No. 6-Heritage. Sydney: Planning Workshop Pty Ltd.

Swanson, B.E., Cohen, R.A., & Swanson, E.P. (1979). Small Towns and Small Towners. Beverly Hills. CA: Sage Publications.

11

Diverging evaluations of the built environment: planners versus the public

Evaluations divergentes de l'environnement urbain: urbanistes contre résidents

Philip J. Hubbard

Il existe un grand nombre de recherches sur les rapports entre l'environnement et le comportement et les différences d'interprétation du cadre bâti entre designers et non designers. En revanche, on ne peut que remarquer l'absence de recherches similaires prennant pour cible les urbanistes. Cet exposé présente les résultats d'une recherche empirique sur ce sujet précis, qui avait pour objectif spécifique les attitudes différentes des urbanistes des autorités locales et des citoyens envers un certain nombre d'aménagements commerciaux du centre de la ville de Birmingham (en Angleterre). On a examiné ces différences au moyen de la méthode de tri multiple et en combinant les échelles multidimensionnelles et les analyses de contenu. L'étude a démontré clairement que les urbanistes et les citadins ont des vues divergentes sur les aménagements, ces divergences apparaissant à tous les stades de l'analyse. Il est soutenu que ces divergences sont liées à la compétence des urbanistes en matière d'environnement. Cette étude a des implications pour les recherches futures et pour l'urbanisme lui-même. La nécessité d'améliorer la participation du public dans les procédures d'urbanisme est particulièrement soulignée.

Mots clé: planification urbaine; esthétique de l'environnement; développement.

Key words: environemntal aesthetics, redevelopment, urban planning

Over the last thirty years there have been a plethora of studies within environment-behaviour research which have examined the interpretation and assessment of natural and built landscapes, with environmental aesthetics now recognised as a self-contained field in its own right. Initial research in this field was heavily influenced by the traditions of experimental and perceptual psychology, with attempts to translate the findings of laboratory- based research to environmental settings. However, it has been increasingly recognised that such studies of austere object perception decontextualise the functioning of individuals from their social and cultural milieu, and therefore provide only a partial explanation of human interaction with the environment (Uzzell, 1989). Indeed, such research largely ignores the variations amongst people, arguing that cognitive processes are common to all individuals as they possess similar nervous systems and perceptual apparatus. In marked contrast to this approach is the idea that environmental assessment is dependent on the meanings ascribed to the environment by virtue of individual histories and experience. As each individual potentially attributes a unique meaning to their environment, it could be considered that scientific investigation of this phenomena is impossible. On the contrary, it has been suggested that environmental meanings are constructed through established codes which are socially transmitted and thus based on learning and culture (Pennartz, 1989). It can be argued that these codes are not individual properties, and that there exist structures of perception, cognition and action common to all members of a group. This can be compared with the concept of **habitus** developed by Bourdieu (1977) which describes the 'socially-constituted system of cognitive and motivational structures' which influence people's world-view.

The idea that there are common perceptual codes shared by members of various groups also suggests why major differences in interpretation may exist between different socio-cultural groups. The logic consequence of this has been a shift to a more socially-constituted environmental psychology in recent years with a commensurate rise in the number of studies examining individual and group differences in the evaluation of the built environment. Bourassa (1991) has suggested that the most important distinction between to be made between social groups in their evaluation of the built environment is in terms of their environmental experience and expertise. Canter (1991) has summed these factors up in the concept of **environmental role**, which he described as 'that aspect of a person's social and organisational role which is related to their dealings with their physical surroundings'. Indeed, the prediction that people of different environmental role will have differing conceptualisations and evaluations of their environment has proved to be a remarkably consistent research finding. In this respect, the most frequently explored distinction is between the 'producers' and 'consumers' of the environment - those who create the environment and those who live in it. Obviously, such a delimitation is rather artificial, as all producers are consumers also, but nonetheless it does appear that the most pronounced differences in environmental perception, cognition and action are between environmental designers and those without any design training.

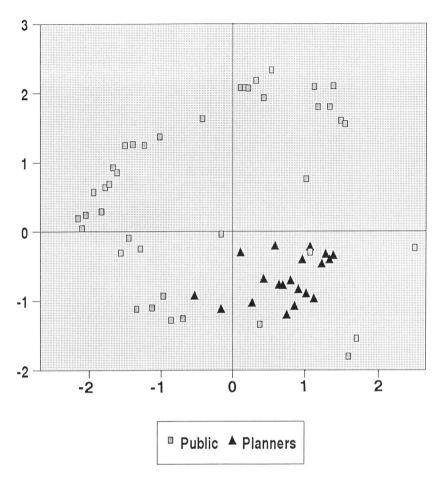

Figure 11.1 Multidimensional scalogram of construct criteria use (STRESS = 0.145, r^2 = 92%).

There have thus been a considerable number of studies investigating the differences in environmental interpretation evident between design professionals and non-professionals. Such research appears to be driven by two main aims, namely the need to understand the effects of professional training and a more pragmatic desire to bridge what has been termed the 'appreciation gap' between designers and the lay public. However, whilst differences in evaluation between experts and non-experts have been well documented with respect to the architectural profession (e.g. Hershberger, 1969, Groat, 1982, Devlin, 1990), there has been a paucity of empirical studies of differences between planners and the public, with evidence for this remaining mainly anecdotal and intuitive. The lack of attention given to planners as a study group is hardly surprising if one considers the background and training of the majority of environment-behaviour researchers. Nonetheless, aside from architects, planners have probably the best opportunity to influence the urban design process, suggesting that such a study would be worthwhile, particularly in Britain with its traditions of central government intervention in the production of the built environment.

Moreover, despite the varied nature of planning practice, the majority of studies of British planners have reached similar conclusions, that planners in general are a fairly homogeneous group who do in fact share distinctive attitudes to a variety of issues such as their environment, their political superiors and their view of society as a whole. Knox and Cullen (1981) have thus described a distinctive professional ideology amongst planners which they describe as 'an amalgam of paternalism, environmentalism, aesthetics (*sic*) and social determinism'. According to Healey (1985), this distinctive ideology is both a result of professional socialisation and selective recruitment (British planners are predominantly white, male and middle-class). Hence there are extensive intuitive grounds for supposing that an appreciation gap exists between planners and the public in much the same way as has been demonstrated with respect to architect and non-architect groups. Specifically, it was expected that the planners' environmental evaluations would not only diverge from those of the public, but would also be qualitatively different than those demonstrated elsewhere for architects. Although planners do share many of the creative concerns of architects, they would be expected to place a greater emphasis on the functionality rather than originality of designs because they are restricted by 'socially-oriented' rules which make them act, at least to a limited extent, in the public's interest.

METHOD

A procedure was thus developed to investigate these hypothesised differences between planners and the public by examining the evaluation of a number of commercial redevelopments within Birmingham city centre. These redevelopments were selected so as to be broadly representative of the type and style of redevelopments completed in Birmingham between June 1988 and June 1991, a period co-inciding with the peak of the property boom. By examining such differences within a case-study format it was hoped to maintain a holistic and meaningful view of these evaluations so that these attitudes could be examined within their wider socio-cultural context. Over one hundred respondents were interviewed, including twenty local authority planning officers of varying experience and forty public participants who were recruited locally. Essentially, the research procedure required that respondents sorted fifteen photographic stimuli, representing fifteen major redevelopment schemes in Birmingham city centre, according to criteria of their own choice. The research procedure employed here was based around the use of the multiple sorting task, a technique that has been recognised as particularly appropriate for identifying inter-individual and inter-group differences in conceptual and categorical systems (Canter *et al*, 1985). The advantage of sorting procedures is that they are sensitive to human ways of thinking, as the act of aligning similar objects is essential to everyday living. Indeed, a number of architectural theorists have argued that the process by which buildings come to have meaning is in itself an act of classification (e.g. Jencks, 1977). As such it was preferred to semantic differential methods which virtually preclude the identification of subtle differences in evaluation. This procedure was supplemented by the completion of an additional questionnaire highlighting specific planning issues, and through the completion of various ranking exercises.

RESULTS

The data generated by the multiple sorting task were analysed through a combination of inferential statistics, content analysis and multidimensional scaling procedures (see Groat, 1982). Initial analysis focused on the themes or types of sorts completed by the respondents, with the total of more than three hundred sorts grouped into twenty construct categories relating to physical, cognitive and functional characteristics, and tabulated to facilitate inter-group comparison (see table one). To maximise the reliability of this technique, a colleague unfamiliar with the objectives of the study repeated this procedure, with a significant level of inter-judge reliability evident. A chi-square analysis was then performed on the table, with the resulting chi-square statistic indicating that there was a significant difference in types of construct categories used at the 99% confidence interval. Specifically, it appeared that over 70% of planners' sorts were concerned with physical aspects of the redevelopments (e.g. materials, detailing, context) whereas 45% of the public's sorts were based on 'ethno-demographic' concepts, for example, preferences, feelings and associations. This concurs with the findings of Hershberger (1969), who suggested that whilst designers respond more to representational meanings, non-designers place more importance on responsive meanings. The use of multidimensional scaling procedures facilitated further examination of patterns of construct use amongst individuals. To implement this analysis, a matrix was constructed matching each respondent to the construct categories that they employed in their sortings, and the resulting matrix entered into the ALSCAL programme running through the SPSS package to produce a multidimensional scalogram. In figure (1), the closer that two people appear in the plot, the more similar they were in terms of the sorting criteria they employed. Although the plot does not partition clearly into planners and public, suggesting there was some overlap in the type of concerns which they emphasised, the planning group is fairly clustered, suggesting the planners assessed the redevelopments according to similar criteria, whilst the distribution of the public group shows a fairly high level of scattering and little homogeneity.

Furthermore, the overall patterns of conceptualisation of the redevelopments were examined through the use of INDSCAL (individual differences scaling), a type of multidimensional scaling analysis which has advantages over other similar statistical methods such as factorial analysis in that it can be used to examine both the commonalties and differences amongst individuals by describing a common mean space as well as describing the variation of individuals and groups with respect to that space (such configurations are indices of underlying perceptual structures). Inter-group differences in patterns of conceptualisation were thus examined by comparing weights which indicated the salience of each dimension of the overall scaling solution to each individual (see Doise et al, 1993 for details). Statistical comparison of the magnitudes of vectors for each of the respondents (i.e. based on the sum of the squares of the subject weights) indicated that there were significant differences in patterns of conceptualisation at the 99% confidence interval. Examining individual stimulus configurations, it appeared that not only did the planning group possess a sophisticated vocabulary for expressing their concerns, but also that their underlying conceptualisation of the redevelopments possessed a more organised and coherent structure, clearly derived from their familiarity with architectural criticism. For example, whilst the public group commonly delimited those redevelopments which they considered to be 'traditional' and 'modern' in style, the planners employed a more sophisticated classification, typically differentiating Post-modern, Hi-tech and neo-vernacular styles of redevelopment.

Given these differences in conceptualisation, it was perhaps not surprising that the planners and the public groups had differing evaluations of the redevelopments used in this study. Indeed, comparison of preference ranks revealed an absence of any significant association between the planners' evaluations and those of the public groups. Furthermore, PREFMAP analysis (a form of multidimensional scaling based on preference data) revealed that whilst the public group had a more positive evaluation of the more derivative architectural styles, the planning group preferred the more hi-tech and late-Modern styles. This lends support for the view that whilst the public tend to appreciate continuity in the townscape, planners, like architects, tend to appreciate more fashionable and 'up-to-date' architectural styles (Jencks, 1977). However, in other respects, the attitudes of planners appeared to be different to those of architects, in that they placed more importance on aspects of the functionality of buildings and their contribution to the public realm, although future research would clearly be required to validate this statement.

DISCUSSION

This is one of the first studies to have convincingly demonstrated the existence of disjunctive attitudes between planners and the public, with quantitative and qualitative differences evident at virtually every stage of analysis. These findings were largely consistent with those identified in previous research, and in line with expectations, suggesting differences in environmental role have a profound influence on the interpretation and assessment of the built environment. Furthermore, whilst in some studies such inter-group differences appear to result because of the inherent bias of verbal measurement techniques such as the semantic differential, specifically, that designers may be more able to express what they can see (Valadez, 1984), the essentially non-verbal nature of the multiple sorting technique means that the differences observed did not merely result from differences in vocabulary, but resulted from fundamental differences in the way that the groups conceptualised the redevelopments.

It is felt that the differences observed here between planners and the public are particularly important if one considers the role of planners within the development control system is to evaluate planning applications in the best interests of the public. Indeed, whilst planners portray themselves as 'evangelistic bureaucrats', it appears because of their distinctive socio-demographic and professional background that planners' evaluations may not be congruent with those of the wider population, and indeed, that they may not always be able to appreciate the wider context in which decisions should be made. This brings into question the extent to which planners are able to conform to Royal Town Planning Institute educational guidelines which stipulate that they must be able to 'identify the aesthetic dimensions of buildings and urban forms, assess symbolic and cultural values in specific situations and evaluate the impact of development and change on built form'.

	PUBLIC	PLANNERS
FORM	8%	3%
AFFECT	32%	6.5%
FUNCTION	10%	10%
AGE	11%	3%
CONTEXT	1.5%	13%
MATERIALS	5%	6.5%
SCALE	6.5%	9.5%
FAMILIARITY	1.5%	5%
STYLE	8%	6%
HUMANITY	3%	7.5%
DETAILS	6.5%	3%
FORM/FUNCTION	1.5%	3%
LOCATION	0%	4%
DESIGN APPROACH	0%	11.5%
ENVIRONMENT	3%	6.5%
OTHER	2.5%	2%
TOTAL	100%	100%

Table (1) - Frequency of construct category use: inter-group comparison.

These results lend support to the view that there should be greater integration of public interests within the planning process, particularly with respect to aesthetic control, where current procedures for participation and consultation are clearly inadequate. Indeed, it has frequently been suggested that studies of environmental perception can act as an important information base for planners, by indicating the values of the public and the different groups who constitute the public (Hubbard, 1992). Although central government advice on aesthetic control in Britain has traditionally been negative, asserting that aesthetics is a subjective matter and not a subject for dogmatism, recently this attitude has changed somewhat, with a more sympathetic attitude to design guidance evident. By showing how the built environment can satisfy the wide range of affective, cognitive and behavioural demands that people make of it, environment-behaviour research is well-placed to play an important role in contributing to the formulation of such guidelines, and can help to produce architecture that satisfies aesthetic, social, cultural and functional criteria.

References

Bourassa, S.C. (1991) The Aesthetics of Landscape London, Belhaven.
Bourdieu, P. (1977) Outline of a Theory of Practice Cambridge, Cambridge University Press.

Canter, D. (1991) 'Understanding, assessing and acting in place: is an integrative framework possible?' in Gärling, T., Evans, G.W. (eds) Environment, Cognition and Action New York, Oxford University Press.

Canter, D., Brown, J., Groat, L.N. (1985) 'The multiple sorting task' in Brenner, J., Brown, J., Canter, D. (eds) The Research Interview London, Academic Press.

Devlin, K. (1990) 'An examination of architectural interpretation: architects versus non-architects' Journal of Architectural and Planning Research 7 (3) pp. 235-244.

Doise, W., Clemence, A., Lorenzi-Cioldi, F. (1993) The Quantitative Analysis of Social Representations Hemel Hempstead, Harvester Wheatsheaf.

Groat, L. (1982) 'Meaning in Post-modern architecture: An examination using the multiple sorting task' Journal of Environmental Psychology 2 (1) pp. 3-22.

Healey, P. (1985) 'The professionalisation of planning in Britain: its form and consequences' Town Planning Review 59 (4) pp. 492-507.

Hershberger, R.C. (1969) 'A study of meaning in architecture' in Sanoff, H., Cohn, S. (eds) Proceedings of the first annual EDRA conference Raleigh, North Carolina State University.

Hubbard, P.J. (1992) 'Environment-behaviour research and city design - a new agenda for research?' Journal of Environmental Psychology 12 (3) 269-273.

Jencks, C. (1977) The Language of Post-modern Architecture London, Academic Press.

Knox, P.L., Cullen, J. (1981) 'Planners as urban managers: an exploration of the attitudes and self-image of senior British planners' Environment and Planning (A) 13 (5) pp. 885-898.

Pennartz, P.J.J. (1989) 'Semiotic theory and environmental evaluation - a proposal for a new approach' Symbolic Interaction 12 (2) pp. 231-250.

Punter, J.V. (1982) 'Landscape aesthetics: a synthesis and critique' in Burgess, J., Gold, J.R. (eds) Valued Environments London, Allen and Unwin.

Uzzell, D.L. (1989) 'Environmental psychology perspectives on landscape' Landscape Research 16 (1) pp. 3-10.

Valadez, J.J. (1984) 'Diverging meanings of development among architects and three other professional groups' Journal of Environmental Psychology 4 (2) pp. 223-228.

12

A spa culture for the nineties and thereafter: health and relaxation in an urban setting.

Une culture des "bains" pour les années 90: santé et détente dans l'espace urbain

David Doughty and Wolf Zwirner

L'exposé considère la possibilité d'une renaissance de la culture des villes d'eau à la fin du 20ème siècle et effectue des comparaisons avec l'âge d'or des bains à la fin du siècle dernier. Trois villes sont citées en exemple: Karlovy Vary, Budapest et Llandrindod Wells. Il est montré comment les vieilles villes d'eau d'Europe Centrale sont restaurées pour servir d'alternative aux stations balnéaires traditionnelles, qui sont menacées par la diminution actuelle de la couche d'ozone et la pollution. Les villes d'eau, sources de santé physique et spirituelle dans l'environnement urbain, profitent également aux revenus touristiques d'un pays. Il semble que la Grande Bretagne ait négligé un tel programme de rénovation, et préfère les vacances-santé "new age" destinées aux classes sociales favorisées. Les possibilités d'une renaissance sont étouffées par la bureaucratie et l'apathie.

Mots clé: Villes d'eau, santé, détente, renaissance, environnement urbain.

Key words: Spa, health, relaxation, renewal, urban environment.

A century ago, the continent of Europe and Britain were filled with Victorian gentlefolk spending their holidays, "taking the waters" at fashionable resorts from Baden Baden and Carlsbad to Llandrindod Wells and Harrogate. Yet, two world wars later, the Spa holiday had all but disappeared in Britain, replaced by the more proletarian "seaside Breaks" at Blackpool, Brighton and Rhyl whilst those still wishing the atmosphere and cure of the old times were forced to travel abroad for their pleasures (Beattie 1992; 240-241). This paper takes a look at the prospects for revival of a Spa culture at the end of the twentieth century, when interests in alternative health treatments are in the ascent and an ever more dangerous gamble with premature aging and skin cancers. In order to show the developments and the future potential for such a growth in the specifically urban Spa, the authors will concentrate on three towns - Karlovy Váry, one of the great nineteenth century Spas, in the Czech Republic, Budapest, capital city of Hungary, and Llandrindod Wells, county town of Powys in Wales.

Karlovy Váry with its tradition of drinking the waters from its twelve springs and Budapest with its ancient hot baths from the Turkish period have been chosen to demonstrate a still thriving spa culture in central Europe. By contrast, Llandrindod Wells was a spa town in the past, still has its spring water, but stands as a typical example of the decline of the spa culture in the UK.

Karlovy Váry

Karlovy Váry (formerly Carlsbad) makes up, together with Marienbad and Franzensbad, the famed Bohemian triangle of Spas which exercised such a fascination on nineteenth century travelers from Goethe to Karl Marx as witnessed by the guest lists in the town library (Fink 1992; 26). Unlike nearby Marienbad (an almost entirely nineteenth century development), Carlsbad was founded as a German settlement as long ago as 1350. Despite its six hundred and fifty years of history, most of the town was rebuilt in the nineteenth century, much of it in the Art Nouveau or Sezession style (Mráz 1991; 49-50 & 51-52). Karlovy Váry today is a flourishing Spa town, host to an international film festival each year and even recently to the international "Jeux sans Frontières" television game show. The town is also a regional shopping centre and within the last few years has seen considerable redevelopment of tourist facilities (hotels and restaurants) as well as high investment on restoration and refurbishment of the historic buildings of the town. The wooden and iron colonnades are being restored to their former glory, new hotels constructed in traditional style, older hotels brought up to international luxury standards. Exclusive shops and boutiques have been created for the influx of wealthy tourists from Germany and Austria and national and international banks are restoring some of the almost derelict architectural gems of the town. The introduction of private capital in the formerly socialist Czech Republic has allowed for an acceleration of development of the town and has also allowed for a more consciously environmental approach to reconstruction (two newly renovated hotels on the river promenade show this new approach to harmony). The socialist government was, however, responsible for maintaining the status of the town as a health resort from 1948 onwards and (despite the inappropriately designed monster Thermal Hotel from those years and the deterioration of the turn of the century housing stock that makes up much of the inner town), Karlovy Váry cannot be said to have gone into a decline after the second world war. Although today's specific treatments take place in special sanatoria, guest accommodation abounds in all classes from the luxurious old fashioned Grand Hotel Pupp (Mráz 1991; 50-51) down to rooms in private homes and the waters from the springs of the town are available free to all visitors who have taken the precaution of bringing a drinking cup along. Karlovy Váry has thus continued since its early days to be a respected and popular Spa resort which nowadays attracts both young and old, Czech and foreign visitors, day trippers and long-term guests seeking relaxation, amusement and the waters. New investment from within and outside the country is ensuring a Spa fit for the twenty first century which still prides itself on its historic, architectural and cultural traditions (Mráz 1991; 52-53).

Budapest

Although Karlovy Váry can be seen as a regional centre as well as a Spa town, it cannot compare in stature with Budapest, which is not only a Spa town but also a capital city. This means that, as well as a health and relaxation centre, the town/city has to work as the commercial and political centre of the country. Hungary has been developing as something of an economic success both within and without the socialist system but recent developments in Europe and in particular, within the former socialist states of eastern Europe may have brought Hungary almost to the brink of bankruptcy. Budapest is the "City of Baths" (Vida 1992; 16 & 23-28) and suffers both the advantage and disadvantage that its main Spa facilities date from the time of Turkish domination some three hundred years ago. This means that the major baths of the city (which lie in Buda on the left bank of the Danube) are not only health resorts, but also historic monuments. Recent drastic cuts in budget, since the privatisation of the Budapest Spas authority, mean that little money is available for modernisation of the basic facilities of the baths, such as showers, tap fittings, changing facilities etc. Despite this, the Baths of Buda (as well as the monumental nineteenth century Széchenyi Bath in Pest) are used regularly by the population for relaxation and for health purposes (bathing, rehabilitation and locomotor disorder therapies, drinking, swimming etc.) both privately and upon medical advice (certain baths, such as Lukács and Czászar are sanatoria and not open to the general public).   The current success story of Budapest is that of the most famous of the Spa Hotels - the Gellért (Csörnyei et al 1970; 9-23). Here, the German Steigenberger Group has bought into the national Danubius Group hotel but not into the adjoining independent Baths company. The result is that foreign (and local) tourists can stay in a famous, historic hotel in the centre of the city and have preferential entrance facilities for the adjoining medicinal Baths and treatments whilst locals are still able to use these health facilities upon payment of a minimal entrance charge. Current opinion in the Spa Directorate is that such a coexistence may provide the answer to redevelopment of the other historic Baths of the city (e.g. Rudas, Rácz, Király (Csörnyei et al 1970; 59-71, 73-79 & 81-86 respectively)) by building hotels adjacent to these facilities where foreign tourists would have a preferential (i.e. free and unlimited) entry to the Baths whilst, at the same time, the local residents of Budapest would retain their right of entrance at current rates. Thus, what is seen in Hungary as a beneficial resource for the Budapest inhabitants remains accessible to locals on lower incomes (in Western terms) whilst also being available to tourists looking for a health holiday who have a higher disposable income. The Spa Directorate would thus hope, from this income, to be able to maintain the status quo as well as to institute refurbishments and improvements to these historic baths.

Llandrindod Wells

Llandrindod Wells is, like Karlovy Váry, a regional centre - it is the county town of Powys (formerly Radnorshire). As such, although it is a small town, it has an importance beyond its size. Llandrindod is a Victorian Spa and its development and time as an elegant watering place is confined to a period approximately from 1870 to the end of the first world war (Bufton 1906; 17-87) Llandrindod is a Spa of drinking waters and was developed as a place for the well to do middle classes to spend a relaxing time taking the waters. This is not to deny that the springs of Llandrindod were known for their medicinal and beneficial health properties and several people came regularly for their cure at the end of the century. The development of the Spa in Victorian times led to the creation of a park housing the springs and Spa buildings in the ironwork style of Karlovy Váry and the railway architecture that was then springing up. Indeed, it was the opening of a railway station at Llandrindod in 1868 that led to the popularity of the town as an inland resort, this together with the building of several impressive hotels, including the Bridge (now Metropole) facing its elegant town park square and bandstand (Anon undated; 1-6). Llandrindod was built for the new wealth of the adjacent Midlands and faced its decline when the world order as it was collapsed after 1918 (Anon undated; 7). In recent times, redevelopment funds (principally from the E.U.) aimed at this neglected part of central Wales have been poured into Llandrindod to restore its Spa. Apart from the obvious aesthetic disasters such as building an soulless indoor bowling hall next to the old Pavilion (still awaiting completion of restoration) by the peaceful Rock garden, much has been done to restore the town to its former glory. The Spa park, an integral feature of all major European Spas where walking off the effects of drinking the waters was considered an integral part of the treatment, has been lovingly refurbished with new paths and the centre of the Spa, the Spa buildings themselves have been brought back to full working order. Visitors should now be able to sit on the terrace or in the cafe and enjoy a glass of one or all of the local waters. The Hotel Metropole has also been restored to fit in with the ambiance of the old town and a new "Health Spa" (Beattie 1992; 7-13) has been added to the hotel in a mock Victorian style conservatory building for guests to enjoy the "modern" Spa treatments of a health farm - heated swimming pool, Jacuzzi, Sauna, Exercise machinery etc., the hotel has also a high class restaurant and is a conference centre (Beattie 1992; 190-191). Llandrindod Wells has thus become a blue print for a modernisation of British Spas to compete with Europe - or has it? On a recent visit (October 1993), unfortunately the cafe in the Spa park was firmly closed, a notice on the entrance door stating that no water could be sold because of enquiries and tests under the Water Act of 1991. The one spring remaining open was the chalybeate spring within the park (difficult to close off as it stand completely in the open) and that was certainly not being patronised. Britain is receiving severe criticism from the E.U. for its standards of water purity and it is ironic that a Spa town revived with the help of E.U. grants should be prejudiced by E.U. water directives. As it is, the Metropole Hotel has a healthy trade in conference delegates and tourists enjoying the clear air and fine scenery of mid-Wales even without the elegance of taking the waters across the railway line in the lower town. Needless to say, it is the lower town where the post war decay of Llandrindod is most evident and it is arguably a matter of concern whether the attempt to revive one of Britain's Spas may founder on bureaucracy and lack of genuine interest.

DISCUSSION AND CONCLUSIONS

Despite the attempts at reopening Llandrindod Wells and projects such as the restoration of the Victorian Turkish Baths at Harrogate, (Donaldson1993) Britain still remains far behind central Europe in taking its Spas seriously. In France and Belgium, whole seaside resorts are gearing up to the new fashion of thalassotherapy - the Spa by the sea (Odent 1990; 38-42, Husson 1993 & Ryan 1993). In the new Czech Republic, the glories of nineteenth century Spa life are being revived in the restoration of luxury hotels and bathing and drinking facilities. In Hungary, joint ventures are showing the way for the invigoration and preservation of a bathing culture which has remained a central part of everyday life since the Turkish period. These are all examples which can and should be taken into account by a weak British tourist industry. Budapest may seem unique as the city of baths, but two hundred years ago, London had a similar reputation - Epsom, Sadlers Wells, Beulah, Lambeth, Clerkenwell and many other "Spas" flourished in those days, all to be walled up or to run dry and be forgotten (for a general view of British Spas see Addison 1951). There is an argument for better use of leisure time and for more alternative health consciousness. In the 1980s, health farms have shown a new and growing demand for water-based health breaks in the countryside (Beattie 1992; 240-248). In the present day urban environment of stress and decay, the Spa complex within the city would offer alternative facilities without the need to travel far. Whilst sunbathers take to their high factor creams and fear polluted seas and beaches, the Spa presents a healthy alternative. Not long ago, the British would never have considered drinking bottled waters, spending a weekend in the jacuzzi of a health farm, or giving birth in water pools in hospitals; the trend towards a revival for the British Spa is already evident, the question is whether the tourist and health industries will be ready and eager to meet the new challenge or whether Karlovy Váry and Budapest will be left to flourish and draw in tourist revenue whilst the doors to Llandrindod Wells remain firmly closed.

Selected References

Addison, W. (1951) English Spas. London, Batsford
Anon. (undated) The Story of the Metropole. for Best Western Hotels
Beattie, C. (1992) Healthy Breaks. Woking, Discovery Books
Bufton, W.J. (1906) Illustrated Guide to Llandrindod Wells. London, F. Hodgson
Croutier, A.L. (1992) Taking the Waters. New York, Abbeville Press
Csoernyei, S. et al. (1970) Heil- und Schwimmbäder in Budapest. Budapest, Pannonia Verlag
Donaldson, L. (1993) Historic spa towns springing back to life. London, in The Independent on Sunday, p21
Fink, H. (1992) Buchers Reisebegleiter - Die Böhmischen Bäder. Munich & Berlin, Verlag C.J. Bucher GmbH
Husson, H. (1993) Spécial - Thalassothérapie. Paris, in Le Figaro, 5th-6th June pp 19-20
Mráz, B. (1991) Karlov∞ Váry & Grand Hotel Pupp. Prague, Nákladatelství Merkur
Odent, M. (1990) Water & Sexuality. London, Arkana Publications, the Penguin Group
Ryan, R. (1993) Opportunity Knokkes. London, in the Sunday Times, Style & Travel p 46
Vida, M (1992) Spas in Hungary in Ancient Times and Today. Budapest, Semmelweis Kiadó

13

Validating contextual urban design principles

Vérifier la validité des principes d'urbanisme contextuel

Arthur E. Stamps III

Plus de 80% de villes aux Etats-Unis prévoient des contrôles de physionomie architecturale, et plus de 75% de ces contrôles prescrivent l'évaluation de la compatibilité des projets proposés avec les bâtiments existants. Pourtant il existe peu de données scientifiques vérifiant spécifiquement la validité des principes sur lesquels sont fondés les contrôles d'urbanisme actuels. De plus, il semble qu'il y ait peu de preuves scientifiques de la validité des méthodes de simulation utilisées pour les expériences de compatibilité contextuelle.

Ce rapport présente les résultats de deux expériences visant à vérifier la validité de la technique de simulation du photomontage et de cinq principes d'urbanisme sur les proportions et le caractère résidentiels. Il s'est avéré que les préférences pour les diapositives d'îlots d'immeubles correspondaient à 0.93 avec les préférences pour les photomontages d'élévations d'immeubles individuels. La technique du photomontage a ensuite été utilisée pour créer des façades artificielles d'îlots d'immeubles résidentiels qui pourraient servir à vérifier les principes d'urbanisme. Quatre principes ont été étayés par les données empiriques recueillies (la compatibilité est plus importante que les caractéristiques des îlots d'immeubles ou des immeubles individuels; les îlots d'immeubles homogènes l'emportent sur les îlots d'immeubles disparates, même si ceux-ci contiennent un immeuble, qui considéré séparément, est préféré par les personnes interrogées; plus une maison partage de caractéristiques avec les maisons voisines, et plus on préfère le quartier où elle est située; les îlots homogènes sont plus appréciés que les îlots hétérogènes). Le seul principe qui n'a pas été validé est celui selon lequel on préférerait les îlots de petits immeubles plutôt que de grands immeubles. En fait, le degré de préférence baissait si l'on ajoutait un grand immeuble à l'îlot, mais augmentait par la suite si l'on en ajoutait plusieurs. Enfin, l'auteur discute des limitations possibles et de la désirabilité des reproductions indépendantes.

Mots clé: urbanisme; dessein contextuel; bâtiment résidentiel.

Keywords: urban design; contextual design; residential infill.

Ever since the publication of Trystan Edwards' Good and Bad Manners in Architecture in 1924 it has been recognized that an important part of the urban experience is the design of buildings which fit into the existing visual context. Clearly contextual compatibility impacts many aspects of the urban experience, including urban quality, urban landscapes, urban planning, urban conflicts, urban policies, urban design, urban housing and urban neighborhoods. Many authors and designers (Cullen, 1961; Brolin, 1980; Bently et al., 1985; Tugnutt & Robertson, 1987) have commented on the need to fit new buildings into existing visual contexts, not to mention architectural critics ranging from the Prince of Wales down to the rest of us. What has not been so widely recognized is the virtual absence of scientific validation for the basic principles of contextual design. For example, most cities in the United States have implemented aesthetic controls on architecture (over 80% of all U.S. cities and 93% of the cities with populations of 100,000 or more have "design review" requirements for new projects) and over 75% of those cities sometimes or always used contextual principles to evaluate new buildings (Lightner, 1993). Yet, in a recent international conference on design review, 49 papers were presented, but only three papers were grounded with scientific data (Preiser & Lightner, 1992). The importance of scientific validation in design review can be ascertained by inspecting the connections between public policy, the judicial system, and the scientific establishment. In the United States, evaluations of architectural aesthetics are required by most urban design codes and, (for projects in natural settings) by environmental impact reports as well (Findley & Farber, 1992, p. 28ff; California Council of Civil Engineers & Land Surveyors, 1991, p 125) . The judicial justification for those controls is that the public welfare includes a beautiful environment, where beauty is judged by ordinary people (Ziegler, 1986, p. 245). Determinations of beauty are often made by experts using personal experience and judgment (for examples see Smardon, 1992), but after 70 years, the rules for admitting expert judgments in the U.S. courts just changed (Mervis, 1993; Stamps, 1994). Where the old standard was whether a scientific technique had been published in a peer-reviewed journal, the new standard requires scientific knowledge to be relevant, reliable, and grounded in the methods of science. Knowledge is specifically stated to connote more than subjective belief or unsupported speculation (Daubert vs. Merrell Dow, U.S. Supreme Court, No. 92-102, decided 28 June 1993). Since common law insists on using the most reliable sources of data, and since for the purpose of predicting the public interest in aesthetics, evidence is beginning to suggest that science is more reliable than expert judgments (Stamps, in press,a), scientific evidence would seem to be the most appropriate grounds for adjudication of aesthetic controversies. The connection to urban design principles is clear: under the new judicial criteria for admitting expert testimony, urban design controls which are based only on professional judgment or personal experience will be vulnerable to legal challenge, while urban design controls which have been validated scientifically will be secure. Thus, at least in the United States, there is a clear and present need for scientific validation of urban design principles.

With specific reference to contextual urban design principles it appears that there are many more principles than scientific validations. A review of the literature generated the following list of hypotheses regarding commonly held or implemented contextual urban design principles: (H1) Contextual fits between individual houses and their surrounding houses are more important than attributes of the houses themselves; (H2) people will like homogeneous blocks over blocks with different buildings even if, in isolation, they like the different building better; (H3) the more attributes an infill house shares with the rest of the block, the more people will like the block; (H4) people will like homogeneous blocks over diverse blocks, and (H5) people will prefer blocks with small houses over blocks with large houses. Only three attempts at scientific validation of contextual design principles were found. Groat (1988) reported data which indicated a very high correlation between expert's and lay judgments for contextual compatibility of a wide range of architectural projects (r = .97). She also reported data indicating that experts' judgments of facade variables predicted more contextual compatibility than experts' judgments of site or massing variables (r's of -.56, -.64, and -.89 for site, mass, and facades respectively). Nasar (1988) investigated effects of different levels of complexity on preferences for street scenes, and found than an intermediate amount of complexity was the most preferred. This finding was a replication of many previous experiments using other types of stimuli (Berlyne, 1960, 1971, 1974; Berlyne & Madsen, 1973). Finally Sanoff (1991) reported several small studies in which contextual fits of new buildings were ascertained by inserting line drawings of the new project into line drawings of existing block elevations. This was called the "best fit slide rule method".

Thus, given the need for scientific validation of contextual design principles and the apparent lack of such studies in the literature, it was decided to begin experimental inquiry into the efficacies of urban design principles with respect to public preferences for urban scenes. Because local planning codes specifically mandated compatibility of new residences with the scale and character of the existing neighborhoods (San Francisco, 1988), and because Groat found that facade variables were the best predictors of contextual fit, it was decided to focus specifically on validating urban design principles for scale and character in residential block facades.

144

EXPERIMENT #1

Methods

Detailed analysis of the experimental literature indicated that the chief methodological weaknesses were the type and number of stimuli. Most experiments used photographs of existing street scenes, and the numbers of photographs were very small in relation to the number of factors under investigation. It is possible, for example, to find published studies of 21 variables based on 25 photographs. Aside from the obvious statistical difficulty of obtaining useful results for 21 variables from 25 stimuli there is also the difficulty of finding actual buildings and block facades which exhibit the desired contextual relationships explicitly enough to support a balanced factorial experimental design. However, as Berlyne (1974, 17 - 21) pointed out, this difficulty could be overcome by creating artificial stimuli which did exhibit the desired relationships. For the purpose of evaluating aesthetic effects of contextual fit in residential block facades, Sanoff's slide rule method seemed promising. However, a recent review of the environmental simulation literature, covering 1200 stimuli, 4200 respondents, and 20 media (Stamps, 1993a), indicated that (a) preferences obtained from colored photographs or slides correlated highly with preferences obtained on site, and (b) photographs of buildings were better simulations than the line drawings used in Sanoff's studies. There was, however, no experimental validation of the use of elevation photographs for elevations of blocks of buildings, and so it was decided to do a preliminary experiment to determine how well preferences for photomontages of house elevations compared to preferences for actual blocks.

Stimuli:

Ten residential blocks, each of which contained 5 stylistically homogeneous, contiguous residences, were photographed using the two photoprotocols shown in Figure 1a and 1b. Use of stylistically homogeneous residences controlled for variables such as fenestration and facade materials. Landscaping was controlled for by selecting houses using the photoprotocols described in Stamps (1993a). The 5 individual photographs obtained using protocol b were pasted up and rephotographed as a block elevation. The experimental stimuli thus consisted of 20 slides: ten perspectives of the actual blocks and ten artificial block elevation photomontages. (For reproductions of the actual stimuli please see Stamps, 1993b.)

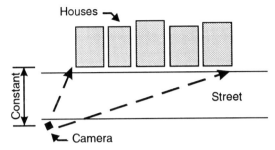

1a. Photo protocol for slides of block facades

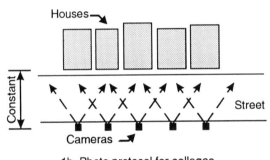

1b. Photo protocol for collages

Figure 13.1 Photoprotocols. 1a shows how to obtain perspective photographs of blocks. 1b shows how to obtain photographs for a photomontage elevation of the block.

Respondents:

Respondents were chosen at random by a professional survey research firm. Based on power analysis, it was estimated that at least 40 respondents would be needed to obtain 80% power with ten blocks, a .05 significance level, and an expected effect size of 1% (Cohen & Cohen, 1983; Cohen, 1988). Due to logistical opportunities the actual number of respondents was 45.

Task:

Each of the 20 stimuli was shown to the respondents. The respondents rated each stimulus on the criterion of personal preference using an 8 point semantic differential scale.

Results

It was found that the Pearson correlation between preferences for the slides and preferences for the photomontages of block elevations was .93.

Discussion

Because previous findings had indicated that preferences for slides correlated highly with preferences obtained on site, and because preferences for the photomontages correlated highly with preferences for slides, it seemed that the photomontages of block elevations were adequate simulations for the purpose of predicting environmental preferences.

EXPERIMENT #2

Methods

Selection of design components

After the simulation method had been validated it was used to test the contextual urban design hypotheses listed above. Those principles required selection of design components for individual buildings. Since the focus of neighborhood planning in San Francisco was on the scale and character of houses, scale and character were chosen as the basic design components.

Moreover, hypothesis H2 required prior evidence that one residential character be preferred over another residential character when each character was viewed in isolation. Identification of appropriate architectural characters was facilitated by previous replicated findings that plain stucco boxes with flat roofs and little trim were liked less than houses with gable roofs and decorative trim (Sanoff, 1991, p. 27-31; Stamps, 1991; Stamps & Miller, 1993). For brevity the levels of the character factor were called "plain" and "fancy". Identification of local houses with different scales was simple because the local planning code had different height limits for R-2 (two unit zoning) and R-1 (one unit zoning) housing. Again for the purpose of brevity the levels of the scale factor were called "small" and "large". Figure 2 shows line drawings of each type of house.

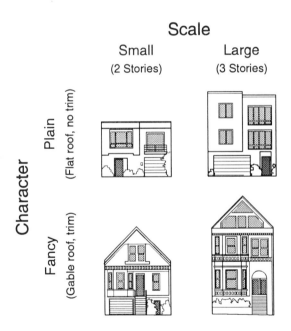

Figure 13.2   Line drawings of four house types: plain small houses, plain large houses, fancy small houses and fancy large houses.

148

Once the four house types were identified (big and small, plain and fancy) the next step was to use the photomontage method to create artificial block elevations. It was decided to use 7 houses on each block, and so 7 houses of each type were identified and photographed. Then the 28 individual house elevations were assembled into 40 artificial blocks. (Space limitations prevent inclusion of the photomontages in this article. The photomontages will be published elsewhere (Stamps, in press, b)). In 16 of those blocks one infill building was inserted into otherwise homogeneous block faces. These 16 blocks are shown diagramatically in Figure 3. For blocks on the main diagonal (AFKP) the infill house matched the block in terms of both scale and character. For blocks on the counter-main diagonal (DGJM) the infill house contrasted with both the scale and the character of the rest of the block. In the remaining 8 blocks the infill house contrasted with only the scale (CHIN) or only the character (BELO) of the rest of the block. These stimuli permitted testing of hypotheses H1 - H3. More artificial blocks were created in order to test hypotheses regarding diversity and degree of development. For diversity blocks were created by inserting none, 1, 2, or 3 houses which differed from the rest of block. Examples of each of these diversity levels are shown in Figure 4. Hypotheses regarding degree of development could be tested with blocks which differed in the number of large buildings. That number ranged from 0 (all small houses) to 7 (all large houses). Figure 13.5 shows diagrams of the blocks used to test development hypotheses.

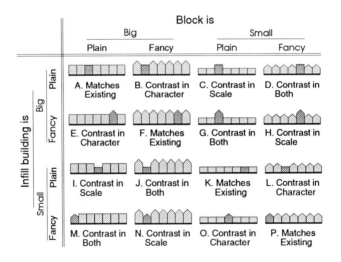

Figure 13.3 Generation of synthetic blocks in which infill houses systematically mix or match with the other houses on the block.

Levels of Diversity

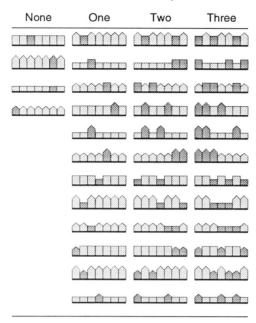

Figure 13.4 Blocks with different levels of diversity.

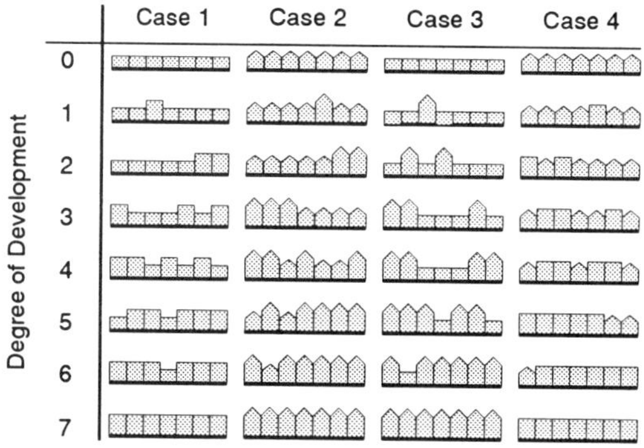

Figure 13.5 Blocks with different degrees of development.

Respondents and task

The respondents and task were the same in both experiments.

Results

(H1) Contextual fits between individual houses and their surrounding houses are more important than attributes of the houses themselves. This hypothesis was tested using variance components analysis of preferences for the 16 stimuli shown in Figure 3. The hypotheses suggested that the block by building interaction would account for more preference variance than either the block main effect or the building main effect, and that turned out to be the case. The variance components for the interaction, block and building effects were 14%, 1.9%, and 7% respectively.

(H2) People would like homogeneous blocks over blocks with different buildings even if, in isolation, they like the different building better. Since previous research indicated that people preferred "fancy" houses over "plain" houses, this hypothesis suggested that people would like homogeneous blocks over the same blocks with one "fancy" infill house. Using "*" to mean "is preferred to" and referring to the stimuli shown in Figure 3, this implies A * M, A * E, K * G, and K * O. These four claims can be combined in the ordinary way to form a simple contrast in preferences (Rosenthal & Rosnow, 1985; Winer et al., 1991). Statistical analysis indicated that the data supported this hypothesis (contrast = .34, t = 2.4, p * .008).

(H3) The more attributes an infill house shares with the rest of the block, the more people will like the block. This hypothesis entails two contrasts among the stimuli shown in Figure 3. The first claim is that people will like blocks in which the infill building matches both the scale and character of the other houses over blocks in which the infill house matches only the scale or only the character of the rest of the block. In symbolic terms, AFKP * BCEHILNO. The resulting contrast was positive and significant (contrast = .5, t = 5.0, p < .0001). The second claim is that people will like blocks in which the infill house matches only the scale or character over houses in which the infill house matches neither the scale nor character. In symbolic terms, BCEHILNO * DGJM. Again the contrast was positive and significant (contrast = .41, t * 4.1, p < .0001).

(H4) People will like homogeneous blocks over diverse blocks. This hypothesis can be tested as a trend among the columns of blocks shown in Figure 4. The trend was positive and significant (trend = 1.96, t = 6.77, p < .0001).

(H5) People will prefer blocks with small houses over blocks with large houses. This hypothesis can be tested as a trend in the rows of the stimuli shown in Figure 5. The trend was negative and significant (trend = -5.77, t = -4.33, p < .0001), indicating that the hypothesis was wrong. These respondents did not prefer the blocks with smaller houses over the blocks with larger houses.

Since the main hypothesis regarding degree of development turned out to be wrong it was decided to further investigate the relationships between preferences and degree of development. A quadratic trend analysis in degree of development indicated the presence of a local minimum (trend = 8.24, t = 6.19, p < .0001). Inspection of the means suggested that the minimum was located at the first large building on the block. Subsequent contrast analysis comparing the blocks with only one large building against the other blocks confirmed that the blocks with only one large building were worse than the rest of the blocks (contrast = .40, t = 4.53, p < .001). The means also suggested that after blocks had one large building, preference would increase with the addition of more large buildings. A trend analysis of the bottom seven rows of stimuli in Figure 4 confirmed this hypothesis (trend = 3.97, t = 8.0, p < .001).

Discussion

First, the simple technique of photomontage simulations appears to be a valid and useful medium for testing contextual urban design principles. Second, it would appear that, for these stimuli and respondents, almost all the contextual urban design principles were valid. Contextual effects were more important than factors of blocks or buildings; people liked homogeneous blocks over blocks with different buildings even if, in isolation, they liked the different building better; the more attributes an infill building shared with its neighbors the more people liked the block, and people liked homogeneous blocks over diverse blocks. Third, the principle that people would like blocks with smaller houses better than blocks with larger houses was not supported; instead, it was found that the first large building on a block reduced the aesthetic merit of the block while subsequent large buildings had the effect of raising the block's aesthetic merit.

In the application of these results some qualifications might be in order. The most important qualification concerns the scope of the stimuli. Valid experimental design requires restricted numbers of factors and levels of each factor. In the present experiment the factors were scale and character and the levels were R-1 and R-2 and plain and fancy respectively. Moreover the characters were chosen based on previous findings that there was a definite public preference for one character over the other. While all these restrictions produce an excellent experimental design they also limit the range of applicability of the results.   The obvious next step, therefore, is to try to replicate the present findings using the same simulation protocols but with different buildings. For example, the lot width in San Francisco is typically 25 feet, so the factor of building height was completely confounded with the factor of building proportion. Only in other cities might it be possible to find the buildings necessary to determine if contextual rules based on the design component of specific overall building proportion are efficacious.

The second qualification concerns the respondents. Possible concerns include the number of respondents and the population from which they are chosen.   Based on previous work on environmental preferences (Stamps, 1992) the number of respondents does not appear to a major concern so long as the samples are really random and the results concerning subpopulations are not desired. Potentially more serious is the fact that these respondents all came from the same city, and a city with a very long and active history of citizen participation in urban design.   (The first date we have for neighborhood participation in this   city is 1850 (Barton, 1985)).   Thus, not only is independent replication desirable, independent replication is   desirable somewhere other than in our city. Therefore should any other researchers care to try out these ideas in their own venues, we would be most pleased to assist them in any way possible.

References

Barton, S. E., (1985). The neighborhood movement in San Francisco. Berkeley Planning Journal 2 (1-2), 85-105.

Bentley, I., Alcock, A., Murrain, P., McGlynn, G., (1985). Responsive environments: a manual for designers. London: Architectural Press.

Berlyne, D. E., (1960). Conflict, arousal and curiosity. New York: McGraw-Hill.

Berlyne, D. E., (1971). Aesthetics and psychobiology. New York: Appleton-Century-Crofts. Berlyne, D. E., (1974). Studies in the new experimental aesthetics: steps towards and objective psychology of aesthetic appreciation. New York: Wiley.

Berlyne, D. E. & Madsen, K. B., (1973). Pleasure, reward, preference: their nature, determinants, and role in behavior. New York: Academic.

Brolin, B.C., (1980). Architecture in context: fitting new buildings with old. New York: Van Nostrand Reinhold.

California Council of Civil Engineers & Land Surveyors, (1991). California environmental quality act: CEQA guidelines. West Sacramento, California: Author.

Cohen, J. & Cohen, P., (1983). Applied regression/correlation analysis for the behavioral sciences.   Hillsdale, New Jersey: Lawrence Erlbaum.

Cohen, J. (1988). Statistical power analysis for the behavioral sciences. Hillsdale, New Jersey: Lawrence Erlbaum.

Cullen, G., (1961). The concise townscape. New York: Van Nostrand Reinhold.

Edwards, T., (1924). Good and bad manners in architecture. London: Philip Allan.

Findley, R. W., & Farber, D. A., (1992). Environmental Law. St. Paul: West.

Groat, L. N., (1988). Contextual compatibility in architecture: an issue of personal taste? In: In: J.L. Nasar (Ed.). Environmental aesthetics: theory, research, and applications. Cambridge: Cambridge University Press, 228-253.

Lightner, B., C., (1993). Survey of design review practices. PAS Memo, January 1993. Chicago: American Planning Association.

Mervis, J., (1993). Supreme court to judges: start thinking like scientists. Science 261 (2 July 1993) 22.

Nasar, J.L., (1988). The effect of sign complexity and coherence on the perceived quality of retail scenes. In: J.L. Nasar (Ed.). Environmental aesthetics: theory, research, and applications. Cambridge: Cambridge University Press, 300-320.

Preiser, W., & Lightner, B. C., (1992). Proceedings of the international symposium on design review. University of Cincinnati, October 8 - 11, 1992. Cincinnati: Department of Architecture, University of Cincinnati.

Rosenthal, R. & Rosnow, R. L., (1985). Contrast analysis: focused comparisons in the analysis of variance. Cambridge: Cambridge University Press.

San Francisco, City of, (1988). Neighborhood conservation interim controls. City planning commission resolution, September 28, 1988.

Sanoff, H., (1991). Visual research methods in design. New York: Van Nostrand Reinhold.

Smardon. R. C., (1992). The legal landscape. New York: Van Nostrand Reinhold.

Stamps, A. E., (1991).Comparing preferences of neighbors and a neighborhood design review board. Environment and Behavior 23 (5) 616 - 629.

Stamps, A. E., (1992). Bootstrap investigation of respondent sample size for environmental preferences. Perceptual and Motor Skills 75, 220-222.

Stamps, A. E., (1993a). Simulation effects on environmental preference. Journal of Environmental Management, (1993) 38, 115 - 132.

Stamps, A. E., (1993b). Validating contextual urban design photoprotocols: replication & generalization from single residences to block faces. Environment and Planning B: Planning & Design 20, 693-707.

Stamps, A. E., (1994). Daubert and peer review. Poster paper, Annual Meeting, American Association for the Advancement of Science. San Francisco, February 18 - 23, 1994.

Stamps, A. E., (in press, a). All buildings great and small: design review from high rise to houses. Environment and Behavior.

Stamps, A. E., (1994, in press b). A study in scale and character: contextual effects on environmental preferences. Journal of Environmental Management.

Stamps, A. E. & Miller, S. D, (1993). Advocacy membership, design guidelines and predicting preferences for residential infill designs. Environment and Behavior 25 (3) 367-409.

Tugnutt, A., & Robertson, M., (1987). Making townscape. London: Mitchell. Winer, B. J., Brown, D. R., Michels, K. M., (1991). Statistical principles in experimental design. New York: McGraw-Hill.

Ziegler, E. H., (1986). Aesthetic controls and derivative human values: the emerging rational basis for regulation. In: J. B. Gailey (Ed.)., 1986 Zoning and planning law handbook. New York: Clark Boardman, 239-252.

14

L'expérience urbaine personnelle: une voie d'accès utile au projet de réaménagement

Personal urban experience: a relevant approach for urban design and renewal

Gilles Barbey

The present study attempts to relate the personal and sensitive experience of the urban milieu to its objective and scientific study, in order to identify relevant criteria for the conservation of existing buildings and the renewal of urban neighbourhoods. An autobiographical and phenomenological survey of various memories of foreign and familiar cities provides a combination of the respective urban visions. Urban experience, which is closely related to place identity, can be seen as the integration of holistic and fragmentary urban images. Their balanced exploration identifies values that will influence the conscience of a specific urban field as well as the choice of the adequate type of urban rehabilitation. The main goal of this research is to indicate a process whereby the fruit of urban experience can become instrumental when applied to various tasks in urban redevelopment.

Keywords: urban experience; place identity; phenomenological autobiography; cognitive images; urban redevelopment.

Mots clés : expérience urbaine; identité des lieux; autobiographie phénoménologique; images cognitives; réaménagement urbain.

La présente étude se propose de combiner la connaissance sensible et individuelle du milieu urbain avec sa compréhension plus systématique et objective fondée sur les sciences sociales et l'histoire en parti culier. Dans cette perspective, la démarche d'exploration historique de la ville est supposée connue et ne sera pas évoquée ici. On formu lera l'hypothèse que l'expérience urbaine, dont nous allons fournir une illustration, constitue un point de passage obligé qui permettra de développer l'exercice du projet urbain. En l'occurrence, nous avons situé notre démarche d'analyse dans notre propre mémoire du champ urbain.

Il s'agit donc d'examiner dans quelle mesure la vision extérieure d'une ville peut rejoindre sa connaissance de l'intérieur; d'examiner aussi où se situe le point de fusion entre la représentation indivi duelle de la ville et son enregistrement dans la mémoire collective. Cette préoccupation de savoir comment aborder la ville avec un niveau suffisant de compétence ne clôt pas le débat entre partisans respec tifs d'une vision intérieure et extérieure. Notre projet consiste en effet à analyser les effets complémentaires de cette double explora tion.

On peut donc dresser un plaidoyer en faveur d'une approche de la ville qui permettra d'allier les visions holistique et fragmentaire résul tant d'une analyse du milieu urbain à laquelle s'ajoute l'expérience personnelle. La perception sensible fournit les moyens de nuancer la connaissance scientifique et d'y inscrire la "coloration" affective indispensable.

Cette familiarisation avec le champ urbain représente à notre avis une nécessité pour déterminer le type et le degré de l'intervention en gendrée par le projet urbain, de manière à en pondérer le déroulement par rapport aux deux extrêmes que sont la conservation intégrale et le renouvellement total.

Ainsi l'expérience urbaine exige-t-elle bien un approfondissement du rapport individuel à la ville, qui va livrer des indices précieux pour la connaissance du milieu. Cette forme de mise à l'épreuve de la cons cience personnelle offre parallèlement un support utile pour cerner les manifestations d'identité.

METHODOLOGIE

L'idée d'une recherche en circuit fermé, à savoir l'exploitation de ses propres souvenirs articulés autour de son monde vécu (lifeworld) nous paraît légitime et conforme à l'orientation phénoménologique. Une expérience de vie de 60 ans de résidence alternée en ville (25 ans) et à la campagne (35 ans) représente un terrain d'analyse d'autant plus utile que la vie campagnarde aiguise la conscience de l'urbain, en offrant le recul nécessaire à l'observation.

Deux dimensions essentielles de l'expérience urbaine retiennent d'em blée notre attention et prêtent à l'approfondissement : d'une part la diversité des expériences récoltées, d'autre part leur profondeur même. En conséquence, nous choisirons d'explorer simultanément les deux champs suivants :

	Perception "scénique"	Implication phénoménologique

AUBE D'HIVER SUR
VILLE EN RUINE

HAMBOURG   1952

Zeitgeist: Immédiat
après-guerre
Genius loci: Canal,
centre-ville
Circonstance: Avant
travail technique

Forte empathie urbaine
présageant une propension
à l'acclimatation, en dépit
d'une ville à l'état de
destruction. Illusion
d'emprise sur la ville

DIMANCHE ESTIVAL DANS
CHAMBRE SUR COUR

VIENNE   1953

Zeitgeist: Période
d'occupation militaire
Genius loci: Wiener Hof
dans le Ring
Circonstance: Congé
dominical, lecture

Impression de déconnection
et dépaysement ressentie
en pleine ville, à portée
du Danube. Sentiment latent
de dépendance

NUIT D'AUTOMNE PRISON-
NIERE D'UNE COURETTE

PARIS   1955

Zeitgeist: Années de
guerre froide
Genius loci: Immeuble
résidentiel à Passy
Circonstance: Immobilisa-
tion pour convalescence

Promiscuité sonore et
visuelle émanant d'un voisinage étranger et quasi
hostile, accréditant un sentiment de confinement carcé-
ral. Résignation acceptée
au cadre de vie

AURORE PRINTANIERE
PRES DE LA TAMISE

LONDRES   1959

Zeitgeist: Nuit de mai
finissante
Genius loci: Rues désertes
à Westminster
Circonstance: Attente de
naissance d'un enfant

Sentiment d'impuissance
face à l'espoir mêlé de
désespoir, errance urbaine
dramatisée par l'annonce
d'une exécution capitale.
Assurance de solidarité
avec la ville et d'un
avenir prometteur

SOIREE FIN D'ETE
MANHATTAN

NEW YORK   1961

Zeitgeist: Après tempête
fin août
Genius loci: Midtown
Manhattan, Eastside
Circonstance: Après
travail actif

Impression d'être assimilé
par une ville tentaculaire
où s'inscrivent des projets
personnels mobilisateurs.
Conviction d'habiter au
centre du monde, quoique
de manière fort provisoire
et précaire

Figure 14.1 Evocation de la diversité des souvenirs associes au sejours successifs dans
diverses villes etrangères.

	Perception "scénique"	Implication phénoménologique
 VILLE SOURCE DE DECOUVERTES	LAUSANNE 1940 Zeitgeist: avant-guerre menaçante Genius loci: Seule plate-forme dans ville en pente Circonstance: Enfant emmené en promenade	Ville comme terrain de découverte et d'aventure ponctué de parcs arborisés
 VILLE OFFERTE EN PANORAMA	LAUSANNE 1950 Zeitgeist: Après-guerre renaissante Genius loci: Symbiose avec panorama urbain Circonstance: Adolescent en semi-liberté	En opposition à sa périphérie banale et morne, le centre-ville est source d'attraction et de sollicitations au plan des rencontres et des ressources. La ville est providentielle
 A LA PORTE DU CENTRE-VILLE	LAUSANNE 1961 Zeitgeist: Années de haute conjoncture Genius loci: Quartier à la limite du centre-ville Circonstance: Activité professionnelle débutante	La ville semble aborder une phase nouvelle de son développement avec des projets de construction pour lesquels il est urgent de prendre parti en vue de l'avènement de la modernité au plan local. Perspectives de contribution à l'urbain
 NO MAN'S LAND SUR ARTERE ROUTIERE	LAUSANNE 1971 Zeitgeist: Ralentissement de la croissance Genius loci: Périphérie sans âme Circonstance: Engagement professionnel teinté de marginalité	Ville menacée dans son intégrité par des extensions chaotiques. La scène urbaine apparaît de plus en plus opaque et contradictoire, au point qu'il est malaisé d'y trouver son rôle. Peu d'emprise potentielle sur l'urbain
A DISTANCE DE LA VILLE	LAUSANNE 1985 Zeitgeist: Années de réévaluation fondamentale Genius loci: Centre-ville réapproprié Circonstance: Reconversion vers une activité théorique	Ville structurellement en état de stagnation. Elle n'offre plus guère de marge d'action hors de la politique. L'urbanité en crise devient un sujet de réflexion. L'emprise sur l'urbain ne peut être que critique

Figure 14.2 Evocation de la profondeur des experiences successive d'une même ville.

1. L'évocation du séjour temporaire dans plusieurs villes étrangères retracée sur un mode synchronique. Laps de temps considéré : une décennie (voir figure 14.1)

2. La narration des observations successives d'une même ville suivant un mode diachronique. Laps de temps considéré : cinq décennies (voir figure 14.2)

Il faut tenir compte d'un obstacle épistémologique attribuable au fait que tout souvenir est automatiquement soumis à un effet de sublimation de ses côtés prosaïques pour revêtir un caractère transposé, voire euphémisé. Nous ne croyons pas qu'un processus correctif quelconque autorise rétrospectivement la saisie de la réalité telle qu'effective ment vécue et nous admettrons d'office les distorsions inévitables et inhérentes à l'expérience urbaine.

L'EXPERIENCE URBAINE : DIVERSITE ET PROFONDEUR

L'évocation de la diversité et de la profondeur de l'expérience ur baine rend possibles des comparaisons à condition d'adopter une ma nière commune d'analyser les impressions ressuscitées par la mémoire. Pour rendre compte utilement de l'expérience de la complexité urbaine, il nous semble admissible d'adopter par analogie le concept de la perception scénique susceptible de se traduire à travers la règle des trois unités théâtrales traditionnelles, à savoir :
1. L'unité de temps qui prend en compte le Zeitgeist
2. L'unité de lieu qui correspond à la notion de genius loci 3. L'unité d'action qui évoque l'usage du milieu étudié et la circonstance d'observation

Ces trois concepts, admis ici dans une acception moins absolue que dans leur application à la tragédie classique, permettent d'envisager pour chaque ville un minimum de cohérence épistémologique. L'examen de la diversité des souvenirs associés aux séjours successifs dans diffé rentes villes est opéré pendant la décennie 1952-1961. Durant cette période, certaines villes temporairement habitées commencent à se relever des années de guerre et présentent encore la trace des ruines et la marque de l'occupation étrangère. (voir tableau 14.1)

On pourrait évoquer à ce propos le souvenir des villes étrangères découvertes au cours d'un séjour de brève durée à travers l'image du kaléidoscope, qui valorise en le décuplant le reflet d'un épisode urbain remémoré. L'instrument sert à enchanter la vision en offrant un spectacle décoratif et abstrait. Les éclats d'objets, insignifiants par eux-mêmes, se reflètent dans le jeu de miroirs au point de subli mer la réalité en composant un tableau. Les prismes recueillant l'image révèlent soudain des profondeurs abruptes. A la jointure des miroirs apparaît un motif étincelant de précision. Cette production artistique est toutefois éphémère et non susceptible de se reproduire à l'identique. La moindre rotation du kaléidoscope remettra en scène une autre image visuelle.

L'expérience fugitive des villes de rencontre prend une tournure com parable. Tandis que le souvenir a écarté toutes les impressions con joncturelles, en particulier les circonstances déplaisantes, il ne reste qu'un substrat optimal, qui symbolise l'épisode vécu, à la ma nière d'une partie pour le tout. L'image saisie dans le kaléidoscope du souvenir est irréversible et ne permet guère de remonter aux fragments qui l'ont engendrée. L'enregistrement de l'épisode vécu ne relève d'aucun calcul d'intérêt. Il s'agit d'une forme de condensation poétique de la réalité urbaine.

Il faut sans doute avoir vécu de nombreuses heures sombres ou joyeuses dans diverses villes pour retirer de ce souvenir une forme de poétique urbaine. La dimension tragique, liée à la souffrance de la condition urbaine, est inséparable de toute expérience de la grande ville.

La perception urbaine semble émaner principalement de deux types d'at titude : d'une part, le sens de l'observation en alerte qui fait tra vailler l'imagination en aiguisant la volonté de se ménager une part d'urbanité et, d'autre part, un sens de l'observation distraite, où l'imagination au repos cède à l'envoûtement du cadre, avec une propen sion empathique à l'urbanité. Les réactions respectives sont bien entendu dictées par les circonstances d'observation de la ville et le rôle dévolu au spectateur. Des moments fugitifs de rapprochement in tense avec une ville peuvent laisser des souvenirs inoubliables et donner l'illusion d'avoir saisi sur l'heure l'essence même de l'ur bain.

De telles impressions appartiennent à la poétique de la ville et viennent enrichir la culture urbaine, à laquelle on fera référence lors de l'exercice du projet d'aménagement.

Par ailleurs, l'évocation de la profondeur des expériences inspirées par une même ville au cours d'une période de 50 ans conduit à des observations bien différentes (voir figure 14.2). L'énumération des divers souvenirs échelonnés dans le temps n'est pas comparable à la superposition de couches distinctes qui se détacheraient aisément les unes des autres pour se prêter à l'analyse.

Contrairement à la vision kaléidoscope des villes étrangères, la ville familière offre l'image d'un panorama. Avec le temps écoulé, le panorama se complexifie, se fragmente, se décompose en parties hétérogènes. Les strates du temps vécu s'amoncellent, indistinctes. L'image de la ville perd progressi vement de son unité et devient composite. Les nouvelles strates ont partiellement recouvert les précédentes, si bien que leur mémoire s'est envolée. Il est d'autant plus malaisé d'opérer une archéologie du souvenir que l'habitant est pris dans une dynamique de projets et de contraintes qu'il ne maîtrise que par épisodes successifs. Sa po tentialité d'action sur la ville lui retire le peu de la vision can dide qui pouvait lui rester. Il ne sera plus jamais un étranger dans sa propre ville.

Dans le cas de Lausanne, ville côtoyée et occasionnellement habitée entre 1940 et 1990, le passage d'une totale naïveté de l'observation dans l'enfance à la progressive découverte des ressources d'urbanité dans l'adolescence reflète une prise de conscience variable. Avec le temps qui s'écoule, l'observateur quitte le terrain d'aventure de l'enfance pour s'engager sur un terrain d'accomplissement socio-professionnel à l'âge adulte. Ce faisant, il passera d'une observation de type exploratoire à une observation spécialisée en fonction des motivations liées à ses activités.

A la fin du XXe siècle, Lausanne évolue "normalement", c'est-à-dire comme bien d'autres cités, vers l'anonymat, la perte d'identité, le laisser-aller dans la planification. Ce constat n'est toutefois pas dépourvu d'ambiguïté, car on peut constater que moins la ville par vient à se ressaisir pour afficher son identité propre, plus elle devient un objet d'étude captivant, puisque révélateur de mutations plus ou moins ténues.

Pour quiconque détient une activité professionnelle, le côtoiement de la ville familière se décompose en périodes de durée variable se pola risant autour d'aspects déterminés. La préoccupation poétique passe ainsi au second plan et l'attention est davantage retenue par l'exis tence même de la ville et de ses ressources que par son essence. On conviendra toutefois qu'essence et existence de la ville sont insé parables et qu'elles médiatisent conjointement l'expérience urbaine.

Si la ville entrevue passagèrement nous harcèle joyeusement de ses messages, la ville familière tente de nous contenir sans chercher à nous apostropher. D'un côté, la fraîcheur d'une liberté ressentie face à l'inconnu, de l'autre une captation ressentie comme un assujettisse ment. Ressortir frais et dispos d'une ville traversée n'a rien d'ex ceptionnel, même après des heures d'errance. La ville d'établissement au contraire est entachée de compromissions et rend en quelque sorte ses habitants impurs.

Dans le creuset prismatique du kaléïdoscope se retrouvent bout à bout des fragments d'images, de positions adoptées, d'instants vécus, qui sont autant d'impressions saisissantes. Ces remémorations subsistent quand bien même tout le reste aura été oublié. Tout le contraire en somme de la vision panoramique de la ville familière, étalée à la manière d'une nappe. Vision plus continue mais aussi plus indistincte, sur laquelle se fondent des épisodes vécus : l'ascension d'une rue, une rencontre longuement attendue, l'accomplissement d'une mission. Le temps pèse alors d'un autre poids sur le souvenir.

Il faut donc de tout pour nourrir l'expérience urbaine, depuis le fugitivement entrevu jusqu'au mûrement subi : la conjugaison des ima ges et des êtres qui ont peuplé nos champs urbains, combinaison iné puisable qui ne saurait être débrouillée au delà d'un seuil à peine sensible. L'expérience urbaine prend corps dans la confrontation de la mémoire personnelle et des souvenirs liés au monde des activités pro fessionnelles.

EXPERIENCE ET IDENTITE URBAINE

L'expérience urbaine évoquée plus haut se circonscrit entre le chaos de la guerre et le constat de l'éclatement des villes à la fin du XXe siècle : l'évolution esquissée passe habituellement par la perception d'une saturation extrême du tissu urbain vers les années 1960/1970, qui déclenche un processus d'effritement suivi de la reconstruction de fragments urbains, avec pour résultat une cohérence toujours plus lâche de l'ensemble.

Ici apparaît un paradoxe : la ville reste la même quoique constamment différente[1]. La question est en fait plus complexe qu'il n'y pa raît. Si l'existence propre de la ville n'est pas menacée de change ment, son essence par contre se modifie constamment. Or pour acquérir une expérience urbaine, il faut aussi exercer l'exploration urbaine à travers diverses visions (voir charte 13.1). Plusieurs perspectives s'avèrent indispensables pour former un spectre adéquat de références sur lequel prendre appui pour passer aux projets de réaménagement.

L'épisode urbain reconstitué dans le souvenir a valeur de partie pour le tout : à travers un moment vécu et remémoré se concentre toute l'expérience urbaine. Cette vision holistique de la ville est le ré sultat d'une réinterprétation personnelle et synthétique, incomparable à la prise de vue photographique. Ce fragment de mémoire urbaine pro cède d'un abrégé des circonstances liées à son enregistrement. Nous avons vu que le lieu précis, le moment considéré et la position de l'observateur sont déterminants dans cette perception. Mais le frag ment de souvenir qui subsiste est le résultat d'une fixation et non d'une déambulation. Cette fixation n'aurait sans doute pas été possi ble sans une exploration préalable du contexte urbain.

Il faut évoquer ici la problématique du lieu et de l'identité en ren voyant aux thèses sur l'identité des lieux (place identity) (Proshansky, 1976) qui ont dans les années 1970 attiré l'attention sur les modes de fixation affective dans l'espace urbain devenu si unifor mément anonyme. Durant les années 1980, la problématique du lieu et de l'affiliation au lieu gagne considérablement en ampleur et indique la diversité des modes d'adhésion et d'ancrage aux lieux de vie (Sime, 1985). Le rôle réconfortant ou déstabilisant joué par les domiciles successivement occupés peut aussi être retracé à partir d'autobiogra phies résidentielles (Barbey & Giuliani, 1993). Il est parallèlement utile d'envisager et d'approfondir les circonstances qui rapprochent le lieu de domicile individuel de la ville familière, où il est englo bé (Cantafora, 1993). Cette brève évocation de travaux de recherche portant sur les relations entre cadre de vie et réactions de l'usager, bien que fort incomplète, indique toutefois de quelle manière l'expé rience de la ville peut se commuer en assurance d'identité urbaine.

PROFIL SCHEMATIQUE DE LA CONSTITUTION DE L'EXPERIENCE URBAINE PERSONNELLE

Situation	Mémoire socio-professionnelle	Mémoire personnelle	Sens révélé
Rapport à la ville	Vision **diachronique** de la ville familière: Lausanne(1940-1985) Cas unique envisagé à long terme	Visions **synchroniques** des villes étrangères: Hambourg, Vienne, Paris, Londres, New York (1952-1961) Cas divers envisagés à court terme	La réalité de l'expérience urbaine est obligatoirement partagée entre ces deux visions complémentaires
Perspective d'observation	LIEUX URBAINS considérés comme constitutifs de la ville et de son EXISTENCE	Ville considérée comme constituée de LIEUX URBAINS reflétant son ESSENCE	Essence et existence de la ville obligatoirement entremêlées
Rôle joué	Etablissement et enracinement socio-professionnels	Installation et fréquentation passagères	Durée et nature de l'implication urbaine sont déterminants
Vision urbaine	Vision instrumentale et évolutive symbolisée dans le PANORAMA urbain	Visions anecdotiques et transitoires assimilables à un KALEIDOSCOPE urbain	Visions complémentaires à combiner
Tendances	Plus la mémoire socio-professionnelle est densément constituée, plus elle conduit à une vision utilitariste et instrumentale de la ville	Plus la mémoire personnelle des villes traversées est riche, plus elle alimente une vision poétique et transposée de la ville	Envers et endroit de la réalité urbaine s'interpénètrent
Expérience propre	Fixation urbaine incontournable. Engagement socio-professionnel entaché de compromissions. Marginalisation et renoncement à une emprise effective sur la ville	Itinérance délibérée et découvertes urbaines. Stimulation et illusion d'une saisie globale de la ville. Complicité avec la ville étrangère	Expériences interne et externe aboutissant à des résultats complémentaires
Emprise potentielle sur la ville	L'illusion d'emprise potentielle sur la ville semble croître proportionnellement à l'engagement socio-professionnel	L'illusion d'emprise sur la ville semble exister indépendamment de l'absence d'implication personnelle	Illusion d'emprise sur l'urbain pas nécessairement proportionnelle au degré de familiarisation avec la ville
Conséquence pour le projet urbain	Capacité de pénétrer les composantes effectives de la ville, du général au particulier	Capacité de schématiser l'essence de la ville, du particulier au général	Degrés de compétence utiles pour instrumenter le projet urbain

DE L'EXPERIENCE URBAINE AU PROJET DE REAMENAGEMENT

Une littérature importante que nous ne pouvons évoquer ici se rapporte à la méthodologie du projet d'urbanisation ou de rénovation urbaine. Rares sont par contre les efforts consentis pour indiquer par quels cheminements le vécu propre d'une ville peut contribuer à étayer la démarche du projet urbain. Il nous paraît du reste déplacé de chercher à codifier un domaine qui résiste heureusement à toute forme de réduc tion méthodologique, laquelle entraînerait inévitablement des effets positivistes.

Nous rappellerons simplement que le projet urbain fait appel au souve nir et par conséquent à l'expérience personnelle. La philosophie de la reprise est ici en cause. La véritable reprise créatrice destinée à retrouver ce qui a été (le "même") doit procéder d'une manière inédite ("autre"). Elle implique un saut qualitatif pour passer d'un ordre à un autre situé plus haut, d'où le postulat d'une transcendance (Kierkegaard, 1843/1990). S'il est aisé de rallier l'adhésion à pareille formulation, il est en revanche malaisé d'en entreprendre une exacte démonstration, sinon par la présentation du développement d'un projet particulier, relativement aisé à commenter. Ici apparaît inévitable ment une limitation à la faculté de formuler une théorie de l'appli cation susceptible de préciser davantage le déroulement de la matéria lisation.

Dans le cas qui nous occupe, la démonstration entreprise a consisté à baliser un cheminement et à retracer quelques-uns des antécédents culturels du projet urbain. Cette démarche-là, qui fera l'objet d'un développement ultérieur, avait pour l'heure comme but principal de démontrer le bénéfice qui peut être retiré de la mise à contribution d'une expérience urbaine étendue. L'expérience urbaine, dans la mesure où elle reste une aventure personnelle et irréductible, débouche sur une culture transmissible quoique non généralisable, sur laquelle asseoir, partiellement au moins, la démarche conceptuelle de réaména gement.

EN CONCLUSION

La question essentielle liée à l'acquisition de l'expérience urbaine est celle de l'emprise potentielle sur la ville à travers le projet considéré au sens large, c'est-à-dire théorique et matériel à la fois. Le préalable de tout projet urbain réside en effet dans l'approfondis sement de l'expérience urbaine propre. Ici, la mémoire personnelle rejoint incidemment l'implication socio-professionnelle au point d'en devenir indissociable. Par ailleurs, l'assujettissement vécu à travers la prise en charge d'un rôle social dans la ville familière de rési dence ne saurait évacuer l'aspiration au sentiment de liberté éprouvé dans une ville de passage : l'évocation de celle-ci contribue à recen trer l'attention sur celui-là. Aussi un effort de topoanalyse (au sens de l'introspection des lieux vécus, telle qu'elle est préconisée par   G. Bachelard) peut-il contribuer à illustrer l'expérience urbaine en   structurant ses composantes sans tomber dans le réductionisme. La poétique de la ville trouve ainsi une raison d'être dans son rappro chement de l'analyse objective du milieu urbain.

Note

(1) L'allemand fait ici une différence que d'autres langues ne font pas (dergleiche / derselbe)

References

Barbey G., Giuliani M.V. (1993) 'Autobiographical Reports of Resid ential Experience: An Exploratory Study' in Housing: Design, Research, Education, M. Bulos & N. Teymur, eds., Ethnoscape, Avebury, Aldershot UK, p. 81.

Cantafora A. (1993) voir à ce propos ses travaux, en particulier 'Città come casa' in Archimade, Lausanne, sept. 1993, no 41, p. 18.

Kierkegaard S. (1843/1990) La reprise, Copenhague, 1843, trad. fran çaise : GF Flammarion, 1990, p. 19.

Proshansky H. (1976) Le concept de "place identity" est approfondi en particulier par l'auteur in 'Environmental Psychology and the Real   World' in American Psychologist no 31, pp. 303-310.

Sime J. (1985) Creating places or designing spaces: the nature of place affiliation, in Place and Placemaking, K. Dovey et al., editors.   Proceedings of the PAPER 85 Conference, Melbourne, Juin 19-22, 1985.

15

Environmental psychology in the PsycLit database (1987-1992)

Psychologie de l'environnement-analyse bibliométrique

Maria Montero y Lopez Lena and Alejandro Muniz Campos

Une étude utilisant l'approche bibliométrique a été réalisée sur le développement conceptuel et méthodologique de la psychologie de l'environnement et les différents niveaux de son application.

On a décrit les données recueillies en analysant 1293 articles, couvrant la période janvier 1983-décembre 1992 et obtenus grâce à la banque de données Psychlit.

Les variables étudiées sont a) le type de publication, b) le pays et l'institution, c) l'auteur et d) les mots clé.

Les résultats sont discutés en tenant compte de la méthode bibliométrique et de ses limites.

Mots clé:Psychologie de l'environnement, analyse bibliometrique

Key words: Environmental Psychology, Bibliometric Analysis

Analyzing information produced within the field of Environmental Psychology may prove a difficult task, especially if the rapid development characterizing the field is taken into consideration. The 1991 reprinting of The Handbook of Environmental Psychology just four years after the first edition, can be seen as the most recent evidence of the current impact of this type of information.

Dr. Stokols's 1978 review of Environmental Psychology stands out among several attempts to provide an overview of the proliferation of literature in this field. Dr. Stokols's reported that more than thirty monographs, ten textbooks and two series on the interaction of human behavior with the socio-physical context had been published within a five-year period. In fact, it is in Dr. Stokols's review that the greatest number of references to Environmental Psychology, (497) can be found.

By means of a retrospective analysis of the development of Environmental

Psychology, four main stages can be distinguished:

1) Gestation, from the late fourties to the late fifties. Specialists in closely related disciplines to Psychology, such as Human Geography or Sociology, "started to examine lay conceptions and evaluations of physical surroundings". (Canter, 1981, p.2).

2) Emergence, as a potentially specific area within Psychology. This happened during the late fifties and early sixties, when the field was given a new name: Architectural Psychology.

3) Recognition, from the late sixties to the early seventies. The field was incorporated into the APA as a formal Division, (number 34) with an entry known as "Population and Environmental Psychology". This period was characterized by the publication of Environment and Behavior, one of the most representative journals in the field, and the establishment of the Environmental Design Research Association.

4) Consolidation, during the seventies and eighties. The growth of Environmental Psychology became evident. There was a boom in publications, both in specialized texts on conceptual (Stokols & Altman, 1987/1991; Freimer & Geller, 1983; Kaplan S.& Kaplan R., 1973; Kaplan R & Kaplan S., 1989; Altman, 1975), and methodological topics (Betchel, R. Marans, R., Michelson W.,1987).

The number of articles on different environmental topics published in the United States, Europe, Asia and Latin America is remarkable. However, there is still a lack of knowledge on systematic information patterns produced in Environmental Psychology in spite of the latter's rapid and continued growth. The most representative periodical publications, schools and institutions are practically unknown outside traditionally leading countries in the field such as the United States, England and Germany. There is a clear need to discover scientific production patterns that can consistently be found in the literature produced within Environmental Psychology; that is, the main purpose of this study.

METHOD

In order to achieve the above-mentioned aim, a bibliometric analysis was carried out. According to Garfield and colleagues, (1978), "Bibliometrics may be defined as the quantification of bibliographical information capable of being analyzed" (p.180). For this study, references classified within the field of Environmental Psychology in the PsycLit Data-Base, covering the period from January 1983 to December 1992, were analyzed.

One thousand two hundred and ninety-three entries were retrieved from

the PsycLit Data-Base and the following variables were analyzed: a) journal type, b) country and institution, c) author, and d) key words. All entries included under Environmental and Applied Psychology were retrieved according to the APA subject classification (Thesaurus, 1991).
Data for this section were selected and classified into three groups:

1) Specialized journals on Environmental Psychology, where at least one concept concerning the environment or architectural design, whether or not combined with a behavioral concept, was included in the title.

2) Psychology journals including titles covering both applied and basic psychology topics

3) Non-specialist journals whose titles did not clearly specify any key concepts (e.g. environment, behavior or architectural design), or aspects of psychology.

RESULTS.

a) Analysis by journals and papers
Of the 320,668 entries in the PsycLit Data-Base, from January 1983 to December 1992, 303 were journal titles concerned with Environmental Psychology, while 1321 were the titles of papers on the subject.

PsycLit
Papers on Environmental Psychology (1983-1992)

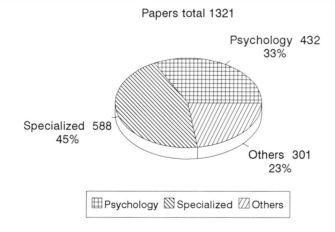

Figure 15.1 Papers on environmental psychology (1983–1992).

Of the 303 journal titles, 172 (56.76%) belonged to publications that regularly included psychological topics, 18 (5.94%) belonged to specialist journals, while 113, (37.29%) belonged to journals that did not specialize in either psychological or environmental issues.

As shown in figure 15.1, out of the total number of entries or papers in the field of Environmental Psychology, (n=1321), 32% (n=432) were published in General Psychology Journals, 45% (n=588) were published in specialist journals while 23% (n=301) were published in non-specialist periodicals.

Environment & Behavior Journal with 174 papers, is the leading specialist publication as can be seen in figure 15.2. This is followed by the Journal of Environmental Psychology, with 127 articles since its publication in 1981. EDRA Proceedings is the third most important, with 59 articles, (50% fewer than the previous journal) specializing in the psycho-environmental field. Publications with moderate frequencies include the Journal of Architectural and Planning Research (n=49), Human Behavior and Environment Advances in Theory Research (n=38) and Journal of Environmental Education (n=32), followed by Man-Environment Systems and Aviation Space and Environmental Medicine with frequencies of 27 and 25 respectively.

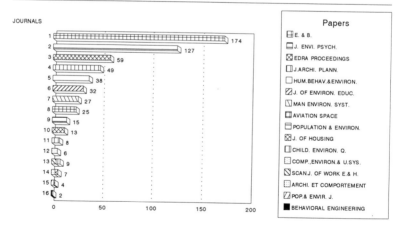

Figure 15.2 Paper frequency distribution of specialised journals.

Finally, the following journals, given in descending order, have publishing frequencies of fewer than 20; Population and Environment, Behavioral and Social Issues, (n=15), Journal of Housing for the Elderly (n=13), Children's Environment Quarterly (n=8), Computers, Environment and Urban Systems (n=6), Scandinavian Journal of Work Environment and Health (n=4), Population and Environment Journal of Interdisciplinary Studies and Architecture et Comportement (n=3) and Behavioral Engineering, Urban Studies, and Ecological Psychology with just one article.

Psychology journals that occasionally accept environmental papers with more than 10 entries include Perceptual and Motor Skills (n=43), Journal of Applied Social Psychology (n=23), Journal of Economic Psychology (n=19), American Psychologist (n=18), Psychological Reports (n=12) as well as Journal of Social Psychology (n=11). Finally, there are only three non-specialist publications with a frequency of over 10; Leisure Sciences (n=34). Risk Analysis (n=18) and Journal of Social Issues (n=11) and Ergonomics (n=10).

Countries by number of publications for their University and Institutions

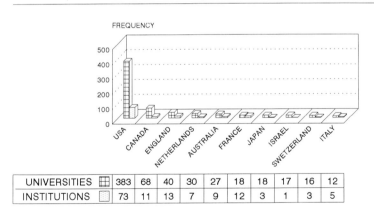

		USA	CANADA	ENGLAND	NETHERLANDS	AUSTRALIA	FRANCE	JAPAN	ISRAEL	SWETZERLAND	ITALY
UNIVERSITIES		383	68	40	30	27	18	18	17	16	12
INSTITUTIONS		73	11	13	7	9	12	3	1	3	5

Figure 15.3   Countries by number of publications for their University and Institutions.

b) Analysis by country and institution
Of the 1321 entries retrived, 837 were published in USA, while 484 were published in the other 41 countries inclued in the sample. figure 15.3 shows the ten countries with the highest frequency of publications in this field. The same graphic shows that Environmental Psychology research takes place more often in universities. The USA's bar represents only the ten most productive states of the Union. California is the leading state in the number of studies produced, followed by New York, Texas, Illinois and Michigan. (figure 15.3).

c) Analysis by author
This section only considers first authors. The majority, (842) have only published one article as first authors, while only 21 researchers have published four or more articles.
d) Analysis by key word.
In this section, it was decided to reduce the number of entries even further. The 1321 original entries were arranged according to a second classification code and 399 of these were eliminated, since they were already cross-referenced to another code besides Environmental Psychology and related topics. Finally, 922 specialist entries for this area were obtained. Key words were arranged in order of range of occurrence, with frequencies obtained for each key word identified.

Key Words Ocurring more than fifty times

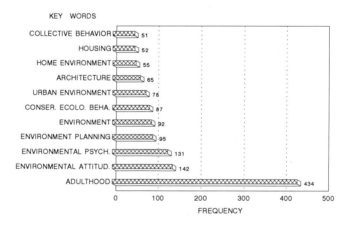

Figure 15.4 Words occurring more than fifty times.

Figure 15.4 shows key words occurring more than fifty times. It should be mentioned that the total number of key words retrieved from the 922 entries was 692.

DISCUSSION.

One of the advantages of Bibliometric analysis is that it gives an overview of scientific production within a specific field published in journals. It also provides an opportunity to observe the direction that a particular field is taking. In other words, it yields scientific indicators describing the necessary changes that a field of study undergoes over time.

The importance of studying the relationship between human behavior and a natural or man-made environment is ratified by the above analysis. In the eighteen years since it was recognized by the American Psychological Association, Environmental Psychology has provided almost 0.4% of all papers published within the field of psychology over the past nine years.

While this can be seen as an attempt to consolidate the area, it also opens up the possibility of analyzing key concepts more in depth. A case in point is the term "environment," that needs to be defined more precisely. It is very clear from reading the Environment and Behavior and Behavior and the Man-Environment Systems Journal that the two do not agree on the definition of "environment". While the former is characterized by greate remphasis on social aspects and architectural design, the latter is more concerned with computerized systems that optimize man's cognitive functions. Obviously, both journals focus on the relationship between environment and behavior, but on different levels of integration, i.e macro (social) versus micro (neural) environment. Work must be done on this delimitation of the central concept of environment to provide conceptual taxonomies to facilitate the systematic study of the "environment" at different levels of integration. Studies by Stokols (1985,1991) and Garling and Evans (1992) are examples of valuable attempts to define the concept of "environment" in both a cognitive sense and in terms of application.

The analysis by countries and institutions confirmed the United States' leading position in promoting Environmental Psychology. It is interesting to note the repercussions that this field has had in both European countries, such as England and the Netherlands, and Middle and Far Eastern countries, such as Israel and Japan, and even as far away as Australia.

This proves the degree of interest in helping to consolidate knowledge in the area, but also highlights the need to encourage more research in Latin American countries, where environmental problems, such as air and water pollution in Mexico, are reaching dangerous proportions.

One way of increasing psycho-environmental research in Latin America would be to carry out crosscultural studies. As well as solving specific regional problems in the area where they are carried out, these studies could also provide evidence to increase the validity of propositions that have already proved useful. They could even suggest new alternatives to solve, control or even prevent new environmental problems.

As for results of the analysis by author, the contrast between the number of researchers with just one publication as first authors and those belonging to the small group of researchers with more than four publications as first authors is easily understood. It points to the stage of development that the field is currently experiencing. Several of those who published a single article may still be looking for their particular line of research, while those with more publications may be working to construct their own theories within this area. In another study, it would be interesting to use the bibliometric approach to explore the lines of conceptual influence and "invisible schools" (Pol, 1988) that develop around prolific writers.

Finally, as regards the analysis by key word, there is a lack of conceptual criteria to enable one to derive semantic networks with hierarchies of inclusion and standards for the definition of concepts. The variety of terms associated with the area points to the complexity of the factors it covers, (physical, social, psychological and architectural) on the one hand, but also to the lack of conventional definitions based on already proven theories or principles.It is remarkable that the most frequently-occurring key word, adulthood, is not exclusive to the area. It also shows the need for more research with other age cohorts, since children and the elderly are known to perceive their surroundings differently.

Given the proliferation of knowledge involving different disciplines, there is a need not only to promote interdisciplinary training but also to formalize a standardized language to act as a support for both the "transduction" (Barker, 1968) of behavioral patterns to architectural design patterns and vice versa, and also the creation of a conceptual base to enable findings from specialist literature to be integrated in a structured way. It is suggested that once they have been standardized, traditional Environmental Psychology concepts should be incorporated into the American Psychology Association's Thesaurus. Alternatively, a special thesaurus for this field could be compiled to help with the standardized handling of information.

Finally, it is also suggested that more bibliometric studies on Environmental Psychology should be systematically produced. This will provide an objective and sensitive resource for transformations that will occur in this field. This proposal implies not only regarding bibliometric research as an effective tool for scientific evaluation, but also a useful resource for:a) proposing specific research to deal with hitherto unstudied aspects of a particular subject, b) establishing areas or schools of influence, whose concepts and methodology are adopted and, c) proposing new lines of research that respond to both social demands and the theoretical maturity achieved within a certain area.

References

Altman, I.(1975). The Environment and Social Behavior. Monterey, CA: Brooks/Cole.
    American Psychological Association (1991). PsycINFO Database (CD-PsycLIT).
    Norwood, MA: Silver Platter Information, Inc.
Barker, R. (1968). Ecological Psychology. Stanford: Stanford University Press.
Bechtel, R., Marans, R, Michelson, W. (Eds.) (1987). Methods in Environmental and
    Behavioral Research.New York: Van Nostrand Reinhold Co.
Canter, D., Craik, K. (1981). Environmental Psychology. Journal of Environmental
    Psychology, 1, 1-11.
Freimer, N. R., Geller, E.S. (Ed.) (1983). Environmental Psychology: Directions and
    Perspectives. New York: Praeger.
Garfield, E. Malin, M. V. and Small, H. (1978). Citation data as science indicators. In
    Y. Elkama, et al. Tow and a metric of science. New York: Wiley.
Kaplan, S., Kaplan R. (1973). Cognition and Environment. New York:Praeger.
Kaplan, R., Kaplan S. (1989). The Experience of Nature: A Psychological Perspective. New
    York: Cambridge Univ. Press.
Garling, T., Evans, G. W. (Ed) (1991). Enviroment Cognition and Action. An
    Integrated Approach. New York: Oxford University Press.
Pol, E. (1988) La Psicologia Ambiental en Europa. Analysis Sociohistorico. Barcelo,
    Espana: Anthropos Stokols, D. (1978). Environmental Psychology. Annual Riview
    of Psychology. 29:253-295.
Walker, A. Jr. (Ed.) (1991). Tesaurus of psychological index terms. Arlington, Virginia:
    American Psychological Association.

Part Two

USER NEEDS AND EVALUATION

16

Introduction

Susan J. Neary

La deuxième partie de la conférence section donne une interprétation de l'expérience urbaine en se plaçant du point de vue des usagers; elle contient une réflexion sur leurs besoins, met en lumière leurs perceptions et évalue divers aspects de l'expérience urbaine passée et présente. Plusieurs chapitres sont consacrés à l'évaluation des interventions en milieu urbain et des politiques de la ville, et discutent des méthodologies permettant une meilleure compréhension des forces en jeu dans la reconfiguration des villes.

Les auteurs se réfèrent à des études de cas réalisées en Bulgarie, en Italie, aux Pays-Bas, en Suède, en Turquie, aux Etats-Unis et au Royaume-Uni. Certaines communications se concentrent sur des questions locales spécifiques liées à une situation nationale, politique ou ethnique particulière, alors que d'autres traitent du phénomène urbain tel qu'on le retrouve de manière universelle.

L'exploration de la satisfaction des usagers semble poser autant de questions qu'elle n'en résout. S'il limite le champ de ses investigations, le chercheur peut dans une certaine mesure comprendre une question spécifique; toutefois, les personnes dont il suscite l'opinion sur cette question l'entraînent souvent dans d'autres directions, qui ne font pas partie du projet de recherche, mais qu'elles jugent plus importantes. Si la satisfaction des usagers peut être mesurée, l'insatisfaction d'un plus grand nombre se fait également entendre.

The second part of the conference interprets the urban experience from the point of view of the user, reflects on their needs, throws light on their perceptions and evaluates various aspects of the urban experience past and present. It also includes a number of chapters which deal with the evaluation of urban interventions and policies and discuss methodologies for increasing understanding of the forces at work in reshaping cities.

The authors cite examples and case studies from Bulgaria, Italy, the Netherlands, Sweden, Turkey, the United States, and the United Kingdom.

Whilst the focus of some of these papers is location specific and relates to particular national, political and racial differences, others deal with more unive rsally recognisable urban phenomena.

Investigating user satisfaction seems to leave unanswered as many questions as it seeks to answer. In focusing research on a narrow area the researcher has the possibility of gaining some insight into a specific topic, but respondents as well as voicing their opinions on that topic, point to other areas of their experience, not under investigation, which they perceive to be even more important. User satisfaction may be measured but dissatisfaction of a wider environment is also clearly heard.

The theme of "User needs and evaluation" is introduced by Vernez Moudon who discusses the responses of residents to their environment. She questions the importance they give to the physical aspects of the built and 'natural' environment, their reactions to design complexity and scale of features in the residential landscape. The relationship between the physical environment of the residential neighbourhood and its occupants is seen to be deeper and more complex than many designers, developers and planners choose to recognize. This criticism of the professionals is a theme which is referred to again by many of the authors who voice a consistent lack of confidence in the role played by professionals in the urban experience. There is a considerable amount of consistency between Vernez-Moudon's findings and those of other authors who focus on each of these aspects of evaluation in detail in different countries and from the viewpoints of different user groups.

Urban home ownership is studied by Rae in relationship to New York City Co-ops. She examines why and how the co-ops came about and identifies the criteria for their success, which is as much about control and security as it is about the physical improvement of housing conditions. Some co-op owners had even changed how they felt about where they lived in a positive way. Rae suggests that research on other forms of tenure such as limited -equity should be researched not only in terms of economic but also psychological factors to understand how they are experienced by people.

Jackson leaves us with a rear view window analysis of city planning in Harlem as he experienced it in the sixties. He was involved in a community action programme as Model Cities Planner. From a distance he is able to explore his role as he saw it then, and to reflect on the other forces at work at the time. He gives us an insight into the overt and hidden agendas being played out in Harlem and reflects on lessons observed but maybe not learnt. Other contributors continue the theme of inquiring into some of the many forces at work facilitating and shaping our cities. Each considers regeneration at a different level in the urban structure - the neighbourhood, the city and the region and each considers evaluation from different viewpoints.

Each holds up a different mirror to the their reality of the city, property development, residents, local and national government. Of necessity each specific social group can voice their needs and evaluate strategies for urban regeneration, but it is difficult to imagine strategies which can satisfy all of their needs or indeed who may be most appropriate to carry out the evaluation.

At the neighbourhood level, Ulusoy proposes a methodology for the study of urban rehabilitation based on property rehabilitation. His paper is based on the premise that 'rehabilitation is significant for neighbourhood change, and its interaction with other measures of change is crucial in understanding the process' He goes on to identify four types of rehabilitation scenario with goals of a)upgrading the property for the incumbent, b)renovation of the property for a new clientele/to collect higher rents, c) make the building match the need of new owner-occupiers/ gentrification and d) profit oriented renovation/ speculation. The methodology aims to disentangle the intricate network of interactions and interpret conflicting indicators of change in neighbourhoods

Cebulla gives details of a survey of the residents assessment of urban change and the economics of city centre regeneration in Belfast. He outlines the special features of that city and describes the interventions which have been used to encourage city centre regeneration. The residents views are then used to evaluate the success of these interventions. Of the lessons learnt in the city centre, most importantly the 'statement' of confidence by a major public sector player, is seen as a pre-requisite to urban regeneration on the periphery of the city.

At a regional level Wong investigates the quality of urban living, using as the basis of case studies the nine TEC areas in North West England. She identifies a "wish list" of infrastructural factors. The infrastructural categories considered are social and cultural, housing/property, industrial structure, knowledge/information, scenery/image transport/communication, utilities, waste/pollution management and the institutional context. From these thirteen indicators are defined and used to measure infrastructural resources. Wong then interprets the data in terms of the quality of life and urban experience in the cities included in the study area.

Two very specific examples of urban change, the forces at work, and the diversity of objectives for change are given by Troeva and Aydin-Wheater. Troeva examines the changing urban values of Bulgarian cities. She states very clearly the changing public and professional awareness and confronts some of the problems of changing from a planned to a market economy. She puts the case for planning, for 'proper urban values, which are basic to the self-realisation of the urban population', the need for regulation and the need for planners to win back the confidence of society and the prestige of their profession. By contrast Aydin-Wheater describes in some depth the plans for regenerating the lost green of Ankara from 1932 until the present. She identifies intrinsic problems in each of the proposals which appear to make it impossible to achieve the stated objectives, even if the plans had been realised. As each new plan is put forward objectives shift and change, but the author constantly questions the outcome. Plainly she feels that there is a hard if not insurmountable task ahead to recreate green in Ankara.

In both these chapters the process of planning and the knowledge and skills of those involved is questioned and confidence in the professional is low.

Alternative ways forward are discussed in relation to urban landscape by Rivlin and Coeterieré. Open places in cities are explored by Rivlin, who examines how public life is lived in those spaces. She identifies the essential qualities of public life as a reflection of the diversity of society, freedom of choice - the ability to exercise public space rights as a member of society. However, these bring with them the necessity to negotiate the rights and freedom of others and to overcome conflicts which will/may occur. The author questions the public space policies of the nineties and asks if they are meeting the needs of urban dwellers. She advocates the use of the participatory model as offering the most promising possibilities for stimulating healthy public lives and the spaces in which to experience them.

Coeterier, using as case studies two cities in the Netherlands, investigates the external conditions for creating liveliness in town centres. Not unexpectedly, there is some overlap between his results and those of Rivlin. He finds that diversity is a most important factor - diversity of people, of functions and of urban detail in buildings and public spaces. He also identifies the need for accessibility and some degree of management and regulation, these last two acting as dissatisfiers or necessary conditions for the use of the spaces. Coeteriere argues that since 'people experience their environment at a scale of 1:1, and not 1:100,000' they have a sharp eye for details, which is far more important to them than the 'clear spatial structure' beloved of the urban planners. Again a criticism of the professional is voiced and questions of what scale of environmental features are most important leave avenues for further research.

The three chapters which examine public space indicate where the answers to some of these questions may be found. In the outcomes of these studies the authors mention different age groups having different perceptions difference by gender etc. They also indicate that context is also important as it colours the value given to specific features.

Meanings and attitudes towards urban green have been studied in some detail by Bonnes. She explores the meaning attached to the urban green from both socio-centred and person-centred perspectives. From the socio-centred perspective the problem of the urban green is considered as strictly connected to the responsibility of planning and management of the environment. From the person-centred perspective the different attitudes towards the man-nature relationship depend upon the characteristics of gender, age, residence, geographical positions and level of education.

Public space is considered by Lieberg as one focus of the appropriation of the city by teenagers. He examines the use of public space by groups of teenagers in Sweden over a three year period, and identifies and defines various types of use of specific spaces in the city. He concludes that teenagers need a variety of different types of space with different spatial and social characteristics. He sees teenagers as 'one of the most important actors in the public space' and goes on to indicate other aspects of the 'dangerous/fun city' as subjects for further discussion of the urban experience.

The concept of place is discussed by Bonaiuto in terms of the relation to other places and sub-places, using as examples the two Italian cities of Rome and Lecce. Inhabitants living there were asked to state how often they performed a series of activities in each the three sub-places considered: neighbourhood, centre and periphery. The resulting analysis of the inter-place activities defines actions which are seen as relating to integration - activities with positive orientation, high specificity, high mobility and high social interchange, and those which are seen as relating to confinement - activities with negative orientation, low specificity, low mobility and low social interchange. Features of the findings specific to the small city include the tendency of the inhabitants to have a more integrated urban experience between different places, for example, home and neighbourhood and to feel less 'urban isolation' especially among the social groups more at risk: older and younger people.

Nakamura looks not only at the public space but at the urban landscape as a whole and investigates the relationship between classification of urban space and overall evaluation. A classification of urban landscapes was built up by asking interviewees to classify photographs of urban landscapes. The differences between the factors that people consider when evaluating the desirability of urban landscapes of each category was compared to those in their association level with overall evaluation. Although the major evaluative constructs varied for the three types of streets investigated, office street, housing street and shopping street, when analyzed along the two axes of "composure and unity" and "cheerfulness and excitement" the influences exerted by these evaluative constructs on the evaluation of the urban landscape were considered not to vary with the type of street.

Asking users about their environment brings not only detailed information in response but triggers reactions about their concerns in other aspects of their lives. Evaluation of the environment remains a rich source of data for analysis and debate.

17

Reading the residential landscape

Lectures de paysages domestiques par les habitants

Ann Moudon and Marion Ryan

Cette recherche concerne l'attitude des habitants envers la complexité du paysage construit en réponse aux tendances récentes sur l'homogénéité du cadre résidentiel. On a choisi trois quartiers ayant une base socio-économique semblable mais des environnements physiques différents, et on les a classés selon leur complexité. On a fait parler les habitants sur leur entourage alors qu'ils suivaient un parcours préétabli à travers le quartier. L'analyse du contenu des 55 "discours" montre des thèmes qui reviennent souvent, mais aussi des commentaires variés, et leurs relations avec les paysages urbains traversés. Les "discours" comportaient relativement peu de thèmes ou de concepts. Les caractéristiques du paysage et de la végétation revenaient dans la plupart des quartiers, suivies de peu par l'esthétique des logements et de l'utilisation des terrains. Il est important de noter que la majorité des commentaires sur le thème de l'utilisation des terrains se rapportait aux attributs esthétiques de facilités prévues pour des groupes de familles. La complexité des plans, la circulation et l'entretien sont ensuite les thèmes les plus fréquemment mentionnés. La complexité des plans était, pour le quartier le plus complexe, le troisième thème le plus souvent mentionné. Ce thème est revenu plus souvent dans le quartier le moins complexe que dans celui à complexité moyenne. La complexité était liée d'une manière positive au nombre total de commentaires faits par les habitants de chaque quartier.
Les résultats confirment les recherches passées et montrent l'importance du paysage et de la végétation dans la perception et l'expérience du cadre urbain. L'expérience esthétique et la complexité des plans sont également des facteurs structurant les relations entre les individus et leur entourage. Ces résultats ont des implications importantes pour la planification des quartiers.

Mots clé: paysages construits; complexité; esthétique; attitude des habitants.

Keywords: Built Landscape, Complexity, Aesthetics, Residents' Attitudes

Are people aware of physical complexity in their environment? How do they perceive it and how important is it to them? These questions became the focus of a research project conducted at the University of Washington. In broad terms, the object of the research was to assess the attitudes and concerns of a sample of local residents toward physical complexity in their local neighborhoods. This paper presents an overview of the results of this research.

The research was prompted by a growing concern that new suburban residential developments tend to provide a limited number of design options. The contemporary trend in new suburban residential design is toward strong stylistic themes: house types and styles adhere closely to a limited range that all too often mask a developer's preference for simple and easily reproducible built forms. In defense of this approach, adherence to stylistic theme results in physical homogeneity, a sense of neighborhood identity and resident control. Furthermore, the use of restrictive covenants used in many new residential environments has ensured the continuance of initial design control into the long-term, and has effectively reduced the ability of home owners to adapt or alter their properties. Developers argue that home owners prefer less rather than more design complexity in the environment because they fear that individual manipulation of color, form, material, landscaping, etc., threaten the identity of the neighborhood and eventually lower property values. They believe, in short, that preference for regularity and order in residential landscapes is a strong motivation for purchase and occupation, one which leads to high levels of occupant satisfaction (Winkel 1982).

The intention of the research project was to examine the validity of these underlying assumptions and to ascertain the extent to which new developments reflect the preferences and requirements of the contemporary housing market.

Indeed, the very success and popularity of older, established residential neighborhoods in American cities appears to challenge the validity of the above assumptions, as these frequently are neighborhoods that reflect high degrees of complexity created by sustained personalization and adaptation over time. Many such areas thrive across the nation and raise the question of what particular physical qualities are sought by suburban families in their search for personal and family satisfaction. How important, in fact, is the element of physical complexity to residents of neighborhood areas? To understand the relative importance of this one element to residents, it became clear that the research would have to address all elements of the built landscape that were considered important to residents, and then to examine the role, if any, of complexity within this broader list. The research process was designed to facilitate an understanding of which aspects of the built landscape drew attention and elicited responses from a sample of residents in several residential neighborhoods.

THE CONCEPT OF DESIGN COMPLEXITY

The concern of the research team was with the role and relative importance of the element of complexity in an environment. The focus was on complexity within the physical environment, as distinct from social, ethnic or economic complexities of the residents within it. "pecific findings of the relative importance of physical complexity to the subjects are discussed in "Residents' Attitudes Toward Design Complexity" (Moudon and Ryan in progress).

Complexity within the physical environment has to do with the relative order found in the elements that comprise it (Bosselmann and Craik 1985). Where little or no order is evident, an environment is perceived as chaotic and irregular. The opposite condition is one of total control and uniformity of components. Most actual environments lie between these two extremes, reflecting different degrees of complexity. The physical manifestation of complexity occurs as a function of both the initial level of complexity built into the neighborhood by the original designers, and the complexity gained organically over time as residents modify their surroundings in response to new needs and circumstances. Both forms of complexity needed to be considered and were the basis for choosing the areas to be studied, as is discussed in more detail later in this paper.

The task of defining complexity within two or more physical environments was made possible through an examination of the material component of the built landscape. A typomorphological model (Moudon 1988), defining elements such as streets and blocks, types of buildings and open spaces, patterns of land subdivision, etc., enabled clear distinctions to be drawn between the levels of complexity exhibited by the chosen case study environments. Variety in the sizes of the elements (e.g. lot size, building size, etc.) as well as variety in the detailed treatment of the material dimension of these elements establish different levels of complexity. Higher levels of complexity are found where elements are small and their material dimension (both mineral and vegetal) is finely detailed. Hence one expedient way to define complexity is to distinguish between "fine- and coarse-grained" environments, indicating high and low levels of complexity, respectively. Grain is therefore a proxy for the distribution of different types and sizes of elements.

THE RESEARCH DESIGN

The choice of research design involved an extensive examination of various options available. The model chosen to guide the research was the psycho-social model of environment:behavior which assumes an interactive relationship between human behavior and the quality and composition of the physical environment (Canter 1977). Given that the concern was with resident's attitudes toward complexity in the design of the built environment, two broad elements are evident in the structure of the research approach: the place and its occupants. A clear definition of potential causality between the two was required, so as to evaluate how components of place affected and were perceived by occupants.

The research design needed to be one that would enable the collection and comparison of residents' attitudes and responses to different levels of complexity - as initially built into the environment or as acquired over time. The method chosen to ascertain resident opinion was one of observation and recording of spontaneous comments rather than a structured survey or predetermined interview. The approach used in "Walk Around the Block" (Lynch and Rivkin 1957, Hardie 1989) was the model on which the study was based. Subjects were accompanied by members of the research team on a twenty- to forty-minute walk along a chosen and constant route within each neighborhood. Their comments and observations were recorded and later incorporated into the information base for the neighborhoods studied.

From the outset it was considered critical that observations made by the residents should not be solicited by the researchers, because their value lay in originating from the residents in direct response to physical elements within the neighborhoods. Researchers were at pains to maintain neutrality in their conversations with the residents and to avoid leading the discussion or influencing the residents concerns in any way. The neighborhood walks had several advantages. One of the most important was that they allowed the subjects to discuss any aspect of the physical environment freely and without the constraints of a structured questionnaire. In this way, preconceptions on the part of the research team as to what may or may not be important to the residents were circumvented.

The use of a walk, rather than exposure to any environment-simulating techniques also ensured that the residents were exposed to the multiple elements of the neighborhood which constitute total experience (Nasar 1988). Photographs can only show single perspectives of a place at any one time, and their selection may reflect a bias or preference on the part of the research team itself. Further, the use of photographs would have thus invalidated much of the value of the responses obtained since photographs remove the effect of movement in the experience of space.

Places: The Choice of Case Studies

The team was interested in assessing differences in the perception of the built landscape by people whose local built landscapes reflected different degrees of

LEGEND: KEY TO BUILDING TYPES

Farm/Pioneer		40's, 50's, 60's House	
Bungalow		Seattle Box	
Colonial		Apartment	
Tudor		Other	

Figure 17.1 Plan of Wallingford building types.

micro-scale complexity - reflecting differences in scale, grain and content (Lynch and Rivkin 1957). Three case studies were selected according to the amount of complexity that each displayed: Wallingford exhibiting the highest level, Upland Green the lowest, and Haller Lake an intermediate level of complexity. Differences in background, status, culture or income-level of the residents were controlled in that the areas selected displayed similar mixes of occupants, offering primarily single-family accommodations for predominantly middle-class families. Market values of housing units in all three areas are similar.

The areas differ from each other in two aspects of complexity. First, the characteristic physical environment or the morphological make-up represents in each case different development histories; one neighborhood dates from the 1920's, one from the 1950's and the third from the 1970's. Dominant house types and architectural styles vary substantially from area to area, reflecting the architectural traditions and tastes of each era. Size of lots vary: the smallest being found in Wallingford and the largest in Haller Lake (Moudon 1992). In addition to differences in the major structuring elements of each neighborhood, the age differences of the three neighborhoods have allowed different degrees of physical changes to occur over the life span of each. Thus, varying degrees of complexity (mostly the consequence of personal adaptations by owners and occupants) are apparent in the fine grain of the built form within each case study area.

Figure 17.2 Wallingford bungalows, 1920s.

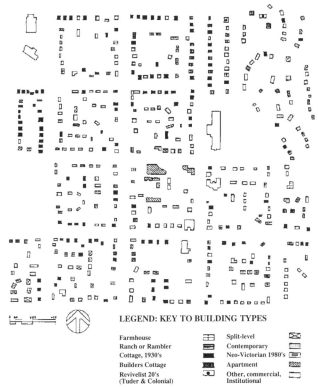

LEGEND: KEY TO BUILDING TYPES

Farmhouse		Split-level	
Ranch or Rambler		Contemporary	
Cottage, 1930's		Neo-Victorian 1980's	
Builders Cottage		Apartment	
Revivelist 20's (Tuder & Colonial)		Other, commercial, Institutional	

Figure 17.3 Plan of Haller lake building types.

Figure 17.4 Haller Lake split-level house, 1960s.

Wallingford is a neighborhood of fine-grained development, and displays a high degree of detail and complexity of elements - both built and -natural at the micro-scale. It was platted (as a 250 x 350-foot grid with streets 60 to 70 feet wide) at the turn of the century and developed in the 1920's by different owners and builders.

Lots are fairly small, typically 40 to 60 feet wide by 100 feet deep. The "California bungalow" house type prevails with 60 percent of the properties within this category (figures 17.1, 17.2). Churches, small convenience stores and apartment buildings are present in small numbers, scattered throughout the area. The general landscape is dominated by detached houses and individual, decorative gardens. The area has adapted to the changing needs and preferences of its population over time, and many design details and finishes have been replaced or altered (Heasley 1986). A proportion of the original single-family houses have been renovated and subdivided as duplexes which have provided accommodation for an aging population and an influx of rental occupants.

Haller Lake This medium-grained neighborhood was platted in the 1930's as a 600- by 600-foot grid. This was gradually broken into smaller blocks and lots, which now tend to be larger than in Wallingford, averaging about 60 feet in width by 150 feet in depth. Most of the original 120 x 300-foot lots have been subdivided, providing a complexity in lot size throughout the neighborhood. A variety of building types - including farmhouses and 1920's styled houses, but dominated by Ranch and Split-Level - is evidence of the fact that houses have tended to be the product of single owners or builders (figures 17.3, 17.4). Once again, evidence of cosmetic and some structural changes to the original buildings is apparent today.

Upland Green is an area of coarse-grained development with a low degree of complexity of component elements at the micro-scale. It was developed in the 1970's as a model affordable community. The area was designed in full, and was developed in entirety by a single developer. The neighborhood is completely residential, with no local commercial or institutional facilities. Lot sizes are typically 40 feet by 100 feet, and houses include single-family detached structures, as well as a number of plexes of various size and configuration (figures 17.5, 17.6).

Although a range of types is evident in the design of the houses, the use of similar construction materials, details, and colors (further controlled with the use of covenants) has created a sense of uniformity which is maintained today.

LEGEND: KEY TO BUILDING TYPES

Single Family
Du-plex
Four-plex
Apartment
Other, commercial,
Institutional

Figure 17.5   Plan of Upland Green building types.

Figure 17.6   Shawnee village garden apartments 1980s.

Occupants: The Choice of a Sample

Letters inviting residents to participate in the study were sent to householders in the three study areas. A total of 55 residents completed the walk. Their general distribution and characteristics are listed in table 17.1.

Two criteria were defined prior to the recruitment of respondents. First, respondents were to be residents of the area. It was decided that the most valuable research would represent people who belonged and related to the neighborhood, because one's perception of a neighborhood is invariably "colored" by emotional attachments and memory. Second, however, respondents should not live immediately adjacent to the study route itself , in order to avoid an excessive amount of emotional association or territoriality influencing the responses.

Respondents were thus required to have a general familiarity with the neighborhood, rather than the specific familiarity associated with living in one of the houses along the route. Within these two requirements, respondents were selected randomly by a sight-unseen invitation to local residents - this invitation outlined the purpose of the study, described the proposed use of the neighborhood walk, and noted that respondents would be free to discuss any of the sights and sounds along the way.

	Wallingford	Haller Lake	Upland Green
No. Subjects	18	18	19
No. Female	11	12	13
Average Age	39.6	45.9	36.9
Renters	9	1	7
Ave. Residence	7.0	13.5	2.9

Table 17.1: Characteristics of Research Respondents

	Wallingford	Haller Lake	Upland Green
Length (linear feet) (3,640 ft average)	4070 (111.81% of ave.)	4170 (114.56% of ave.)	2680 (73.63% of ave.)
Time (minutes)	25 - 35	30	20 - 25
No. of buildings.	120	72	73
No. of lin.ft per bldg	33.9	57.9	36.7
No. of dwellings	NA	NA	99

Table 17.2: Characteristics of Each Route

Selection of Routes

A number of criteria guided the selection of the routes along which the walks were to be conducted. First, routes were to be of similar length, so that the time of exposure to the environment in each case would be approximately equal. This meant, however, that the number of buildings adjacent to the route varied because of the different lot sizes in each neighborhood. As a compromise, the length of routes in Wallingford and Haller Lake are similar, but the number of properties in Wallingford substantially higher due to the higher density of the area. Haller Lake and Upland Green, in contrast, have the same number of buildings along their routes but the length of the route in Upland Green is approximately one third-shorter than in Haller Lake. The repetitious nature of buildings in the former neighborhood, however, can justify this difference.

Second, each route was also carefully selected so as to include representative groups of building types, land-use pattern, as well as architectural styles (see figures 17.1 to 17.6). These groups reflect the typical conditions of each neighborhood.

THE RESEARCH PROCESS

Data Collection

Volunteer respondents in all three areas were accompanied on a walk, averaging eight blocks in length. They were instructed to relay their impressions of the environment and to point out the elements that they noticed, liked, or disliked, or were significant to them in any way. No questions were asked by the researchers, so that each commentary was made only in response to the landscape.

All observations were tape-recorded, and were later transcribed exactly as they had been made. No changes were made to either content or grammar. These transcripts formed the raw information of the research. They were then processed and analyzed with the using a factor analysis method and categorizing gross information according to dominant subject areas or issues (factors) that had been raised repeatedly. In this more manageable form, the information could be interpreted, and the three neighborhoods compared with each other.

194

Data Analysis

Three areas of specific information were considered; first, the distribution of comments by theme; second, the scale at which comments were directed, and third, the evaluative quality of the comments (whether these comments were positive, negative, or neutral). Each of these aspects, and their relative importance, are discussed in more detail below.

The Subject Matter of Comments: Themes

Comments and observations made by each of the subjects were analyzed by applying the principles of factor analysis selecting key concepts used by the respondents (Babbie 1989). Recurring concepts were grouped into categories of themes, to which discrete comments and observations were allocated. This task was complicated by the heterogeneity in the subject's perceptions, their evaluation of places, and the difficulties in expressing complex ideas and opinions in simple conversation . Comments encompassed such topics as general neighborhood characteristics, concrete attributes of specific physical elements, spatial features, and functional characteristics. Under closer examination, however, several recurrent themes ran through the comments in all three areas; seven such themes were identified and their relative significance was ascertained through an evaluation of the frequency of comments with which they had been raised.

The seven most common themes identified in the analysis included the following:

1 Design Complexity, which encompassed comments relating to differences or similarities in the environment, themselves identified through the use of such words as "variety, sameness, uniformity, conformance, difference, uniqueness, fit/non-fit," etc.
2 House Aesthetics, which grouped comments related to the specifics of individual homes along the route. This set of comments tended to be substantive and indicative of fairly strong personal preferences. 3. Landscape and Vegetation, the subject of many comments which also reflected strong personal preferences.
4 Land-Use, which included comments about the introduction of non-residential uses in the (primarily) residential fabric. Multi-family buildings, new developments, and increases in density were part of this theme.
5 Upkeep and Maintenance.
6 Traffic and Parking.

The comments which did not fit into any of the above themes fell into the following categories:

Miscellaneous comments related to diverse, often non-physical features of the neighborhood, such as children, views, community organizations, etc. Unclassified comments were unrelated to the physical landscape or the general characteristics of any of the three areas - mostly portraying personal histories or attitudes of the individual respondents.

Relative Scale at Which Comments Were Directed

The individual observations were directed at one of three broad categories of scale. There were comments about particular properties (including house and yard), about streets (the public space between properties), and about the neighborhood in general. As they walked and talked, respondents indicated a clear awareness and understanding of the different scales in the landscape and of their relationship with personal concerns.

Several reasons underlie the importance of the scale at which comments were directed. First, personal interactions with an environment comprise experiencing elements at a wide range of scales. Second, because planning intervention itself is scale-specific, an examination of residents' attention toward scale relates to professional concerns. The team wanted to assess the degree to which people were focused (or specific) in experiencing and describing their environments, particularly so that complexity was expected to be perceived at the smaller scales of the built landscape.

Level of Evaluation

Once the range and distribution of comments had been assessed, it was possible to examine the qualitative nature of individual comments within each theme. It was considered important to ascertain which elements had been responsible for the most positive or negative comments.

GENERAL FINDINGS

The number of comments made in each neighborhood, the scales at which these comments were addressed, and the evaluative contents of the comments constitute the general set of research findings.

Number of Comments

In absolute numbers, Wallingford residents showed the strongest response to their environment - they have the highest scores in the total number of comments, in the average number of comments per subject, and in the frequency of comments. Adjusting the figures for the different lengths of the routes and the number of subjects, however, responses in Wallingford and Upland Green gain a similar intensity, with Haller Lake trailing behind. These adjusted figures indicate that variations in the number of comments made in each neighborhood are limited and therefore do not lead to strong conclusions except to the extent that residents had a substantial number of "things" be related to the density of development and to the frequency of buildings along the route - see table 17.2. These figures support the theory of buildings as important stimuli in the behavior:environment model (Appleyard 1969, Heath 1988). Finally, the figures also appear to relate to the relative complexity of the built landscape insofar as the most and least complex environments generate significantly more responses than the environment of medium complexity.

	Wallingford	Haller Lake	Upland Green	Totals
Number of Comments	592	470	398	1,460
	(529)	(410)	(512)	(1,451)
Percent Total Comments	40.5	32.2	27.3	100
	(36.5)	(28.3)	(35.3)	(100)
Number of Subjects	18	18	19	55
Ave. Number of Comments/Subject	32.9	26.1	20.9	26.3
	(29.4)	(22.8)	(28.4)	(26.9)
Frequency of Comments by Subject**	123.7	159.8	128.2	137.2**

* Absolute numbers. Numbers in parenthesis are adjusted for the different lengths of the routes and the different numbers of respondents.

** In linear feet (Total length of walk/total number of comments/number of subjects).

*** Walking speeds vary between 180 and 270 feet per minute. On average, respondents talked for the duration of the walk.

Table 17.3: Number of Comments per Area and Subject*

Further caution is necessary to interpret the relative intensity of comments in the three neighborhoods without regard for the nature of the individual comments. For example, while the average number of comments per building along the route is similar in Wallingford and Upland Green, the majority of comments in Upland Green are directed not at the individual building but at the neighborhood in general. It is therefore appropriate to focus the analysis of comments on the different themes under which the comments are made and to concentrate on the relative distribution of these comments by neighborhood.

Dominant Themes

The distribution of comments by major themes is discussed below. Some comments belonged to more than one theme, resulting in higher totals of comments by thematic content than there were actual comments.

	Wallingford		Haller Lake		Upland Green		Totals	
	Total	%	Total	%	Total	%	Total	%
Design Complexity	102	17.2	36	7.7	40	10.1	178	12.2
	(91)		(31)		(51)		(173)	(11.9)
House Aesthetics	198	33.4	74	15.7	45	11.3	317	21.7
	(177)		(65)		(58)		(300)	(20.7)
Landscape and	145	24.5	106	22.6	135	33.9	386	26.4
Vegetation	(130)		(93)		(173)		(396)	(27.3)
Upkeep	72	12.2	60	12.8	51	12.8	183	12.5
	(64)		(52)		(65)		(181)	(12.3)
Traffic and Parking	57	9.6	68	14.5	58	14.6	183	12.5
	(51)		(59)		(75)		(185)	(12.7)
Land Use	93	15.7	113	24.0	134	33.8	340	23.3
	(83)		(99)		(172)		(354)	(24.4)
Miscellaneous	45	7.6	34	7.2	62	15.6	141	9.7
	(40)		(30)		(80)		(150)	(10.3)
Unclassified	25	4.2	40	8.5	15	3.8	80	5.5
	(22)		(35)		(19)		(76)	(5.2)
TOTALS	737	124.5	541	115.1	540	135.7	1,738	119.4
	(658)		(464)		(693)		(1,815)	(124.8)

* Absolute numbers. Numbers in parenthesis are adjusted for the different lengths of the routes and the different numbers of respondents.

Table 17.4: Distribution of Comments Per Theme*

Although some themes appeared to be more important than others, one important finding was the common distribution of all of the themes in the three neighborhoods. The team concluded that these six elements - landscape and vegetation, house aesthetics, complexity, traffic, upkeep and maintenance, and land use - represent a short list of themes which would appear to be common concerns in all of the neighborhoods studied. A preliminary conclusion of the research is that these themes may be valid as generic concerns regarding the built landscape which are common to all neighborhood residents.

The predominance of themes for each neighborhood reflected interesting overlaps as well as deviations. Landscape and vegetation emerged as a common and important theme in all three areas, indicating a high awareness of the natural component of the environment, and its general appearance, in all respondents. This concern with appearance was also evident in the high incidence of comments regarding house aesthetics in Wallingford and Haller Lake. Here, too, the theme of complexity was high. In Upland Green, on the other hand, a high number of comments regarding land use and miscellaneous points to a general concern directed at the scale of the neighborhood as a whole, rather than at the individual elements within it. This focus of interest, general in Upland Green, more specific in Haller Lake and Wallingford, was reiterated by an analysis of the scale at which comments were directed in all three areas.

As a general observation, it was felt that the relative importance of the themes related to three specific and important elements of the behavior:environment model: the aesthetic quality of the neighborhood (appearance), comfort of and convenience to the residents themselves, and the degree of interest that the presence of physical features elicited. The relative dominance of the themes of landscape and vegetation and house aesthetics in Wallingford and Haller Lake corroborates past research in behavior: environment (Ulrich 1986). Further, however, the relative frequency of comments regarding complexity may be considered the result of the level of interest which each neighborhood generates. In Upland Green, where the focus on land use was high, the concern appears to be more with the degree of comfort and convenience. Similarly, the significance of and upkeep and traffic in Haller Lake may have been a consequence of the level of convenience and comfort that these elements would facilitate in a neighborhood in which the street and vehicle played important roles.

In all three areas, the incidence of miscellaneous and unclassified comments was notable: approximately 12 percent in Wallingford, 16 percent and Haller Lake and 19 percent in Upland Green. That these occurred in all three areas led the team to the conclusion that all of the subjects perceived the built landscape to be more than the aggregate of physical parts, and that non-physical elements such as community organizations, children, etc., were significant and perhaps even integral to their response to the physical environment. In addition, the fact that the residents of Upland Green made significantly more of this type of comments than those of Wallingford is believed to be a function of the lower degree of physical complexity in Upland Green, which caused residents to respond with fewer specific comments, and thus to incorporate elements such as those categorized as miscellaneous and unclassified.

Scales

Analyzing the predominance of scale-specific comments and observations in each of the three study areas allowed the research team to extract an understanding of which scale had most impact on the residents perceptions. Results of this analysis are summarized in table 17.5.

	Wallingford		Haller Lake		Upland Green		TOTALS	
	Total	%	Total	%	Total	%	Total	%
Property-directed Comments	376	**63.5**	234	**49.8**	76	19.1	686	47
Street-directed Comments	48	8.1	141	30.0	45	11.3	234	16
Neighborhood-scale Comments	168	28.4	95	20.2	277	**69.6**	540	37
TOTAL	592	100	470	100	398	100	1460	100

Table 17.5: Distribution of Comments Directed at Properties, Street or Neighborhood Level.

From these figures it was possible to calculate the average number of property-related comments per building along the route. Results were as follows: 3.1 comments per property in Wallingford, 3.3 comments in Haller Lake and only 1.0 comments per property in Upland Green (adjusted figures are similar at 2.8 comments per building in both Wallingford and Haller Lake, and 1.3 in Upland Green). Hence approximately three times as many comments were made about the more complex buildings in Wallingford and Haller Lake than about the homogenous buildings found throughout Upland Green. Further, twice as many of the total number of property-related comments were made on atypical buildings as on buildings that were commonly found in the neighborhoods. The implications of this finding on residents' responses to complexity will be elaborated on later. For now, however, it explains why Upland Green residents had less comments about properties in their neighborhood since Upland Green buildings are all of the same style and differ only in terms of the building footprint and of the number of dwellings contained in one structure.

Most comments in Upland Green were general rather than property-specific. Of the three areas, then, Upland Green generates the least attention to specific details, with most comments raised by residents of this neighborhood directed at the neighborhood level.

Comparing the relative physical complexity of the built landscapes of the three areas and the dominant scale of the comments raised in each one, an unsurprising, though still speculative, relationship may be seen between environmental complexity and comment specificity. As a preliminary observation - one which conforms to many of the presumptions of the stimulus:response theory of environmental psychology (Heath 1988) - higher degrees of complexity in an environment elicit site and detail-specific comments from observers, while less complex environments generate fewer specific comments, and more observations about the neighborhood as a whole.

Evaluative Contents

Most specific - both positive and negative - comments were directed to the scale of the individual property, while descriptive - and essentially -neutral comments were usually directed to the neighborhood level. Personal opinions regarding preferences were thus largely given in response to specific elements at the micro-scale. More general comments with fewer personal biases tended to reflect neighborhood qualities or characteristics at the macro-scale. In areas which offered a large array of specific, noteworthy elements (Wallingford and Haller Lake) comments reflected a greater degree of evaluation than mere description.

Generally, perceptions of the built landscape can be expressed (and therefore measured) more precisely and more richly at the smaller scales of the environment than at the large scale. Conversely, small scale elements in the built landscape elicit more specific and qualitatively defined reactions from people than elements at the large scale.

FINDINGS RELATED TO THEMES

The following is a discussion of findings related to comments associated with each one of the themes. The analysis includes the distribution of comments by neighborhood, the scales at which the comments were made, and the characteristics of the comments themselves.

	Wallingford		Haller Lake		Upland Green	
	Total	%	Total	%	Total	%
Property-directed Comments	92	63.4	58	50.9	22	16.3
Street-directed Comments	26	17.9	38	32.1	42	31.1
Neighborhood-scale Comments	27	18.6	19	17.0	71	52.6
TOTAL	145	100	115	100	135	100

Table 17.6 Scale of Comments Regarding Landscape and Vegetation

	Wallingford		Haller Lake		Upland Green	
	Total	%	Total	%	Total	%
Property-directed Comments	178	89.9	67	90.5	32	71.1
Street-directed Comments	9	4.5	5	6.8	2	4.4
Neighborhood-scale Comments	11	5.5	2	2.7	11	24.4
TOTAL	198	100	74	100	45	100

Table 17.7: Scale of Comments Regarding House Aesthetics

Comments Regarding Landscape and Vegetation

Residents in all three neighborhoods addressed more than 22 percent of their comments to the landscape features along the route. Landscaping and vegetation were discussed primarily at the level of the property in Wallingford and at the level of the neighborhood in Upland Green (table 17.6). In all three areas, however, landscaping details of the street along which the walks were conducted were considered important.

The range of comments made was extensive. Individual elements such as trees, plants and lawns as well as observations about maintenance, seasonal variations, etc., were recorded. In Wallingford, the emphasis was on individual yards, and specific design elements or maintenance problems within them. Respondents also clearly related landscape and vegetation to the overall appearance of the individual house.

In Haller Lake, subjects commented most frequently on trees and the general greenery of the neighborhood. The environment was perceived to be more of "natural" than in Wallingford, where it had distinctly been considered a "man-made" element. Although there was less attention paid to individual yards or gardens in Haller Lake, many comments addressed the issue of garden maintenance, showing distaste for yards that had been neglected. Residents were especially positive about the landscaping of a particular school along the route.

In Upland Green most comments addressed landscaping at the level of the neighborhood, focusing largely, and mainly in positive terms, on the common green space and trails. A number of respondents suggested improvements to the open space system, the erection of picnic tables, more trees etc. Overall, in all three areas, awareness of the vegetation as an integral part of the streetscape was high.

Comments Regarding House Aesthetics

The number of comments related to this theme was greatest in Wallingford and smallest in Upland Green. As expected, and in all areas, most of these comments were made at the scale of the house, even in Upland Green (table 17.7).

Opinions were directed to three aspects of the house: those that referred to the house as a whole: those that highlighted particular design features such as colors, windows, etc., and those that indicated a general responses. In all three areas most comments raised about house aesthetics were specific (table 17.8).

One interesting observation regarding this table is that the "specific" comments (including elements such as house style, color, presence of porches, construction materials, windows and doors, ornamentation etc.) made about house aesthetics in Upland Green reflects exactly the percent of property-related comments in this theme for this area (table 17.7). In contrast, comments in Wallingford and Haller Lake show greater variation, and specifically lower degrees of "specific" comments than may have been expected by the high property-directed comments for these areas.

Style and color appeared to be important to residents in all three areas. Interestingly, comments regarding style were almost uniformly positive in Wallingford and Haller Lake, whereas comments regarding color were primarily negative. The reverse situation was true in Upland Green. The high degree of awareness of color as an element in the physical environment has drawn the attention of the research team to the fact that further research into this specific element is necessary. Clearly, however, is that observations about house aesthetics were richest and more diverse where the built landscape reflected the greatest number and variety of elements.

Comments Regarding Design Complexity

Wallingford elicited many more direct references to design complexity than the two other neighborhoods; 17.2 percent of all comments in Wallingford related to this theme, with lower figures of 7.7 percent and 10.1 percent in Haller Lake and Upland Green, respectively. While the fairly high incidence of comments regarding complexity in Wallingford confirmed the research assumption of the team, the incidence of this theme in Upland Green was far higher than anticipated.

Related to complexity, the concept of relative appropriateness of elements was raised in discussions of the relative RfitS and Rnon-fitS of features. They suggested that residents understood the presence or absence of complexity to be an underlying theme in the neighborhoodUs physical character. In Wallingford, where it existed at the smallest scale of development, complexity of elements was understood to be a contributory factor in the overall character of the neighborhood. In Upland Green, on the other hand, the lack of small-scale complexity was acknowledged as an equally important component of the neighborhood character, in that its absence became a feature in itself. Hence, the scale at which comments regarding complexity were made in the three areas points to the significant difference between complexity comments from Wallingford residents, and those from Upland Green residents (table 17.9). In Wallingford, complexity comments dominated at the scale of the individual property with 77 percent of these comments, while comments addressing the neighborhood represented only 12.6 percent. The opposite situation existed in Upland Green, where property-specific comments measured only 35 percent against a 45 percent total of comments directed to the neighborhood scale.

This suggests that awareness of complexity as a contributory factor in neighborhood structure is evident among all neighborhood residents. When complexity is present, it is referred to at the scale of the property, where it is most noticeable. And the absence of complexity is noted at the scale of the neighborhood at large.

As far as the content of the complexity comments was concerned, a mixture of positive and negative comments added to the interpretation of the information. Property-related comments on complexity were primarily positive - in Wallingford, 42 percent positive, 31 percent negative, and 28 percent descriptive; in Haller Lake, 50 percent positive, 36.4 percent negative, and 13.6 percent neutral; and in Upland Green, 40 percent positive, 40 percent negative, and 20 percent neutral. The positive nature of these comments is especially significant that most addressed properties that were atypical - a finding suggesting that physically complex neighborhoods are indeed attractive.

	Wallingford		Haller Lake		Upland Green	
	Total	%	Total	%	Total	%
Specific Comments	116	58.6	42	56.8	32	71.1
General Comments	67	33.8	26	35.1	10	22.2
Other Comments	15	7.6	6	8.1	3	6.6
TOTAL	198	100	74	100	45	100

Table 17. 8: Relative Specificity of Comments Related to House Aesthetics

	Wallingford		Haller Lake		Upland Green	
	Total	%	Total	%	Total	%
Property-directed Comments	77	75.5	22	61.1	14	35.0
Street-directed Comments	12	11.8	7	19.4	8	20.0
Neighborhood-scale Comments	13	12.6	7	19.4	18	45.0
TOTAL	102	100	36	100	40	100

Table 17.9: Scale of Comments Regarding Complexity

With regard to comments on complexity at the street and neighborhood scales, Wallingford displayed 56 percent positive, 36 percent negative, and 8 percent neutral comments; Haller Lake, 42.9 percent positive and negative comments, and 14.3 percent neutral; and Upland Green, 38.5 percent positive, 26.9 percent negative, and 34.6 percent neutral. These figures indicate a higher level of satisfaction with environmental complexity in Wallingford than in Upland Green.

Comments Regarding Land Uses

The issue of mixing different land-uses was a common concern to residents of all three areas, especially in Upland Green and Haller Lake. Various aspects of land use were discussed, including density, mixed use, multi-family developments and open space. From a planning point of view, one of the most interesting conclusions arose from discussions of mixing single-family dwellings with multi-family units, as all three study areas included a selection of such buildings along the route - 12 in Wallingford, 3 in Haller Lake, and 16 in Upland Green. Most comments suggested less of a general distaste for the mixing of uses than for the aesthetic qualities of some of the multi-family buildings themselves. The significantly lower number of comments on land use in Wallingford where most multi-family structures are older and hence better detailed than modern plexes in Upland Green reinforced this finding.

Other land uses that raised comments included churches: of these, 75 percent were either positive or descriptive. In Haller Lake, where the walk by-passed six commercial properties, 48 comments were directed at these specific sites, totaling more than 40 percent of land-use-related comments (and 10 percent of all comments) made in the area. Interestingly, more than 60 percent of these comments were positive: respondents indicated an appreciation for the convenience of these neighborhood businesses, which included a daycare, a dentists office, and an old public school converted into a private junior-high and high school. Also significant was the fact that these commercial properties raised more interest than the multi-family properties in the area.

Comments Regarding Upkeep and Maintenance

This theme appeared to be important in all three case studies, with equal emphasis in each. It drew 12.2 percent of the comments in Wallingford and 12.8 percent in both Haller Lake and Upland Green.

Comments about upkeep did not fall as easily into the three scales established earlier. Rather, they related most often to individual properties. In

Wallingford, the majority of the comments related to specific features of the houses and individual yards. In Upland Green and Haller Lake, comments were more general,. and few comments directed at the neighborhood level were raised by residents of these two areas. The upkeep of streets, alleys, and open spaces appeared to be of greater concern to residents in Haller Lake and Upland Green.

Generally, at least half of the comments were positive in all three case studies. The amount of detail included within the comments themselves differed significant between neighborhoods. In Wallingford, respondents were highly descriptive, addressing specific features that appeared well-kept or unkempt. Comments in Haller Lake and Upland Green tended to be far less specific, perhaps as a result of the comparatively coarser grain of these neighborhoods.

Comments Regarding Traffic and Parking

Automobile and pedestrian traffic, parking and noise were addressed fairly frequently by respondents in all three areas, though to a slightly lower degree (9.6 percent of total comments) in Wallingford than in Haller Lake or Upland Green (14.5 percent and 14.6 percent respectively). It is interesting to note the higher incidence of these comments in Upland Green, the "planned" neighborhood, where streets are strictly internal to the neighborhood, and hence not useful to outsiders, and where streets and parking are largely controlled by the community. In Wallingford, on the other hand, where streets are narrower and overall gross density higher than in Upland Green, this theme raised less interest.

Traffic and parking issues were broken down into the following categories: automobile traffic, street and intersection design, parking, pedestrian traffic and sidewalks, noise, and access to public transportation. Except for the element of parking, which was generally property-specific, comments in this theme were most commonly addressed to the scales of the street or the neighborhood.

In Wallingford, parking shortages, especially given the small garages built prior to World War II, noise from small aircraft landing at nearby Lake Union, and the need for sidewalk repair were elements frequently mentioned. In Haller Lake, lack of sidewalks (this was a common source of complaint), noise and safety issues related to the freeway nearby, and the several arterials in the vicinity were important. In Upland Green, topics included the worsening of the parking problem as the neighborhood matured, the fact that local streets were unsafe for children and the lack of sidewalks (although this was not perceived to be as much of a problem as in Haller Lake).

Miscellaneous Comments

Frequently raised comments regarding non-physical aspects of the neighborhoods included: children, especially in Upland Green where concerns were raised about safety in the other two areas, the absence of children was noted; views, with positive comments made in Wallingford and to a lesser degree, in Haller Lake; community associations; a number of Upland Green respondents made mention of their "Homeowners Association" and the governing covenants that this body regulated (2.8 percent of the total comments fell within this topic in Upland Green, but very few comments of this nature were raised in Wallingford or Haller Lake.

INTERPRETIVE SUMMARY

This research highlights people's perceptions of the important aspects of their residential landscape. The research was designed to determine how residents respond to different neighborhood morphological structures, and specifically, to different levels of design complexity.

What residents talked about as they walked through their neighborhoods was organized through analysis in sets of discreet comments, each focusing on one specific concept or theme. The total number of comments generated in each neighborhood appeared to relate to the morphological make up of the environments studied in that it was commensurate with the number of properties or structures along the route taken by the respondents. A close correspondence appeared to exist between the frequency of large elements in the landscape and the frequency of comments made.

Buildings with rich architectural composition and detailing stimulated many more comments than homogeneous ones. Similarly, atypical structures generated significantly more responses than the ones that were commonly found in the neighborhoods.

Residents talked primarily of elements at the scale of the property or the buildings in the neighborhood exhibiting design complexity, and at the scale of the general neighborhood in the least complex study area. Further, residents' responses were more specific and defined at the small scale than at the large scale of the built landscape: comments were less descriptive and more opinionated at the former than at the latter scale.

Comments and observations collected showed that neighborhood residents do have common interests, attitudes, and concerns. These emerged as six recurring themes present in all of the interviews: landscape and vegetation, house aesthetics, land use, design complexity, upkeep and maintenance, and traffic and parking. Different themes dominated in the different neighborhoods indicating that residents are keenly attuned to the character of their surroundings and that different built landscapes generate different responses which are shared by the residents. Comments   made under the six themes included the following:

Landscape and vegetation grouped the highest number of comments in all three neighborhoods studied. The prvations that people discuss in describing their neighborhood's physical setting. Variations in the degrees of relative importance of these themes allowed us to draw some preliminary conclusions about resident perceptions of the built landscape and the element of complexity within it.

The themes most commonly mentioned in all three neighborhoods were "landscape and vegetation" and "house aesthetics." Surprisingly, themes that are now central in neighborhood planning such as "traffic" and "upkeep and maintenance" appeared to be of relatively low importance to the respondents. Only "land use," a common concern in neighborhood planning, was emphasized and mentioned consistently. Ironically, the only planned neighborhood, Upland Green, yielded the lion's share of comments on land use. Further, however, residents appeared to be less concerned about mixing uses than about the appearance of uses other than the dominating single-family residences. They liked the convenience of nearby stores and the "quaintness" of old apartment buildings. They disliked not the small, but the large new apartment buildings.

The findings beg for a re-examination of the focus of the planning profession in addressing the provision and satisfaction of common themes. Contrary to the findings of this research, land-use and traffic have long been considered suitable concepts to be tackled by planners, while house aesthetics has been considered almost exclusively the domain of the individual architect, builder or developer. Landscaping of new developments is controlled, homogeneous, and low in aesthetic variation.   Greater congruence between resident opinion and the roles and attitudes of the planning profession seems to be needed. Planners need to focus more on small-scale appearance and content of built landscapes.

Residents appeared keenly attuned to the character of their neighborhoods, responding readily to the different grains of the built landscapes. Respondents apparently reflected both the need and the ability to seek out satisfaction from their environments. Where complexity was present, residents appeared to appreciate the richness of experience that it offers. Where it was lacking, however, as in many new residential areas across the nation, residents appeared to compensate for its absence by an appreciation - at some level - of the harmony and order generated as a result. This study did not facilitate a relative evaluation of which of the two situations was "better" or "worse," but it did show that complexity is not only an important consideration in environment:behavior relationships, but also a structuring one in the way people perceive their environments.

The research highlighted certain areas in which further investigation is essential. First, the notion of a relationship between the level of complexity within an environment and the level of satisfaction and the residents' attachment to place should be researched further. The importance of landscape and vegetation features to neighborhood residents must now be integrated into the ways that planners and designers conceive and shape urban areas, with an emphasis on the specific design elements and to include such features as color, detailing and adaptations. Possible impacts of gender, age and income status on response patterns and preferences should also be investigated further.

CONCLUSION

This research initially focused on the element of physical complexity within the built landscape - its presence, absence and the residentUs awareness of it. However, the format and method used to collect the data yielded an expanded list of themes which emerged as common interests and concerns in all of the neighborhoods studied. These themes may be viewed as a basic cluster of ideas, thoughts, and observations that people discuss in describing their neighborhood's physical setting. Variations in the degrees of relative importance of these themes allowed us to draw some preliminary conclusions about resident perceptions of the built landscape and the element of complexity within it.

The themes most commonly mentioned in all three neighborhoods were "landscape and vegetation" and "house aesthetics". Surprisingly, themes that are now central in neighborhood planning such as "traffic" and "upkeep and maintenance" appeared to be of relatively low importance to the respondents. Only Rland use," a common concern in neighborhood planning, was emphasized and mentioned consistently. Ironically, the only planned neighborhood, Upland Green, yielded the lion's share of comments on land use. Further, however, residents appeared to be less concerned about mixing uses than about the appearance of uses other than the dominating single-family residences. They liked the convenience of nearby stores and the "quaintness" of old apartment buildings. They disliked not the small, but the large new apartment buildings.

The findings beg for a re-examination of the focus of the planning profession in addressing the provision and satisfaction of common themes. Contrary to the findings of this research, land-use and traffic have long been considered suitable concepts to be tackled by planners, while house aesthetics has been considered almost exclusively the domain of the individual architect, builder or developer. Landscaping of new developments is controlled, homogeneous, and low in aesthetic variation. Greater congruence between resident opinion and the roles and attitudes of the planning profession seems to be needed. Planners need to focus more on small-scale appearance and content of built landscapes.

Residents appeared keenly attuned to the character of their neighborhoods, responding readily to the different grains of the built landscapes. Respondents apparently reflected both the need and the ability to seek out satisfaction from their environments. Where complexity was present, residents appeared to appreciate the richness of experience that it offers. Where it was lacking, however, as in many new residential areas across the nation, residents appeared to compensate for its absence by an appreciation - at some level - of the harmony and order generated as a result. This study did not facilitate a relative evaluation of which of the two situations was "better" or "worse", but it did show that complexity is not only an important consideration in environment:behavior relationships, but also a structuring one in the way people perceive their environments.

The research highlighted certain areas in which further investigation is essential. First, the notion of a relationship between the level of complexity within an environment and the level of satisfaction and the residentsU attachment to place should be researched further. The importance of landscape and vegetation features to neighborhood residents must now be integrated into the ways that planners and designers conceive and shape urban areas, with an emphasis on the specific design elements and to include such features as color, detailing and adaptations. Possible impacts of gender, age and income status on response patterns and preferences should also be investigated further.

Footnotes

"Environment," "physical environment," "residential landscape," "built landscape" are used interchangeably to describe all the physical and formal elements which constitute neighborhoods, including "man-made" as well as "natural" features. "Built environment" generally connotes a focus on elements that are built, in opposition to "landscape" which suggests elements that are grown. These distinctions are only partially useful since most physical elements in a neighborhood are designed by people and form an interdependent system of things which define "place." Hence it can be argued that in the residential context, either "built environment" or "landscape" include elements that are built as well as those that are grown.

The research was funded in part by the National Endowment for the Arts, Design Arts Program, a Federal Agency. The project's co-principal investigators were Drs. Anne Vernez Moudon and Judith Heerwagen. Two additional papers are being developed based on this research to discuss in greater detail the residents' attitudes toward landscape and vegetation and design complexity (Moudon and Ryan in progress). Lynch introduced the term "grain" to refer primarily to the mix of different uses in the environment (Lynch 1981). In this research, land use mix is obviously less of a significant factor for defining grain than are building types, lot size, and material treatment. The concept of grain also relates to Rapoport's theory of "noticeable differences" (Rapoport 1982).

A distinction is made between structures or buildings and properties. Properties related to lots and ownership structure, while buildings describe discreet structures. In single-family detached areas, the number of properties coincides with the number of buildings, while in areas of duplexes or triplexes each building contains several dwellings which may be owned individually or collectively.

Initial responses were categorized in terms of the subject matter that they addressed. Early attempts to define categories with the use of key words only gave way to the use of key concepts or themes which the subjects were discussing. Themes were identified from the verbatim transcripts as sets of comments made recurrently by the respondents. Comments were defined groups of words or sentences made under a particular concept or theme. Some comments related to more than one themes and were therefore counted as appropriate.

For a more comprehensive analysis and discussion of this theme, refer to "Residents' Attitudes Toward Landscape and Landscaping"(Moudon and Ryan in progress).

For a more comprehensive analysis and discussion of this theme, refer to "Residents" Attitudes Toward Design Complexity"(Moudon and Ryan in progress).

Bibliography

Appleyard, D. 1969. "Why Buildings Are Known,"Environment and Behavior (December):131-56.

Babbie, E. 1989. The Practice of Social Research.5th ed. New York:Wadsworth Inc.

Bosselman, P. and K. Craik. 1985. "Perceptual Simulations and Environments," in Bechtel, R.B., ed. Behavioral Research Methods in Environmental Design. New York: Van Nostrand.

Canter, D. 1977. The Psychology of Space. New York: St. Martins Press. Hardie, G. ed. 1989. "Changing Paradigms," Proceedings of Annual Conference on Environmental Design. EDRA. School of Design, North Carolina State University.

Heath, T.F. 1988. "Behavioural and Perceptual Aspects of Urban Environments," in Nasar, J. L., ed. Environmental Aesthetics. London:Cambridge University Press.

Heasly, A.E. 1986. "The Front Yard, Wallingford Landscapes, 1937 - 1985." Masters Thesis. Department of Landscape Architecture, University of Washington University, Seattle.

Lynch, K. 1981. A Theory of Good City Form. Cambridge, MA: MIT Press. Lynch, K. and Rivkin, M. (1957). "Walk Around the Block," in Landscape 8, Spring.

Moudon, A. Vernez. 1992 . "The Evolution of Twentieth-Century Residential Forms: An American Case Study," in Whitehand, J.W. R. and Peter J. Larkham, eds.Urban Landscapes: International Perspectives. London: Routledge. Moudon, A. Vernez and M. Ryan. In progress. "Residents' Attitudes Toward Design Complexity, and "Residents' Attitudes Toward Landscape and Landscaping.

Nasar, J. L., ed. 1988. Environmental Aesthetics. London: Cambridge University Press.

Rapoport, A. 1982. The Meaning of the Built Environment. Beverley Hills, CA: Sage Publications.

Ulrich, R.S. (1986). "Human Responses to Vegetation and Landscapes,"Landscape and Urban Planning, 13: 29- 44 Winkel, G.1982. "Perception of Neighborhood Change," in Harvey, J., ed. Cognition, Social Behavior and The Environment. New York: Hillsdale.

18

Urban home ownership: a study of New York city co-ops

Posséder une maison urbaine: une étude des co-ops de la ville de New York

Ruth A. Rae

Tandis qu'à travers les Etats Unis les gens possedent leurs maisons privees, dans la ville de New York, la plupart sont des locataires. L'opportunite de posseder sa propre maison existe toujours, mais traditionellement les habitants de la ville de New York preferent un type de residence mieux conforme a la vie urbaine: une sorte de residence pouvant loger plus d'une famille. Cooperative, ce genre de residence, permet a ces locatiaires de devenir proprietaires. Cette etude examine particulierement cette forme de devenir proprietaire par le cooperative, très courant dans la ville de New York. Deux types de cooperative sont actuallement en vigueur a New York. Le but du premier, la grande majorite, c'est pour le proprietaire original d'un edifice d'offrir a des gens de haut ou de moyen revenus d'assumer la possession de la maison comme proprietaires par là, partager le coût et les frais de l'edifice. Le second type represente des locataires de faibles revenus qui acceptent de prendre en main la direction d'un building abandonné par le proprietaire et de ce fait devenir proprietaries eux-memes par le cooperative et surtout eviter le tracas du délogement. Cette dissertation aura pour principal but d'etudier la phenomene par ou ces gens de faible revenus deviennent proprietaires de cooperative. Tous les recherches, investigations et entrevus centreront sur l'importance et la valeur de ce type de proprietaire. Le focus sera de demontrer comment, devenir proprietaires de cooperatie à un profound effect sur la vie sociale et economique de ces gens. La dissertation essaiera de comprendre les sentiments de ces nouveaux proprietaires et les facteurs psychologiques qui ont influence ces sentiments.

Mots Clé: Residence; proprietaire de maison, proprietaire par le cooperative

Keywords: housing, home ownership, cooperative ownership

It is assumed that given the choice, most people would prefer to own their homes. Home ownership is thought to be the superior form of tenure which provides financial, psychological and societal benefits. It is regarded as a dream all Americans aspire to and should be able to achieve. Home ownership is thought to be a natural desire, and to result in a superior way of life (Borgos, 1986; Duncan, 1982; Kemeny, 1981; Saunders, 1990; Stone, 1986). It is related to people's sense of identity, and important as a symbol of self or status (Agnew, 1982; Cooper, 1976; Dean, 1945; Duncan, 1986; Saegert, 1986; Turner, 1972). A home owned is suppose to offer security, control and independence (Depres, 1989; Gilderbloom & Appelbaum, 1988). Supposedly, given accessibility and adequate resources all households would choose to own (Kemeny, 1981).

Across the United States most people own their homes, while in New York City the majority rent apartments. While ownership opportunity exists in New York City, it is primarily a type better suited to urban areas with a preponderance of multi-unit dwellings. Cooperative ownership is a particularly urban form of ownership found concentrated in New York City. Cooperative ownership is usually created through the conversion of rental housing, and intended to offer home ownership opportunities.

In New York City there are two types of cooperative conversions. The majority are sponsored by the building owner and aim to offer home ownership opportunities to middle and upper income people. Low income tenants also sponsor cooperative conversions, but these are typically a response to landlord abandonment and an attempt to prevent their own displacement.

This paper examines the phenomenon of low income tenant sponsored cooperatives in New York City and reports preliminary results from this author's dissertation research. The research investigated what cooperative home ownership means to low income people, and how it has affected their lives. Its was focus to understand how low income people feel about home ownership, and identify the economic and psychological factors that influenced those feelings.

BACKGROUND

Historically, the favored form of tenure in the U.S. has been the private home ownership of a detached single family home (Johnson, 1982;

Lundqvist, 1986; Snyder, 1971). It is linked both to the democratic ideal of individual ownership of property, and the capitalist principles of private enterprise. Detached homes dominate the housing market and are usually privately owned. The tendency is for single family or detached dwellings to be owned, and for flats or apartments to be rented.

Overall in the United States, sixty-four percent of Americans owned their homes in 1986 (Schwartz, Ferlauto & Hoffman, 1988). New York City, unlike other cities, is primarily a city of renters. As of 1991, seventy percent of the occupied units in New York City were rented and only thirty percent were owned (City of New York, 1993).

Cooperatives have been referred to as a middle ground between owning and renting. They are usually created through the conversion of rental housing, and are intended to offer home ownership opportunities (U.S. Department of Housing and Urban Development, 1980). In the United States, the cooperative form of ownership has not been popular. This is partly because it is usually found in multi-unit apartment buildings which are typically seen as inferior to single family homes. Yet cooperatively owned housing provide an opportunity to achieve home ownership when the private ownership of detached single family homes is not an available option.

Landlord sponsored cooperative conversions resulted in an increase of home ownership in New York City. From 1978 to 1987 the home ownership rate grew from 27 percent to 30 percent (Weitzman, 1989). Yet home ownership rates, consistent with income, vary substantially by race and ethnicity. Consistent with their higher incomes, White and Asian households are more likely to own their homes than Afro-American or Hispanic households. In 1991, 41 percent of all White and 32 percent of all Asians were home owners compared to 23 percent of Afro-American and 25 percent of Hispanic households (Stegman, 1991).

Conversions in metropolitan areas are characterized by a strong market demand for home ownership (U.S. Department of Housing and Urban Development, 1980). Landlord sponsored conversions are motivated by the desire to profit through the sale of apartments, and in part to escape the restrictions of New York City's rent control laws. Tenant sponsored cooperative conversions arise out of difference circumstances with different motivations than landlord sponsored conversions. In the case of landlord sponsored conversions, both the buyer and seller are primarily profit or investment motivated. Tenant sponsored cooperative conversions are usually prompted by the landlord abandonment of rental property which is not economically viable or profitable.

The majority of housing abandonment has been in low income and minority neighborhoods, where it was estimated that 270,000 housing units were lost through abandonment (Sullivan, 1982). When landlords abandon their buildings and no longer provide services, low income tenants often find themselves forced to take control of their buildings in order to keep their homes. The threat of their displacement is intensified by the lack of affordable housing and the possibility of racial discrimination in the housing market (Heskin, 1983; Kolodny, 1973; Sullivan, 1982). Both the fear of losing their homes, and limited housing options have prompted tenant actions to convert previously rental buildings to cooperative ownership (Kolodny, 1973; Sullivan, 1982). In the last 10 years, over 400 buildings were sold in New York City to tenants as low income cooperatives (Saegert & Clark, 1989).

Control, security and attachment to place were found to be psychologically important to low income owners in tenant sponsored cooperative conversions,(Kolodny, 1973: Leavitt & Saegert, 1989; Sullivan, 1983). Residents' control over their living situations was a more important motivating factor in the conversion than ownership per se (Kolodny, 1973; Sullivan, 1982; Zimmer, 1977). In fact, low income people who have rented all their lives can sometimes be reluctant to accept the responsibilities of ownership (Stegman, 1970; Sullivan, 1982; Zimmer, 1977). While pride, satisfaction and feelings of security can grow out of a conversion to cooperative ownership, ownership was seized as a way to preserve people's homes, not because of the belief that ownership in itself is superior than renting (Kolodny, 1973).

RESEARCH DESIGN

This study examined low income cooperative ownership in buildings converted to cooperative ownership by the tenants with the assistance of the Ownership Transfer Program (OTP). OTP is a program of the non-profit Community Service Society of New York. Its purpose is to prevent displacement, preserve housing and promote low income home ownership. OTP assists tenants in purchasing buildings being abandoned by their owners, but before the City of New York forecloses on the properties (Drummond & Shiffman, 1984). As of 1990, the Ownership Transfer Program helped tenants purchase 49 buildings with 1,000 apartments.

In order to understand how low income owners in OTP buildings felt about cooperative ownership, and how it affected their lives, interviews were conducted with 52 cooperative owners in 15 buildings. Since building specific differences could influence how people felt about cooperative ownership, a decision was made to interview a small number of people in a variety of cooperatives, each with their own unique story and internal dynamic, rather than to interview a large number of people in a small number of buildings. From each selected cooperative under 20 units, 3 owners were interviewed, and from each selected cooperative 20 units or greater, 4 owners were interviewed. Cooperative buildings were sampled by size and length of ownership, and only buildings which achieved legal limited-equity cooperative ownership were included. Interviews were conducted with owners who had previously been tenants in the building, and included both Board of Directors and non-Board members.

In-depth personal interviews were conducted with respondents in their homes and took approximately 2 hours each. Although conducting long interviews limited the sample size, this was the most thorough way to investigate the meaning of cooperative ownership. The questionnaire contained both scaled and open ended questions, and the data will be subject to both content and statistical analysis. Analysis of the data will identify differences between individual cooperatives and respondents, as well as compare cooperative size and length of ownership categories.

Topics explored in the interview included the building's cooperative conversion, changes in physical building conditions and maintenance, the cooperative's management practices and structure, and how people experienced and felt about cooperative ownership. Specifically examined were feelings of control, security, responsibility commonly related to cooperative home ownership. Also explored was how cooperative ownership, which involves shared financial responsibility, and limited-equity ownership, which puts a limit on the profit, affected how low income people feel about cooperative ownership.

Since in general buildings had gone through radical physical changes, an exploratory and optional photographic method was included at the end of the interview. To determine if feelings related to becoming home owners were reflected in the perception of their physical environment, residents were asked to take Polaroid photographs of physical changes in the apartment or building they considered important or meaningful. Thirty-three people (55%) took photographs of changes in their apartment or building. Although the content analysis of these photographs has yet to be conducted, many photos were taken of changes in kitchens or bathrooms, or involved the personalization of space.

FINDINGS

Since analysis has just begun, results from the content and statistical analysis of the data is not yet available. Only the summary percentages from the scaled questions are reported below (due to some yet uncoded data, a few percentages do not equal 100). Although clear conclusions cannot be made without complete qualitative and statistical analysis, these preliminary findings begin to depict the experience of low income cooperative home owners.

Of the 52 people interviewed, 73% were women, and 27% were men. Racially, 21% were Afro-American, 29% Hispanic and 50% were White. The average age was 45, but residents interviewed ranged from 23 to 74. Forty-four percent of the respondents were currently employed, while 56% were not. One-half of the respondents had annual incomes of $20,000 or less. Sixty-three percent of those interviewed were currently on the cooperatives's Board of Directors. Respondents tended to be long time residents, for the average tenure in the building was 15 years and 22 years in the neighborhood.

Because of neglect by the building owner, most of the OTP buildings in this study were in poor physical condition before the tenants took over. Building violations were numerous, windows or even walls could be missing, and some tenants reported using umbrellas inside to protect them from leaks. Building conditions at the time of initial occupancy were rated as very poor or poor 52% of the time, with 21% reporting fair conditions and only 17% stating the building was in good or very good condition. Ninety-four percent reported that physical changes were made in their building, and 71% had made physical changes in their apartment. Overall, 77% of the respondents rated general building conditions as having improved, 17% stated they stayed the same and only 4% believed they had worsened. Finally, when asked if ownership made them feel more, the same or less responsible for building maintenance than before they bought, 60% stated they felt more responsibility while 36% felt the same.

When asked about the affordability of their apartments, everyone interviewed believed their monthly housing cost was reasonable. Compared to similar apartments in the neighborhood 65% found it inexpensive while 35% found the cost to be very inexpensive. This was found even though 65% of the respondents experienced a rent increase when the building was converted to cooperative ownership. The average rent had been $164 and the average current monthly cost was now $337.

In general, people were satisfied with their apartments (79%) and buildings (67%) but less so with their neighborhoods (31%). About half of those interviewed reported that ownership changed the way they felt or thought about their apartments (50%) or buildings (56%), while less stated it affected how they felt about their neighborhoods (29%). Of those who reported a change, the majority stated their feelings or thoughts had changed in a positive way in terms of their apartments (92%), their buildings (83%) or neighborhoods (67%).

A comparison was made between feelings of personal control and security while as a tenant and later as a cooperative owner in the same building. Respondents were asked how much they felt a sense of security, in the sense that they wouldn't lose their homes, first as a tenant and then as a cooperative owner. As a tenant, about half of the respondents felt no (40%) or little (17%) security, while as a cooperative owner everyone interviewed felt some (21%) or a lot (79%) of security. When asked how much personal control respondents felt they had over conditions in the building as a tenant over half felt none (42%) or a little control (19%), while as a cooperative owner the majority felt some (39%) or a lot (50%) of personal control.

When questioned as to the type of ownership they preferred more than half (62%) preferred the private ownership of a detached house, yet 38% stated a preference for the cooperative ownership of a apartment. Forty-six percent reported that as a cooperative owner they felt more like an owner, while another 44% felt like something 'in between' an owner and a renter. When asked if owning the apartment had affected their life in any way, the respondents were essentially split in half; 48% said it did while 52% stated it did not. However of those who said ownership had affected their life, 60% said it was in a positive way, 36% said it was mixed and 4% reported the effect was negative.

DISCUSSION

The results of this study, though very preliminary, begin to depict how low income people experience and feel about cooperative ownership. The majority of respondents saw conditions in their buildings improve, and felt that costs were affordable. Residents were satisfied with their apartments and building, and for some ownership had even changed how they felt about where they lived in a positive way. As cooperative owners, respondents felt more control and security in their homes than they had as tenants, and long time residents were not displaced from their homes.

The study validated the perspective that the cooperative ownership of housing is experienced as a 'middle ground' between owning and renting. Almost one-half of the respondents felt that as a cooperative owner they were something 'in between' an owner or renter. This has to do with the fact that cooperative ownership is a more social form of ownership where responsibility and control are shared. It is interesting that, although the cooperative ownership of an apartment does not bring with it the assumed advantages of the private ownership of a detached home, thirty-eight percent of the respondents of this study still preferred it.

Although home ownership assumes a variety of benefits, little is actually known about how people experience it. This research project examined what cooperative ownership means to low income people, and how it has affected their lives. As more alternative forms of tenure are developed in urban areas, they may not have the traditional benefits associated with the private ownership of a detached home. Yet these more shared forms of tenure, such as cooperative ownership, may have additional social benefits that are not found in private ownership. Limited-equity or non-profit cooperative ownership is designed to make housing affordable, yet in doing so removes some of the traditional financial benefits of home ownership. Studies of home ownership must broaden to examine the costs and benefits of alternative forms of tenure. It is important to investigate both the economic and psychological factors that influence how home ownership, in its various forms, is actually experienced and what it means to people.

References

Agnew, J. (1982). Home ownership and identity in capitalist society. In J. S. Duncan (ed.), Housing and identity (pp. 60-97). New York: Holmes and Meier.

Borgos, S. (1986). Low-income homeownership and the ACORN squatters campaign. In R. G. Bratt, C. Hartman, & A. Meyerson (Eds.), Critical perspectives on housing (pp. 428-446). Philadelphia: Temple University Press.

Cooper, C. (1976). The house as symbol of self. In Proshansky, H. M., Ittelson, W. H., & Rivlin, L. G. (eds.), Environmental psychology: people and their physical settings. (pp. 435-449). New York: Holt, Rinehart and Winston (2nd Ed.).

City of New York (1993). Proposed comprehensive housing affordability strategy (draft). New York: City of New York, Department of City Planning.

Dean, J.P. (1945). Home ownership: is it sound ? New York: Harper.

Depres, C. (1989, August). The meaning of home: literature review and directions for future research and theoretical development. Paper presented at The Meaning and Use of Home and Neighborhood, International Housing Symposium, Sweden.

Drummond, A. and Shiffman, Y. (1984). Saving home for the poor: low income tenants can own their own apartments. New York: Community Service Society.

Duncan, N. J. (1982). Home ownership and social theory. In J. S. Duncan (ed.), Housing and identity (pp. 98-133). New York: Holmes and Meier.

Gilderbloom, J. I. & Appelbaum, R. P. (1988). Rethinking rental housing. Philadelphia: Temple University Press.

Heskin, A.D. (1983). Tenants and the American dream. New York: Praeger.

Johnston, J. (1982, May). Home ownership within a national housing policy. Unpublished masters thesis, North Texas State University, Danton, Texas.

Kemeny, J. (1981). The myth of home ownership: private versus public choices in housing tenure. London: Routledge & Kegan.

Kolodny, R., assisted by Marjorie Gellerman. (1973). Self help in the inner city: a study of lower income cooperative housing conversions in New York. New York: United Neighborhood Houses of New York.

Leavitt, J. & Saegert, S. (1984, Summer). Women and abandonment: feminist praxis in housing. Social Policy.

Lundqvist, L. (1986). Housing policy and equality: a comparative study of tenure conversions and their effects. London: Croom Helm.

Saegert, S. & Clark, H. (1989, August). The meaning of home in low-income cooperative housing in New York City. Paper presented at The Meaning and Use of Home and Neighborhood, International Housing Symposium, Sweden.

Saegert, S. (1986). The role of housing in the experience of dwelling. In Altman, J. & Werner, C. (Eds.), Human Behavior and Environment: The Home. New York: Plenum.

Saunders, P. (1990). A nation of home owners. London: Unwin Hyman.

Schwartz, D.C., Ferlauto, R.C. & Hoffman, D.N. (1988). A new housing policy for America: recapturing the American dream. Philadelphia: Temple University.

Snyder, K. L. (1971, September). Ideological views of home ownership. Unpublished dissertation, business administration., University of Eugene, Oregon.

Stegman, M. A. (1970). Home ownership opportunities for the poor. In M.A. Stegman (ed.) Housing and economics: the American dilemma. (pp. 317-325). Cambridge: MIT press.

Stegman, M.A. (1991). Housing and vacancy report: New York City, 1991. New York: City of New York, Department of Housing, Preservation and Development.

Stone, M. E. (1986). Housing and the dynamics of U.S. capitalism. In R. G. Bratt, C. Hartman, & A. Meyerson (Eds.), Critical perspectives on housing (pp. 41-67). Philadelphia: Temple University Press.

Sullivan, B. T. (1982). Analysis and assessment of the alternative management programs for New York City's In-Rem properties. New York: Pratt Institute for Community and Environmental Development.

Turner, J. F. C. (1972). Housing as a verb. In Turner, J. F. C. & Fichter, R. (Eds.), Freedom to build (pp. 148-175). New York: Macmillan Company.

U.S. Department of Housing and Urban Development. (1980). The conversion of rental housing to condominiums and cooperatives: a national study of scope, causes and impacts. Washington, D.C.: U.S. Government Printing Office.

Weitzman, P. (1989). Housing, race/ethnicity and income in New York City, 1978-1987. New York: Community Service Society.

Zimmer, J.E. (1977). From rental to cooperative: improving low and moderate income housing. Beverly Hills, Ca.: Sage.

19

The legacy of the Harlem model cities program

Le leg du programme "villes modeles" à Harlem: un urbaniste communautaire examine ses travaux depuis les années soixante

Barry Jackson

Un architecte noir, qui fut l'urbaniste communautaire dans le programme "Villes Modèles" à Harlem-Harlem Est à New York, se penche sur le programme lancé dans les années soixante pour revitaliser des quartiers entiers de taudis à travers l'Amérique, et le nouveau processus d'urbanisme dans la communauté récemment mis en vigueur. L'exposé rappelle le contexte des années soixante, l'évolution de l'action communautaire, et le délabrement des quartiers urbains. Il explore la dichotomie entre l'urbanisme à l'échelle de la communauté et les vastes programmes mis en oeuvre au niveau gouvernemental, ainsi qu'entre la perception qu'a la communauté du problème et la façon dont le gouvernement perçoit la solution. Il définit un nouveau cadre conceptuel pour l'urbanisme à petite échelle. L'exposé suit le développement d'un projet, un complexe de logements à Milbank-Frawley Circle, jusqu'à sa réalisation.

L'auteur conclut que le programme "Villes Modèles", loin de créer une société plus humaine, n'a fait que renforcer la nature de la société existante. L'échec du programme dans la communauté a été causé par le manque de réelle gestion des ressources. En outre, les "idées novatrices, nouvelles et audacieuses" que la législation appelait et que le projet mettait en oeuvre, ont été rejetées par les hauts fonctionnaires gouvernementaux, qui ne pouvaient apparemment pas les concilier avec leurs préjugés. Le programme était condescendant, et incapable de réconcilier la perception qu'avait la communauté de ses besoins et la perception que le gouvernement avait des besoins.

Mots clé: urbanisme communautaire; programme "Villes Modèles"; quartiers de taudis.

Keywords: Community Planning; Model Cites Program; Slum
Neighborhoods.; Advocacy

In 1966, in the midst of America's urban chaos, the United States Congress
passed PL89-754, The Demonstration Cities and Metropolitan Development
Act, which stated partially that "bold new innovative programs... must be
designed to 1) renew entire slum neighborhoods by the combined use of
physical and social development programs and 2) increase substantially the
supply of standard housing of low and moderate cost" (United States
Congress, 1966). Each city designated for the program was to choose its
own area to renew based upon the criteria of the program. New York City
designated Harlem-East Harlem as one of the areas.[1] In New York City, the
Model Cities program was under the aegis of the Housing and Development
Administration, a newly created "super agency" developed in a major effort
to deliver housing to the city.

New York City was clearly in need of an improved housing stock. In
1968, Paul Davidoff reported that New York required "one million new and
rehabilitated low- and moderate rent units" (Davidoff, 1968, p.11). The rate
of new construction, while sufficient to meet middle- and upper- income
demand... fails to provide new units, or liberate enough existing units
through market operation, to satisfy more than a small portion of the city's
need for low-income families" (Davidoff, 1968, p.12).

HISTORICAL CONTEXT

In the early sixties a new energy burst upon America. There was a moment
of peace between two Asian wars, the tough quality of a new, young
President, new musical sounds in the air. The potential of the America of the
future, stymied by the Great Depression and World War II, seemed about to
be realized.

But that period of which we speak became, suddenly, with the death of
John Kennedy, a moment of dashed hopes. The pent-up expectation,
particularly in the black communities across the country, finally burst into
flames and struggle, and that strife caught the energy of the nation either to
sustain it or to oppose it. One after the other riots flared up: Harlem, Watts,
Detroit, Newark. Those previously muted forces spilled over. *"Everything
must change."*

The movement of blacks from the rural south to the urban north was
one of the great transforming demographic events in the second half of the
twentieth century. This movement profoundly effected urban geography,
education, popular music, politics and government social policy. This was

not the only transformation going on; it couples with, for example, the movement of whites from the cities to the suburbs. These two not unrelated events helped transform the image of America.

THE WAR ON POVERTY

The War on Poverty emerged in 1964 as Lyndon Johnson's effort to both establish a domestic policy and set his own domestic agenda. The legislation passed without a clear understanding of how the Office of Equal Opportunity (OEO), which was formed under the enabling law, intended to operate. The attitude regarding the need for social services was quite varied. These attitudes were formed more from the literature about the black neighborhoods than from experience in the neighborhoods. Such writers as Galbraith, Harrington, Cohen and Cloward and Ohlin collectively set the intellectual framework for the period. "The War on Poverty was planned in a time of much greater national harmony and propriety... with an optimism that seems reckless, and carried out in a time of much greater tension and violence" (Lehmann, 1988, p.38).

To blacks, though, everything had the feeling of paternalism. To a large extent, whites didn't bother to differentiate between the attitudes of poor and middle class blacks. Blacks were considered to have a monolithic point of view. Each side referred to the other as "*they*". To the extent that whites differentiated, it was a statistical differentiation, which seemed, most often, to extrapolate to all blacks the behavior and attitude of the statistical majority.

COMMUNITY ACTION

The centerpiece of the War on Poverty was community action. And flawed thought it was, once the community action genie was let out of the bottle, there was no getting it back in. Starve it, emasculate it, put it under siege, but back into the bottle it would not go. For the Model Cities program, which developed later, also had, as part of its mandate, a community action component. The concept of community action began to change the feelings in the black neighborhoods, began to raise the possibility that the government cared. Some would later argue that "...small material advances, by raising the expectations of blacks, may actually have spurred greater demands. In this sense, the federal strategy for the cities, and especially the poverty program, may have contributed to a growing discontent and turbulence in the ghetto, at least in the short run" (Piven, 1974, p.45).

In the meantime, community action introduced into the discourse the idea that urban poverty could be solved from within the neighborhoods. This idea became much more appealing politically when decoupled from the OEOs tendency to engage in confrontation with the power structure" (Lehmann, 1989, p.45). With community action came the community advocate. The concept behind the community advocate was that poor people had neither the knowledge nor the access to the processes which would aid them. Not everyone, was in favor of it. The power structure relied on the lack of sophistication in poor neighborhoods; providing advocates began to level the playing field, and the poor were not so easy to fool.

But other forces were gathering. In 1964, the first summer race riot of the decade took place in Harlem. Outside New York this was not seen as the precursor of calamity in the black neighborhoods. In Harlem, the action was more on a political level. With the introduction of the large sums of OEO money into the anti-poverty program, the community action agency, HAR-YOU, was formed and the political turf battles, which lasted for the remainder of the decade, began. Locally, the tone was being set with the activists and the politicians lining up for a piece of the action.

The OEO had by-passed the controlling political structure in Harlem. The Harlem congressman "...Adam Clayton Powell demanded a piece of the action at HAR-YOU, a project whose guiding spirit was the black psychologist Kenneth B. Clark; HAR-YOU became HARYOU-ACT, Clark resigned in protest, and almost from the moment it received its first OEO grant, of $1.2 million, in June of 1965, HARYOU-ACT was under investigation for financial irregularities" (Lehmann, 1989, p. 61).

In Harlem, much of the anxiety centered around whether the community would explode again, as if it were a local phenomena. The Watts riots, in the summer of 1965, made it obvious to everyone that the urban neighborhoods were in severe difficulty. Riots in other cities followed. Immediately, the cities became the leading domestic issue. For the next three years the rioting worsened, and the country seemed strained to near bursting. This was the climate in which the Model Cities Program and advocacy planning was introduced.

THE MODEL CITIES PROGRAM IN NEW YORK CITY

The Model Cities program spearheaded a major effort to change the nature of planning and implementation in New York City. The Housing and Development Administration (HDA) was created in 1967 in order to streamline and coordinate the housing transactions in the City. The agency was administered by Jason Nathan. HDA brought together the Housing and

Redevelopment Board, the Rent and Rehabilitation Administration, the
Building Department, the Relocation Department, and some elements of the
Real Estate Department, but excluded the Housing Authority and the City
Planning Commission. The restructuring added the Model Cities
Administration, among others, to the mix. In its initial years some of the old
line agencies improved little while under the super agency umbrella, but
conceptually, the agency was designed to streamline the decision-making
process.

THE MODEL CITIES PROGRAM IN HARLEM-EAST HARLEM

Milbank-Frawley Housing Council. In order to create a decision-making
body for the planning process, the Model Cities Administration,[2] created a
local housing council. Since there was to be one planning district it was
designed to overlap the two planning boards in existence: one in Harlem and
one in East Harlem embracing the black and Hispanic communities
respectively. This initial decision created the framework for the fragmented
political and turf battles which ensued.[3] Among other critical political and
organizational battles waged by the community, including leadership and
location of meetings, was who was to be the planner. After being
interviewed by both the community and the Model Cities Administration, I
was chosen for the position.

ADVOCACY

The question arises: who can be an community advocate without being an
outsider? Most people raised in a neighborhood who go away to college
begin to take on the values of their educated peers. My argument has always
been that neighborhood people can sense the needs of the neighborhood with
more clarity. The only people able to be true advocates for a neighborhood
are those who stay in the community, go to college there and remain
connected to the values of the community. In some sense, all the rest of us
are carpetbaggers. Even the Davidoffs sensed this difficulty when they said,
"If the planners for minority groups are middle-class white professionals
...then manipulation of the clients by those professionals and imposition of
the professionals' ideas upon the clients will always be a potential
danger."(Davidoff, 1974) The Davidoffs contention is true even if the
planners are middle-class black professionals.

WORKING WITH THE COMMUNITY

At that time, the prevailing viewpoint was that the community merely needed technical resources. The counter argument was that advocates were preventing traditional community actions. Both of these are true. In some ways my role in the Model Cities program was quite complex. I was under contract to the Model Cities Administration. I appeared at community meetings as an individual, but in reality I was backed by a well-trained staff that I had assembled.[4] My assignment as Model Cities planner, aside of from lending technical support to the community, was to determine *the location* of several hundred units of housing, in an appropriate mix and with certain additional constraints.

THE ROLE OF THE PLANNER

In order to establish that the process was open, that the plan wasn't "rolled up in City Hall", I started the planning processes from scratch, as if teaching a course called *Introduction to Planning*. Week by week a committee of the Housing Council worked on discovering how we could change the neighborhood. We drew maps, located vacant lots and buildings, and investigated what physical changes might be made. My strategy was to go to the weekly meetings and use my office staff as the support for what was going on in the committee meetings. To test the validity of some of the ideas coming under discussion at the program, my office worked designing prototype housing, developing test cases for rehabilitation through the FHA programs, and engaging in supportive research. As I gathered information and insight I slowly revealed the information to the neighborhood in a manner that tried to give the impression that it was new and fresh. Street logic had to merge with technical back-up information.

From the outset, there were plenty of preconceptions about what to do. At one of the first planning meetings, Mrs. Coleman, a community resident, pointed at the map and turned to me: "We want a park on that corner. We don't need no housing. When they put up that school they never put in a playground and they promised us a park. I've been living on this street for twenty years and I've been coming to meetings for twenty years. Nothing but a park goes there." I called it Coleman's Corner from then on.

The problem was that issues such as child care, jobs, training kept coming up, and there was nothing in the planning process that included those things, except when there was a physical manifestation.[5] We discussed the economical viability gained through construction: each new building not only creates a person who has learned a skill and can continue this in the neighborhood, each building requires some small business to take care it; each new daycare center required a staff. The economic viability of the neighborhood can be changed dramatically if the programs are coordinated, comprehensive, and continuous. That means that the State, City or Federal programs have to coordinated, comprehensive and continuous. Needless to say they are not.

The community, in general, didn't want any new construction. There was a belief that in order to create new construction something always had to be demolished. There is irrefutable logic in that observation, since the amount of vacant land was very limited. Several other points were made:
1) "They is n'ver gonna build no new houses for black foax."
2) If they tear down sumpin', they is nevah gonna put it back.
3) Therefore, "Let's fix up what we have."

That sounds very logical, except that under the FHA guide-lines which were operating at that time, the minimum property standards did not allow putting back the same number of units in an old law tenement (which was the main housing stock) as were presently in it. The square footage requirements allowed only three units for every four. Therefore, all rehabilitation of the tenement housing stock *reduced* the total number of units. And thus the relocation issue entered the equation. Historically, relocation causes social disruption. People rarely return to their old neighborhood, because the time lag between planning and implementation is usually so long that people have grown roots in a new neighborhood. The relocation and rehabilitation issues were central to the discussion. The committee establish principles of action regarding one move for relocation not more than two blocks.

The anti-advocates

Some of the professionals, particularly those who worked for planning agencies developed a decade earlier under Urban Renewal, didn't much care for advocacy. There was a certain arrogant stance that I noted. I perceived a resentment from the white liberals, too, especially toward the black professionals as if we were getting in their turf.

Some of the intellectuals didn't care for advocacy either. As Frances Fox Piven voiced it, "In one city after another, local groups in Model Cities neighborhoods are involved in the technical dazzlements of planning, some to prepare plans, others to compete with counterplans. But there is little being built in these neighborhoods. Nor are locally prepared plans likely to change the pattern. A plan, of itself, is not a force; it is not capable of releasing the necessary federal subsidies or of overcoming the inertia of the city agencies. Quite the contrary, for those people who might otherwise have become a force by the trouble they made are now too busy. As one advocate planner for a Harlem neighborhood that is still without construction funds proudly said, "They are learning how to plan" (Piven, 1974, p.47). I guess she was talking about me. In general, the planners didn't have much respect for the communities. Scott reports the community as being "inarticulate, timid, suspicious, or indifferent" (Scott, 1969, p.629). On the other hand, I found the community perceptive, adamant, realistic, but overwhelmed.

To answer Piven: advocacy began the understanding in the community of not only the how's of planning, but also the shortcomings of it; that it is control of the resources, not only control of the plan, which is essential. In the sixties, the learning process started. The Davidoffs had the foresight to realize that "bringing poor people into the process of preparing and presenting demands is not, as Piven unfortunately seems to imply, involving them in something that is beyond their intellectual capacity. It is part of building a movement whose leaders are capable of seeing what is wrong with their society and of organizing to do something to change it."(Davidoff, 1974, p.57) And in the nineties, the *modus operandi* has changed.

On one point Piven is right. The city officials were trying to coax people off the streets, trying to avoid, in the phrase of the time, "the long, hot summer". But the community also knew how to work both sides of the street at the same time. Advocacy did not inhibit activism; there were plenty of people to go around.

Plans and Counterplans

Meanwhile, other events were happening "offstage" as it were. Other groups, not recognized by the city, but with just as much right to organize, became "the opposition". The Puerto Ricans, more overtly political, developed a both/and attitude: work with the Housing Council and work outside of the Housing Council. In other words, cover as many bases as possible. The opposition had either to overthrow the Housing Council or set up an organization which took over its function. Meanwhile, the Housing Council, after it was successfully organized and operating smoothly, received a contract from the City to provide the community services component of the project, but the Puerto Ricans, organized now as United Residents of East Harlem, unsuccessfully sued the city to take over the operation.

The effect of opposition groups is to slow the process. The government, in these situations, either uses the emerging countervailing point of view to delay the process or reallocate resources. The political astuteness of the community was at stake. Eventually, the Housing Council effectively used both front and back channels to reach its goals.

The United Residents of East Harlem, with its own advocate planner, as evenhandedly reported later in *Architectural Forum,* (Perry, 1968) developed a counterplan which was, in my opinion, very unrealistic. It was, I can say now, over designed and under thought. However, I was not in a political position to object or criticize the plan publicly at the time because criticism at that point would seem self serving. Admittedly, the plan had more character and pizzazz, than the simple, plausible, realistic planning concepts and building designs which I developed.

Computers and Urban Models: The Basic Housing System

In a parallel process, I was developing a mathematical model of the neighborhood called the Basic Housing System (Jackson, 1968) that I hoped would support any answers that came out of the planning process. I was trying to develop a mathematical answer to Jane Jacobs four principles of planning.

Complex questions were being raised. For example, what is the correct mix for new and rehabilitated housing in a neighborhood? Politics and attitudes aside for the moment, the answer lies in the economic goal that community wishes to reach and the resources the community wishes to use. The answer shifts dramatically as the amount of resource changes. If the goal is to provide ten units of housing at the least cost with the least relocation, the answer is to rehabilitate an empty building. As the amount of resource increases, vacant land enters as a resource and when the vacant land is used up a complicated mix of rehab and new construction proves to be the answer. Ownership (or cost of acquisition) is also a major variable. I constructed a computer model to work out all the available economic paths because the answer, particularly when looking at a real community with a mixed housing stock, a variegated zoning map, and mixed ownership of land, is in many ways counter-intuitive. When the issue of relocation came up in the planning meetings I added zero relocation as a boundary function to the mathematical model. My objective function was maximum number of units *gained* at the least cost for a given resource with zero relocation. At the end of the process, the model reflected all of the requirements of the project from both the government's point of view and the community's point of view. The concept of the model was to analyze the trade-offs. The ideas behind the model turned out to be quite acceptable to both the Model Cities Administration and the Housing Council when it was clear that the computer was not indiscriminately picking out housing sites.

Early runs of the model immediately flagged the question "What are our resources?" I asked that question of the Model Cities Administration. HDA didn't really know. The agency's goal was to put about two thousand housing units into the neighborhood. My report then was based upon a sliding scale of potential resources. When the model was run with a small resource certain sites were picked up in the model; as the amount of resource increased new sites were added. Some sites were clearly always economical (e.g. a vacant, city-owned parcel). The Basic Housing System was one of the earliest uses of the computer in the planning process.

The final meetings

After months of meetings the members of the official site committee reached some agreement among themselves. It was time to present *the plan* to the entire Housing Council. The proper procedure for the committee was to report back to the Housing Council. I was prepared with maps, charts, slides and other paraphernalia to act as the technical support person for the committee. My homework had been to teach enough planning logic to the committee to assure that the technical report matched the community needs and ideas. To be viable, the report had to come from the committee, for ultimately, the advocate had no power, but acted only as broker, interpreter or communicator. The advocate brought only skill and integrity. Much to my amazement, after considerable discussion, the plan - which was merely the designation of sites - was accepted (Jackson, 1967). While I felt that I had retained some measure of trust among all groups, later when I asked a leader of the opposition why she had not opposed to the plan, she said, "It was too early. And anyway," she continued, "the money isn't here yet." In other words, there was plenty of time for opposition.

AFTER THE PLANNING

The Urban Development Corporation: The scale of ideas

Meanwhile, the newest force at work, was the emergence of the Urban Development Corporation (UDC) under the direction of Ed Logue. Logue was ready to participate within the context of the change of political climate in New York State. UDC is an example of how centralized government worked to solve the urban crises. There should be a corollary to Gresham's Law which states that "big ideas" chase out "little ideas". By "little ideas" I mean "small scale" ideas. An example of big ideas in planning are: "let's tear down these blocks....", of small scale ideas are "let's put in vest-pocket housing...." From the viewpoint of the Housing Council and its planner, a super bulldozer, reminiscent of urban renewal, was lurking over the horizon.

Ed Logue, who is nationally known for his work in Boston with the Redevelopment Agency (BRA) and in New York with the Urban Development Corporation (UDC), was a man with big ideas. Working with "virtual immunity from local controls; (UDC) could condemn property, override local zoning and building codes and plan, build, manage and promote its own projects" (Goodman, 1972). Conceptually, UDC was going to cut through the bureaucratic red tape that cast a pall over urban renewal and take an *action oriented* approach to planning and development. "Cities must organize themselves to fight slums efficiently and matter-of factly as they now organize to fight fires", suggested Logue.

In some instances, I have liked the concept of some of his big ideas,[6] but in Harlem they were in conflict with some of my own notions about the Jane Jacob approach to planning which had to do with small scale ideas. Small scale ideas are very compatible with community action, because - as one community activist said, "You can monitor small scale projects....". Some examples of "small scale ideas" are: rehabilitating sound structures, vest pocket housing, and daycare centers on empty lots.

Ed Logue and I met just after he was appointed to his post at UDC. His offices weren't even open yet. Already he had a map of Harlem up on the wall of the unrenovated space. At our meeting he drew a checkerboard of x's on the map and said: "We'll tear down every other block, put up high rise housing, relocate the people from the remaining blocks....". I had long stopped listening, had long since become an enemy. I knew Ed Logue was wrong (particularly from the community point of view), and only right from the point of view of "downtown" where "the power brokers" wanted the beautiful brownstones - the real estate - of Harlem back. Ed Logue was all about power and money.

SPONSORING AND BUILDING MILBANK FRAWLEY CIRCLE

In the fall of 1969, UDC began quietly meeting with other representatives of the community to develop a Harlem subsidiary that would handle the development of all the designated sites in Harlem. Logue wanted to avoid working with the existing citizen's groups because they were too militant and belligerent. "He had been an outspoken critic of the Model Cities program, perhaps because its citizens groups were self-appointed, unstable, and often recalcitrant..." (Brilliant, 1975, p.87). He thus rejected a suggestion that the Milbank-Frawley Housing Council be utilized as the basis for the subsidiary and that he use UDC monies to help these groups form a viable, independent community corporation. If at all possible UDC would have avoided working with the communities at all, since its commitment was directly to the City

234

through HDA. The problem, as I see it, was one of strategy and policy.[7] The Milbank-Frawley Housing Council battled to be designated the sponsor of the Frawley Circle site. The more militant community groups, including the Housing Council, feared gentrification of the borders of Harlem, and viewed the encroachment, based on previous activities, as the neighborhood policy of the City Planning Commission. In fact, the sites bordering the Park were designated by the City as "joint interest sites".[8] Although the site had been approved by Board of Estimate in 1967, the privilege of sponsorship of the project had not been resolved. A raging turf battle had evolved in the community, and HDA (and other city officials) seemed unwillingly to decide between the two foremost groups. In some sense the city was able to capitalize upon the factionalism and inexperience of local community groups to prevent major realignments of decision-making about resource allocation. In a city like New York, which has a very complex political structure, there are always fewer resources than needed to solve all the problems. When one community is not ready to move forward, it is very easy to move - or threaten to move - the resources to a competing community. One aspect of planning which the community knew least about was resource allocation and budgeting. "They've got the money downtown," was a continuous community litany.

The Milbank-Frawley Housing Council lost its bid - after all its planning effort - to become the sponsor for the site. It has also been suggested that "...Logue was undoubtedly interested in developing an integration-oriented Harlem. Such a goal would be closely tied to economic factors and entirely compatible with them. Harlem would be more valuable as real estate if it retained more of its black middle class and if, in addition, white and other racial groups at its fringes were retained there". (Brilliant, 1975, p.118). This concept was not voiced, however, except as I have noted in my conversation with Logue who favored, quite clearly, large scale development. This image plays out the impression the community had that *"They have the plan rolled up in City Hall."*

Logue wished to use people further up the chain of power, people more educated, more middle class. At any rate, the rival groups fought over the potential of sponsoring the Frawley Circle site. Finally, with much behind the scenes maneuvering, the sponsorship was given to the Central Park North group, which had expressed prior interest. Apparently, Logue favored a group more interested in an integrationist approach to developing Harlem. The theory was quite simple. "Harlem might become more valuable real estate if it retained more of its black middle class and if, in addition, white and other racial groups at its fringes were retained there." (Brilliant, 1975, p. 118)

The partnership between UDC and the City was fundamentally a viable one. The City had the power to condemn, clear and "write-down" land costs. Clearly the agency couldn't afford to bring in middle income housing at economically feasible costs without the partnership. All this was quite clear right from the beginning of the planning effort, for the first runs of the Basic Housing System computed the necessary write-downs to make each project economical. There were no economically feasible projects without "write-downs".

With difficulty UDC, nearly unable to escape the financial constraints of building in New York City or the inherent political obstacles with the community groups, among the various city and state agencies, between the city and the state and ultimately with the federal government, built the Frawley project. It took two more years to resolved these issues, even though UDC was fast tracking the project, and it was finally completed in 1973.

The entire procedure, from the first site selection process to the opening of the project had taken seven years.

CONCLUSIONS

Part of the failure of the Model Cities program was its main premise: *that the solution to the problem of neighborhood deterioration lies in the rebuilding of the neighborhood.* Urban programs that concentrate their funds largely on efforts within the city boundaries were bound to be unsuccessful. The fundamental flaw was that it was not possible to lure large numbers of the black middle class back into the city through urban renewal efforts. In one of my earliest presentations to the City Planning Commission I was asked to outline my strategy for solving the housing problem in Harlem. My answer, facetiously, was "Build new, affordable housing in Rockland County." which is a few miles north of Harlem. One of the administrators looked quite startled at my answer, so I elaborated. "The assumption, a priori, that the solution to the planning problem exists *within* the boundaries of the project area is not valid. Of course, I understand quite clearly that that's not the answer you expect...."

Another way of looking at it is this: the Model Cities program formulated the wrong questions on a micro level and rejected any answer which was not preconceived by the "*powers that be*". The perception of the program in its proper political context was also understood by the community. One community person stated it properly, although I was surprised at the time. "*They just sent you up here to help them take it away. They got the plan all rolled up down at City Hall, You just think you're drawing in the plan."* Yes, I thought I was drawing the plan.

While one might conclude that adding to the centers of decision making at the local level resulted in favoring the status quo because conflicting goals prevented major actions from being taken, in the long run the community consciousness was raised and the responsibility of knowing and controlling the process was, to some extent, realized.

The question that is raised - and Herbert Marcuse posed this problem - how can revolutionary political change be created without changing the language of culture? "It has been said that the degree to which a revolution is developing *qualitatively* different social conditions and relationships may be indicated by the development of a different language: the rupture with the continuum of domination must also be a rupture with the vocabulary of domination" (Goodman cites Marcuse, 1972, p.33). As long as the poor, black neighborhoods of America were labeled *the ghetto*, then that was the perception that was created. All efforts to generate Model Cities, imaginative as they might be, were doomed to failure.

End Notes

1. The other two areas were the South Bronx and Bedford-Stuvesant.
2. The Model Cites Administrator, responsible for all three plnner areas, was Eugenia Flatow.
3. Later, when I questioned straddling the black and Hispanic communities with the planning boundary the explanation was simple: it was not politically expedient to put two planning districts in Manhattan. In other words, New York already had three Model City areas.
4. The back-up team was Fisher/Jackson Associates, a joint venture operation between John Fisher and myself.
5. In theory other committees of the Housing Council were supposed to be discussing these other issues, which made them outside of the jurisdiction of the Site Committee. They were also beyomd the scope of my assigment.
6. The Welfare Island Project, for example.
7. I am relying heavily on Brilliant's account of things after I left the project, and recognise that the account may be one-sided.
8. It should be noted that this process of planning and building in the public domain was being repeated at several locations within the city, so that each group benefited from the collective understanding from observation of other projects.

References

Alexander, Christopher, "The City is Not a Tree". This has been published several times, but was originally given as a lecture at the University of California, Berkeley, in the Fall of 1963.

Bellush, J. and Hausknecht, A., *Urban Renewal: People, Politics and Planning*, Doubleday, 1967.

Brilliant, Eleanor L., *The Urban Development Corporation: private interests and public authority*, Lexington Books, 1975.

Cloward, Richard A. and Ohlin, Lloyd E., *Delinquency and Opportunity: a theory of delinquent gangs*, Free Press, 1960.

Cloward, Richard A. and Piven, F.F., *The Politics of Turmoil, Essays on Poverty, Race, and the Urban Crises*, New York, Pantheon Books, 1974.

Cohen, Albert K., *Delinquent Boys*, Free Press, 1955.

Davidoff, Paul "Advocacy and Pluralism in Planning", *American Institute of Planners Journal*, Vol. 31, 1965.

Davidoff, Paul, *A Housing Program for New York State*, New York, 1968.

Galbraith, Kenneth, *The Affluent Society*, Houghton Mifflin, Boston, 1976.

Gans, Hebert J., *The Urban Villagers*, New York, Free Press, 1982.

Gans, Hebert J., *People and Plans*, Basic Books, 1968.

Goodman, Robert, *After the Planners*, New York, Simon and Shuster, 1972.

Harrington, Michael, *The Other America; poverty in the United States*, New York, Macmillan, 1962.

Jacobs, Jane, *The Death and Life of the Great American Cities*, Random House, New York, 1961.

Jacobs, Jane, *The Economy of Cities*, Random House, New York, 1969.

Jackson, Barry, "Basic Housing System", *The Applications of Computers to the Problems of Urban Society*, The Annual Symposium of the Asssociation for Computing Machinery, 1968.

Jackson, Barry, *Preliminary Report*, Vest Pocket & Rehabilitation Housing Study for Housing Development Administration and Milbank-Frawley Circle Non-Profit Housing Corporation, New York, 1967.

Jackson, Barry, "Practice at the Edge: Working at the Boundary Between Black and White", *Proceedings of Crossing the Boundaries in Practice*, Cincinnati, Ohio, 1993.

Lehmann, Nicholas, "The Unfinished War, Part I", *The Atlantic*, Vol. 262 No. 6, December, 1988.

Long, Louella Jacqueline and Robinson, Vernon (Ben) *How much power to the people? A study of the New York State Urban Development Corporation's Involvement in Black Harlem*, The Urban Center at Columbia University, 1971.

MacDonald, Malcolm, "Review of The Other America", *The New Yorker*, January 1963.

Matusow, Allen J. *A History of Liberalism in the 1960s*, New York, Harper&Row, 1984.

Perry, Ellen Berkeley, "Vox Populi: Many Voices From a Single Community", *Architectural Forum*, May 1968.

Piven, F.F. and Cloward, R.A., *Poor People's Movements: Why They Succeed, How They Fail*, New York, Pantheon Books, 1977.

Scott, Mellier Goodin, *American City Planning Since 1890*, Berkeley, University of California Press, 1969.

United States Congress, *Demonstration Cities and Metropolitan Development Act of 1966, Public Law 89-754*, U.S. Government Printing Office, Washington, 1966

20

A methodology for the study of urban rehabilitation

Méthodologie pour l'étude de la réhabilitation urbaine

Zuhal Ulusoy

La plupart des études consacrées aux transformations du voisinage, et en particulier celles sur la question de l'embourgeoisement, concentrent leur analyse sur l'évolution de la population, les changements sur le marché de l'immobilier ou les modifications des conditions physiques des bâtiments, sans prêter beaucoup d'attention à l'interaction entre ces aspects différents, mais liés, de la transformation des zones résidentielles. En outre, les variations au sein d'une même zone géographique passent inaperçues puisque l'on utilise des données statistiques pour des zones beaucoup plus larges que les voisinages eux-mêmes. La méthodologie proposée dans cet exposé combine les trois aspects de la transformation du voisinage, c'est-à-dire les changements dans le stock, le marché de l'immobilier, et dans la population. Les données pour chaque catégorie sont réunies au niveau des habitations individuelles et leur interaction est étudiée. Il est soutenu que l'ordre dans lequel s'enchaînent ces trois aspects du changement résidentiel révèle les différentes intentions des protagonistes. En conséquence, la méthodologie proposée nous permet de clarifier la complexité du processus et de mettre à jour les dynamiques se cachant derrière les transformations de voisinage.

Mots clé: réhabilitation urbaine; transformations de voisinage; méthodologie.

Keywords: Urban rehabilitation; neighborhood change; methodology

Rehabilitation activity is one of the most visible forms of neighborhood change, yet the qualitative and quantitative aspects of the physical stock and variations therein are not paid their due attention. Studies of neighborhoods emphasize changes in the demographic and socio-economic aspects of neighborhoods and the activity of the residential property market (DeGiovanni, 1983; Goetze, 1979; Pattison, 1983; Smith, 1979). While one needs to study and interpret secondary data on geographical areas to assess signs of changes in socio-economic composition and property values, renovated buildings are direct indications of investment and change. Here, it is argued that the effects of rehabilitation are not limited to the visible improvement of the physical stock but also extend to increases in the property values, and that property values affect socio-economic composition. Thus, rehabilitation ultimately connects to the types of changes normally emphasized in neighborhood theory.

Studies that focus on the characteristics of rehabilitation and its connection with other aspects of neighborhood change are limited (Clay, 1979; Galster, 1987; Jager, 1986; Maher et.al., 1985). Nevertheless, the condition of the physical stock is an important factor in determining a neighborhood's status: while a declining neighborhood is characterized by run-down properties, physical deterioration and lack of investment, an improving neighborhood exhibits tangible signs of investment, ranging from basic maintenance to major rehabilitation (Hoover and Vernon, 1962; Birch, 1971; Grigsby et.al., 1977; Downs, 1981; LaGory and Pipkin, 1981). Actions that qualitatively change the physical condition of buildings, then, have a role in neighborhood change.

The premise of this paper is that rehabilitation is significant for neighborhood change and its interaction with other measures of change is crucial in understanding the process. The purpose is to propose a methodology that is capable of analyzing and clarifying the intricate relationship among various indicators of change within a neigborhood. While doing this, the role of rehabilitation in neighborhood dynamics and the particularities of renovation in an upgrading neighborhood need also be studied. In order to attain this objective, the research should incorporate an in-depth analysis of the quantitative and qualitative aspects of renovation activity and its interaction with property sales and the turnover of residents. This interaction, in turn, needs to be discussed in relation to changes in the larger neighborhood and the city and in connection to the public policy framework. This will enable us to uncover the dynamics of rehabilitation activity in a particular area and to relate them to forces set by its urban context and to the contingencies defined by the agents directly or indirectly involved in rehabilitation. The approach proposed here aims to enable us to answer three major questions. First, what happens to the housing stock in a neighborhood undergoing significant upgrading? Second, what kinds of renovation activity occur? And third, what consequences do they have for property sales and turnover of residents.

METHODOLOGY

Neighborhood change cannot be studied singularly at the neighborhood level; the changes that are manifested at the level of individual properties need to be considered as well. Neighborhood data essentially give aggregate information, where most of the changes are levelled out, especially when the neighborhood covers a large area. Variations among individual cases that make up the whole, the range of these variations and their geographic distribution are lost. This becomes particularly a problem in neighborhoods where renovation activity is uneven. There are cases in which renovation activity is clustered on some blocks and not in others, and even clustered in parts of blocks. In such cases, what happens at the property level can not be directly reflected by neighborhood level data and variations are lost. Yet, most of the times the trends of change can only be observed by studying these variations in the whole over a period of time.

The purpose of property level analysis is to identify the particularities of each property and its uniqueness, rather than reducing the complexity of events to simplifying generalities. Here, intensive research methods to understand how causal processes work out in a particular case or a limited number of cases are proposed to be used in conjunction with extensive methods, i.e. descriptive and inferential statistics and numerical analyses to discover common properties and general patterns of a group as a whole.

TYPES OF DATA

Three types of data are suggested for property level analysis; renovation activity, the sale of property, and the residents. Renovation activity data consist of information on renovation type, date and cost. Records on building permits, such as the records of Building Inspection Offices, can be used to study how different aspects of physical change -- the type, degree, and cost of the renovation -- are related to residential turnover and property sales; and also whether there is any predominant ordering among these measures of residential change.

Information on property sales, including the date of sale and the sale value, are the second category of data. They can be obtained from the deed registry records of local governments. For each property, it is possible to study variations in sale values and to relate this trend with the history of recorded renovations of the property. Through this property-based information, trends of property value changes in the aggregate, and the relation between these trends and those in renovation activity can be studied to find whether they are related, and, if they are, to explore the nature of this relation in terms of their timing, and the type and cost of renovation.

The third data set is on occupants and their turnover for each property over the study period. Reverse directories that list the inhabitants by their address can be used as sources of secondary data, if collecting primary data about the inhabitants using inteviews or questionnaires is not desired. Information on the length of stay of each resident at a particular address, frequency of turnover of residents, subdivisions of properties, thus trends in residential turnover, especially if data on the socio-economic characteristics of the past and present residents are available, are strong clues for the nature of changes in an area. Also, the way these trends relate to renovation activity and sale of property can be analyzed.

MAJOR QUESTIONS CONSIDERED

The proposed methodology should have the potential to answer some of the questions that are central to neighborhood change: What happens to the housing stock in a neighborhood that is undergoing significant upgrading? What kinds of renovation activity occur in such neighborhoods? What are its qualitative and quantitative characteristics? How is renovation activity distributed in time? What consequences does it have for property sales and residential turnover? Are they related directly and significantly? If they are, is there a regularity to this relationship in terms of types, costs, and timing of renovation? Does this interaction change with respect to the stage of the rehabilitation process? Are there predominant patterns of occurrence among renovation, property sale and turnover of residents? What can be the intentions behind renovation, assuming that these patterns are clues for the intentions?

TECHNIQUES OF ANALYSIS

Different analytical techniques need to be applied in order to clarify changes in a neighborhood. First, time series analysis of number and types of renovation, money spent for renovation, number of sales, and the sale values of renovated and non-renovated properties in the neighborhood need to be performed to identify trends in the area over the study period. Then, renovation, property sale and residential turnover should be analyzed non-sequentially in order to see whether there is significant relationship among them. Cross tabulations between the number of instances of renovation and sale, renovation and turnover, and sale and turnover can be used for this purpose. Yet, as discussed earlier, such descriptive information falls short of uncovering the interaction and causal relation among individual events. Thus, the analysis should be taken a step further and focus on the timing of the occurrences of renovation, sale and turnover of residents -- their sequencing. This would show which incidence preceeds the others and which ones occurred at the same time; hence, what might be the underlying intention behind the actions.

The proposed methodology enables us to discuss the nature of intervention using the findings of descriptive statistics together with those of sequential analysis. Hence, statistical information about the type, degree, and cost of renovation, sale price, occupants and their turnover, accompanied with information about their timing all become clues to explain different aspects of neighborhood change, and solve the puzzle of this complex process. A number of possible outcomes are discussed below.

Renovations that do not accompany property sale and turnover of residents are done by owner-occupants and are taken as examples of 'incumbent upgrading', that is, people rehabilitating their own houses without moving out (Clay, 1979). Instances where there are no changes in ownership but turnover of residents occur after renovation may indicate a change in the occupancy status -- rental property turned into owner-occupied or vice versa. If the property is rented after renovation, we may assume increasing the rent is the motive behind action.

Property sales that occur simultaneously with resident turnover without any renovation, might be speculative since the appreciation of property, if there is, is not due to the investments made. The intention in such instances is to collect value increases due to the spill-over effect of renovations on nearby properties.

If the properties are sold and renovated at the same time and this was accompanied by a change in occupants, then it indicates that the renovation potential of properties attract a new group of households into the area. Depending on the socio-economic characteristics of the newcomers and the previous residents, these instances might be examples of gentrification (Beauregard, 1986; Laska and Spain, 1979).

The type and degree of renovation is assumed to reflect the intention of the agent who does the renovation. If the renovation is done by the original owner-occupants, it is expected to be basic maintenance or moderate renovation to increase the building's utility. Renovations that follow a change in ownership and probably a turnover of residents also imply a desire to increase the fit between the building and the occupants' needs and tastes, hence are not speculative. People buying property in older neighborhoods to renovate and then inhabit them are examples of this case. If the renovation is done by an agent who does not occupy the building, the primary intention is expected to be to increase its market value, hence, to increase either the rent or sale price. Thus, if the prospects of selling the property at a price higher than the previous sale price or renting it at a level higher than the current rent are high, then the renovation will target a different clientele than the existing one, and it will be qualitatively more extensive and exterior oriented, and quantitatively more costly. Extensive renovation could be done by an owner, but usually just after purchase and before the unit is occupied. This has been the case with households buying "shells" in gentrifying neighborhoods.

Qualitatively, renovation activity in the early years of neighborhood rehabilitation is expected to be more modest; extensive and more elaborate renovations are expected to occur later in the process. Hence, renovations would get more expensive throughout the study years. Similarly, sale values are expected to increase with time. Verification of these hypotheses will support the stage theories of neighborhood revitalization.

The sequential or simultaneous occurrence of events are suggested to indicate the intention behind renovation. Based on the discussion above, four types of "scenarios" -- actors and their objective in renovation -- are developed:

Type A - Cases where there is no change in ownership or turnover of occupancy at the time of renovation. These might be instances of incumbent upgrading. Renovation is done either by the owner-occupant or an absentee-owner, but the goal is not to attract a different type of household.

Type B - Renovation leads to a turnover of the residents but the property is not sold. This change in residents might be the turnover of tenants, or turning a rental property into owner-occupancy, or an owner-occupant moving out to rent the place. Nevertheless, the objective of renovation is to make the property fit a new clientele and, if it becomes completely rental after renovation, to collect higher rents.

Type C - Renovation occurs after a property is purchased and occupied by the new owner. The intention is to make the building match the needs and tastes of the new owner-occupants. Depending on their socio-economic characteristics and on the characteristics of the larger neighborhood, these new residents might be gentrifiers.

Type D - Property is renovated and sold after or during renovation. Renovation is profit oriented, and might be speculative. Instances where renovation starts after a purchase and the property is sold after renovation also fit in this category.

DISCUSSION AND CONCLUSION

The methodology introduced above enables us to discuss the changes in an area at a level of detail that cannot be attained using conventional methods of neighborhood research. While analysis based on aggregate data of a neighorhood can reveal overall trends of change, it falls short of uncovering the spatial differences within the area and variations that occur over time. Such differences can be captured by incorporating data at a scale smaller than the scale of a neighborhood. Moreover, interaction among different measures of neighborhood change necessiates a method that enables a detailed analysis of the intricate network of relationships. The qualitative differences among renovations done by different actors involved in the process need also be discussed.

The method of analysis introduced in this study can be expanded into a model for neighborhood analysis. Such a model can be used to determine the direction and the nature of changes in a neighborhood, and, depending on the extensiveness of information and the changes in the larger context, can be used to make predictions for potential changes. Three indispensible variables in such a model are (1) the timing of renovation in relation to property purchase, (2) the cost of renovation, and (3) the type of renovation. Integration of these three variables enables a discussion of motives behind each renovation activity, and, in the aggregate, hints at the nature of changes at the neighborhood level.

Other information on the demographics of the neighborhood and the policy dimensions of rehabilitation enrich the analysis, elaborate the discussion and provide support for the conclusions. The changes in population in terms of overall number of residents, the racial make-up of the area, income and educational characteristics of households are also important for assessing the direction of changes in a neighborhood. The socio-economic characteristics of the renovators are clues to discussing whether an area is upgraded by its original residents and/or households of similar status, or by people of a higher socio-economic status; that is, whether it is a case of incumbent upgrading or gentrification. The source of investment is significant in determining the involvement of public and private monies in the rehabilitation of an area, and eventually discussing the extent of governmental motivation behind it, as well as the types of developers involved in renovation.

This method is based on the hypothesis that renovation can be manifested in quantitatively and qualitatively different forms. One has to be attentive to these variances in order to arrive at credible conclusions regarding the nature of changes in a neighborhood. A modest renovation that is done without any change of property ownership has completely different

motives than an extensive and costly renovation which follows the purchase
of property. Thus, the existence of various forms of renovation in a
neighborhood imply totally divergent trends. The methodology introduced
here aims to allow an in-depth neighborhood study to undo the intricate
network of interactions, interpret the conflicting indicators of change, and
uncover geographical variations in an area. As such, this approach can be
turned into a tool which might be used to shape future actions and policies
not only for individual neighborhoods but also a network of neighborhoods
in cities.

References

Beauregard, Robert A. (1986) "The chaos and complexity of gentrification", in
    Gentrification of the City, Neil Smith and Peter Williams (eds) Boston: Allen and
    Unwin, pp.35-55.

Birch, David (1971) "A Stage Theory of Urban Growth," Journal of the American
    Institute of Planners, vol.37, pp. 78-87.

Clay, Phillip L. (1979) Neighborhood Renewal - Middle-Class Resettlement and
    Incumbent Upgrading in American Neighborhoods. Lexington, Massachusetts:
    Lexington Books.

DeGiovanni, Frank F. (1983) "Patterns of change in housing market activity in
    revitalizing neighborhoods", American Planning Association Journal, Winter 1983,
    pp.22-39.

Downs, Anthony (1981) Neighborhoods and Urban Development. Washington, D.C.: The
    Brookings Institution.

Galster, George C. (1987) Homeowners and Neighborhood Reinvestment. Durham: Duke
    University Press.

Grigsby, William G.; Sammis B. White, Daniel U. Levine, Regina M. Kelly, Marsha
    Reines Perelman, and George L. Claflen, Jr. (1977) Re-thinking Housing and
    Community Development Policy. Philadelphia, Pennsylvania: The University of
    Pennsylvania.

Goetze, Rolf (1979) Understanding Neighborhood Change - The Role of Expectations in
    Urban Revitalization. Cambridge, Massachusetts: Lexington Press.

Hoover, Edgar M. and Raymond Vernon (1962). Anatomy of a Metropolis. New York:
    Doubleday-Anchor.

Jager, Michael (1986) "Class definition and the aesthetics of gentrification: victorian
    Melbourne", in N. Smith and P. Williams (eds.) Gentrification of the City.
    Boston: Allen and Unwin, pp. 78-91.

La Gory, Mark and John Pipkin (1981) Urban Social Space. Belmont, California:
    Wadsworth Publishing Company.

Laska, Shirley Bradway and Daphne Spain (eds.) (1979) Back to the City - Issues in
    Neighborhood Renovation. New York: Pergamon Press.

Maher, Timothy; Ain Haas, Betty Levine and John Liell (1985) "Whose neighborhood?
    The role of established residents in historic preservation areas", Urban Affairs
    Quarterly, vol.21, no.2, pp.267-281.

Pattison, Timothy (1983) "The stages of gentrification: The case of Bay Village", in Neighborhood Policy and Planning, Phillip L. Clay and Robert M. Hollister (eds.), Lexington, Massachusettes: Lexington Books, pp.77-92.

Sayer, Andrew (1984) Method in Social Science. London: Hutchinson.

Smith, Neil (1979) "Toward a theory of gentrification: A back to the city movement by capital not people", Journal of the American Planning Association, vol.45, no.4, pp.538-548.

21

A residents' assessment of urban change and the economics of city centre regeneration in Belfast: lessons for the urban periphery

L'opinion des habitants sur la transformation urbaine et les aspects économiques de la régénération du centre ville de Belfast.

Andreas Cebulla

En l'espace de seulement dix ans, la politique de développement urbain à Belfast s'est détournée de la construction de logements en banlieue pour se concentrer sur l'aménagement commercial du centre ville. Elle est maintenant sur le point de se concentrer à nouveau sur la régénération économique des zones désavantagées de la ville. Une enquête locale a révélé que si la régénération du centre-ville suscitait en général des réactions favorables de la part des habitants de Belfast, ils éprouvaient néanmoins une certaine insatisfaction envers la qualité de l'environnement en dehors du quartier des affaires. Cet exposé présente les résultats les plus importants de l'enquête et les leçons de la régénération du centre-ville qu'il faudrait retenir pour faciliter l'aménagement de la ceinture périphérique de la ville et répondre aux besoins des habitants.

Mots clé: régénération du centre-ville; satisfaction locale; développement de la périphérie urbaine.

Keywords:city centre regeneration; local area satisfaction; urban peripheral development

In the 1970s, the improvement of private and public sector housing was on top of urban planners' policy agenda in Belfast. Ten years later, when the housing renewal strategy was under review, policy makers felt that not only did the strategy need revised (McGivern 1989), but that it was time to consider new initiatives beyond housing.

During the '70s, Belfast's city centre had been extensively damaged by a paramilitary bombing campaign directed against commercial property. When, in the early 1980s, the Department of the Environment (NI) responsible for physical planning in Belfast embarked on a policy of city centre regeneration, it was emulating national policies but also responding to calls from the local retailing sector to provide incentives for property investments and to improve the environment of the city centre in order to attract shoppers back into Belfast (Brown (1987)).

Until then, urban policy had mainly been concerned with meeting the needs and demands of the two ethnic communities in the city (cp Project Team (1976); Wiener (1980)) which led to the duplication of many public sector provisions in the city. In the 1980s, regenerating the city centre was seen as an opportunity to finally plan for social and economic improvement in *one* place. The city centre would "offer(s) easy accessibility to all sections of the urban population" (DoE(NI) 1987) and, hence, everyone could partake in new economic and social activities. This paper contrasts the overwhelmingly positive public assessment of city centre regeneration -as highlighted in a survey of Belfast residents - with its failure to spread employment and environmental benefits to the urban periphery[1]. Moreover, city centre regeneration had negative side-effects on the quality of life in other parts of the city. Yet, there are valuable lessons to be learned from a study of the economics of city centre regeneration which could inform peripheral development strategies.

Government office relocation policy and the provision of Urban Development Grants formed the backbone of city centre regeneration. Their contribution to city centre regeneration is discussed with reference to the question of promoting peripheral economic development.

URBAN POLICY EVALUATION

Inspired not least by a review of urban regeneration initiatives in Great Britain (National Audit Office (1990)), the Belfast Development Office of the DoE(NI), in 1990, commissioned a review of the impact of its policy initiatives and their public perception (DoE(NI) (1994)). Part of the study was a survey of businesses in Belfast including businesses which had received an Urban Development Grant (henceforth: UDG). The UDG was one of the principal policy instruments used in the process of urban regeneration. Between 1983 and 1992, over £50m of UDG were paid to property owners and investors in Belfast, generating over £200m of construction and property improvement work. In expenditure terms, UDG programme was the single most important DoE(NI) urban development initiative.

In addition, a survey was undertaken asking residents about their views on environmental changes in the city centre and their own local areas. The survey involved face-to-face interviews with some 2500 individuals in their homes. The sample was collected so to allow the disaggregation of results, along planning boundaries, frequently co-inciding with social and ethnic population patterns, by Northern, Eastern, Southern and Western sub-areas in Belfast's inner and outer cities.

THE RESIDENTS' VIEW

The survey found wide-spread approval of city centre regeneration in Belfast. Over 90% of residents welcomed the visual and functional improvements in the city's retail and office cores, above all the improved range and quality of shopping facilities, pedestrianisation, and the upgrading of buildings.

Local area satisfaction was less outspoken, but still 80% of Belfast residents were *satisfied* with the area in which they lived (Table 21.1). Over 40% of all Belfast residents considered the appearance of, and the amenities and functions in their area to have *"changed in the last few years"* (the survey was conducted in early 1992). Over 50% of inner city residents expressed this opinion, whereas in the outer city, the city average of 42.7% was surpassed only in the western sub-area. Since planning policy in the 1980s focussed on central Belfast with some overspill of outputs into inner city parts, this inner/outer city divide was not unexpected.

Residents were asked to more specifically name factors which had contributed to change in their local areas. The choice and quality of shopping facilities and housing, and the volume of traffic were mentioned most frequently. Less than one in five residents thought the quality of the environment had played a part in change in the local area.

There also were intra-city variation in perception. A greater number of residents noted changes in the provision of *shopping* facilities in the city's east, north and Outer West than elsewhere in Belfast. Predominantly inner city residents observed changes in the provision of *housing*, whereas largely residents in the east and south of Belfast said local *traffic* volumes had changed.

Table 1
Area Satisfaction and Change
Very and Fairly Satisfied - Change Observed
(% of respondents)

	Belfast	Inner East	Inner North	Inner South	Inner West	Outer East	Outer North	Outer South	Outer West
Satisfaction	80.1	77.8	68.1	79.4	62.9	90.7	74.1	88.6	79.6
Observed Change	42.7	51.7	54.1	54.5	57.4	33.2	37.2	38.8	47.5

Source: Belfast Residents Survey 1992 (database)

Table 2
Problems with the Area
(% of respondents)

	Belfast	Inner East	Inner North	Inner South	Inner West	Outer East	Outer North	Outer South	Outer West
Litter	55	59	65	77	60	44	51	42	65
Dogs	44	49	29	49	29	50	44	49	44
Damage or Theft	31	24	24	49	35	29	33	39	24
Vacant Houses	27	52	39	58	28	19	28	21	12
Traffic Noise	26	33	20	37	31	26	19	34	22
Disturbances from Teenagers	19	18	21	17	31	15	18	14	25
Air Traffic Noise	17	32	10	19	13	24	7	24	13
Rowdy Children	16	15	22	21	20	15	20	9	14
Derelict Sites	13	18	23	22	21	13	13	8	9
Empty Commercial Properties	11	17	15	16	11	9	12	13	5
Industrial Smells	10	12	9	16	8	8	10	11	11
Violence	10	9	12	15	16	5	11	7	13
Building Sites	9	11	17	16	11	7	10	4	8
Industry	8	8	2	17	5	14	4	13	2
None	13	6	11	6	14	14	14	13	15

Source: adapted from Belfast Residents Survey 1994

These changes were almost uniformly judged *either* an improvement *or* a deterioration of area conditions. A striking exception was the Inner East where residents were more inclined to judge observed changes in the local environment as improvements. Across the city, housing and - in particular in the Outer West - shopping provisions were judged to have improved. Traffic, on the other hand, was overwhelmingly perceived as having deteriorated, as was employment and, to a lesser extent, the environment.

POLICY ACHIEVEMENTS AND LITTLE PLANNING DISASTERS

The results of the Residents' Survey lend support to the Department's view that significant improvements had been made during the 1980s (and before) in the provision of shopping facilities and (public) housing.

Yet, residents identified new problems, above all, dirty streets, vacant houses and increased traffic (Table 21.2). Concern about increased traffic was greatest in the city's east, and the outer arterial routes leading into the city centre.[2]

A cornerstone of city centre regeneration had been the relocation of government offices from suburban and other locations across the city to the city centre. The stategy helped sustain property demand and, hence, commercial rents. It also provided public sector anchor tenants to or near shopping complexes. Retailers perceived office workers relocated into central Belfast as additional customers sustaining their business. Moreover, new private office developments in excess of 2000 sq ft of floorspace replacing ageing stock across the city were restricted to the Central Business District (henceforth: CBD), adding more potential shoppers and again maintaining property values. One side-effect of concentrated development was to increase into-town-commuting by private motor car. In particular, Government office workers and civil servants have over the years chosen the east of or to the city (where also the larger government offices were located) as their area of residence. A more recent cluster of "service class" residents has emerged in the south of the city. These people now commute "downtown" for work, passing through (various parts of) East and South Belfast. Thus, the greater concern about traffic is a "real" experience for many East and South Belfast residents and is - at least in part - an outcome of the city centre regeneration strategy.

The perception of declining environmental qualities, except in the Inner East, echoes the Department's policy of committing few financial resources to areas outside the CBD (DoE(NI) 1994). Expenditure incurred outside the CBD focussed on the upgrading of existing environmental features, i.e. forests and parks at the outskirts of the city. Little was directed towards improving the physical infrastructure in residential or commercial parts of the inner and outer city.

EMPLOYMENT AND THE PERIPHERY

The Belfast Residents Survey also highlighted concerns about local employment opportunities, including the question of personal safety restricting access to employment.

Asked to express agreement or disagreement with a series of statements, over half of the respondents felt that "the only jobs that people in this area can get are low paid" (Table 21.3). A sizeable minority across the city also found that "an address in this area" prejudiced against being given a job interview (32%) or that jobs were available only "in parts of Belfast where it is dangerous to work" (33%). These perceptions were most pronounced in the Catholic west of Belfast.

These responses reflect the reality of urban segregation. An increase in employment in the "neutral" city centre during the 1980s - while most other parts experienced employment decline (DoE(NI) 1994) - has shown little impact on the employment outlook and prospects in the west of the city. The office concentration strategy pursued by the DoE(NI) above all "relocated" employment. Hence, a separate analysis of Residents Survey data found that East Belfast residents - pulled into the CBD by relocations - were proportionately over-represented among city centre employees. Changes in the retail sector were characterised by the modernisation rather than the expansion of provisions. In particular, multiples of British retail chains replaced the declining stock of locally-owned department stores.

LESSONS FROM THE CITY CENTRE

The renewed search by the DoE(NI) for urban regeneration opportunities in disadvantaged areas has raised once again the question of how to improve the quality of life of residents by employing area-based strategies. The experience of city centre revitalisation - based on a combination of public sector grant assistance and an office concentration policy - provides an example of how physical and economic regeneration in the urban periphery could be encouraged by a Government policy of improving demand side conditions.

The contrast to-date between regeneration in the city centre and in the periphery could hardly be stronger. Whereas high yields and profit margins achieved in Belfast (Management Horizons 1989) persuaded retail chains from Great Britain to set up in Belfast's CBD, development projects in the periphery were mainly driven by local interests and interest groups. These often narrowly focussed on the provision of public and private sector housing, reinforced by sectarian divisions and the claim for "territory". Yet, this policy helped maintain population levels in the Catholic west of the city relative to other parts of Belfast, while over-spill occurred into South Belfast. This again encouraged new retail developments along the main arterial routes - hence the survey finding that shopping had improved in the Outer West - which showed that there was nothing inevitable about the decline of commercial activity in west Belfast.

A central weakness of urban policy in the 1980s was its inability to overcome the low take-up of its main plank, the Urban Development Grant in the urban periphery by both speculative investors and owner-occupiers[3]. The fear among property owners in the west was that the cost of development and upgrading could not be recouped given the stagnant property market. If the periphery's property market was stimulated, shopkeepers argued, investment would be much more likely and so would be associated employment spin-offs. Speculative investors, on the other hand, had their eyes clearly focussed on the city centre.

Table 3
Attitudes to Training and Employment in the Area
(% in Agreement with Statement)

	Belfast	Inner East	Inner North	Inner South	Inner West	Outer East	Outer North	Outer South	Outer West
The only jobs that people in this area can get are low paid	54	59	82	31	85	29	50	25	81
The only jobs available are in parts of Belfast where it is dangerous to work	33	29	36	38	66	14	32	13	61
An address in this area makes it difficult for young people to obtain job interviews	32	10	58	25	78	4	26	5	79

Source: adapted from Belfast Residents Survey 1994

Developers and business owners sought government signals of commitment to an area to instill confidence that investments will be secure. Environmental improvements were a useful ingredient helping to create conditions conducive to investment in the CBD. However, on their own, it is unlikely they would have triggered economic regeneration. Even in the demand-led regeneration environment of the city centre, for investment to come forward, the DoE had to *actively* facilitate the stabilisation of land values and the property market (to attract the property developer).

In September 1993, the University of Ulster announced a feasibility study of a new campus to be located in a redevelopment area in the west of the city. This announcement gave new life to a large scale regeneration project which had become entangled in a traditional development model of housing and training-cum-workshop provisions[4].

In the absence of a city-wide strategy for regeneration, or perhaps as a first phase, **major** public sector "statements" would appear an alternative or indeed prerequisite to urban regeneration in the periphery. For "pockets of regeneration" to have wider social benefits, they must be given an economic base. This base requires public commitment to an area to provide a secure environment for private investors.

Bibliography

Project Team (1976) , Belfast Areas of Special Social Need, Belfast: HMSO
    DoE(NI) (1987) Belfast Urban Area Plan 2001, Belfastt: HMSO
Brown, S. (1987), "Shopping centre development in Belfast", *Land Development Studies*, 4, 193-207
DoE(NI) (1994), Belfast Urban Policy Evaluation Study, Belfast: DoE(NI)
    Management Horizons (1989), Castlecourt Belfast - A Summary Report, Management Horizons: Twickenham
National Audit Office (1990), Regenerating the Inner Cities, London: HMSO
McGivern, W (1989), The Belfast Experience - A Perspective of housing renewal programmes in the inner-city, NIHE: Belfast
Wiener, R. (1980), The Rape and Plunder of the Shankill, Belfast: Farset

22

Quality of urban living: an infrastructural dimension

Qualité de la vie urbaine: la dimension de l'infrastructure

Cecilia Wong

Depuis les années 1980, les priorités politiques ont mis en valeur la régénération du tissu économique et social des zones urbaines en déclin de la Grande-Bretagne. Il est admis depuis longtemps que le concept de régénération contient plusieurs questions différentes. La Commission de la Communauté Européenne, reconnaissant l'existence de liens entre différents facteurs pour déterminer le potentiel de régénération urbaine d'une région, a réuni plusieurs indicateurs afin de réaliser un "index synthétique" pour son troisième "rapport de l'état des régions". De même, en Grande-Bretagne, les décideurs politiques ont cessé de croire en une "recette unique" pour réussir, et plusieurs ministères ont commissioné des études visant à identifier les points forts et les faiblesses des différentes régions pour leur permettre de mieux comprendre le contexte général des économies locales. Une région donnée tirera profit de telle ou telle opportunité de régénération en fonction de la combinaison unique des ressources dont elle dispose. L'objectif de cet exposé est de discuter l'utilisation d'indicateurs qunatitatifs, fonder qch sur des proposer mesures identifier pour un de ces études, pour évaluer les points forts et les faiblesses de la qualité de la vie dans les zones urbaines du point de vue de leurs ressources en infrastructures. Les études de cas de quinze administrative locales et de deux conurbations du nord de l'Angleterre illustrent les variations dans les différentes dimensions de qualité des infrastructures.

Mots clé: régénération urbaine; administrative locales, ressources en infrastructures; qualité de vie.

Keywords: urban regeneration; Local Authority Districts; infrastructural resources; living quality

Cities are seen as dynamic places which provide a wide variety of lifestyles, a great range of choices for both work and play, and a stimulating atmosphere. However, cities are also associated with crime, vandalism, deprivation, unemployment and all sorts of socio-economic problems. The economic restructuring since the 1970s has eroded the traditional manufacturing base of urban areas. Cities have suffered not only from the loss of employment but also from a rapid decrease in population. The counterurbanisation process has been evident with a tendency for population and employment growth to be concentrated in small and medium-sized towns and rural areas. However, in the 1980s, there have been suggestions of a trend towards re-urbanisation in most British cities. Statistics from the National Health Service Central Register show that the net out-migration rate of inner cities tended to be lower in the 1980s than the 1970s. This is partly related to the 'yuppie' culture as young single professionals have rediscovered the dynamics and excitement of city life. Also, the rapid increase in the number of dual career households means young couples prefer to stay in a metropolitan location to maximise the range of job opportunities available to both partners (Snaith, 1990). More importantly, the 1980s has been a decade when policy priorities have emphasised the regeneration of the social and economic fabric of declining urban areas in Britain.

Urban regeneration as a concept captures the problems of social and economic decline as well as the challenge of finding new ways to improve the social and environmental quality of living. Physical decay, social disadvantage and economic decline are often seen to be interlinked with each other. European policy-makers have not been slow to appreciate this diversity of influential factors shaping an area's regeneration potential. The Commission for the European Communities has commissioned a range of studies on how to improve the competitiveness of urban regions (eg. Biehl, 1986; NEI, 1992). In Britain, the key objectives of urban regeneration has been set out in 'Action for Cities' (Cabinet Office, 1988 & DoE, 1993). Policy-makers have abandoned their belief in a single 'recipe' for success. Different government departments have commissioned or carried out studies to identify the strengths and weaknesses of different areas to improve their understanding of the wider context of the local economy (eg. DTI et al, 1993; Coombes et al, 1992). It is the distinctive mix of indigenous resources which makes an area more or less likely to benefit from different types of regeneration opportunities (Fielding & Halford 1990).

The living quality of urban areas is identified as one of the influential factors affecting an area's regeneration potential (Coombes et al, 1992; IFO, 1990; NEI, 1992). Recent research development for 'rating places' using indicators of quality of life or economic prosperity has attracted much media attention and public interest (eg. Breheny et al, 1987; Champion & Green, 1990; Rogerson et al, 1989). The use of indicators to evaluate quality of life in different countries has long been an academic concern (eg. Cantril 1967, Liu 1976, Pacione 1980, Smith 1973). There has been much debate on the range of indicators to be included and their relative importance to the overall measurement (Carley, 1981).

This paper aims to discuss how to use appropriate quantitative indicators to assess the strengths and weaknesses of the living quality of urban areas in terms of their infrastructural resources. Fifteen Local Authority District (LAD) areas[1] in the two urban conurbations of North West England, Greater Manchester and Merseyside, are used as case studies to illustrate the variations in different dimensions of their infrastructural quality. The indicators used here are based on the proposed measures identified in the infrastructural component study (Coombes & Wong, 1993), which is one of a series of studies commissioned by a UK Government Department to develop an overall index to reflect the variations of local socio-economic conditions in terms of human, infrastructural, financial and locational resources.

INFRASTRUCTURE AND QUALITY OF LIFE

It is far from easy to achieve a single and generally accepted definition of infrastructure (Diamond & Spencer, 1989; Frey, 1979). In this study, a broad range of infrastructural types including, cultural, social and environmental amenities, are taken into account. This definition echoes the widely accepted definition of the Biehl report (1982) which defines infrastructure as the "public or social overhead capital element of the overall regional capital stock". One of the distinctive characteristics of infrastructural resources is that they are immobile, long-term features of an area (Coombes et al, 1992) which demarcate them from other more mobile factors of production such as labour and entrepreneurship. Nijkamp (1986) suggests that another defining feature of infrastructure is its *polyvalance* in terms of its multiple use for different activities. This emphasises the dual nature of infrastructure as both public goods and capital goods (Biehl, 1982). For instance, the presence of some public utilities may be seen as a form of infrastructure as they play a central role in facilitating the development of other enterprises or economic activities.

Quality of life is a multi-dimensional concept which aims to represent different aspects of the well-being of residents in an area. Liu (1977) identifies five goal areas (economic, political, environmental, heath and education, and social), from which indicators are chosen to measure the quality of life performance of American cities. The broader notion of different infrastructural resources in this study aims to reflect the relative prospects of an area's social, economic and environmental development in terms of its endowment of potentiality factors. Improvements in infrastructure can directly enhance the more intangible aspects of living quality in relation to one's social and environmental well-being (Bökemann, 1990; Coombes & Wong, 1993). Infrastructure provisions broaden the location-linked options of individuals such as where they live and where they work. With better accessibility to the infrastructure networks of road, rail, and air, interpersonal communication opportunities can be increased at both local and global levels (Bruinsma & Rietveld, 1993). The social and environmental living quality of individuals can also be affected by the provision of better housing, and the availability of cultural and heritage facilities.

The presence of infrastructure is not usually a sufficient condition for economic development, but it does provide a necessary resource basis for economic activity (Van Gent & Nijkamp, 1988). The positive externalities of infrastructural resources can trigger spin-off effects to the local economy in three different ways. Firstly, improvements in infrastructure can enhance the efficiency of other production factors, and is significant in explaining growth in productivity, income and employment (Biehl, 1986). Secondly, an area with a well balanced set of infrastructure (eg. good quality housing and other public facilities) is more likely to attract and maintain other mobile factors of human and financial capital (Diamond & Spencer, 1989). Thirdly, the transaction costs of industries and firms in an area can be reduced by improved transport and communication facilities (Bruinsma et al, 1990).

Following an extensive review of literature, an analytical framework was derived to provide a full coverage of different dimensions of infrastructural quality. However, any form of infrastructure which is ubiquitously available in Britain has been explicitly discounted, as such resources do not indicate any variations in local quality of living. Nine categories of infrastructure are identified in the analytical framework to establish an overall measurement. A 'wish list' of 20 candidate indicators (see Table 22.1) for each infrastructural category was then compiled . Nevertheless, the quality and specificity of these indicators vary considerably. This means it is necessary to filter these indicators through a rigorous selection process by using six specific criteria: (a) each indicator has to be relevant to the measurement of infrastructure; (b) data availability is another obvious constraint of indicator selection; (c) the data sources used have to provide a complete geographical coverage of Great Britain to enhance comparison and be available at the appropriate spatial scale; (d) the timeseries of data sources will affect an indicator's updatability and the possibility of monitoring changes; (e) the measurement of indicators has to be easily implementable; and (f) there is a preference for the indicators to be readily interpreted.

Twelve indicators under six infrastructural categories were finally chosen for the study after applying the above six principles of indicator selection, and going through a consultation exercise with policy-makers. Due to the difficulties of obtaining appropriate statistics, indicators of three infrastructural types (utilities, pollution/waste management, and institutional context) were discarded. Though this results in measurement gaps in a few infrastructural categories, it is more important to avoid any distortion that is likely to arise from defective measures. Table 22.2 provides a summary account of each of the twelve selected indicators.

A CASE STUDY OF THE CONURBATIONS IN NW ENGLAND

Similar to the fate of other British conurbations, Greater Manchester and Merseyside have suffered from massive industrial decline and undergone a process of economic restructuring since the mid-1960s. In spite of these common economic problems, each area within these two conurbations have gone through a specific regeneration experience and they exhibit variations in terms of their potential for future development. This study aims to investigate the variations in local infrastructure of the fifteen LAD areas in the two conurbations. In the Greater Manchester there are ten LADs: Bolton, Bury, Manchester, Oldam, Rochdale, Salford, Stockport, Tameside, Trafford and Wigan. There are five LADs in Merseyside: Liverpool, Knowsley, Sefton, St. Helens and Wirral. Table 3 shows the values of the 12 infrastructural indicators for all these LADs with Great Britain as a benchmark.

Both Merseyside and Greater Manchester are cosmopolitan areas with a mix of different ethnic and social groups. Most of the LAD areas in the conurbations have a good social mix of different occupational groups which is indicated by values in the social polarisation indicator that are similar to or above the national average. It is interesting to find that the three more "wealthy" areas, Stockport, Sefton and Wirral have a higher degree of social segregation. This is because pockets of areas in these three LADs are affluent suburbs where the professional middle class tends to concentrate. However, in the case of Liverpool, the slightly stronger tendency of spatial segregation probably reflects its state of depression which reinforces the north-south divide in the City. Another aspect of social infrastructure is the enterprise climate of an area. As residents in professional and managerial socio-economic groups are the major dynamics of small firm start-up, the indicator thereby standardises for this main social structure influence to account for the effects of local enterprise culture. Manchester City stands out as an area with a very strong enterprise culture, the level of new VAT registrations in the area is far higher than the national average. Salford, Trafford and Liverpool also exhibit their dynamics in new firm formation. Rochdale, Oldham and Tameside in Greater Manchester, are performing well in terms of new firm fertility rates. This may be partly related to the local culture of setting up small textile factories, and partly explained by a high concentration of Asian population which tends to have higher self-employment rates than the white population (Campbell & Daly, 1992). Areas that have a sluggish enterprise climate tend to concentrate in Merseyside, including the more depressed area of St. Helens as well as the more well-off areas of Sefton and Wirral.

The presence of science parks does not only signify the availability of very prestigious industrial sites, but also the strong linkage with Higher Education Institutions (HEIs) to enhance the transfer of technology and business skills. All the LADs in the two conurbations have good access to science parks in the region. However, LADs located in the east of Manchester also enjoy accessibility to science parks in South and West Yorkshire whereas Wirral benefits from easy access to parks in North Wales. This locational advantage of the conurbations is echoed by the high value of accessibility to potential research contacts. The two conurbations have a high concentration of HEIs: there are four universities in the Manchester area and two in Merseyside. LADs that located at the periphery of Greater Manchester also benefit from the accessibility to institutions outside the conurbation, Wigan is the best example as it can access to HEIs in Merseyside as well. In comparison, Wirral is losing out in terms of quick access to potential research contacts in the region.

Turning to domestic property, it is important to look at the range of choice in an area in terms of house and tenure types to meet with the diversified market demand. The three Cities, Manchester, Salford and Liverpool, in the two conurbations provide a far wider range of choice than the national average. This is because these areas tend to have a larger private rental sector and more public housing provision. The advantage of these is to encourage young single people and unskilled labour to take up jobs in the area. On the other hand, the more affluent areas of Stockport, Trafford and Sefton tend to have a less diverse housing market.

After two decades of economic restructuring, the industrial mix of most areas has tended to converge towards the national structure, this is especially true of Stockport, Trafford, Salford, and Bolton in the Greater Manchester conurbation. The favourable industrial structure in these areas is reflected in their forecasted employment growth by the year 2000. However, places like Knowsley, Oldham, Tameside and Rochdale still have a relatively specialised economy, especially in those declining industrial sectors such as engineering, textile and clothing, which leads to a slight forecasted decline in total employment. In general, a more diversified economy is seen to be healthier and less vulnerable to the decline of any particular industrial sector. However with a slightly specialised structure, Manchester, Bury, Liverpool, Sefton and Wirral are forecasted to have an above average growth rate. This is attributable to the concentration of growth sectors (such as health and education, other services) and the lack of a presence of large mining, metal or engineering industries.

Table 1 A 'Wish List' of Infrastructural Factors

Infrastructural Categories	Candidate Indicators	Chosen Indicators
G Social and Cultural	G1 social polarisation G2 enterprise climate G3 theatres & concert halls	* *
H Housing / Property	H1 science parks H2 house price H3 lower earning owner occupiers H4 mix of housing	* * *
I Industrial Structure	I1 employment forecast I2 industrial diversification I3 establishment size	* *
K Knowledge /Information	K1 potential research contacts K2 key information facilities	*
S Scenery / Image	S1 heritage scenery S2 heritage facilities	* *
T Transport / Communication	T1 access to seaports T2 access to airports T3 public transport usage T4 telematics use	* * *
U Utilities	U1 cost of gas to industry	
W Waste / Pollution Management	W1 waste management services	
X Institutional Context	X1 local authority structure	

Table 2   Indicators of Infrastructural Resources

Indicators	Description of Indicators
G1 social polarisation	this measures the degree of spatial segregation of two social groups (the semi-skilled and unskilled versus the remaining classes). High value means more social harmony.
G2 enterprise climate	this is a standardised birth rate of small firms (the number of new firms registering for VAT per 100 economic active Social Class I and II residents).
H1 science parks	this measures the accessibility to science parks which can provide strong linkage with HEIs and can facilitate the transfer of technology; the index is weighted by the acreage of the parks. High values imply good accessibility.
H2 house price	this is a 'housing mix weighted' average representing 1991 housing price for an area.
H4 mix of housing	this measures the degree of variety of housing in terms of eight categories (by separating out some house types within the tenure groups). High values indicate a good range of choice.
I1 employment forecast	this indicator directly implements the Warwick University forecasting model which applies national prediction of employment change by 17 industrial sectors to the local sectoral mix.
I2 industrial diversification	this measures the divergence of an area's industrial mix from the national structure. High values indicate areas with industrial structure similar to the country as a whole, which is interpreted as a diversified economy.
K1 potential research contacts	this measures the accessibility to HEIs which is a potential source of expertise and research capacity; the index is weighted by the number of academic staff.
S1 heritage scenery	this measures an area's accessibility to the designated national heritage scenery (ie. National Parks, Areas of Outstanding Natural Beauty, Heritage Coastlines). High values mean good accessibility.
S2 heritage facilities	this measures the relative attractiveness of an area (ie. the number of visitors to facilities such as museums, historic buildings, stately homes and galleries standardised by the number of local residents). High values represent the local presence of tourism-related attractions.
T1 access to seaports	this measures the relative accessibility of each area from Britain's ports; and the index is weighted by the tonnage throughput (excluding petro-chemicals) of each port. High values signify good accessibility.
T2 access to airports	this measures the accessibility to airports; the index is weighted by the capacity of the airport (ie. the number of scheduled international flights). High values imply good accessibility to large airports.
T3 public transport usage	this measures the number of public transport commuters who live in car owning households. High values suggest that the local public transport provision is more adequate than elsewhere.

Table 3 Indicator Values for the Nine TEC Areas in NW England

	Bolton/ Bury	CEW TEC	Manchester	Merseyside	METRO TEC	Oldham	QUALI TEC	Rochdale	Stockport / High Peak	Great Britain
G1	79.06	72.95	78.25	73.24	83.17	77.87	83.18	81.51	75.52	78.70
G2	3.23	2.78	4.66	3.33	3.12	3.52	2.67	3.66	3.38	3.39
H1	48.57	66.08	49.96	48.79	49.04	51.07	49.51	50.81	50.79	48.61
H2	50416	58097	50034	49499	48973	38395	50450	45088	65108	62508
H4	80.05	80.46	33.38	82.51	78.64	78.93	78.73	81.58	79.05	81.30
I1	1.29	2.56	2.50	3.63	-0.1	-0.9	0.14	0.0	0.97	1.87
I2	89.71	89.83	92.40	92.25	88.04	81.12	85.82	83.27	90.70	100.00
K1	52.02	44.24	52.00	46.40	56.45	52.92	52.09	52.21	52.66	47.43
S1	34.68	28.02	32.88	27.97	31.85	34.21	29.72	35.34	31.59	41.76
S2	1.17	8.33	2.80	6.33	3.03	0.71	0.31	0.93	4.19	5.84
T1	50.86	54.51	50.37	55.19	55.90	49.82	56.58	49.47	51.04	56.87
T2	19.71	12.86	20.25	13.21	18.24	20.23	16.78	19.14	20.70	29.15
T3	10.96	11.58	14.11	17.91	8.82	12.52	10.92	10.63	9.74	12.65

Environmental quality, both natural and built, affects an area's amenity and quality of life as well as its image to outsiders. The two conurbations are not well endowed with natural heritage, which is clearly reflected from the LADs' below average accessibility scores to heritage scenery. Fortunately, the built heritage of Manchester and Liverpool do create a magnet to attract a massive number of visitors to the North West. The Granada Studio Tours and G-Mex Centre in Manchester have attracted 1.5 million visitors in 1992. The successful regeneration story of Albert Dock (with Tate Gallery and Maritime Museum) in Liverpool have drawn in another million. Another well-performing area is Sefton because of the seaside amusement attraction of Southport. With the flagship project of Wigan Pier, Wigan has attracted more tourists than the remaining areas in the two conurbations.

The transport networks of an area are extremely important to personal and business mobility. Accessibility to seaports is increasingly important to trade with the European market (Diamond & Spencer, 1989). Nearly all LADs in Greater Manchester have below average accessibility to large seaports, whereas Merseyside enjoys the locational advantage of the coastline. In spite of Greater Manchester districts' below average scores, they enjoy good air transport accessibility. The national average value is largely skewed by the concentration of three large airports in Greater London. Bearing this in mind, Manchester Airport does provide one of the best service outside the South East. Merseyside tends to perform worse in this indicator because of its distance from Manchester Airport. Both conurbations have a well developed public transport network especially with the considerable success of the Merseyrail system. It is also important to point out that the index values of some Greater Manchester areas will have been underscored because the Metrolink service was in operation just after the conduction of the 1991 Census. This indicator shows that quite a large proportion of car-owners actually commute by public transport. This high level of usage will both help to preserve the viability of the infrastructure and contribute to the greening of the environment.

CONCLUSIONS

The analysis of the twelve infrastructural indicators demonstrate the wide variations in the operating environment and the living quality of the fifteen LADs in the two North West conurbations. Areas such as Rochdale, Oldham and Tameside have suffered from a specialised economy concentrating on declining industrial sectors, but they also have a strong enterprise culture. This means policy-makers can focus their development on channelling indigenous resources to diversify the local economy. Both Manchester and Liverpool have shown their dynamics as a city in terms of the range of facilities and choices they provide, such as better public transport networks, a wide range of heritage facilities and wider house choice. On the other hand, one cannot neglect their inner city problems, such as their poor accessibility to scenic countryside and the problem of social polarisation in Liverpool. However, the employment prospects of these two areas look positive with their changing industrial structure. Stockport, Sefton and Wirral are better-off areas with pockets of attractive suburbia which provide the most popular environment for living and investment. Nevertheless, their remoteness from the typical urban problems also implies the existence of other difficulties, for instance, Sefton and Wirral's lack of immediate accessibility to HEIs, and the problem of spatial segregation in Stockport. The value of such analysis is to identify the strengths, weaknesses, opportunities and threats of an area which can then provide a basis for policy-makers to structure their development strategies.

Acknowledgements

This paper arises from part of the work undertaken on a research project funded by a UK Government Department. The author acknowledges the inputs of other researchers, in particular Mike Coombes and Simon Raybould of CURDS at Newcastle University.

Notes

[1] Local Authority District areas are demarcated by the administrative boundaries of local governments. In the metropolitan areas of Greater Manchester and Merseyside, the fifteen local authorities are responsible for a wide range of local services which include education, housing, planning, transport, social services, environmental services, local taxation etc.

References

Biehl, D (Coordinator) (1982) *The Contribution of Infrastructure to Regional Development* Final Report to Infrastructure Study Group, Brussels
Biehl, D (1986) *The Contribution of Infrastructure to Regional Development* Commission of the European Communities, Luxembourg
Bökemann, D (1990) The importance of infrastructure in regional evolution, in *Infrastructure and the Space Economy* (edited by Peschel, K) Springer-Verlag Berlin, Heidelberg, 81-100
Breheny, M, Hall, P and Hart, D (1987) *Northern Lights: a development agenda for the north in the 1990s Derrick Wade & Waters*, Preston

Bruinsma, F, Nijkamp, P and Rietveld, P (1990) Employment impacts of infrastructure investments: a case study for the Netherlands, in *Infrastructure and the Space Economy* (edited by Peschel, K) Springer-Veriag Berlin, Heidelberg, 209-226

Bruinsma, F and Rietveld, P (1993) Urban agglomerations in European infrastructure networks *Urban Studies* 30(6), 919-934

Cabinet Office (1988) *Action for Cities* HMSO, London

Campbell, M and Daly, M (1992) Self-employment: into the 1990s *Employment Gazette*, June 1992, 269-292

Cantril, H (1967) *The Human Dimension: Experience in Policy Research* Rutgers University Press, New Jersey

Carley, M (1981) *Social Measurement and Social Indicators* George Allen & Unwin, London

Champion, A and Green, A E (1990) *The Spread of Prosperity and the North-South Divide Booming Towns* Gosforth & Kenilworth, Newcastle-upon-Tyne

Coombes, M G and Wong, C (1993) *Local Environment Index: Infrastructural Resources Dimension*, an unpublished report to a UK Government Department, CURDS, University of Newcastle-upon-Tyne

Coombes, M G, Raybould, S and Wong C (1992) *Developing Indicators to Assess the Potential for Urban Regeneration* HMSO, London

Department of Employment (1988) *Employment for the 1990s* (Cm. 540) HMSO, London

Department of Employment (1993) *Annual Report on Research* DE, Sheffield.

Department of the Environment (1993) *The Government's Action for Cities Initiatives* DoE, London

Department of Trade and Industry, The Scottish Office, The Welsh Office (1993) *Regional Policy Review of the Assisted Areas of Great Britain* DTI, London

Diamond, D and Spencer, N (1989) *Infrastructure and Industrial Costs in British Industry* HMSO, London

Fielding, A and Halford, S (1990) *Patterns and Processes of Urban Change in the United Kingdom* HMSO, London

Frey, R L (1979) *Die Infrastruktur als Mittel der Regionalpolitik* Bern

IFO (1990) *An Empirical Assessment of Factors Shaping Regional Competitiveness in Problem Regions* Commission of the European Communities, Brussels

Liu, B-C (1976) *Quality of Life Indicators in US Metropolitan Areas: a statistical analysis* Praeger, New York

Liu, B-C (1977) Economic and non-economic quality of life *American Journal of Economics and Sociology* 36, 226-240

NEI (1992) *New Location Factors for Mobile Investment in Europe* DGXVI, Commission of the European Communities, Brussels

Nijkamp, P (1986) Infrastructure and regional development: a multidimensional policy analysis *Empirical Economics* 11, 1-21

Pacione, M (1980) Different quality of life in a metropolitan village *Transactions, Institute of British Geographers*, NS5, 185-206

Rogerson, R J, Findlay, A M, Morris, A S and Henderson, J W (1989) *Britain's Intermediate Cities: a comparative study of quality of life* Glasgow Quality of Life Group, Department of Geography, University of Glasgow

Smith, D M (1973) *The Geography of Social Well-Being in the United States* McGraw-Hill, New York

Snaith, J (1990) Migration and dual career households, in *Labour Migration* (edited by Johnson, J H and Salt, J) David Fulton, London, 155-171

Van Gent, H A and Nijkamp, P (1988) Mobility, transportation and development *I.A.T.I.S. Research* 11, 62-68

23

The changing urban values of the Bulgarian cities

Changements des valeurs urbaines des villes Bulgares

Vesselina Troeva

L'étude du développement des villes bulgares est le résultat d'une recherche scientifique de l'auteur sur les fonctions écologiques, esthétiques, psychologiques et utilitaires des espaces urbains. Elle présente deux étapes, liées aux changements politiques et socio-économiques du pays après la Seconde Guerre mondiale.

L'analyse porte sur les changements de la structure urbaine et sociale, ainsi que sur le comportement des protagonistes de la réforme urbaine - les politiciens, juristes, urbanistes, promoteurs et entrepreneurs, ainsi que l'individu et la société en général. On étudie les défis présentés par la période de transition et leur influence sur la conception des valeurs urbaines les plus importantes - la nature d'où nous puisons la force de vivre en milieu urbain, les monuments culturels et historiques qui conservent la mémoire de la nation, les structures et les relations sociales qui assurent le développement de la société.

Les conclusions tirées portent sur les conséquences de la politique urbaine centralisée et sur les problèmes prévisibles de la démocratisation de la planification urbaine et de la décentralisation du contrôle de l'aménagement du territoire. L'auteur présente aussi les principales tâches à entreprendre dans la gestion administrative, la législation, et l'urbanisme, ainsi que dans les domaines professionnels et éducatifs.

Mots clé: milieu urbain; régénération urbaine; valeurs urbaines.

Keywords: built environment, urban renewal, urban values.

The political, social and economic changes in Central and Eastern Europe have their inevitable impact on the land use and planning and on the methods for urban development management. This is due not only to the transition from planned to market economy and the restitution measures. The changing forms of property and the new attitudes towards planning increase substantially the number of decision makers involved in development of Bulgarian cities. In this new environment, it appears necessary more than ever before, to face the current problems from a completely new perspective, borrowing on both the positive as well as the negative urban experience in the developed countries, whose route Bulgaria is trying to follow.

At the outset, it appears very important to consider changing the public and professional awareness and understanding of few basic and simple truths:

* The transition from planned to market economy does not mean in the least denying the need for planning;
* Democratization in urban planning does not mean uncontrolled land use and management;
* Private initiative liberalization does not mean encouragement of uncoordinated individual initiatives at the societal expense; * Property and land restitution does not mean neglecting the social mission of urban policy;

Among all other principles for sustainable development, the professionals should find the way to enhance those proper urban values, which are basic in relation to the self-realization of the urban population. In this respect means should be found to control socially unjustified manifestations of personal creativity and initiative.

RETROSPECTIVE ANALYSIS

The general development of the Bulgarian cities after the Second World War follows the traditional pattern of East European cities. The fast growth of cities like Sofia, Varna, Plovdiv, Bourgass, Rousse, Stara Zagora, Pleven etc. is due mainly to the neighboring industrial locations, which brought escalating increase of the population and the accompanying housing crisis. The alluring perspective to use the industrial enterprise investments for public utilities, city centres renewal and technical infrastructure was limited to partial implementation of social programmes, which included social housing and culture houses construction. These housing estates with predominating small flats were designed to meet the needs of young specialists or couples without children. The so called culture houses duplicated the existing culture, communist party or youth houses with their analogous functions, forms, volume and architectural image. This was one of the reasons for ineffective use of this expensive complexes, which consumed impressive financial resources, badly needed for education and health services.

The solution of the acute housing problems in big cities was carried out at the expense of agricultural fertile land, suitable for the construction of prefabricated industrial systems. In this way were created the unified housing estates on the urban fringe which destroyed the link with the natural environment and ignored the microclimate, the land forms, the character of the city. Planned according to the urban theory rules, they rarely reached full completion and all the necessary elements of public and administrative services. The public utilities and housing landscaping actions were carried out only in some prestigious complexes. Journalists, painters, researchers, lecturers and workers, among others, had to survive in this featureless, monotonous and grey environment and also to preserve their emotional and creative potential, to educate and bring up their children. Bringing together inhabitants with different cultural background and lifestyle - those seeking better self-realization in the big city and the old city dwellers, forced to leave their homes in the central parts because of the planned public construction actions, is by itself a precondition for serious social and psychological problems, for apathy, hostility and alienation.

At the same time the central parts of some cities were left intact or half-rebuilt because of the redevelopment plans that never came into life for lack of sufficient investments. Witnesses to this are the still existing abandoned bare constructions in the centres of Shumen and Bourgass. In other cities the imposed stale models for the city centres with the compulsory set of communist party, local council and cultural buildings resulted in the destruction of the historical heritage and individuality throughout the country. The situation is somewhat different in those cities, which had the chance to be on the route of the annual diplomatic corps country tours as Blagoevgrad, Lovetch, Smoljan, where the government spent lavishly on the urban centres reconstruction. Put simply, at the expense of sacrificed historical values and professional compromises, the so called "corps urban design" provided the impressive party, cultural and office ensembles with surrounding enormous open public spaces - fully organized and landscaped, yet exceeding by far the scale of the town and the needs of its population.

"Art synthesis" was to be part of the overall architectural designs. At the same time the efforts of scores of Bulgarian architects, painters, sculptors and designers to make the urban environment more aesthetically acceptable and more humane had short term effect. The impressive monuments, which are the focal points of almost every central urban place and park and which are so hotly debated to-day, demonstrate their grave and strong presence in everyday societal life and stand like eternal symbols of totalitarianism and communism.

The retrospective assessment of the urban development in Bulgaria is a very contradictory subject, both from professional and social points of view. The professionals can not accept the overall rejection of the large scale interdisciplinary plans, such as the National unitary development plan, the development plan of the Black sea coast, the landscape plans for national parks, the city centres urban renewal and some separate prestigious projects, ordered and financed by the Government. The public opinion on these issues is contradictory and usually too strongly influenced by the political partialities to be accepted as a valid criteria.

The social, ecological, aesthetic and economic consequences of the centralized urban policy could be summarized as follows:
- concentration of population in the big cities and depopulation of the small towns and villages, situated predominantly in remote and frontier regions;
- destruction of social structure in the city centres;
- urban ecology aggravation caused by inappropriate transport, industrial and other developments;
- intensification of the housing crisis, despite the construction of a great number of small flats, yet unsuitable for the real needs of the population;
- destruction of urban structures, scale, character and townscape; - worsening of the quality of life in the cities due to the destroyed urban values and creation of negative attitudes in the population towards the everyday environment.

The urban development results of the last few decades are yet to be reevaluated. The main aim of the conferences organized by the National club of Urbanists and the discussions held in the Ministry for Regional Development and Construction was to draw the general requirements about new legislation and to determine the directions of urban policy in the period of political and socioeconomic transition.

THE CHANGES TODAY

The conditions for the urban planning reform in Bulgaria are complicated and conflicting. In addition to the well known phenomena, accompanying economic crisis, the specific features include political and legislative uncertainty, political and social polarization, lack of professional ethic in the competitive environment, land and property speculations, decreased control on the urban development, destroyed institutional structures of urban planning . It is difficult to foresee the models of social behavior, once the euphoria of newly won freedoms fades away and the illusions for fast and easy solutions of the major economic, political, social and ecological problems get replaced by the realities of life. One can expect and to some extent acquit the negative public overreactions, which come to compensate for long deprived freedoms, identity and individuality, initiative and participation in decision making.

The changes in Bulgarian cities during the last five years are a result of these specific conditions of transition. They are not large scale and impressive, but have a considerable impact on the social, natural and cultural urban values.

The extension of the circle of participants in urban planning and construction presented the state, planners and local administration with many contradictory challenges. Few people are capable of making good choices in conditions of prevailing negativism and disruptive forces. In the urban environment it is almost impossible to obliterate the past and start everything from scratch. It is even more impossible to change overnight the public consciousness and the professionals' way of thinking.

As pendulum effects tend to work, one alternative to large scale planning initiatives are the current private initiatives. They started timidly from the ground floors of houses, flats, from garages and backyards, reconstructed to supplement the inefficient enterprises in the sectors of retailing, social services and catering. This tendency spread gradually to the bigger stores, restituted architectural monuments, public open spaces, parks, public transport facilities etc. The most alarming cases are those of functional transformation of the restituted cultural, educational and health service buildings. We still don't think enough about the consequences of destroying large parts of the green system and its aesthetic and ecological impact upon the built up environment. There is also the phenomenon of mushrooming glossy, colourful boutiques and cafes all over the cities, usually in full operation well beyond official approval, providing otherwise badly needed services at the expense of general disorder and disturbed living comfort.

The private initiative in the housing areas has varying dimensions in the different regions. The largest scale is typical for the areas with recreational resources and traditions in the tourism development. The delay of the Black Sea Coast Development and Management Act resulted in the uncontrolled construction of too many big private hotels and enterprises in that part of the country. Housing developments in the centres of bigger cities provided opportunities for both owners and architects. The owners, having waited too long for the implementation of the development plans can thus solve their housing problems. The architects have also the chance to demonstrate their abilities beyond the boundaries of prefabricated construction systems. The aspiration for prestige and self-expression led to the spread of illogical and environmentally strange buildings, sometimes contravening the urban acts and regulations with the local authorities illegal permission. The vicious circle of disloyal competition, lack of professional ethic and corruption the assigning, design, approval and construction produces not necessarily the best buildings that Bulgarian architects are capable of creating. And they are long there to stay.

In the capital and cities, alluring to the foreign investor with their strategic position, the owners face another challenge. They have to decide between staying in the heart of the city, providing the local authorities want to preserve the main living function, and assigning construction rights to the rich investors against appropriate compensation. The latter will probably create the full range of financial, business, retailing and animation complexes, hotels and offices according to their own taste and vision. In the situation of escalating inflation and restrictive state financial policy for housing loans, the local dwellers have no real choice. The local authorities have not many options either, because of budget restrictions and lack of rules and procedures for the increase of their financial resource.

Problems in urban development are created also by the restitution of land, which was until recently reserved for big urban park developments. It is impossible to limit the rights of the original owners even when the respective spaces are very important for the urban ecology and population health and recreation. The situation is similar in areas expropriated for construction of schools, universities, hospitals, clinics and buildings of great social importance. This is one reason why the new legislation foresees the limitation of private interests to the benefit of society. The monuments of totalitarianism, like those of Lenin, Soviet liberation army, the Mausoleum of George Dimitrov etc. have recently been the focus of many controversial public and professional disputes. These monuments, awkward as they appear to many people, are also creations of outstanding Bulgarian artists, sculptors and architects. Not the professionals, whose mission and professional ideology is to create, face the difficult and delicate choices: to accept the demolition of these "creative" symbols of communism, to find new functions for the monuments and their environment or to leave free the choice to the next generations, unencumbered by political prejudices. In the meantime these monuments are objects of unheard of vandalism, that increases the political tension and polarization. Maybe they play also an important role as outlets of the popular frustration and tension.

In the near future the country will face another fact it is hardly prepared for - the unexpectedly short life span of the prefabricated housing. The inevitable future collapse of the prefabricated concrete constructions in a short period of time, almost all over the country, is bound to create enormous social, technological, financial, organisational and ecological problems. The rehousing of a great number of dwellers, demolition of the buildings, the transportation, deposit and reuse of the construction waste are just a small number of the tasks for which we have no clear strategy and programme.

The less important problems for the moment include the maintenance of the urban environment - buildings, complexes, streets, parks, open spaces with the accompanying natural and cultural values, which give us the strength to survive in contact with history, culture, urban liveliness and the beauty of Nature.

CONCLUSIONS

It is true that high quality of the urban environment is a creation of a prosperous society. It is also true that the development of society is possible only if such high quality of life is provided and if the natural, cultural and social values of the cities are preserved. This reflects on the mission of the planners today. They have to win back the confidence of society and the prestige of their profession by helping the placement of urban development issues on an equal footing with the economic and ecological priorities in government policy.

The distribution of responsibilities for making and renovating the Bulgarian cities have to guarantee the integration and coordination of the different and sometimes mutually incompatible interests of the participants in the urban planning activities - individuals, public administration, planning teams, developers, government, society as a whole. To achieve this a full set of laws and regulations are necessary, including mechanisms that will allow control over all spontaneous initiatives through the planning programmes on an operational level. Solutions to these tasks are inconceivable without coordination between urban planning practice and education reforms. Special knowledge and skills should be developed for the specialists in the area of urban policy, applied urban theory, administration, land and estate management. These specialists have to establish and enhance the urban values which provide the psychological balance, emotional experience, cultural development, self-realization and prosperity of urban society.

References

Dikov, P. "Urban planning in the period of change" Sofia, Arch & Art bull. 21/1993 and 22/1993

Hiss, T. "The experience of place" Vintage Books edition, New York, 1990 ISBN-0-679-73549-1

Parkinson, M., Folex, B. and Judd, D. (ed.) "Regenerating the cities. The UK crisis and US experience." Fulbright Papers 4 Published by Manchester University Press, 1988 ISBN 0-7190-2475-7

Thornley, A. "Urban planning under Thatcherism" Routledge, London and New York 1991, ISBN 0-415-05538-5

Tonev, L. "Urban planning in Bulgaria", Sofia, Edited by "Technic" 1984

24

Regenerating the lost green of Ankara: a hard task ahead

Faire d'Ankara une ville à nouveau verte: une tache difficile

Nazan Aydin-Wheater and Gaye Culcuoglu

Cet exposé se base sur l'inventaire des espaces verts et des mesures visant à appliquer la politique urbaine de ceinture verte à Ankara, capitale de la Turquie. Cet inventaire révèle un manque de structure nationale et conceptuelle nécessaire à la mise en oeuvre des décisions.

La population d'Ankara a fortement augmenté depuis les années 1920, et la ville a souffert des conséquences d'une urbanisation rapide. Pendant ces quarante dernières années, les espaces verts, entre tous les plus vulnérables, ont continuellement cédé du terrain face au développement urbain. Les premières initiatives pour remédier à ce phénomène sont apparues au début des années 1980 et se sont concentrées sur la création de "ceintures vertes" visant à combattre la pollution. La question "verte" apparaissait ainsi à l'ordre du jour des urbanistes.

Des études de cas, l'étude d'écrits sur le sujet, de plans, de projets et des entretiens avec des urbanistes, nous permettent penser que la création d'une capitale turque "vraiment verte" s'avèrera difficile. Les parcs urbains sont le plus souvent négligés, et de simples parcelles boisées sont considérées comme des "ceintures vertes". Il faudrait adopter une approche plus large, holistique et interdisciplinaire pour pouvoir envisager des solutions.

Mots clé: régénération; vert; ceinture verte; Ankara.

Keywords: regeneration; green; green belts; Ankara.

Ankara is the capital city of Turkey. However, it is still Istanbul that has the leading position in capital market activities, trading, finance and information technologies. Ankara has recently also started to lose its unique character as the centre of Turkish media to Istanbul. Istanbul views the world as a smaller place, and asserts itself to be more global, more cosmopolitan. Ankara, on the other hand, is currently in search of a reinforced identity, as opposed to that of Istanbul, the imperial capital of the past. Ankara aims at strengthening its well respected image as the voice of nationalism and Kemalism, but at the same time an enlightened positivism and westernism. It is above all, the capital city of the seventy year old Turkish Republic. This must be the core of the image it intends to promote.

Seventy years ago, in 1923, Ankara was announced to the nation as the new capital city by the leaders of the independence movement. Selecting a new capital in Central Anatolia to counter-balance the power of Istanbul superimposed some necessary duties for the new regime: Ankara, in the early 1920's, was no more than a small Anatolian town of which economy was based on mohair production and population reached only about 20 000 (Akcura, 1971; Gunay, 1988.). The physically inadequate and desolate small Anatolian town was to be reconstructed to properly present the image of a capital city, and injected new functions to serve the nation politically and economically as well as geographically.

PLANNING AND DESIGNING THE IMAGE OF CAPITAL CITY

There are four major planning processes in the planning history of Ankara:
The Jansen Plan (1932-1957)

Due to a shortage of qualified professionals in the field of urban planning, an international competition was held in 1928 to generate an ideal scheme for Ankara's prospective 'capital city like' development. The jury selected Hermann Jansen's master plan as the best alternative amongs the others. 'Jansen was realistic and modest with no bias to the Baroque planning principles. He considered the neighbourhood unit as the element making up a city rather than avenues and plazas. In this respect, he is somewhat different compared with urban design approaches which are two dimensional and dependent solely on 'road planning'. The design of neighbourhood units with garden city principles, provision of large green belts are all reminiscent of the English garden city.' (Gunay, 1988). Oztan, on the other hand, reported that 'Jansen in his plan for Ankara reflected his determination for protection but at the same time development of the city's natural, topographical, morphological and microclimatic features in reference to functional recreational green and also emphasized his sensitivity on such issues' (Oztan, 1991). The natural green belts within the periphery of the capital which mainly consisted of vineyards were indeed largely intact on the paper.

Jansen missed one important point in his analyses: the input from the likely consequences of a massive urbanization process by which Ankara's macroform was to be shaped. 'This was a period of unprecedented increase in rural-urban migration countrywide and Ankara got much more than its share of it. The 1980 population target of the Jansen plan was reached 30 years before time' (AMPO, 1978). Implementation of the plan proved difficult as there already occurred '... density increases in the city and opening of new land for urban development. Furthermore, there were signs of squatting in certain portions of the city' (Gunay, 1988). Another international competition was to be organized in 1955 to find a remedy for the capital's unexpected ill-development.

The Uybadin-Yucel plan (1957-1969):

The Uybadin-Yucel plan was, by and large, an extension of the Jansen plan. The Turkish planners team were careful to retain the theme of 'garden city' for the new Ankara. But unfortunately their plan was to be out of date in the face of rapid developments. As some planners would like to phrase it the Uybadin-Yucel plan was 'born dead' (as was Jansen's), because first of all their population projection of 750,000 for the year 2000 was reached long before that date, in the early 1960's. In this plan period squatting further spread around the city. Due to limited development space within the master plan boundaries, high-rise apartment blocks were built and formed speedily the residential parts of Ankara by individuals and small contracting companies. The green set aside on the plan was shared between the squatters, apartment block dwellers and the developers. The idea of the green garden city was to wither away. Administrative control over the urban green and urban land in general weakened. Speculative pressures, instead of governmental apparatus shaped the market price of the land.

Air pollution, on the other hand, was to begin creating real problems for Ankara during the late 1960's. The unplanned developments, thus gave the first signal in this plan period towards moving to a more rational and flexible thinking in planning. This time hopes were to be fostered for the activities of the Ankara Metropolitan Planning Office- AMPO which was founded within the ministerial structure of the Ministry of Reconstruction and Resettlement in 1969.

The AMPO plan (1970-1985)

The AMPO Plan is the first not to draw up precise development boundaries for Ankara. In this respect, it is to be distinguished from the previous plans which were both master plans in character. The AMPO plan, although formally named as master plan, was in effect a 'structure plan' in employing certain techniques for decision making and implementation processes. A number of proposals made by the AMPO planning team was implemented quite effectively by the local government such as the organized industrial and housing developments and squatter prevention zones in the western stretch of the city. Having been once pre-disposed to the effects of rapid urbanization which was organic and natural, the macroform of the capital could still not be freed from the shaping power of the prevailing speculative pressures in this plan period, either. In this state of affairs and under the catalyst effect of the financial and administrative reorganization of the local authorities in 1985, AMPO was eventually to be closed.

Green deficiency re-visited

In the decades of high density urban development of Ankara came the usual story. The late 1970's and early 1980's witnessed re-awakening for the sight of green both in the centre and periphery of Ankara. As the AMPO plan summary pointed out there was '... a great deficiency in the provision of urban and local public open space' and the deficiency was '... as high as 95% and 86% at the local and urban levels respectively measured by the plan standards' (AMPO, 1978). Furthermore the available large swath of green was almost all owned by the military institutions, universities, foreign embassies and some first rank public institutions. Then it follows that the ordinary inhabitants of Ankara were dismayed also from not having access to what we may call the 'invisible green' on top of the visible green deficiency problem. Planners had to tread carefully though, as regards the latter part of the whole issue, the access question, since it would have been a herculean task to perform if any promises had been made towards solving this problem. Compensation for green defficiency therefore was to become a feature of the AMPO plan period. This also provided the incentive to undertake a collaborative work between the Ministry of Tourism and Information and AMPO. Having been, up until then, in a state of ambivalence about the 'recreational potential' of the city in general, this study was a material advance to guide the public open/green space provision. Three main objectives of the project were as follows:

* 'Urgent measures must be taken to ensure the conservation and optimal development of the environments of valleys, lakes and water reservoirs in the vicinity of Ankara,
* The natural environment of valleys, mountains and water reservoirs in the farther region must be preserved,

* The open space wedges penetrating the urban area as proposed by AMPO must be studied and developed for urban recreational use' (AMPO, 1978)

As can be noted, the search for green was now directed towards the outer skirts of Ankara since there were only small left overs of recreational green space in the centre. One significant shortcoming of this study was that it didn't bring a mix of related disciplines together for decision making activity other than planning. This is not surprising given the fact that many fields of inquiry were then in the process of academic maturity and even professional acceptability such as Landscape Architecture.

The Ankara Green Belt Afforestation Project-AGBAP

The air pollution problem was not a new threat to Ankara's health in the early 1980's, but the situation had worsened so much that the whole population of the city was almost convinced that the quality of their urban life was doomed to an irreversible decline. Something had to be done. Alongside other forms of measures, AGBAP was basically designed as a tool to tackle air pollution. The forestry management division of the Ministry of Agriculture, Forestry and Rural Affairs-MAFRA, the architect of the project, succeeded in having official approval for implementation in 1984. In a little, modest booklet the primary objectives of the project are given as follows:

* 'To protect the city of Ankara from floods,
* to establish a vegetation cover in order to decrease the level of air pollution, reaching dangerous levels during recent decades,
* to increase the areas of recreation sites in the neighbourhood of Ankara, for the physical and psychological rehabilitation of people,
* to establish a barrier against the rapid expansion of the unplanned settlement areas,
* to contribute the provision of sufficient amount of good quality water, by controlling the situation in watershed areas, with the establishment of plantations and erosion control measures' (MAFRA, 1987).

The project encompasses 20,408 hectare land and aims at planting 40,816,000 trees on the designated green belt area. A common error made in putting these numbers into analyses is to think that the given quantity of both land and trees represent the future existence of public asset. Project applications from 1985 to 1990, de facto, reveal that half of the afforested land belonged to universities, military organizations, municipality and top-ranking public institutions (4500 ha of the 9000 ha planted area), and the other half was owned by the Treasury (Ankara Metropolitan Municipality-AMM, 1990). The planners must not fail to appreciate that the project may not achieve much in reference to the third objective item listed above, as the question of 'access' still remains to be answered.

AGBAP proposes a system of three separate green belts encircling Ankara and specifies the species of the afforestation scheme as Pinus nigra, and Cedrus libani in the category of evergreen; and Robinia pseudoaccacia, Acer negundo, Eleagnus angustifolia and Ailanthus altissima of deciduous. The project, which is still in implementation is basically a product of the forestry field.

A structure plan for Ankara: 'Ankara from 1985 to 2015'

The municipal authorities were empowered administratively and financially to carry out their own planning activities in 1985. Having the autonomy to govern this transition period, AMM first delegated the colossal problem of transportation system of Ankara to a team of six academics from the Urban and Regional Planning Department of the Middle East Technical University-METU. This work, linked with alternative land use decisions, perhaps inevitably widened its horizon to a 'structure plan' for Ankara. The METU team prepared a report for a thirty year perspective ahead of 1985, containing a plan program which was based on the 'systems approach'. In crude terms, the multidimensional analyses carried out by the team underlined a long over-due shift from 'centralization' to 'decentralization' in development terms. As such, collective housing developments which were initiated in the vicinity prior to this plan period, were to be served with modern and competent network of transport, metro and rapid rail system as well as improved social services. At the other end of the spectrum, the question of 'green', laid in front of the planners was approached by first reaching an agreement on the functionality of AGBAP. Then it was proposed that the depth of the green belt had to be 8-10 kms to achieve the desired air circulation over the city. But no information as to how and by whom 8-10 kms thickness had been determined was given. The planners team also could touch on the potential value of the valley formations as future urban regeneration areas and physical extensions of the green belt idea. Today, a number of Ankara valleys are included in regeneration programmes. Legal control over green belts could be imposed by a 'green belt legislation' according to the package of policies put forward by the METU planners team.

Ankara City Afforestation (Master) Plan- ACAP

As the activity horizon of the local governments widened already, the Municipality's incentive for investing into the idea of a 'greener Ankara' for a civilized urban living could find expressions in a variety of green practices. ACAP was designed as a complementary project to AGBAP in 1990. ACAP in four years time period, promises to provide an extra 1.58 sq mts green per head. Objectives of acap are listed as the facilitating of air circulation, regulation of moisture and oxygen in the air, absorption of dust and subsequently assisting the alleviation of ankara's air pollution. To this end, highways, ring-roads, city approach roads, railway corridors, valley formations, city streets and avenues, schools, parks, gardens of apartment blocks and collective housing settlements are all to be planted.

CONCLUSIONS AND DISCUSSION ON THE RE-GENERATION OF ANKARA'S GREEN: EXPERIENCE AND HOPES

We must admit that we have been so far a couple of worried bystanders in the context of the green experiences of Ankara, but this doesn't necessarily mean that the Turkish capital is not breeding its way to a better future urban life as regards the green issue. We in fact see the official flirtation of today with open/green space and green belts partly as a reflection of the ordinary Ankara dweller's wish for recovering from the nightmare of the mass of grey concrete. 'Partly' is a cautiously chosen term here as there exists a number other discernible elements underpinning such flirtation.

First comes the image of Ankara as the capital city of a nation in the run up to the year 2000. Administrators and planners will probably never produce heaven on earth in Ankara, but they appear to be convinced that the idea of establishing an identity as a contemporary, modern service city with good quality urban life; an attractive diplomatic centre for the Middle East and the former Soviet Republics (many of which are considered as members of the Turkish family) seems feasible. Istanbul's hegemony also adds to that pressure. One result of this image problem is the multiplication of green both in the centre and the vicinity of the city. Secondly, increased quantity of green is expected to mitigate air pollution. As pointed out, earlier AGBAP and ACAP are both officially directed afforestation programs primarily improvised for creating green lungs for the capital. Leaving aside the argument that green fabric of cities indeed improve the air quality anyway, as forcefully questioned by J. Jacobs in the 1960's, we are more concerned with the nature of the greenery being generated, be it under the title of afforested land or green belts. The afforestation applications, as far as the political pressures can be resisted, are also utilised as a tool to rescue land from urban development for a period of time.

'Better pasture and brighter days ...' is that what is all about the green phenomena, assuming that the pasture of Ankara will be better? Is the pasture really getting better? Why is it that the green of Ankara would not look really green to a green lover's eyes? What should be done to overcome the difficulties that planners are facing today?

Shortcomings of the provisional agenda: a lack of a rationale

* No conceptual framework seems to provide guidelines for either urban open/green space or green belt applications. The existing green belt afforestation scheme does not quite fit into the definition of 'green belts' or 'greenways' in their isolated and disconnected designations. No analysis appears to have been carried out into the recreational, ecological, natural, historical, cultural and visual aspects of the green belts/greenways planning and design issue. As for the city and neighbourhood parks of the city, firstly the design process draws our attention. In general, the city parks mirror either the municipality's or the designer's individual taste in parks. The necessary infrastructure and a pattern of user oriented provision are mostly lacking. For the sake of Western modernization some park facilities and equipment look out of place in an area densely populated by rural migrants user group.
* Numbers in reports, projects and books on how much Ankara's greenery has increased or is to be increased can be deceptive. As touched on earlier, land owned by the governmental institutions, for example, are counted in. Majority of such greenery is totally inaccessible to public and even invisible. Square meter per person type of standardized policies also distracts attention away from analysis of the access issue alongside such variables as distance, travel, user needs and satisfaction. In addition, the present provisional attitude does not appear to question the democratic distribution of open/green space. What's more, large hardscaped park areas are quantified as green with no distinction in reports and included in inventories of green for the 7 sq mts/per head objective. This standard was introduced in 1957 with the 6785 numbered 'Improvement' legislation, and for almost 40 years, it's never changed denying the different needs, tastes and socio-economic characteristics of today's society.

* Politics can at times interfere with the whole process. Approaching the elections a fury of green activities may even find locations joined to a busy road system to facilitate recreation under dense smoke, smell and noise. Politics can also be a powerful factor to cancel out former municipality's planning policy and adopt a completely different one. Under such circumstances a steady elevation of the quality of urban green can be a difficult task.

* Economic limitations cause counter-productive adjustments and can lead to breakdowns of the green order. Local authorities are largely subsidized by the central government in Turkey. Nevertheless, their financial strength to exercise expropriation of land is overpowered by the soaring prices of urban land which is shaped by a speculative market where individual land holders play great roles. Administrative control of large portion of urban land is necessary.

* Environmentalists and especially landscape architects/designers are somehow marginalized in decision making processes. However this seems to be partly due to their scale of activities which are removed from comprehensive planning issues. Planning areas like green belts require specific, professional consultation. Landscape planning as a planning field in its own right, needs to be recognized and its expertise matured for the interest of both landscape architecture profession and the capital city.

* No one official report, structure plan or master plan or a single volume of academic study has, to date, elaborated the issue of culture and its relation to 'green'. No research has been carried out on inquiry areas such as what sort of behaviour would Turkish people display in the open green, what they would wish to see there and what they would not. According to the 1990 census the population of Ankara is 2,900,000 and is expected to reach 3,500,000 in 1995.

Whatever form of green we provide, they are the users, the clients. Our task, as planners, to consult them is long overdue. A new research paradigm has to start.

According to the preliminary results of an interview we have carried out among planners and landscape architects, a number of other alternatives are also given emphasis:

* The existing urban open/green space system has to be reconsidered in a revision programme,

* Not only green belts but also 'agricultural belts' must be taken into consideration to connect the human factor to his/her environment,

* Collaboration between professions as well as organizations is necessary. The Landscape Architecture profession needs to strengthen its organizational and institutional framework to function more assertively.

Based on what we see in the present, we believe that there are two distinct scenarios for Ankara: The first includes the perpetuation of the existing planning tradition with problem solving orientation and is prone to dissolving under pressures of modern life, politics, demography and technology. The second scenario includes the hard task ahead: We use our minds and knowledge well. We think, analyse, plan, imagine, create and explain. To do that, we broaden our professional horizons and learn when and how to consult the specialized knowledge. We establish guidelines and a legislative base. We go and absorb the green in its natural habitat. We no longer create plans and design parks or green belts removed from the human factor. This may be an all too rosy view and implausible in practical terms, but there is always the hope.

Acknowledgements

We are grateful to Professor Ozcan Altaban, Professor Yuksel Oztan, Dr. Turkay Ates and Zeki Ulkenli for their useful comments and advice on different aspects of the subject matter. We also would like to thank those who have read and provided their opinion on drafts of this paper.

References

Akcura, T. (1971) Ankara: A Monographic Study, Middle East Technical University Publications, No. 16, Ankara.
Ankara Metropolitan Municipality (1990) Ankara City Afforestation (Master) Plan, Ankara.
Ankara Metropolitan Plan Bureau (1978) Urban Development Strategy-A Summary Ankara 1970-1990, Publication No. 8, Ankara.
Elson, M. J. (1986) Green Belts, William Heinemann Ltd., London.
Gunay, B (1988) Our Generation of Planners: the Hopes, the Fears, the Facts, Scupad 88, 20th Anniversary Congress Submission, Salzburg.
Little, C. E. (1990) Greenways for America, John Hopkins University Press, Baltimore.
Ministry of Agriculture, Forestry and Rural Affairs (1987) Ankara Green Belts Afforestation Project, Forestry General Management Major Application Projects No. 1, Ankara.
Oztan, Y.: 'The Potential of Open/Green Space System of Ankara City for the 21st Century', Peyzaj Mimarligi Journal, No 30 (2): 32-36, 1991.

25

Public spaces and public life in urban areas

Espaces publics et vie collective en zone urbaine

Leanne G. Rivlin

Ce plan se veut un effort de clarification des rapports qualitatifs réciproques entre les espaces publics et la vie collective dans la société urbaine contemporaine. S'appuyant sur les recherches historiques et empiriques de l'auteur, cette analyse se propose d'étudier l'écart entre vie collective et vie privée; elle souligne également l'importance de la prise en compte de certains paramètres: diversité des populations, liberté de choix, mesures à adopter pour essayer de résoudre le problème. Les qualités essentielles de l'espace public dont elle dresse la liste incluent la facilité d'accès, l'aspect fonctionnel, la liberté d'action, la création de réseaux d'espaces et les rapports à eux. La tendance accrue à privatiser les espaces publics a soulevé aux Etats-Unis une vague d'inquiétude, et une approche concertée des projets urbains peut se révéler une alternative à l'attitude actuellement adoptée.

Mots clé: espace public; vie collective; découverte d'espaces; politique d'aménagement des espaces publics; squatters.

Keywords: public space; public life; found spaces; public space policies; squatters.

The social structures and economies of many if not most countries have been changing over the past century, raising some troubling and challenging questions concerning cities, the role of their public spaces and the nature of public life. This paper will draw on experiences, largely in the United States, but the issues may resound with those in many other parts of the world.

In the late 1980's a series of struggles began in a small park in a gentrifying neighborhood of lower Manhattan, 10 1/2 tree-lined acres called Tompkins Square Park. This park had existed in the area for many years (by U.S. standards)--back to the nineteenth century. Photographs from the early 1900's reveal a benign image of children in a playground supervised by women. The controversy that ignited the local community in 1988, one that regularly found its way into the newspapers, resulted from the presence in the park of a number of squatters, homeless people who had built various kinds of tents as shelter. They had created a small community that sharply contrasted with other users and areas of Tompkins Square Park. Police entered and removed the squatters after "the most violent conflict between the police and a crowd in New York City in years" (Purdum, August 14,1988). This initiated a series of disputes that ended on May 31,1991 when the police went into the park, destroyed the homes of squatters, and sealed off the area for future renovation. Now reopened, the homeless residents are gone but the anger remains, raising some serious questions regarding public space rights.

While one can question whether a meager shelter in a public place is an adequate home for people, and whether the designation of public land includes the right to live there, the removal of people from a park raises concerns about the nature of public space and public life. In addressing these issues I will draw on a number of sources--research on public spaces including observations and interviews in mini-parks (sometimes called vest-pocket parks), as well as "found" or informal spaces, a study of homeless squatter communities in the Lower East Side of Manhattan (Rivlin & Imbimbo, 1989), collaborative work in conceptualizing the functions of public spaces (Carr, Francis, Rivlin & Stone, 1992) and considerable historical research on homelessness, public life and public spaces.

THE NATURE OF URBAN PUBLIC LIFE

For most persons, there is some distinction between public and private life, sometimes a sharp one. Private life generally takes place in people's homes, their workplaces or recreational areas--settings that are defined as private property. (For a comprehensive historical perspective on private life, the series under the general editorship of Aries and Duby offers a remarkable view into people's experiences, over twenty centuries.) The legal definition of "private" is only one perspective for clarifying the nature of private and public spaces and private and public life.

Both interviews and observations reveal that people often seek privacy in public places. Many of the people using the public areas in front of the

New York Public Library or the vest-pocket Greenacre Park were deeply into their own thoughts, while others were involved in intimate conversations with one or more persons, also private. When interviewed, people said that they went to public places to be alone, to think about things, and sometimes to grieve. Conversely, many spaces defined as private property regularly become public arenas--the various sections of Rockefeller Center in mid-Manhattan are a prime example, especially at holiday time. Both from an individual and legal point of view, the public and private distinctions are far from clear and a reflection on their nature is useful as we address contemporary concerns.

A particularly insightful analysis of public life has been provided by Michael Brill, first in an address to the 1987 meeting of the Environmental Design Research Association and later appearing as a chapter in the Altman and Zube book (Brill, 1989). He examined a set of his assumptions about public life and then proceeded to critique them. At the heart is a recognition that much of what we believe about public life today is, in fact, nostalgia and romanticized illusion. The forms of public life people in the United States yearn for from the past--or from other cultures--may never have existed or if they did exist, they served the specific needs and geography of those times, climates and areas. Conversely, there is considerable contemporary public life that is ignored or unrecognized. Brill described many forms, including a technological kind. The increasing use of computers and electronic mail systems of communication suggest some of these new forms, albeit ones available to a privileged few. Whether the communication possible in this "virtual space" represent a real form of public life is a question requiring attention. For some persons computers offer a lifeline to the world and some sources of collegial contacts and satisfaction but they may not meet all of the requirements for a true public life.

QUALITIES OF CONTEMPORARY URBAN PUBLIC LIFE

In understanding the role of contemporary urban public life it is useful to outline some of its essential qualities.
*   Public life should reflect the diversity of the society in which it is exercised. This includes the presence of males and females, representation of the various social, cultural, sexual preference and ethnic groups encompassed in the society, and should enable a range of ages to locate appropriate places. This does not mean that one place must serve everyone, but particular groups such as elderly persons, women, children, and

homosexuals should not be excluded either by implicit or explicit rules of enforcement.

* A critical element in public life is freedom of choice which we early saw as enabling the exercise of privacy, territoriality and avoidance of a sense of crowding (Proshansky, Ittelson & Rivlin, 1970). In the realm of public life freedom of choice represents the ability to exercise public space rights as a member of society without restrictive rules and management policies.

* Public life presumes life-in-public, which necessitates negotiation with the lives, and the rights and freedoms of others. This can be very difficult, especially in areas where diversity rather than similarity of users prevail. However, too often we ignore the complex articulation of users and uses, the remarkable choreography that enables diversity to exist without colliding. The streets of a busy city provide one example with pedestrians, peddlers and people engrossed in conversation able to share the limited sidewalk space.

* It is essential to recognize that conflicts will occur and there must be peaceful ways of addressing them. The example of Tompkins Square Park described earlier is a poor model for the resolution of conflicting interests and values in public life. If people are involved in the location, design and management of local public spaces they may be more inclined to obey the rules set for their functioning than regulations set without their input.

THE NATURE OF URBAN PUBLIC SPACES

In the same sense that the boundaries of public and private life can be blurred, the distinction between public and private space is not always clear or consistent. The stereotypic images of public places are the parks, plazas, playgrounds, streets and other settings monitored and supervised by public authorities and designed to accommodate public activities. Although streets are used by pedestrians they must share the space with other functions, cars, trucks, taxis, bicycles, roller-skaters, runners and people pushing many different wheeled objects from baby carriages to carts. Although this broad access is an essential characteristic of urban public places it carries with it a range of shared demands including those of safety and security.

At the most basic level urban public spaces must be public, a tautology that raises some troubling questions. What is public about public spaces? One need is for clear messages that users can enter and when they do go in they will be welcome. However, the criteria for the public qualities of spaces, their publicness (Forrest & Paxson, 1979), are not always clear.

They also can be manipulated to restrict access making the availability of public space a powerful political issue. When particular groups are refused use of public areas for mounting protests or are prohibited from joining a parade, their rights may be at risk.

QUALITIES OF URBAN PUBLIC SPACES

There are specific qualities of public spaces that draw people to them, or repel them. Our research findings have identified a number of them.

* Convenience is an important quality, especialiy of found spaces. This involves minimal commitment to enter and use a space, although people often spend considerable time there. They fit into people's lives in an easy and casual manner, largely because of their locations.

* The spaces that are heavily used often are sited at a crossroad that is part of a network of places used by a person. They may be near a workplace, a residence, a shopping area or tourist attractions. For some persons they become an integral part of daily life. Others may travel some distance to get to the site but ease of access, including available transportation, and the compelling quality of the place are the attractions.

* Safety is an essential quality of public place and is especially salient to people in urban areas. The centrality of found spaces and some designed ones make the places open to scrutiny, facilitating the eyes on the street so valued by Jane Jacobs (1961). However, there is a subtle distinction between friendly observation that offers a sense of security and extensive rules and surveillance that act to restrict people's freedom. In fact, many public places are not safe, especially the underused ones or those whose designs obscure the view inside them.

* Freedom of action is the space-related parallel to the freedom of choice in public life. Perhaps the most problematical of qualities it raises questions around the troubling conflicts that occur when the goals of people conflict with each other. On one level it may be the desire of parents with young children and older people to locate a comfortable place for themselves in a park or playground that is filled with active, boisterous teenagers playing soccer or basketball. On another level the competition may be between the needs and desires of different ethnic groups or specific interest groups within the population. Where the freedom of action extends to those violating the law, for example, competition for use by drug dealers or other criminals, the protection of public rights may assume another dimension.

Balancing people's "spatial rights" (Lynch, 1981) or rights of action is a complex task, even when the public policies support this aspect of urban life. Urban areas, by their very nature, are likely to have heterogeneous populations and efforts to enable them to co-exist are not often successful. In some instances the timing of use may facilitate the process, with different users and uses occurring at different times of day and night. Sensitive designs may also facilitate co-existence, for example if those seated on benches are shielded in some way from flying balls and bodies. Reasonable management of urban spaces also can enable the appropriation of sites in a sharing manner that supports the diverse interests of diverse users.

The exercise of rights presumes freedom of action that is supported by political authorities. Even where access may appear to be free, if particular uses are discouraged, not on the grounds that they are dangerous or illegal, as in the case of drug dealers, but because they are seen as unacceptable, the public quality of the space is compromised. This is especially true when governments restrict access to public areas to political protesters, with examples from many parts of the world testament to this condition.

Urban public places also can facilitate the creation of invisible networks of contacts and stopping points that weave together the fabric of relationships to people and places. On a cognitive level, this assists in creating the legible cities that Kevin Lynch (1963) described. The ability to image places also enhances memories of places, something that accumulates over time and contributes to the identities of people. These are components of the place identity that Harold Proshansky and his associates have described (Proshansky, Fabian, & Kaminoff, 1983). They also are some of the ingredients of "rootedness" (Tuan,1980) that can enrich urban life and make the anonymous city comprehendible, familiar and manageable.

Spaces can support this process in both obvious and subtle ways. Seating surfaces can facilitate connections by enabling people a degree of comfort that may encourage lingering in a place. The necessity for seating in public places, chairs, benches and ledges, has been William H. Whyte's message, for many years (Whyte, 1980; 1988), and he has documented urban people sitting or perching on a range of surfaces, many of them far from comfortable.

An essential quality of urban public spaces is that they meet the needs of users (Carr, et al., 1992). They must have some value to the people who might use them, some reason to use them. One of the attributes of found spaces is their functionality, even the simple functions of a resting place, a corner to tap into neighborhood news or a place to buy things from a peddler.

Public spaces can be both sources of stimulation and relief from high levels of stimulation that characterize urban life. For many users interviewed in public spaces these dual qualities appeared. Some sought the opportunity to look at the passing scene or to enjoy the formal and informal entertainment available. For others the public space was an escape, a respite from the hectic activities and pressures of urban life.

However, too many urban public places are bleak, underused stretches of space with little of interest that would draw users to them. New York City has a number of settings of this kind, many of them the result of the public space zoning provision that offered developers increased bulk and height if they included public space in the design. Manhattan now is dotted with these tokens of bonus planning, most of them plazas but some indoor atria, as well. Those drawing users often contain programmed activities such as concerts or questionable forms of recreational shopping. All use various space management devices to discourage the so-called "undesirables" from lingering.

If private developers can be given rights previously restricted to parks departments and other city agencies the publicness (Forrest & Paxson, 1979) of these spaces can be compromised. Increasing acres of land that appear to be public space are in the hands of private groups. Although there are some limits to what they can do there is a very real question whether the developers--sometimes corporations, sometimes "Business Improvement Districts" (consortia of private businesses located in an area)--are really using the precious urban space in the interests of the public. This privatization of public space is changing the landscape of many areas and is in need of serious reflection and public action.

A FINAL VIEW

As we approach the twenty-first century it is appropriate to reflect on public space policies for urban areas and question whether they are meeting the needs of urban dwellers. Public spaces are scarce resources in most areas, especially so in cities. It is essential to examine the nature of contemporary life and consider whether it is supported by available public space. This kind of reflection can offer important directions for the future.

A major one is the recognition that public space policies are cornerstones in the lives of societies and that they need to be recognized as such by both the public and by political authorities. Access to public space is an essential spatial right. Through the involvement of the public in public space planning the needs of the different populations may be reflected in the spaces. The participatory model is not new but still offers promising possibilities for stimulating healthy public lives and the spaces in which to experience them. It may also help to create "a future public environment that is in all senses barrier-free, with public spaces that are both open-minded and open-hearted" (Carr, et al., 1992, p. 368).

Bibliography

Brill, M. (1989). Transformation, nostalgia, and illusion in public life and public place. In I. Altman & E.H. Zube (Eds.). Public places and spaces (pp.7-29). New York: Plenum.

Aries, P., & Duby, G. (Gen. Eds.). (1987, 1988, 1989, 1990). A history of private life (Vols. 1-4). (A. Goldhammer, Trans.). Cambridge, MA: Harvard University Press. (Original work published in 1985, 1986, 1987 as Histoire de la vie privée. Paris: Sevil.)

Carr, S., Francis, M., Rivlin, L.G., & Stone, A.M. (1992). (Eds.). Public space. New York: Cambridge University Press.

Forrest, A., & Paxson, L. (1979). Provisions for peoples: Grand Central Terminal/CitiCorp study. In L.G. Rivlin & M. Francis (Eds.). Grand Central Terminal study. New York: City University of New York.

Jacobs, J. (1961). The death and life of great American cities. New York: Vintage.

Lynch, K. (1963). The image of the city. Cambridge, MA: MIT Press.

Lynch, K. (1981). A theory of good city form. Cambridge, MA: MIT Press.

Purdum, T.S. (1988, August 14). Melee in Tompkins Sq. Park: Violence and its provocation. New York Times, pp. 1, 38.

Proshansky, H.M., Fabian, A.K., & Kaminoff, R. (1983). Place identity: Physical world socialization of the self. Journal of Environmental Psychology, 3, 57-83.

Proshansky, H.M., Ittelson, W.H., & Rivlin, L.G. (1970). Freedom of choice and behavior in a physical setting. In H.M. Proshansky, W.H. Ittelson, & L.G. Rivlin (Eds.), Environmental psychology: Man and his physical setting (pp.173-183). New York: Holt, Rinehart & Winston.

Rivlin, L.G., & Imbimbo, (1989). Self-help efforts in a squatter community: Implications for addressing contemporary homelessness. American Journal of Community Psychology, 17(6), 705-728.

Tuan, Yi-Fu (1980). Rootedness versus sense of place. Landscape, 24(1), 3-8.

Whyte, W.H. (1980. The social life of small urban spaces. Washington: DC: The Conservation Foundation.

Whyte, W.H. (1988). City: Rediscovering the center. New York: Doubleday.

26

Liveliness in town centres

Des villes vivantes

J.F. Coeterier

Une enquête a été faite sur l'animation des villes. Quelles conditions sont nécessaires pour obtenir une cité vivante? On a tout d'abord mis au point un modèle théorique. Les individus ne peuvent se sentir à l'aise que lorsque l'environnement satisfait leurs besoins profonds. Cette satisfaction peut être obtenue avec deux types de conditions externes: celles dont la présence est source de satisfaction; celles dont l'absence est source d'insatisfaction ("satisfiers" et "dissatisfiers" selon Hetzberg). La phase suivante était d'identifier les conditions nécesaires pour qu'une ville soit animée. Dans ce but, on a interrogé 22 habitants d'une ville moyenne hollandaise sur leurs expériences de l'animation en ville. Ces discussions ont été suivies d'une enquête parmi 462 habitants d'une grande ville (Utrecht). On a identifié cinq types de conditions externes: la diversité des habitants, des fonctions, des détails urbains, l'accessibilité et la gestion par la municipalité. Les trois types de diversité sont des "satisfiers"; les deux dernières conditions sont des "dissatisfiers".

Mots clé: animation des villes; expérience urbaine; psychologie de l'environnement.

Key words: liveliness, urban experience, environmental psychology.

Environmental psychology studies the relationship between man and his environment. This relationship has three aspects: causes, effects, and conditions. Causes and effects are internal or personal (=man), conditions are external (=environment).

Causes

A person is characterized by a number of needs. Certain needs are linked to the external environment, such as the need for privacy. Needs may be seen as causes.

Effects

Satisfaction of this kind of "environmental" needs results in feeling at home in an environment; dissatisfaction leads to alienation. Feeling at home or alienation may be seen as the effects of need fullfillment. Feeling at home, however, is more than the sum of a number of separate need fullfillments. It is the result of an *integration* of these fullfillments, whereby the integration has properties which the separate fullfillments have not, such as the development of roots.

External conditions; the environment

In people's experience, the environment is characterised by a number of attributes or qualities. These qualities may be seen as the conditions for need fullfillment, and thus for alienation or for the development of ties. The extent to which an environment offers opportunities for need fullfillment determines the nature of the relationship between man and his environment. It is important to note that there does not exist a one to one relationship between a need and the external conditions fullfilling this need. Privacy may be found in a library, at a quiet town square, or in a forest. In fact, although the number of needs is small and fairly constant, there is a great variety of external conditions influencing need fullfillment.

In this study on a man-environment relationship, 'man' is a resident or a visitor of the city centre, 'the environment' is the dutch city centre, and 'the relationship' concerns the liveliness of the centre as experienced by visitors and residents. The object of the study was to determine the external conditions that influence liveliness. First, a short theoretical framework will be given. Then, the results of the study will be presented, followed by a discussion of some implications for town planning.

Causes: Needs

In psychology, there are several methods to map needs. One is by Maslow (1954), who orders five fundamental needs into a hierarchy: the needs for food and drink, safety, social contacts, recognition, and self-realization (the highest). Higher needs can only be satisfied if first the lower ones are fullfilled. Another model is a variant of Berlyne's arousal theory. According to this model, man does not strive for the fullfillment of only one need; he strives to maintain an equilibrium between two mutually opposed needs, one reducing arousal, the other inducing arousal, e.g. the needs for rest and stimulation (Schellekens 1976), or for privacy and contact. The deviation from Berlyne (1973) is that Berlyne considers only one need at a time, while here it is the *relationship* between two needs that matters. The equilibrium is a dynamic one, not a steady state, continually shifting between the two poles. This is, because the level of arousal contained in a steady state is not constant, it changes in time. After a good rest one gets bored and needs some excitement. Further, the degree of shifting is restricted. Arousal is only stimulating within certain margins. In the extremes, however, both high and low, arousal becomes stress and is experienced negatively. Contrary to Maslow, the needs in this model are not ordered hierarchically. They are equivalent but polar, or complementary as Stephen Carr calls it. Carr speaks for instance of "the complementary needs for comprehension and for novelty".

> "They are complementary because they call on the one hand for sufficient order in the environment to facilitate comprehension and on the other for sufficient complexity and change to stimulate curiosity and exploration."

The term 'complementary', however, is misleading. What *seems* to be complementary are the induction ('stimulating curiosity') and reduction ('facilitating comprehension') of arousal, but this is only superficially so. It is not the one *because of* the other; *both* are necessary, independent of each other. People have a need for comprehension *and* for exploration, for privacy *and* for contact, but not privacy because of too many contacts. The state of privacy has its own goals and activities, not only recovering from too many contacts. So, more of one need does not imply less of the other. On the contrary, if one need works very strongly, the opposite pole must work very strong too in order to maintain an equilibrium. For instance, children want to explore their environment but their mother must be near by. The farther they venture out, the nearer the mother must be.

One must beware of not interchanging needs and external conditions. There is a need for a high or a low level of arousal; order and complexity are only some of the many external conditions that may satisfy this need. But it would be wrong to speak of a need for order or complexity (Vocht, 1978), or 'visual needs' (Lozano, 1974). That this is a real danger is evident from Arnheim. Arnheim, a psychologist, also starts from the presumption that needs are complementary, but he then transfers this complementary character to the external conditions. He states:

"Order and complexity are antagonistic, in that order tends to reduce complexity while

complexity tends to reduce order",

as if order and complexity lead a life of their own.

Examples of paired needs are:

* The need for the known versus the need for the unknown.

This may also be called the need for certainty versus the need for risk-taking, for safety versus mystery. External conditions regarding this need are for instance complexity and order.

* The need for freedom versus the need for developing ties, or roots.

This pair of needs finds its expression in a wish for freedom of choice (between activities, environments, or modes of behaviour, i.e. the presence of alternatives), but within a clearcut framework, i.e. a structured situation with manifest rules and an overview of the alternatives which must not be too many. In psychiatry, these needs are called the needs for invitation and for inhibition. They require different environments. External conditions include the surveillance of rules.

* The need for privacy versus the need for contact.

In psychiatry, this are the needs for ego- and other-involvement. External conditions include having a private and a communal territory (Jonge 1970). An example of a communal territory are the sandy paths around villages in the south of Holland. On these paths, there is a frequent contact among the local residents, with little chance of meeting outsiders. This is one of the reasons why local people are strongly opposed to the paving of these paths.

Both models are useful in environmental psychology because they can easily be linked to external conditions, the arousal model directly (the environment provides arousal) and Maslow's needs via the concepts of satisfiers and dissatisfiers (see below).

Effects: Developing ties or alienation

Alienation is the combined effect of insufficient fullfillment of different needs. The effect is that one cannot develop a relationship with the environment, one feels like a stranger, excluded. Fullfillment leads to "attachment" behaviour, as it is called in psychiatry. According to Bowlby, attachment behaviour in children is enhanced by an environment that:

• stimulates thinking, feeling and the development of volition or conation, in the sense that it must make possible adaption and action directed by thinking and feeling;

• does not provide ready-made solutions for every type of behaviour;

behaviour must not be programmed too much. The playing with boundaries must be possible.
This applies to adults as well.

In order to avoid alienation, three types of external conditions must be fullfilled

Existential conditions.
For instance, an environment must provide feelings of safety, stability, and security. (The concepts 'habit' and 'habitation' have the same root). For a building this means that it must not be too big, one must have an overview.

Functional conditions, conditions of use.
For an environment or a building this means for instance:
- its function must be part of the daily activities of people. Large office buildings or banks are experienced negatively (except may be for the people working there);
- behaviour must not be programmed too much (Bowlby's second condition) and alternatives for behaviour must not be too limited. Negative examples are for instance practically all buildings for public services, especially the social services;

Visual conditions.
An environment or a building must stimulate curiosity. This is not the case if there is too much order or too little complexity. Neither must they be too ugly, for instance a building must not be made of an ugly material, such as concrete; people don't like it.
Of these three, the visual conditions have gotten most attention (Coops 1976, Steffen 1978, Van Rijn 1976), Hertzberger 1982) while they are the least important. Most important are the existential conditions, of which three subtypes are mentioned in literature (Blauner 1964). These subtypes correspond with Maslow's need hierarchy. They are:
• The environment must provide *safety and protection.* This means, among other things, that it must not change too fast or too drastically and that there must be surveillance of rules. (This are Maslow's two "lowest" needs).
• The environment must provide opportunities for *making contact,* for communication, isolation must be avoided. Alienation may occur when there are no social contacts, no group goals or activities, no possibilities to develop a feeling of togetherness. (This is Maslow's third need for affiliation).
• The environment must *not* induce feelings of *powerlessness* or helplessness. This occurs when a person has too little influence on the design

or the management of his environment. It includes getting information about future changes in the environment and having a say in it. This is also called: perceived control (Rotter 1981), or dominance (Mehrabian and Russell 1974). (Maslow's two highest needs: ego needs and self realization). (The same subtypes are stipulated in a new dutch law on working conditions).

In order to develop roots, or to avoid alienation, all three types of conditions must be fullfilled, and at different levels: at home, in the neighbourhood, and in the town centre.

Environmental conditions: Satisfiers and Dissatisfiers

In the relationship between a person's needs and the external conditions, there are two types of conditions according to Herzberg, an industrial psychologist: dissatisfiers and satisfiers (Herzberg 1968). Dissatisfiers are attributes the presence of which is taken for granted, they are considered as normal; for instance safety in a town centre. A certain amount of the attribute has to be present but after that, more of it does not necessarily give more satisfaction (it may even lead to a decrease of satisfaction). Its absence, however, leads to dissatisfaction.

Satisfiers are attributes the presence of which gives satisfaction (the more the better) but their absence does not lead to dissatisfaction. An example are historical buildings.

Satisfiers and dissatisfiers show a different relationship between the amount of need satisfaction and the amount of the attribute (see figure 26.1).

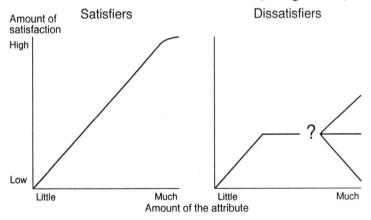

Figure 26.1 The relationship between need satisfaction and environmental attributes for satisfiers and dissatisfiers.

The attributes function differently too. Dissatisfiers determine if you go to the town centre at all. Satisfiers determine how long you will stay and how agreeable your stay will be; dissatisfiers determine the frequency of visits, satisfiers their duration. The absence of historical buildings will not prevent people from visiting the town centre but they will enjoy their stay more when there are historical buildings, or a diversity of urban detail (Pennartz 1990, Karsten 1981, Knol 1993). If the town centre is unsafe, however, people will not go at all, notwithstanding the presence of historical buildings.

There is a relationship between (dis)satisfiers and Maslow's need hierarchy. His two lowest needs work as dissatisfiers. The environment must possess the necessary attributes to fullfill these needs, but enough is enough. The two highest needs work as satisfiers: the more attributes to fullfill them the better. The middle one, the need for affiliation, works out in two ways; it has a personal and an impersonal aspect. The impersonal aspect is that an environment must offer opportunities for making contact, for seeing people. This works as a dissatisfier, a certain amount of contact is enough. The personal aspect is the attitude and the mentality of other people, e.g. the attitude of the employees in shops and offices, or the mentality of the other visitors of the town centre. This works as a satisfier: the friendlier the better.

THE STUDY

In two cities in the Netherlands, Amersfoort and Utrecht, the external conditions for creating liveliness in the centres were investigated. Liveliness is considered to be arousal inducing, so, only one side of the equilibrium. Important in itself but not presenting the whole picture.
There were four steps:
• a literature review;
• interviews with experts (town planners, architects, scientists);
• exploratory in-depth interviews with the inhabitants of Amersfoort, a middle-large town;
• an opinion poll among 462 inhabitants of ten districts of Utrecht.
Utrecht is the fifth town of the Netherlands. One of the districts was the town centre itself, so there are data on visitors as well as on residents of the town centre. The results are summarized below.

RESULTS

Objectives for a visit

Usually, when people visit the town centre, they have more than one objective (Wardt 1991). There are implicit and explicit goals. The explicit goal is the main reason for their visit, e.g. buying something that is not available in neighbourhood shops, or going to a concert or a restaurant. But besides, there are a number of other goals as well, some explicit too, such as window shopping and visiting a gallery, and some implicit. The implicit goals are at least as important, but probably more important than the explicit goals. They are for instance:

* Gathering information.
The town centre is the culmination point of our culture. "Our culture is mainly rooted in the urban community" (Dekkers 1983). Taking note of this culture, its manifestations and its latest developments, is such an implicit goal (Stoppelenburg 1979, Ganzeboom 1981, Brunt 1989). It is done by observing people, what they wear, how they behave; or by noting what is announced on bill boards or advertising columns (the secondary structure).

* A second implicit goal is to reach an equilibrium between relaxation and exertion, the objective of recreation. Relaxation by passively absorbing all kinds of interesting scenes, e.g. seeing other people at work. Exertion by walking through the crowd, adapting to high noise levels, avoiding traffic, and in general being alert. To partake in liveliness is a form of recreation and for many people, the town centre as a place for recreation is at least as important as is the countryside or a nature reserve for other people. (Naturally, recreation may be an explicit goal too).

* Probably even more important is the need to belong to, or to feel part of a greater whole; to be among other people (Graaf 1979). In nature, one feels a part of Life, in the town centre one feels a member of the great Family of Man. This is a passive form of Maslow's third need of affiliation.

* A fourth implicit goal is to partake in, or to be able to partake in, the richness of the many possibilities for action. For what is appreciated is not *doing* things but having the *possibility* of doing things. Doing things may even be boring and tiresome, as many men think for instance of shopping. Many activities have a higher preference than is evident from the actual time spent on them (Wardt 1991).

External conditions; environmental qualities of the town centre as determinants of liveliness

People mentioned five categories of external conditions leading to an increase of liveliness. (The categorizing was done by the author).

I. A diversity of people

According to Jacobs (1972), a diversity of people, or groups of people, is the only condition for liveliness. Having a crowd is not enough. A one-sided crowd, e.g. visitors of pubs, or football supporters, are threatening for other people. A diversity of people is obtained by:
● stimulating the organisation of happenings in the centre by the municipality, or at least not obstructing them by imposing high costs, difficult and tardy applying procedures, etc.;
● maintaining the dwelling function in the city centre; building houses for different groups of people, not only young bachelors or the poor but also for well to-do people;

II. A diversity of functions

This is: having choice; both between braches and inside a branch. A diversity of functions attracts a diversity of people. A diversity of functions is enhanced by:
● having not only shops in the town centre, but other functions as well;
● having not only jeans shops but specialized shops as well;
● a choice of routes, each route with a multi-functional lay-out. Not only one long straight shopping street, or separate districts for pubs, shops, and culture, but a large area with everything combined, where you can walk safely;
● coffee shops and little restaurants where you can sit in the sun and watch people go by;
● streetlife, e.g. people making music, markets;
● the presence of public services, e.g. a post office, banks, health institutions;
● business and commercial firms, the exercising of trades;
● culture and recreation, e.g. galleries, a library, sporting activities.

It also implies:

● the protection, or financial support, of economically weak functions; not only stimulating economical growth.

III. A diversity of urban detail in buildings and public spaces

This includes the presence of:
• greenery, e.g. urban parks, canals with trees along them, trees in the streets (not in the shopping centres) and on quiet squares; this stimulates feelings of having contact with nature and temporary being far from the madding crowd;
• historical buildings and places, e.g. market squares, quays, the historical street pattern, canals; this implies: rather conserving and restoring old buildings than demolishing the old and building new ones, no great traffic break-throughs, fitting new elements into the existing environment, maintain the different styles of building; there must be continuity of the stream of culture and an equilibrium between the old and the new;
• spatial differentiation; no large-scale projects but spatial intimacy by curved lines and openness on squares; a good proportionality between the height and the width of streets and squares; space not becoming emptiness, not a hole between two walls, but space where it is agreeable to be; no uniformity of elements or absence of detail (Steffen 1980);
• decoration; e.g. street furniture, decorative pavement, ornaments on houses and buildings, lanterns for street lighting,
• an extensive secondary (information) structure of mobile and/or temporary objects, posters, advertisement boards, placards.

IV. Accessibility

This has two aspects, a physical and a social one, the latter including the rendering of services, especially by the municipality: is there an easy access to public services, is there customer-relatedness.
Physical accessibility includes:
• possibilities for parking your car, but also your bicycle, preferably with surveillance;
• a frequent bus service
• good traffic regulation, especially the planning of traffic, e.g. not too many one-way streets, by which one gets easily lost.

V. Management and Regulations
This includes:
• maintenance: no dilapidated structures, especially no neglect of historical buildings and greenery, no streets continually under repair, no filth in the canals;
• safety: surveillance on the observance of rules by the police and in the form of social control of different groups on each other, safety for

pedestrians from motorized traffic;
• squares for pedestrians and not for parking cars; for organizing markets and happenings;
• freedom for private citizens to organize things; more possibilities for them to have a dialogue with civil servants about procedures, for doing things by mutual arrangement; a different way of planning, not only controling the environment by making regulations and forbidding things but planning by creating conditions so that things may happen. This is the only way to create diversity.

The categories I-III are satisfiers, IV and V are dissatisfiers.
However, for diversity to be a satisfier it must be diversity of a special kind. Not every diversity works positively, it must fit in a narrowly defined frame. This frame is very important. It marks the difference between the abstract concept of diversity, often mentioned in literature, and the actual meaning people ascribe to it. For instance, many different nationalities add to a diversity of people, but 'nationality' works as a dissatisfier in 'a diversity of people'; a certain amount of differentiation may contribute positively to the liveliness but too many nationalities thrown together disturbs a potential group coherence, or a feeling of togetherness, and is experienced negatively. It is a diversity between narrowly constricted bounds. The same goes for the other satisfiers. Only special kinds of people, functions, and details are acceptable, but those falling outside the framework have a contrary and negative effect.

There were some differences between the visitors and the residents of the centre. Although a number of satisfiers and dissatisfiers were the same for both groups, what was functioning as a satisfier (=something extra) for the visitors could be a dissatisfier (=a necessary condition) for the residents, for instance the presence of green areas, or quiet places in general (e.g. for children to play), or shops for daily purchases.

DISCUSSION. CONSEQUENCES FOR URBAN PLANNING AND DESIGN

An environment is experienced positively if it provides opportunities for need fullfillment; there must be a link between people's needs and the external conditions by which these needs may be satisfied. Only then people can feel at home. Several comments in the interviews, however, are suggestive of a discrepancy between the ideas of architects or urban planners and the wishes of the "ordinary" users of the city centre.

1. What designers advocate as *'a clear spatial structure'* does **not** form part of the external conditions for ordinary people; or, in popular but unscientific language, people have no need of a 'clear spatial structure'. 'Structure' has two aspects: the differentiation of places and the connection between places. A differentiation of places is highly appreciated but a clear connection between these places is not, if that takes the form of broad and straight highways through the city. People experience their environment on a scale of 1:1, and not 1:10.000. They see the tree in the street, not the "green structure" of a town. This means, among other things, that they have a sharp eye for details, and for the fittingness of an element in its surroundings. Non-fitting elements (falling outside the framework) raise the arousal in a negative sense, they cause annoyance.

So, the term 'a clear spatial structure' is architect's language, not corresponding with people's needs. It does not provide a sense of adventure, nor of order, but rather of disorder and stress by the traffic it generates (Krük 1989). Further, it leads to a structural oversimplification. For, in time, people learn to find their way in any environment and then a highly differentiated network of place connections is appreciated higher than 'a clear spatial structure'. It is difficult to make a long and straight highway rich on urban details, or to give it an element of surprise.

2. Neither does what designers call *'a clear identity'* form part of the external conditions for need fullfillment. Everything has an identity and is "legible", in time. In this respect too, arousal is often strongly diminished by urban designers because they make things too simple, too uniform, too poor in detail. Less clear situations are often more challenging.

3. What designers call *'a special expression of buildings'* does not form part of the external conditions if that means: a special expression of the architect. Ordinary people and architects have a completely different interpretation not only of beauty but also of the function of urban elements. For ordinary people, buildings must not stand apart, they must not isolate themselves, but they must be integrated into the other components of the centre and into the daily life of the citizens (Maki 1979). Their 'expression' is accidental; first envelopment, then demarcation. Another example are modern urban parks. According to some designers, nature need no longer be present in parks, while for ordinary people it is its main function, because nothing reduces arousal so much as nature, or even the suggestion of nature.

4. Prefab meanings and strict rules for behaviour should be avoided. People like to have some freedom in the way they interpret and use their environment. An environment elicits attachment when it offers opportunities for creativity and self-regulation (Bowlby).

Liveliness corresponds to the arousal inducing side of needs. A town centre, however, must also provide the means for arousal reduction, otherwise it becomes hectic. This need not only take place in quiet corners. On the contrary, it can be very relaxing to *watch* liveliness, to see people at work, for instance watching a performance by street artists, watching boats in the canals of Amsterdam, drinking a cup of coffee and watch people go by. For relaxation needs not take long. Partaking in liveliness is arousal inducing, watching liveliness can be arousal reducing.

The main problem in urban planning and design is not doing new research again and again, but to apply the results of research. By studying the literature, one cannot help feeling that everything about people's experience of the city centre has already been explored, studied, mapped, and documented. Their feelings and wishes are clear, only the consequences are not drawn by planners, architects, and urban designers.

References

Because the object of the study was conditions for liveliness in *dutch* city centres, mainly dutch literature was studied. Many reports are university studies and in the grey circuit, not published in journals or books. This does not mean, however, that the research methods are inferior or the data invalid.

Arnheim, R. (1972). Toward a psychology of art. Originally written in 1960 for a handbook of landscape architecture.
Berlyne, D.E. (1973). The vicissitudes of aplopathematic and the lematoscopic pneumatology. In: D.E. Berlyne and K.B. Madsen, Eds. Pleasure, reward, preference. New York, Academic Press.
Blauner, R. (1964). Alienation and Freedom. University of Chicago Press. Chicago.
Brunt, L. (1989). De magie van de stad. Inaugurale rede. Amsterdam University.
Carr, S. (?) The city of the mind. In: E. Ewald (ed), Environment for man: the next twenty years. Midland Books.
Coops, R.H., Kremer, A.A. and Mulder W. (1976). De belevingswaarde van de binnenstad van Groningen. STAP, Instituut voor sociale en bedrijfspsychologie. Groningen University. Follow-up study in 1979 in Arnhem.
Dekkers, H. and K. Kuijstermans. (1983). Stad in Beeld. Vakgroep Sociologie van de Ruimtelijke Ordening. Tilburg University.
Ganzeboom, H. (1981). Beleving van monumenten, 1 + 2. Vakgroep Sociologie. Utrecht University.
Graaf, J. de, Habets, A. and Nijenhuis, W. (1979). Meten en regelen aan de stad. Sunschrift 170. Socialistische Uitgeverij, Nijmegen.
Hertzberger, H. (1982). Het openbare rijk. Samenvatting colleges 1973-1982. Deel A. Delft University Press, Delft.
Herzberg, F. (1968). Work and the nature of man. Stapleton, London.
Jacobs, Jane (1972). The death and life of great american cities. Harmondsworth.
Jonge, D. de (1970). Perceptie, Plaatskeuze en territorialiteit. Capita Selecta. Voordrachten 1969-1970. Afdeling Bouwkunde, Delft University Press, Delft.

310

Karsten, L. (1981). Recreatie van binnenstadsbewoners. Instituut voor stedebouwkundig onderzoek. Delft University.

Knol, F.A. (1993). Ruimtelijke kwaliteit en bewoners. Planologische Discussiedagen, Deel 1, pp. 329-337.

Krük, P.R. (1989). leefbaarheidsonderzoek toont manco's in beleid aan. De Nederlandse Gemeente, 41, pp. 1016-1017.

Lozano, E.E. (1974). Visual needs in the urban environment. Town Planning Review, 45, pp. 351-374

Maki, F. (1979). The city and inner space. Ekistics, 278, pp 328-334.

Maslow. A.H. (1954). Motivation and personality. Van Nostrand. New York.

Mehrabian, A. and Russell, J.A. (1974). An approach to environmental psychology. MIT Press.

Pennartz, P.J.J. (1990). Belevingswaarde van binnenstedelijk gebied. Vakgroep Huishoudstudies, Agricultural University, Wageningen

Rijn, H.T.U. van, (1976). Geintegreerd milieu onderzoek. Deel I. Rijnmond.

Schellekens, H.M.C. (1976). De straat. Dissertatie. Eindhoven University.

Steffen, C. (1980). De Stadsvoorstelling. Centrum voor Architectuuronderzoek. Delft University.

Steffen, C. and Voordt D. van der, (1978). Belevingsonderzoek in Antwerpen. Centrum voor architectuuronderzoek, Delft University.

Stoppelenburg, P.A. (1979). Achtergronden van niet-deelname aan cultuur en recreatie. Instituut voor sociaalwetenschappelijk onderzoek, Tilburg University.

Vocht, C. van der, (1978). Beleving van monumenten. Sociologisch Instituut, Nijmegen University.

Wardt, J.W. van de, and H. Staats. (1991). Veranderend binnenstadsgebruik. ROV, Leiden University.

27

Meanings and attitudes towards urban green: an approach to urban ecology

Significations et attitudes vis à vis des espaces verts urbaine: un approche à l'écologie urbaine.

Mirilia Bonnes, Antonio Aiello and Rita Grazia Ardone

On étudié les significations et les attitudes des habitants vis-à-vis des espaces verts dans la ville, en se référant à la théorie des Représentations Sociales (Moscovici, 1976; Bonnes, Secchiaroli, 1992). Une attention particulière a été portée aux significations les plus et les moins consensuelles qui fondent cette représentation sociale.

A partir d'un échantillon de 519 sujets d'âge, de sexe, de niveau scolaire et de lieux de résidence différents, on a dégagé deux principales dimensions de signification: l'une à dominante "socio-centrée", l'autre à dominante "individu-centrée"; chacune se rapporte différemment aux diverses representations selon qu'elles sont plus ou moins répandues. Pour les significations les moins consensuelles, deux nouvelles tendances dans les attitudes sont apparues, qui différencient les sujets et qui sont liées aux variables socio-démographiques et socio-culturelles qui les caractérisent.

Mots clé: écologie urbaine; vert urbain; représentations urbaines.

Key words: urban ecology, urban green, urban representations .

Within an ecological approach to the urban environment (Giacomini, 1981; Di Castri, Baker, Hadley, 1984; Bonnes, 1987, 1991), one of the most relevant topics is the relationship people have with the natural features of the urban environment and, in particular, with its green aspect (Altman, Wohlwill, 1983; Knopf, 1987; Burgen, Harrison, Limb, 1988; Bruce, Hull, Harvey, 1989; Ardone, Bonnes, 1991).

Some studies have pointed out the clear preference people have for urban settings, including natural features and, in particular, greenery; on the other hand, many studies have shown how the presence of green features in the urban environment affects inhabitants' residential satisfaction (Fried, 1982; Bonnes, De Rosa, Ardone, Bagnasco, 1990; Ardone, Bonnes, 1991). Taking into account the social psychological perspective (Canter, Correia Jesuino, Soczka, Stephenson, 1988; Bonnes, Secchiaroli, 1991) of the people-urban environment relationship and, in particular, the theory of social representations (Moscovici, 1976; Breakwell, Canter, 1993), it seems important to study people's attitudes towards urban green, giving particular attention to both the more and the less shared meanings attributed to these environmental features in order to understand the process of forming and changing these environmental representations.

The aim of the present study is to investigate the meaning people attach to green features of the urban environment in order to discover i) the more and the less shared features of these environmental representations, and ii) to point out how these different meanings attributed to the urban green may be affected by the socio-demographic and socio-cultural characteristics of the people involved.

METHODOLOGY

Research population

The sample was composed of 519 subjects. The breakdown of the sample by socio-demographic variables was as follows: gender, 264 males (50.9%), 255 females (49.1); age, 93 SS between 14 and 18 years of age (17.9%), 137 SS between 19 and 30 years of age (26.4%), 111 SS between 31 and 45 years of age (21.4%) and 178 SS between 46 and 80 years of age (34.3%); educational level, 208 SS (40.1%) have a middle school educational level, 240 SS (46.2%) have a high school educational level, 71 SS (446.2%) are graduated; geographical areas, 80 SS (15.4%) come from northern Italy, 387 SS (74.6%) from central Italy, 52 SS (10.0%) from southern Italy; place of residence, 383 SS (73.8%) live in big cities, 136 (26.2%) live in towns.

Questionnaire

A questionnaire was developed on the basis of results of a previous explorative study, which involved interviewing 30 SS on the theme of urban green. The instrument is composed of a Likert-type scale consisting of 78 items, each with a 6-point response scale.

Statistical Analyses

Using the SPSS-X statistical package, an analysis was carried out of the percentage distributions of the frequencies of responses provided by the Likert scale for each affirmation. Further, a factorial analysis was made, which included items whose responses were not found among the first or last two points of the scale with a frequency equal to or greater than 80%. Also, variations in the evaluative orientation, with respect to several socio-demographic and socio-cultural characteristics of the sample, were verified by means of ANOVAs.

RESULTS

More and less shared meanings

Analysis of the percentage distribution of the frequencies of the scores on the Likert scale shows the items that obtain a high level of sharing both in the sense of agreement and disagreement with each affirmation (80% on the first or the last two points of the scale).

The qualitative and comparative analysis of these items, with reference to the other items which have more differentiated answers, allows for the singling out of two main perspectives of meaning attached to the urban green. On one hand, a more "socio-centered" perspective is defined; according to these items, the social value of the presence of the green features of the urban environment is emphasized. These items stress the importance that urban organization and planning pay particular attention to these environmental features, pointing out how the presence and the good quality of green in the urban environment must be considered as an indicator of urban and social quality.

On the other hand, a more "person-centered" perspective is defined, which refers to a variety of items emphasizing different perspectives of meaning attached to urban green features, more related to individual preferences and evaluations.

The prevalence of items referring to the "socio-centered" perspective can be noted in the group of items receiving more shared answers; on the other hand, the more differentiated answers refer to a prevalence of items emphasizing the "person-centered" perspective.

The subsequent statistical analysis permitted the further differentiation of this "person-centered" perspective into two main attitude orientations, as well as the enhancement of individual differences of these attitudes according to the various socio-demographic and socio-cultural individual characteristics.

Different attitude orientations

As far as the different attitude orientations are concerned, the scree-test of the factor analysis, with varimax rotation, carried out on all items (n=53) not showing maximum agreement or disagreement, pointed out the presence of two main factors. Following this first analysis, the items with saturations of less than 38 were discarded. At the end, 38 of the 53 original items remained. The total of the explained variance of the two factors was 28.2%. The two main and different attitude dimensions (see Table 27.2 for the two factors), which are independent from each other, regard, on one side, (I Factor: 21.3% of explained variance) a dimension which can be defined as "Attitude of integration between man and nature"; this is based on a general tendency toward "positively evaluating the presence of urban green with multiple perspectives." On the other side (II Factor: 6.9% of explained variance), an additional and different dimension, which can be defined as "Attitude of opposition, man vs. nature," with parallel desire to control over nature, and the consequent need for nature to be subordinate to man.

As can be observed in the table, the first attitude orientation appears to be supported on the basis of different evaluations, which are centered on the evaluation of urban green and nature in a person-centered perspective; according to this, urban green is held to be (1a) a source of psycho-physical well-being and psychological recovery, as (1b) a possible means of access to "naturalness" and, thus, (1C) as a potential for enriching the capacities of the self (experience of intimacy, non alienation, solidarity, desire to explore, awareness of one's own limits); however, there is also an evaluation of nature in the socio-centered perspective (urban green as promoting sociability (1d)), with an attribution of possibility of bettering social relationships at both the interpersonal level and the level of social organization.
With regard to the second dimension of the exclusively person-centered attitude, on one side, the tendency is clearly shown toward admitting the need to subordinate nature to man (item 2a) and, on the other side, the existence of an implicit fear of nature ("man modifies nature because he fears it"); the consequent desire to control would seem to be based on this (item 2b).

Figure 27.1   Main effect of gender.

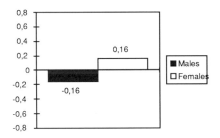

Figure 27.4   Main effect of place of birth.

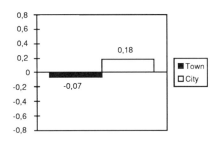

Figure 27.2   Main effect of age.

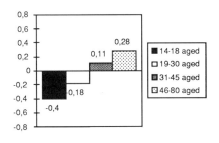

Figure 27.5   Interaction place of birth and place of residence.

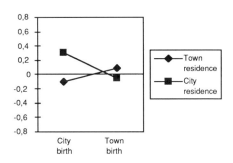

Figure 27.3   Interaction gender and age.

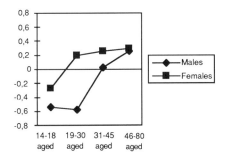

Figure 27.6   Main effect of geographical area of residence.

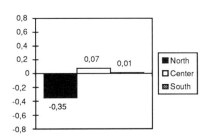

Figure 27.7 Main effect of age.

Figure 27.10 Main effect of place of residence.

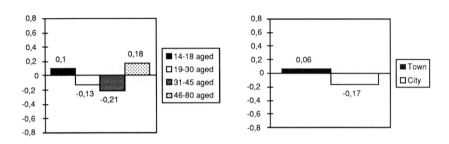

Figure 27.8 Interaction gender x age.

Figure 27.11 Main effect of educational level.

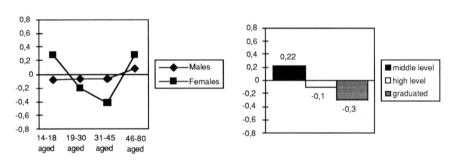

Figure 27.9 Main effect of place of birth.

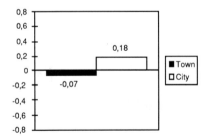

Individual differences in attitude orientations

As far as the individual differences in attitude orientations are concerned, the analysis of variance was carried out on factorial scores obtained by the various subjects relative to each factor, or dimension of attitude (attitude scores), in relation to the following variables: gender (males, females), age (recodified into four classes: 14-18 years of age; 19-30 years of age; 31-45 years of age; 46-80 years of age), diploma of study (middle school; high school; graduated), place of birth (city, town), geographical area (north, center, south), place of residence (city, town).

With regard to the man-nature integration attitude (1st dimension), according to the ANOVA gender (2) x age (4), above all a more marked attitude can be seen in this sense in females than in males (gender: $F(1.510)=14.49$, $p=0.0001$) and in the less young age group than in the young one (age: $F(3.510)=12.95$, $P=0.0001$). These gender differences appear more marked (interaction gender x age: $F(3.510)=4.16$, $P=0.007$) in the 19-30 year olds and the 14-18 year olds, and they decrease and disappear in the less young groups (over 35 and over 45 years of age) (see figuresfrom 1 to 3).

According to the place of birth (2) x place of residence (2) design, those born in the city (interaction place of birth x place of residence: $F(1.514)=3.99$, $P=0.05$) and currently residing in a town show more of an attitude of integration than those who choose the city as their place of residence. On the contrary, being born in a town does not result in differences regarding a different place of residence (see figures 4 and 5).

Also, the geographical area of residence (3) factor affects this attitude. It is shown that residents in the north are significantly less orientated toward "man-nature integration" than residents in the south and, above all, than those in the center (geographic area: $F(2.515)=6.03, P=0.003$) (see figure 6).

With regard to the second dimension of psychological orientation, in agreeent with the gender (1) x age (4) design, it is interesting to note how the attitude of "man-nature opposition/subordination" (interaction gender x age: $F(1.510)=2.95, p=0.03$) is less marked for the women in the intermediate age range (19-45 years of age) rather than in the very young (14-18 years of age) and the less young (over 45 years of age); the latter two groups are both oriented in a contrary and differentiated way. The male group of subjects does not show differences either compared with the female group or with respect to the different age groups (see figures 7 and 8).

Place of birth in a town rather than a city (place of birth: $F(2.514)=13.11$, $P=0.0001$) and place of residence in a town rather than a city (place of residence: $F(1.514)=11.87$, $P=0.01$) seem to affect the

318

"man-nature opposition/subordination" attitude, according to the place of birth (2) x place of residence (2) design (see figures 9 and 10)

Also, a more marked attitude of man-nature opposition appears to significantly and systematically increase with the decrease in subjects' level of education (diploma of study: $F(1.515)=9.76$, $P=0.0001$) (see figure 11).

CONCLUSIONS

Overall, from our study it emerges that the meanings inhabitants attribute to different aspects of the urban green appear heterogeneous and also differentiated depending on whether the analysis focuses on the more or the less shared aspects of this social representation.

The tendency to consider the problem of urban green as strictly connected to the responsibility of planning and management of the environment is one of the most shared aspects of representation, and the different perspective considering the man-nature relationship as integration or opposition appears to be the part of the representation destined to present the greatest inter-individual differences; thus, the characteristics of gender, age, residence and geographical position and level of education seem to be determining.

TABLES

Table 27.1
More shared meanings: items with more than 80% of agreement/disagreement on the first or last two scale points.(25 items/78 total)
1) Socio-centered perspective (15 items)
1a) Urban green as indicator of quality of social organization:
prescribed/normative perspective on aspects of management
of the environment (12 items: agreement average percentage=88.6).
1b) Urban green as promoter of sociability
(3 items: agreement average percentage=88.5)

2) Person-centered perspective (10 items)
2a) Urban green: need for subordination, man vs. nature
(3 items: agreement average percentage=83.6).
2b) Urban green as evaluation of nature as a means of self enrichment
(3 items: agreement average percentage=88.3).
2c) Urban green as source of psycho-physical well-being:
relaxing function, decrease of urban anxiety/stress.
(4 items: agreement average percentage=81.7).

Table 27.2
Less shared meanings: different attitude orientations.(38 Items/78 total)
First dimension: 29 items.
Attitude of integration between man and nature: evaluation
of urban green with multiple perspectives (21.3% explained variance).

PERSON-CENTERED PERSPECTIVE (22 Items)
1a) "Urban green as source of psycho-physical well-being:
relaxing function, decreasing urban anxiety/stress" (9 items).
1b) "Urban green as means of access to/relationship with nature."
(7 items).
1c) "Evaluation of nature as means of self enrichment." (6 items).
SOCIO-CENTERED PERSPECTIVE (7 Items)
1d) "Urban green as promoter of sociability" (7 items total)
1d1 interpersonal level (4 items)
1d2 level of social organization (3 items)

Second dimension: 9 items
Attitude of man-nature opposition, subordination man vs. nature
(6.9% explained variance).

PERSON-CENTERED PERSPECTIVE (9 Items)
2a "Need for subordination man vs. nature" (6 items)
2b) "Fear of nature/desire for control" (3 items)

References

Altman I., Wohlwill J.F. (eds) Human behaviour and the environment. Behaviour and the natural environment, New York: Plenum.

Ardone, R.G., Bonnes, M. (1991). The urban green spaces in the psychological construction of the residential place. In M. Bonnes (a cura di) Urban ecology applied to the city of Rome. UNESCO M.A.B. Project 11 (pp. 149-173). Roma: M.A.B. Italia, progress report (4).

Bonnes M., Secchiaroli G., (1992), Psicologia Ambientale. Introduzione alla Psicologia Sociale dell'ambiente. Nuova Italia Scientifica. Roma.

Bonnes, M., De Rosa, A.M., Ardone, R.G., Bagnasco C. (1990) Perceived quality of residential environment and urban open green areas. Blraum-Blauguetia, 3,54-62.

Breakwell G. M. , Canter D. V. (1993). Aspects of methodology and their implications for the study of social representations. In G. M. Breakwell, D. V. Canter (eds.) Empirical Approaches to Social Representations. Oxford: Clarendon Press.

Bruce Hull, R., Harvey, A. (1989). Explaining the emotion people experience in suburban parks. Environment and Behavior,21, 323-345.

Burgen, J., Harrison, C.M., Limb, M. (1988). People, parks and urban green: a study of popular meaning and values for open spaces in the city. Urban Studies, 25, 455-473.

Canter D. A., Correia Jesuino J., Soczka L., Stephenson G. M. (1988) (eds.).

Environmental Social Psychology (NATO ASI Series). Dordrecht: Kluwer Academic Publishers.

Di Castri F., Baker F., Hadley M. (1984) (eds.). Ecology in Practice. Dublin: Tycooly.

Giacomini V. (1981) Rome considered as an ecological system. Nature and Resources, 17, 13-19.

Herzog, R.R. (1989). A cognitive analysis of preference for urban nature. Journal of Environmental Psychology, 9, 27-43.

Knopf, R. (1987) Human behaviour, cognition and affect in the natural environment. In

Stokols D., Altman I. (eds.): Handbook of environmental psychology, pp. 783-826. New York: Wiley.

Moscovici S. (1976) Social influence and social change. London: Academic press.

Whyte, A. (1977). Guidelines for field studies in environmental perception. MAB technical note 5, Unesco, Paris.

28

Appropriating the city: teenagers' use of public space

L'appropriation de la ville: les adolescents et l'utilisation de l'espace public

Mats Lieberg

Cette étude montre comment les adolescents utilisent les espaces publics de leur banlieue et leur ville pour donner une signification et un contexte à leur vie. Pendant une période de trois ans, plusieurs groupes d'amis, provenant d'une banlieue suédoise typique dans une ville moyenne au sud du pays, ont été suivis. Les méthodes utilisées étaient à la fois quantitatives et qualitatives, les plus importantes étant l'observation participative et la conduite d'entretiens-conversations structurés. Les travaux indiquent quels sont les endroits publics utilisés par les jeunes, leurs caractéristiques et la manière dont les jeunes les utilisent.

L'utilisation symbolique et l'utilisation factuelle sont toutes deux décrites. Une discussion intervient sur l'importance de la vie citadine et de la ville sur le développement des jeunes, à l'aide des théories actuelles sur la jeunesse, la modernisation et l'individualisation. Les résultats montrent que les jeunes se rencontrent dans les endroits publics parce que leur âge et manque d'argent ne leur permettent pas d'aller ailleurs. Cependant ils utilisent l'espace public d'une manière active et créative, pour se "qualifier" et se préparer à la vie adulte. Ils crèent leurs propres espaces et territoires dans les lieux publics, où ils peuvent être ensemble sans être dérangés, poursuivre leurs intérêts et développer leurs compétences. Ils veulent être vus et créer quelque chose leur appartenant en propre. Ainsi, ils apparaissent comme des acteurs importants de l'espace public.

Mots clé: Jeunesse; mode de vie; espace et endroits publics; environnement urbain; rapports personne-environnement.

Key words: Youth, life-style, public space and places, urban environment, person-environment relations.

A lot of studies discuss the consequences of suburban living on small children but little has been written about the effects of this particular physical environment on teenagers. This study seeks to determine how teenagers, 13-17 years old, use public spaces in their residential areas and their city, to create purpose and context in their existences. During a three-year period, different groups of friends from a suburb of Lund, Sweden were studied both in their housing area and in the downtown area[1]. The various places used by these young people are described and characterized. The purpose of the study was to investigate how teenagers relate to the built environment in relation to 1) their real use of different places and environments in public areas, and 2) the symbolic significance this use has for the youths. The reason the study was limited to teenagers is because this period is an important transition in the lives of young people, who are now leaving the parental home and entering the public environment. The following issues are taken up:
-       Where in the public environment do the young people congregate? What is characteristic for just these places? How do these places relate to their area and to the city as a whole?
-       What kind of activities and actions do the teenagers engage in in these places? Why do they seek out these places? Does their use of these places differ from that of adults and other groups?
-       What idea do youths have of their city, their immediate surroundings and their residential area?
-       In what way do the young people use the physical environment for their development? What symbolic significance do public places and spaces have for different teenagers?

YOUTH AND MODERNIZATION

'Youth' as a category is far from uniform. It consists of many different groupings and subcultures of which each and every one has its own more or less individual styles, interests and directions (Hebdige 1979, Forns & Bolin 1992). In my study I chose to focus on the 'usual' teenager, the one who in modern literature belongs to the 'mainstream' culture (Brake 1987). An important starting point is to consider the young people as individuals who are active, creative and able to act, who (re)create their own environments and contexts (Willis 1990). Based on the background of sociological theories about youths, modernization and individualization (Gillis 1981, Bjurstrm &

Forns 1988, Ziehe 1989), and supported by theory building in social psychology and developmental psychology (White 1956, Blos 1962, Piaget 1973, Silbereisen & Noack 1988, Nielsen & Rudberg 1991), I claim that young people today must prepare themselves for adult life. It is the task of youth (March 1985), rather than a specific, chronological period in one's life span that should be the basis of the definition of 'youth'.

This task of youth is made more difficult by the fact that this is a period of transition for them, full of contradictions: on the one hand, they are breaking with their childhood and their parents, while on the other, they are qualifying and integrating themselves into the adult world. As a teenager, one shall both liberate oneself from one's parents and the values of childhood and prepare oneself for the responsibilities and demands of adulthood. It is in connection with this that the city, city life and its various environments and contexts become important. In public life and when with one's pals, teenagers are confronted with different people, situations and values. This can act as a kind of learning process to help prepare them for what awaits them as adults.

THE NEIGHBOURHOOD CASE STUDY

The case study, which I report on in this paper, had as a starting point a neighbourhood on the outskirts of Lund, called Norra Fladen. This part of the town was chosen because it exemplifies a typical Swedish, residential suburb. It is located about 2 km. from the heart of the city. Its design was greatly influenced by the same 'neighborhood ideal' which was the foundation for many of the housing areas built in Sweden during the 60's and 70's[2]. Closest to the shopping center, in the middle of the suburb, is a green area (park) immediately behind which the various housing enclaves are located. Since the first buildings went up in 1967, rental apartments, tenant-ownership, terraced and free-standing houses, and student houses have been added. This part of Lund quickly became a rather independent part of the city, with shops, schools, day-care centers, an indoor swimming pool, library, out-patient clinic and other municipal services. There is also a stable, tennis hall and soccer fields in the immediate vicinity. Of the 67,141 inhabitants in Lund as of January 1, 1992, c. 8,500 of them live in Norra Fladen. Of these, over 8% are teenagers.

METHODS

Data were collected in different ways, the most important being a teen survey (questionaries), essays, personal interviews and participant observation. The approach can be described as a type of triangulation (Denzin 1978:28), where the choice of method for data collection was determined on the basis of the concrete issues and on which resources and possibilities were available. The investigation was facilitated by the fact that I have lived in the area for more than 10 years. My role as researcher varied during the various phases of the study and changed gradually during the three years it took: in the beginning I was an observer and regarded the young people from a distance. As time went on, I became more and more involved in their activities and the role of passive observer gradually changed to that of active participant.

At an early stage in the investigation I asked 75 teenagers in three high school classes from N Fladen to write essays about themselves and answer a questionaire about their free time activities and how they valued their physical environment. I also asked them to draw mental maps (Lynch 1960, 1977) of the housing area and to point out their most important places. At a later stage this was repeated for the center of the city. From this quantitative part of the study, three main categories of teenagers crystalized, from which I then chose the small groups (gangs) which I followed close-up through behavior traces and participant observation in the qualitative part of the study. I call the three categories 'home-oriented', 'association-oriented' and 'friend-oriented'[3]. The type of interviews I conducted can most closely be characterized as structured conversations (Taylor & Bogdan 1984). They were based on a plan or set of questions determined in advance about a number of themes and aspects. With few exceptions, the interviews were conducted in the teenagers' own surroundings. They were made both individually and in a group, depending on the aim of the interview. They were taped and then transcribed verbatim. Following this they were reviewed and sorted into different themes. In total, I interviewed 42 teenagers within the three groups. Furthermore I made interviews with another 15 teenagers and with 15 key persons (parents, teachers, youth recreation leaders, local police-officers and other adults in the housing area). Public and semi-public places in N Fladen and downtown were intensely observed over a 8-month period (although I had been informally observing them for many years).

CLOSE-UP STUDY OF TWO GROUPS

The most important part of the field work consisted of following two groups of teenagers from the area as a participant observor[4]. The one group consisted of eight girls between 14 and 17 years of age who were active in a sports club and belonged to what I earlier referred to as the association-oriented teenagers. Five or six other teenagers of both sexes were part of the group on and off. Most of them were active in the club but they also met often at each other's homes. They put in much time on their homework, but were also out a lot, both in their own area and downtown. The other group consisted of a core of four boys and four girls, 15-17 years old. They met regularly at the recreation center or elsewhere in the housing area. None of them was active in any kind of association or club, and they did not spend much time on their home^_work. This friend-oriented group was not as stable in composition as the group of association-oriented girls: ten to fifteen other girls and boys at one time or another hung out with this group. I followed both these groups for a total of three years. Through participant observation in their most important places and with the help of repeated personal interviews, individual as well as collective, I gradually got a good picture of their everyday-life and activities at different public places.

RESULTS

The mental map study and the essays indicated that the teenagers' individual knowledge and idea about their immediate vicinity was very good. To be sure, there were individual differences in both depth (richness of detail) and breadth (spatial spread), but the great majority presented integrated maps which were easy to interpret and orient oneself from. In general the boys made maps with more details, while the maps of the girls generally had a more artistic design. The personal relation - that is, what one has personal experience of - was important for the knowledge of the area and what they drew on the maps. The fact that male teenagers spend more time outdoors in the housing area partly explains why their maps contained more details than the female maps. The results correspond to a great deal with findings from other similar studies (Appleyard 1970, Ladd 1970, Maurer & Baxter 1972).

The results of the survey indicated that the N Fladen teenagers were very local in their use of public and semi-public places. They spent most of their time during the week within the suburb - preferably at home or at school (fig. 1). In general, they only spent about 10 % of their free-time in public or semi-public places. But the differences between individual persons and groups were considerable. Some teens spent almost all of their leisure-time at the local sport-club or recreation center, while others stayed home most of the time. It was almost only on weekends and holidays they went downtown. When asked to name their five most important places in order of preference, a higher percentage named private spaces - either their own or a friend's home - than public or quasi-public places (table 1). A gender comparison shows a slight female preference for private and semi-public places and a small male preference for public places, but the differences were not significant.

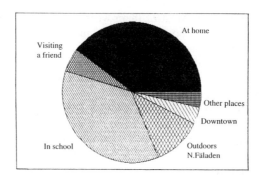

Figure 28.1 Teenagers' use of time during a week.

Table 1. Most important teenage places in order of preferences

	Class			
Place	7 (n=23)	8 (n=23)	9 (n=21)	Total (n=67)
Outdoors near home	18	12	11	41
Friend's home	11	14	10	35
Shopping mall	6	12	12	30
Park/green area	9	11	3	23
Bus station	9	5	7	21
Tennis courts	6	3	7	16
Recreation center	3	4	8	15
Indoor swimming pool	3	5	6	14
Sport grounds	3	4	5	12
Tennis hall	1	3	3	7
The stable	3	-	3	6
The library	-	1	3	4
Sum	72	74	76	222

From the interviews and behaviour observations in the qualitative study I learned that the major meeting place for the association-oriented teenagers was the sports club and its premises. By participating in the club's trips, they came into contact with many other young people and places outside of N Fladen and Lund. They also spent time regularly at different places downtown. When they wanted to be undisturbed, they either met at someone's home (they all have their own rooms) or some less public place outside in the housing area. The friend-oriented group of teenagers used the recreation-center and the out-of-doors as their primary arena. They were well acquainted with the neighborhood and moved around freely in the entire area. In the warm months they could often be found in the square in the shopping center, where other young people from the neighbourhood also gathered. Furthermore they had different 'hiding places' and 'secret places' which they could go to if they wanted to be undisturbed. They seldom went downtown.

According to the results of the qualitative part of the study - particularly concerning the young people's relationship to the built environment - the following can be stated: teenagers often try to get away from this type of one-dimensional space or else redefine it in terms of their own interests and needs. The spatial exploration of the environment was made more intensely by some teenagers than others, who instead chose other ways of finding out about social life. Also, what seems to be very important at this age is the distinction between privacy and publicy. By preference teenagers keep to stairwells, basements, corridors, corners and alleyways - areas that I call close-to-home places. They also flock to border areas or localities situated 'between' different spaces. These are 'neutral' localities which connect clearly defined places, something I call fringe areas. Examples of such places in my material are the areas on the outskirts of N Fladen and the areas between the various housing groups or enclaves. A third type of place in the suburb where teenagers congregate is what I call hiding places and retreats. These are private places away from the public eye and control, for example, basement rooms, shelters, garages or concealed places out-of-doors, where the youths can be alone and create and develop their own thoughts and talents. Of particular importance for teenagers is what I call social and spatial free zones. These are created by the teenagers themselves and in general lack permanent borders. They are characterized by three things: first, there is no adult supervision and control. Second, there is no purpose or goal for anything they do. It is places for pronounced 'do nothing' culture (Corrigan 1979) but where the unexpected suddenly could happen. Third, the free zones are characterized by emancipatory patterns of action : that is, the actions taking place there are not interpreted or acted out in advance. Preferably all the actions are unique. It is not easy to give examples of teenage free-zones because what is a free-zone to one group does not have to be one for others. But in my study some of the boys in the friend oriented group had found the secret entrance to an underground culvert system for rainwater transportation. During summertime, when the system was almost empty of water, these boys used to walk and creep into the immense pipes to explore the system and to find out who could penetrate longest (the record was 2 km). The exaltation of exploring a unique place where no-one has put his feet before and the ambition to get the record are both important factors in this kind of emancipatory patterns of action.

The downtown area offers many possibilities which do not exist in the suburbs, for instance freedom from the watching eyes of parents, teachers and neighbours. It also offers opportunities to make acquaintance with other faces, and other threats; new scenes and games, with other rules to be learnt. Here there are also 'free zones', but they are of another nature than the ones in the suburbs. If one, like Goffman (1963), believes that the free spaces in the suburb act as retreats 'back stage', the time spent in the downtown area is rather confrontational and 'on stage'. In this way the center of the city becomes the teenagers' theater. Here they can appear in front of an 'audience'. Here they can feel the pulsating heartbeat of the city with its street life and the world of adults (at least during office hours). There is also entertainment and commerce here. The social and pedagogic function of the street must be stressed. Jane Jacobs (1965) underlines that the densely populated and functionally varying city core and city street is a positive antithesis to the monotony of the suburbs. These kinds of places develop a sense of belongingness, at the same time as they are safe and permit freedom of choice in contacts. Peter Noack (1988) suggests that public streets and sidewalks can provide the middle ground needed between private homes and teen hangouts - particularly for the sensitive group of adolescents - who might be overstressed in more active teen hangouts. Teenagers of N Fladen - especially when they appear in big groups - look sometimes strangely suspicious loitering on sidewalks "floating" between the shopping center and large parking lots, because there does not seem to be any legitimate reason for them to be there.

The youths in my two groups had completely different relations with the downtown. While the teenagers in the friend-oriented group stayed almost exclusively in the suburb where they felt secure and could act like "kings", the association-oriented girls in the girls' group stayed in the center of the city or in other places outside the suburb much more often. In this way they acquired a different view of the world around them and a different spatial experience than the more locally oriented teens. The girls often took the bus downtown to go window-shopping or just stroll around. They were drawn in particular to places with life and movement, gathering places for other people, what I call strips; for example, pedestrian streets and passages. Sometimes they joined the crowds at one of the city's discotheques, cafes or hamburger joints, some being 'in' places. I call these hang-outs.

Due to their age and their lack of funds, teenagers are often excluded from different entertainments and places. All that remains for them is the streets and public places, which they take over and temporarily turn into their own 'living rooms' or home areas (Lofland 1973). This phenomenon of temporarily converting parts of public areas to private ones often causes irritation and conflicts with adults and other groups who feel they also have the right to be there. One example is a square in the middle of the city which has become the special stamping grounds for a gang of punks. Motorcycle gangs and 'hot-rodders' hang out in other squares in the city. At times, and especially on Friday and Saturday nights, they more or less take over the entire square. The same phenomenon occurs in N Fladen when the teenagers in the friend-oriented group turn the square in the shopping center into their home area. The mechanisms of this process and how the youths in different ways defend the home area from intruders is developed with the help of the term territorialization (Lyman & Scott 1967; Pettersson 1990).

The different places I have described above can be more or less public. They are more or less open and accessible for teenagers and their endeavour to come in contact with other groups. The variety of places the teenagers seek, have spatial as well as social qualities that to a greater or lesser extent fulfil the requirements and needs of the group. Hiding places, close-to-home places and fringe areas are backstage places teenagers seek primarily to avoid public control and adult observation. The most important activities that may appear at these places is about the relations within the teenage group. The spirit of community and time together with other teenage friends have high priority. Hang-outs, strips and favourite places are the kind of on stage places where the teenagers themselves want to control adult observation and public entrance. At these places the group as a collective is emphasized. Potential conflicts tend to be about the relations between the group and other groups of teenagers or adults outside the collective.

One of the most important aspects of teenagers' use of public spaces is the possibility to control and shape their own existence without adult control. This is a part of the modernization and individualization process in the sense that young people today must take their own responsibility for their future life[5]. Because of their relative lack of free space (they have not yet reached the age of driving-licenses) they are more dependent on the neighbourhood and the local spaces than most other groups. To be sure, my results show that different kinds of teenage groups can be more or less limited in space. The members of the friend-oriented group were much more bound to the local environment than for instance the association-oriented teenagers. But whether they stay in the neighbourhood or in the city centre the teenagers almost always find places and situations that correspond to their needs and preferences. If there are no such places, they "recreate" the existing places, to give them new meanings and contents.

IMPLICATIONS FOR DESIGN AND PLANNING

There is a lot of open space in N Fladen, especially compared with the usual residential area. Foot and bike paths criss-cross through the area. There are open, free spaces and parks between the different housing enclaves. Parks represent a gathering place for a specific group of teenagers but with most parks hidden behind a curtain of trees, bushes and other vegetation, they do not provide a place for teenagers to look out and not be seen - no one can see in or out. Also, the large amount of space covered by parks in N Fladen serves no legitimate function at night and thus becomes deserted. One thing that all these spaces and areas share is that they are permanent, often functionally one-dimensional and intended for one specific type of activity. As I earlier stated, teenagers often try to avoid or redefine this type of places. They value a variety of places including natural and undeveloped landscapes, places where they can be alone and where they can look out and not be seen, gathering places, unsupervised yet safe places, accessible places and places they can call their own[6].

The problem with N Fladen, from the teenagers' point of view, is not that it is over-designed and that it really needs less design. Rather it is that N Fladen is poorly designed, both for teenagers and for human public interaction in general. Places where teenagers can feel independent while in an adult setting should be located within walking distance of their homes and should be safe. Commercial areas and streets, with a mixture of people and a diversity of activities, are ideal settings for these objectives. But when a commercial area or shopping center is separated from housing areas, public streets or main foot paths and left deserted during evenings and nights, the opportunity is lost for them to become truly legitimate hangouts. Instead, it is of great importance that these places have close contacts with a street or main foot paths where people are moving. Parks as well should not be hidden from view. Illegitimate behavior and criminal activities would be less likely in highly visible places.

CONCLUSIONS

To a great extent the analysis has consisted of characterizing the different places young people use. This characterization ultimately resulted in a number of new concepts and categories. The terms used previously can be called 'sensitizing concepts' (Blumer 1954) and can be gathered under two umbrella terms: places for retreat and places for interaction. Places for retreat are places where you can get away, both from other teenagers and from adults. Places for interaction are associated with places where you can see and be seen and where there is life, variation and possibilities to meet with other people, strangers as well as friends. The stability and the pattern of the local teenage environment depend a great deal on the access to this type of place.

One conclusion which can be drawn from the study is that young people need different types of places with different spatial and social characteristics. From the teenagers point of view and with references to Norberg Schulz (1980), I think it is relevant to talk about the city as an "existential room", as a sequence of multifunctional places. Alexander (1966) and Gehl (1987) are some of those who have emphasized the importance of such gradual transition zones in the urban context. Despite the home-centred Swedish culture, the 'over-planning' in the cities and the poor planning in the suburban housing areas, my study has shown that teenagers still find backstage places for retreat and onstage places for interaction. They create their own home areas and free zones in the public environment, to a large extent dependent on the fact that they have nowhere else to go. Together with a few other groups (immigrants and yuppies), youths appear as one of the most important actors in the public space. According to this there are two major developments of the the public city life that should be discussed. The first is what can be called "the dangerous city" (Brunt 1992), where the picture of the street as a breeding ground for destructive actions, criminality and violence emerges. An interesting question is what happens if we minimize or exclude the presence of free-zones and back stage places for young people. Probably, not all of them will go into the "norm zone", engaging themselves in institutionalized activities. On the contrary, some of them will probably enter the "forbidden zone" and land up in criminal activities. The second development of city life, sometimes referred to as the "Fun city" (Oosterman 1992), is one of an enriching environment where young people can meet, be together and get inspiration and strength to meet the demands and expectations of adult life. Young people have discovered more and more possibilities in the city. They see it as a resource and use it for many different things - to see and be seen, to hide, to learn and to acquire qualifications in order to create something of their own.

Notes

1 The complete results from this study are presented in my doctoral dissertation (Lieberg

332

1992).
2 The master plan was developed by Fred Forbat and Stefan Romare, based on the "Neighbourhood Unit" concept.
3 It should be pointed out that the majority of young people could not be placed unconditionally in any of the three groups; therefore, the divisions should be considered rather as general categories.
4 The reason why I didn't follow the "home-oriented" group of teenagers was that they usually don't create gangs and because they took the most cautious attitude to the use of public places.
5 The implication of the modernization and individualization process to youth is developed by Forns & Bolin (eds) (1992) and Ziehe (1989).
6 See also Owens (1988) and Nordstrm (1993).

References

Alexander, C (1966): The City as a Mechanism for Sustaining Human Contact, Berkeley: Center for Planning and Development Research.
Appleyard, D (1970): "Styles and Methods Structuring a City" in Environment and Behavior nr 2, pp 100-118.
Brunt, L (1992): "Coping with Urban Danger", paper presented at the conference on European Cities, Growth and Decline, Haag 1992.
Bjurström, E & Fornäs, J (1988): "Ungdomskultur i Sverige" (Youth Culture in Sweden), in U Himmelstrand & G Svensson (eds): Sverige - Vardag och struktur (Sweden - Everyday Life and Structure) Stockholm: Norstedts Förlag.
Blos, P (1962): On adolescence. New York: The Free Press.
Blumer, H (1969): Symbolic Interaction. Perspective and Method. Los Angeles/London: University of California Press.
Brake, M (1987): Comparative Youth Culture. The Sociology of Youth Culture and Youth Subcultures in America, Britain and Canada. London: Routledge & Kegan.
Corrigan, P (1979): Schooling the Smash Street Kids, The London: Macmillan Press.
Denzin, N (1978): The Research Act. A Theoretical Introduction to Sociological Methods, New York: McGraw-Hill.
Downs, R M & Stea, D (1973): Image and Environment, Chicago: Aldine.
Fornäs, J & Bolin, G (Eds) (1992): Moves in Modernity, Stockholm: Almqvist & Wiksell International.
Gehl, J (1987): Life between Buildings: Using Public Space, New York: Reinhold.
Gillis, J (1981): Youth and History. Tradition and change in European age relations 1770-present, New York: Academic Press.
Goffman, E (1963): Behavior in Public Places, New York: The Free Press of Glencoe.
Hebdige, D (1979): Subculture - the Meaning of Style, London: Methuen.
Jacobs, J (1965): The Death and Life of Great American Cities, New York: Random House.
Ladd, F (1970): "Black Youths View Their Environment. Neighbourhood Maps", Environment and Behavior, nr 2.
Lieberg, M (1992): Att ta staden i besittning. Om ungas rum och rörelser i offentlig miljö (Appropriating the City. Teenagers Use of Public Space), Lund University:

Department of Building Functions Analysis (R3:1992).

Lofland, L (1973): A World of Strangers. Order and Action in Urban Public Space, Illinois: Waveland Press.

Lyman S & Scott M (1967): "Territoriality - A Neglected Sociological Dimension". Social Problems, bd 15/1.

Lynch, K (1960): The Image of the City. Cambridge: MIT Press.

Lynch, K (1977): Growing Up in Cities. Cambridge: MIT Press.

Maurer, R & Baxter, J (1972): Image of the Neighbourhood and City among Children. Environment and Behavior, December 1972.

Mörch, S (1985): At forske i ungdom. En socialpsykologisk essay. Köpenhamn: Rubikon.

Moore, R C (1990): Childhood's Domain. Play and Place in Child's Development, Berkeley, California: MIG Communicatins.

Nielsen, H & Rudberg, M (1991): Historien om pojkar och flickor. Könssocialisation i ett utvecklingspsykologiskt perspektiv. (The story about boys and girls. Gendersocialization in psychological perspective) Lund: Studentlitteratur.

Norberg-Schulz, C (1980): Genius Loci. Towards a phenomenology of architecture. New York: Rizzoli.

Noack, P (1988): "Adolecent Development and Choice of Leisure Settings", Children's Environments Quarterly, Vol. 5, No 2, pp 25-33.

Nordström, M (1993): "The Fundamental Importance of Outdoor Space in the Experience of the Built Environment", Architecture & Behaviour, vol 9 (1993), No. 1.

Oosterman, J (1992): "Welcome to the Pleasure Dome", in Built environment vol 18, no 2.

Owens, P E (1988): "Gathering places and Prospect Refuges: Characteristics of outdoor places valued by teens", Children Environments Quarterly, Vol 5, No. 2, pp 17-24.

Petersson, K (1990): Ungdom, livsvillkor, makt (Youth, living-conditions and power). En studie av erfarenheternas rum i det moderna. University of Linköping: Tema kommunikation.

Piaget, J (1973): The Child's Conception of the World. St Alban: Paladin.

Silbereisen, R & Noack, P (1988): "Adolescence and Environment" in Canter, D (eds): Environmental Policy, Assessment & Communication . Ethnoscapes: Vol 2. Avebury, Atheneum Press Limited, Newcastle.

Taylor, S & Bogdan, R (1984): Introduction to qualitative research methods, New York: John Wiley & Sons.

White, R (1956): "Motivation reconsidered: The concept of competence" i Psychological Review. Vol 66, Nr 5.

Willis, P (1990): Common Culture. Open university Press, London.

Ziehe, T (1989): Kulturanalyser. Ungdom, utbildning, modernitet (Cultural Analysis. Youth, Education, Modernity), Stockholm/ Stehag: Symposion Bokförlag.

29

Pragmatics of urban places according to the size of the city

Pratiques des lieux urbaines selon la taille de la ville

Marino Bonaiuto, Mirilia Bonnes and Anna Rita Mazzotta

On a étudié les rapports des habitants avec leur environnement urbain, en faisant une comparison entre une grande ville (Rome) et une petite ville (Lecce). A partir de la theorie du lieu qui considère les activités comme une des composantes principales de celui-ci, on a etudié les activités poursuivies par deux echantillons d'habitants de Rome (434) et de Lecce (120) dans trois differents lieux urbaines: le centre-ville, le quartier de résidence, la peripherie. Le rapport des habitants avec la ville a ètè examiné aux niveaux intra-lieu et inter-lieux (Bonnes, Mannetti, Secchiaroli & Tanucci 1990; Bonnes, Secchiaroli & Mazzotta 1992).

On traitera seulement ici de l'analyse inter-lieux pour comparison entre les deux villes. Des similarités et des différences entre les habitants des deux villes ont ètè mises en evidence. Celles-ci se refèrent a la manière dont la ville est connue comme "systeme multi-lieux" dans les experiences des residents, è travers leurs pratiques urbaines. Elles varient galement en fonction des caracteristiques socio-demographiques, essentiellement l'age et le sexe. Dans la petite ville les habitants ont tendance avoir (1) une expérience urbaine plus intègré entre les différents lieux et entre maison et quartier, (2) un plus fort engagement dans les activités de socialisation inter-personnelles au niveau du quartier, une pratique urbaine moins orientée vers le repli domestique.

Le mots clés: lieux urbaines; quartier de résidence; analyse inter-lieux; pratiques urbaines; ville comme systeme multi-lieux des activités

Keywords: urban places; neighbourhood; inter-place analysis; urban pragmatics; city as multi-place system of activity

During the last fifteen years the concept of "place" has taken on an increasingly central role in the works of several social and environmental psychologists like Canter (1977, 1988), Stokols (1981), Russel and Ward (1982), Proshansky, Fabian and Kaminoff (1983), Holahan (1985), Altman (1986), and others. Particularly, many authors have attempted to identify this construct and to acknowledge the place-specific nature of all human behaviour. Generally speaking "place" may be defined as an "experience unity" or psychological unity referring to specific physical settings (Canter, 1986; Russell & Ward, 1982). It has three main components: physical properties, evaluative conceptualization, and activities carried out in it. Thus, place theory considers actions, carried on by people in relation to a specific setting, to be one of the main components of the psychology of place and of person/environment relationship. Looking for a more complete place theory, some authors recently stressed the importance to consider a perspective defined as "place system" (Rapoport, 1986, 1990) or "inter-place system" (Bonnes, Mannetti, Secchiaroli & Tanucci, 1990; Bonnes, Secchiaroli & Mazzotta, 1992; Bonnes & Secchiaroli, 1992).

The starting point of such a perspective pertains the consideration about the existence of organized modalities in the construction of the individual place experience: places are connected each other both at the individual and collective experience level. An inter-place perspective should reconstruct such multi-place organization modalities of the place systems, in relation both to the specific places considered and to the involved persons.

This means that each place is not isolated from other places. Rather, each place is "constructed", at the psychological level, in relation to other places and sub-places, and according to organized relations between these places (like hierarchical super-place or sub-place relations between places linked by spatial or category inclusion/exclusion). For instance, we may assume that persons using and living in the place "city" tend to break down their experience according to a set of smaller sub-places (neighbourhood, centre, and periphery); those can be re-aggregated into larger places according to patterns which vary with the characteristics of either the sub-places or the individual concerned. Thus, persons would organize their own place experience according to a multi-place perspective.

Therefore our understanding of the place-specific character of human activity should be increased by extending the scope of the relevant research to cover also such interdependence, i.e. by progressing from intra-place analysis to inter-place analysis. Our research is intended as a step in this direction, taking the construct of place as the basis for studying individual/environment relationship, particularly transactions between the inhabitants and their urban environment. Thus we will focus on the type of activity they perform in each sub-place or better on the "system of activities"

(Rapoport, 1990) carried out in the city considered as a multi-place system.

This contribution focuses on the inter-place analyses carried out on the inhabitants' systems of activity of two different cities: Roma (see Bonnes et al., 1990) and Lecce (see Bonnes et al., 1992). We will compare the analyses carried on for the large vs. the small city to seek out similarities and differences according to the size of the two cities: (i) in the construction of the urban experience as multi-place system; (ii) in the specific relationships between the inhabitants' "urban pragmatics" and the inhabitants' characteristics (their age, gender, socio-economic and educational levels, and length of residence in the neighbourhood).

METHOD

Subjects

The two considered samples consisted of 434 inhabitants of the city of Rome and 120 inhabitants of the city of Lecce. The inhabitants of each sample lived in one neighbourhood of the city, which was located mid-way between the city-center and the periphery (quartiere Aurelio in Rome, quartiere Santa Rosa in Lecce). Both samples were selected taking into account first of all age and gender; the Rome sample had different socio-economic level (medium-upper, medium, medium-lower), while the Lecce sample was fairly homogeneous around the medium level.

Procedure and tool

Each resident was interviewed through a structured questionnaire. They were asked to state how often they performed each of the listed activities (previously identified through the exploratory phase of the study) as being personally performed in the three main sub-places considered: neighbourhood, centre, periphery. These responses were given through a frequency four interval scale (never to always) and were subsequently rated on a four point scale (1 to 4). Only in the city of Lecce the residents also answered to other groups of question devoted to measure a range of attitudes towards the same urban place.

Analysis of data

A principal component analysis was applied in each city on the frequency with which each activity is carried out in each of the three urban places (S.P.A.D. software; Lebart & Morineau, 1982): First considering each place separately (separated intra-place analyses for neighbourhood, centre, periphery) and then considering activities carried on in the three places together (inter-place analysis). Here only inter-place analyses results will be reported (for intra-place analyses results see Bonnes et al., 1990, and Bonnes et al., 1992).

Then, for each city a cluster analysis of the residents was developed on the basis of the main components obtained from the previous inter-place analysis of the activities carried on (active variables). Socio-demographic, residential, and attitude (only for the Lecce sample) characteristics of the residents have been used as illustrative variables to describe the identified clusters of residents (passive variables).

RESULTS

Dimensions of inter-place activities

In each city, inter-place analysis of the activities has shown the existence of four main dimensions of inter-place activities tending to link together the intra-place activities (Tables 1 and 2). In the small city all four dimensions include activities related to two places. While in the large city there is one dimension pertaining to only one place (4th dimension refers to a mono-place use of centre), in the small city there is a more systematic tendency toward the integration among the three urban places with respect to the large city. However in both cities inter-place analysis shows the integration between the main intra-place activities characterizing the neighbourhood and some of the intra-place activities characterizing the city-centre (1st and 3rd inter-place dimensions in Rome, 1st and 2nd inter-place dimensions in Lecce) or the periphery (2nd inter-place dimension in Rome, 4th inter-place dimension in Lecce). Only in the small city, one dimension links periphery and centre activities (3rd inter-place dimension in Lecce).

In both cities, 1st dimension indicates that the numerous activities involving specific and non-specific uses performed in the course of multiple utilization of the centre are positively associated to the performance of physical activity in the neighbourhood (i.e. 1st intra-centre dimension joins 1st intra-neighbourhood dimension); besides, in the small city this is opposed to home confinement. On the whole it is a sort of extension at the city level of the residential or home openness/closedness: thus "Residential closedness vs. Urban openness" seems a fairly stable urban activity dimension independent of the size of the city (14% and 16.5% explained variance). The other three dimensions result to be more different between the two cities.

Table 1. Inter-place activities dimensions (*city of Rome*). Principal component analysis of activities carried out in neighbourhood, centre, periphery (only items with factor loading higher than .40 are reported).

1st dimension			
Multi-uses of the centre + sports in the neighbourhood			
Positive pole	*c.a.*	Negative pole	*c.a.*
Neighbourhood			
Playing sports	.42		
Centre			
Meeting friends	.67		
Visiting exhibitions	.65		
Going in for no special reason	.63		
Spending spare time there	.62		
Going to bookshops or libraries	.62		
Looking at beautiful things	.61		
Looking for a link with the past	.59		
Walking	.59		
Going to the pictures	.59		
Going to the theatre	.58		
Visiting museums	.56		
Walking at night	.56		
Going to a restaurant	.55		
Going to public meeting places	.54		
Shopping (general things)	.53		
Shopping (special things)	.51		
Discovering the old town	.51		
Celebrating special days	.49		
Being together with other people	.48		
Going to cultural centres	.45		
Meeting new people	.45		
Facilities lacking in neighbourh.	.45		
Window-shopping	.43		
Finding quiet places	.43		
Visiting acquaintances	.42		
Visiting antique shops	.41		
Getting out of the house	.41		
2nd dimension			
Many discretionary uses in the periphery + social commitment in the neighbourhood			
Positive pole	*c.a.*	Negative pole	*c.a.*
		Neighbourhood	
		Participate in political committee	- .46
		Periphery	
		Walking	- .53
		Looking for parkland, green areas	- .50
		Meeting friends	- .43
		Visiting relatives or acquaintances	- .43
		Going for a pic-nic	- .41

continued on next page

Table 1 — *continued*

3rd dimension			
Home centred in the neighbourhood + escape use of the centre			
Positive pole	*c.a.*	Negative pole	*c.a.*
		Neighbourhood	
		Spending most of the time at home	- .57
		Spending spare time at home	- .56
		Just staying at home in evening	- .49
		Window shopping	- .47
		Centre	
		Getting out of the house	- .43

4th dimension			
Cultural activities and non-escape use in the centre			
Positive pole	*c.a.*	Negative pole	*c.a.*
Centre		*Centre*	
Visiting churches and monuments	.56	Being together with other people	- .40
Visiting exhibitions	.47		
Visiting museums	.45		

Large city. The 2nd dimension (5.7% explained variance) shows that discretionary activities in the periphery (green areas, walking, meeting acquaintances, friends) are associated with the participatory and socially committed activities in the neighbourhood (1st and 3rd intra-periphery dimensions with 3rd intra-neighbourhood dimension: "Many discretionary uses in the periphery and social commitment in the neighbourhood"). The 3rd dimension (5.3% explained variance) reveals the home-centred activities in the neighbourhood are associated with the use of centre for the purpose of escape (2nd intra-neighbourhood dimension with 2nd intra-centre dimension: "Home centred in the neighbourhood and escape use of the centre"). The 4th dimension (4.7% explained variance) refers only to cultural activities in the centre (it corresponds to the 2nd intra-centre dimension: "Cultural activities and non-escape use in the centre"): The centre of a big city like Rome seems to have an independent status from the other two urban places, as far as cultural activities are concerned.

Small city

The 2nd dimension (7% explained variance) associates non-specific visual-evoking use of the centre with multiple integrate and social use of the neighbourhood vs. multiple specific use of centre with non-use of neighbourhood (2nd intra-centre dimension with 2nd intra-neighbourhood dimension: "Non-specific use of the centre and multi-use of the neighbourhood / Specific use of the centre and non-use of the neighbourhood"). The 3rd dimension (6% explained variance) opposes multi-use of periphery (discretionary and non-discretionary activities) to specific multi-use of centre for acquisitive and escaping activities (1st intra-periphery dimension with 2nd intra-centre dimension: "Multi-use of the periphery and non-discretionary use of centre / Specific multi-use of the centre"). The 4th dimension (5.7% explained variance) shows that a home-confined life in the neighbourhood is associated with looking for green and open spaces in the periphery and opposed to use open and green spaces in the neighbourhood (1st intra-neighbourhood dimension with 1st intra-periphery dimension: "Residential closedness and use of green areas in the periphery / Use of green areas and social activity in the neighbourhood").

On the whole, these results point to a tendency for the inhabitants to use the city by integrating different sub-places, that is in a multi-place sense through the kind of activities they perform in each sub-place.

Inter-place activities and residents' characteristics

With reference to the four inter-place activity dimensions illustrated above for each city, the subsequent cluster analysis of the residents in each sample indicates that the inhabitants could be divided into six groups in the large city (44% explained variance), and into five groups in the small city (61.6% explained variance). Each group of residents is significantly characterized both by the activities performed or not in each of the three places and by a number of characteristic socio-demographic patterns based on age, gender, socio-economic and education levels, length of residence and attitude characteristics. Tables 29.3 and 29.4 summarize the results of cluster analyses showing the six Rome groups and the five Lecce groups according to the inhabitants urban pragmatics. On the left side there are differences in inhabitants urban pragmatics. The urban pragmatics oriented toward urban integration is characterized by positive oriented activities (to do instead of not to do), by specific activities (specific use activities instead of non-specific uses), by high mobility and social exchange: Partial or total integration according to "bi-place" or "multi-place" pragmatics.

Table 2. Inter-place activities dimensions (*city of Lecce*). Principal component analysis of activities carried out in neighbourhood, centre, periphery (only items with factor loading higher than .35 are reported).

1st dimension Residential closedness / Multi-uses of the centre + sports in the neighbourhood			
Positive pole	*c.a.*	Negative pole	*c.a.*
Neighbourhood		*Neighbourhood*	
Just staying at home in evening	.58	Playing sports	- .46
Spending most of the time at home	.49		
Spending spare time at home	.46	*Centre*	
		Meeting friends	- .79
		Meeting new people	- .74
		Going to public meeting places	- .71
		Being together with other people	- .69
		Window-shopping	- .68
		Going for a walk	- .68
		Celebrating special days	- .65
		Getting out of the house	- .65
		Going to bar	- .63
		Going to the theatre	- .59
		Looking at beautiful things	- .56
		Going to the pictures	- .53
		Walking at night	- .50
		Visiting exhibitions	- .47
		Going to a restaurant	- .43
		Visiting museums	- .43
		Seeking to be seen	- .43
		Joining in political demonstrations	- .39
		Visiting antique shops	- .39
		Going to cultural centres	- .37
2nd dimension Non-specific use of centre + multi-uses of neighbourhood / Specific use of centre + non-use of neighourhood			
Positive pole	*c.a.*	Negative pole	*c.a.*
Centre		*Centre*	
Looking for a link with the past	.62	Going to public meeting points	- .45
Discovering the old town	.40	Working or studying	- .44
Looking at beautiful things	.40	Going to the pictures	- .41
		Joining in political demonstrations	- .40
Neighbourhood			
Meeting neighbours	.57	*Neighbourhood*	
Window shopping	.50	Staying there only to sleep	- .44
Just staying at home in the evening	.48		
Joining in parish activities	.41		
Going to the gardens	.35		

continued on next page

3rd dimension
Multi-use of the periphery / Specific multi-use of the centre

Positive pole	c.a.	Negative pole	c.a.
Periphery		*Centre*	
Meeting friends	.57	Shopping (general things)	- .39
Going to public offices	.43	Shopping (special things)	- .36
Going for a pic-nic	.42	Going to the pictures	- .35
Looking for parkland, green areas	.41		
Walking	.41		
Visiting relatives or acquaintances	.40		
Playing sports	.39		

4th dimension
Residential closedness + use of green areas in the periphery / Use of green areas and social activity in the neighbourhood

Positive pole	c.a.	Negative pole	c.a.
Neighbourhood		*Neighbourhood*	
Spending spare time at home	.59	Going to the gardens	- .56
Spending most of the time at home	.54	Going for a walk	- .53
		Going into friends homes	- .36
Periphery			
Going for a pic-nic	.47		
Looking for parkland, green areas	.46		
Shopping in supermarkets	.45		

The urban pragmatics oriented toward urban confinement is characterized by negative oriented activities (not to do instead of to do), by low specificity (more non-specific uses than specific uses), by low mobility and social exchange: It corresponds to partial or total confinement according to "bi-place" or "mono-place" pragmatics.

On the left-higher cell of each table, the full urban openness and integration is located, where all the three urban places are used. In both cities only a minority of residents are found on this cell.

Rome Group 6 (n=35) displays intense activity in all three urban places considered: it shows interest in socializing activities (both political commitment and interpersonal encounters), discretionary activities both in the periphery and in the centre; in the neighbourhood the less frequent activities are those of staying at home. The socio-demographic features significantly different in this group, compared to the whole sample, are male gender and degree level of education ("hyperactive males, socially oriented, fully integrated in the city").

Lecce Group 3 (n=21) uses all three urban places: home use and social activities in the neighbourhood, both non-specific use of centre (visual-evoking activities and social-escaping activities) and specific use of centre (cultural and acquisitive activities), discretionary activity in periphery (open space, acquisitive, social activities). They are "medium-age working". In the central-higher cell of each table, we found two groups of residents in each city, using two of the three urban places.

Rome Group 3 (n=63) is the most active in the use of city-centre (specific and non-specific activity) but few activities are performed in the neighbourhood (the use of which is restricted to sport and open-air activities). Young age coupled with degree level of education characterize this group defined as "Young city-centre multi-users, with physical activities in the neighbourhood, not home centred". Then, Rome Group 2 (n=126) is also very active in the city-centre, particularly as far as cultural dimension is concerned. The use of neighbourhood is limited to parks, and mainly to spend considerable time at home avoiding activities of interpersonal and community nature in the neighbourhood. High cultural and socio-economic level characterize this group defined as "Social elite, quality users of the centre, home centred in the neighbourhood".

Lecce Group 2 (n=21) has mainly city-centre uses for many different activities both specific and non-specific (entertainment, escape, specific services) but also discretionary periphery uses (open-space and interpersonal activities). They are young (18 to 34 years) and lived there for more than 10 years ("Young long term residents"). Then, Lecce Group 1 (n=21) has mainly entertainment and escape activity in centre (specific and non-specific use), coupled with neighbourhood use limited to interpersonal encounters.

Table 3. The city as a multi-place system according to the residents' urban pragmatics (*city of Rome*). Cluster analysis identified 6 different groups of inhabitants on the basis of their inter-place activities and of the related socio-demographic characteristics.

Type of urban pragmatics	Multi-place system features: - spatial extension - differentiation - complexity		
	High (Multi-place)	*Medium* (Bi-place)	*Low* (Mono-place)
Toward Integration Activity with: - positive orientation - high specificity - high mobility - high social interchange	*Full-integration* *Group 6 "hyperactive males degree education"* - neighbourhood - centre - periphery	*Semi-integration* *Group 3 "young degree education"* - neighbourhood - centre *Group 2 "social elite"* - home - centre	--------
Toward Confinement Activity with: - negative orientation - low specificity - low mobility - low social interchange	--------	*Semi-confinement* *Group 4 "housewives low education and socio-econ. level"* - neighbourhood - centre	*Full-confinement* *Group 5 "very young"* - centre *Group 1 "old poor"* - home

They are young, medium socio-economic level and mainly students or housewifes ("Young non-working long term residents").

In the central-lower cell of each table, we found one group of residents in each city, using two of the three urban places.

Rome Group 4 (n=95) has intense use of the neighbourhood (acquisitive, entertainment, social activities) and the home; in connection it has a totally non-specific use of city-centre limited to a physical presence for the sole purpose of entertainment / escape. Low education and socio-economic levels, over 35 years of age or elderlies (over 55 years) and female gender, characterize this group defined as "Housewifes of low socio-economic level, home centred and neighbourhood multi-users, escape users of the centre".

Table 4. The city as a multi-place system according to the residents' urban pragmatics (*city of Lecce*). Cluster analysis identified 5 different groups of inhabitants on the basis of their inter-place activities and of the related socio-demographic characteristics.

Type of urban pragmatics	Multi-place system features: - spatial extension - differentiation - complexity		
	High (Multi-place)	*Medium* (Bi-place)	*Low* (Mono-place)
Toward Integration Activity with: - positive orientation - high specificity - high mobility - high social interchange	*Full-integration* *Group 3 "medium-age working"* - neighbourhood - centre - periphery	*Semi-integration* *Group 2 "young long-term residents"* - centre - periphery *Group 1 "young non-working long-term res."* - neighbourhood - centre	*Low-integration* *Group 5 "females short-term residents"* - neighbourhood
Toward Confinement Activity with: - negative orientation - low specificity - low mobility - low social interchange	--------	*Semi-confinement* *Group 4 "old-males long-term residents"* - neighbourhood - centre	--------

Lecce Group 4 (n=21) uses almost only the place neighbourhood, rarely periphery (only discretionary use) and centre (only evoking use); however they are well integrated in the neighbourhood, where they perform several activities: entertainment and social activities both indoor and outdoor. They are male, between 55 and 65 years of age, long term residents ("Old males long-term residents").In the right-higher cell we found one group in the small city.

Lecce Group 5 (n=36) is confined in the neighbourhood. They spend most of their time inside the home, but they also use the neighbourhood to do daily shopping. They are mainly "female short-term residents".
In the right-lower cell we found two groups in the large city.

Rome Group 5 (n=55) is practically absent from the neighbourhood; it stays there only to sleep. This lack of activity in and absence from the neighbourhood is accompanied however only by scanty generic activities in the centre, limited to uses involving social meeting and entertainment (without more specific use of this sub-place). Very young age (18-25) and medium-high educational level (or still studying) characterize this group of "Very young limited users of the centre, absent from home and neighbourhood". Then, Rome Group 1 (n=60) is characterized above all by the absence of the activities in each of the three urban places, except for the neighbourhood. Here, however, the only activities are those involving spending all one's time at home. It is the oldest group in Rome (over 55 years) with low socio-economic and educational level: "Old, poor, home-confined".

DISCUSSION

The inter-place analysis shows similarities (the first dimension is the same for the two cities), but it also shows differences between the two cities. In the small city there is a stronger tendency to integrate the different places, both in the inter-place dimensions (two places are always present), and in the inter-place activities performed by the various groups of inhabitants (virtually no one with mono-place urban pragmatics if we consider the Lecce Group 5 as acting in both the home and the neighbourhood).

The large as well as the small city appears to be constructed by the inhabitants as multi-place system according to specific modalities referring to its spatial extension, differentiation, and complexity (Tables 3 and 4). Results from cluster analysis indicate in both cities only one group of residents having a full urban integration, with "multi-place pragmatics" and thus with a highly extended, differentiated, complex multi-place system. In both cities the most frequent groups are characterized by a "bi-place pragmatics" (at least two places) with a multi-place system with average extension, differentiation, complexity.

In the large city two groups (1 = "old poor", 5 = "very young") are fully confined through "mono-place pragmatics" with low extended, differentiated and complex multi-place system. In the small city two groups tend to have multi-place activity systems oriented toward confinement (4 = "old males", 5 = "females short-term residents"), but such confinement conditions seems to be not so extreme as in the large city. The urban life condition of elderly people appears to be particularly different: while in the large city they appear to be completely isolated and confined at home, in the small city their life condition seems more outside oriented. It is enriched by social exchange occasions in the neighbourhood and it does not loose contact with the centre.

Similarly, in the large city young people escape from residential place and are confined in the centre, showing a special case of urban confinement. Again in the small city, notwithstanding their preference for the city-centre, the younger are able to maintain links with other urban places (periphery for group 2, neighbourhood for group 1), thus avoiding the particular kind of urban confinement of the young people in the large city.

About residents' gender, both the two cities tend to show a stronger urban isolation (in the neighbourhood) for women than for men. This tendency appear more clearly in the small city (group 5). This result should be interpreted in relation not only to the lower extension but also to the southern geographical position of Lecce (with respect to Rome). In Italy the woman role is usually associated with traditional cultural models and life styles both in small cities and in southern regions.

On the whole the study, conducted on the large city (Rome) and then replicated on the small one (Lecce), shows both the generality of the results across the cities and some specific features of inhabitants-city relationship depending on the size of the city.

Particularly, the generality of the results pertains to:
i) the multi-place integrate modalities through which inhabitants tend to construct their urban experience;
ii) the relevance both the residential places (home and neighbourhood) and the city-centre have to organize such experience;
iii) the influence mainly of age and also of sex to determine the extent of spatial extension, complexity and differentiation which characterizes the city as a "multi-place system" for its inhabitants.

At the same time, some specific features characterize the small city (vs. the large one):
i) the tendency of inhabitants to have a more integrated urban experience between different places, first of all between home and neighbourhood;

ii) the higher frequency and relevance of interpersonal socialization activities, which result to be realized mainly in the neighbourhood life;
iii) the conditions of less "urban isolation" especially for the social groups more at risk: older and younger people.

On the whole, the inter-place perspective seems useful to comprehend the inhabitants-urban environment relationships in different size cities. Inter-place analysis affords us insight into the links between the dimensions of place-specific actions and it reveals the close interdependence between the various dimensions of activities referring to the various urban places considered. By means of this perspective it is possible to gain a better "molar" understanding of individual intra-place activities, and to identify more general modalities through which the experience of the place "city" is constructed by the residents with reference to the various sub-places.

The place of residence (neighbourhood/home) seems to play a crucial role in the organization of the inter-place activities performed. Each of the main intra-place activity dimensions of the centre and the periphery tend to be regulated in accordance with the specific dimensions of activities carried out in the place of residence: the inhabitants do or do not carry out certain specific activities in non-residential urban places according to the type of activity preferentially carried out in their place of residence.

The close relationship between person and urban places becomes evident by analysing the various types of inter-place activity associated to socio-demographic variables and by referring to the different groups of residents. Different modalities of action characterize the residents "multi-place urban pragmatics" through which the city is constructed in the residents' experience as a place or, better, as an integrated multi-place system. It tends to take on features defined and modified according to the features assumed by its residents/agents.

The place-specific nature of human behaviour appears with its distinctive features of purposive, goal directed activity above all at the inter-place level. The agents plan and pursue their actions not only in the situations or in the places but above all "among them".

Acknowledgements

We are grateful to Dr. Pino Bove for statistical analyses of data and to Paola Fazzi for help in data gathering.

References

Altman, I. (1986). Theoretical issues in environmental psychology. Paper presented at the 21st IAAP Congress, Jerusalem.

Bonnes, M., Mannetti, L., Secchiaroli, G. & Tanucci, G. (1990). The city as a multi-place system: An analysis of people-urban environment transactions. Journal of Environmental Psychology, 10, 37-65.

Bonnes, M. & Secchiaroli, G. (1992). Psicologia ambientale. Introduzione alla psicologia sociale dell'ambiente. Roma: La Nuova Italia Scientifica.

Bonnes, M., Secchiaroli, G. & Mazzotta, A.R. (1992). The home as an urban place: Inter-place perspective on person-home relationship. In M.V. Giuliani (ed.), Home. Social, temporal and spatial aspects, pp. 199-214. San Giuliano Milanese: Progetto Finalizzato Edilizia.

Canter, D. (1977). The psychology of place. London: Architectural Press.

Canter, D. (1986). Putting situations in their place: Foundations for a bridge between social and environmental psychology. In A. Furnham (ed.), Social behaviour in context. London: Allyn and Bacon.

Canter, D. (1988). Action and place: An existential dialectic. In D. Canter, M. Krampen & D. Stea (eds.), Ethnoscapes: Environmental perspectives, vol. 1, pp. 1-18. Aldershot, Hampshire: Gower.

Holahan, C.J. (1985). Environmental psychology. Annual Review of Psychology, 37, 381-407.

Lebart, L. & Morineau, A. (1982). S.P.A.D.. Paris: CESIA.

Proshansky, H., Fabian, A.K. & Kaminoff, R. (1983). Place-identity: physical world socialization of the self. Journal of Environmental Psychology, 3, 57-83.

Rapoport, A. (1986). The use and design of open spaces in urban neighbourhoods. In D. Frick (ed.), The quality of urban life, pp. 159-176. Berlin: de Gruiter.

Rapoport, A. (1990). System of activities and system of settings. In S. Kent (ed.), Domestic architecture and the use of space, pp. 159-176. Cambridge: Cambridge University Press.

Russell, J.A. & Ward, L.M. (1982). Environmental psychology. Annual Review of Psychology, 33, 651-658.

Stokols, D. (1981). Group x place transactions: Some neglected issues in psychological research on settings. In D. Magnusson (ed.), Toward a psychology of situation: An interactional perspective, pp. 393-415. Hillsdale, N.J.: Lawrence Erlbaum.

30

Relationship between the classification of urban streetscape and overall evaluation

La classification des paysages urbains et l'évaluation globale

Yoshiki Nakamura, Kiwamu Maki and Masao Inui

Les paysages attrayants ne sont en général pas ceux des rues, qu'elles soient résidentielles ou commerçantes. En partant de ce point de vue, nous avons examiné la manière dont les individus classent les paysages urbains pour voir si les différences de constructions interviennent sur l'attrait des paysages, et l'importance qu'elles ont pour chaque catégorie.

 Lors de la classification des paysages urbains, trois groupes (rues d'affaires, rues commerçantes et rues résidentielles) sont apparus comme des catégories de premier ordre. Nous effectué des interviews pour déterminer quelles constructions influençaient l'évaluation globale dans chaque groupe, et nous avons trouvé des différences entre les groupes. Une expérience à l'aide d'échelles de classement a permis d'identifier quantitativement les relations entre les constructions et l'évaluation globlale. Les résultats ont montré que les relations entre les constructions d'un même groupe peuvent changer, mais que cela peut être dû aux déséquilibres des impressions entre les groupes. L'influence exercée par les constructions sur le jugement des paysages urbains ne change pas avec le groupe.

Mots clé: paysage urbain; paysages de rues; évaluation globale; classement.

Keywords: urban landcsape, streetscape, overall evaluation, clssification

Diverse types of landscapes exist in Japanese cities. Just taking townscapes, for example, we find that the elements constituting townscapes vary greatly according to the function of the individual townscape such as office street or shopping street. This makes us doubtful about classifying them into the same group under the name of townscape. Further, as we consider this great variety of landscapes in cities, we become skeptical about evaluating all those landscapes crosswise by applying only one scale to every one of them. This skepticism naturally lead us to consider the use of different scales for different groups, with each group sharing a certain level of similarity.

The authors carried out a preliminarily experiment in which 33 subjects were asked to freely describe the conditions constituting desirable streets. The result of this experiment revealed that the conditions of desirable streets are often listed for each function of streets including office streets, shopping streets, and residential streets. When we discuss urban landscapes featuring wide variation, should classify them into groups according to their functions? And if we should, what categories should be established?

The same problem applies to general research into landscapes. For instance, the landscapes are categorized when we divide landscapes into natural landscapes and urban landscapes like Kaplan does or when we perform analysis on each category of content as Herzog does. This means that both Kaplan and Herzog emphasize the importance of such categorization for review and analysis.

This paper organizes various aspects of the categorization. In this paper, the authors discusses how people instinctively classify diverse urban streetscapes and also discusses, for each category group, the preferable urban streetscapes and the differences in the association level among the evaluative constructs that they consider when evaluating preferable urban streetscapes.

Landscapes involve comprehensive experiences. Photographs cannot fully represent the landscapes, but the authors used photographs as the stimuli for the experiment which was intended for identifying problems with the categorization. Only students served as subjects for the experiment.

INVESTIGATION BY INTERVIEW 1: CLASSIFYING URBAN STREETSCAPES

We carried out the investigation through interviews to determine how people classify urban streetscapes. For this investigation, we prepared 125 photographs of urban streetscapes which were taken in Tokyo and its environs (Figure 30.1) and showed them to 33 subjects (15 males and 18 females). The subjects were asked to subdivide the photographs. The viewpoints on which they were based for classifying the photographs and the number of photographs of each category group were all left up to the subjects. The subdividing work were carried out by stages until the subjects decided that they could no longer subdivide. Table 1 shows the investigation procedures taken. Every subject completed the classifying work within five steps.

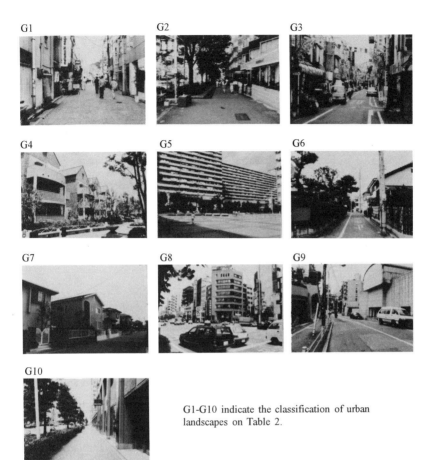

G1-G10 indicate the classification of urban landscapes on Table 2.

Figure 30.1 Examples of streetscape photographs in interviews.

Table 1 Procedure for Investigation by Interviews

This is an experiment on urban landscapes. We would like you to let us know how you classify them.

(1) First, roughly classify the 125 photographs of streets. You are free to set any standard for classifying them. You are also free to set the number of category groups and the number of photographs which fall into each group.

(2) Then, regarding each group you make, let us know what kind of group it is.-----> Extraction of classifying constructs

(3) Of the groups you have established, do you think that there are some that can be subdivided? If there are, subdivide them in the same manner as you did for the rough classification.

* Repeat the steps (1) through (3) listed above until it becomes impossible to subdivide any further.

Based on the results of the classification by the subjects, we prepared a matrix of the frequency of each photograph being classified into the same category group. Taking this as the similarity of urban streetscapes, we performed cluster analysis based on the furthest neighbor method. As a result, we obtained the clusters shown in Table 30.2. The majority of the subjects first classified the streets into shopping streets, residential streets, and office streets which belong to the left hand cluster of Table 30.2, then worked on the right hand cluster. The clusters thus obtained showed good matching with the processes through which most subjects went. The top group on the left is the category group based on the function of streets; as the level goes down from the top to the bottom, the category group tends to be based on the constituents and the impressions of streets.

From the results, we found that people first classify urban streetscapes according to their functions, then they use the commonality of impressions and constituents for subdividing. The following describes the changes in the evaluation standard for each of the three categories based on the functions of streets which are commonly used by people and which are considered to most influence the commonality in the evaluation standard for urban streetscapes.

Table 2 Classification of Streetscapes

Level 1	Level 2	Level 3
Shopping streets <37>		G1 Back-street shopping areas <7> (Narrow streets)
		G2 Front-street shopping areas <11> (Bustling streets)
		G3 Drinking shop streets <19> (Disorderly streets)
Residential streets <49>	Apartment streets <19>	G4 Low-rise or small-scale <11> apartment houses
		G5 High-rise or large-scale <8> apartment houses
	Independent house streets <30>	G6 New residential streets <19>
		G7 Old residential streets <11> (e.g.,the old quarter)
Office streets <39>		G8 Streets of mixtures of offices <12> and commercial buildings
		G9 Low-rise building streets <6>
		G10 Medium- to high-rise building streets <21>

INVESTIGATION BY INTERVIEWS 2: EXTRACTING EVALUATIVE CONSTRUCTS

To find whether different categories have different constructs that are considered when the desirability of streets is evaluated, we carried out the investigation based on interviews by using the method suggested by Sanui (Sanui & Inui, 1984, 1986). The investigation procedure used is as shown in Table 30.3. The stimulants presented were the same photographs as those used for the interview investigation 1. 16 subjects were interviewed to extract evaluative constructs of each category group using the photographs subdivided into the three categories.

We totaled the frequencies of the words used to evaluate the urban streetscapes which were obtained from the investigations. Table 30.4 shows the constructs that were used by three or more subjects. Further, to identify the connection among the evaluative constructs, we drew the network charts shown in Figure 30.2. In the network charts, specific evaluative constructs (lower constructs) are shown on the right, while abstract evaluative constructs (higher constructs) are shown on the left. The lines with arrowheads connecting the constructs represent the relationship between the constructs, and it shows that the evaluative constructs at starting points are essential factors for satisfying the evaluative constructs at terminating points.

Table 3 Investigation Procedure for Extracting Evaluative Constructs

1. Divide these photographs of streets into five ranks with the most desirable ones at the top.
2. Of the differences between the 5th group and the 4th group, let us know which of them you think are related to the evaluation of "desirability". The differences may not necessarily apply to the entire group.
3. (About the differences among the groups the subject has described.)
Which characteristics of the streetscapes make you feel as you do?
On what do they exert an influence?
---> The subject is asked to describe the relationship between the constructs.

* Steps 2 and 3 above are repeated four times for each rank of "desirability."

The frequencies at which the evaluative constructs are mentioned show that there are differences among the groups in terms of "organization," "excitement," and "the sign of people's life." Also, the evaluative construct "there is greenery" was mentioned very frequently, indicating that it is basically an important factor.

The characteristics of each category group are summarized as follows:

a. **Office streets**

A distinct network has been obtained, of which the higher constructs were "unity" and "organization," the main lower constructs were "unity of buildings," "harmony of colors," "signboards are less conspicuous," "there are fewer objects," and "the roads are wide." The impression of "easy to walk along" has been connected primarily with "unobstructed view," "spacious," and "presence of greenery," suggesting that an emphasis is placed on the visual impression.

b. **Shopping streets**

Many subjects selected "beauty" and "composure" and also evaluative constructs concerning "signboards" in relation to the two evaluative constructs. The evaluative construct "looks exciting" was selected frequently, however it did not appear in the networks. It is probably caused by the variety of estimation "looks exciting" from person to person.

Table 4 Major Evaluative Constructs

O	S	R	Affirmative evaluative constructs	Negative evaluative constructs	O	S	R
4	7	2	Peaceful	Not peaceful	3		
9	5	3	Organized	Disorderly	6	8	4
1		4	Disorderly	Organized	2		
8	2	3	Unified	Ununified	5	3	2
	2	6	Characteristic	Plain	1	1	3
3	8	5	Beautiful	Not beautiful	1		2
3	9	3	Exciting	Boring	5	3	2
2	2	4	Warm	Cold	3	3	4
2	4	3	Cheerful	Cheerless	6		1
4	2	2	Relaxing	Unrelaxing		1	1
9	7	3	Easy-to-walk	Hard-to-walk	3	2	1
3	4	3	Encourages us to walk	Discourages us from walking	3	4	1
3	1	1	Unobstructed view	Obstructed view	1		
5	5	8	Show the sign of people's life	Does not Show the sign of people's life		2	2
1		4	Good association among neighbors	Poor association among neighbors			1
2	3	6	Associated with my memories and experiments				
15	9	13	There is greenery	Little greenery	2	3	2
7	4	5	Trimmed greenery,moderate greenery	Poorly trimmed greenery	3		4
7	2	4	Unified look of buildings	Ununified look of buildings	4	1	1
3	4	1	Harmony of buildings with their surroundings	Buildings not matching the surroundings	2		2
5	3	2	Harmonized colors	Inharmonious colors	1		
4	6	5	Wide roads	Narrow roads		5	3
2	7	8	Maintained sidewalks	Poorly maintained roads	3	1	2
4	4	1	Wide sidewalks	Narrow sidewalks	1	1	1
5	4		Inconspicuous signboards	Conspicuous signboards	3	6	
1	6		Characterisitc signboards				

O: Office Street , S : Shopping Street , R : Residential Street

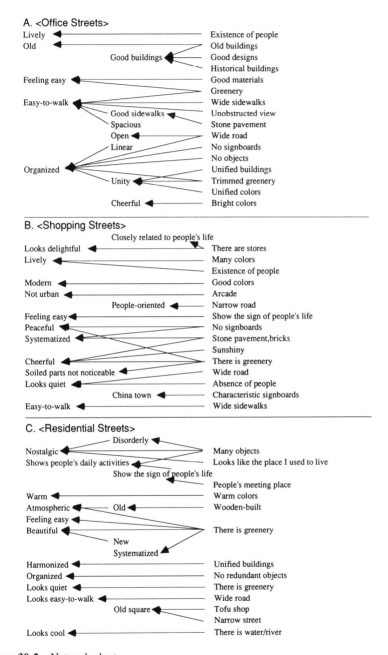

Figure 30.2 Network charts.

c. **Residential streets**

Many constructs such as "it shows the sign of people's life" and "it looks like the neighborhood in which I used to live" which are related to people's life and human relationships were often selected. Also, the word "disorderly" was often used in a positive meaning, which is considered to be associated with people's life and nostalgia.

Thus, it has been determined that, in evaluating urban streetscapes, visual impressions such as "organization" and "unity", or the factors connected with the images of life, which are typically represented by "the sign of people's life," are influential depending on the category group of the streets. It has been proved that the evaluative constructs for overall evaluation differ from one category group to another.

EXPERIMENTS WITH RATING SCALES: RELATIONSHIP BETWEEN OVERALL EVALUATION AND EVALUATIVE CONSTRUCTS

Next, to identify the differences in the association level among the evaluative constructs, we made 68 slides out of the 125 photographs used for the interview investigation and showed them to the subjects who then rated the urban streetscapes using the same scale. The slides presented to the subjects included 25 scenes from residential streets, 22 scenes from shopping streets, and 21 scenes from office streets. The scale used for the rating was obtained by converting a total of 36 constructs of the evaluative constructs extracted in the interview investigation 2 and the overall evaluation, i.e., "desirability," into a 7-step rating scale. There were 40 subjects, 21 males and 19 females.

Based on the obtained data, the authors made two analyses. In Analysis 1, an attempt was made to identify the differences in the association level among evaluative constructs by using the data on each category group. In analysis 2, an attempt was made to identify the differences among the category groups in analyzing the overall data.

Analysis 1: Correlation among the evaluative constructs in a category group

Using Kruskal's multidimensional scaling, we attempted to show the levels of connection between rating scales for each category group. Each group was represented two- dimensionally under small stress values (see Fig. 3). Analyzing the results given in the charts, from which the connection of each scale was determined, shows that office streets and shopping streets, for example, exhibit a high level of correlation between "composure," "organization," and "harmony of colors" while residential streets exhibit a low level of correlation.

Thus, the relationship between the scales varies according to the category group, and the scales which are closely correlated to the overall evaluation "desirability" also vary depending on groups. As far as correlation among the scales is concerned, the decisive factors in overall evaluation vary according to category groups.

Analysis 2: Analysis across the category groups

First, to obtain visual understanding of the stimulus variations in the rating values of each rating scale, the authors carried out a factor analysis to organize the scales and create a factor score chart.

As a result of the factor analysis, three factors represented by the scales of "composure, " "cheerfulness," and "spaciousness" were selected. The factor scores were as shown in Figure 30.4. It is seen from the figure that some groups project similar impressions, and unevenly distributed.

When we correlated the factor scores to overall evaluation, we found that the scores of the first and second factors are correlated to overall evaluation. When we expressed the rating in terms of "desirability" on the factor score chart, as shown in Figure 30.4, the scores of "desirability" increased as the scores of the first and second factors increased. This trend was found to be constant in all category groups.

We then carried out a multiple regression analysis with the two factors used as the explanatory variables. The correlation between the estimated values and the rating values was high at 0.944. Judging from the high level of correlation, it was decided there was no need for classification. The same multiple regression analysis was performed on all category groups and the analysis results were compared with the results of the whole.

The comparison result indicated that the estimation accuracy stayed almost unchanged and the weighting also stayed the same for all category groups. This means that there is almost no difference among the category groups when we assume that the overall evaluation is defined by the evaluative constructs represented by the two factor axes.

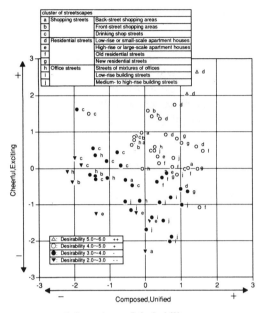

Figure 30.3 Factor scores and the ratings of desirability.

DISCUSSION

As described above, the results of Investigation by Interview 2 and the results of Analysis 1 indicate significant differences among the groups. The results of Analysis 2, however, indicate that there are not significant differences among the groups. These conflicting results imply that similar data are interpreted differently depending upon whether all or part of the data are analyzed. Dividing into groups means that each group has a certain characteristic, which is, after all, directly related to the unevenly distributed data. And if it is decided that the data are unevenly distributed, then it is necessary to carefully discuss whether grouping should be carried out and what categories should be established to group them once it is decided to divide the data into groups. It is also indicated that we need to carefully examine what should represent the whole.

It is also quite difficult to group actual landscapes even when the differences among the individual categories are distinct. This posed a problem in working on this research. There are only a few typical office streets and typical shopping streets and most streets are mixtures of offices and shops. The same probably applies to the categories of natural landscapes and urban landscapes. When the unevenly distributed data in each group are considered, the result of the analysis heavily depends upon the group into which those "not clearly defined" landscapes are classified.

On the other hand, however, it can hardly be said that overall determination is important. For instance, "signs of human life" which was recognized as a very important factor for residential streets indicates lower correlation in the overall analysis and loses its influence. Most multivariate analyses are based on correlation coefficients, but their calculation method causes those data, which exhibit high correlation only under specific conditions, to lower the correlation in the overall analysis. It is doubtful, therefore, that merely using correlation coefficients or making a regression analysis is adequate for identifying the factors that influence the overall evaluation of a landscape. Some kind of grouping is necessary.

It is concluded that merely applying the correlation analyses or regression analyses to the data obtained is not adequate for determining what kind of landscapes is preferred. It has also been shown that it is necessary to group the obtained data according to some kind of categories and that utterly different results are likely to be acquired depending on how the data are grouped. In the future, it is necessary to consider a grouping method which does not depend on the subjectivity of an experimenter. The authors are considering the adoption of a method in which subjects themselves evaluate landscapes and, at the same time, also determine the categories to which the landscapes should belong.

References

Herzog, T. R. (1985). A cognitive analysis of preference for waterscapes. Journal of Environmental Psychology, 5, 225-241.

Herzog, T. R. (1989). A cognitive analysis of preference for urban nature. Journal of Environmental Psychology, 9, 27-43.

Herzog, T. R. (1992). A cognitive analysis of preference for urban spaces. Journal of Environmental Psychology, 12, 237-248.

Kaplan, S. (1987). Aesthetics, affect, and cognition; environmental preference from an evolutionary perspective. Environment and Behavior, 19, 3-22.

Kaplan, R., Kaplan, S., and Brown, T. (1989). Environmental preference: A comparison of four domains of predictors. Environment and Behavior, 21, 509-530.

Sanui, J. and Inui, M. (1984): Towards a phenomenological model of place evaluation. Paper presented at the IAPS 8th international conference in Berlin, W-Germany.

Sanui, J. and Inui, M (1986): Individual Differences in the Evaluation of Living Rooms. Paper presented at the IAPS 9th international conference in Haifa, Israel.

Part Three

ENVIRONMENTAL EDUCATION AND URBAN THEORY

31

Introduction

Frank E. Brown

La troisième partie de la conférence comprend des communications qui, bien que n'ayant pas toujours un contenu "théorique" ou "éducatif", contribuent de diverses manières à expliquer ces questions importantes. Les questions de théorie et de méthodologie doivent être le pivot de toute recherche sur l'expérience urbaine. Comment explorons-nous et interprétons-nous les réactions de l'individu face à la ville? Quelles sont les forces critiques qui forment notre conscience et donc notre perception de l'environnement bâti? Si "l'expérience" doit être notre point de départ, la formule de base "relations homme-environnement" doit être considérée comme une problématique à part entière.

The third part of the conference encompasses a range of papers which, if not always explicitly "theoretical" or "educational" in their content, nevertheless help, in their different ways, to highlight these important issues. Questions of theory and methodology have to be central to any enquiry into the urban experience. Just how do we go about investigating and interpreting human responses to the city? What are the critical forces that shape our consciousness and hence our perception of the built environment? If we are to take "experience" as our starting point, the basic formulation "people-environment relations" has to be seen in itself as inherently problematic.

Peter Dickens, who sets the keynote for this session, directs his attention squarely at the "people-environment" framework and finds it wanting. Put bluntly, the point at issue here is whether such a perspective represents a scientific approach or an ideological category. Dickens clearly sees it as the latter: as a skewed picture that tends to reflect, rather than illuminate, contemporary social life. This is not to say that the dichotomy is totally invalid. On the contrary, Dickens is at pains to emphasize the reality of the people-environment divide as an aspect of consciousness and day-to-day existence. But for him the crucial point is that this a product, not a cause of social relations, and hence can only be properly understood, and explained, by reference to the underlying structures and processes of society itself.

Taking his cue from the general theme of "people-environment" relations, Dickens develops his analysis around Marx's concept of alienation. Interestingly he draws principally on Marx's early writings, rather than his fully-fledged "scientific" output, which is normally the stuff of marxist analysis. This is presumably because the questions of social being, of history and human nature are dealt with more directly, and centrally, in these humanistic texts than in his later works of political economy. They certainly provide Dickens with effective tools for dissecting both the person / person and person / environment relation. But in the latter part of his paper he goes beyond orthodox marxist analysis, bringing in post-modern concerns with signs and symbols, and the way these distort our perception. Ultimately, the issue that has to be addressed is how we are to achieve emancipation from the alienated, mediated relations of late capitalism. The way may not be easy, but Dickens finds hope in both new technology and new forms of production.

Dickens' keynote address is not the first time the IAPS perspective has been taken to task. Some twenty years ago Hillier and Leaman (1973), in an influential critique of what was then referred to as the "man-environment" paradigm, saw the concept of "environment" as the principal obstacle to environmental analysis. Rather than trying to seek causal relations between the individual and environment, the proper path, they argued, was to study concepts and cognitive operations as they are embodied in the built environment itself. It was buildings, and more specifically spatial relations, that mediated social relations, not behaviour or subjectivity.

Hillier's formulation is very different from that of Dickens, who would almost certainly regard space as a contingent, not a necessary phenomenon. But Hillier's redirection of the field of study away from people-environment relations and towards architectural and urban morphology has been enormously productive. As operationalized in the form of space syntax, the approach has stimulated an increasing amount of work within IAPS itself, where there is now a large and flourishing "spatial analysis" network. The fruits of space syntax work are illustrated in this volume in two papers, one focussing on the urban level, the other on domestic space.

Zacharias highlights the issue of urban pedestrian movement in his study of the Parisian *passage*. This is a very pertinent study, given the current emphasis in space syntax on the representation of urban systems and public space more generally. In Hillier's analysis pedestrian movement is determined primarily by spatial configuration, i.e. by the pattern of integration of the spatial network, expressed as a set of axial lines. While land-use and local characteristics play a part, the prime generator is always this topological network, producing what is termed "natural movement". Yet in the case of the historic *passages* of the second *arrondissement*, so much of the literature points to the very opposite - to the draw exercised by social custom and the qualities of place.

The alternative explanations are compared here by use of axial mapping of the global network and by reference to videotape recording of actual pedestrian movement. While yielding a broad correlation with spatial integration, Zacharias points also to the inadequacies of axiality as a spatial tool, underlining the role of functional arrangements, of distance and geometry in generating movement. This is a valuable study, which could usefully be repeated elsewhere.

Space and social interaction are central also to Evans' enquiry, though in quite a different context. His concern is to elucidate the relationship between overcrowding and psychological stress by reference to a specific spatial property: that of "depth". Topological depth (i.e. the number of spaces through which it is necessary to pass in order to reach the one concerned) figured strongly in Hillier's early work, and was arguably one of the most suggestive of the graph-theoretic measures employed in space syntax. The social implications of access and depth, however, have seldom (if ever) been tested in quite this way. Evans' conclusion - that spatial subdivision of the interior offers a "coping strategy" that may diminish the need for social withdrawal - appears significant, and lends weight to the importance of space as a variable. How far the link between space and interaction can be taken as trans-historical, or trans-cultural, remains, however, to be seen.

Grouped with the paper by Evans are two others - by Purcell, Lamb, Peron, and Falchero, and by Gabidulina, respectively - which also provide case-studies in environmental psychology. Purcell et al. look at cognitive categorization as applied to outdoor scenes, and, in so doing, reveal a much more diverse and articulated domain than suggested by previous studies. The authors' principal aim is to see how far there are common views of "naturalness" and "builtness" in landscape perception, and their study is given an interesting cultural dimension by being carried out in two, very different countries - Italy and Australia. The results of the experiment point, not only to cultural (or at least geographical) differences between the participants, but also to a nuanced perception of landscape, in which a crude division between the natural and the built is clearly inadequate as a predictor of preference.

Gabidulina's study was carried out in a suburb of Moscow, and assesses children's preferences in the built environment by reference to a fixed scale of parameters. A questionnaire was supported by a drawing test to help overcome deficiencies in verbal communication. Clear favourites emerge from her study (park being top of the list) but certain features, most notably the absence of figures from the drawings, are taken to be particularly significant. The fact that Gabidulina interprets this in terms of estrangement seems to make for analogies with the social phenomenon of alienation proposed by Dickens in his introductory essay. But it equally highlights the conceptual (and epistemological) gulf between the two.

The piece by Ohno and Kondo is an interesting attempt to characterize aesthetic experience by focussing on a particular artefact renowned for its beauty - the Japanese circuit-style garden. One of the main dangers of such a study is that it can only too easily become reductive: complex interactions are lost, and the problem is simplified out of existence. Though concerned with objective analysis, Ohno and Kondo respect the different facets of aesthetic experience - tactile, and kinaesthetic as well as visual. The suite of computer programs they developed are an attempt to embody information on touch, pressure, etc. alongside the more familiar visual data. This is a potentially richer approach to aesthetics as far as the built environment is concerned.

The papers by Wolschke-Bulmahn and Schneider both pursue the theme of landscape, but do so firmly in a historical context. The first paper, by Wolschke-Bulmahn and Groening, traces developments in garden design in Germany before and after the First World War, pointing to the conflicting trends - rational, future-oriented versus backward-looking and romantic - that emerged at this time. The ferment of ideas after the Great War and the eventual suppression of internationalism and functionalism during the 1930's in favour of folk art closely mirror developments in architecture, having the same political roots. The German experience seems to embrace trends that are both general and specific. Against this background, there is no doubting the importance of the project outlined by the authors, i.e. to clarify the relationship between landscape design and ideology.

Schneider and Groening take a similar historical viewpoint with regard to the allotment garden, in this case distinguishing two different lines of development - one leading to the proletarian allotment or *Laubengarten*, the other producing the Schrebergarten or allotment adopted by more wealthy tenants. Though the authors' historical sketch points to an intended merger of types in the twentieth century, with a programme of "gardens for all", this, like other democratic ideals, remains an unfulfilled programme.

There follows an excellent group of papers on the theme "Urban Cultures and Conflicts". If Dickens has argued for a *theoretical* re-orientation to give proper weight to the social factors that affect our response to the environment, these studies show *empirically* how it is possible, and necessary, to bring society back into the "man-environment" equation. The problematic nature of environmental perception is admirably illustrated by Chattopadhyay in his probing analysis of British attitudes to two Indian cities, Calcutta and Bombay. While Bombay gained in esteem during the nineteenth century, Calcutta was increasingly denigrated for its ugliness and squalor. Rather than take contemporary descriptions at face value, the author turns our attention to political and social relations between the British and the natives in the two cities. It was, he argues, the conflict of interests between the Bengalis and the Raj that were critical in shaping British impressions of the city. In Bombay, by comparison, the political and economic interests of the native Parsees appear to have been well aligned with those of the colonial government.

If the Calcuttans seem to have been in a "no-win" situation as far as the British were concerned, this is certainly true of the Irish in Manchester. The account by Busteed and Hodgson shows how readily the early Irish immigrants became scapegoats for general urban ills. Their distinctive culture, religion, and politics all militated against them. Demographic statistics can be telling: there were, according to the authors, only 15 Catholics in the entire township as late as 1744; by 1851 13%

of Manchester's population was Irish, most of them Catholics. The Irish were plainly in a cleft stick in their relations with the English: they were both strike-breakers and trouble-makers. Small wonder that stress and alienation are clearly identifiable here.

Focussing on a suburb of Sydney, Australia, Armstrong too addresses the question of immigrant experience, though in a modern context. Despite (or because of) the emergence of heritage culture, many immigrant communities in Australia find little or no place in public life or the built environment, where ethnicity is increasingly reduced to stereotyping or, in the phrase the author aptly borrows from Eco, "hyper-reality". The main charge of her argument is that stories matter as much as artefacts, and that discussion can help to elicit the concepts and beliefs that fail to find their way into the domain of "urban heritage".

Germain, Blanc, Charbonneau, and Dansereau take much more of a spatial slant in their study, which looks at another country with a large, and growing immigrant population - Canada. Concerned with the use of public space, they examine social interaction at a number of points within Montreal, all of which are in multi-ethnic neighbourhoods. Despite initial pointers to their significance in social terms ("espaces privilégiés de socialisation à la différence"), these spaces progressively emerge as places of segmentation - of social separation rather than contact. This outcome seems to be far removed from notions of "communitas", and comparative studies (in Vancouver or Toronto, perhaps?) could be informative.

With Brierley we move back once again to an historical perspective. Like Wolschke-Bulmahn and Schneider, he directs our attention to design and ideology, though in this case at the larger scale of urban design. The subject here is Amsterdam in the early part of the twentieth century, and Brierley usefully examines the ideas and "philosophies" that underpinned the work of the main protagonists - Berlage and van Eesteren. Though confined essentially to design discourse, this brief account provides insights into the different aesthetic principles that were at work at this time - a diversity that resists any simple mapping of base on to superstructure.

The final paper, by van Andel, brings into focus a different issue - not the production of knowledge but the communication and application of that knowledge. This is a topic of long standing within IAPS. Van Andel tests systematically the transfer of information by both maps and tables, and compares the efficacy of the two. The findings clearly have implications for environmental education, although, as the author himself recognizes, the application of social science is also vitally dependent upon other factors - most notably on the learning styles and values, in short the ideology, of architects. But that is another story.

Reference

Hillier, B. and Leaman A. (1973): "The man-environment paradigm and its paradoxes", Architectural Design, August, pp. 507-511.

32

Alienation, emancipation and the environment

Alienation, emancipation et environnement

Peter Dickens

La plupart des informations sur l'environnement urbain sont basées sur des façons de penser dichotomiques. Voici quelques exemples: société/nature, urbain/rural, construit/naturel, individu/société, sciences/sciences sociales.
Les dichotomies résultent en partie de la définition limitée de certaines matières. Les études sur l'environnement, tout comme les relations de cause à effet de ces dichotomies, sont caractérisées par:

(1)   une hostilité toujours présente de la part des partisans du mouvement écologiste envers la science moderne.
(2)   d'éternels impérialismes disciplinaires: un défaut commun aux sciences sociales et naturelles.
(3)   la fragmentation de la vie moderne elle-même. La nature, par exemple, n'est pas seulement conçue de façon distincte de la société humaine. On la <u>traite réellement</u> comme si elle était indépendante, distincte.

Le résultat de toutes ces fragmentations s'avère tout à fait inutile et désastreux. Ainsi, par exemple, les relations sous-jacentes et le processus qui en est la cause restent inexplorés.
Ce document aborde ces problèmes en encourageant une vue d'ensemble conceptuelle qui permet une meilleure perspective des relations hommes/environnement. Il montre aussi comment l'on peut créer des liens importants entre plusieurs disciplines. En outre, l'objectif est d'informer les professionnels. Comment peut-on, dans nos sociétés modernes, donner aux individus un certain pouvoir de manière à ce qu'ils puissent à nouveau se comprendre, et comprendre l'environnement?

Mots clé: science; sciences sociales; environnement; aliénation; émancipation.

Keywords: science, social science, environment, emancipation.

This paper presents a general theory of people-environment relations in modern society. The first part argues that the natural and social environment is integral to peoples' well-being. And yet, due mainly to the way in which production-processes are organised in capitalist society, people remain alienated from their environment and from one another. The second part suggests that people increasingly rely on signs and symbols of the environment. These provide people with packaged and partial understandings of their environment. And in the end these only further contribute to the process of alienation. The final section offers some preliminary ideas as to strategies which might start overcoming peoples' estranged relations with their social and physical surroundings.

This conference, with its special emphasis to the relations between people and their environment, has long been sensitive to human consciousness. On the other hand, what are sometimes called 'man-environment studies' have systematically under-emphasised the relations and processes associated with advanced capitalist societies. The purpose of this paper is therefore to effect a merger; one which continues to appreciate the importance of peoples' consciousness but which at the same time recognises the underlying social processes affecting such awareness.

The paper will develop this theme with particular reference to the relations between people and their environment. There is a central methodological point here, however. While there is of course no reason why relations between humans and their environment should not remain our immediate focus, an adequate understanding of these relations cannot afford to remain fixed on this people-environment dichotomy. Such stubbornness will lead to a seriously flawed appreciation of the relations between people and their environment. To put this another way, the most significant factors affecting our relationships with the environment will not be elucidated unless or until we have a reasonable understanding of how modern capitalist society itself works. So we must proceed, initially at least, at some distance from some the more visible and obvious manifestations of contemporary social life (this including 'man-environment relations') to give consideration to how capitalism actually operates and how people are caught up in this process.

There are many ways, of course, in which this could be achieved. This paper takes much of its inspiration from Marxian political economy. Even taking this 'cut' at the problem, there are many ways in which such a perspective could be laid out and developed here. But bearing in mind the aim of this paper as outlined above, this paper will give special emphasis to Marx's theory of alienation. This recognises underlying social relations and processes while at the same time remaining concerned with how human beings respond to these features of capitalism. And, again, it sheds new light on the often problematic link between humans and the physical environment.

ON COMMODITY-PRODUCTION AND THE ALIENATION OF HUMAN CAPACITIES

What we are pleased to call 'the environment' is a product of society. More specifically, it is intimately locked into the production and consumption of commodities in a society dominated by capitalist social relations. Thus any understanding of 'man-environment relations' must address itself to a general understanding of how commodities are produced and peoples' relationship to these commodities.

Buildings and what is sometimes referred to as 'the natural environment' are, like all commodities, caught up in complex social relations and processes. Typically, capital purchases peoples' labour power (their capacity to work) and combines it with the means of production (various types of technology) and raw materials drawn from nature to produce commodities for sale. Included amongst these commodities are various forms of 'environment', buildings and so forth. Again, the 'natural' environment; is an integral component of this; money, labour power and various forms of machinery being combined to produce the things that people need; food, clothes and a vast array of other commodities. Once the combination of money, people and technology is in place, a complex labour-process takes place; one whereby commodities (including of course buildings) are produced and sold on the market. The cash resulting from such selling is either returned with interest to those who originally invested their money or is ploughed back into buying still more labour power and technology.

This general process of commodity-production and sale of commodities contains a number of important features. First, it is predicated on certain key social relations. There is, in short, a necessary system of social power built into the process. If those making commodities (and, by extension those selling these commodities) were themselves owners and controllers of capital the system would immediately break down. Furthermore, if they were able to exercise control over what was made and sold, the whole process could again come under very serious threat.

Thus seen from the individual's viewpoint, there are important forms of alienation involved.(Marx 1973, Ollman 1971, Dickens 1992). The person invests large amounts of her or his labour power in a product. Yet this individual has virtually no control or influence over what happens to this product. The problem can be elucidated by referring to what Marx called 'man's species being'. Part of this being is a creative capacity, one which is largely denied by contemporary labour processes. More disturbing still, this person has very little understanding of what happens to the product of her or his life's work. This denies the human species' advanced capacities for conceptualising and planning their place in the world. And, as Marx argued 150 years ago, the object which the individual makes or sells becomes even more alienated from the subject the individual works on it. In other words, the more effort that goes into the object, the more the individual becomes dominated by the object he or she is constructing. Much the same might apply to an individual who is selling a product in what is known as a 'service' industry. The more effort that goes into this process, the more the individual becomes alienated from the item involved.

Alienation from the product of one's work is perhaps the best-known form of estrangement in modern society. But there are other forms, and, as I hope to have indicated by the end of this paper, they are all relevant to an understanding of 'people-environment' relations. The technology which is introduced into the labour process has a steadily de-skilling process. And again, as Braverman (1974) argued some time ago, this applies as much to workers in modern 'services' employment as it does to the manufacturing workers which occupied much of Marx's thinking. This technological de-skilling is a further alienating process. Again, human beings have well-developed capacities for creative thinking, for stepping back from their work, for learning and planning alternative courses of action. Technological innovation (at least as it tends to be deployed by capital) tends to undermine these capacities or leave them unrealised.

A third dimension of alienation, or what Marx sometimes called 'estrangement', concerns peoples' relations with one another. The social and the technical divisions of labour are the key factors here. The social division of labour is that between particular crafts, trades and professions. The detailed division of labour concerns the workplace itself; individuals being assigned to particular, often very repetitive, tasks. Not only does this undermine the individual's creative capacities, it alienates people from their own species. People are, like many other animals, a social and communicating species. This is another aspect of their 'species being'. The division of labour, whether social or technical, systematically separates people from one another.

Fourth, and of particular relevance to environmental questions, human beings become systematically estranged from nature in modern society. This refers not to the fact that fewer people live in the countryside. (It need hardly be said that people living in towns have as much contact - even if it is disastrous contact - with nature as those living in 'rural' areas). The alienation from nature of which Marx wrote and on which we must concentrate is again of a primarily social form. Social relations, private property and labour-processes are again the main culprits. All societies have of course depended on the use of nature (and on the manipulation of the powers of nature) to reproduce themselves. Modern industrial systems have greatly developed this process. The non-human world is not only increasingly manipulated by human societies but is broken down into units and formed into the production-process. This in turn means that every element of the natural world (including now even its genetic structure) can now be worked on and modified. Even more importantly, each element can now be invested in by capital. In these ways that nature is increasingly broken down and treated as a mere 'input' of raw materials into production. People are disconnected from it in the sense that do not appreciate its own independent value.

They also fail to understand the complex environmental and ecological systems of which they remain part. Their relationship is restored, or seemingly restored, through the market. But this is at best an ambiguous form of reintegration with the natural world. The market is itself largely responsible for the original destruction of the natural world.

Why does the separation of people from nature matter? Marx argued, in a way which has become more recently echoed by elements within the environmental movement, that 'nature' is man's inorganic body.' (1973 op.cit.) By this he meant that nature was needed by man; not just in the sense of requiring it for food and other physical necessities but for aesthetic and spiritual nourishment. Yet, as we have seen, capitalism systematically estranges people from their 'inorganic body' Recent work in the natural sciences stresses the extent to which all organisms depend on their environment to develop.(Kauffman 1993, Wesson 1993) Human beings are the only species which has devised ways of life which systematically place obstacles between itself and the physical and natural environment. The same goes between relations between members of the human species. As outlined earlier, the social and technical division of labour amongst human beings means that this social species has devised very advanced ways of separating its individuals from one another. For the natural and social environment alike, it is again the social relations of production rather than 'man-environment relations' to which we must look for an adequate explanation.

A fifth type of alienation is one hardly covered by Marx. It is, however, one which has received considerable recent coverage from geographers and from sociologists with a particular sensitivity to physical space. Giddens (1984) uses the term 'time space distanciation' to refer to the spreading of social life over the globe. This, he argues, leads to 'ontological insecurity', a form of anomie which is particular to late 20th century society. The anomie stems, he argues, not simply from an inadequate understanding of our relations with global society. Rather, this peculiarly modern form of alienation stems from our knowing about our global impacts but remaining relatively powerless to do anything about it.

A final source of alienation concerns forms of knowledge. There are three important issues here. And again they are highly relevant to an adequate understanding of the relations between people and environment. First, we have knowledge divided into relatively watertight disciplines; a result which is in large part the product of the social division of labour alluded to earlier. Perhaps the most important is the division between the social sciences, the sciences and 'the arts'. Such separations are almost guaranteed to obfuscate understanding and, more particularly, make over-clinical distinctions between 'rational' and 'emotional' appreciations of the social and natural world. Peoples' 'species being' enable them to think flexibly. These divisions between different areas of social life again alienate people in the sense that they deny an adequate understanding. Furthermore, such distinctions now seem desperately inadequate given the extent to which human society is impinging on science - and vice-versa. Marx, alluding to the division between science and 'philosophy' referred to the eventual need for 'one science' ; a form of understanding which would adequately reflect the extent to which the natural world is becoming increasingly humanised. His appeal for a single science (or at least a set of inter-linked sciences which would connect understandings of the human to the non-human world) now has even greater urgency. The urgency derives, of course, from the growing and increasingly disastrous effects of advanced human society on the physical environment and other species.

A second form of alienation stemming from inadequate knowledge concerns the separation of abstract from concrete or practical knowledge. Here is another form of dichotomy which needs proper understanding if people are to start feeling 'at home' in their social and natural world. Knowledge of the concrete world can easily be disparaged. Abstract theory, by contrast, tends to be retained and held 'close to the chest' of academics, scientists and 'experts' often on behalf of powerful vested interests. What is needed here is a conceptual framework which recognises the relations between these two forms of knowledge and thus breaks the rigorous dichotomy. Such a framework is now under active development by philosophers and others working within a 'critical realist' mode of analysis.(see, for example, Sayer 1992 Collier 1994) Briefly, this again recognises the real and underlying causal mechanisms and powers underlying what we can observe in the real world. At the same time, however, it recognises contingent factors which to varying extents affect what can be observed. The net effect of such a conceptual framework (which cannot be outlined at length in this paper) is to recognise that there are indeed processes and relations affecting what we can observe. As such, it overcomes some of the difficulties of positivism which rely entirely on 'facts' as self-evident things which can be used for the testing of theories. At the same time, critical realism recognises different types of knowledge, some indeed more abstract, some being more contingent to particular places and times, and other forms which are the result of direct sensuous experience.

To sum up here, then, human beings in modern capitalist remain essentially alienated from their 'environment.' This includes the commodities they make, other people, and the non-human world. Alienation also stems from inadequate and fragmented understanding; especially that between abstract and concrete knowledge and between scientific and social scientific appreciation. Furthermore, people are progressively alienated from their own nature; that of communicating and creative human beings. And the globalisation of social life and environmental problems provides another form of alienation, one in which people may be aware of the global impacts of their actions, but stand few chances of doing a great deal about it. And, to rub the main theoretical or analytical point in further, an understanding of such alienation entails not so much looking at 'man-environment relations' but at the structures, processes and tendencies of capitalism itself.

COMMODITY FETISHISM: THE CULTURE OF COMPETING SIGNS

So far this paper may have left the impression of people as dumb, unwilling and passive dupes in the face of the underlying processes and structures of capitalist society. This is not an accurate picture, however. The other side to the coin portrayed above is one in which people assert their own understandings of their predicament. There are two somewhat opposing impulses here. One celebrates an aspect of the labour-process, the technology involved, the commodities produced and the regulation of nature in the pursuance of human purposes.

All these, it seems, offer emancipation or at least a better way of life in the future. A second is an essentially backward-looking vision, one which attempts to restore what has been alienated by harking back to versions (especially sanitised versions) of older, apparently less alienated forms of social life. These incorporate symbols of human community, close relations to nature and pre-industrial, or early industrial, forms of work. Both these impulses represent human reconstruction's of the social world, images which help in either a futuristic or nostalgic way to restore the various forms of alienation to which people are subjected.

It was again Marx, with his analysis of commodity fetishism, who first spotted what was taking place. If people remain alienated in all these ways in the sphere of industrial production there is, within the two broad categories of symbols outlined above, a vast number of ways in which they can restore, or at least appear to restore, their selves and the various forms of relationship they have lost. But, and this is crucial to any understanding of alienation, this takes place predominantly in 'civil society'; the sphere of social life outside employment.

What, for Marx, does such commodity fetishism entail? It means that we start to misunderstand commodities. Now we see them as apparently not as produced under definite types of social relation and with definite effects on the individuals involved in their production but as things in themselves. They become simply items which are purchased and sold in the market. What Marx called the 'silent' sphere of production becomes lost in the process. But this type of commodity fetishism provides at best a partial picture. Commodities are, of course, things which are bought and sold. But, as should be clear from the above, to fetishise them as if that was all they are is to provide a largely illusory picture of how modern society is organised.

But it is writers since Marx's day who have carried forward his original analysis of 'commodity fetishism' in contemporary capitalist society. Lash and Urry (1994), for example, have recently emphasised the extent to which commodity production and social life more generally is now organised around not only the production and consumption of commodities but of signs and symbols.

> What is increasingly produced are not material objects, but signs. These signs
> are of two types. Either they have a primarily cognitive and are post-industrial
> or informational goods. Or they have primarily an aesthetic content and are

what can be termed postmodern goods. The development of the latter can be seen not only in the proliferation of objects which possess a substantial aesthetic component (such as pop   music, cinema, leisure, magazines, video and so on), but also in the increasing component of sign-value or image embodied in material objects. The aestheticization of material objects takes place in the production, the circulation or the consumption of such goods.(p.4)

Lash and Urry argue that such 'economies of signs and symbols' do not simply to lead to a social life which is evacuated of meaning, abstraction and homogenisation. Rather,

these processes may open up possibilities for the recasting of meaning in work and in leisure, for the reconstitution of community and in particular for the reconstruction of a transmogrified subjectivity, and for heterogenization and complexity of space and of everyday life.(p.3)

But, bearing in mind the theoretical perspective of this paper, the significance of modern economies of signs and symbols can be taken rather further than this. What is taking place through the production and consumption of such signs and symbols (including the acquisition of the new home-based technologies allowing access to these forms of communication) is nothing less than the means by which alienated men and women attempt to restore their selves, their relation to their creative capacities, their relation to one another, their relation to nature and their relation to knowledge of the social and natural world.

In short, the modern culture of signs and symbols seems to offer for human beings forms of reality and authenticity, these being largely denied to them by the world of work and employment. Such authenticity also provides, apparently at least, a sense of order and continuity in a society which is simultaneously fragmenting relations between people and their human capacities, between people and other humans and between people and nature.

Such a culture inevitably reflects the economic and social structure responsible for their production. The alienated individual experiencing or consuming these signs and symbols is obviously confronting one aspect of the material reality of how modern capitalism it is organised. In addition to alienating people it is offering at least plausible ways in which their alienation can be overcome. Furthermore, as the above quotation from Lash and Urry suggests, it is indeed possible to lead a life which is oriented around such a modern culture. But the images of modernity which such signs and symbols offer (this taking the form of apparently un-alienated relations) is simultaneously illusory. The forms of community, relationships to nature and so on which they offer remain largely 'packaged' and are predominantly offered on capital's terms. As such they offer at best partial and limited prospects for overcoming the types of alienation outlined at the beginning of this paper. Furthermore, debate on the future of modern society focuses on (or in Marx's word 'fetishes') the signs and symbols of modern culture rather than on the social relations underlying them and peoples' need for them.

But finally, the continuing contradiction between material processes of alienation on the one hand and apparent emancipation on the other should be emphasised. The forms of alienation first spelt out by Marx are as deeply engrained in modern society as ever. Commodity fetishism or engagement in the world of signs and symbols may make such alienation more palatable but it does not overcome it. Furthermore, the apparent authenticity offered by contemporary culture remains just that, apparent. So the 'two sides of the coin' alluded to in this paper exist in an unstable relationship. A genuinely 'authentic' understanding of contemporary society would attempt to reveal the relations and processes outlined at the beginning of this paper. But this, for obvious reasons, it is unlikely to do. The authenticity offered by signs and symbols is therefore constantly under challenge and re-negotiation. I will now illustrate some of these themes.

SOME CONTEMPORARY IMAGINED COMMUNITIES

Of more direct relevance to this conference are the various and overlapping symbols of place, community, environment and nature which seem to be acquiring a special significance in modern society. The 'forward-looking' and 'backward-looking' symbols are again very much in evidence.

Harvey (1989) and Lash and Urry (1994) and a number of contemporary writers on postmodern or late modern culture have referred to the particular role of space in the reassertion of human identity and meaning in human society and economy. The underlying explanations here are is again the various forms alienation outlined in the first part of this paper. These authors offer, however, an explanation almost wholly in terms of spatial alienation, or what we have earlier found Giddens referring to as the 'time-space distanciation' of modern life. As Harvey puts it: 'as spatial barriers diminish so we become much more sensitized to what the world's spaces contain.' But, bearing in mind the facets of estrangement originally outlined by Marx, this seems at best a partial picture.

While capital is alienating people from their species being, it is simultaneously investing in spaces which people consume in an attempt to overcome such alienation. Lash and Urry outline, for example, the present tendency towards arcadian or 'backward-looking' visions of the past. They refer to:

> the production of simulacra, replications of originals more real, or hyper real, than the original. Almost everything can now be reproduced, including apparently authentic ancient buildings as in Quinlan Terry's neo-classical Richmond development on the banks of the Thames in England; and 'natural' features of the landscape, such as the pink and white terraces which were located above Lake Rotomahana in New Zealand are to be 'recreated' elsewhere a century after they were destroyed by a volcano. (1994: 302-3).

Here, then, are further examples of signs and symbols representing 'tradition' and 'nature', this time a highly packaged example. They combine, albeit in complex ways, with the apparent restoration of an arcadian community-life; such as that of an imagined upper class 18th century England. Space, according to Urry, is now being divided into thematic units, with new place-names being constructed especially for the tourist industry. The tourist industry, including so-called 'soap tours' is where these tendencies are most acute. In the North of England, for example, we find:

'Last of the Summer Wine Country', 'Emmerdale Farm Country', 'James Herriot Country', 'Robin Hood Country', 'Catherine Cookson Country', 'Bronte Country' and so on. (1990:145)

To these can be added 'Lovejoy's East Anglia' and 'Poldark's Cornwall.' And the small town of Stamford in Lincolnshire has been the focus of an influx in tourists, this being the setting of the TV series, Middlemarch. Nevertheless, it is important to stress once more that these simulations of a lost past exist in parallel with other forms of simulated environment. The 'Granada Studios Tour', for example certainly includes 'The Coronation Street Experience' but other contrasting simulations.

Climb the stairway to the stars and find yourself gazing over the glittering L.A. skyline from the 39th floor of Los Angeles Skyscraper. One minute you're having a close encounter with alien spaceships on a Hollywood rooftop, the next a chat with a friendly policeman outside Number 10... Finally, we'll take you far away to the rain forests of the darkest Amazon, a place of fireflies, slithering snakes, gorillas and earth-shattering volcanoes.(Granada Studios Tour brochure, 1994)

These simulations and allusions to lost combinations of community, nature, pre-industrialism and futurism are an increasingly common feature of contemporary culture. But it is difficult to understand these somewhat bizarre cultural forms the parallel investments in alienating work and consequent separations from community and nature. It is predominantly the latter, and peoples' attempt to restore their identity and their selves as consumers which leads to their apparently avid consumption of such pre-packaged commodities.

The other main thing to point out here is that these symbols are only representations of material reality. They do not in themselves of course restore the various forms of alienation which generate the need for them. They do not, in short, 'deliver' their promises of an unalienated life. Furthermore, they can of course be interpreted (or re-created) in various, perhaps conflicting ways by the people experiencing them. All this makes them unstable and subject to constant change by their producers.

The arguments above may lead to obvious rejoinder. Who exactly are these 'consumers' reasserting their citizenship in modern societies by engaging in these packaged forms of culture? Research in this area seems quite limited. Urry (1990) argues, persuasively, that it is an array of middle class groups who are probably in the most advantageous position in this respect. It is they who, for example, have been the most active in the organisations devoted to the preservation of the landscape and of 'heritage'. The situation is more complex, however, than any assertion that the 'middle classes' or 'the service class' are the leading devotees to this type of consumption. The 'middle classes' are in a broad sense most likely to realise, or be able to realise, their natural and species being in these ways. But it is important to recognise the potentially wide spread of classes engaging in consumption of this kind. Possibly the groups visiting 'The Rover's Return' in Coronation Street would be distinct from those visiting the set for the making of Emily Bronte's Middlemarch.

CONCLUSION: AWAY FROM ESTRANGEMENT AND THE CULTURE OF SIGNS.

There are two comments to make as a conclusion. The first concerns the adequacy of the conceptual framework used here; one which combines classical Marxist theory with contemporary theories of postmodernism or late modernism. The most significant critique of the argument will probably come from a feminist position. If our prime concern is with human alienation as a result of work, then there are other spheres of work where such alienation takes place. Specifically, of course, work (including 'emotional work') in the home. This may have its own rewards, particularly if can be made into a zone of recovery and self-determination outside the workplace. But if we are interested in how people are estranged from their creative capacities, from the product of their labour, from other people and from nature then we should surely turn to the home-place as well as the workplace. This, then, is a major gap in Marx's theory of alienation; estrangement of the kind he outlines can also take place in this particular part of civil society.

The second comment concerns the implications of this paper's analysis for practical and political action. Are modern alienated people permanently committed to live out their lives in worlds of simulated hyper-reality, consuming video games, TV reconstructions of 'authentic' communities, 'real' holidays in 'real' places or engaging in technological futures in which the enemies are not the real social ones on earth but unspecified 'aliens' supposedly attacking the earth as a whole. Can we envisage more profound forms of emancipation than this? 'Profound' in the sense that non-experts can emancipate themselves and others not through a simulated reality but through the material reality in which they spend the rest of their lives

First we must recognise that the kinds of alienation outlined above have been recognised, at least in part, by capital. New management methods, especially in the more dynamic sectors of industry, recognise 'human resources' and the need to replace some of the worst excesses of the 19th century workplace with systems which recognise that repetitive and uncreative labour is no way to create a satisfied and productive workforce.   Such innovations place stress on the worker's creative capacities, working as a team and planning at least part of the labour-process.   As Morgan and Sayer (1988) argue, these social experiments cannot be simply dismissed. They can bring real, material benefits to those concerned.   On the other hand, these initiatives are of course aimed not simply at having a more contented workforce but a more productive workforce.   They remain highly subordinated to the demands for profitability.   As a result they usually they bring little influence to the operatives as regards what is produced, how it is produced and for whom it is produced.   The interactions between employment and 'natural resources' has hardly started to be considered by these innovations.   Peoples' relation to the raw materials which form the basis to the objects on which they are working remain as disastrously alienated as ever.   In short, the underlying and alienating relations first outlined by Marx have not been profoundly changed by developments during the 20th century, though we should not decry the efforts of groups (such as the Greater London Council during the 1980s) to restructure working practices and forms of production which were intended to overcome many of the forms of alienation to which this paper is addressed.

Are there more immediate prospects for emancipation, especially within civil society?   Are there ways in this sphere of social life in which peoples innate creative abilities can be recovered and developed?   Are there ways in which collective and communal work can be restored?   Can some more direct or unmediated understanding of the natural world be acquired?   Are there ways in which locally-based action can be better understood in relation to global developments?   Can anecdotal or practical knowledge be related to more general or abstract knowledge?

It is difficult to be over-optimistic here either.   One interesting development is the emergence of so-called 'community architecture.'   The idea here is to create collective and communal ways of working, with non-experts using kits of parts to create houses to build their own houses.   The user/expert relation is different from that in conventional building, with the experts working in close alliance to the end-users instead of at arm's length.   The method overcomes, potentially at least, many of the forms of alienation associated with the creation of the built environment.   And this includes alienation of nature, with use of local resources, buildings with low energy needs and using re-cycled materials.(Wates and Knevitt 1987)   The danger of such innovations is that once they become successful they are moved in on by capital and the original aims become steadily subverted, trivialised.   The close link between the producer and the consumer) become more distant and professionalised.   The consumers become the well-off and 'community architecture' becomes another purely symbolic item purchased by those who can afford it.

Nevertheless, there are a number of ways in which such movements within civil society could continue to be developed.   And they do not necessarily mean turning their backs on modern developments.   Another possible way forward is via the 'democratisation' of new interactive communications technology.   These, and the software associated with them, are again usually pre-packaged by the large corporations which produce them. As such they continue to provide further packaged and simulated understandings of material reality. On the other hand, these technologies are becoming a familiar part of domestic life and are in principle capable of being 'subverted' for alternative, more creative, uses. Compact discs, for example, can in principle be used by non-specialists for the collection and manipulation which they (and not some software programmer working for a corporation) have undertaken. This technology could be used, for example, to collect, manipulate and share practical and more general information about physical and social environments. And, since CD discs and in due course so-called electronic 'super-highways' can carry vast amounts of information, they offer prospects for making soil networks and linking local to global information. Work, at least work as it is carried out by some schoolchildren, is now being organised in this way.(Dickens and Parry 1994) The subversion of technology therefore does not entail some blind belief in technological determinism. Rather, the object must be that of challenging its control and the uses to which it is put.

In the end the aim must be to challenge the dichotomy between employment and civil society. It is this division which lies behind the kind of alienation of which Marx originally wrote and which lies behind the argument of this paper. It is short-sighted (as, for example, Gorz 1982, 1985 has suggested) to argue that since emancipation and autonomy are more achievable in civil society the sphere of production should be abandoned as a site of freedom. Rather, and as I have implied above, civil society is now offering progressive forms of social, political and technological relationships which could pre-figure how forms of less-alienated production might also start to be developed. And, once such material changes are in place, the need to consume simulated and apparently unalienated forms of reality should start to evaporate.

References

Braverman, H. (1974) Labor and Monopoly Capital, London & New York, Monthly Review Press.
Dickens, P. (1992) Society and Nature, Hemel Hempstead, Harvester.
Dickens, P. (1993) 'Society and Nature' in M Haralambos (ed) Developments in Sociology Vol.9, Ormskirk, Causeway Press.
Giddens, A.(1984) The Constitution of Society, Oxford, Polity. Gorz, A. (1982) Farewell to the Working Class, London, Pluto Gorz, A. (1985) Paths to Paradise, London, Pluto
Kauffman, S.(1993) The Origins of Order. Oxford University Press.
Lash, S and Urry, J. (1994) Economies of Signs and Space, London, Sage.
Marx, K. (1973) Early Writings, Pelican, Harmondsworth
Morgan, K., Sayer A.(1988) Microcircuits of Capital, Oxford, Polity.
Ollman, B. (1975l ()Alienation, Cambridge University Press Savage, M. et a1992) Property, Bureaucracy and Culture, London, Routledge.
Sayer, A.(1992) Method in Social Science, London, Hutchinson. Urry, J. (1990) The Tourist Gaze,

London, Sage.
Wates, N and Knevitt, C. (1987) Community Architecture, Harmondsworth, Penguin.
Wesson, R (1993) Beyond Natural Selection, MIT Press, Cambridge, Mass.

33

Pedestrian behaviour and the Parisian *passage*

Le comportement pietionnier et le passage parisien

John Zacharias

Le passage parisien fournit un laboratoire idéal pour l'étude de l'utilisation variable des réseaux piétonniers dans un contexte local de choix multiples. Les caractéristiques de réseau sont-elles déterminantes des niveaux d'activité ou, alternativement, les variations observées dans le comportement piétonnier sont-elles signes de l'influence d'autres facteurs? L'utilisation par des piétons de cinq groupes de passages a été capturée à l'aide d'un camescope. Des comptes de présence et de mouvement ont été effectués et comparés aux niveaux d'utilisation attendus d'une modélisation du niveau d'intégration du réseau. Les études de mouvement ont révélé le rôle primordial des liens dans le système de déplacement piétonnier.

Mots clé: comportement piétonnier; modélisation urbaine; environnement urbain.

Keywords: urban planning, pedestrians, arcades, behaviour

The theoretical interest of studying the Parisian passage revolves around the arrangement of pedestrian networks. Can a pedestrian network be augmented by inserting additional links of equivalent length? Can the observed use of these particular spaces be explained by a graph-theoretic interpretation of the urban pedestrian network or is there more to pedestrian behaviour? In this respect, the literature on the Parisian passage returns insistently to the themes of place: the social life and customs, the shop-owners, artisans, residents and habitués, the architectural frame and the goods on offer [Lemoine, 1989]. The on-going restoration of the passages is inspired by this rich social and literary history and guided by the imperative to preserve the architecture, but has so far failed to reproduce a brief but glorious hey-day (Figure 33.1). Is the passage primarily an urban room, a public space for exchange, commerce and social life, or does its use depend mostly on the movement of people from one street to another, incidentally passing through the short-cut provided? It has been claimed that it was usually a failure to provide a natural channel for existing movement patterns in the city and specifically to shorten one's trip from place to place that led to the failure of many of them [Geist, 1962].

Figure 33.1 Examples of the Parisian *passage*.

This paper compares pedestrian presence and directional movement within and around the passages with a graph-theoretic interpretation of the Parisian urban fabric. It also considers the role of functional linkages across the urban fabric and block geometry in supporting the use of particular urban spaces.

THE URBAN FABRIC OF THE PASSAGES

The area studied corresponds closely to the limits of the second arrondissement and is delimited by the Avenue de l'Opéra in the west and the Boulevard de Sébastopol in the east. The northern limit is the Rue Richer while the southern edges are roughly those areas immediately south of the Rue des Petits Champs and generally above the Louvre. While this area most certainly constitutes more than one and probably several distinct walking environments with a variety of functional characteristics, it includes several of the passages developed in the first half of the nineteenth century.

The western part of the second arrondissement is dominated by office activities, retailing and financial services while the eastern portion is more intensively inhabited. In addition, the eastern half hosts an important clothing manufacturing and wholesaling activity as well as street markets related to the former Halles de Paris [Mairie du IIe Arrondissement, 1993]. Partly as a consequence of this arrangement, the strongest functional connections exist in an east-west axis along the boulevards and the Rue Réaumur. A second pattern of exchange is evident from the north-west to the south-east, principally along the rues Montmartre and Montorgueil. Additional strong north-south movement associated with the Gare du Nord and de l'Est onto the ôle de la Cité and across the Seine can be seen along the Rue St-Denis and the Boulevard de Sébastopol. In spite of the availability of several north-south channels in the western half of the arrondissement, there is no compelling reason to travel in these directions and as a result these streets are generally the quietest of the entire sector.

Within this large-scale morphology, one can identify five distinct groups of passages [Figure 33.2]. While all of them lie adjacent to these major functional connections and the movement patterns associated with them, none of them offers a key link or even parallel path to the major flow. Moreover, they all lie within distinct functional areas and have little physical or functional connection, although perhaps an associative one, with each other. Given this analysis it is to be expected that these spaces will share with local streets the purpose of conveying people locally and purveying goods and services. If they were to capture some of the large flows on neighbouring and parallel streets, then perhaps the architectural design or social character might explain this pedestrian behaviour.

1 - Galerie Vivienne
2 - Galerie Vivienne 2
3 - Rue de la Banque
4 - Rue des Petits
   Champs
5 - Galerie Colbert
6 - Galerie Colbert 2
7 - Rue Vivienne
8 - Galerie Feydeau
9 - Rue St-Marc
10 - Pa. des Panoramas
11 - Galerie Montmartre

12 - Galerie St-Marc
13 - Rue Montmartre
14 - Pa. des Panoramas
15 - Boul. Montmartre
16 - Galerie des Variétés
17 - Rue Vivienne 2
18 - Passage Jouffroy
19 - Passage Verdeau
26 - Rue St-Denis

27 - Pa. du Bourg-l'Abbé
30 - Passage du Caire
33 - Pa. du Grand Cerf
34 - Rue Réaumur
35 - Passage Choiseul
36 - Rue St-Augustin
37 - Rue Ste-Anne
38 - Rue Choiseul
39 - Rue Monsigny
46 - Rue Richer
47 - Rue du Faubourg

Figure 33.2 Five groups of *passages* studied in the second *arrondissement* of Paris.

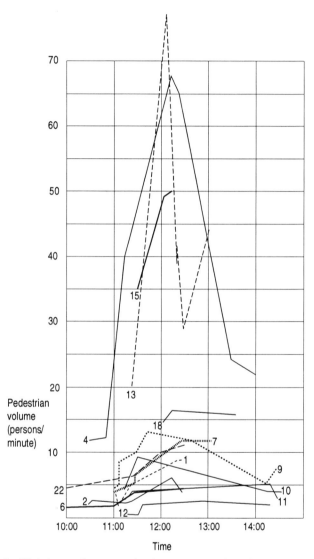

Figure 33.3 High integration scores for the western section of the study area are shown by line weight (a). Average pedestrian volumes are represented by line weight (b).

Could the actual level of pedestrian use of the passage be predicted from an analysis of its importance in the network of paths across the district? Space syntax [Hillier and Hanson, 1984] provides a topological measure of how closely connected any pathway is to all other pathways in an urban area. An integration score or the degree of connectedness of any street length is derived from the number of straight street lengths required to reach it from all other points in the urban area. This measure has been shown to be reasonably well correlated with the level of patronage in the streets of several cities.

The functional linkages across the local environment around the passages also need to be examined to see if they might explain the flows within these spaces. Two intersecting flows could be relatively large but unconnected. Two flows might also share part of a path and remain unconnected although coincidental in space. In a complex, multiple path, multiple link system, aggregated paths may overlap but have little to do with each other.

It could also be that pedestrians are attracted from a number of directions and simply circulate within a space, generating a high internal flow and volume of individuals but where there is no significant external linkage associated with this important human presence. Thus, in addition to an analysis of the entire pedestrian network, one should also examine the direction of flows.

METHODS

Portions of the second and ninth arrondissements of Paris were used to derive measures of integration, following methods described in detail first by Hillier and Hanson [1984] and subsequently by others (Figure 33.3).

Sections of the passages and the adjacent streets were videotaped beginning at 10.00 and ending at 14.30 on several consecutive weekdays. The camera operator stood at a point on the street where passing pedestrians on both sides of the street would be captured along with movement into, out of and within the passage itself. A circuit was repeated several times so that 5-8 film segments would be available for each space. It will be seen from Figure 33.3 that portions of the network were thus observed from two or three vantage points.

The film was then examined and each person's trajectory through the space was transferred to a plan view. For the map of actual pedestrian volumes (Figure 33.4b), everyone passing through the space was counted, even though some individuals passed through only a part of the space. The film was viewed several more times in order to record individual paths.

AN ANALYSIS OF PEDESTRIAN MOVEMENT DATA

The volumes recorded in various parts of the same spaces from single videotaped records of 5-minutes duration were compared. Within each of the local environments studied, there is a distinct hierarchy of use. One can observe clearly as many as four pathways in one video record and the associated volumes can be compared over time to see whether they maintained their ranked positions with regard to each other. A ranking of individual pathways within these areas by intensity of use is consistent over time. A three-level hierarchy can easily be established within each area such that the adjacent street experiences by far the heaviest use while only one path within the passage complex achieves a second order of use, followed by several channels of low intensity use. The differences in the averages derived from the volume studies are statistically significant at the 95% confidence level.

But how good is this videotaped record for the purposes of estimating level of use? Previous studies using still photos of sidewalks [Sandrock, 1988] have been shown to achieve acceptable counts for modeling. Volume counts over periods as short as 5 minutes have yielded a useful estimate [r2=0.67] of two-hour pedestrian volumes [Davis et al., 1988]. Sampling error has also been established in relation to pedestrian volume and sampling time in one city [Hanes, 1977]. If our individual five-minute counts based on the videotape record are applied to this last model, then the maximum error (at 95% significance level) would vary between 15% and 50%, with most falling around 30%. If the total videotaped record for each location is used, then the error should drop to a range between 5% and 18%. Apparently such estimates of error will vary considerably depending on the predominant land use [Hocherman et al., 1988]. However it will readily be seen that there are considerable fluctuations over time for the same space and a small budget did not permit simultaneous filming at all locations.

These studies and our results show that the rank order of some of the spaces is preserved while the recorded volumes varied. This will be sufficient for correlating measures of integration with our field record.

Very small samples are sufficient to determine how the individual segments of the pedestrian network are used. The above analysis shows that fluctuations in pedestrian volumes over time in the vicinity of the passages are much greater than the differences in volume between different parts of the same complex of streets and passages. The data suggest that in the common peak period between 12.15 and 12.30 there exists sufficient variation among the data at different locations to distinguish the spaces studied.

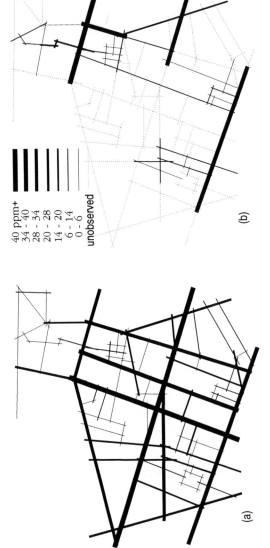

Figure 33.4 Pedestrian volumes derived from videotaped sequences at a sample of locations in the second and ninth *arrondissements* in Paris.

RESULTS OF INTEGRATION STUDIES

Integration scores were developed [Teklenburg, 1993] and correlated with individual, average and peak volumes as drawn from the videotape survey. Pearson and Spearman correlation coefficients were derived from this data. The Pearson coefficients for correlation were modestly positive [r=0.463; r=0.421] but substantially less so than has been found in other studies [Hillier, 1993; Peponis, 1989]. The Spearman r statistic converts the data to ranks before the correlation is computed. The relatively large volumes on certain streets [Figure 33.4b] reduce the predictability of a linear model such as the Pearson, while the Spearman eliminates this effect. Nevertheless, the Spearman coefficients were similarly and modestly positive [r=0.444; r=0.412]. While the integration scores clearly associate all the high volume channels with high integration scores, these measures do not distinguish well among the passages and the adjoining streets. The strong functional connections from one side of the area to the other help explain certain high volume streets and their similarly high integration scores. Others with high integration scores do not serve this everyday function - the rues Vivienne and Richelieu, for example - and have relatively low pedestrian volumes. Parallel paths show greater differential pedestrian volumes than their integration scores would suggest and this includes many of the passages. Even in an urban fabric of relatively uniform and high density, functional arrangements over a wide area may be more important in distinguishing the strength of pedestrian presence in streets than a graph-theoretic interpretation.

The integration measures themselves are topological and so do not take into count distance or geometry. In a relatively uniform grid, these latter factors may be less important. In Paris, a great range of block sizes and corresponding variation in actual distances traversed may be important factors in use. Similarly, nearly every block is irregularly shaped so that, unlike the orthogonal grid, there is only one shortest path around them. Using these measures the frequent jogs within the passages accentuate their segregation from the urban fabric, whereas it is somewhat doubtful that these minor deflections from straight-line movement have direct negative consequences on the level of use. Distance and geometry are suppressed in topological measures but direct observation suggests they have an important role to play in many instances in this urban area. Frequent "use" of the axial boulevards for deriving the integration values correlates in a reasonable fashion with actual use levels. While path minimization by pedestrians may take place, the arrangement of commercial activities along the boulevards makes movement in these directions necessary in any event. Strong north-south movement along the rues Montorgueil and St-Denis is also explained by the daily service needs of local residents although these streets do not have especially high integration values. On the other hand, the discontinuity of east-west streets in the eastern half of the study area inhibits a commercial vocation.

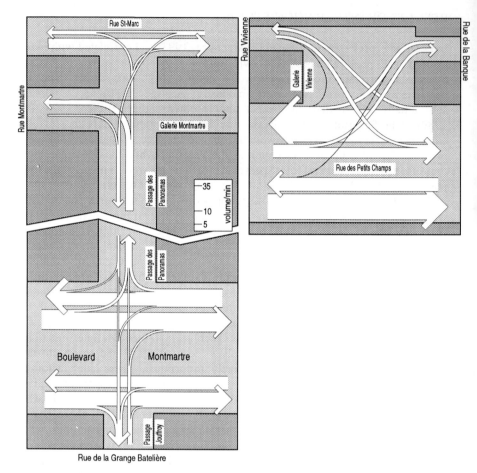

Figure 33.5 Average turning movements between 1200 hours and 1300 hours. Turns are almost invariably made so that the direction of movement is maintained.

LOCAL LINKAGES IN THE VICINITY OF THE PASSAGES

Inferences on the particular role of the passage or street in its local environment can be derived from a study of the directionality of pedestrian movement. Figure 33.5 illustrates two of these studies, that of Galerie Vivienne and the Passage des Panoramas and Passage Jouffroy. It will be seen first of all that the directional flows on the major streets are sensitive to time, underscoring the point above concering the functional linkages. In the case of the Rue des Petits Champs, where narrow sidewalks border an already narrow and heavily trafficked street, the pedestrian flows during peak periods sort themselves directionally on the two sides of the street.

In the case of the Vivienne, it will be clear that the passage is almost never used as a detour from a predetermined path. Nearly all the travel through the Vivienne is directionally consistent with travel on the neighbouring street. The two halls depicted at the top of the figure may be perceived as short-cuts to the Bibliothèque Nationale, to the Rue de la Banque or to the Place des Victoires. The saving in time and distance is marginal over the use of the streets to reach the same destinations. Yet the turning movements at the nearby corners are smaller than those recorded within the passage. There may be a preference to use the passage to reach the same destination and there may be perceived saving in time but a longer, less direct route is almost always avoided, except by tourists.

The same pattern can be observed at the Passage des Panoramas. In this case the Jouffroy (c.1845) was built as a prolongation of the Panoramas (1800) [Geist, 1969, p.340], although people traveling between the two today account for less than half the pedestrians within each passage. The rest are made up of individuals diverted from their paths on the boulevard with destinations within or beyond. That is the case of the Galerie Montmartre linking up with the busy Rue Montmartre and the Jouffroy leading through the Verdeau to the Rue Richer. As a result the areas nearest the boulevard are those most intensively used. These studies demonstrate the highly local nature of the linkages within the passage system.

DISCUSSION

The actual levels of use of the passages correlate approximately with expected levels derived from an examination of the network. However, the distinct hierarchy of paths at the local level is a consequence of the geometry of the streets and public ways as well as the location of major activities. The propensity for individuals to follow a shortest path itinerary appears to be the critical explanatory factor in the local pattern of movement. A model for cumulative density and movement patterns would seem to call for a consideration of the level of integration, block geometry and relative distance along paths between major urban generators.

Acknowledgements

The author wishes to thank two anonymous reviewers for their helpful comments and the Social Sciences and Humanities Research Council of Canada for financial support.

References

Davis S E, King L E, Robertson H D (1988)   Predicting pedestrian crosswalk volumes. Transportation Research Record 1168:25:30.

Geist J F (1969) Le Passage. Paris: Pierre Mardaga, 1969. [Forschungsunternehemen der Fritz Thyssen Stiftung, Arbeitskreis Kunstgeschichte, Bd 5, 1962].

Hillier B, Hanson J (1984) The Social logic of space. Cambridge: Cambridge University Press.

Hillier B, Penn A, Grajewski T, Xu J (1993) Natural movement: or, configuration and attraction in urban pedestrian movement.   Environment and Planning B: Planning and Design, 20:29-66.

Hocherman I, Hakkert A S, Bar-Ziv J (1988) Estimating the daily volume of crossing pedestrians from short-counts. Transportation Research Record 1168:31-38.

Mairie du 2ème Arrondissement (1993).   Le recensement de 1990 dans le 2ème arrondissement.

Peponis J, Hadjinikolaou E, Livieratos C, Fatouros D A (1989)   The spatial core of urban culture. Ekistics, 56, 335:43-55.

Sandrock K (1988) Heuristic estimation of pedestrian traffic volumes. Transportation Research, 22A, 2:89-95.

Teklenburg, J A F, van Andel J A (1993)   Urban morphology and children's use of public space.   Environmental Design Research Association, 24th Annual Conference, March 31-April 4.

34

Crowding and spatial syntax

Surpopulation et syntaxe spatiale

Gary W. Evans, Stephen J. Lepore and Alex Shroeder

La profondeur architecturale, qui fait partie de la théorie de la syntaxe spatiale, peut atténuer les effets psychologiqes néfastes de la densité résidentielle. La profondeur se réfère au nombre d'espaces discrets que l'on peut traverser à l'intérieur d'une structure donnée pour se rendre d'un endroit à un autre. Le retrait social semble intervenir dans l'interaction de la profondeur et de la surpopulation sur le malaise psychologique. Les habitants de logements surpeuplés et sans profondeur adoptent davantage une attitude de retrait vis-à-vis de leurs congénères que les personnes vivant dans des endroits non surpeuplés. Cependant, cette attitude n'apparaît pas dans les logements qui, bien que surpeuplés, présentent une certaine profondeur.

Mots clé: densité; syntaxe spatiale; santé mentale.

Keywords: crowding; spatial syntax; psychological health

This article examines the potential utility of space syntax theory (Hillier & Hanson, 1984; Zimring & Gross, 1991; Peponis, Zimring & Choi, 1990) to study the relations among residential crowding, design elements, and human well being. Dormitory rooms with greater sunlight are perceived as less crowded than same-sized rooms with less natural light (Schiffenbauer, Brown, Perry, Shulack & Zanzola (1977). Baum and Davis (1980) modified a long-corridor dormitory to create a smaller subunit of rooms. This change significantly reduced perceived crowding. Self-reports of excessive, unwanted social interaction dropped; more pro-social behaviors were observed; and laboratory experiments outside of the dorm indicated more social engagement and less withdrawal.

In prisons, Schaeffer, Baum, Paulus and Gaes (1988) found that inmates in open dormitories had higher stress (urinary catecholamines) than inmates with partitioned private space. Square footage was comparable. Cox, Paulus, Mc Cain and Karlovac (1982) showed that spatially enclosed sleeping accommodations largely ameliorated the negative impacts of crowding on health complaints among crowded inmates. Both cross-sectional (Evans, Palsane, Lepore, & Martin, 1989) and prospective, longitudinal data (Lepore, Evans, & Schneider, 1991) have shown that residential crowding can negatively effect psychological health. These field studies, plus laboratory experiments (Evans & Lepore, 1993) indicate that a major reason for residential crowding's adverse psychological effects on people is the disruption of socially supportive relationships among occupants of crowded homes. The disruption of social support systems among crowded residents appears to be an unintended consequence of social withdrawal, which is a typical coping strategy for dealing with chronic crowding.

In the present study, we examine whether an architectural factor that provides greater opportunities to regulate social interaction might also reduce the necessity to socially withdrawal as a way to cope with crowded living accommodations. Spatial syntax describes some interior design characteristics associated with the layout of rooms within a residence that may influence social interaction patterns in the home (Hillier & Hanson, 1984). One of these design characteristics, depth, was selected because of promising, preliminary findings by Hillier and Hanson (1984) linking this construct to social interaction. Furthermore, depth could be reliably estimated from residential blueprints.

Depth can be conceptualized as the number of spaces one must pass through in order to get from one point in a structure to one or more specific termini. For example, in the simple schematic shown in Figure 34.1, the depth of the Master Bedroom would be 2, starting from the front door; whereas the Master Bedroom bath depth would be 3.

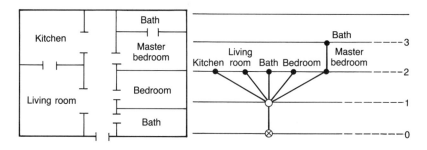

Figure 34.1 Schematic for depth calculation.

Residential interiors with greater depth in general will afford greater opportunities to regulate social interaction because inhabitants can more easily alter the degree of physical separation among themselves. Thus crowded residents in homes with greater depth may not need to socially withdraw because of a surfeit of unwanted, social interactions. Thus we predict that structures with greater interior depth will buffer some of the harmful effects of residential crowding on psychological distress.

In addition to the predicted interactive effects of density and depth on psychological distress, this interactive process should be associated with less social withdrawal from roommates in more crowded homes. That is, social withdrawal from roommates should function as a significant mediator of the predicted interaction effects (density by depth) on psychological distress.

METHOD

Subjects

Two hundred and twelve college students (96 men, 116 women) participated in a study of housing quality and social relationships. The average age of the sample was 20.4 years (SD=2.3). Sixty eight percent of the sample were Caucasian, 18% Asian-American, 6% Chicano or Latino, 4% African-American and the remaining sample ethnicity not provided. Their average monthly income was $704 (SD=$332.62). In exchange for their participation, respondents were eligible to win cash prizes in a lottery. Less than 5% of individuals refused to participate. At the time of the study all respondents had lived in off campus housing for at least eight months. In order to insure independence of responses, only one participant per household was eligible to participate in the study.

Measures

Psychological distress was measured by the Demoralization Index of the Psychiatric Epidemiology Research Instrument (PERI; Dohrenwend et al., 1980). A standardized, 25 item symptom checklist, the PERI measures everyday symptoms of distress (e.g., nervousness, anxiety, mild depression) among nonclinical populations. Respondents indicated on a five point scale (0=never - 4=very often) how frequently they had experienced symptoms during the prior week. The PERI has undergone extensive psychometric development and evaluation.

Social withdrawal was measured by an eight item scale indicating thoughts and actions to avoid social interaction (e.g., felt like withdrawing from your roommates) on a 0 (never) to 4 (very often) scale for the prior week. The scale is reliable (alpha=.93) and was significantly related to housemate's ratings of withdrawal (r=.83) in a pilot study (Lepore, Merritt, Kawasaki, & Mancuso, 1990).

Household density was measured by the ratio of persons per room in the home. Interior depth was operationalized as described in the Introduction. We utilized the front entrance of the residence as the fixed starting point. Rooms interconnected without a wall (e.g., dining room and kitchen) are counted as one room. Depth for the entire residence was calculated.

Depth was calculated by one rater blind to both the density and psychological distress levels of the respondents. His calculations were identical to those of the senior author who independently calculated depth for 10% of the sample.

Procedure

Household density, the PERI, the social withdrawal scale, and additional measures (e.g., sociodemographic data) were collected in a structured telephone interview. Interviewers were blind to respondent's crowding conditions until the end of the interview and had no knowledge of the interior design of the respondent's residence. Respondents were informed that the study addressed issues of housing and social relationships. They had no knowledge of our interests in crowding and/or its relationship to specific design features of the home.

We were able to obtain blueprints and/or floorplans for 151 subjects in the sample from either real estate companies or the cities in which the residences were located. These diagrams were used for the interior design calculations for depth. Different experimenters conducted the interviews and floorplan analyses, respectively.

RESULTS

Interaction Analyses

Table 34.1 shows the descriptive statistics for depth. Density and depth are dichotomized for descriptive purposes only in Table 34.1. As is apparent in Table 1, residential density has a significant and positive relationship with psychological distress, $F (1, 150) = 9.35$ $p < .02$. Overall individuals living in more crowded homes have higher levels of psychological distress. The association between depth and psychological distress is not significant, $F (2, 149) < 1.0$. The interaction of depth and household density is significant in the predicted direction, $F (3, 148) = 3.94$ $p < .05$. The positive relationship between chronic residential crowding and psychological distress only maintains in residences with lower levels of architectural depth.

Neither gender or race interacted with either density or the architectural variables to influence psychological symptoms. Therefore all analyses collapsed across gender and race. Statistical controls for age or income had no effect on the results, lacking any relationship with PERI scores.

Mediator Analysis

In order to demonstrate that social withdrawal functions as an intervening construct that mediates the interactive relationship of crowding and depth on psychological distress, a series of regression analyses are required. The initial regression equation regresses the outcome of interest (herein psychological distress) onto the interaction term (herein Crowding X Depth). This is the same interaction analysis already presented but is repeated to illustrate the logic of the overall analytic approach to testing mediated moderation effects. The interaction term shown in Table 34.2 has already had the main effects of each factor (Crowding and Depth) removed. Equation 2 regresses psychological distress onto the hypothetical mediator (herein social withdrawal). Equation 3 repeats the initial interaction equation regressing psychological distress onto the Crowding X Depth interaction term except that social withdrawal is forced into the equation prior to the interaction term.

Table 1
Crowding X Depth Interaction Results.

	Crowding	
	Low	High
Depth Low	17.63	21.62
Depth High	16.30	17.79

Table 2
Regression Equations Predicting Psychological Distress from the Crowding X Depth Interaction, Social Withdrawal, and the Crowding X Depth Interaction, controlling for Social Withdrawal.

Predictor	Total R	F(total R)	R	F(R)	df	b	SE
Crowding X Depth	.09	4.80*	.03	3.94*	3,148	.69	.34
Social Withdrawal	.18	30.73*	.18	30.73*	1,150	1.07	.19
Crowding X Depth with additional control for Social Withdrawal	.22	10.02*	.00	< 1.0	4,147	.29	.33

* p < .05

The mediating role of social withdrawal is demonstrated by three findings. First, the regression of psychological distress onto the mediator, social withdrawal, (Equation 2) should be significant. Second, the previously significant interaction effect (Equation 1) should become nonsignificant when the hypothetical mediator of social withdrawal is forced into the equation prior to the interaction term (Equation 3). As can be seen in Table 34.2, there is evidence of mediated moderation. The initially significant interaction term (Line 1 of Table 34.2) becomes nonsignificant when the effects of social withdrawal are partialled out (Line 3 of Table 43.2). The statistics of primary interest are the significance tests for the change in R square (see Evans and Lepore, in press, for more detailed discussion of the analysis and interpretation of mediated moderation models).

A third requirement for mediated moderation is that the hypothetical mediator regress onto the interaction term. The interaction of depth and household crowding is significantly related to social withdrawal (b = .42, p < .003).

DISCUSSION

Architectural depth may be a salient design feature in regulating household reactions to crowding. Persons living in homes with greater depth appear to be buffered from some of the harmful psychological health effects of crowding. Furthermore, this significant buffering effect appears to be mediated by social withdrawal. Individuals in crowded homes socially withdraw from their roommates significantly more than those from uncrowded homes. This does not occur, however, amongst roommates in crowded homes with greater structural depth. Moreover, the significant Crowding X Depth interaction is significantly attenuated when the effects of social withdrawal on psychological distress are partialled out of the equation.

These findings are consistent with previous research showing that a primary mechanism for explaining the relationship between residential crowding and psychological distress is social withdrawal. People living under crowded conditions appear to adapt to this situation be employing cognitive strategies to reduce unwanted social interaction (Baum & Valins, 1979; Baum et al., 1981; 1982; Evans et al., 1989; Evans & Lepore, 1993). We suggest that when environmental opportunities to regulate social interaction are readily available, use of cognitive strategies to minimize social interaction will be curtailed. This explanation also fits with some anecdotal reports suggesting that children living in crowded homes who have a space where they can retreat or who can easily play outside apparently suffer fewer ill effects from residential crowding (Saegert, 1982).

Although the correlational design of the present study precludes causal conclusions, the specific interaction predicted is nearly impossible to explain by the usual array of threats to internal validity such as self-selection facing a static, correlational design (Cook & Campbell, 1979). Nonetheless a valuable adjunct to the present study would be prospective, longitudinal field research on spatial syntax, density, and psychological health. Another approach that would strengthen the present suggestive results would be an intervention study wherein architectural depth was changed among crowded and uncrowded households.

Environmental psychologists have focused almost exclusively on intra- or interpersonal processes to understand crowding and human behavior. An additional objective of the present article is to further enjoin social scientists and designers to study the role of interior and exterior design elements directly as they influence human well being. In addition to room brightness, subunit size, degree of private enclosure and structural depth, several other design elements may influence human responses to crowding. Sound attenuation, visual access and exposure, window views, and proximity to open spaces (particularly those with restorative elements) are some potential interior design elements warranting further exploration. External design features such as functional distance to adjacent dwelling units and characteristics of defensible space (e.g., building height and size, well bounded spaces, semi-private small group interaction spaces) may also prove fruitful in influencing human responses to crowded living conditions.

Acknowledgement

This research was partially supported by grants from the National Science Foundation (BNS-892 0483), Hatch Grant NY(C) 327407, and the College of Human Ecology, Cornell University.

References

Baum, A., & Davis, G. (1980). Reducing the stress of high-density living: An architectural intervention. Journal of Personality and Social Psychology, 38, 471-481.

Baum, A., Gatchel, R., Aiello, J., & Thompson, D. (1981). Cognitive mediation of environmental stress. In J. H.

Harvey (Ed.), Cognition, social behavior, and the environment (pp. 513-533). Hillsdale, NH:Erlbaum.

Baum, A., & Valins, S. (1979). Architectural mediation of residential density and control: Crowding and the regulation of social contact. In L. Berkowitz (Ed.), Advances in experimental social psychology, vol. 12 (pp. 131-175). New York:Academic Press.

Cook, T., & Campbell, D. T. (1979). Quasi-experimental design. Chicago: Rand Mc Nally.

Cox, V. C., Paulus, P., Mc Cain, G., & Karlovac, M. (1982). The relationship between crowding and health. In A. Baum & J. E.

Singer (Eds.), Advances in environmental psychology, vol 4 (pp. 271-294). Hillsdale, NJ: Erlbaum.

Dohrenwend, B. P., Shrout, P., Egri, G., & Mendelsohn, F. (1980). Non-specific psychological distress and other dimensions of psychopathology. Archives of General Psychiatry, 37, 1129 1236.

Evans, G. W., & Lepore, S. J. (1993). Household crowding and social support: A quasi-experimental analysis. Journal of Personality and Social Psychology, 65, 308-316.

Evans, G. W., & Lepore, S. J. (in press). Moderating and mediating processes in environment-behavior research. In G. T. Moore & R. Marans (Eds.), Advances in environment, behavior, and design, vol. 4. New York:Plenum.

Evans, G. W., Palsane, M. N., Lepore, S. J., & Martin, J. (1989).Residential density and psychological health: The mediating effects of social support. Journal of Personality and Social Psychology, 57, 994-999.

Hillier, W., Hanson, J. (1984). Social logic of space. New York: Cambridge.

Lepore, S. J., Evans, G. W., & Schneider, M. L. (1991). Dynamic role of social support in the link between chronic stress and psychological distress. Journal of Personality and Social Psychology, 61, 899-909.

Lepore, S. J., Merritt, K., Kawasaki, N., & Mancuso, R. (1990). Social withdrawal in crowded residences. Western Psychological Association, Los Angeles, CA.

Peponis, J., Zimring, C., & Choi, Y. K. (1990). Finding the building in wayfinding. Environment and Behavior, 22, 555-590.

Saegert, S. (1982). Environment and children's mental health: Residential density and low income children. In A. Baum & J. E. Singer (Eds.), Handbook of psychology and health, vol. 2 (pp. 247-271).

Schaeffer, M., Baum, A., Paulus, P., & Gaes, G. (1988). Architecturally mediated effects of social density in prison. Environment and Behavior, 20, 3-19.

Schiffenbauer, A., Brown, J., Perry, P., Shulack, L., & Zanzola, A. (1977). The relationship between density and crowding: Some architectural modifiers. Environment and Behavior, 9, 3-14.

Zimring, C. & Gross, M. (1991). Searching for the environment in environmental cognition research. In T. Garling & G. W.

Evans (Eds.), Environment, cognition, and action (pp. 78-95). New York: Oxford.

35

Cognitive categorisation and preference for places

Catégorisation cognitive et préférence pour les lieux.

R. Lamb, A. Purcell, E. Peron and S. Falchero

On a examiné dans leur Pays deux groups d'étudiants (moitié mâles and moitié femelles), l'un de L'Université de Padoue, située an nord de l'Italie, l'autre de l'Université de Sydney, située dans l'Australie Occidentale. Les sujets ont jugé les mêmes 17 types de scènes - chacun représenté par quant à préférence pour chacun example, et en plus s'il était naturel ou construit; en outre ils devaient en choisir le nom parmi 3 possibles. Seulement pour un certain nombre de cas tous les sujets ont été daccord â définir la scène comme ou bien naturelle ou bien construite. Seulement deux scènes ont été jugées "naturelles" sans aucune doute (forêt et lac), tandis que la plupart a été jugée "construite", et là où toutes deux les résponses étaient présentes, la majorité des sujets a toujours vu ces scènes comme "construites". Ça malgré le fait que très souvent plusieurs aspects "naturels", comme eau et végétation, étaient présents. En outre, le noms choisis indiquent que les sujets ont prêté attention à des aspects différents, et souvent naturels, des scènes, sans que ça change leur jugement quant à "naturel/construit". D'autre part, une scène clairement naturelle (forêt) a été nommée par presque la moitié des sujets avec un nom "construit" (sentier). Les résultats sont discutés à la lumiére de l'étroitesse ou moins des critères, des attributs et des rapports existant dans les representations mentales des scènes pour ce qui se réfère à la categorisation naturel/construit, et aussi à la nature de ces attributs et rapports. Les différences observées entre les deux groupes de sujets quant aux scènes jugées naturelles ou construites, selon les cas, sont discutées en relation á l'extension des changements de l'environnement naturel dûs à l'intervention de l'homme dans les deux Pays examinés.

Mots clé: Cognitive; catégorisation; préférence; naturalité; descripteurs.

Keywords:cognitive; categorisation; preference; naturalness; descriptors

406

The research to be reported represents a first step in investigating the types of cognitive categorisations people use when experiencing landscapes, or more generally outdoor scenes, and whether or not the categorisation chosen is a predictor of preference. This is a significant question because, in much previous environmental perception research, the notion of "landscape" has been treated as though it was a single, coherent category. However, there is evidence that "landscape" treated in this way does not give a good account of the experience of the range of scenes often included in this type of research. Rather, it may be that landscape can be thought of as an articulated category including different kinds of cognitively definable places, and, most often, as a series of mixtures of these (Ward and Russell, 1981; Herzog, 1984, 1987; Purcell and Lamb, 1984; Falchero, Mainardi Peron, Lamb and Purcell, 1992). The questions this possibility raises concern the types of categories that can form the basis for the experience of an outdoor scene or landscape and whether or not categorising the same scene in different ways produces changes in other types of experience such as preference.

In the research literature it has often been argued that people prefer natural over built landscapes (Kaplan, Kaplan and Wendt, 1972; Ulrich, 1981; Purcell and Lamb, 1984; Herzog, 1987) and that this is so frequent as to be a general rule of landscape perception. However, few studies have involved specific judgements of the natural/built qualities of the environments for which preference judgements are being obtained, either in terms of the whole scene or the parts of scenes which are mixtures of natural and built elements. Rather, the importance of naturalness has been inferred from the analysis of the preference judgements (Lamb and Purcell, 1990). As a result one way in which scenes can be categorised, and which would appear to be relevant to preference, is in terms of whether they are natural or built. The first aim of this experiment is to specifically investigate subjects' classification of a range of scenes into natural or built types, with the range that was used corresponding to the range of scenes which in previous work have been referred to as landscapes. This will establish whether there are scenes where there is a generally shared conception of "naturalness" and "builtness" and the characteristics of scenes that can be categorised in this way. Similarly it is of interest to determine whether there are scenes which are classified by different groups as either natural or built and their characteristics relative to scenes that are classified as unambiguously natural or built. Preferences for these scenes can then be examined to determine whether categorising scenes in these differing ways are a predictor of preference.

While the possible importance of naturalness on preference has been widely discussed in previous work there would appear to be another possible way in which landscapes can be categorised. While a generic term, such as landscape, can be used to refer to a scene, examination of the types of scenes used in previous research indicates that there are generally a number of other, often more specific, terms which describe a scene. For example, a type of landscape used regularly in previous research involves a water body, such as a lake, in a mountainous setting with large areas of natural forest (eg. Herzog, 1985). Similarly a landscape scene can consist of views of fields with scattered buildings such as farmhouses with a background of forested hills (eg. Herzog, 1984). In the context of the built environment, a typical suburban street scene will consist of housing units together with a road and its surrounds (eg. Kaplan, Kaplan and Wendt, 1972; Herzog, 1989; Schroeder et al, 1986). In the first case, the scene could be referred to and categorised as a landscape, a lake, mountains or forest; the second as country, hills, fields or farmhouses and the third as suburbs, road or houses. These different ways of looking at the same scene in effect involve differing cognitive categorisations of the scene which could in turn influence preference for the scene.

Finally, an issue of general significance in the area of the experience of the landscape (Tips and Savisdisara, 1986; Kaplan and Herbert, 1987; Chokor and Mene, 1992) concerns the possibility of similarities and differences between cultures in terms of landscape preferences. In this experiment, both this issue and the additional questions of whether or not there are differences in landscape classifications between cultures and how these influence preference were examined by having groups from two widely different geographic locations judge everyday examples of the same types of scenes from each location.

METHOD

Stimulus Material

Seventeen types or categories of scenes which are found in both the Padua region of northern Italy and the Sydney area in eastern Australia were identified. Each type was represented by two slides, giving a total of 34 landscapes, one from each of the two regions considered. The scene types selected were :
1) Housing (apartment buildings in grassy surroundings and with a street).
2) Apartments (suburban buildings with trees and lawns in the foreground).
3) City street (inner city scenes of buildings on both sides of the street)
4) Arcades or porches (views of arcades or building porches from beneath)
5) River (river with greenness in the foreground and a small town in the background)
6) Canal (mixed commercial/industrial development and housing near a waterway)
7) Industrial area (industrial building and street)
8) Hills (cultivated land in the foreground with hills in the background)
9) Country (country land with country houses in the background)
10) Vineyard or orchard (flat foreground view of vineyard or orchard)
11) Fields (large scale view of flat cultivated land)
12) Suburbs (flat uncultivated land in the foreground and town buildings in the

background)
13) Country/city edge (cultivated fields with housing in the background)
14) Landscape (wide scale elevated views of mixed natural and agricultural
    land with scattered buildings at a distance).
15) Farms (wide scale elevated views of green hills with scattered farms)
16) Lakes (wide scale views across lakes with wooded hills in the background). 17)
Forests (views from within forests with a track in one case and small,
    unmade road in the other).
For each category a series of three names were selected in such a way as to be
reasonably equivalent choices of possible descriptors of the category for Italian or
Australian examples.

Subjects

Two groups of 96 undergraduate students, half males and half females, took part in
the experiment. One group of Ss came from the Padua region of Italy and the other
group was from the Sydney region of Australia, subjects ages ranging fro 20 to 30
years. Ss were presented with the slides from both countries however this preliminary
analysis of the data is based on the judgements of scenes from the country of origin
of the Ss. The effects of making judgements about scenes from a different geographic
location will be the subject of a subsequent paper.

Procedure

Each group of Ss was tested in their own country. Ss were told they would be asked
for their own opinions in a series of colour slides of outdoor scenes. The slides were
projected in a darkened room at a mean distance from the viewers of 2.5m, with an
image size of 1.5m in width. Eight different random orders of slides were used.
Each slide was shown for 5 seconds, and then Ss recorded their responses. At the
beginning all slides were shown, to let Ss become familiar with them. Ss were given
a booklet with one page for the results of each slide, and told they could change their
responses at any time during the session. All subjects were presented, always in this
order, with the following questions:
1)   "How much do you like this place"?
     Ss had to answer on a 7-point scale on which 1 denoted not at all, and 7, as
     much as possible.
2)   "Is it natural or built"?
     Ss had to answer by circling the correct choice in the booklet.
3)   "This is an instance of"   and here followed the three possible descriptors
     for the place in question, always in the same order. The alternative names or
     descriptors for each category are shown in the frequency tables. In addition Ss
     were asked to indicate in a brief written statement why they chose that level of

preference for the scene. Once again because of space limitations this aspect of the data is not discussed here.

RESULTS AND DISCUSSION

In this exploratory analysis of the data we have simply presented descriptive statistics in the form of tables of percentages for the different types of categorical judgements and means and standard errors for the preference judgements rather than engage in detailed statistical analyses. We consider this appropriate as the effects we wish to discuss are large in terms of differences in frequencies as are the differences in mean preference judgements particularly when the size of the standard errors associated with these judgements are taken into account. More detailed statistical analyses will be presented in subsequent papers.

For a number of the scene types both groups of Ss essentially unanimously judged the scenes to be either natural or built indicating great similarity between the groups of participants from the two countries. Given the similarity between the two groups of Ss, Table 1 presents the results for these types of scenes for the combined Italian and Australian Ss for each scene descriptor. Where significant numbers of Ss chose either the natural or built categories, the frequencies of each group choosing the natural or built categories are shown in Table 35.2. While there are significant differences between the Italian and Australian groups when the interaction between choice of natural/built and scene descriptor are examined in this Table, only the differences between the two groups for their natural/built choices will be discussed. The detailed analysis of this data will be presented in a subsequent paper. Table 35.3 shows the means and standard errors of the preference judgement for each type of scene averaged across the two groups of participants.

From Tables 35.1 and 35.2 it is apparent that many more types of scenes are judged to be built than natural. Only two types are judged to be unambiguously natural - the forest and the lake types, while there are eight scene types that are judged to be built. For the mixed scene types in Table 35.2, where different subgroups of Ss perceived the scenes as natural or built, it is apparent that, except in one case where there is an even split between the numbers judging the scene as natural or built, the larger group is always the group perceiving the scene as built. Two possible ways of interpreting this broad result are either that it reflects the sampling of the different scene types, or that the criteria for perceiving a scene as natural are much stricter than for judging a scene as built. At first glance, the names and descriptions of each scene type would appear to favour the first possibility. However an analysis of the content of the examples of the differing scene types that were perceived as built provides significant evidence for the second possibility. For example, there are only two scene types where there were no elements present that have been considered as important in the experience of naturalness - vegetation and water. These were the city street and arcade/porches scenes. In the housing and apartment scenes, there are significant amounts of vegetation in the form of grass areas, trees and shrubs. Even in the industrial scenes there are distinct areas of similar types of vegetation and in the canal, country/city edge and suburb scenes there are very large areas of vegetation in the form of trees, fields of grasses or agricultural crops. This interpretation is reinforced by an examination of the choices of descriptors chosen for the one scene (canal) with a strong and significant water element present. Here the dominant choice was for the canal descriptor and not for the alternatives of industrial area and small town. In this case the Ss appear to have been paying attention to what would be thought of as the natural element in the scene rather than the built elements, while perceiving the scene to be unambiguously built.

Scene type (natural or built)	Descriptors		
2. Apartments (built)	Suburb 34	Street 4	Apartments 62
1. Housing (built)	Suburb 50	Street 10	Houses 40
3. City street (built)	City 12	City street 66	Buildings 22
7. Industrial area (built)	Industrial area 75	Road 6	Factories 19
4. Arcade or porches (built)	Street 56	Footpath 14	Arcade/porches 30
6. Canal (built)	Canal 76	Small town 20	Industrial area 5
13. Country/city edge (built)	Country 10	Small town 41	Suburbs 49
12. Suburbs (built)	Country 37	Suburbs 52	Houses 12
17. Forests (natural)	Track 47	Forest 48	Bushes 5
16. Lakes (natural)	Lake 94	Hills 6	Forest 0

Table 1: Percentages of choice, across both groups of subjects, of each of the possible descriptors for scene types which were judged to be unambiguously either natural or built.

Origin of Subjects	Natural/ built	Scene types						
		River	Hills	Country	Vineyard/ orchard	Fields	Landscape	Farms
Italian	Natural	52	63	39	40	40	28	39
	Built	48	37	60	60	60	72	61
Australian	Natural	48	24	29	27	21	22	39
	Built	52	76	71	73	79	78	61

Table 2: Percentages of categorisation of scene types as natural or built for scene types in which subjects split into two distinct groups.

This contrasts sharply with the lake scene which is perceived to be unambiguously natural (94% from both groups of Ss) . For this scene type, the descriptor chosen was lake rather than forest or hills. Participants were therefore paying attention to the body of water in this scene but, unlike the canal scene, it is perceived as unambiguously natural. For the forest scenes a similar paradox also occurs. Trees may be thought of as the archetypal natural form of vegetation and forests as the type of scene which should be judged to be natural. This is clearly borne out in this case as this scene type is judged to be unambiguously natural. However, while these scenes were dominated by trees, each had a track leading through the trees. Examination of the descriptors chosen for this scene in Table 35.1 indicates effectively an equal split (48% versus 47%) between the forest and track descriptors. This represents a similar result to that found with the canal scene except that, in this case, a built element is being paid attention to with the scene being judged to be unambiguously natural.

Two conclusions can be drawn from this discussion. First it would appear that, for scenes to be perceived as natural, stricter criteria have to be met than for a scene to be perceived as built. This may involve, in the case of vegetation, the presence of certain types of vegetation: vegetation in the form of cultivated trees and shrubs, grassy fields and agricultural crops do not meet this criterion. However the results with the forest scenes indicate that a natural scene does not have to be exclusively natural because elements such as tracks can be present, again indicating that it may be the form or type of vegetation that is important. The criteria for a built scene are however much wider or more "tolerant" and include many forms of vegetation. What appears to differentiate between the natural and the built scenes is, not so much simply the presence of built elements, but also the presence of man induced change. For example, various types of artefacts and various forms of cultivated vegetation, as well as buildings, can occur in built scenes.

The second conclusion concerns the implications of the way in which a dominant water element can occur in two different scene types, with one being perceived as natural and the other built. Participants chose the descriptor "lake" for the natural scene and "canal" for the built scene. Both descriptors refer to significant water bodies in the scene but this may not be the determining factor. Rather what may be important is the set of attributes and relationships which are indexed by these words. A "canal" may be, not just a water body, but a water body of a particular type which itself represents a human artefact and which also includes among its features many other types of human artefacts and human produced change. By contrast a "lake" is a water body that appears not to have been created by human means and is associated with other elements such as "natural" vegetation in the form of forests and significant natural landforms. As a result the descriptors "lake" and "canal" access different cognitive categories. It may be that a significant shift in the focus of landscape research should occur towards examining the nature, number and characteristics of the cognitive categories we use to interact with the environment.

The scene types which were associated with mixed natural and built categorisations (Table 35.2) both reinforce the discussion of the types that were categorised unambiguously as either natural or built and also raise other interesting issues. Seven scene types were responded to in this way and all of them contain major areas of vegetation. Some of these scenes (the hill and farm types) contain significant areas of what was referred to above as "natural" vegetation in the context of the forest and lake scenes, as well as significant areas of cultivated vegetation and built artefacts. Others (the river, country, vineyards and fields types) are dominated by cultivated vegetation and other human artefacts. To be unambiguously natural therefore it is apparent that it is not sufficient that significant areas of "natural" vegetation be present. Either all elements must be natural, or, (and this is the interpretation we currently favour), all of the attributes within a scene and the way they relate to each other must be consistent with a type of cognitive category, such as forest or lake, which is regarded as natural, but which can contain some human artefacts. There is however a problem with this explanation - why are some of the scenes which contain only cultivated natural elements perceived as natural by some of the Ss?

One possibility is that two distinct types of naturalness are involved. The first relates to types of scenes that are perhaps universally seen as natural, evidenced in this experiment by the lake and forest scenes being seen as unambiguously natural by two groups from quite different geographic locations. The same type of naturalness is present in other scene types about which Ss differed in categorisation, in combination with elements from the built category and other artefacts. Whether or not a scene will appear natural or built in this situation depends on the aspect of the scene the individual pays attention to. Where attention is paid to the natural elements, it is judged to be natural and reflects the same criteria for naturalness as is present in the lake and forest scenes. The second type of naturalness relates to scenes which combine a cultivated naturalness with other types of artefacts and human induced change. In this case the group differences may reflect thresholds associated with the amount of this type of naturalness which is required for a scene to be classified as natural. Both of these possibilities are open to experimental examination. For example the amount of the different types of vegetation could be systematically varied to determine how such changes effect the classification of the scenes into natural or built and this represents a significant area for future research.

The data for this group of scene types also illustrates a potentially significant difference between the Ss from the different geographic locations. This is most apparent in the data for the hill type in Table 35.2. Here 63% of the Italian respondents judge these scenes to be natural while 76% of the Australian Ss judge them to be built. Both the Italian and Australian examples are very similar in composition in terms of the types of elements and their relationships which are present in the scene. The same difference is apparent, although not in such a striking form, in the country, vineyard and field scenes, where in each case more Australian Ss perceive the scenes as built and more Italian Ss perceive them as natural. One possible basis for this difference may lie in a cultural or, perhaps more appropriately, a geographic bias resulting both from the differing contact with nature the two groups have and also the difference in nature itself in the two countries. This latter difference relates to the fact that in Italy practically all nature is to some extent domesticated or affected by human induced change; that is there is no true "wild" or "savage" nature. As a result Italians, having this experience of naturalness have a more "tolerant" conception of naturalness. By contrast the greater extent and frequency of experience of truly wild or savage nature in Australia produces a more "conservative" classification of naturalness which is associated with a narrower or more strict set of attributes and relationships which are necessary to identify a natural scene than is the case for a large group of the Italian Ss. This in effect represents the same hypothesis to that advanced to account for the difference between the unambiguously built and natural scenes but in this case relates to the response to mixed scene types.

Table 35.1 also demonstrates another interesting aspect of the way in which people categorise scenes. The descriptors for the first four scene types have been arranged so that the descriptors go from generic terms to specific terms relating to particular focused aspects of the scene. It is apparent that the frequency of choice of generic or specific descriptors depends on the type of scene. For the apartment scene type, the specific term referring to the building type is chosen most frequently (62%) with the generic term being chosen much less frequently (34) and the strong street element being chosen very infrequently. With the houses type this pattern begins to change with the generic term, suburb, being chosen more frequently (50%), the specific term, housing, less frequently (40%) and the street descriptor again being chosen very infrequently. With the industrial scene type it is the generic descriptor which is chosen most frequently (75%) with the specific building type being chosen much less frequently (19%) and the street element receiving very little attention (6%). By contrast with the city street scene, it is the street element which is chosen most frequently (66%) with the generic descriptor, city, being chosen very infrequently (12%) and the more specific descriptor, buildings, being chosen with intermediate frequency (22%). Similar differences occur with other scene types, for example, with the canal scene the dominant descriptor relates to the specific element of the canal (76%) rather than the more generic terms industrial area (5%) and small town (20%). The basis for this interesting effect is not readily apparent and clearly is another significant area for future research.

Finally Table 35.3 illustrates the relationship between scene type and preference with the scene types arranged in rank order of preference. If the various scene types are related to the preceding discussion of the way they are classified, it becomes apparent that there is a complex relationship between the way a scene is categorised and preference. The highest preference is related to natural scenes and from the classification results these have to be the types of scenes that are unambiguously natural in the terms of the preceding discussion. Similarly the lowest preferences are associated with unambiguously built scenes. Both of these results appear to confirm previous findings that relate builtness and naturalness to variations in preference (eg. Lamb and Purcell, 1982; Purcell and Lamb, 1984; Kaplan and Kaplan, 1989). However the scene types that occur between these two extremes are either those which were classified as either natural or built or were unambiguously built. For example city street and arcades/porches are quite highly preferred and these are unambiguously built scenes. It must also be remembered that the most frequent response category for the mixed scenes was built. The landscape scene type represents a particularly interesting example in this context. For both groups of Ss this was perceived as an example of a built scene (72% for the Italians and 78% for the Australians) and it is the third highest in terms of preference.

Rank	Scene type	Preference (s.e.)	Possible descriptors
1	7	1.7, (.07)	Factories. road, industrial Area
2	12	2.3, (.09)	Country, suburbs, houses
3	13	2.6, (.09)	Country, small town, suburbs
4	1	2.9, (.10)	Suburb ,street, houses
5	6	3.0, (.10)	Canal, small town, industrial area
6	2	3.1, (.10)	Suburb, street,apartment
7	11	3.4, (.09)	Country, hills, landscape
8	10	3.8, (.09)	Country. cultivated fields, vineyard or orchard
9	4	3.9, (.11)	Street, arcade or porches, footpath
10	9	3.9, (.11)	Country. hills, country houses
11	3	4.0, (.11)	City, city street, buildings
12	14	4.0, .10)	Landscape, hills, small town
13	5	4.0, (.11)	Canal or river, country, small town
14	8	4.1, (.09)	Country. hills, farms
15	15	4.2, (.11)	Landscape, farms, trees
16	16	5.3, (.08)	Lake, hills, forest
17	17	5.7, (.08)	Track, forest, bushes

Table 3: Means and standard errors for preference for the 17 scene types in rank order from least to most preferred. Also shown are the possible descriptors Ss could choose to describe each scene type example.

In conclusion these results demonstrate first that consistent categorisations of different scene types occur both in terms of whether or not a scene is perceived as natural or built or mixed and in terms of the descriptors chosen to apply to the scene. Further it is apparent that there is considerable similarity in the categorisations made by groups from quite different geographic locations and that where differences occur they appear to be related to recognisable differences between the two geographic locations. It is also apparent that naturalness is not a good predictor of preference when it is viewed as a dimension that occurs across different types of scenes. Rather preference appears to be more a function of identifying an example as belonging to a scene type with different scene types being associated with different levels of preference. What we have identified as unambiguously natural types of scenes are highly preferred but it is not the case that unambiguously built scene types are low in preference. These scene types can vary widely in preference, for example from 1.7 for the industrial scene type to 4.0 for the city street scenes, indicative of the major role that scene type plays in preference and, as a result, the role that categorisation processes play in our preference for places.

References

Chokor, B.W., and Mene, S.A. (1992). An assessment of preference for landscapes in the developing world: A case study of Warri, Nigeria, and environs. Journal of Environmental Management, 34, 237-256.

Falchero, S., Lamb, R.J., Peron, E.M. & Purcell, A.T. (1992). Is our experience of the world more complicated than we think? In Aristides, M. and Karaletsou, C. (Eds) Socio - Environmental Metamorphoses : Builtscape, Landscape, Ethnoscape, Euroscape - Proceedings of 12 th. IAPS International Conference, Aristotle University of Thessaloniki, Thessaloniki, Greece, 102-106.

Herzog, T.R. (1984). A cognitive analysis of preference for field and forest environments. Landscape Research, 9, 10-16. Herzog, T.R. (1985). A cognitive analysis of preference for waterscapes. Journal of Environmental Psychology, 5, 225-241

Herzog, T.R. (1987). A cognitive analysis of preference for natural environments : mountains, canyons, deserts. Landscape Journal, 6, 140-152.

Herzog, T.R. (1989). A cognitive analysis of preference for urban nature. Journal of Environmental Psychology, 9, 27-43.

Kaplan, S., Kaplan, R. & Wendt, J.S. (1972). Rated preference and complexity for natural and urban visual material. Perception and Psychophysics, 12(4), 354-356. Kaplan, R., and Herbert, E.J. (1987). Cultural and Sub-cultural comparisons in preference for natural settings. Landscape and Urban Planning. 14, 281-293.

Kaplan, R., and Kaplan, S. (1989). The experience of nature: A psychological perspective. Cambridge, Cambridge University Press.

Kaplan, S., and Kaplan, R. (1982). Cognition and environment: functioning in an uncertain world. New York, Praeger Publishers.

Lamb, R.J., & Purcell, A.T. (1990). The perception of naturalness in vegetation and its relationship to vegetation structure. Landscape and Urban Planning, 19, 333-352.

Purcell, A.T. & Lamb, R.J. (1984). Landscape perception: an examination and empirical investi gation of two central issues in the area. Journal of Environmental Management, 19, 31-63.

Schroeder, H.W., Buhyoff, G.J., and Cannon, W.N. (1986). Cross-validation of predictive models for the aesthetic quality of residential streets. Journal of Environmental Management, 23, 309-316.

Ulrich, R.S. (1981). Natural versus urban scenes; Some psychological effects. Environment and Behavior, 13(5), 523-556.

Ward, L.M. Russell, J.A. (1981) The psychological representation of molar physical environments. Journal of Experimental Psychology: General,

36

Children make assessments of the urban environment

Evaluations de l'environnement urbain par des enfants (exemples de petites villes)

Svetlana E. Gabidulina

Cet exposé présente une recherche empirique sur l'étude psychologique de l'évaluation que font les enfants de leur environnement. Différents emplacements d'une petite ville (une banlieue de Moscou) ont été classés dans quatre groupes selon leur style architectural et leurs fonctions. Les sujets étaient des enfants de 7, 8 et 9 ans, tous élèves de gymnasy; ils ont évalué leurs endroits favoris à l'aide des tests suivants: dessins, échelles de Technique Sémantique Différentielle et Questionnaire mis au point par l'auteur lors de ses précédentes recherches. Les dessins ont été analysés pour trouver les critères de Confort/Malaise et Dépression dûe à l'environnement. Les échelles sémantiques et les réponses ont été utilisées pour construire des images d'endroits confortables et inconfortables. Les groupes de sujets ont été comparés pour découvrir les différences d'âge dans les évaluations.

Mots clé: évaluations; critères d'analyse de dessins; image de la ville; différences d'âge.

Keywords:assessments, criteria of analysis of drawings, image of the city, age differences

Recent interests in environmental psychology include topics such as neighbourhood, retirement, delinquency and child development. The present paper is devoted to the last item. It was noted by Th. Laike (1990) that the child development is generally described in terms of either social or physical environment. Many children get a large portion of their daily care outside their homes and hence are affected by several environments (yards, parks, streets etc.).Their behaviour depends on their ages and interests. A classification of various types of leisure activities and corresponding places was developed by the Russian sociologist I. Bestuzhev-Lada (1972). The models of leisure behaviour are as follows:- places for contemplation (churches, parks, embankments) - places to obtain new information (museums, libraries, exhibitions) - places for creative activities (clubs, daily centres, etc.) - places for sports activities (stadiums, sports centres) - places for entertainment (dancing/concert halls, theatres) - places where the public holidays are celebrated such as the Days of City, etc. (squares, streets)

These models of leisure behaviour are projected on different types of built-environments. The people live and act in a specific architectural environment rather than in a blank space. Therefore the distinct types of the environment can be proposed to promote the distinct types of behaviour. They could also be classed into the following four groups (N. Kunitskaya, 'to be published").

1   Lengthy form of built environment. It features the closed yards limited by houses (so-called wells)
2   Latticed form with streets as main forming elements. Houses are considered as the nodes of a lattice
3   Point form with low-storeyed houses. The houses are spaced by the   distances which are greater than their heights
4   Open air. An open space with elements of natural landscape. Houses are separated from each other by natural elements (trees, bushes, etc.)

The empirical research was carried out in a small town (a suburb of Moscow). Its urban environment generally has latticed and point features with some elements of open air. There is a park with a pond and toddlers' playground in the centre of the town. The urban environment is characterised by modern houses, low traffic flow and good landscaping We have proposed that child development is affected by some parameters of the urban environment.

These parameters were obtained using Semantic Differential Technique by for example, R. Kuller et al., (1972). They are as follows: pleasantness, complexity, unity, enclosedness, potency, social status, affection, originality. Similar results were also obtained for the Russian population by S. Gabidulina (1989), who used a modified Semantic Differential Technique.

The main dimensions of Semantic Space found were: aesthetic appraisal, comfort, simplicity. At the beginning of this project it was necessary to solve some problems. Children are not usually able to express their opinions accurately by verbal means. Also, it was very difficult to use the Semantic Differential Technique for children of 7-9. Furthermore, the emotionality of children was another factor which can strongly influence on the results.

Therefore, a combined test was developed, including a drawing test and a questionnaire. Some questions of this questionnaire were based on the modified scales from the Semantic Differential Technique (these questions are marked by "*"). This combined test aimed to investigate the attitude of children to their environment. The subjects were pupils of gymnastics ages 7-9 years. The total number was 30.

METHODS

Drawing test

Drawing tests are well-known and have been actively used from the XIX century. Drawings enable a person to express their attitudes to other people, situations and events. They help a child to create his own graphic information system when his language is rather poor. We consider drawings as a story which is presented in terms of pictorial means and can be interpreted. According to the classification of psychological methods, drawing tests are the projective ones. They enable people to project personal traits and feelings and to interpret reality in some way. We used a modification of a drawing test. The instruction was as follows: "Please, draw your favourite place adjacent to your house".

Questionnaire

1) Why do you like this place?
2) What are the differences between this place and the others?
3) Are there a lot of trees there?
4) Is it crowded?
*5) Is it funny or gloomy?
*6) Is there a lot of, or a lack of, room there?
7) Is there an "open sky"?
*8) Is it noisy or quiet?
*9) Is it dark or illuminated?
10) How often do you find yourself there?
11) At what time of day do you usually get there?
12) With whom do you spend time there?
13) What do you do there?
14) Are there windows overlooking at this place?

RESULTS AND DISCUSSION

The drawings were grouped by their plots according to the classification by I. Bestuzhev-Lada. The most favoured places were: PARK (1/2 of total number of subjects), YARDS and STADIUM (1/3), and the child's own ROOM (1/6). These are places dealing with sports and playing activities, recognition and contemplation. The results are represented in Tables 1-3.

Table 36.1 Park

No.of
question   Description

1/2   Quiet place, closeness to nature, there are friends, it is funny,   this place is nice and cosy, it is not noisy, it is cool, there are a lot   of trees, it is good for walking across puddles and climbing trees, there are many nice stones, there are a river and hills. You can do whatever you like

3   A lot of trees (1/2 of total number of subjects), a lack of trees (1/2)

4   A lot of people (1/3), a lack of people (2/3)

5   It's funny (90%), gloomy (1 answer), both (2 answers)

6   There is a lot of room (80%), there is a lack of room (20%)

7   There is an "open sky" (90%)

8   It's noisy (1/2), it's quiet (1/2)

9   It's illuminated (90%)

10   I find myself there often (1/2), I find myself there seldom (1/2)

11   I get there in the afternoon and in the evening

12   I spend time there with my friends (1/2), with my parents (about 1/2), alone (1 answer)

13   I play, collect little stones, walk, swim, speak with Nature, toboggan 14. There are windows overlooking the place (about 100%), there are no windows (2 answers)

Table 36.2 Yards and stadium

The yards and the stadium in the suburb feature desolation and the lack of organised activity (e.g. sports activity). They appear as covered with trees and bushes or deserted spaces, and children readily find themselves as independent and "wild" in these places.

1/2   It's nice, cosy, interesting, quiet. It's like a Paradise. My grandparents live there.

3   There are a lot of trees (90%), there is a lack of trees (10%)

4   It's crowded (100%)

5   It's funny (100%)

6   There is a lot of room (90%)

7   There is an "open sky" (100%)

8   It's noisy (1/2), it's quiet (1/2)

9   It's illuminated (100%)

10   I find myself there every day (100%)

11   I usually get there in the morning, in the afternoon and in the evening

12   I spend time there with my friends and with my parents

13   I play, run, speak with my friend

14   There are windows (100%)

Table 36.3 Own room

Possibly, children who chose room feel themselves uncomfortable everywhere except private space. Urban environment seems to them hostile and dangerous.

1/2	It's warm. There are a lot of books and electric fixtures there. My doll lives there
3	There are no trees there
4	Nobody is there
5	It's funny
6	There is a lack of room, but I feel myself like a King
7	There is no sky
8	It's quiet
9	It's illuminated
10	I find myself there everyday
11	Usually I am there throughout the day
12	I spend time there alone, with my mother, with my sister, with my dog 13 I play, read and do whatever I like
14	There are no windows overlooking the place.

The questions were formulated in terms of "physical properties". The objective was to analyse the emotional assessments of the answers. The analysis of the results of Table 36.1 (Park) revealed the following emotional characteristics:

1   Freedom of expression (we use this term following K. Korpela, 1989). In his favourite place, a child can do whatever he likes.

2   Comfort (relaxation). The favourite place is described as "nice, cool, cosy, etc." It enables the person to relax and/or to have a rest.

3   Aesthetics assessments

Answers to Question 13 deal with various types of activities (games, sport competitions, etc.). In this place a child can express his emotions and regulate his psychic balance. Answers to Questions $12+13$ illustrate the fact that at the age of 7-9 children prefer to spend their time in a company. That is why 1/2 of all subjects like public places (park). Other characteristics of the place varied (noisy or quiet, funny or gloomy, etc.). The same place was assessed in different ways depending on the individual. In this place every child can choose his own type of behaviour.

Answers to Question 14 were a little bit surprising. All answers, excluding two, were "yes", in spite of the fact that the houses were quite far away from the park. This question deals with public monitoring the place. It seems that even in the situations with no external monitoring an internal feeling arises that the place is nevertheless monitored. Another favourite place, a yard, is also characterised in terms of relaxation and aesthetic assessments. The freedom of expression is less than in the previous case. A yard is a place with stronger monitoring (100% of answers to the 14th question). Most of the activities relating to yards are outdoor games. A yard is considered by children as a funny place. The elements of contemplation are absent. It is also more "open" and illuminated than the park. There is a lack of a romantic and mysterious atmosphere which is the distinctive feature of a park. The third favourite place is a room. It was mentioned by the minority of subjects.

Based on the results of the drawing test and observation, these children could be characterised as introverts. Their answers reflect their need for privacy and closeness of space. A room is described as a warm, illuminated, narrow space. A child allows a very limited number of people to be present (a mother, a sister, a dog). Isolation and freedom of expression are emphasised (I do whatever I like, I feel myself like a King). External monitoring is absolutely absent. A child entirely controls the situation by his own means. All drawings can also be analysed as projective tests. They demonstrate a diversity of graphic and colour means. But these results are of interest mostly for psychotherapists and teachers. It is of importance that there were essentially no human figures in the pictures. Human figures were in only four pictures. Some authors think that at the age of 7-9 a human figure is a central item. This fact can be interpreted as an insufficient identification with the favourite place which is an important part of self-regulation (e. g., K. Korpela). The phenomenon of estrangement combined with the feeling of strong external monitoring may be considered to be a result of pressing education and insufficient attention to the self-realisation of a child.

CONCLUSIONS

The experimental results demonstrated the suitability of technique based on the drawing and the questionnaire. These two methods are complementary. E.g., provided a drawing exhibits depressive features (i.e., fine details, lack of human figures, etc.), the answers to the questionnaire show that the child tends to the isolation, he likes "bounded" or private places without any public control. This enables one to diagnose the environmental effect on the psychological status of a child.

Also, the choice of favourite places and their exploration demonstrate that the majority of children exhibit an interest to non-structured or "wild" places where they could feel free. This is probably a compensation for the strict determinism and severe control in their usual life. The responsibility of teachers and city authorities is to create the spaces which combine freedom with cultural landscape.

References

Bestuzhev-Lada I. V. Sociologist Tells About Needs // Science and Technology. Riga, 1972, No. 9 (in Russian)

Gabidulina S. E. Psychosemantic Approach to the Environment //Environment. Suzdal, 1989, vol. 2, p. 42-51 (in Russian)

Korpela K. M. Place-identity as a product of environmental self-regulation // Journal of Environ mental Psychology. 1989, Vol. 9, No3, p. 241-256 4. Kuller R. A semantic model for describing perceived environment // National Swedish Institute for Building Research. Stockholm, 1972, 204 p.

Laike T. Using old methods in a new way to help understand the impact of the environment on child development // Proceedings of the 11th IAPS, Ankara, 1990, METU, p.217-227.

37

Measurement of the multi-sensory information for describing sequential experience in the environment: an application to the Japanese circuit-style garden

Mesure de l'information multi-sensorielle pour la description de l'experience sequentielle de l'environnement: application aux jardins de promenade

Ryuzo Ohno and Miki Kondo

Les paysages dans les villes modernes au Japon sont remarqués pour leur pauvreté visuelle: ils sont souvent si chaotiques et quelquefois si monotones qu'on souffre d'un excès et d'une dépravation sensoriels. Les jardins de promenade au Japon ont depuis longtemps été appréciés pour leur beaux points de vue séquentiels. Si nous pouvions retirer des enseignements de leurs arrangements spatiaux, nous pourrions concevoir nos espaces urbains de façon à offrir aux piétons des expériences esthétiques plus riches et un niveau optimal d'information. Pourtant, l'expérience esthétique du jardin a rarement été étudiée de manière scientifique. Cette recherche va tenter d'analyser l'expérience séquentielle par la mesure de l'information multi-sensorielle de l'environnement afin de révéler un ordre caché ou un rythme d'arrangement spatial. On a mis au point une série de programmes informatiques que l'on a appliquée aux données sur l'environnement de trois jardins de promenade célèbres, afin de mesurer les trois aspects suivants de l'information sensorielle: 1) l'information visuelle ambiante; 2) l'information visuelle focalisée; 3) l'information non visuelle, par exemple l'information tactile et kinésique. Les caractéristiques de chaque aspect sensoriel sont obtenus en mesurant les points consécutifs tous les 0.5m (un pas de promeneur) le long du sentier du jardin. Ainsi, les changements dans les caractéristiques d'information sensorielle sont utilisés pour examiner l'expérience séquentielle à mesure que les individus se déplacent dans le jardin.

Mots clé: jardins de promenade au Japon; information multi-sensorielle; expérience séquentielle.

Key words:Japanese circuit-style garden, multi-sensory information, sequential experience

Urban landscapes in Japanese modern cities are notable for their poor visual scenes: they are often chaotic and sometimes too monotonous where people suffer sensory overload and sensory deprivation (Rapoport, 1980). On the other hand the Japanese circuit-style gardens have long been appreciated for their sequential scenes of beautiful landscapes. If we can learn from the spatial arrangements of the garden, our urban spaces could be designed to provide pedestrians with richer experiences and optimal levels of information. The aesthetic experience in the garden, however, has rarely been analyzed based on physical or objective data because it is difficult to explain by the characteristics of particular elements.

In the present study, the aesthetic experience is postulated to depend on the multi-sensory information from the environment, and a method for measuring the relevant variables was developed. By applying the method to circuit style Japanese gardens, the aesthetic value of which has traditionally been recognized, the changes of the physically measurable sensory variables as people moved through the path were objectively described. The changing profile was analyzed to reveal the hidden order or rhythm of the sequential experience.

Research Background

The present study mainly stemmed from Thiel's (1970) " notation ", which is a time based description method of sequential experiences in the environment analogous to a musical score for an orchestra. His method was employed in this study to describe the profiles of multi-sensory information from the environment. Although some researchers (Miyauji ,1992; Kitamura et al ,1989) applied similar methods to such pedestrian spaces as a shopping mall, urban street and river-side landscapes, they did not quantitatively analyze environmental components.

An attempt to quantitatively describe spatial sequences was made by Funakoshi et al. (1988) for the approach path in the Japanese shrines, and Zaino et al. (1992) and Miyagishi et al. (1992) for the Japanese gardens. Although we share similar research interests, these studies dealt only with limited environmental components which were somehow arbitrarily chosen. In addition, the measured unit of spaces was too broad to examine the details of space sequence, and the research was mainly argued on visual sensory information. By contrast, Shinji et al. (1982) measured the curvature of the Japanese garden path and suggested the importance of non-visual factors in the experience of the gardens.

Although there are several descriptive analyses and explanations on the fascinations of the circuit-style gardens (e.g. Watsuji,1958; Hall, 1970), there is no scientific research analyzing the aesthetic experience based upon objective data. This lack of scientific research led to our present study.

METHOD

A set of personal computer programs was developed and applied to the environmental data extracted from the survey maps of three famous circuit-style gardens in order to measure the following three aspects of sensory information: (1) ambient visual information perceived from surrounding scenes; (2) focal visual information taken when focusing on symbolic objects; and (3) non-visual information such as tactile and kinesthetic senses perceived when walking through the garden paths. The profile of each aspect was obtained by assessing consecutive points every 0.5 m (one step of a pedestrian) apart along the garden path. Then, all of the profiles of the multi-sensory information were displayed in parallel like a musical score to reveal a hidden pattern or rhythm of the sequential experience as people moved through the garden.

Garden Selection and Environmental Data Creation

Three "noted" gardens were selected after considering the size and the era in which they were built: Katsura-rikyu villa, Shugakuin-rikyu villa (only the upper area was used in this study), and Saiho-ji temple (Figures 37.1 to 37.3). For convenience sake, we shall call them hereafter as Katsura, Shugakuin, and Saiho-ji respectively. The survey maps of these gardens (Shigemori, 1971; Shigemori, 1976; Takahashi et al., 1978) were used to generate the following data.

(a) Land configuration data and site plan data
Based on the survey map, the graphic data of land configuration was created in the frame memory of a personal computer by using an image scanner and CAD. The land height differences in every 0.5 m (1.0 m in the case of Shugakuin) change was identified by coded colors as shown in Figure 37.4. As for the site plan, building shapes and borders between different land covering materials were first drawn on the display, and then painted according to a color code to identify building height and land covering materials such as path, grass, and water as shown in Figure 37.5.

(b) Observation points data
The data of observation points (location and direction of movement) was created along the garden path every 0.5 m (one step of a pedestrian) apart.

Figure 37.1 Katsura-rikyu villa.

Figure 37.2 Shugakuin-rikyu villa.

Figure 37.3 Saiho-ji temple.

(c) Tree data

Trees in the site were first classified into 14 types (7 different shapes, two different kinds: indeciduous and deciduous trees) with reference to the Landscape Handbook (JILA, 1978). Tree data such as its type, size of crown and location was then put into computer memory. Figure 37.6 shows the indeciduous tree data in Katsura.

(d) Symbolic elements data

Graphic data was created in the frame memory for the symbolic elements (tea pavilions, gates, bridges and others) in the gardens which would attract the attention of people who walk through the garden.

(e) Garden path texture data

Graphic data was created for the garden path textures which were classified into 10 types such as soil, gravel, or stepping-stones as shown in Figure 37.7.

MEASUREMENT AND DESCRIPTION OF SENSORY INFORMATION

Ambient Visual Information

In a previous study by one of the authors, a personal computer program was developed to assess an array of visual surfaces which surround an observer (Ohno, 1991). A part of this program was improved to apply to the Japanese garden. The measurement procedure of the program is as follows.

(1) From the observation point around which the visual state is to be assessed, a scanning line is drawn in each of the colored site plans on the display, and the land height, land covering materials and building heights along the line are identified by color code.

(2) With this data, a vertical section along the scanning line is drawn on the other plane of the display. Using the tree data, a vertical section of trees cut along the scanning line is calculated and drawn on the above obtained section. In this section, many scanning lines radiate from the station point at eye level (1.5 m high). Each of the scanning lines extends until it reaches the outline of the sectional surfaces and reads the color code to identify whether it is, for instance, a path, building, water or tree. At the same time, the length of the scanning line is calculated (see Figure 37.8).

(3) These operations are repeated by changing the azimuth of the scanning line by five degrees until all directions around the station point have been assessed.

(4) A chart is generated which shows the array of visible surfaces of various components. Figure 37.9 shows an example of the results of these assessments. Two numerical measures were taken from the charts relevant to ambient information: a ratio (%) of total area of solid angle for each visible component and a measure of spatial volume shown by mean distance (m) from the surrounding surfaces.

Figure 37.4 Land configuration plan data in Katsura.

Figure 37.5 Site plan in Katsura.

Figure 37.6 Tree data: evergreen trees in Katsura.

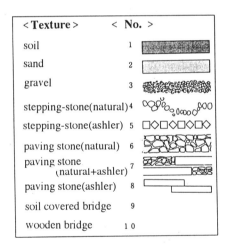

Figure 37.7 Classified textures of the garden path.

432

Figure 37.8 An example of the measuring process section analysis.

Figure 37.9 An example of the assessment results.

The program was applied to a sequence of observation points along a typical path in the gardens. Figure 37.10 shows a part of the result which describes changing profiles of the solid angle for some visible components as we move through consecutive points every 0.5 m apart. Figure 37.11 shows a profile of the spatial volume. This figure, as an example, shows a sequence of the garden path from the Maple Path to Shokin-tei, a tea pavilion in Katsura. Leaving from the Maple Hill (a decrease of visible solid angle of deciduous trees), we pass through the Cycas Hillock, which is in front of a roofed bench, (an increase of building and decrease of indeciduous trees). Soon we begin to see the garden pond (a gradual increase of water surfaces). By following the pond side path we pass under the maple tree (an increase of deciduous trees) and cross a stone bridge until finally we reach the open space in front of Shokin-tei (an increase of the spatial volume).

Focal Visual Information

The presence of symbolic elements in the visual field strongly affects spatial experiences in the garden. It depends upon their visibility rather than on how large they appear because these symbolic elements tend to attract the attention to people who move through the garden. Using the data, (a), (b), and (d), a program was developed which could identify visible elements and measure both direction and distance .

As an example, Figure 37.12 shows the case of Shokin-tei's visibility of the Miyuki-lane from the Miyuki-gate to Shoin, main house, in Katsura. In this figure, the direction where the element can be seen is shown by the relative angles from the direction of movement (top), and its distance (bottom). The distance 0 m in the bottom figure indicates that the element cannot be seen. In this example, one can peep at Shokin-tei 90 degrees to the left through the Maple Path for several steps after the 155 step-point. Upon reaching the soil covered arched bridge, one can see it again over the hedge from the raised viewpoint. As one follows the garden path which turns to the left, it now appears again in the front. The visual line to the Shokin-tei then moves to the left when one makes a turn to enter the Chumon gate.

Every symbolic element in the garden was measured in the same way. This data, having both distance and direction, is regarded as the vector of visual line which connects the observation point and the focal element. The vector is drawn on the site map by an arrow.

Non-visual Information

The senses of touch and pressure experienced by foot when we walk through garden paths of different surfaces and the motion or kinesthetic sense experienced when following the change of the direction and the height of garden paths are also significant factors of the sequential experience. Thus, we developed a program which could identify changes of texture, altitude and directions of garden paths.

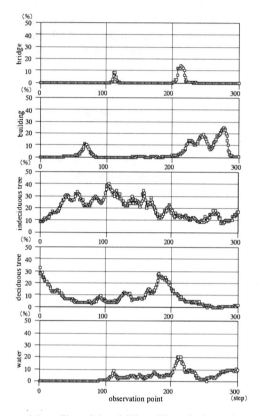

Figure 37.10 Sequential profiles of the visible solid angle for each component.

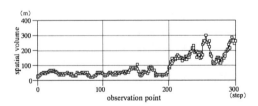

Figure 37.11 Sequential profiles of the spatial volume.

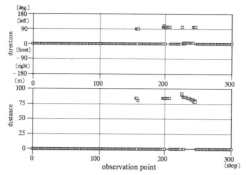

Figure 37.12 Sequential changes of visibility of Shokin-tei in Katsura.

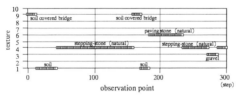

Figure 37.13 Sequential texture changes in the path.

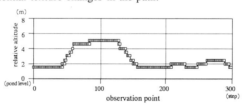

Figure 37.14 Sequential relative altitude changes in the path.

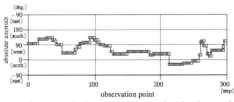

Figure 37.15 Sequential directional changes of the path (absolute azimuth).

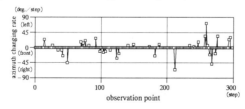

Figure 37.16 Sequential directional changes of the path (azimuth changing rate).

(i) Textures of the garden path

Ground textures were measured by using the observation point data (b) and the garden path textures data (c). Figure 10 is an example showing the garden path from the soil covered bridge in the Valley of Firefly to Shoin through Shoka-tei, a tea pavilion. The numerical value of the vertical axis of this figure is a classification number shown in Figure 4. This figure clearly shows the changes of textures from the soil covered bridge, soil, stepping-stones, soil covered bridge, soil, and finally to the paving stone.

(ii) Height differences of the garden path

The changes of relative altitude as we move through the garden path were measured by using the observation points data (b) and the land configuration data (d). Figure 37.14 shows up-and-down changes of the garden paths in the vertical axis by a relative altitude (m) to the garden pond level. This figure shows changes from the soil covered bridge to Shoka-tei on the top of the small hill which is raised 5m from the garden pond level, and then goes down to the Shoin. It can also show the pitch of an upward and downward slope.

(iii) Direction of garden path

The direction of movement along the garden path was measured in absolute azimuth (north: 0 degree) by using the observation point data (b). In addition, it was expressed by the relative azimuth difference from the previous point (right: +, left:-) in order to show the curvature of the garden path. Figures 37.15 and 37.16 show examples of a result by absolute azimuth (degree), and by the azimuth changing rate (degree/step) respectively. This example shows that it first makes a turn to the left from the soil covered bridge in the Valley of Firefly, then turns to the right, then passes in front of Shoka-tei along the gentle curve, then curves gently to the right, then proceeds practically in a straight path to Shoin, then turns to the right in front of Shoin, and finally swings largely to the right and to the left.

CONCLUSION

This paper proposes a method of measurement for the multi-sensory information in the environment. It was applied to consecutive observation points along the garden paths to measure ambient visual information, focal visual information and non-visual information based upon environmental data extracted from the survey map. Thus, profiles of multi-sensory variables were obtained for each garden.

In order to formulate general rules of spatial arrangements in the garden, further examination of the profiles is necessary concerning the patterns of periodic appearances of each variable and the correlation between variables. Although the present study is still in its infant stage, the method proposed here may be a useful tool for environmental researchers and designers to evaluate the quality of the environment based on objective data.

References

Funakoshi, T., Tsumita, H. & Shimizu, M. (1988): A study of partitive point-analysis and physical-analysis on approach spaces of SHINTO Shrines, Study on approach space of SHINTO Shrines (Part 1) , Proceeding of the Journal of Archit. Plann. Environ. Engng, AIJ, No.384, pp. 55-62. (In Japanese)

Hall, E. T. (1966) : The Hidden Dimension, NY, Doubleday, pp. 51-52.

JILA. (1978) : Zoen Handbook (Landscape Handbook) , Giho-do, pp. 356-347. (In Japanese)

Kitamura, K., Kawasaki, M. & Sasaki, T. (1989): Description of sequence landscape by analogy of music style, Proceeding of the Journal Conference of JJSCE, pp. 252-253. (In Japanese)

Miyagishi, Y. & Zaino, H. (1993) : The relation on sequence of landscape between open-close, impact in space, and walker behavior in landscape : A study on visual sequence of landscapes from the view point of walker behavior in landscape, Proceeding of the Journal of Archit. Plann. Environ. Engng, AIJ, No.440, pp. 119-125. (In Japanese)

Miyauji, K. (1992) : A study on the sequence of visual environment with human movement. Part 1: Case study on shopping malls, Proceeding of the Journal of Archit. Plann. Environ. Engng, AIJ, No.440, pp. 99-109. (In Japanese)

Ohno, R. (1991) : Ambient vision of the environmental perception: Describing ambient visual information, Proceeding of EDRA22, pp. 237-252.

Rapoport, A. (1977) : Human Aspects of Urban Form, New York: Pergamon Press, pp. 195-201.

Sigemori, M. (1976) : Jissokuzu Nihon-teien (Survey Map of Japanese Garden) , Seibun-do, p. 13. (In Japanese)

Shigemori, M. (1978) : Zoku Jissokuzu Nihon-teien (sequel to Survey Map of Japanese Garden) Seibun-do, p. 49, p. 66. (In Japanese)

Sinji, I. (1982) : Studies on characteristics of Japanese gardens : On the scale analysis and the basic modules of the garden a spaces, Proceeding of the Journal of the Japanese Institute of Landscape Architects, No.4, Vol.5, pp. 236-246. (In Japanese)

Takahashi, R., Ide, H., Watanabe, S., Kameyama, A., Katuno, T. & Koshizumi, H. (1986) : Zoen-gaku (Landscape architecture) , Asakura-shoten, p. 72. (In Japanese)

Thiel, P. (1970) Notes on the description, scaling notation and scoring of some perceptual and cognitive attributes of the physical environment, (H. M. Proshansky et al. eds.), Environmental Psychology, the City University of New York, pp. 593-619.

Watsuji , T. (1958) : KATSURA-RIKYU, Chuo-koron. (In Japanese)

Zaino, H. & Miyagishi, Y. (1992) : Relation of sequence landscape of fundamental space structure and sequence landscape of visual behavior, Proceeding of the Journal of Archit. Plann. Environ. Engng, AIJ, No.438, pp. 79-85. (In Japanese)

38

From rationalism to romanticism in landscape architecture: a German phenomenon?

Du rationalisme au romantisme en architecture paysagiste: un phénomene allemand?

Joachim Wolschke-Bulmahn and Gert Groening

Cet exposé a deux objectifs. Le premier est de remettre en question la présomption selon laquelle le jardinage est une activité apolitique, en soulevant quelques points sur les développements politiques, économiques, sociaux et scientifiques dans le secteur de la conception de jardins en Allemagne au début du 20ème siècle. En deuxième lieu, nous montrons comment s'est opérée la transition entre l'approche rationnelle de la conception et l'approche romantique. Nous faisons référence à des exemples en Allemagne; le pays est passé, en un demi-siècle, des dernières années de sa période impériale, s'achevant en 1918, à son premier gouvernement démocratique (1919-1933), et enfin à une dictature de douze ans, qui s'est terminée en 1945.

Notre recherche a suivi deux directions. La structure démocratique de la République de Weimar soutenait les récents développements dans la conception de jardins urbains. La rationalisation était ici un objectif prioritaire. La dictature nationale-socialiste soutenait les idées nationalistes, racistes et romantiques du "jardin naturel", concept qui a joué un rôle contradictoire dans le développement de la conception de jardins en Allemagne.

Mots clé: conception de jardins urbains; rationalisme; romantisme.
french abstract to be completed

Keywords: urban garden design, rationalism, romanticism

The paper is based on the hypothesis that changing modes of garden design do not occur incidentally and do not only reflect individual tastes of designers but are due to changing political, economic, and social conditions. If there are highly political and ideological motives behind seemingly apolitical garden design, then early 20th century Germany should provide excellent case studies. Within a few decades Germany went through an authoritarian period, the Imperial Reich, which ended in 1918, the first

Socialist dictatorship from 1933 to 1945. The impact of political and social changes on ideas of garden design should therefore be clearly recognizable in these parts of German history.

METHODS

After World War II landscape architects many of whom were involved in National Socialism, showed no interest to discuss impacts of Nazi ideology and Nazi politics on landscape architecture in general and on garden design particularly. This is the main reason why substantial works on the recent history of garden design in Germany were not published until the late 1980s and much research remains to be done still today. The analysis presented here is mainly based on the study of primary literature relating to the time under consideration. In particular contributions to important journals on garden design, such as the Gartenkunst and Gartenschoenheit were systematically searched and evaluated. Also books on garden design that reflect theoretical and practical approaches to landscape architecture in those days were examined and evaluated.

Primary literature as a source of research can offer important but somewhat insufficient insights into history. Therefore our analysis is based on additional research in archives such as the Berlin Document Center and the Federal Archive (Bundesarchiv) in Koblenz, Germany where we examined thousands of personal files and documents which allowed to focus more clearly on the ideological and political ideas various landscape architects had about the design of gardens and landscapes. Further information yielded personal interviews, which we conducted with numerous significant landscape architects who had worked professionally during the Weimar Republic and during National Socialism and who left their stamp on the development of garden design in Germany in the 1950s and 1960s.

RESULTS

In late 19th century the most important fashion in urban garden design, one that had enjoyed great popularity for several decades, was the imitation of what was seen as the English landscape garden on a tiny scale in the garden of the urban middle class. The aristocratic predecessors of these imitated "landscape" gardens had resulted from changes in the perception of nature and society as well as from changes in the economic situation of aristocratic families. To apply this garden style on a tiny scale in an urban garden did not correspond to the garden interests of the new middle class. The gardens were considered to be of limited use to their owners.

In Europe the first reactions to this unsatisfactory situation came from England.

Architects, especially those associated with the Arts and Crafts movement, demanded the application of consistent aesthetic principles to the house, its rooms and the adjacent garden which became defined as an enlarged housing space.

The influence of the Arts and Crafts architects was not limited to England (cfl. for Denmark Hauxner 1993 and Stephensen 1993, for Sweden Bucht 1985). Beginning in about 1900 they particularly influenced the development in Germany. The book "Country House and Garden", published in 1907 by the German architect Hermann Muthesius[1], had a revolutionary impact on garden design. According to Muthesius the main idea in future garden design is "that garden and house are a unit of which the main features must be thought out by the same genius...The corresponding aim in the smaller house garden is to replace the landscape garden with the formal garden" (Muthesius 1907:XXV)[2]. Peter Behrens, also an architect, described how this new garden type became formally separated into distinct garden units: "What we want today also for the garden is a genuine room. It should shelter us as does a house or the rooms of the house, which complement one another and work together. This will lead automatically to the three-dimensional arrangement of the garden. We recognize the unthought-of beauty of axial views, of the various levels of the terraces, of the enclosure by high and low walls...It would be highly desirable to extend formal reminiscences of the rooms of the house into the garden" (Behrens 1930:17).

Members of the emerging profession of landscape architecture soon took part in the discussion of how to raise the standards of garden design (cf. Wolschke-Bulmahn and Groening 1988). After 1900 numerous articles and books were published in Germany carrying programmatic titles such as "Gardens of Today", "The German Garden", and "The Modern Garden". In 1908 a competition to predict future developments in garden design was organized by the magazine "The Week".

This development towards a more rational design of gardens came to a temporary halt, however, with the beginning of World War I, which caused considerable social, political, and economic changes in Europe. In Germany it brought about the end of the Imperial period marked by the forced resignation of the last emperor Wilhelm II.

The following period of the first democracy in Germany exposed great social and political tensions and contrasts. Nationalism and racism were opposed to internationalism and socialism. Romantic and emotional harking back to a preindustrial society stood against progressive and rational assessment of technological advancement. Also there was a deep disappointment because of the breakdown of the Imperial Reich. On the other, large groups of the population in Germany hoped for a democratic, social, and even socialistic future with more personal freedom, more political power and greater rights for the lower social groups. Scientific progress should transmit social progress. If the same rationality which yielded the fascinating results of scientific progress would guide society then social progress would be inevitable.

These attitudes were also reflected in garden design. There were proponents of

442

a rational and future-oriented approach as well as advocates of a garden design based on reactionary ideas about society who pleaded for romanticism in garden design.

It is difficult to categorize unambiguously these developments in the field of garden design in the 1920s in Germany. Expressionist concepts, like the one of the "coming garden" presented by landscape architect Gustav Allinger at the "Jubilee-Horticulture-Exhibition" in Dresden, Saxonia in 1926, stood besides symbolist, cubist and functionalist approaches.

The new political order established in the Weimar Republic was associated with "New Realism" in architecture and garden design. As one part of mass housing programmes initiated by city administrations and building co-operatives, concepts for small productive gardens (and parks) (see Migge 1930) were developed in order to improve the housing situation especially for lower income groups.

The stimulating effects and the aspirations which came with the introduction of democracy should also bring art into everyday life. So the rational schemes designed for these gardens took aesthetic considerations into account also (cf. Groening and Wolschke-Bulmahn 1985). Leberecht Migge, a strong proponent of these gardens set clear priorities: "To open up the path for many gardens, for the garden of everybody - that is the genuine garden architecture we need. For that not so much aesthetic abilities and learned disciplinary formulae are required, but rather knowledge of people's economy and the social and technical conditions, this is the basis which brings gardens into existence" (Migge 1927:64). Being aware of the bad living conditions for many, Migge suggested to apply advanced gardening techniques in the "New Garden" which "will be a productive garden, a work garden and...a glass garden" (Migge 1927:65). For Migge glass symbolized a highly technical garden. This may have been inspired by expressionism, which had taken one of the architects of "New Realism", Bruno Taut, "to the hight of Alpine peaks with his Scheerbartian version of a world of coloured glass and concrete" (Sharp 1966).

Landscape architect Georg Georgsen thought about garden types (Georgsen 1923:27) and a garden theory which would be easy to understand for everybody. The types of gardens should be in accordance with aesthetic, economic, and social needs of the people. Similarly another Danish landscape architect, Gudmund Nyeland Brandt, whose thoughts were also published in the German journal "Gartenkunst" in the 1920s, advised that "the garden should be inexpensive to lay out...easy to maintain...usable...a toy...(and)...should meet the delight in flowers" (Brandt 1927:92). With his fourth demand -the garden as a toy- Brandt rejected both a garden "in which the main focus is formal" and also "a garden which consists of delicately matching plant associations" (Brandt 1927:92) and reintroduced into gardens for everybody what had been an unquestioned part of earlier gardens but had become explained away in the productive gardens for less affluent people, pleasure. His own design for what he called the "coming garden" perhaps best illustrates his ideas.

Whereas Brandt's approach to the garden for everybody opened up a new perspective, landscape architects Gustav Allinger and Otto Valentien felt the garden perspective, landscape architects Gustav Allinger and Otto Valentien felt the garden should allow for experiments and expressionism as architects Bruno Taut (cf. Volkmann 1980) and Hans Scharoun (cf. Pfankuch 1974, 19932) had shown with their sketches of utopian projects. Valentien's demand that landscape architects should "designate expressionism simply as the 'New'" (Valentien 1924:17) is rather meaningless and conceals his artistic qualification[3]. The attempts to be avant-garde were caricatured by the architect Alwin Seifert, who had turned to landscape architecture .

Other garden architects, such as Georg Belá Pniower, Wilhelm Hirsch, Hans Friedrich Pohlenz, Heinrich Schmitz, and Heinz Wichmann, tried to strip garden design of romanticism (cf. for example Wichmann 1924). So did the architect Ernst May, who interpreted his home and garden as a unit. Neither garden nor house should be understood as works of art, "but as a beautifully designed community" (Schuster 1928:168).

In a book on modern gardens and terrasses by the French architect Andre Lurcat, May's garden was included (Lurcat n.y. 1929?). Lurcat's collection clearly demonstrated that rationalism in garden design was not restricted to Germany. Even more important, Lurcat presented in his book a way to design gardens, which seems to have drawn attention in Germany. A few weeks after an article (cf. Winternitz 1930) on Lurcat's garden had been published in the German journal "Gartenschoenheit", landscape architect Wilhelm Huebotter published his redesign of the same garden in a more romantic way (cf. Huebotter 1930).

It seems as if such French rationalist examples of garden design were more provocative to German romantic and expressionist landscape architects than were those of their rationalist German contemporaries. Valentien for example commented on a Lurcat and a Corbusier garden: "The results of both design principles remain strange to us; the result is no garden, but a piece of decoration or shapeless side by side placements of plants and paths" (Valentien 1930:104).

With the end of the Weimar Republic and the rise of National Socialism the meaning of an assumed emotional connection between nature, soil, German landscapes, and German people, i.e. German blood, gained considerable ideological authority. The new "romanticism" in landscape architecture fitted nicely into this ideology.

With the concept of a "nature garden", which had been advocated much earlier by the garden architect Willy Lange, many professionals tried to fight rational and international trends in garden design. A genuinely German garden style should become created. In England the garden writer William Robinson and others searched for the truely English garden. In France Andrɵ Vera looked for the true French garden. In the United States of America the landscape architects Jens Jensen and Wilhelm Miller tried to pull away from the garden design of the Old World and wanted to establish a genuinely American garden style which would be clearly distinguishable from European garden design.

In Germany this development in garden design turned into a radical nationalistic movement during national socialism. According to Alwin Seifert, who had introduced the term "rootedness to the soil" into garden design, the struggle between "rootedness in the soil and supra-nationality" was "a fight between two opposing Weltanschauungen: on one side the striving for supra-nationality, for levelling down of huge areas, and on the other the elaboration of the peculiarities of small living spaces, emphasizing that which is rooted in the soil" (Seifert 1930:162f). Seifert probably echoed Lange, who some years earlier had praised the "re-discovery of so-called folk art; the stressing of one's own folk character - in opposition to the glorification of the international, in reality non-national" (Lange 1928:14). Here nationalistic thinking is evident in the seemingly apolitical field of landscape architecture.

From 1933 on, freedom to experiment in the field of garden design no longer existed. Solutions that could be interpreted by National Socialists as "degenerated", un-German or peculiar could endanger one's career, one's freedom, and even one's life. Landscape architect Erik Pepinski, for example, was no longer allowed to work as such under the Nazis, because his wife was of "fully Jewish origin"[4] .

Where romanticism still would have allowed for sensations in a garden, garden design according to National Socialism resulted in a programmatic decline unknown before. The first national garden show under the Nazis was held in summer 1933 in Hannover, Lower Saxony, under the title "Year's Exhibition of German Garden Culture". "Of all the great German garden exhibitions" as the leading Nazi landscape architect Heinrich Wiepking full-mouthedly wrote, he "liked that in Hannover most" and praised it because "nothing had happened there" (Wiepking-Juergensmann 1933:162).

Some of the landscape architects who had tried for a rational approach towards garden design had to emigrate in 1933 or later, were persecuted by the Nazis, were barred from practising as landscape architects or otherwise lost their influence on professional development. After 1945 they could not regain their former status.

Rational and critical analyses of the social and historical meanings of gardens are needed. Rather than to glorify individual landscape architects, their ideologies and works should be scrutinized. That could be part of the foundation upon which an international future of everyday gardens in democratic societies may evolve.

Bibliography

-BEHRENS, Peter 1930: Neue Sachlichkeit in der Gartenformung,
Jahrbuch der Arbeitsgemeinschaft fuer Gartenkultur, Berlin
-BRANDT, Gudmund Nyeland 1927: Vom kommenden Garten, Die
Gartenkunst, 40, 89-93

-BUCHT, Eivor 1985: The Naturalistic Tradition in Swedish
Urban Landscape Design, GROENING, Gert (ed.), Open Space
Planning and Open Space Politics, 7-20, Hannover
-GEORGSEN, Georg 1923: Der moderne Garten als Gartentyp, Die
Gartenkunst, 36, 24-27
-GROENING, Gert and Joachim WOLSCHKE-BULMAHN 1985: Zur
Entwicklung und Unterdrueckung von freiraumplanerischen
Ansaetzen der Weimarer Republic, Das Gartenamt, 34, 6,
443-458
-HAUXNER, Malene 1993: Fantasiens Have, Copenhagen
-HUEBOTTER, Wilhelm 1930: An die Schriftleitung der
Gartenkunst, Die Gartenkunst, 43, 7, 105-106
-LANGE, Willy 1928: Gartengestaltung der Neuzeit, Leipzig
-LURCAT, André n.y. (1929?): Terrasses et Jardins, Paris
-MIGGE, Leberecht 1930: Rentable Parks, Zentralblatt der
Bauverwaltung, 50, 4, 93-97
-MIGGE, Leberecht 1927: Der kommende Garten, Gartenschoenheit,
8, 64-65
-MUTHESIUS, Hermann 1907: Beispiele neuzeitlicher Landhaeuser
nebst Grundrissen, Innenraeumen und Gaerten, Munich
-PFANKUCH, Peter (ed.) 1974, 1993: Hans Scharoun, Bauten,
Entwuerfe, Texte, Schriftenreihe der Akademie der Kuenste,
Band 10, Berlin
-SCHUSTER, Fritz 1928: Der Garten am Wohnhaus Stadtrat May,
Die Gartenkunst, 41, 161-168
-SEIFERT, Alwin 1930, Bodenstaendige Gartenkunst, Die
Gartenkunst, 43, 10, 162-164
-SHARP, Dennis 1966: Modern Architecture and Expressionism,
New York
-STEPHENSEN, Lulu Salto 1993: Tradition og Fornyelse i Dansk
Havekunst, Lund, Sweden
-VALENTIEN, Otto 1930: Neuzeitliche Gartengestaltung, Die
Gartenkunst, 43, 104-105
-VALENTIEN, Otto 1924: Expressionismus und Gartenkunst, Die
Gartenkunst, 37, 17-19; 46-47
-VOLKMANN, Barbara (ed.) 1980: Bruno Taut 1880-1938, Akademie
der Kuenste, Akademie-Katalog 128, Berlin
-WICHMANN, Heinz 1924: Ein Wohngarten, Gartenschoenheit, 5,
169-171
-WIEPKING-JUERGENSMANN, Heinrich Friedrich 1933: Jahresschau
Deutscher Gartenkultur Hannover, Gartenschoenheit, 14, 9,
162-167
-WINTERNITZ, Lonia 1930: Ein franzoesischer Hausgarten,
Gartenschoenheit, 11, 5, 88-89

-WOLSCHKE-BULMAHN, Joachim und Gert GROENING 1988: 1913-1988,
75 Jahre Bund Deutscher Landschafts-Architekten (BDLA),
Teil 1, Zur Entwicklung der Interessenverbaende der
Gartenarchitekten in der Weimarer Republik und im
Nationalsozialismus, BDLA (ed.), Bonn

Notes

1 Muthesius had been assigned to the German embassy in London
  solely to study modern English architecture and house
  -building
2 The idea of a unit of house and garden takes up an old
  motive in Italian garden architecture, masterly displayed
  in the 16th century house and garden of Villa d'Este in
  Tivoli, e.g.
3 Later in his life Valentien gave up landscape architecture
  and turned to painting only
4 see file of the ReichsChamber of Fine Arts, in which
  everyone who wanted to work as a landscape architect during
  National Socialism had to be enrolled

39

The allotment garden as a countryhouse garden

Les jardins ouvriers et les jardins de maisons de campagne

Gert Groening et Uwe Schneider

L'objectif de l'exposé est de montrer comment les jardins ouvriers urbains sont devenus, pendant une période assez courte, une partie importante de l'architecture paysagiste. Ce qui pourrait être interprété comme un processus de démocratisation - un projet "populaire" attirant un certain intérêt - est en fait ambivalent. Par exemple, le "Schrebergarten" de Leipzig, en Saxonie, préconisait une idée bourgeoise du jardin avec une conception relativement élaborée et impliquait une attitude de loisirs. En outre, la notion de "culture de jardin" a été le point de départ d'une théorie exigeant un jardin ouvrier utile et beau. Cette revendication, ainsi que l'incorporation de caractéristiques des jardins bourgeois, s'est révélée inadéquate pour la plupart des usagers du prolétariat.

Mots clé: jardin ouvrier; conception; signification sociale.

Keywords: allotment garden, design, social meaning

By the end of the 19th century two different kinds of allotment gardens had developed (Brando 1965: 12-19, Groening 1974: 9-15, Goettlicher 1981: 16-17). One had emerged as a concomitant of industrial development in large cities during the last decades of the 19th century. This "Laubengarten", was proletarian and had to serve primarily to secure survival. Some years earlier and under completely different economic and historical circumstances the "Schrebergarten" of Leipzig had come into existence. It was a type of allotment garden with a solid infrastructure for all gardens and the community of the garden tenants. The founders of allotment gardens elsewhere, for example at Breslau, Silesia, refered to the "Schrebergarten" idea in Leipzig (Dannenberg 1901: 118-119). The location, the infrastructure, and the rents point to relatively wealthy tenants. The design of the individual gardens shows similarities to contemporary designs for house and villa gardens (Hampel 19022: 1). Such lots were good for amateur gardening and leisurly pursuit. In Stettin petty bourgeois and bourgeois people (teachers and public servants) had rented the gardens (Schulze 1909: 61-66).

Allotment gardening was only a side issue in the bourgeois garden journals around 1900. Proletarian gardens were not mentioned or if so were depreciated because of the improvised impression they gave. This, however, would change soon. During and after World War I allotment gardens became a topic which attracted leading garden designers of the time. From the Weimar Republic up to present their design was characterised by a middle-class attitude which demanded order and beauty for these gardens. The allotment garden was, subtilizely expressed, regarded as a country house garden. At the same time this attitude prevented a self-determinated proletarian garden-culture.

METHODS

The research is based on a systematic analysis of books and articles which relate to theoretical and practical approaches in garden design during the first half of the 20th century in Germany. The theoretical concept of the higher evaluation of allotment gardens is explained by the work of two leading garden architects before World War I. The middle-class oriented tendencies in allotment garden design after World War I and II can be better understood on this basis.

RESULTS

"Garden Culture", the contribution by Leberecht Migge

In his book "Garden culture of the XXth century" (Gartenkultur des XX. Jahrhunderts) Migge developed a theoretical frame for open space planning which should relate to the interests of low-income groups of the population. He demanded a garden for everybody. The garden was to become a "social matter" (Migge 1913: 153). Also allotment gardens were supposed to become part of city planning and receive long-term leases. His programme envisaged a promising development for allotment gardens. It even bore a utopian vision of a better future, since allotment gardens would be a step towards a "new, more just, and more beautiful community of people" (Migge 1913: III).

The main demands of Migge's "Garden Culture" were formulated in an article in 1911. Migge seceded from historical "aristocratic" and from contemporary garden art, which he named "superficial and decorative" (Migge 1911: 108). For him garden art should become part of culture, should dedicate itself to real life and real issues. As "garden culture" it should "serve the real use of a new individual" (Migge 1911: 108). Before one could plan and implement real issues, such as allotment gardens and public parks, preliminary examinations would have to be made which were outside the genuine artistic process of designing. Plans would have to be scrutinized for their economic and social fundaments. Ultimately "garden culture" would have to be subordinated to national issues. It should become " a true daughter of greater Germany and its cultural mission" (Migge 1911: 110).

It is surprising to learn that a traditionally educated landscape architect considered "economic and social factors" for the solution of issues. Likewise it is surprising that horticulture was given a role in the context of a "Greater Germany", the "Germany of the future and of its cultural mission" (Migge 1911: 110).

As Migge had pointed out in his book he felt encouraged in this project by the architect Hermann Muthesius. After a seven-year residence in England, Muthesius had become a well known expert for contemporary development in villa architecture as well as villa garden architecture. Migge's book, "Gartenkultur des XX. Jahrhunderts", leaned toward the planning principles described by Muthesius (Migge 1913: 58-63). The "Deutscher Werkbund" - an arts and crafts association Migge had joined in 1912 (Jahrbuch des Deutschen Werkbundes 1912: n.p.; see "Mitgliederverzeichnis") - and its programme which had been essentially developed by Muthesius, was of fundamental significance for the "garden culture".

The consideration of economic and social factors for the programme of "garden culture" were literally taken from a speech Hermann Muthesius had given at the first annual meeting of the "Deutscher Werkbund" in 1908 in Munich (Verhandlungen des Deutschen Werkbundes 11. und 12. Juni 1908: 41-53).

With respect to allotment gardens, two basic assumptions were important. First of all, Muthesius believed "mass production" to be inevitable. He demanded, however, that its "quality must rise". Secondly, Muthesius, assisted by the "Deutscher Werkbund", demanded a "new design for all human ways of expression". This should follow "the innate need of humans for beauty". The egalitarian programme of "garden culture", i.e. gardens for everybody, was comparable to the goal of the German Werkbund to establish a mass culture. The "products" of "garden culture" had to be designed "useful and beautiful" (Migge 1913: 6; cf. Groening 1992).

A plan by Migge for Ruestringen shows that Migge's egalitarian claim was not far-reaching. On that costly furnished site with playgrounds, water areas, sports- and tennis grounds, open air baths etc. (Westheim 1914: 181-182), the allotment gardens were named "Schreber- und Buergergaerten", i.e. "Schreber- and Citizen's gardens". Migge had explained the term "Buergergarten" in his aforementioned book. Such gardens should provide for "the higher social strata of our work centers, like civil servants, craftsmen, and small trade". He also mentioned that "these leased gardens would most likely be somewhat larger, more solid and more decorated, equivalent to the stronger economic power of this stratum" (Migge 1913: 9).

"The German people's park", the contribution by Harry Maasz

The landscape architect Harry Maasz is another significant representative of a new, seemingly "egalitarian" concept of open space planning. Maasz introduced himself to the field of "social" open space planning in 1911 with a newspaper article on "zoning plan and allotment gardens" (Bebauungsplan und Laubenkolonie) (Maasz 1911). He demanded allotment gardens be included in zoning plans in order to secure their long-term existence. Looking at the design and his explanations, his "social" attitude requires some further comments.

The design Maasz presented for Hamburg in 1911 contains a complicated system of roads and paths with many place-like amplifications and a large number of differently sized lots (Maasz 1913: 26). Several alleys cut the irregular site at oblique angles. Two play grounds, a grove, and a decorated area form the center. Further small places relate to various buildings and separated groups of lots. The allotment gardens themselves are of a most varied shape. Maasz had taken into account already existing paths on the site. His system of paths as well as the numerous place-like openings were consciously aimed at a more complicated structure of the project. In an earlier study of 1908 he had designed a place in a garden city as "artistic city planning" would have it. He designed this project with "the example of old city landscaspes" in mind "with their salient and receding corners, which lend them picturesque beauty" (Maasz 1908: 38). Maasz had argued for a "more beautiful" image of the city (cf. Sitte 1889: 186), ultimately a merely aethestic perspective, which would stress the economy and the financial feasibility of the above mentioned project in Hamburg.

In 1913 Maasz published a programmatic piece "The German people's park of the future" (Maasz 1913). In it he wanted to show the path to "deal with the wants of the garden-hungry people". His attempt to deduce this people's park idea from a seemingly "German garden life in the Middle Ages" (Maasz 1913: 5) reveals Maasz' retrospective attitude which also served to refuse contemporary attempts to profit from park politics in America and in England. Maasz cited as model sites the allotment gardens in Leipzig, Lueneburg, and Kiel and praised them as "exemplary in their rich aesthetic values" (Maasz 1913: 13; 23). He had provided his "people's park of the future" for the working classes of the urban population, for "low civil servants and workers" (Maasz 1913: 11). Nevertheless he also looked after more affluent groups of the urban population, for whom he demanded a so-called "Laubenpark", i.e. a park with allotment gardens, in "better-off" city quarters (Maasz 1913: 11). For the specific design of the allotment gardens he refered to the model subdivision and use of plants in farmers' gardens (Maasz 1913: 60-61). His closeness to the German Werkbund to which he belonged since 1913 (Jahrbuch des Deutschen Werkbundes 1913: n.p.; see "Mitgliederverzeichnis"), is expressed in his attempt to connect "the shape of usefulness with the shape of beauty".

Maasz' blue prints for allotment gardens demonstrate the idea of a "beautiful" garden (Mahn 1917: 54-60). His design for an "allotment garden as a play garden" (Laubengarten als Spielgarten) of 1914 has the character of a garden for leisure or a house garden with a small productive section quite similar to the garden of a single family home. Flower beds accompany the entrance path sided by a large recreation meadow, interpreted as separate space bordered by a hedge and additionally planted decorative shrubs. Close to the arbour (Laube), flowers decorate the space. On one side, a bench and a sand box is provided, on the other side a gymnastics area. Behind the arbour, another separate "room" is located, again bordered by high hedges, named "air and sun bath". The productive garden proper with vegetable beds, small livestock sheds, compost, espalier fruit, and a neighbouring apple tree copmprise about one sixth of the entire garden space.

Similarly, the design for an "allotment garden as a flower garden" (Laubengarten als Blumengarten) of 1914 displays a residential and a decorative garden. To the side of the path there is an area bordered by hedges and a sundial in its center. The inner sides of this garden space are formed by broad flower borders. In front of the arbour there is a round sunken garden space with a seating area surrounded by a little dry wall. Finally there is a small productive garden.

Maasz designed garden spaces deliberately separated by trellises which due to their height evoked a three-dimensional impression. Like a model, the designs represent the idea of the "garden as an amplified home". The search for the right shape of the garden also questioned the functionality of the various spaces. As a result, the bourgeois programme for the rooms of a villa became imposed upon the garden. "The main point is that the garden shall be linked up to the rooms of the country house, or even shall perpetuate them" (Muthesius 1905: 25). Applied to allotment gardens, this plan would require a more precise definition of garden activities according to a bourgeois standard. In contemporary villa gardens garden elements like the air and sun bath, play grounds, gymnastics grounds, as well as costly decorative and flower gardens were quite common.

The sunken garden had been adopted from English country house gardens. The 1909 excursion to England of the "German Association for Garden Art" (Deutsche Gesellschaft fuer Gartenkunst) seems to have been particularly influential in this adoption. In German garden art, flower borders and a path accompanied by flower borders became one of the most favourite motives after this excursion. For comparatison design elements of contemporary country house gardens include: a "light and sun bath for a larger house garden by Theodor Ott (Hardt 1914: 111), a playground for a house garden by Kurt Winkelhausen (Hardt 1914: 74), a path with flower borders for a house garden by Theodor Ott (Hardt 1914: 30), a playground and a bleaching area for a garden at a house for a director by E. Hardt (Hardt 1914: 87), a sitting place surrounded by flowers for the house garden Fr. Schlenter by Theodor Ott (Hardt 1914: 34), and a lawn with a solitary sculpture, surrounded by a rose border, for the house garden of Dr. Hensch, also by Theodor Ott (Hardt 1914: 31).

Assessment of the works by Migge and Maasz

Both authors departed from a new evaluation of open spaces. With respect to Migge's "garden culture" this led to questioning the traditionally bourgeois and feudal garden art. This is significant for non-priviledged ways of gardening thus came into focus for landscape architects. Progressive at that is the interest to integrate people's parks and allotment gardens into zoning plans. However, other elements of Migge's "garden culture" point to future problems in the implementation of this programme. Consequently applied, the programme of "garden culture" demanded an optimal connection between useful shape and the beauty of a garden, thus raising the standard for allotment garden planning considerably.

Migge and Maasz both refered to the model "Schrebergaerten" in Leipzig with a good infrastructure of the gardens and a well-ordered site with playgrounds, decorative places, and promenades. Massz also harked back to a tradition of bourgeois garden culture which he claimed dated back to the Middle Ages.

Migge and Maasz saw their "gardens for everybody" especially apt for civil servants, white collar workers, and more affluent members of the working class. They tried to impose their bourgeois concept of a garden as the center of family life. The idea of a people's park and of "garden culture" pretended to satisfy open space needs of less affluent people but ultimately only offered a perspective for a petty bourgeois existence in a one-family home. Within the thus "reconstituted" family lay the new significance of a non-working wife, which was contradictory to the prevailing conditions for work and living of the poor.

DISCUSSION OF THE RESULTS AND FURTHER DEVELOPMENT

Ultimately the claim for a useful and beautiful design in the "garden culture" programme proved too ambitious for a garden for everybody. This could only become achieved by improved legal, organizational and economic foundations. Legal basis for allotment gardens was reached when the KGO (Kleingarten- und Kleinpachtlandordnung), the "allotment garden and small-leaseland act" had been issued in 1919. When organizational difficulties were overcome and cities had established authorities for allotment gardening, basic structures had been created which allowed for a discussion of the difficulties involved in providing a democratic basis to allotment gardens. Nevertheless, bourgeois designers tried to implement their elitist claims. Karl Heicke, editor of the journal "Die Gartenkunst", frankly demanded that upper class attitudes should influence the allotment gardeners. Allotment gardens should be dealt with like the large private house garden: "The allotment garden is the lowest link, the large private house garden is the upper link of a succession. The same means shall be applied to all of them." (Heicke 1918: 69).

In Germany, during National Socialism, the demands for the urban integration of allotment gardens, for their uniform planning, and for their typified and aesthetically pleasing design had a political dimension. "The uniform outlook is therefore so important, because it expresses the uniform mind of all holders of allotment gardens, it is the realization of the community ideal", as Max Kaempfer, a german garden architect, had written (Kaempfer 1939: 67). Josef Pertl, director of the communal park department in Berlin demanded a number of restrictions for the design of allotment gardens: the beautiful design was decreed. Self-determined, individual design was undesired (Groening 1984: 756-758).

In German post-war development the uniform and beautiful design of allotment gardens was still esteemed. The municipalities justified the "sanitation" of aesthetically "insufficient" allotment garden colonies. Many new planned allotment gardens were planned in a uniform manner (Poblotzki 1992: 249-262). The middle-class private house garden still served as standard for the tenants of allotment gardens (Poblotzki 1992: 65-71). A self-determined allotment garden-culture instead of an overly planned one could prove to be an alternative to the development sketched here (Groening 1984: 756-758; Crouch 1993: 1-7).

Bibliography

Brando, Paul. Kleine Gaerten - einst und jetzt: Geschichtliche Entwicklung des deutschen Kleingartenwesens. Hamburg: Christen, 1965.

Crouch, David. "British Allotments: Landscapes of ordinary people". Landscape 31.3 (1993): 1-7.

Dannenberg, P. "Schrebergaerten in Breslau". Die Gartenkunst 3.6 (1901): 118-119.

Goettlicher, Manfred. Gaerten im Staedtebau. Dokumentation zum 1.-14. Bundeswettbewerb. Schriftenreihe 'Bundeswettbewerbe' des Bundesministers fuer Raumordnung, Bauwesen und Staedtebau 05.011. Bonn, 1981.

Groening, Gert. "The idea of land embellishment". Journal of Garden History, 12.3 (1992): 164-182.

Groening, Gert. Tendenzen im Kleingartenwesen dargestellt am Beispiel einer Großstadt. Landschaft und Stadt. Beiheft 10. Stuttgart: Ulmer, 1974.

Groening, Gert. "Gestaltung im Kleingarten". Das Gartenamt 33 (1984): 755-760.

Hampel, Carl. 125 kleine Gaerten: Plan, Beschreibung und Bepflanzung, entworfen und bearbeitet fuer Gaertner, Baumeister und Villenbesitzer. Berlin: Parey, 19022.

Hardt, E. Hg. Deutsche Hausgaerten. Handbuch fuer buergerliche Gartenkunst. Wiesbaden: Heimkultur-Verlag, 1914: 31.

Heicke, Karl. "Kleingartenbau und Siedlungswesen in ihrer Bedeutung fuer eine kuenftige deutsche Gartenkultur. I. Allgemeines". Die Gartenkunst 31 (1918): 64-70.

Jahrbuch des Deutschen Werkbundes 1912. Jena: Diederichs, n.p. (see "Mitgliederverzeichnis").

Jahrbuch des Deutschen Werkbundes 1913. Jena: Diederichs, n.p. (see "Mitgliederverzeichnis").

Kaempfer, Max. Der deutsche Garten, seine Geschichte, Aufgabe und Gestaltung. Grundlagen und Fortschritte im Garten- und Weinbau 52. C.F.Rudloff. Hg. Stuttgart: Ulmer, n.y. (1939): 67.

454

Maasz, Harry. "Studie zu einem Gartenstadtplatz". Die Gartenkunst 10.3 (1908): 37-39.

Maasz, Harry. "Bebauungsplan und Laubenkolonie". Neue Hamburger Zeitung. 16 September 1911.

Maasz, Harry. Der Deutsche Volkspark der Zukunft: Laubenkolonie und Gruenflaeche. Frankfurt a.O: Trowitzsch, 1913.

Mahn, H. "Kleingaerten und Kriegersiedelungen". Die Gartenkunst 30 (1917), 54-60.

Migge, Leberecht. Die Gartenkultur des XX. Jahrhunderts. Jena: Diederichs, 1913.

Migge, Leberecht. "Wirtschaft und Kunst in der Gartenkultur". Die Gartenkunst 13.6 (1911): 105-110.

Muthesius, Hermann. "Die Anlage des modernen Landhauses". Die Werkkunst 1 (1905): 25-27

Schulze, O. "Wie sind die staedtischen Anlagen fuer die Bevoelkerung praktisch nutzbar zu machen". Die Gartenkunst 11.4 (1909): 61-66.

Sitte, Camillo. Der Staedtebau nach seinen kuenstlerischen Grundsaetzen. Wien: Graeser, 1889.

Verhandlungen des Deutschen Werkbundes am 11. und 12. Juni 1908. Leipzig, n.y. (1908).

Westheim, Paul. "Sozialisierung der Gartenkunst". Die Gartenkunst 27 (1914): 181-182.

40

Nineteenth-century British attitudes toward Calcutta and Bombay

Les dispositions d'esprit britanniques du xixe siecle vis-a-vis de Calcutta et de Bombay

Swati Chattopadhay

Dans cet article, j'examine la façon dont les dispositions d'esprit britanniques vis-à-vis des indigènes Bengalis de Calcutta influencèrent la conception et la représentation de cette ville. En comparant la Calcutta du XIXe siècle à Bombay, une autre ville coloniale britannique, je soutiens que les différentes attitudes adoptées à l'égard de ces villes étaient plutot causées par l'antagonisme culturel et politique des indigènes de Calcutta par rapport à leur contemporains plus coopérateurs, les Parsis de Bombay, que par le milieu physique des deux villes.

Mots clé: Bombay; Calcutta; villes du XIXe siècle; histoire urbaine; représentation urbaine

In the nineteenth century the native Bengalis of Calcutta had a profound influence on how the city came to be represented. British attitudes towards the Bengalis permeated ways in which the city was experienced and imagined by its British rulers and thus framed the discussions and representations of the city itself. These British impressions of nineteenth century Calcutta are particularly important because they became "evidence" in the writing of the history of Calcutta and the Raj. The image-making assumes significance because this trend of portraying Calcutta continues to present times, and has deeply influenced the way insiders (Calcuttans) and outsiders (Indians as well as foreigners) see the city and its problems and prospects. To understand Calcutta, one must include that which is seen and unseen, that which is both permanent and passing. In examining the historical evidence of Calcutta much has been neglected, thus generating a static historical account, leaving too many questions unanswered.

For the purpose of studying attitudes towards Calcutta in the nineteenth century, I have chosen to discuss Calcutta in comparison with another British colonial city, Bombay. Besides, both having important colonial ports, the two cities shared similar urban characteristics, and most importantly, they both played significant roles in the larger imperial aims of the British in colonial India.

Most British impressions of Calcutta at the turn of the nineteenth century were on the whole positive. However, by the middle of the nineteenth century there seems to have been a discernible shift towards a more denigrating view of the city. Rudyard Kipling's sinister verse stuck indelibly to the city of palaces -- in popular imagination Calcutta became if not the "city of dreadful nights," then at least a city without a future. The picture the British visitors portrayed "laid emphasis on over-building and dilapidation, on disease, dirt, stench" although "such appalling living conditions characterized many nineteenth century metropolises, and even in the richest and most industrially advanced nations, cities were marked by primitive municipal services, recurrent epidemics, inadequate housing, and widespread poverty" (Evenson 1989, p.25). In contrast, after 1860 Bombay seems to have gained in esteem as a city and by the end of the 19th century has surpassed Calcutta in status. Reviewing the historiographic evidence I shall argue that the differing dispositions had primarily to do with a reading of the cultural and political aspirations of the native Calcuttans as compared to their contemporaries in Bombay, and much less to do with the physical condition of the two cities.

That an experience of a city would be infused with an impression of its people is not surprising, but the frequency with which Indians and Europeans are referred to, and the context in which they appear are significantly different in the discussions of Calcutta as compared to Bombay. For Europeans, a discussion of Calcutta and its inhabitants necessarily began with the members of their own community, supplemented with cursory remarks on a few notable Bengali zamindars, and more commonly the babus, or the clerks in government offices. Aside from the numerous servants employed in their households, it were these babus and zamindars that the Europeans typically encountered in Calcutta, and the domains of these encounters left discernible effects in the writings.

"Babu-ridden Calcutta"/ "City of Palaces"

Perhaps the best known example of portraying Calcutta through the role of its inhabitants is Kipling's verse:
> Where the cholera, the cyclone, and the crows
>> Come and go;
> Where the merchant deals in indigo and tea,
>> Hides and ghi;
> Where the babu drops inflammatory hints
>> In his prints;
> Stands a city -- Charnock made it -- packed away
>> Near a Bay --
> By the sewerage rendered fetid, by the sewer

Made impure,
By the Sunderbans unwholesome, by the swamp
Moist and damp . . .
Let the babu drops inflammatory hints
In his prints . . .
Let the City Charnock pitched on -- evil day! --
Go her way (1913, pp. 156-159).

The manner in which Kipling weaves in the issue of the babu dropping "inflammatory hints" within a narrative of the city, the seditious babu appears almost as a part of the city's physical fabric -- the very "evil" stuff the city is made of. But in the first part of the century, not so many people found Calcutta such a horrible place. What the European visitors found attractive and took pride in was clearly British Calcutta. Most visitors found the city impressive, and approaching its public buildings and palatial residences most thought it deserved the title "The city of palaces."[1] It is also clear from their descriptions that they were very conscious about the difference between the "white" town and the "black" town. The visitors mostly agreed that the black town was "dirty, crowded, ill-built, and abounding with beggars and bad smells" (Roberts 1835, p. 580), whether they ever had the occasion to visit that part of Calcutta or not.[2] In the accounts before 1830-35, references to native lifestyles in Calcutta are scant, and only appear as general descriptions of the bazaar, and more typically the scenes of Kalighat. But around 1840 specific people find place in the accounts e.g. Rammohun Roy, Dwarakanath Tagore, Radhakanta Deb, et al., and Bengalis as a social group appear in the landscape of the British imagination of Calcutta.

A visitor to Calcutta in 1857, noted that the "influence which the British sway exerts upon the higher circle of Hindoo society, and the gradual transformation which it is producing is remarkable" (Nair 1989, p.1012). He went on to say:

One of the wealthiest men in Calcutta, Tagore, of the Bramin caste, gives balls, soirees, and dinners in his palace, which in splendor and taste rival those of the governor; and the Europeans invited on such occasion, beholds, with surprise, an assembly of Hindoos conversing upon politics, science, and philosophy with a freedom, adroitness, and saneness of judgment, that would do honour to the best society in Europe (Nair, p.1013).

However, such optimism was more commonly hedged with sufficient apprehension, which found expression in two attitudes. One was the idea that although the Bengalis took to English education "as a duck takes to water," they are not fit to progress very far because of their inherent disabilities (Low 1906). The second attitude derived from the distinct social divisions that existed in Calcutta society.

The first reason for apprehension grew around the characterization of the

Bengalis, and no single person perhaps contributed more to it than Thomas Macaulay. Macaulay disliked Bengalis as much as he disliked Calcutta. His aim was to train a small group of upper class Indians in the English language and European ideas so that they could perform the role of "intermediaries" between the Raj and the native population. He did not see English education as a threat to colonial power as long as it was confined to a minority, and this minority did not overgrow their role as "intermediaries." These intermediaries in Calcutta were the Bengali babus, and Macaulay held intense contempt for this class.[3] And three quarters of a century later Sidney Low (1906) remarked along the same lines of Macaulay, putting the uncordial relationship between the babus and the English in unequivocal terms:

> The typical Bengali is the babu, the man of the clerky, semi-educated, class.
> . . He has shown little capacity of the indigenous native in Bombay for
> asserting himself successfully in trade. . . In some other parts of India . . .
> you may find plenty of Englishmen expressing real regard for the natives of
> their district. But you may be a long time in Bengal without hearing a good
> word spoken for the Bengali. The Englishman frankly does not like him, nor
> does he for any part entertain any profound affection for the English (pp.
> 212-222).

The problem with the Bengali as Low (1906) noted was more than one. They were derided for not having succeeded in business in Calcutta as the Parsis did in Bombay,[4] and with his "superficial" knowledge of the English language he was seen as suitable only as a "minor official," without reaching far in his career. He was considered clever but not brave ("if not all cowards they are certainly unwarlike"), and with his small build and bare head ("a mode which seems scarcely decent to an eye that has become habituated to the graceful folds of the many colored turban") was not "picturesque" at all "like the wild man of the North with his martial air and swashbuckling swagger, nor simple and manly like the sunburnt cultivator of the Central districts" (Low, p.222). In other words the Bengali was a problematic category that did not comfortably fit into any preconceived notion of the exotic Orient. While establishing why the Bengali "be he a peasant or pleader is not the kind of person who naturally wins his way to the Anglo-Saxon heart," Low himself cites plenty of examples which contradict the above characterizations. But in his refusal to modify the characterizations themselves, Low exposes another layer of the problem to suitably categorize the Bengali -- not all of them complied with the cowardly, sedentary, half-educated, underachiever image.

The second reason for discomfort surfaced in the writings due to the growing class differentiation in Calcutta society -- the European community's apparent disregard for any kind of social interaction with the Indians and vice versa. The few encounters are explained as curious images, or as spectacles like the dinners given by the Tagores and the"nautchs" presented by the Debs and Mullicks. A London missionary visiting Calcutta in 1848, noted:

The greater part of the English . . . evince no regard whatever to the real interests of the natives . . . provided they can accomplish their own worldly objects, and leave the country with the least possible delay. . . The measures of the government, are, by such, objects of praise, or of censure, merely as they happen to the affect the interests of the small class to which they belong; and if their opinion take the form of kindness to the natives; it is generally only when the interests of both classes happen to be the same (Nair 1989, p.929).

And in contrast to Bombay, the interests of the natives and their English rulers in Calcutta were seldom the same. Lack of common interest reflected in the nature of daily social intercourse as well. Commenting on evening drives William Russell noted in 1858:

The only spectators by the sides of the drives are Europeans. Perhaps a few sleek fat young baboos, with uncovered head, white robes which allow the brown calf and leg to be seen. . . are walking about with umbrellas under their arms; But it is evidently for the walk, and not to look at the sahibs. The high capped Parsees, who are driving about in handsome carriages are in better terms with the Europeans, as far as interchange of salutations go; but the general effect of ones impression, derived from a drive in the Calcutta Course, is, that not only is there no rapprochement between the Indian and the Englishman, but that there is some actual barrier that neither wishes to cross (pp. 960-961).

Russell's description is telling of the perceived status difference in the juxtaposition of "bareheaded" babus "walking" and the Parsi in his "handsome carriage." Although Russell does not elaborate on what these barriers were, it is evident form the accounts that the social barrier was well understood among the English inhabitants and visitors. The picture of a society becoming increasingly differentiated may seem contradictory to the earlier portrayal of a society in which the natives and Europeans were meeting on apparently equal terms (e.g. parties at the Tagore Palace). However, it is not contradictory, and the Britishers likely reconciled such apparent contradiction in one out of the two following ways. First, possibly these dinners and other displays of wealth and erudition did not threaten the English as much because they were not pervasive among the native population as a whole. These were isolated events, spectacles, which by virtue of lying outside the realm of everyday could be treated at best as amusing aberrations and not threatening the status quo. Second, one may argue that it was precisely such increasing erasure of class lines, or rather apprehension about erasure of class lines that necessitated the invention of new categories and fresh efforts to make differentiation along lines of race, in this case by stereotyping the Bengali.[5]

Such uneasiness about ambiguity in class structure echoes the mid-nineteenth century anxiety of Parisians about dissolving differences between the working class and the bourgeoisie in terms of sociability and modes of consumption.[6] This anxiety is clearly manifested in the writings of Sidney Low (1906), about his experience of "babu-ridden" Calcutta in the later part of the nineteenth century:

> Calcutta is an English city which owes its very existence to English adventure, and its greatness to English rule. We are not here inheriting past stories or treading in the steps of fallen dynasties. . .It is a great native town, too, though it is not one of which white Calcutta affects to be proud. It has the squalor of the East, without its picturesque colour -- a nest of mean streets, unpaved, dirty, and shabby, lined with dingy shops and malodorous hovels. . . There are busy thoroughfares, which are as ugly as the working-class suburbs of an English seaport. . . And there are back alleys which have the shiftless untidy aspect of Southern Europe. Native Calcutta is like some of her own citizens: she has departed from the ways of the East only to produce a very poor travesty of the West (pp. 211-221).

The passage not only sums up the various attitudes about Calcutta, it evokes a deep anxiety that the British, even after securing almost complete economic control from the Bengalis, have failed to allay all threats from the native population. Calcutta, as Low proclaims, in spite of being a very British city (and he was not the only one who thought so), has failed to meet the equation -- it kept on reminding the Englishman something familiar that he or she was not willing to encounter in this far corner of the empire. In his very characterization of native Calcutta, Low brings out, perhaps unknowingly, the crux of the problem in the British imagination of Calcutta. The city mirroring its inhabitants, was perhaps not sufficiently different from European towns.[7] While similarity of the white town with its European counterparts bred familiarity and pride, a mere semblance of working class Europe in the physical characteristics of "black" Calcutta bred not only contempt but uneasiness. This uneasiness arose from reminiscences of a part of western life that has not yet been reformed by a Victorian sense of order, and also from the inability to neatly categorize native Calcutta in a manner that unequivocally established its difference from the West, something that other Indian or Eastern cities afforded to some degree. In short, the mortification of seeing in Calcutta the image of the European working class, which in itself was a problematic category was objectionable to the Englishman.

There is, however, no evidence to support a belief that Bombay's working class neighborhoods looked much different from those of native Calcutta, but curiously, such comparison to Europe were seldom used by Britishers to describe Bombay. What Low was reacting to perhaps had little to do with the physical characteristics of the city itself, but more with the image of the people he had -- half European, producing "a very poor travesty of the west." While Kipling's verse implied that the "pestilential" nature of the town was an essential characteristic of Calcutta, and that such a city is doomed by its very nature, Low makes no such claim. In his very acknowledgment of its similarity to European towns, he indicates the underlying reason why such similarity is abhorrent.

In contrast Bombay did not excite such extreme reaction. Although not as splendid as Calcutta in the early nineteenth century, Bombay was considered more picturesque by many. Bombay, a seaport, did have a distinct physical advantage of a natural harbor over a city like Calcutta with its port located far inland. But there were other qualities about Bombay that European visitors found delightful, in spite of its lack of grand architecture in the early days of the nineteenth century.[8]

Bombay -- "A place of generous people"[9]

Norman Macleod visiting Bombay in 1838 thought the city was ill-equipped in terms of architecture, and its bazaars contained scarcely "anything more picturesque than calico," and yet he acknowledged that the city "deserved" better and did not fail to mention the merchants of Bombay who were most liberal "in the exercise of princely hospitality," and "in subscribing to useful institutions" (p.24). In spite of their great wealth (they along with the rest of the native mercantile community owned most of Bombay), the Parsis were considered amiable because of their lenient customs (compared to those of Hindus or Muslims) and because of their philanthropy.[10] Similarly, most memoirs of nineteenth century Bombay are profusely punctuated with affectionate memories of its wealthy mercantile class, who seemed to personify the city itself. In many ways this was justified, because the Parsis were the pioneers in Bombay, and maintained their commercial foothold till the later parts of the nineteenth century, when Bombay finally developed its full-fledged British puckah-sahib infrastructure. To the Parsi community goes the credit of the first postal system, shipbuilding firm, and the first cotton mill.

The Parsi community formed the apex of this mercantile community with merchants like Jamshetji Jeejeebhoy, Hormasji Bomanji Wadia, Dadabhai Pestonji Wadia, Kavasji Jehangir Readymoney. There were also a few Jains, Hindu banias and Baghdadi Jews who established themselves in the business community, e.g. Jugganath Shankersett, Premchund Roychand, et al. These were names that were revered among British circles for their business acumen and sheer wealth.[11] The native mercantile community of Bombay adopted themselves to the colonial situation better than any other community in India, and donated generously to civic improvements, and the educational and cultural sphere of Bombay. They worked with the colonizers.

Contributions to civic improvement

In the context of nineteenth century British imperial aims, Bombay was expected to act as an "urban crucible" where urban legislation and civic experiments could be implemented and then replicated in other colonial cities. Numerous civic plans regarding land reclamation, drainage, supply of potable water were drafted. The work of land reclamation and building of docks and railways went hand in hand with opening up space for more factories and mills as well as for widening roads, building officers quarters, etc. By 1875 the urbanscape of Bombay had been significantly restructured (Dossal 1991).

Among other problems, Bombay suffered from bad drainage and sanitation, and was considered responsible for transmitting cholera and other dreaded diseases to Western countries. However, it is unclear from the nineteenth century descriptions of the physical state of the two cities, why Bombay's sanitary condition was given higher priority, if it did not have to do with how the authorities envisioned the future of these two cities. Although several schemes for road improvement and drainage were conducted in Calcutta, none of them were as extensive as that of Bombay's. Going by the accounts of British visitors and government reports the "problems" of Calcutta were certainly not less in magnitude, and in fact very similar in nature -- swamps, bad drainage, excessive humidity, etc.[12] While Indians in Calcutta were blamed for doing nothing for the improvement of the city except building tanks, ghats and temples (Dowlean 1860), Indians on their part, resisted hikes in municipal taxes as they felt the revenues went into the improvement of solely the European part of Calcutta (Evenson 1989, p.29). Most Britishers in Calcutta actually felt the white's needs and black's needs were different and the two towns should be treated separately:

> The interests of the Europeans and natives ought to be weighed separately. To fuse both into the same category is absolutely impossible. In a sanitary point they will never be identical; in commerce and trade Europeans enterprise and capital will maintain their supremacy; in politics the lead must be retained by Government (Dowlean 1860, p.9).

Lord Elphinstone, Governor of Bombay, had similar sentiments regarding capital investment in Bombay. He made it clear that his government was "against the use of English capital on guaranteed railways or any such enterprise in India. It was rather 'native' capital which should be employed and thereby contribute to the improvement of the country" (Dossal 1991, p.181), And unlike the native population of Calcutta, the merchants of Bombay saw little problem in such a policy. Both the Bombay mercantile community and the British authorities realized that they depended on each other for mutual benefit. Lord Elphinstone remarked in 1859 that the reason the wealthier classes amongst the native were favorable to the British because they enjoyed a degree of security under British rule that they had not experienced before. Echoing Elphinstone, Bartle Frere, who succeeded Elphinstone as Governor commented that the mercantile community is by "necessity" loyal (Dobbins 1972).

So one of the major reasons for favoring Bombay over Calcutta , it may be reasonably conjectured lay in the preference for Bombay's native population. Although this rich mercantile community did not represent the whole Indian community and did not often speak for them either, they were the ones with enough capital who could make or break relations with the British, and as long as their allegiance was assured the British authorities had little to fear. There was considerable disagreement within the Indian ranks on a number of issues in which the younger generation of reformists did not agree with their rich elders. Some of this conflict found expression in the role played by the Bombay Association and the reactions to the organization's actions.

"Not in a material position to lead"

In 1852, the Bombay Association, the city's first political organization came into being at the behest of the youthful intellectuals of the Parsi community and found financial approbation from men like K.R. Cama and Jugannath Shankersett. The chief objective of this organization was to ascertain the needs of the natives of India living under the Government of the Bombay Presidency, and advance to the authorities measures that were necessary for the advancement of the people and welfare of the country. But when the association sent a petition to the Parliament urging it to act on the promise that no Indians should be disqualified from the office of the state "by reason only of religion, place of birth, descent or colour," many rich leaders of the organization including Jamshetjee Jeejeebhoy and Mohamed Roghay resigned from the association in fear of reprisal and of discrediting themselves in the eyes of the British (Albuquerque 1985). Also, at a later date considering the License tax on trades and professions unlawful, Bhau Daji sent a petition to the parliament which was boycotted by his wealthy opponents, led by Jugannath Shankersett. In reference to this disagreement the Rast Goftar editorial noted:

> We cannot help thinking that our community is unhappily pulling at two different ends, to the great detriment to this country. One part which we believe, represents the greater part of the capital of this place does not appear to be, as yet, wide awake to what is going on in the world; while the others (whose ranks we hope are increasing) is probably not yet in a material position to lead (as cited in Albuquerque 1985, p. 52).

It was precisely this condition that deemed Bombay as un-threatening . In comparison, the situation in Calcutta was significantly different. The manner in which the rich mercantile class in Bombay and the British authorities were accommodating each other for mutual benefit was not forthcoming in Calcutta, and the Bengalis were gaining more political ground than the British wished to see. In fact increased participation of Indians in the Calcutta Municipality in the 1870's, coincided with the decline in the city's positive image in the British imagination. In the latter parts of the century, the Bengalis were no longer a benign threat, merely dropping "inflammatory hints" as Kipling had imagined,13 prompting him to declare in 1899:

It seems not only wrong but a criminal thing to allow natives to have any voice in the control of such a city -- adorned, docked, wharfed, fronted, and reclaimed by Englishmen, existing only because England lives. . . All India knows about the Calcutta Municipality. . . The damp, drainage-soaked soil is sick with the teeming life of a hundred years, and the Municipal Board is choked with the names of natives -- men of the breed born in and raised in the muck-heap! They own property, these amiable Aryans on the Municipal and the Bengal Legislative Council. Launch a proposal to tax them on the property and they naturally howl. They also howl upcountry, but the halls for mass-meetings are few, and the vernacular papers fewer, and with a zubardasti Secretary and a President whose favor is worth the having and whose wrath is undesirable, men are kept clean inspite of themselves. . . Why, asks a savage, let them vote at all? They can put up with this filthiness. They cannot have any feelings worth caring a rush for (pp. 8-11).

Kipling's implication was clear -- a people born out of a "muck-heap" cannot possess the right faculties to decide for a "British" city, and he like many others despised their encroachment on municipal affairs. The "official" view of the situation was not far removed, but merely tempered with authority. Although sanitary improvement of Calcutta was slow, in the early years (before 1876) the slow progress was attributed to lack of funds and the habits and reluctance of the natives. But once the control of the Municipal Board moved in favor of Indians, the representative form of election to the Board was blamed as the chief cause for inadequate sanitary work. A Resolution of the Bengal Government quoted in the Sanitary Report for 1877-78 noted:

The hope formerly expressed that . . . the work of sanitary reform, as well as the general business of the municipality, (be) carried on vigorously and earnestly has been disappointed; prolonged and unprofitable discussion has been the chief characteristic of municipal administration. . . The experiment of what is often called a representative system of municipal administration of Calcutta may, as is frequently asserted, be a very interesting experiment; but after all it is only an experiment, and having regard to the enormous outlay and heavy liabilities of the town, it is certainly a very dangerous experiment, . . . If the year 1879 does not show a very much more favorable working of the municipal administration, it will be the imperative duty of the government to place control of the affairs of the town in other hands (p.24).

While the political conflict between the British and the Bengalis heightened in the last two decades of the nineteenth century,14 the atmosphere was brewing for a whole century in the mutual distrust of the English and the Bengalis, that resulted in the disinterest to conduct civic improvements, and a city that was decaying as a physical plant.

Conclusion

To take the perceptions and imageries of Calcutta at face value and as reliable representations of the physical condition of the city and as clues to its development is an oversight. Rather the descriptions and commentaries on Calcutta reveal to a large degree attitudes towards the indigenous population, apprehensions and anxieties about that part of the landscape that was scarcely familiar to most British residents of the city. Whether Kipling's account, for example, was "truthful" or not, is not the point in question. The issue is that these imageries were not simply innocuous passive commentaries, but were actively informing the vision of Calcutta in the nineteenth century, of what appeared Calcutta's possible future options. After all, nineteenth century London itself, with the Thames fetid with the city's sewerage, could just as easily have been labeled the "City of Dreadful Nights."

Calcutta is certainly not the only city that has suffered from inadequate attention to historiographic detail. The example of Calcutta simply illustrates the necessity for an urban history that attends to attitudinal subtleties, and the political and cultural contexts that shaped the experience of the people from whom we inherit the evidence to construct history.

End notes

1 See Valentia 1809, Graham 1810, Nugent 1812, Parks 1850 for positive descriptions of the "white" town as "the city of palaces."

2 For unfavorable description of the "black town," also see Valentia, p.236.

3 The term "babus" in the eighteenth century and among the Bengalis even in the nineteenth century meant the wealthy merchants, bankers and brokers. Not until the second quarter of the nineteenth century did the term come to refer the clerical staff employed in government service.

4 Contrary to popular assumption, Bengalis were a strong mercantile force even in the beginning of the nineteenth century, and some of the most wealthy merchants in the eighteenth century were Bengalis, like the Seths, Basaks and Mullicks. In the nineteenth century the wealthy Bengalis started switching their investment to landed property, but not until the later parts of the nineteenth century did the Marwaris conduct large-scale purchases of the city's wholesale market (see S. Chaudhuri 1990).

5 One indication of how clearly social boundaries were drawn according to race is that Dwarakanath Tagore who hosted some of the balls and dinners in his palace for his European and Indian business partners and friends (see p.2) was nevertheless denied admission to the Bengal Club on grounds of race and religion.

6 For an excellent reading of such class anxieties see Clark (1984).

7 A similar but less biased opinion of the similarity between native Calcutta and European towns is found in Macleod 1871, p.199.

8 Bombay in the early years of the nineteenth century was derided for its lack of grand architecture by both visitors and residents. For a general description of the city of Bombay see Young 1838,

pp.1-45 and Wacha 1920, pp. 47-145.

9 Quoted from a verse written specially for Bombay, by Dave Carson, a performer in the San Francisco Minstrels (Times 1863, as cited in Albuquerque 1985, p.93)

10 Speaking of the native community of whom "a large majority are Parsis" Edwards (1909) remarked:

        The Parsis are . . . far less intolerant in their principles than either the   Hindu or the Mussalman, and will, therefore, perform a greater variety   of work, and are more agreeable to live with. . . The greater portion of   the wealth is in the hands of Parsi merchants, who are a hospitable   race, and, though not extravagant, liberal in their expenditure. The   houses of these persons will be   found filled with European furniture,   and they have adopted many customs and habits which remain   unthought of by the Mussalman and Hindus (p.150).

11 It is however interesting to notice that Britishers used the label "Parsi" as a blanket term to refer to the native mercantile community in Bombay as a whole. This may be interpreted as the Britishers magnifying the role of the Parsis more in relation to others in the native mercantile class.

12 For similar readings see Evenson (1989), Chaudhuri (1990).

13 The native Calcuttans virtually controlled the Municipal affairs from 1875 onwards until in 1899 the Government legislated to change the form of representation to the Municipal body to reduce the number of elected Indians.

14 For a political history of late nineteenth century Calcutta see Ray (1979). In the late nineteenth century, Bombay's native population was becoming politically troublesome too, but most of these dissenters were Chitpavan and Saraswat Brahmins and very few banias or Parsis. So the threat could have been viewed as less than that of Calcutta's. But the major anxiety about Calcutta was the fact that as the second capital of the empire there was simply more at stake there.

References

Albuquerque, T. 1985. Urbs Prima in Indis: An Epoch in the History of Bombay, 1840-1865. New Delhi: Promilla & Co.

Bose, N. 1975. Calcutta: People and Empire. Calcutta: India Book Exchange.

Chowdhury, S.(ed.). 1990. Calcutta: The Living City. vol.1. Calcutta: Oxford University Press.

Clark, T.J. 1984. The Painting of Modern life: Paris in the Art of Manet and his Followers. Princeton: Princeton University Press

Dobbin, C. 1972. Urban leadership in Western India: Politics and communities in Bombay City, 1840-1885. Oxford: Oxford University Press.

Dossal, M. 1991. Imperial Design and Indian Realities: Bombay, 1845-75. Bombay: Oxford University Press.

Edwards, S. M. 1909. By-ways of Bombay. Bombay: Taraporvala & Co.

Evenson, N. 1989. The Indian Metropolis. New Haven: Yale University Press.

Graham, M. 1989. "Calcutta in 1810." Excerpts from "Journal of a Residence in India" In Nair, P.T.(ed.) Calcutta in the Nineteenth Century. pp.86-109. Firma KLM Pvt. Ltd.

Kipling, R. 1899. The City of Dreadful Night. New York: Alex Grosset & Co. 1913 (original pub. 1899). "A Tale of Two Cities." In Departmental Ditties and Barrack-Room Ballads. New York: Doubleday.

Low, S. 1907. A Vision of India. London: Smith, Elder & Co.

Macleod, N. 1871. Peeps at the Far East. London: Strahan & Co.

Nair, P.T. 1989. Calcutta in the Nineteenth century. Firma KLM Pvt. Ltd.

Nair, P.T. 1989. Calcutta in the Nineteenth century. Firma KLM Pvt. Ltd.

Nugent, M. 1839. "Calcutta in 1812." Excerpts from "A Journal from the year 1811 to the year 1815, including a Voyage to India, with a Tour of the Northwestern parts of the British Possessions in that Country, under the Bengal Government." In Nair, P.T.(ed.) Calcutta in the Nineteenth Century. pp.110-185. Firma KLM Pvt. Ltd.

Parks, F. 1850 (repr. 1975). Wanderings of a Pilgrim in Search of the Picturesque. Oxford: Oxford University Press.

Ray, R. 1979. Urban Roots of Indian Nationalism. New Delhi: Vikas Publishing House.

Roberts, E. 1837. "Calcutta in 1835," Excerpts from Scenes and Characteristics of Hindostan, with Sketches of Anglo Indian Society. In Nair, P.T.(ed.) Calcutta in the Nineteenth Century, pp.574-603. Firma KLM Pvt. Ltd..

Russell, W. H. 1860. "Calcutta in 1858." Excerpts from "My Diary in India in the year 1858-59," v.1. In Nair, P.T.(ed.) Calcutta in the Nineteenth Century, pp.952-978. Firma KLM Pvt. Ltd.

Report on Sanitary Measures in India in 1877-78, v. XI. In British Parliamentary Papers. 1879. Printed by George Edward Eyre & William Spottiswoode for Her Majesty's Stationery Office.

Valentia, G.V. 1809. Voyages and Travels to India, Ceylon, and the Red Sea, Abyssinia, and Egypt in the year 1802, 1803, 1804, 1805 and 1806, v.1. London: William Miller.

Wacha, Sir D.E. 1920. Shells from the sand of Bombay, being my Recollections and Reminiscences 1860-1875. Bombay: Bombay Chronicle Press.

Young, M. (ed.). 1839. Western India in 1838, by Mrs. Postans, v.1. London: Saunders and Otley.

41

Coping with urbanisation: the Irish in early Manchester

S'en tirer a l'urbanisation - les irlandais a manchester au vieux temps.

Mervyn Busteed and Rob Hodgson

Les èmigrants irlandais à la Grande-Bretagne au début de l'ère industrielle ont découvert que les villes nouvelles des usines représentent un environnment menaçant. Les problèmes de s'ajuster de la part des irlandais s'étaient accrus à cause de leur milieu surtout rural et pré-industriel et à cause de l'avis de l'opposition prise par la population indigène à laquelle ces immigrés représentaient une menace. Les réactions des irlandais sont débattues d'après diverses documents. Tout se réfère à Manchester qui est devenu la première complexe industrielle pendant les premières et moyennes décennies du dix-neuvième siècle. Pour la plupart, les irlandais ont réagi d'une manière positive à cause de leur sentiment de solidarité communitaire. Cette-ci s'était representée par une forte ségrégation résidentielle qui a offert la possibilité de se rassurer d'une manière psychologique et a aidé la mobilisation de tout le monde en face des menaces. Les irlandais à Manchester se sont servis de l'église catholique comme un système d'appui. Cependant il y a aussi des indications que quelques-uns des émigrants irlandais ont rencontré des difficultés à s'en tirer aux contraintes de la vie urbaine. Il s'était montré de diverses régions de l'Irlande, et par les pourcentages très élevés des irlandais parmi ceux qui ont été arrêtés pour des crimes de violence et d'ivresse.

Mots clefs: les irlandais de Manchester; milieu menaçant; la ségréΘgation résidentielle; l'église catholique; les crimes de violence.

Key words: Manchester Irish; hostile environment; residential segregation; Catholic church; violent crime.

Adjustment to urbanisation can be a painful process for migrant groups from a rural background, and the coping strategies they adopt are a crucial area of scholarly investigation into past societies as well as an important aspect of contemporary political, social and economic life. The sizeable Irish populations that were found in most of Britain's towns and cities by the middle decades of the nineteenth century provide some particularly vivid case material (Collins, 1993; Davis, 1992). The considerable Irish presence in nineteenth century Manchester is of special interest, not least because of the many native and foreign visitors who in the 1830s and 1840s came to this, the first, great industrial city, and carried away adverse stereotypical images of the Irish that were to travel the world. It is possible, however, to give a more balanced and sympathetic view of the urban experience of Irish people. Using a wide range of contemporary sources, it will be shown how the Irish confronted and attempted to cope with an alien and hostile environment.

THE HOSTILE ENVIRONMENT

Manchester was the place where the rapidly accelerating processes of machine manufacturing and urbanisation first converged to create the modern industrial city. The resulting paradox, of general economic wealth amid mounting social problems, stirred deep unease in many contemporary observers. The population, which grew at an unprecedented rate, from 76,788 in 1801 to 316,213 by 1851 (Kidd, 1993), contained a large working-class element, among whom the usual agencies of social control which had operated in traditional rural and small town Britain were absent or inadequate (Briggs, 1968). Manchester was also notorious for its radical working-class politics, and support for trades' union rights and parliamentary reform, as shown in the Peterloo incident of August 1819, when a demonstration dispersed by the militia left eleven dead and at least 600 injured (Bee, 1989; Belchem, 1989). Equally frightening were the occasional economic depressions which created widespread unemployment and hunger, as in the early 1840s, and the periodic outbreaks of infectious disease such as the cholera epidemics of 1832 and 1848. The impact of all these events was profound in both establishment circles and the populace at large. An air of nervousness, bordering on moral panic, set in.

In this volatile population of notably diverse origins, the Irish were the most visible and distinctive and as such quickly became objects of suspicion. The factor which above all others set them apart from the native population was their Roman Catholicism. English popular nationalism had always contained an element of anti-Catholicism and this was given new life during the first decades of the nineteenth century by the immigration of the overwhelmingly Catholic Irish. In the case of Manchester there had been only fifteen Catholics in the entire township as late as 1744 (Blundell, 1939), but by 1841 there were over 30,000 Irish-born people living in the city, the great majority of whom were Catholics. Popular prejudice was also exacerbated when the Catholic community began to adopt a more active, high-profile role in British public life after the granting of full civil rights in 1829 and the restoration of the Catholic hierarchy in England and Wales in 1850. The Irish were also politically distinctive, some supporting repeal of the Union of Britain and Ireland, while others were active in radical working-class politics. A meeting supporting both causes, held on St Patrick's Day 1848, was reported in dismissive and resentful fashion by the local press (Manchester Guardian, 18 March 1848). Adding to Irish cultural distinctiveness was their quite frequent use of Gaelic; Frederick Engels (1845), for instance, remarked upon the amount of Irish he heard spoken in the most densely populated parts of Manchester in the 1840s. Finally, the Irish had long been regarded with xenophobic suspicion. As early as 1791 a magistrate from Hope, Manchester, while remarking upon the general prosperity of the district, also noted 'attendant evils: amongst these I include a very numerous and foreign population (especially from Ireland)'. (Aspinall, 1949)

It is hardly surprising therefore that the Irish also became scapegoats for the poor living conditions, low wages and bad housing endured by many working people in early Manchester. Dr J. P. Kay, who had been active in combating Manchester's cholera outbreak of 1832, believed that Irish 'lack of moral forethought and economy' was partly responsible for the overcrowding and insanitary living conditions endured by most of the urban working class. In a widely read and influential pamphlet, he asserted that they had 'discovered, with the savage, what is the minimum of the means of life upon which existence may be prolonged... and this secret has been taught the labourers of this country by the Irish' (Kay, 1832). Their low expectations of comfort merely encouraged the building of poor quality housing, because 'if it had not been for the Irish, there would have been no class of persons on whose willingness to put up with so small amount of convenience, and so large a subtraction of comfort, it would have been prudent to speculate.' (Report on the State of the Irish Poor in Great Britain; hereafter Irish Poor Report, 1836). This was merely the most rational articulation of what quickly became a common conviction.

The Irish were also held responsible for undermining the wages and living conditions of native workers by their readiness to accept low pay. This was a widespread view at all levels of society even though it is at variance with recent work suggesting that their impact on wage levels was probably neutral (Williamson, 1989). Fellow workers such as Richard Sheridan, a Manchester hand-loom weaver who gave evidence in 1834 to the investigation into the Irish poor in Britain declared: 'I have no doubt that the Irish have lowered the rate of wages in Manchester by the numbers that come over.' Most of the city mill owners declared that they welcomed the Irish for this very reason (Irish Poor Report, 1836). Situations arose in which the Irish could not win whatever they did. Some employers, for instance, were prepared to use them as strike breakers: 'The moment I have a turnout...I send to Ireland for 10,15, or 20 families' (Irish Poor Report, 1836). Other employers, however, were convinced that the Irish were the worst trouble-makers, being 'more disposed to turn out, to make unreasonable demands, to take offence at slight causes, and to enforce their demands by strikes and ill language, than the English..' (Irish Poor Report, 1836: evidence of J.Taylor and J.B.Clarke, Manchester).

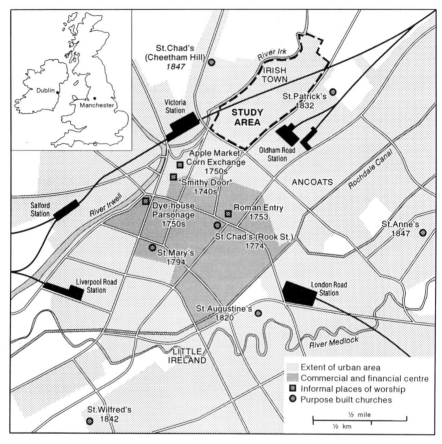

Figure 41.1 Location of Irish districts and Catholic places of worship in Manchester in first half of nineteenth century.

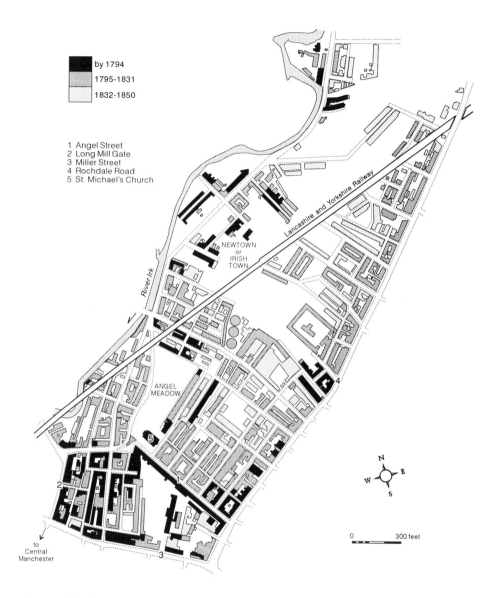

Figure 41.2 Stages in the development of Irish Town to 1851.

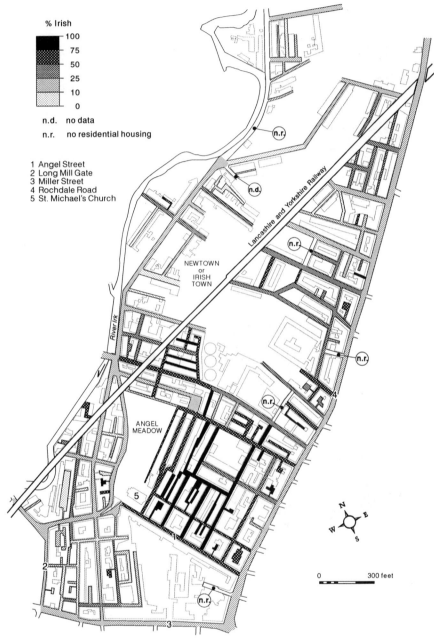

% Irish

100
75
50
25
10
0

n.d.   no data

n.r.   no residential housing

1 Angel Street
2 Long Mill Gate
3 Miller Street
4 Rochdale Road
5 St. Michael's Church

NEWTOWN
or
IRISH
TOWN

Lancashire and Yorkshire Railway

River Irk

ANGEL
MEADOW

0   300 feet

Figure 41.3   Proportion of Irish residents (by street) in Irish Town, 1851.

IRISH STRATEGIES

The responses of the migrant Irish were largely derived from an assertion of various forms of communal solidarity, particularly as based upon residential segregation and the institutions of Catholicism. But for some the urban experience was so disorienting that violent anti-social behaviour erupted.

By the 1830s the Manchester Irish were concentrated in three districts whose popular names, in two instances at least, reflected their already dominant presence: 'Little Ireland' off Oxford Road; Ancoats; and 'Irish Town', behind Victoria station (Figure 41.1). Detailed investigation of the last-named district reveals the extent to which residential segregation was a key Irish response to the new hostile environment, especially following the Famine influx of the late 1840s (Busteed, Hodgson, & Kennedy, 1992). Most of this district grew up between 1790 and 1830, at the peak of Manchester's development, when it became a mosaic of factories and working-class housing (Figure 41.2). The 1851 census revealed that 52,801 or 13.1% of Manchester's population was Irish born. In Irish Town there were 18,347 people, of whom 8,048 (44.1%) were Irish born or had two Irish parents. Of these 5,840 (72.6%) lived in streets which were 50% or more Irish. Moreover, almost all of these Irish majority streets were to be found in a distinct cluster in the south eastern part of the study area, with some streets over 75% Irish (Figure 41.3).

Some contemporary observers realised how this clustering provided a base for varied forms of mutual support. 'On account of the number of Irish in Manchester, they feel almost as if they are coming to an Irish town,...they will take in a family of fresh immigrants, when they have only one room.' (IPR,1836). There was also an economic motive. Since the great majority of the Irish had only the skills of the agricultural peasant to offer, they were generally employed on the poorest paid jobs where only physical strength was required. Multiple occupation was one way to reduce rent, and ethnic compatibility an obvious criterion in the selection of tenants and accommodation. Consequently, in houses in Irish Town that had an Irish majority the density of occupation (8.7 persons per house) was greater than in those with a non-Irish majority (6.4 per house).

Residential segregation also enables rapid mobilisation of community resources in the face of outside threat (Boal, 1972). The Superintendent of the Manchester Watch ruefully paid tribute to the strength of Irish communal solidarity in 1834: 'It repeatedly happens that, in order to apprehend an Irishman in the Irish parts of the town, we are forced to take from ten to twenty, or even more watchmen; the whole neighbourhood turn out with weapons, even women, half naked, carrying brickbats and stones for men to throw' (Irish Poor Report, 1836).

The Catholic Church paid a key role in sustaining communal life amongst the migrant Irish (Lowe, 1976, 1989). Aside from spiritual comfort, it was a landmark of cultural identity and a source of leadership and facilities even for the significant numbers who had lapsed from their religion (Gilley, 1985). Since the clergy were virtually the only people with any education and leadership experience, they were frequently lay leaders as well as spiritual guides, regularly visiting even in the midst of infectious epidemics (Faucher, 1844), and calming and defending their flock in times of stress. In July 1834, when several parishioners were on trial following a disturbance, Father Daniel Hearne, the Irish-born priest of St. Patrick s Church, off Rochdale Road, gave character references for several of the accused and described how 'he had been engaged until the evening keeping things as quiet as he could' (Manchester Guardian, 19 July 1834).

Originally Manchester's Catholics had worshipped in private houses or in two small churches in the old city centre, but as the city expanded and the Catholic population grew, large new churches appeared (Figure 41.1). Initially, they tended to follow the location of the Catholic community, but once established, they reinforced the nature of a district. This effect was amplified by the agglomeration of facilities and organisations. Irish Town, for instance, was served by the significantly named St.Patrick's, founded in 1832. By 1845 the church had, nearby, a cemetery, an orphanage, and schools for both boys and girls run by Irish teaching orders. The redoubtable Father Hearne also boosted parish life by founding a Temperance Hall and four guilds (Leetham, 1965).

But there were also indications that for some Irish the novel stresses of urban life were severe enough to rupture the bonds of community solidarity and result in group and individual violence and drunkeness. Intra-group violence took the form of faction fights between people from different parts of Ireland. This had been a feature of life in rural Ireland since the late eighteenth century (O'Donnell, 1975), when it probably reflected growing population pressure on land. Transferred to the urban context it seems a likely response to the pressures of life in the hostile urban environment, and one source of the constant local newspaper references to the 'wild Irish' (e.g. Manchester Courier, 30 March 1830) and 'Another Irish Outrage' (e.g. Manchester Guardian, 14 July 1832). One shopkeeper in a Manchester Irish district asserted that in the summer of 1832 there had been a running fight between men and women from Roscommon and Leitrim which lasted two weeks and, significantly, was not ended until the local priest called a meeting in the Sunday School (Irish Poor Report, 1836).

To some extent the level and nature of Irish involvement in crime may be interpreted as further evidence of stress and alienation. The common perception of a high level of violence has already been noted. Recent work (Swift, 1990) suggests that the Irish were most likely to be arrested for drunkenness, disorderly behaviour, assault and some categories of petty theft. Data on arrests in Manchester in 1845, the first year when returns were broken down by country of origin, largely bears out this pattern (Table 1). Irish people were arrested for a notably large proportion of crimes associated with illicit distillation, breach of the peace (whether drunk or sober) and common assault on both civilians and police. By contrast, larceny and vagrancy were more frequent reasons for arresting English people.

Table 1: Five most significant crimes for which Irish and English arrested in Manchester, 1845

Reason for Arrest	Total Arrests	Percentage Irish	Reason for Arrest	Total Arrests	Percentage English
Illicit distillation	24	41.7	Larceny by servants	112	84.8
Breach of peace (sober)	294	31.0	Larceny (miscell)	247	78.5
Common assault	771	30.2	Vagrants reputed thieves, suspicious characters	465	78.5
Breach of peace (drunk)	2003	28.4	Vagrants wandering about etc.	234	75.6
Assault on Police Constable	165	27.9	Larceny in dwelling houses, warehouses etc.	623	75.4

Source: Manchester Police Returns, 1845, Table 8, p.21

CONCLUSIONS

Manchester's population in the first half of the nineteenth century was a mosaic of native residents and migrant groups from far and wide, but the Irish were undoubtedly perceived as the most exotic and most suspect. Since their arrival was largely caused by industrial expansion and coincided with growing alarm over urban working and living conditions, it is hardly surprising that they became scapegoats for many of the ills of early manufacturing cities. In the Manchester case they responded by falling back on communal solidarity, as expressed in residential segregation and reliance on the facilities of the Catholic Church. However, faction fights and the high levels of individual violence and drunkenness suggest that for some the strains of urban industrial life were occasionally too much to bear, leading to social and personal disintegration.

When viewed in this context certain aspects of the social geography of early industrial cities, including known patterns of anti-social behaviour, can be seen as important and relevant dimensions of the urban experience.

Acknowledgements

We would like to express our appreciation to the Manchester and Lancashire Family History Society, the Local Studies Unit of Manchester Central Library and Chetham's Library for access to their microfilm copies of the 1851 census enumerators returns and their newspaper and other files, and to the Manchester Geographical Society for financial support.

References

Aspinall, A. (1949) The Early English Trade Unions: Documents from the Home Office Paps in the Public Record Office (Batchworth, London)

Bee, M.&W. (1989) 'The Casualties of Peterloo', Manchester Region History Review 3/1: 4351

Belchem, J. (1989) 'Manchester,Peterloo, and the Radical Challenge', Manchester Region Hky Review 3/1: 9-14

Blundell, F.O. (1939) Old Catholic Lancashire (Burns, Oates & Washbourne, London)

Boal, F.W. (1972) 'The Urban Residential Sub^^Community: a Conflict Interpretation', Area 4/3: 164-68

Briggs, A. (1968) Victorian Cities (Pelican,Harmondsworth)

Busteed, M.A., Hodgson, R.I. & Kennedy, T.F. (1992) 'The Myth and Reality of Irish Migrants in mid-nineteenth century Manchester', in O'Sullivan, P. (ed) The Irish World Wide. Vol.2:The Irish in The New Communities (Leicester University Press, Leicester)

Collins, B. (1993) 'The Irish in Britain,1780-1921', in Graham,B.J.,& Proudfoot,L.J.,(eds.) A n Historical Geography of Ireland,(Academic Press, London) chapter 11

Davis, G. (1991) The Irish in Britian 1815-1914 (Gill & Macmillan,Dublin)

Engels, F. (1845) The condition of the working class in England (Translated and edited by W.O.Henderson & W.H.Challenor, Blackwell, Oxford, 1971)

Faucher, L. (1844) Manchester in 1844: its present condition and future prospects (Simpkin Marshall, London)

Gilley, S. (1985) 'The Irish', History Today 35:17-23

Kay, J.P. (1832) The moral and physical condition of the working classes employed in the cotton manufacture in Manchester (Cass, London. new impression, 1970)

Kidd, A. (1993) Manchester (Ryburn, Keele)

Leetham, C.R. (1965) Luigi Gentili: his work in Manchester in the 1840s (Burns & Oates, London)

Lowe, W.J. (1976) The Irish in mid-Victorian Lancashire: the shaping of a working class community (Lang, New York)

Lowe, W.J. (1976) 'The Lancashire Irish and the Catholic Church 1846-71', Irish Historical Studies 20: 129-55

Manchester Courier

Manchester Guardian

Manchester Police Returns, 1845

O'Donnell, P. (1975) The Irish faction fighters of the nineteenth century (Anvil, Dublin)
    Report on the State of the Irish Poor in Great Britain, Appendix G (1836, Parliamentary Papers, London)

Swift, R. (1990) The Irish in Britain 1815-1914: perspectives and sources (Historical Association, London)

Williamson, J. (1989) 'The impact of the Irish on British Labour markets during the industrial revoluation', in Swift,R & Gilley,S. (eds) The Irish in Britain 1815-1939 (Pinter, London) chapter 5

42

Sustaining urban heritage in multicultural cities

Preserver le patrimoine urbain dans les villes multiculturelles

Helen B. Armstrong

Les quartiers en bordure du centre des villes les plus anciennes d'Australie regorgent de groupes complexes d'immigrés. Ces groupes sont tellement concentrés que leurs quartiers réflètent leur culture. A la faveur d'une amélioration de leur niveau de vie, les générations suivantes se dispersent davantage à l'extérieur. Cette évolution périodique des quartiers du centre peut provoquer une perte de sites d'une valeur inestimable - le patrimoine - pour différents groupes d'immigrés. US ICOMOS a reconnu que les attitudes à l'égard du patrimoine sont passées des valeurs traditionnelles de l'antiquité et de la structure interne à des notions qui réflètent l'évolution vers une société plus ouverte, surtout le pluralisme culturel et la valeur du patrimoine non matériel. Dans les villes australiennes, l'aménagement identifie les sites de valeur culturelle en suivant les données objectives de la Charte ICOMOS de Venise, notamment les lieux appréciés par la culture dominante anglo-celtique. De telles méthodes ne permettent pas d'identifier facilement les endroits qui possèdent une valeur culturelle dans les quartiers ethniques. Une étude récente a reconnu l'importance des récits attachés à ces lieux, surtout ceux dont la valeur historique réside dans leur association avec les expériences de l'immigration. Le maintien d'un tel patrimoine dans les villes multiculturelles est sapé, premièrement par une interprétation inadéquate de l'importance de certains lieux pour les groupes d'immigrés si les assesseurs sont étrangers à leur culture; deuxièmement, par la simplification stéréotypée de sites ethniques à des fins touristiques (ce qui est surtout catastrophique dans les villes australiennes où le pluralisme culturel consiste à métisser les pratiques culturelles du pays d'origine avec la culture australienne); troisièmement, par la modernisation. Les caractéristiques qui attirent les promoteurs dans les quartiers ethniques reposent sur les loyers peu élevés et sont économiquement fragiles. Les rues commerçantes ethniques sont particulièrement vulnérables devant les grands centres commerciaux, la modernisation et l'aménagement urbain. Cet essai propose de nouvelles méthodes pour identifier les sites du patrimoine urbain, et le défi qui consiste à préserver de tels lieux dans les villes multiculturelles.

Mots clé: défi urbain, patrimoine culturel, passé urbain.

Key Words: urban challenge, cultural heritage, neighbourhoods, urban histories.

Urban heritage is a broad and encompassing term. It may refer to aspects of an urban way of life or to urban heritage places. Urban designers refer to it as an inherited identity or sense of place while cultural geographers consider it to be the customs and traditions which sustain meaning and value to an urban community.

Urban places in Australia have a short history of 200 years. The first cities were created by British settlers and successive waves of immigrant groups have added to the accumulated urban heritage. Today most Australians tend to live in large cities scattered around the coast. The largest and oldest city, Sydney is a multicultural city which abounds in inner suburbs of complex mixes of ethnic groups, Anglo-Celtic Australians and Aboriginal Australians.

Sustaining urban heritage raises the question - heritage for whom? Australia is an example of a modern society with indigenous people, a dominant British culture and a significant cultural fabric created by people from many other countries. Current heritage interpretations are derived from the ICOMOS model[1] where antiquity, excellence and rigorous evaluation criteria prevail. Australia has shown extensive commitment to the conservation of natural environments, but the desire to sustain cultural heritage places in cities has been constantly contested, resulting in the loss of many 19th and early 20th century places. Heritage assessment emphasises historic, scientific and archaeological value in places rather than social value [Burra Charter 1979]. The concept of social heritage significance[2], what is valued by the community, is poorly understood; whereas sustaining places which facilitate a way of life or continuing cultural practices has not been addressed at all. Into this tenuous notion of urban heritage values has been added the cultural pluralism derived from the massive immigration programmes since the 1950s. Much of the cultural richness of older Australian cities today is derived from the complex blendings and transformations of the culture of European, Middle East, Asian and South American immigrants.

The concept of heritage in the New World is different from heritage in the Old World where meanings associated with heritage places are collectively understood globally and locally. In Australia the recent heritage of the last 200 years lies in the stories as much as the artifacts, many of which are still being told. This is particularly true for the immigrant groups since 1950s. There is a need to understand the narratives of Australian urban heritage places. Significant oral history programmes were undertaken for the Bicentennial in 1988, but there has been little value given to such histories by the heritage professionals who determine what is an urban heritage place. Instead they rely on objective methods of assessment because so many heritage places are contested in courts of law. It is suggested that objective assessments are not only limited forms of assessment of heritage value, they are also ineffective in protecting places legally [Commissions of Inquiry 1981-1993].

Urban heritage needs to be reconsidered in terms of the stories about cities.

Teasing out the resonant stories of urban places allows for a more responsive approach to cultural heritage. In Australia this is particularly important because of the massive immigration programmes. Australia has become the repository of cultural practices no longer sustained in the Old World and of unusual cultural transformations. Despite this, little is known about immigrant heritage because conventional heritage practices do not give value to stories in case they are distorted. As David Lowenthal suggests

> We must reckon with the artifice no less than the truth in our heritage. Nothing ever made has been left untouched, nothing ever known remains immutable; yet these facts should not distress us but emancipate us[Lowenthal 1985 p.26].

The concept of cities as cultural landscapes provides alternative assessments of value. Cultural geographers see the cultural landscape as patterns and forms derived from the interaction of people, culture and environment [Relph 1976, 1981; Meinig 1979; Lowenthal 1985]. They have also pioneered alternative ways of identifying valued places which privilege local, familiar and everyday places [Clifford 1985, Burgess 1988]. Cultural landscapes can be seen as providing clues to human values and practices. In multicultural cities, urban landscapes - all external space - provide a myriad of clues to the overlay of cultures and suggest that urban heritage places have highly complex meanings and values to the community.

This paper describes a research project which contrasts existing methods used to identify heritage places with in-depth focus group methods which identify community values [Morgan 1988]. The research has been undertaken in one inner city neighbourhood which abounds in different immigrant groups. Conventional methods of heritage planning have been undertaken in the area and while such methods have effectively identified the physical fabric of the place, the vibrant multicultural qualities have only briefly been acknowledged. The study suggests that heritage values need to be understood at both expert and community level. It uses a methodology which investigates heritage values for the different immigrant groups grounded in experiences, concepts and beliefs held by people whose views are rarely heard in the public arena [Armstrong 1990]. This is achieved through the medium of conversation. In contrast to objective assessments, the study suggests that there is a relationship between researcher and subject which can be used in the research. Small group qualitative research emphasises the empathetic understanding between people. The researcher is engaged in understanding the small group while at the same time the small group is engaged in understanding the research. The interpersonal knowing between researcher and subject enables all to transcend the gulf between 'insider' and 'outsider' [Morgan 1988, Silverman 1985]. The interpretive phase of the research uses transcripts of the small group meetings to identify individual and group perceptions. Narratives are then constructed around session themes. Such techniques provide an assessment of heritage places in terms of social value to communities.

Using the inner city suburbof Marrickville in Sydney as the study area, the project compares the heritage expert's assessment of heritage places with other methods of identifying heritage values including the in-depth discussion groups and community arts projects and presents them as a set of narratives to suggest that urban places are many authored realms. The narratives also draw from Lyotard's discussions[3] about knowledge [Lyotard 1979].

The first narrative is derived from an Australian Aboriginal group, the Koories, who are one of the many groups who live in the area. The heritage experts stated that there is little evidence of Koorie culture prior to the first land divisions in 1820. They refer to the middens[4] beside the Cooks River, but they make no reference to the fact that Koories have continued to live in the area and have a history since 1820. The Koories revealed through a Community Arts mapping project that there are numerous heritage places in the area including the cemetery around one of the oldest churches which contains graves of the first Aboriginal people to receive a Christian burial. Community arts can be highly effective in revealing locally valued places. In Britain, a group known as Common Ground has developed innovative ways of revealing local community values [Clifford 1985]. Clearly knowledge about the Koorie history in urban places is very important, but existing techniques to identify heritage are unlikely to be able to access such knowledge.

The Anglo-Celtic narrative of urban heritage in the area can be read in the built form, road layouts and open parks all of which are cultural responses developed over the last 180 years. Urban heritage does not lie solely in the physical fabric of places but this paper concedes that the physical fabric derived from the Anglo-Celtic community provides the prevailing structural framework for the Australian stories and subsequent narratives of different immigrant groups. The road layouts reflect the early subdivisions of the 1820s. The railway with its ornate stations, the elaborate villas and terraces and prestigious town halls and the large industrial areas reflect the urban heritage of the 19th century. This also includes a grand shopping area known as a 'regional emporium' in the 1900s [M.H.S.1986]. The Anglo-Celtic heritage continues into the early 20th century with small Federation cottages of 1910-20, 1930 Art Deco blocks of flats decorated with intricate brick detailing and 1940s Californian bungalows. By the end of World War 2, the Anglo-Celtic narrative starts to fade when a vibrant change occurred in the area initiated by a massive immigration program. Many immigrant groups came to Marrickville because the area provided cheap housing near the large industrial areas. In the 1950s Greeks and Italians settled; in the 1960s Lebanese and Yugoslavs; in the 1970s a second wave of Lebanese and Vietnamese; in the 1980s Portuguese and Pacific Islanders and the middle class Australian gentrifiers. In the late 1970s, 47 different nationalities were enrolled in one local school. Meanwhile the Anglo-Celts continue to live in the area sustaining their way of life in the pubs and clubs, churches and to a lesser extent in the shopping areas. The Anglo-Celtic urban heritage can be summarised as one which reflects the prevailing culture since 1820 in the buildings, public spaces and road layouts, however the heritage of cultural practices and traditions has receded to be one of many different traditions practiced in the area.

It is interesting to compare the Anglo-Celtic narrative with the heritage professional's narrative which reflects the prevailing cultural values of the decision makers and planning authorities. The heritage professional's narrative is similar to the Anglo Celtic narrative, however the reading is slightly different in that it is the objective outsider describing the urban heritage in terms of historic themes and ranking the urban heritage into categories of conservation worth. Their theme for Marrickville is the 'theme of change' [M.H.S.1986]. Their categories are residential heritage, retail heritage and industrial heritage. Each of these categories is then interpreted within the theme of change. In terms of the residential heritage the theme of change refers to the remnants of each residential era. They speak of the remnants of the first country estates as place names and a pair of castellated gates which led to an 1820s version of a Norman castle. They also refer to the dominant villas and terraces of the building boom of the 1880s and pockets of other eras such as the modest cottages of the 1920s, 30s, 40s and the Art Deco flats. The unusual changes effected on the existing residential character by the waves of immigrant groups are not described, presumably because they are not considered to be urban heritage by the heritage professionals.

In terms of retail heritage, the heritage professionals highlighted the interesting urban fabric created by the Victorian era shopping emporia and the small corner shops developed for the 1900s worker housing, however the vibrant ethnic shopping streets were not included as urban heritage. This omission is unfortunate as ethnic shopping streets are vulnerable to current corporate economies and need planning protection. The theme of change was not adequately explored within the category of retail heritage; instead they concentrated on shop fittings as evidence of retail practices during different historical periods. Similarly the industrial heritage was seen in terms of archaeological significance rather than social significance. This is in contrast to the Greek and Lebanese narratives which speak of the industrial places as the reason why they came to the area and their stories tell of the pain and humiliation experienced in the factories. Within the theme of change, heritage professionals acknowledged the presence of the Greeks identifying a Greek milkbar and the Greek church as part of the urban heritage, however they did not include other immigrant groups. The heritage professionals provide an important historic understanding of the urban heritage of the area. The narrative contains the expertise of the heritage professional and provides particular interpretations of the place, but it is a limited interpretation. Urban heritage consists of more than the physical fabric of a place.

To understand other interpretations it is valuable to look at one Greek narrative about the urban heritage of area; stories told by a group of Greek men and women who came to Marrickville in the 1950s. This narrative is derived from the qualitative focus group process which includes subjective responses, opinions, anecdotes and conversations. Such contemporary community input would be resisted by heritage professionals because of its subjectivity. Community values which are incorporated into professional assessments of heritage places come through published histories, archival material or old newspapers. They are only allowed to enrich the history if they are history themselves. Contemporary discourse is treated with suspicion because it is subjective, emotive and therefore unreliable.

If urban heritage is to be sustained in its fullest sense, different multicultural groups need to be able to consider and discuss what it is about a place that has value for them. Urban heritage needs to include cultural pluralism and the value of intangible heritage. It is not enough to revise the heritage professionals brief so that ethnic heritage is considered. As long as the heritage expert needs to be an objective assessor there is a high risk of misinterpretation and stereotyping of ethnicity. Multiculturalism is a mutually altering process of interactive exchange rather than a stereotypic display of difference.

The Greek narrative is derived from meetings with 10 men and women over 65 years of age, who came to Marrickville directly from Greece after the civil war. The meetings discussed notions of cultural heritage, how this Greek group made Sydney feel more familiar and what the group would like to see sustained in Marrickville as urban heritage. The Greeks consider that their heritage is strongly related to the experience of migration, namely issues of hardship and humiliation, issues of the language barrier and how Marrickville was a place where one could hear Greek being spoken and ways in which they created a sense of 'Greekness' in their local environment. Finding the food with which one is familiar was one of the first concerns mentioned by the Greeks. Australia in the 1950s reflected a British approach to cuisine, however the Mediterranean migrants were quick to grow herbs, import olive oil and bake their own bread. They created food shops which serviced their needs in local shopping streets. They also changed their houses and gardens, planting grapevines, lemons, figs and olives in their gardens and modifying their houses with elements which evoked Mediterranean villas transposed onto worker's terraces of the Victorian era. The church was an important aspect of Greek heritage, but not the church designated by the heritage professionals which the Greeks considered to be of poor architectural design. The Greek cinemas were a vital aspect of their migrant experience. Greek films were screened in the local Art Deco cinemas. On weekends entire Greek families gathered in the cinemas during the 1950s and 1960s. Unfortunately most of Sydney's Art Deco cinemas were demolished during the speculative boom of the 1980s.

The sequence of steps taken to settle into a new country - food, shops, places of worship, modified houses and recreational places - have similarly emerged in discussions with the Lebanese and the Vietnamese in the area. The Greeks considered that their urban heritage lay in the Church, the library which kept Greek books and newspapers and the old Australian houses which they saw as the heritage of their new country, but they particularly valued the local shopping streets which are now a dynamic mix of Greek, Lebanese and Vietnamese shops.

The urban heritage in ethnic retail areas is important to understand. When a particular ethnic group establishes their shops, they not only provide goods and services that are related to their cultural practices, they are also creating small business opportunities which provide a strong sense of community. Local ethnic shopping centres are now threatened by new large internalised shopping complexes and they are threatened by gentrification. The diverse, dynamic and locally specific shopping streets are an important part of Sydney's urban heritage and they need planning protection. The challenge of the continued facilitation of small scale, marginal activities is as much an issue for heritage planning as the designation of conservation items.

Sustaining urban heritage in multicultural cities in the face of gentrification is more difficult to address. The dynamic qualities which attract gentrifiers are often associated with low rents and the process of gentrification inevitably raises rents and drives out marginal uses. Of more concern is the commodification of ethnicity in urban places which is often associated with gentrification. In Sydney, there is a Chinese area, a Vietnamese area and an Italian area each of which has commodified the ethnic character into highly selfconscious and hyper-real[5] interpretations of Chineseness, Vietnameseness and Italianness. These places are interesting phenomena in that the exploitation of ethnicity is being done by the ethnic community itself. But in terms of sustaining urban heritage there is the concern that much that is subtle and which reflects complex cultural transformations will be lost in the exuberant commodification of ethnic cultures.

SUMMARY

Using narratives to describe the different urban heritage values held by a number of groups for one inner suburban place has revealed that sustaining urban heritage in multicultural cities is complex. Heritage experts provide informed opinions about the physical fabric of Anglo-Celtic heritage, however they are limited in their understanding of immigrant heritage and Aboriginal heritage. The issues of misinterpretation and stereotyping can be addressed by using small indepth focus groups to reveal the subtleties of the immigrant experience and the unusual cultural transformation which have evolved. The issue of holding marginal uses and low rent areas is more complex, however with innovative planning this aspect of urban heritage may be sustained. But the issue of gentrification and commodifying ethnicity as the exotic 'other' is much more difficult to address. Many of the qualities of multicultural neighbourhoods reveal a lack of self consciousness and authenticity derived from trying to create a place in a new country. It would seem that authenticity is one of the first casualties of gentrified inner urban areas and that urban heritage becomes a superficial representation of what is a highly complex culture not yet understood by the Australian community.

Endnotes

1. International Council on Monuments and Sites (associated with UNESCO).
2. Social significance is one of the criteria of cultural significance developed by ICOMOS. Social value embraces the qualities for which a place has become a focus of spiritual, political, national or other cultural sentiment to a majority or minority group.
3. Lyotard contrasts narrative and scientific knowledge and privileges narration as the 'quintessential form of customary knowledge'(Lyotard.1979.p19).
4. Middens are sites of large collections of crustacean debris associated with gathering places for Aboriginal groups. They are thought to be thousands of years old.
5. Hyperreality is taken from Umberto Eco's 'Travels in Hyperreality' 1986 Pion:UK.

References.

Armstrong, H. 1991. Environmental Heritage Survey 1990, Cultural Landscape Research Unit monograph, UNSW.
Burgess, J. Limb, M. Harrison, C. 1988, 'Exploring environmental values through the medium of small groups: 1. Theory and practice.' in Environment and Planning A. V.20,pp309-326.
Burra Charter 1979, see Marquis-Kyle.
Clifford, S. & King, A. 1985, Holding Your Ground. Wildwood House: UK.
Commissions of Inquiry Reports, S41 Heritage Act(NSW) 1981-92. AGPS: Sydney.
Lee, A. 1987, 'Discovering Old Cultures in the New World: The Role of Ethnicity' in American Mosaic.Stipe, R. & Lee, A.(eds) US/ICOMOS publ: USA
Lowenthal, D. 1985, The Past Is Foreign Country, Cambridge University Press : UK.
Lyotard, Jean-Francois 1979, The Postmodern Condition: A Report On Knowledge, Manchester Uni. Press: UK.
M.H.S. Marrickville Heritage Study. 1986. publ. by Marrickville Municipal Council: Sydney.
Marquis-Kyle,P. & Walker,M. 1992, The Illustrated Burra Charter. Australia ICOMOS: Brisbane.
Meinig,D.W (ed), 1979, The Interpretation of Ordinary Landscapes, Oxford Uni. Press : UK.
Morgan, D. 1988, Focus Groups as Qualitative Research, Sage Publ : UK
Relph, E. 1976, Place and Placelessness. Pion: UK.
Relph, E. 1981, Rational Landscapes in the Age of Humanism. Croom Helm: UK.
Silverman, D.1985, Qualitative Methodology and Sociology. Aldershot: Hants.

43

L'éxperience de l'espace public en quartier pluri-ethnique: rassemblement ou segmentation?

The experience of the urban spaces in multi-ethnic neighbourhoods: cohesion or segmentation?

Annick Germain, Bernadette Blanc, Johanne Charbonneau and Francine Dansereau

The assimilation process of immigrants is in part an urban issue involving housing patterns, participation in community life, the use of public service etc. How is the urban presence of immigrants reflected in the use of public space and what kind of specific social dynamic is emerging in this kind of space - a space which is in principle universally accessible? Does it encourage social cohesion, as many urban planners believe, or does its use reflect the loosening of social bonds, as some social scientists argue? In order to discuss these issues, we present the results of a study carried out in six neighbourhoods of the metropolitan region of Montréal, selected for there multiethnicity (in terms of numbers and of ethnocultural diversity), for their location (in the centre and in the periphery), and for their socioeconomic profiles (middle class suburb, low-income enclave, old socially heterogeneous neighbourhood). In each neighbourhood, we conducted interviews with key informants from about 15 local associations (sometimes perceptive observers of the social life of the neighbourhood). We made systematic observations of the sociability of the main public places (parks, metro [underground] station, shopping centre, café etc.) and conducted brief interviews with the users of these places. In this paper we will mainly discuss issues such as social segmentation of space and patterns of cohabitation by types of users, as well as the different connotations of the concept of appropriation.

Key words: Public space, neighbourhood life, immigration, sociability.

Mot clé:Espace public, vie de quartier, sociabilité, immigration.

L'immigration est (re)devenue une question urbaine non seulement du fait de la concentration des immigrants dans les grands centres métropolitains mais aussi et

488

stratégique dans l'insertion des nouveaux arrivants. L'école, le travail et l'habitat représentent les pôles principaux de cette expérience et font l'objet de travaux de recherches importants. On s'est par contre moins penché sur les espaces publics comme espaces où peut se jouer la construction de l'inter-ethnicité. Ce sont en effet par définition des lieux ouverts à tous, où l'on choisit de passer ou de séjourner alors que l'habitat et le travail nous imposent, à des degrés divers un certain voisinage. On peut donc y voir se déployer librement le jeu des échanges et des exclusions, des indifférences et des interactions entre groupes et individus socialement et ethniquement différenciés. Pour Jean Rémy, ce type d'espace renvoie au paradoxe de l'inconséquence : les lieux publics peuvent être d'autant plus importants dans la construction de l'inter-ethnicité que les rapports entre les usagers "sont sans conséquence sur les grands enjeux de la vie sociale" (Rémy, 1990). Ils peuvent donc fonctionner comme des espaces privilégiés de socialisation à la différence. Mais ils peuvent aussi être l'enjeu de conflits d'appropriation comme le pensent Toubon et Messamah : "...c'est au niveau des espaces d'interconnexion que sont les rues, les places, les commerces que les tentatives d'appropriation sont les plus fortes, en fonction des acquis culturels et de la volonté de signifier une identité, d'autant plus menacée que la distance sociale à la société d'accueil est plus grande" (Toubon et Messemah, 1990 : 28).

Les espaces publics semblent donc offrir un terrain de choix à l'analyse de l'insertion urbaine des immigrants ainsi qu'à l'étude des transformations du tissu urbain de villes de plus en plus cosmopolites[1]. Ce choix s'avère particulièrement pertinent à Montréal où une étude avait clairement montré il y a une dizaine d'années que les immigrants anciens et récents étaient de grands consommateurs d'espaces verts et qu'ils fréquentaient les parcs urbains davantage que les membres de la société d'accueil (Samson, L'Ecuyer et Gaudreau, 1981). Par ailleurs, tout observateur de la vie urbaine montréalaise peut noter aisément le regain de faveur dont jouissent actuellement de nombreux espaces publics.

Nous avons donc choisi d'explorer la sociabilité publique dans une série de quartiers montréalais caractérisés par leur pluri-ethnicité, en faisant l'hypothèse que cette analyse apporterait un éclairage particulier à la question de l'interculturalité devenue aujourd'hui le leitmotiv de nombreux intervenants. Les lieux publics sont-ils fréquentés par des populations d'origines ethno-culturelles variées, ces populations se mélangent-elles, échangent-elles, comment se partagent-elles l'espace, telles sont les questions principales à l'origine d'une vaste enquête entreprise l'hiver dernier dans sept quartiers de la région montréalaise[2].

L'ENQUÊTE

Ces sept quartiers pluri-ethniques[3] présentent des cas de figure variant en termes de localisation[4], de statut socio-économique, de profil ethnique, de modèle résidentiel et d'histoire de peuplement[5] Dans chaque quartier, nous avons sélectionné les espaces publics les plus significatifs dans la dynamique inter-culturelle. Au total, nous avons retenu une trentaine d' espaces publics dont 18 parcs, 4 centres commerciaux, 3 stations de métro, des cafés ainsi qu'un ensemble de secteurs (comprenant entre-autres des rues commerciales) régulièrement "balayés" par nos enquêteurs. La plupart sont des espaces de proximité, sauf les centres commerciaux de banlieue où par définition prévaut un zonage des fonctions urbaines . Les quartiers résidentiels y sont donc éloignés des espaces commerciaux.

Ces espaces ont fait l'objet d'une douzaine d'observations systématiques (en semaine et en fin de semaine, en début et en fin d'après-midi, en période scolaire et en période de vacances, en hiver et pendant la belle saison), puis d'entrevues avec des usagers et avec des observateurs privilégiés(allant des intervenants communautaires aux épiciers, employés de métro, chauffeurs de taxis etc).

Les observations portaient sur les activités de séjour (et non de passage) et visaient à faire un portrait des usagers[6], à identifier les formes de coprésence dans l'espace, à dégager la constitution éventuelle de territoires et à déceler les pratiques d'exclusion.

LIEUX DE LA DIVERSITÉ.

Si comme le pensent Brezger et Quéré (1992), la qualité de publicité d'un espace urbain tient à la variété de ses usages et de ses usagers, plusieurs parcs observés au cours de notre enquête se sont avérés éminemment publics!

La diversité ethno-culturelle et socio-démographique de leurs usagers est en effet remarquable. Dans ces lieux se côtoient des immigrants d'Europe du sud, d'Europe de l'est des Caraïbes, d'Asie du sud et de l'est, d'Amérique latine, du Moyen Orient etc, et bien sûr des non immigrants.

Mais la variété de leurs usages doit également être soulignée. Plusieurs servent à la fois de raccourci, de lieu de détente, d'oasis de tranquilité, de terrains de sport, et se transforment à l'occasion en scènes de spectacle ou salle de fêtes communautaires. Il faut dire qu'ils sont, pour bon nombre d'entre eux, programmés pour être polyfonctionnels, quelle que soit leur taille. Ils illustrent la victoire remportée par les tenants de l'école des parcs comme espaces récréatifs, donc à équiper, sur la conception associant les parcs à des jardins publics favorisant la détente et la tranquillité (Laplante 1990). Chose certaine, à Montréal, les espaces libres sans équipements et sans arbres n'ont guère de succès. Notre échantillon comprend cependant aussi certains parcs fonctionnant en fait comme des squares : ce sont des espaces verts équipés de bancs et jouissant d'une localisation centrale. Ces parcs-squares ont eux aussi une clientèle diversifiée sur le plan des origines ethno-culturelles. Par contre, la variété des usages est évidemment plus limitée, ce qui n'est peut-être pas sans incidence sur leur accessibilité, comme on le verra plus loin.

Les centres commerciaux se veulent eux aussi de plus en plus polyfonctionnels. Certains ambitionnent même une certaine centralité dans la vie socio-culturelle de la municipalité. On peut y trouver des équipements récréatifs et des expositions pour enfants, ainsi qu'une panoplie d'activités et d'èvénements destinés aux familles. A cet éventail de fonctions programmées, s'en ajoutent d'autres, cette fois sur le registre de la sociabilité. Ainsi ces centres commerciaux deviennent-ils, par exemple, le lieu de rendez-vous de groupes de personnes âgées des pays de l'est, d'Europe du sud ou encore d'Asie de l'est. Les rigueurs du climat et la relative pénurie d'espaces publics dans certains quartiers résidentiels expliquent en partie la fonction sociale que remplissent ces espaces auprès des aînés.

DES LIEUX DE DIVERSITÉ À DOMINANCES

Ce constat de diversité doit immédiatement être assorti d'un autre. Plusieurs groupes ont des lieux de prédilection où ils se rassemblent volontiers entre gens de même origine, voire aussi du même groupe d'âge. Des femmes indiennes se retrouvent souvent au parc de Lestre dans Parc Extension, des hommes grecs dans le parc Athéna, des Libanais âgés au parc Painter dans le quartier Chameran, de jeunes noirs au parc Campbell-Centre dans la Petite-Bourgogne,etc. La plupart du temps, la conversation tient une grande place dans ces rencontres souvent régulières.

Dans certains cas, ces lieux de rassemblement intra-ethnique finissent par marquer le profil socio-ethnique des publics qui fréquentent ces parcs. Ainsi les noirs anglophones sont-ils beaucoup plus présents au parc Campbell-Centre que les autres catégories ethno-culturelles du quartier qui ne sont pas pour autant absentes du parc. Les habitudes, le nombre et la fréquence peuvent à la longue imprégner l'identité du lieu sans pour autant qu'il y ait eu une véritable appropriation exclusive de l'espace par une catégorie donnée. Mais dans ce cas, où finit l'appropriation, où commence l'exclusion, la question est difficile à trancher. Il n'en reste pas moins que ces espaces restent des lieux de diversité.

Par ailleurs, il faut préciser que les lieux de prédilection ne se muent pas nécessairement en espaces à dominance, loin de là. Le parc de Lestre n'est pas fréquenté uniquement par les femmes indiennes, son image n'est pas non plus associée à la leur.

En fait, plusieurs dominances dans l'occupation des espaces doivent aussi être mises au compte de la composition du voisinage. Par exemple, il est évident qu'à proximité du parc Campbell-Centre vit une concentration importante de noirs anglophones qu'on peut donc s'attendre en toute logique à retrouver dans les espaces publics.

Mais dans quelle mesure la loi du nombre n'a-t-elle pas parfois des effets dissuasifs à l'égard d'autres groupes comme peut en avoir une forte cohésion ethnique exprimée dans les lieux de prédilection évoqués précédemment? Plusieurs entrevues réalisées avec des groupes d'habitués de certains lieux laissent entrevoir un jeu complexe de repli sur le "nous" et de mise à distance des autres sans geste de rejet ou même de dissuasion explicite. A la limite, c'est la quasi-intimité que secrète un groupe d'usagers de même origine qui semble contredire la "publicité de l'espace" et éloigner d'autres usagers éventuels qui ne seraient pas à court d'alternatives.

Le parc Athéna présente à cet égard une dynamique particulièrement complexe. Ce parc-square situé en plein coeur du quartier Parc Extension, au bord d'une artère commerçante majeure fort animée, fonctionne un peu comme un bistro à ciel ouvert mais sans débit de boissons! Des hommes se retrouvent entre gens de même origine (grecque surtout, mais aussi indienne) et occupent en habitués, par petits groupes, une grande partie de l'espace. Le partage d'un banc public avec un habitué des lieux n'est pas particulièrement bienvenu et ne peut s'effectuer que le dos tourné. Les entrevues avec les usagers se sont avérées particulièrement difficiles à obtenir, étant perçues comme une intrusion malvenue dans un espace dominé par les retrouvailles entre pairs ou par le plaisir de regarder en solitaire la foule des passants. En principe ouvert à tous, ce parc n'attire en fait ni les femmes ni les jeunes.

Au parc Painter, les habitués libanais se retranchent dans un petit pavillon central pour jouer aux cartes.Ici aussi l'enquêteur est perçu comme un intrus mais qu'on n'éconduit pas pour autant et à qui on tente même de répondre fort civilement.

UNE SOCIABILITÉ INTERCULTURELLE?

Si comme le répètent à l'envi architectes et urbanistes, les espaces publics sont des lieux de rassemblement, voire comme le pensait Frederic Law Olmsted, des lieux de réconciliation sociale, force est de constater ici que cette fonction ne s'exerce qu'à l'intérieur de groupes ethno-culturels donnés. Tout au long de nos observations, les formes de sociabilité interculturelle sont l'exception plutôt que la règle. Le mélange des populations et les échanges inter-culturels ne se font que dans le cas des jeunes enfants, autour d'une pataugeoire par exemple, ou dans le cas d'activités organisées. Les garderies qui utilisent les parcs que nous avons observés accueillent parfois des clientèles pluri-ethniques. On retrouve alors des enfants d'origines différentes partageant leurs jeux, et des contacts se font à l'occasion entre les parents à l'heure de fermeture de la garderie. Mais on dénombre aussi nombre de cas où les jeunes enfants d'origines différentes s'évitent plutôt que de se rapprocher. Les écoles constituent aussi un bassin potentiel de sociabilité inter-culturelle pour les parcs qui les jouxtent.

Un autre type d'exception notable à signaler est le cas d'un organisme de loisirs pour jeunes dans Parc Extension, qui s'est donné une mission explicitement interculturelle. Fait remarquable, les activités sportives réunissant des jeunes d'horizons ethno-culturels différents induisent des habitudes de sociabilité qui se poursuivent par la suite sur le registre de l'informel. Les interventions communautaires n'ont cependant pas toujours le même succès. Dans plusieurs quartiers, la vie associative est dense et plusieurs organismes communautaires tentent chacun à leur manière de promouvoir «l'interculturel». Mais beaucoup d'organismes sont avant tout mono-ethniques et se soucient avant tout de leur propre clientèle.

Certains types d'espaces pressentis au départ pour être des lieux de sociabilité interculturelle se sont avérés plutôt décevants à ce chapitre. C'est le cas notamment des jardins communautaires dans deux quartiers, qui attirent quantité d'amateurs de jardinage mais qui s'adonnent à leur activité en solitaire et des cafés. Contrairement aux villes européennes, le café n'est pas une institution majeure de sociabilité semi-publique. Ce genre d'établissement est moins répandu qu'en Europe et dans nos quartiers les cafés sont clairement identifiés à une communauté culturelle donnée. Une exception toutefois qui se présentait au départ comme résolument ouvert à la diversité culturelle. Sa clientèle est effectivement assez diversifiée (encore que majoritairement non immigrante) mais on y observe fort peu d'échanges entre clients de diverses origines. La courtoisie qui y règne frôle souvent l'indifférence.

Dans certains quartiers, les fêtes et les spectacles sont des moments privilégiés où se mélangent des populations d'origine variées. Ce n'est donc qu'à l'occasion d'événements particuliers que la sociabilité publique semble se faire interculturelle.

Si donc on n'assiste guère à des interactions positives entre catégories ethno-culturelles différentes, comment se déroule la coprésence de ces catégories dans les mêmes espaces?

La coprésence indifférente à l'autre semble être la figure dominante que prennent les relations sociales dans les espaces publics. Les gestes d'exclusion sont rares, les attitudes d'évitement ne sont pas fréquentes. Certes, les jeunes manifestent parfois une certaine rivalité dans l'occupation d'un espace. Mais en général, c'est sans conflit ouvert que se fait la coexistence dans l'espace public. Dans leurs entrevues, nos interlocuteurs prennent acte de la fréquentation pluri-ethnique des espaces publics sans porter pour autant de jugement de valeur sur ce constat.

C'est autour du thème de la sécurité que font surface les malaises, les appréhensions et les jugements.

Dans un quartier se remettant d'un passé pas si lointain de quartier à problèmes, la sécurité dans les espaces publics fonctionne dans l'imaginaire collectif comme un baromètre de la santé du quartier. L'insécurité ayant été associée plus ou moins directement au commerce de la drogue et à une communauté ethnique donnée, on se félicite aujourd'hui de la sécurité retrouvée comme pour signifier que la cohabitation interethnique ne fait plus problème. L'espace public fonctionne jusqu'à un certain point à la confiance. Le thème de la sécurité est donc stratégique.

SEGMENTATION DES PUBLICS

L'ensemble des espaces observés présentent donc l'image d'une forte segmentation des publics de ces lieux, et ce quel que soit le quartier observé ou le type d'espace public considéré. Cette segmentation se fait non seulement selon les origines ethno-culturelles, mais aussi selon les groupes d'âge, le sexe et les types de ménage.

Beaucoup d'immigrants récents se rendent volontiers en famille dans les centre commerciaux où l'on voit fréquemment déambuler trois voire quatre générations. Ces sorties n'ont pas que les achats comme seul but. La sociabilité publique fait partie des plaisirs de l'expédition même si elle se vit sur un mode très réservé, notamment dans le cas des familles asiatiques.

Dans les parcs, les sorties en famille sont d'abord motivées par les activités des jeunes enfants. La solidarité éventuelle susceptible de rapprocher des parents au-delà des origines ethno-culturelles ne semble guère s'exercer dans les parcs observés si ce n'est à l'occasion d'échanges furtifs. Encore ici, la spécialisation des parcs en fonction de leurs équipements renforce certainement la segmentation des clientèles.

Mais c'est davantage avec son groupe d'âge que l'on se rend au parc, entre filles/femmes ou entre garçons/hommes. La fréquentation des espaces publics étant une pratique culturelle, il y a certains liens à faire entre les conduites dans la société d'accueil et dans le pays d'origine. Dans les pays méditerranéens par exemple, ce sont les hommes qui occupent l'espace public au premier chef. Le parc Athéna, lieu de prédilection d'hommes adultes grecs, ne serait probablement pas aussi achalandé si ne vivaient à proximité que des non immigrants!

Il y a cependant des cas où ce sont bel et bien ces derniers qui occupent l'espace, alors que les immigrants ne les fréquentent guère. C'est le cas notamment du parc Lahaye dans le Mile End qui attire surtout des hommes âgés que l'on qualifierait de Québecois de souche. Ces personnes viennent généralement seules au parc et pratiquent "l'équidistance" dans l'occupation des bancs publics, pour reprendre l'expression de Brezger et Quéré (1992). Les clientèles ethniques en grand nombre dans le quartier (du reste un des quartiers pluri-ethniques les plus conviviaux) ne semblent guère attirées par ce parc, mal localisé et qui ne répond pas aux besoins de leurs familles (aires de jeu pour enfants etc).

Quant aux stations de métro observées dans nos quartiers, l'une d'entre elles présente le même genre de segmentation des clientèles. En tant qu'espace de transit, la station-Côte Vertu voit certes défiler des populations de tous âge et de toutes origines. Mais comme lieu de sociabilité où l'on s'attarde, où l'on converse avec d'autres, où l'on se donne éventuellement rendez-vous, elle s'avère fort prisée par des groupes d'adolescents (noirs, asiatiques et moyen-orientaux). Les deux autres stations semblent peu fonctionner comme lieux de sociabilité publique. Sans doute les opérations policières dissuasives face aux rassemblements parfois tumultueux des jeunes y sont-elles pour quelque chose.

494

LE PARTAGE DE L'ESPACE

Les types de sociabilité observés dans les espaces publics présentent donc un certain nombre de traits communs, au-delà de la diversité des quartiers et des types de lieux. La segmentation des publics et la coprésence relativement indifférente à l'autre ressortent comme deux traits majeurs des pratiques d'espaces publics dans les quartiers pluri-ethniques montréalais. De plus, plusieurs parcs fonctionnent comme espaces de rassemblement entre gens de même âge et de même origine.

Le partage de l'espace semble s'opérer sans hostilité, du moins à première vue. La polyfonctionnalité des espaces et la quasi-absence de pratiques d'appropriation exclusive expliquent sans doute en partie ce type de modus operandi. Mais il se pourrait aussi que ce qui apparait comme accomodement réciproque cache des tensions larvées qui pourraient faire surface en situation de crise. Les observations faites dans les espaces publics correspondent à une coupe dans le temps. La période actuelle se caractérise, à l'échelle de la ville entière, par un climat de paix sociale relative. Mais l'analyse de l'histoire des quartiers a fait ressortir dans certains cas des conjonctures conflictuelles encore présentes dans la mémoire des lieux et qui se sont soldées par des exclusions de certains groupes.

Par ailleurs le constat de cette coexistence relativement pacifique dans l'espace public doit également être mis en rapport avec une appropriation plutôt lâche des lieux au plan symbolique, ce qui est bien somme toute dans la logique même de l'espace public. Si dans certains quartiers les rues commerçantes témoignent du marquage de l'espace urbain par les communautés immigrantes et sont valorisées en tant que telles, il n'en va pas nécessairement de même dans les parcs qui ne semblent guère l'enjeu de conquêtes identitaires. Celles-ci se déroulent sans doute sur d'autres terrains que ceux que nous avons examinés ici.

Références

Brezger, Dietrich et Louis Quéré, La matrice pratique du caractère public des espaces urbains., Rapport de recherche pour le Ministère de l'équipement, du logement et des transports. Paris: Centre d'études des mouvements sociaux, 1992.
De Laplante, Jean, Les parcs de Montréal. Des origines à nos jours, Montréal, Méridien, 1990, 255p.
Rémy, Jean, "La ville cosmopolite et la co-existence inter-ethnique", dans Immigrations et nouveaux pluralismes. Une confrontation de sociétés, Albert Bastenier et Felice Dassetto, éds., Coll.Ouvertures sociologiques, Editions universitaires, Université De Boeck, Bruxelles, 1990, pp.85-106.
Samson, Marcel, Daniel L'Ecuyer et Marcel Gaudreau, De l'utilité des parcs urbains dans la ville centrale : le cas de Montréal, INRS-Urbanisation, Etudes et documents, n°21, Montréal, 1981, 132p.
Toubon, Jean-Claude et Khelifa Messamah, Centralité immigrée, le quartier de la Goutte d'Or. Dynamiques d'un espace pluriethmique : succession, compétition, cohabitation, Paris, l'Harmattan-CIEMI, 1990, 2 tomes, 764p.

Notes

1   C'est le cas de Montréal qui, avec Toronto et Vancouver accueille depuis quelques années un nombre élevé d'immigrants arrivants au Canada. 70% des quelques 45 000 immigrants qu'accueille chaque année le Québec se retrouvent sur l'île de Montréal. Au niveau de la région cette fois, la proportion d'immigrants à Toronto et à Vancouver est plus du double de celle de Montréal.

2   Cette enquête commandée par le ministère des Communautés culturelles et de l'Immigration et par la Ville de Montréal comprend aussi un volet sur la dynamique communautaire, dont il ne sera pas question ici.

3   Ces quartiers multi-ethniques peuvent avoir de 20 à 90% de leurs habitants qui ne sont d'origine ni française ni britannique. La plupart comptent plusieurs dizaines d'ethnies différentes parmi leur résidents.

4   Banlieue ou quartier central.

5   Il s'agit de Brossard, de Côte-des-Neiges, du Mile End, de Parc Extension, De la Petite-Bourgogne et de deux quartiers dans Ville St-Laurent, Norgate et Chameran.

6   A cet égard, l'identification approximative de l'origine ethno-culturelle des usagers s'est avérée ardue dans bien des cas.

44

A comparison of the Berlage and van Eesteren plans for the extension of Amsterdam

Une comparaison entre les projets de Berlage et de van Eesteren pour l'agrandissement d'Amsterdam

Edwin Brierley

La signification des projets de Berlage ainsi que de ceux de Van Eesteren pour l'agrandissement d'Amsterdam tient à ce que que les images urbaines formelles qui s'ensuivirent peuvent être considérées comme ayant été plus influenccées par l'art et la culture que par les questions d'ordre social. Le projet de Berlage pour Amsterdam Sud, à l'origine un développement des idées de Camillo Sitte, a été revu en 1915 de façon à inclure des concepts de plan civique et de rationalisme géométrique. Par contraste, on a eu tendance à considérer le projet de Van Eesteren pour l'agrandissement général d'Amsterdam de 1935 en termes d'influence de De Stijl ainsi que du CIAM des années d'avant guerre; cependant, Van Eesteren considéra que l'approche conceptuelle du projet et, dans une certaine mesure, les caractéristiques indéterminées de sa réalisation étaient d'une plus grande importance. Il est possible de conclure que le développement en conception urbaine qui a résulté des deux projets a conduit ainsi que renvoyé aux changements plus généraux intervenus dans les notions de développement urbain de la première moitie de ce siècle. Cette communication est le résultat d'une étude des types de logement contrastés qui se sont développés à partir de l'Ecole d'Amsterdam, dont il exist de nombreuses illustrations à Amsterdam Sud, ainsi que De Stijl, dont Van Eesteren était membre. Cette étude, qui a été subventionnée par une bourse universitaire Leverhulme a été basée sur une recherche archiviste, un travail sur le terrain et une étude de la littérature sur le sujet.

Les mots clés: histoire urbaine; projets d'agrandissement; rationalisme géométrique; plannification indéterminnée; environnements urbains

Keywords: urban history; extension plans; geometric rationalism; indeterminate planning; urban environments

THE PLAN SOUTH AND THE GENERAL EXPANSION PLAN

The various development plans which have been proposed for Amsterdam throughout this century in a way reflect the development in attitudes to notions of urbanity during this century. Berlage's plan for Amsterdam South originally indicated an influence from Camillo Sitte and the final plan of 1915 was based upon geometric rationalism and a formalised conceptual approach. In contrast the work of Van Eesteren, from 1927, which led to the extension plan for Amsterdam of 1935 reflected to an extent indeterminate notions on design.

Both designers showed a concern for a social approach to design but the urban appearances of the two ideas are as contrasting as the architectural styles which they contain. Berlage's plan has many good examples of the decorative Amsterdam School . On the other hand Van Eesteren, who had worked with Van Doesburg, the founder of De Stijl, reflected in his work the ideals of both De Stijl and of the International Congress of Modern Architecture, CIAM. Berlage's plan was concerned with idea and style, whereas Van Eesteren's concept was of an 'abstract reality', a 'mental image' (Van Eesteren 1927).

The nature of the Berlage plan for Amsterdam South was that the layout was. in part, determined by notions of geometry. The overall planning concept could be related to two pentagons, which in turn produced the main axes of the development. The urban quality of the scheme is based upon generously proportioned avenues that are derived from the geometric layout. The areas which evolved from this form of thinking are less picturesque than those of the earlier plan derived from Sitte, but arguably they are more civic in overall effect.

The block forms of the dwellings are contained in a perimeter arrangement with walk-up access to the flats. Berlage's plan was both a grand design and one that indicated a social concern. The dwellings, although relatively meanly planned were of reasonable design and the appearance of the blocks were controlled by the 'schoonheidscommissie'. Schoonheid is a Dutch word which can mean both beauty and cleanliness and the commissions which controlled the design of sections of Berlage's plan and indeed other areas in Amsterdam would select the architects who would implement Berlage's plan.

The result of this procedure was that the housing associations who managed and developed the proposals used standard plan types and the architects were , in the main, employed as facade architects. In the early phases of the implementation of the proposals (Figure 44. 3), that is up to 1923, several of the Amsterdam School of designers were employed, including De Klerk and Kramer who were the leading exponents of the style.

Figure 44.1   H.P. Berlage: the Explansion Plan for Amsterdam South 1917 (from *Het Nieuwe Bouwen Amsterdam 1920–1960*, Delft University Press).

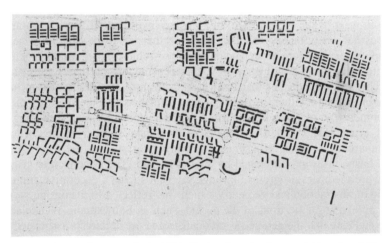

Figure 44.2   C. van Eesteren, Paris 1924. Design for a business neighbourhood (from *Het Nieuwe Bowen Amsterdam 1920–1960*, Delft University Press).

In contrast,the urban experience which resulted from Van Eesteren's plan is on the whole of openness in the spatial character and of variety in the dwelling blocks that are produced. The two sources which are often quoted to be precedents for the plan are ideas which result from both De Stijl and CIAM thinking. Clearly the implementation of the plan was originally influenced by socio-economic, functionalist precepts. Van Eesteren's approach was obviously influenced by CIAM, of which he was the president from 1930, but in terms of theoretical approach he understood the processes of the time scale of implementation. He envisaged that before the 'work of art' could be achieved, the time that was needed was in a way comparable to the construction of cathedrals in earlier centuries which took several decades (Hellinga 1983). This would in fact be an advantage, for Van Eesteren's plan was concerned with anticipating future needs which should reflect the culture of the times.

THE CONTEXT OF THE STUDY

The concept upon which the study of the origins and developments of the extension plans is based was the dual notion of abstraction and empathy (Worringer 1963) which was current at the turn of the century. The work in Holland at that time is reasonably well documented[1]. In particular the contrasting housing forms that resulted from the decorative Amsterdam School, of which several examples can be found in the Plan South, and of the work of De Stijl[2]. Upon investigation, Berlage's rational approach does not easily belong to either group, rather his work should be seen in the context of the Architectura group and the society Architectuur et Amicitia. Further study indicated the general influence of De Bazel and his partner Lauweriks on Berlage. Archive study indicates that Lauweriks had more of a theoretical influence and De Bazel a design influence. Berlage was influenced by the German theorist Gottfried Semper who placed an emphasis upon technical innovation providing new architectural types. De Bazel and Lauweriks who had worked in the office of Cuypers, the architect of the Rijksmuseum, were interested in the symbolic and proportional basis of design developed by Viollet-le-Duc. The Architectura group of which they were members progressed through the 1890s from a decorative attitude to design to one of abstraction and geometry which was reflected in the design work of Berlage. To an extent publications of the period, such as Bouwkundig Weekblad and Architectura indicate that the geometric rationalists and the architects associated with De Stijl had similar interests in abstraction. Van Eesteren's work reveals the elementary phase of De Stijl. This he acknowledged in the De Stijl magazine (Van Eesteren 1925). His connection with CIAM resulted from membership of the Opbouw group of functionalist designers, whose work was reported in the magazines i 10 and de 8 en Opbouw. It is from this documentary evidence that the significance of the Berlage and Van Eesteren extension plans may be considered.

INFLUENCES UPON THE PLANS

The basis of Berlage's thinking on urban issues can to a large extent be traced to Sitte's book Der Stadte-Bau which stressed that Town Planning should be derived from 'artistic principles' (Sitte 1889). Berlage further developed his ideas on style in two articles: 'Art in Town Planning' (Berlage 1892) and 'Architecture and Impressionism' (Berlage 1894). That thinking led to Berlage's first plan for Amsterdam South of 1900 in which several compositional devices appear to have been drawn from Sitte. The final plan of 1915, arguably with a clearer structure, was more rational in effect and clarified the formal identity of the plan. The area to the east of the plan, which had been laid out as parkland, became a neighbourhood of urban housing and it would be this part of the plan in which the decorative expressionism of the Amsterdam School was to be particularly effective (Searing 1972).In many ways there are parallels between the changes in the design for Berlage's plan for Amsterdam South with that of Berlage's most renowned architectural work, the Amsterdam Stock Exchange of 1896 to 1903. Both the Stock Exchange and Plan South were originally based upon picturesque or romantic notions as well as upon ideas on the monumental scale of building. The changes in both designs are in some ways due to the work of De Bazel and the influence of De Bazel's partner, Lauweriks, who was a friend of Berlage. De Bazel and Lauweriks and indeed Berlage were associated with the Nieuwe Kunst style of design which acknowledged the influence of proportional systems and geometry upon design. The Stock Exchange was influenced by a competition design by De Bazel of 1895 and the Plan South by De Bazel's design for a world capital which Berlage drew upon for his 1908 plan for the extension of The Hague. De Bazel's design of 1905 was influenced by Ebenezer Howard's diagram for a garden city of 1898 and also by the utopian plans of Renaissance Italy; De Bazel's work is reminiscent of Filarete's plan for Sforzinda (Reinink 1993).The change in Berlage's thinking from the approach of Sitte to the geometric form was facilitated by a decision to incorporate a railway station at the southern perimeter of the Plan South. This effectively changed the focus in Berlage's plan from being an additive one to the old centre to the idea of a complementary urban form. In effect, the Plan South turned its back on the old centre and by means of the broad avenues achieved a civic scale rather than a romantic quality (Figure 44.1). Although the plan of Berlage has in part been identified with the Amsterdam School of design, Berlage's own architectural style of this period was similar to the standardisation of block forms and limited decorative work which occurred in Amsterdam South after 1933 until 1938 (Fraenkel 1974).

502

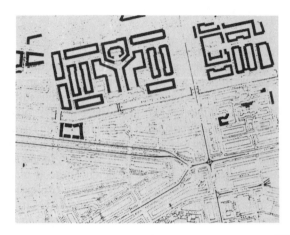

Figure 44.3 The Slotermeer district resulting from the implementation of van Eesteren's General Expansion Plan (from Sociale Woningbouw Amsterdam, Gemeentelijk Dienst Volkuisvesting).

Figure 44.4 Part of Berlage's plan for Amsterdam South, indicating areas developed by the Amsterdam School of Architects (from Sociale Woningbouw Amsterdam Gemeentelijk Dienst Volkhuisvesting).

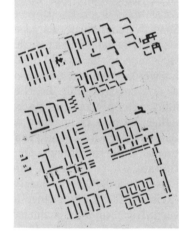

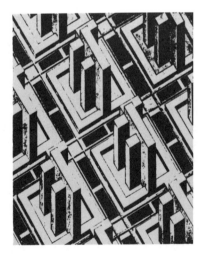

Figure 44.5 The Osdorp district resulting from the implentation of van Eesteren's General Expansion. Plan for Amsterdam (from Sociale Woningbouw Amsterdam, Gemeentelijk Dienst Volkhuisvesting).

The Plan South grew out of a moral concern that society had an obligation to provide improved living conditions for the people and was a reaction that was aimed at alleviating the poor conditions and overcrowding that existed in the old centre of Amsterdam. The reason for Van Eesteren's plan was originally a legislative one. Following the 1921 amendment to the 1901 Housing Act, towns were required to draw up expansion plans that were concerned not only with public spaces and transport routes but also with the spaces in between. A more urgent need for a plan was that by annexing surrounding areas the size of Amsterdam was to grow to four times its pre- 1921 size (Van der Woud 1983, a). The requirement of the planners, which determined Van Eesteren's flexible approach to the design solution, was that a population of almost one million people was envisaged by the year 2000.

Discussions on Van Eesteren's work have to a large extent focused on the effect of De Stijl and CIAM thinking on his work. Van Eesteren was not present at the inaugural meeting of CIAM at La Sarraz in 1928 which Berlage attended for part of the time to present a lecture on the relationship of government to architecture. In 1930, however, Van Eesteren was appointed president of CIAM and the tone of his approach, which represented the mood of CIAM members, is illustrated by his opening address to the fifth meeting of CIAM in Paris 1937: 'CIAM has become a great laboratory of urbanism and architecture' (Van der Woud 1983, b). Van Eesteren's thinking prior to his work on the Expansion Plan was influenced by Le Corbusier's Plan Voisin for Paris of 1922-25. An indication of Van Eesteren's approach to urban design at that time, 1924, can be seen in a design of which he was the co-author for a business centre in Paris (Figure 44.5). It is in this context that his note in De Stijl of 1927 was made in which he reconciled the idea of abstract reality with a mental image (Van Eesteren 1927). Certainly a conceptual approach resulting from objective and abstract notions were of equal importance to the universal values and ideas on harmony derived from De Stijl.

By the time the General Expansion Plan for Amsterdam was produced in 1935 Van Eesteren had been president of CIAM for five years. The first meeting he attended was that at Brussels in 1930 which was concerned with a rational approach to urban development. In that context rational implied a balance between economic and social issues (CIAM 3 1930).To an extent CIAM has become identified with the functional, social and economic thinking of the Athens Charter which resulted from the 1933 congress, whose theme was 'The Functional City'. Van Eesteren considered that the Athens congress represented the conclusion of the analytical phase of CIAM's work (De 8 en Opbouw 1935). The next phase was intended to be of illustrative examples . The difference in approach of the two phases which Van Eesteren identified are in effect those of the pre-war and post-war phases of CIAM. The former which was current during the design stage of Van Eesteren's plan had been analytical, deductive and socio-economic. The latter, contemporary with the implementation of the plan, was more inductive and reflected ideas on society and culture.

A COMPARATIVE NOTE

The formal characteristics of both Berlage's and Van Eesteren's plans are a result of the interactive nature of the spaces about the buildings and the contrasting block forms. That contrast is one of the experiential nature of the urban environment, which in another context has been identified as, 'the city, where what was once walled and intimate, the confirmation of community... has been rendered strange by the spatial incursions of modernity' (Vidler 1992). The facet of the designs where this is most apparent is in Berlage's use of the perimeter block form and the development in the Van Eesteren plan of the form giving principle of the 'strokenbouw'. Implicit from the use of the perimeter block form is the concept of a public and a private realm in which the architectural style and grouping of entrances to the flats is used as an effective formal device. Whereas the public facade was generally a well detailed composition, the private court elevations were of repetitive standard units. The development of the 'strokenbouw' (or in German, the 'zeilenbau') idea of parallel rows of housing blocks was a central feature of rationalist, functional design. The idea, which in a way defined the detail plan of 1939 for the Slotermeer district of the General Expansion Plan (Figure 44.2), can be traced to the new objectivity of Hilberseimer's work at the Bauhaus (Hilberseimer 1927) and also to the 'siedlungen' built by Ernst May in Frankfurt. May's approach was reflected in the theme of the second congress of CIAM held at Frankfurt in 1929 which was based upon the notion of the minimum dwelling in an urban context (Die Wohnung fur das Existenzminmum).

CONCLUDING OBSERVATIONS

Although the need to alleviate overcrowding in the old centre of Amsterdam had been a social one, the Plan South of Berlage evolved due to aesthetic principles and possibly utopian notions of urban design. Van Eesteren's work represented a different culture, of values determined by modernity that could be observed in an analytical approach to data and empirical study of land use. The urban design was expected to be based upon a scientific approach and detailed reports were presented. Yet, in practice, once the quantification of needs and projections for the future had been published in 1935, 'the city began to acquire style' (Barbieri 1983). Whilst Berlage's plan was clearly influenced by precedent, the results of Van Eesteren's work should not be considered to be a development from that of Berlage. Manfred Bock has made a perceptive comment on this point: 'The way from De Stijl to modern urban construction was not seen by Van Eesteren and his fellow-members of the architects association "De 8" and the Dutch CIAM group as a gradual replacement of Berlage by De Stijl ... but the realisation of De Stijl in urban construction' (Bock 1982). That was not meant to imply that the literal forms of the figurative images of De Stijl would be applied to the plan, rather the conceptual approach of new objectivity was to be realised. That approach was based upon analytical functional values which had formed the central theme of the 1930 Brussel's congress of CIAM. The concept, which was the principal idea of pre-war CIAM thinking, was one which was both social and analytical. It was an attitude to design that was reflected in the work of the De 8 group in Amsterdam who contributed to the implementation of Van Eesteren's plan (Figure 44.4). The essence of De 8's work, which was originally developed in theoretical terms in the magazine i 10, was that the aim of design was efficient construction rather than aesthetics. A particular attribute of the plans was that the appearance of the proposals would be regarded to be aesthetically neutral. In contrast to the formal expression of the architects of the Amsterdam School which was developed in Berlage's plan, the style of architecture of the expansion plan of Van Eesteren was derived from the units of constuction of the repetitive 'strokenbouw ' blocks which were arranged in landscaped settings. The influence of De Stijl was that of universal values and of harmony in the formal arrangement of the plans. The architectural expression that resulted from the development of Van Eesteren's plan was consistent with that advocated by the functionalist magazine de 8 en Opbouw of the 1930s. With the post-war years of CIAM, there was a reaction to the economic and analytical values of the pre-war years and some emphasis was then placed upon artistic and cultural values.

Notes

1 The documentary and archive material of designers of this period, including work by Berlage, Van Eesteren, De Klerk and others which could be referred to at the Documentation Centre for Architecture, Amsterdam are now transferred to the Netherlands Architecture Institute in Rotterdam.
2 The study of the contrasting housing forms of the Amsterdam School and De Stijl was supported by a Leverhulme Fellowship, other research awards enabled study of both the works of Lauweriks and of aspects of CIAM.

References

Barbieri, Umberto 1983, 'The City has Style', Het Nieuwe Bouwen: Neo Plasticism in Architecture, Delft University Press, p 134.
Berlage, H.P. 1892, 'De Kunst in Stedenbouw', Bouwkundig Weekblad, 12: pp 87-91, 101-02, 121-24, 126-27.
Berlage, H.P. 1894, 'Bouwkunst en Expressionisme', Architectura, 2: pp 93-95, 98-100, 105-06, 109-10.
Bock, Manfred 1982, 'De Stijl and the City', De Stijl: 1917-1931. Visions of Utopia, Minneapolis, Walker Art Centre, p 200.
Bock, Manfred 1983, Anfange einer neuen Architektur, s'Gravenhage, Staatsuitgeverij.
CIAM 1930, Rationnelle Bebauungsweisen, Brussels.

De 8 en Opbouw, 1935, no. 10/11, p 107.

Fraenkel, F.F. 1974, H.P.Berlage's plan for the southern extension of Amsterdam, Alphen aan den Rijn, Canaletto.

Hellinga, H. 1983, 'The General Expansion Plan of Amsterdam', in: Het Nieuwe Bouwen: Amsterdam 1920-1960, Delft, Delft University Press, p 70.

Hilberseimer, Ludwig 1927, Grosstadtarchitektur, Stuttgart, Bauhausbucher Band 3.

Reinink, W. 1993, K. P. C. de Bazel- Architect , Tweede met een Nawoord Vermeerderde Druk, Rotterdam, Uitgeverij 010, p 115.

Searing, Helen E. 1972, Housing in Holland and the Amsterdam School, (Phil.Diss. Yale University 1971) Ann Arbor Michigan, University Microfilms.

Singelenberg, Pieter 1972, H.P.Berlage, Idea and Style: the Quest for Modern Architecture, Utrecht.

Singelenberg, P., M.Bock, K. Boos, 1979, Berlage 1856-1934, Amsterdam, Van Gennep.

Sitte, Camillo 1889, Der Stadte-Bau nach seinen kunstlerischen Grundsatzen, Vienna.

Van der Woud, Auke 1983, Het Nieuwe Bouwen International: CIAM, Housing, Town Planning, Delft, Delft University Press, (a) p 55, (b) p74.

Van Eesteren, Cornelis 1925, 'Modern Stedebouwbeginselen in de Practijk', De Stijl, VI 10/11, p 162.

Van Eesteren, Cornelis 1927, '10 jaar "Stijl", Kunst, Techniek en Stedebouw', De Stijl, vol VII, 79/84, p 96.

Van Rossem, V. 1993, Het Algemeen Uitbreidingsplan van Amsterdam Geschiedenis en Ontwerp, Rotterdam, NAi; Den Haag, EFL Stichting:Bock, M. 1993, Editor, Deel 2, Cornelis van Eesteren, Architect-Urbanist, Rotterdam, NAi; Den Haag , EFL Stichting.

Vidler Anthony 1992, The Architectural Uncanny, Cambridge Mass., The MIT Press, p 11.

Worringer, Wilhelm 1963, Abstraction and Empathy,: A contribution to the Psychology of Style, Routledge and Kegan Paul Ltd., first published Munich 1908.

45

Behavior mapping and urban design: graphic versus non-graphic information about environment-behavior relations.

Cartes de comportement et conception urbaine: information graphique et non-graphique sur les relations environnement-comportement

Joost van Andel

La visualisation et l'information graphique jouent un rôle important dans le processus de conception. Cela pourrait aussi être le cas dans le transfert de connaissances entre concepteurs et chercheurs. Les 'cartes de comportement' relient le comportement (observé) des utilisateurs à une carte de l'environnement. Ceci peut être une technique de valeur pour rendre les résultats de recherches en environnement-comportement accessibles et utiles aux concepteurs.

Cette étude exploratoire porte sur les effets de différentes formes de présentation de données relatives aux cartes de comportement. Plus spécifiquement nous avons comparé trois groupes d'étudiants en architecture travaillant sur un problème de conception et utilisant des cartes, des tableaux ou une combinaison de ces deux formes. Pendant la période de recherche d'informations les données étaient présentées sur un logiciel qui permettait aux étudiants de parcourir les différentes parties de l'information. Les variables dépendantes étaient le temps passé dans les différentes parties du système d'information et la qualité de l'information extraite.

Dans la condition tableaux-seuls, les étudiants utilisaient moins d'écrans et passaient moins de temps à la consultation de l'information. Le fait que les étudiants étudiaient les cartes individuelles plus souvent mais pour une durée plus courte que les tableaux, suggère une façon plus globale de traiter l'information. Dans la combinaison tableaux-cartes, les étudiants utilisaient plus d'écrans et passaient plus de temps que dans les conditions tableaux-seuls et cartes-seules. Ils semblaient aussi obtenir plus d'informations et des données plus détaillées, suite à leur consultation du système.

Notre communication finit par une discussion des résultats et présente des suggestions pour des recherches futures.

Mots clés: transfert de connaissances, conception urbaine, cartes de comportement, présentation d'information graphique, formation à la conception urbaine.

Keywords: knowledge transfer; urban design; behavior mapping; graphic information display; urban design education

Communication is a key issue in the collaboration of designers and social science researchers. Several differences between designers and researchers in method and approach of problems seem to account for communication problems between the two groups. Researchers and designers seem to differ on: point of view (behavior vs. environments); method (analytical vs. synthetical); presentation (words vs. images); pattern of values (theoretical vs. ideological) and role conception (advisor vs. integrator) (van Andel, 1988). In their review of the transfer of (technical) information to designers and architects Lera, Cooper, and Powell (1984) mention the need for well-structured, relevant, and well-presented information. But they doubt if the presentation and organization of the information are the essential elements of successful information transfer. "They may be essential but they are not sufficient. It is necessary to stress that decisions are rather complex, emotionally demanding human processes, not just individualized intellectual analyses" (op. cit., p. 119). Newland, Powell, and Creed (1987) focus on the effect of learning styles, perception, and cultural biases on information transfer. These factors cause individual differences in the communication with architectural designers.

Given this more general framework, the form and structure of information are important elements in many studies of architectural design processes. Oxman (1990), for instance, explores the role of prior knowledge in design, which might be organized as integrated prototypes. These prototypes could organize design knowledge at a high abstraction level. It is not yet clear whether semantic or graphic modes play a role in this representation. Christiaans and van Andel (1993) found indications of a fixation effect using visual examples of design principles with industrial design students working in the information gathering phase.

Based on the assumption that visual information is an important aspect in the design process, several computer tools have been developed such as the visual problem-solving environment GISMO by Pracht (1986). Although Gross, Ervin, Anderson, and Fleisher (1988) focus on 'constraint programming' as a way to computerize design processes, they also mention diagrams as powerful tools in conceptual design. Diagrams combine advantages such as the expression of important spatial relationships and retaining useful uncertainty and ambiguity.

So in the transfer of knowledge from social science research to architectural designers, visualization of research data appears a promising way to overcome at least part of the communication problems between social scientists and designers. General guidelines on the visualization of research data are available, such as Tufte (1990). But systematic information about the effects of this type of information in the design process is scarce.

Behavior mapping is a specific technique, developed within environment-behavior studies to register, analyze and present data about the behavior of people in direct relation with their physical environment. Usually some kind of map of the environment represents the observed behavior of people (see for instance Bechtel & Zeisel, 1987). Behavior mapping seems to be a useful technique in communicating the results of environment-behavior studies to environmental designers. But it is not clear in what exact form this information should be presented. An important dimension in this respect is: graphic versus numeric/tabular representation. Is it preferable to present only graphic maps of the data, losing exact, numeric information?; or should the 'traditional' way of tables be used as a condensed but not always easy to read mode of presentation? Or is it more helpful to present the same data both in graphic and in tabular form, to give both a maximum of information and more freedom to use both forms of data presentation?

Therefore, the **main research question** of this study was:
"What are the effects of type of presentation on the transfer of information about environment-behavior relations to designers?"

These presentation effects are studied in different fields. For instance Larkin and Simon (1987) and Kosslyn (1989) focus on the differences between diagrams and text. Kosslyn presents a detailed scheme to evaluate charts and graphs, based on both principles of human visual information processing and on the interpretation of symbols. He distinguishes three levels of analysis: syntactic (how is the chart perceived?), semantic (how are the elements understood?) and pragmatic (what information does the chart convey?). The evaluation study by Pracht (1986) shows that a graphic presentation of a complex problem makes it easier to 'see' the different elements and relations of the total problem, which might help problem solving. This effect was mainly found for highly analytic problem solvers. Levie and Lentz (1982) reviewed research on the effects of text illustrations. They found that illustrations facilitate the learning of information in the written text. The positive learning effects of illustrated texts over non-illustrated texts were stronger if the illustrations were specific and closely related to the text.

Only a few studies focus on spatial information or on the specific differences between maps and tables. For instance Bartram (1980) compared different methods of presenting information about bus routes. Spatial information, in a schematic, color-coded map, appeared to help the task of finding a route between two places better than textual lists of bus stops. Anoskey and Catrambone (1992) compared textual, graphic, and combined instructions in a hypertext related task. They expected subjects in the graphics only condition, to perform faster than in the text only condition, but with more errors. In the combination condition the researchers expected both faster and more accurate performance. The experiment did not show significant differences between the conditions, which the authors attribute to the small number of subjects and the difficulty of the task. Hoadley (1990) studied primarily the effects of color in information presentation. She also compared tabular presentation with several types of graphs, such as pie-, bar-, and line-graphs. Subjects using graphs performed better as to the speed, and worse as to accuracy of information extraction. While the use of colors improved performance on the graphs, it confused the situation more for tables.

These results suggest a trade-off between speed and accuracy in the use of either graphic or textual modes of presentation. The aim of the present study is to explore if these effects exist also with architectural design problems. Compared to the tasks used in most studies, design tasks are more complex, involving the analysis of many different aspects, which is typical of the early stages of design.

Based on the above-mentioned studies, the following expectations for the effects of the form of presentation of behavior mapping data were formulated:

* Maps will be viewed during a shorter time, and will generate more global and less correct answers than tables.
* An information system with a combination of maps and tables will be used longer than the maps-only or tables-only condition, but not as long as the sum of their individual usage times. The combination version will generate more correct answers. And the combination version will lead to both global and detailed answers.

METHOD

Subjects

Three groups of 15 architecture students participated in this experiment. Most of them were graduate students of the College of Environmental Design, UC Berkeley.

Procedure

Each student worked individually on the following assignment: "Suppose you have to redesign this playground for a school for physically disabled children. [The students received some introductory information such as a map with legend, photos, information about size, number of pupils etc. to clarify the problem and to make the situation as realistic as possible]. In the initial phase of the design analysis you can consult information from a study on the use of the present playground by the children. This information is presented through a computer system. Try to find out as much as possible about these users. Make a summary or annotations for future use, as if you were going to use this in a realistic design".

All groups received behavior mapping information about the (play) behavior of children using the school playground that had to be redesigned. Information was available about four aspects of the children's behavior: sex-, age-, mobility-and activity-related differences. These differences were focused on the use of different places, either in a table or on a map.

The students were free to take as much time for the task as they thought was necessary to get their information. They were allowed (and encouraged) to take notes during their consultation with the system. After several pilot-sessions it was decided to give each student the following set of five questions to be answered while consulting the information system. This was done mainly to focus the search for information and to make the answers mutually comparable.

1.   What is the over-all pattern of use of the playground?
2.   What places are used, by whom and for what?
3.   What are differences in use between boys and girls?
4.   What are differences in use between younger and older children?
5.   What are differences in use between mobile and disabled children?

Conditions and materials

The three conditions in the experiment were: tables-only, maps-only, and a combination of tables and maps.

In all conditions the information was available through a computer system. Using a GIS-program (MapInfo) and a hypermedia-program (Guide), three versions of an information system were built, with a simple menu-structure and icons to navigate among the four different behavior maps and tables respectively. Figure 1 and 2 show examples from the combination version of sex-related information as a table and a map respectively.

The program logged the time the students spent with different screens. The dependent variables in this study were the time in seconds spent at each screen, and an evaluation (on a 3-point scale) of the answers on each of the five questions. This evaluation concerned the following three aspects: amount, correctness, and detail of the answers.

RESULTS

Screens and viewing times

The general results for the number of screens visited, and viewing times are presented in table 45.1. The differences among the three conditions are significant on both number of screens visited ($F=23.18$, $p<.001$) and total time ($F=19.20$, $p<.001$). In the table-condition students visited both a smaller number of screens ($t=8.14$, $p<.001$), and spent less time in total consulting the system ($t=3.08$, $p<.005$) than in the map-condition. This difference between tables and maps is not as expected. Probably the maps used in this task are rather complicated and need more time to be understood. As expected, the total task in the combination condition took a longer total time both compared to the tables-only ($t=6.88$, $p<.001$) and to the maps-only ($t=2.84$, $p<.001$), but definitely not as much time as the sum of table and map condition. The average time per screen shows a, non-significant, reversed effect.

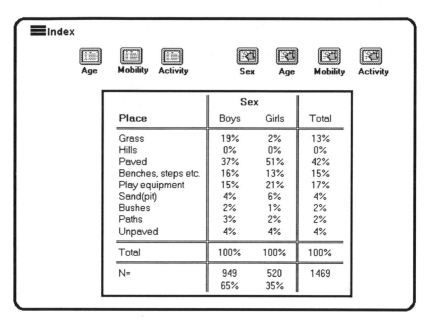

Figure 45.1 Table of sex by place.

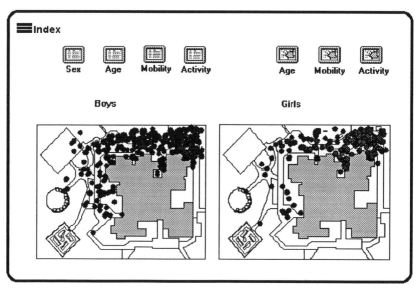

Figure 45.2 Map of sex by place.

In other words, the students see the different maps more often but look at them for a shorter time than the tables, which might suggest a more global way of information handling. The combination-version appears the most complicated in use, because students use both many screens and they need the longest time for the total task.

Tables 45.2 and 45.3 give more detailed information about the use of the different screens per condition. Except for activity, the general trend of tables being viewed longer than maps, can be found in the combination version as well.

Combining maps and tables appears to have complicated effects: Compared to the 'singular' versions, the number of times a particular screen is viewed, decreases; the average viewing time increases for sex and age, and decreases for mobility and activity.

Table 45.2 shows on which subjects the students spent their time as a percentage of the total session time. Table 45.3 gives more details about the average time spent on different screens, accounting for the fact that students do return to the same screen several times during a session. Tables 45.2 and 45.3 indicate that the complexity of the table or map is a relevant factor. In the material used in this study, sex and mobility are variables with only two classes, generating relatively simple tables and maps. Age and activity have more classes (resp. 4 and 12), and consequently lead to more complicated tables and maps. Especially the average time per screen (table 45.3) is higher for more complicated subjects and lower for more simple ones. The combination version does not show these effects.

Another noteworthy result is that the average time spent in the main menu appears to increase from table, via map to combination version ($F=9.33$, $p<.001$).

Comparison of the first, the middle, and the last period of information gathering shows that in the last period always fewer screens are viewed and consequently for a longer time. In the earlier periods of the task students seem to explore the information and come back later in a more focussed way.

Content

Table 45.4 shows the average scores of the five content-related questions. The answers to each question are judged on a 3-point scale for amount, correctness, and level of detail.

Only the differences between the three conditions for detailed answers was found to be marginally significant ($F=2.61$, $p<0.10$). Against the expectation, the answers in the map condition show higher scores than those in the table condition. As expected, there seems to be a trend for higher scores in the combination version.

Table 45.1
Mean number of screens visited and viewing times

	Condition		
	Table	Map	Combination Table / Map
N=	15	15	15
Mean number of screens visited	17.80	27.93	34.20
Mean total time in sec.	1525	2035	2509
Average time per screen	90.14	79.47	78.39

Table 45.2
Mean percentage of time spent on different screens / subjects.

	Condition		
Type of screen	Table	Map	Combination Table / Map
Menu	3%	3%	2%
Sex	19%	19%	11/14%
Age	28%	20%	18/16%
Mobility	25%	22%	10/10%
Activity	24%	36%	12/8%
Total (ave. # sec.)	1525	2035	2509

Table 45.3
Average time per screen as function of screen content.

Type of screen	Condition		
	Table	Map	Combination Table / Map
Menu	20.70	26.36	35.00
Sex	76.56	58.38	100.57 / 74.97
Age	104.74	91.80	121.15 / 113.35
Mobility	94.85	68.02	61.57 / 53.42
Activity	121.23	96.77	55.35 / 80.28

Table 45.4
Evaluation of answers, average over five questions.

Feature of answer	Condition		
	Table	Map	Combination Table / Map
Amount	1.68	1.90	2.01
Correctness	1.81	1.97	1.81
Detail	1.47	1.76	1.91

CONCLUSION AND DISCUSSION

The results of this study show that graphic and non-graphic modes of information presentation certainly have different effects when used in the preliminary phase of a design task. Tables with numeric information allow students to work faster, with fewer repetitions than maps with a graphic representation of the same information. Students consult maps more often but for a shorter time than the tables, which could indicate a more global way of information handling. But the content of the information collected by the students from the tables appears to be less detailed compared with infromation based on the maps. The combination of the two modes of presentation, tables and maps of the same information, appears to have interesting effects. Although the number of screens doubles from four to eight, both the total usage time and the amount of screens used do increase also as expected, but by a much smaller amount of about 45%. The combination has positive effects on the content as well: students' answers based on the combined version are more detailed and slightly more elaborate.

Especially the longer total time for the map version was not as expected. A possible explanation is the high complexity of the behavior maps used. Interpretation of this kind of maps might be more difficult than expected. Another unexpected result was the lack of detail in the answers of the students working with the tables in comparison with the other conditions. Here the translation from numerical, detailed information in the tables to the solution of a spatial design might have caused the differences. Another clue for the importance of the complexity of the tables and maps comes from the comparison of the four separate tables and maps respectively. The students looked longer at tables and maps representing complex information, for instance comparing many different subgroups, than at the simpler ones.

Therefore, in further research the exact influence of the complexity of the information material should be examined and controlled more precisely. A distinction in abstraction level as proposed by Goel & Pirolli (1992) and used by de Vries (1993) is useful in this respect. Repeating a similar study with other design tasks and/or in other design domains seems necessary to account for the large variety in situations and for the differences with more 'standard' problem solving tasks usually found in cognitive studies. Finally it seems of interest to explore the role of other presentation modes such as animation, realistic images, and video that are more available and therefore used more frequently in architectural design practice.

References

Andel, J. van (1988). Expert systems in environmental psychology. In H. van Hoogdalem, N.J. Prak, T.J.M. van der Voordt, & H.B.R. van Wegen (Eds.), Looking back to the future. Proceedings IAPS10 Conference (pp. 303-312). Delft: Delft University Press.
Anoskey, A.M. & Catrambone, R. (1992). Text and graphics in instructional design. In I. Tomek (Ed.), Computer assisted learning. Proceedings 4th Int. Iccall'92 Conference (pp. 74-87). Berlin: Springer Verlag.

Bartram, D.J. (1980). Comprehending spatial information: The relative efficiency of different methods of presenting information about bus routes. Journal of Applied Psychology, 65, 103-110.

Bechtel, R.B. & Zeisel, J. (1987). Observation: the world under a glass. In R.B. Bechtel, R.W. Marans, & W. Michelson (Eds.), Methods in environmental and behavioral research (pp. 11-40). New York: van Nostrand Reinhold.

Christiaans, H. & Andel, J. van (1993). The effects of examples on the use of knowledge in a student design activity: the case of the Flying Dutchman. Design Studies, 14, 58-74.

Goel, V. & Pirolli, P. (1992). The structure of design problem spaces. Cognitive Science, 16, 395-429.

Gross, M.D., Ervin, S.M., Anderson, J.A., & Fleisher, A. (1988). Constraints: Knowledge representation in design. Design Studies, 9, 133-143.

Hoadley, E.D. (1990). Investigating the effects of color. Communications of the ACM. 33, 120-125.

Kosslyn, S.M. (1989). Understanding charts and graphs. Applied cognitive psychology, 3, 185-226.

Larkin, J.H., & Simon, H.A. (1987). Why a diagram is (sometimes) worth ten thousand words. Cognitive Science, 11, 65-99.

Lera, S., Cooper, I., & Powell, J.A. (1984). Information and designers. Design Studies, 5, 113-120.

Levie, W. H., & Lentz, R. (1982). Effects of text illustrations: A review of research. Educational, Communication, and Psychological Technology Journal, 30, 195-232.

Newland, P., Powell, J.A., & Creed, C. (1987). Understanding architectural designers' selective information handling. Design Studies, 8, 2-16.

Oxman, R. (1990). Prior knowledge in design: a dynamic knowledge-based model of design and creativity. Design Studies, 11, 17-28.

Pracht, W. (1986). GISMO: A visual problem-structuring and knowledge-organizing tool. IEEE Transactions on systems, man, and cybernetics, 16, 265-270.

Tufte, E. (1990). Envisioning information. Cheshire: Graphic Press.

Vries, E. de (1993). The role of case-based reasoning in architectural design: Stretching the design problem space. In W. Visser (Ed.), Proceedings of the IJCAI'93 workshop on Re-use of designs: An interdisciplinary cognitive approach (pp. 28-40). Chambèry, France.

ENGLISH KEYWORD INDEX

This index uses keywords assigned to the individual chapters by the authors. The numbers are the page numbers of the first page of the relevant chapter.

INDEX DES MOTS-CLEFS FRANCAIS

Cet index répertorie les mots-clef sélectionnés par les auteurs de chaque chapitre. Les numéros font référence au numéro de la première page de chapitre concerné.